🖂 Let's Go writers travel on your budget.

"Guides that penetrate the veneer of the holiday brochures and mine the grit of real life."

—The Economist

"The writers seem to have experienced every rooster-packed bus and lunar-surfaced mattress about which they write."

—The New York Times

"All the dirt, dirt cheap."

—People

🖂 Great for independent travelers.

"The guides are aimed not only at young budget travelers but at the independent traveler; a sort of streetwise cookbook for traveling alone."

—The New York Times

"A guide should tell you what to expect from a destination. Here *Let's Go* shines."

—The Chicago Tribune

"An indispensible resource, *Let's Go*'s practical information can be used by every traveler."

—The Chattanooga Free Press

🖂 Let's Go is completely revised each year.

"A publishing phenomenon...the only major guidebook series updated annually. *Let's Go* is the big kahuna."

—The Boston Globe

"Unbeatable: good sight-seeing advice; up-to-date info on restaurants, hotels, and inns; a commitment to money-saving travel; and a wry style that brightens nearly every page."

—The Washington Post

🖂 All the important information you need.

"*Let's Go* authors provide a comedic element while still providing concise information and thorough coverage of the country. Anything you need to know about budget traveling is detailed in this book."

—The Chicago Sun-Times

"*Let's Go* guidebooks take night life seriously."

—The Chicago Tribune

Let's Go Publications

Let's Go: Alaska & the Pacific Northwest 2002
Let's Go: Amsterdam 2002 **New Title!**
Let's Go: Australia 2002
Let's Go: Austria & Switzerland 2002
Let's Go: Barcelona 2002 **New Title!**
Let's Go: Boston 2002
Let's Go: Britain & Ireland 2002
Let's Go: California 2002
Let's Go: Central America 2002
Let's Go: China 2002
Let's Go: Eastern Europe 2002
Let's Go: Egypt 2002 **New Title!**
Let's Go: Europe 2002
Let's Go: France 2002
Let's Go: Germany 2002
Let's Go: Greece 2002
Let's Go: India & Nepal 2002
Let's Go: Ireland 2002
Let's Go: Israel 2002
Let's Go: Italy 2002
Let's Go: London 2002
Let's Go: Mexico 2002
Let's Go: Middle East 2002
Let's Go: New York City 2002
Let's Go: New Zealand 2002
Let's Go: Paris 2002
Let's Go: Peru, Ecuador & Bolivia 2002
Let's Go: Rome 2002
Let's Go: San Francisco 2002
Let's Go: South Africa with Southern Africa 2002
Let's Go: Southeast Asia 2002
Let's Go: Southwest USA 2002 **New Title!**
Let's Go: Spain & Portugal 2002
Let's Go: Turkey 2002
Let's Go: USA 2002
Let's Go: Washington, D.C. 2002
Let's Go: Western Europe 2002

Let's Go Map Guides

Amsterdam	New Orleans
Berlin	New York City
Boston	Paris
Chicago	Prague
Dublin	Rome
Florence	San Francisco
Hong Kong	Seattle
London	Sydney
Los Angeles	Venice
Madrid	Washington, D.C.

EGYPT
2002

Joey Shabot editor
Dave Newman associate editor
Elizabeth Ogburn associate editor

researcher-writers
Christiaan Highsmith
Adam Kampff
Eban Lee

St. Martin's Press ♒ New York

HELPING LET'S GO If you want to share your discoveries, suggestions, or corrections, please drop us a line. We read every piece of correspondence, whether a postcard, a 10-page email, or a coconut. Please note that mail received after May 2002 may be too late for the 2003 book, but will be kept for future editions. **Address mail to:**

> Let's Go: Egypt
> 67 Mount Auburn Street
> Cambridge, MA 02138
> USA

Visit Let's Go at **http://www.letsgo.com**, or send email to:

> feedback@letsgo.com
> Subject: "Let's Go: Egypt"

In addition to the invaluable travel advice our readers share with us, many are kind enough to offer their services as researchers or editors. Unfortunately, our charter enables us to employ only currently enrolled Harvard students.

ABOUT LET'S GO

FORTY-TWO YEARS OF WISDOM

For over four decades, travelers crisscrossing the continents have relied on *Let's Go* for inside information on the hippest backstreet cafes, the most pristine secluded beaches, and the best routes from border to border. *Let's Go: Europe*, now in its 42nd edition and translated into seven languages, reigns as the world's bestselling international travel guide. In the last 20 years, our rugged researchers have stretched the frontiers of backpacking and expanded our coverage into the Americas, Australia, Asia, and Africa (including the new *Let's Go: Egypt* and the more comprehensive, multi-country jaunt through *Let's Go: South Africa & Southern Africa*). Our new-and-improved City Guide series continues to grow with new guides to perennial European favorites Amsterdam and Barcelona. This year we are also unveiling *Let's Go: Southwest USA*, the flagship of our new outdoor Adventure Guide series, which is complete with special roadtripping tips and itineraries, more coverage of adventure activities like hiking and mountain biking, and first-person accounts of life on the road.

It all started in 1960 when a handful of well-traveled students at Harvard University handed out a 20-page mimeographed pamphlet offering a collection of their tips on budget travel to passengers on student charter flights to Europe. The following year, in response to the instant popularity of the first volume, students traveling to Europe researched the first full-fledged edition of *Let's Go: Europe*. Throughout the 60s and 70s, our guides reflected the times—in 1969, for example, we taught you how to get from Paris to Prague on "no dollars a day" by singing in the street. In the 90s we focused in on the world's most exciting urban areas to produce in-depth, fold-out map guides, now with 20 titles (from Hong Kong to Chicago) and counting. Our new guides bring the total number of titles to 57, each infused with the spirit of adventure and voice of opinion that travelers around the world have come to count on. But some things never change: our guides are still researched, written, and produced entirely by students who know first-hand how to see the world on the cheap.

HOW WE DO IT

Each guide is completely revised and thoroughly updated every year by a well-traveled set of nearly 300 students. Every spring, we recruit over 200 researchers and 90 editors to overhaul every book. After several months of training, researcher-writers hit the road for seven weeks of exploration, from Anchorage to Adelaide, Estonia to El Salvador, Iceland to Indonesia. Hired for their rare combination of budget travel sense, writing ability, stamina, and courage, these adventurous travelers know that train strikes, stolen luggage, food poisoning, and marriage proposals are all part of a day's work. Back at our offices, editors work from spring to fall, massaging copy written on Himalayan bus rides into witty, informative prose. A student staff of typesetters, cartographers, publicists, and managers keeps our lively team together. In September, the collected efforts of the summer are delivered to our printer, who turns them into books in record time, so that you have the most up-to-date information available for your vacation. Even as you read this, work on next year's editions is well underway.

WHY WE DO IT

We don't think of budget travel as the last recourse of the destitute; we believe that it's the only way to travel. Our books will ease your anxieties and answer your questions about the basics—so you can get off the beaten track and explore. Once you learn the ropes, we encourage you to put *Let's Go* down and strike out on your own. You know as well as we that the best discoveries are often those you make yourself. When you find something worth sharing, please drop us a line. We're Let's Go Publications, 67 Mount Auburn St., Cambridge, MA 02138, USA (feedback@letsgo.com). For more info, visit our website, www.letsgo.com.

HOW TO USE THIS BOOK

Welcome to **Let's Go: Egypt 2002**. This book is a backpacker's guide to Egypt, incl-duing coverage of Petra, Jordan (an easy daytrip from Egypt). If *Let's Go: Middle East* were an animal, it would be a camel. Like a camel, this book is rugged, intel-ligent, dependable, and a delightful shade of yellow. Unlike a camel, this book does not spit; please do not spit on it.

ORGANIZATION OF THIS BOOK

INTRODUCTORY MATERIAL. The first chapter, **Discover Egypt** provides you with an overview of travel in the region, including four **suggested itineraries** that give you an idea of what you want to see and how long it will take you to see it. The **Essentials** chapter outlines all the practical information you'll need to prepare for and execute your trip. The **Life and Times** chapter provides you with a general introduc-tion to the history, religion, and culture of Egypt.

COVERAGE. The chapters are organized by region, beginning with **Cairo** and its environs, including the Pyramids at Giza and the Nile Delta. After Cairo comes **Alexandria** and Egypt's Mediterranean coast. Next we send you to the **Nile Valley**, where you can cruise from temple to temple in the comfort of a *felucca* boat. After the valley comes coverage of the **Western Desert Oases.** Next is the **Suez Canal,** fol-lowed by the **Sinai Peninsula,** a backpacker's paradise of Bedouin camps and scuba dive clubs. In the final chapter, we cover **Petra** in Jordan, which can be conve-niently visited from the Sinai Peninsula. In each destiniation within the chapters, **Transportation** gets you from point A to point B (and tells you how to get around B once you're there). **Orientation** untangles city streets, while **Practical Information** tips you off on how to get your laundry done, and change your currency. The **Accommodations, Food, Sights, Entertainment,** and **Nightlife** sections guide you to the Bedouin camps, shawarma stands, *sheesha* parlors, tombs, camel markets, and watering holes that will give you the most bang for your buck.

APPENDIX. The appendix contains a table of useful measurement **conversions** for the metrically-impaired, a **phrasebook** of handy phrases in Arabic, and a **glossary** of foreign words and Middle Eastern foods.

A FEW NOTES ABOUT LET'S GO FORMAT

RANKING ESTABLISHMENTS. In each of the accommodations and food sections, we list establishments in order from best to worst. Our absolute favorites are denoted by the highest honor we give: the *Let's Go* thumbs-up (🖾).

PHONE CODES AND TELEPHONE NUMBERS. The **phone code** for each region, city, or town, appears opposite the name of that region, city, or town, and is denoted by a ☎ icon. **Phone numbers** are also preceded by the ☎ icon.

GRAYBOXES AND WHITEBOXES. Sometimes **grayboxes** provide cultural insight or historical background; other times they are simply an excuse for crude humor. **Whiteboxes** provide important practical information, such as warnings (🚺), helpful hints and further resources (🖾), border crossing information (🛫), etc.

A NOTE TO OUR READERS The information for this book was gathered by *Let's Go* researchers from May through August of 2001. Each listing is based on one researcher's opinion, formed during his or her visit at a particular time. Those traveling at other times may have different experiences since prices, dates, hours, and conditions are always subject to change. You are urged to check the facts presented in this book beforehand to avoid inconvenience and surprises.

CONTENTS

MAPS

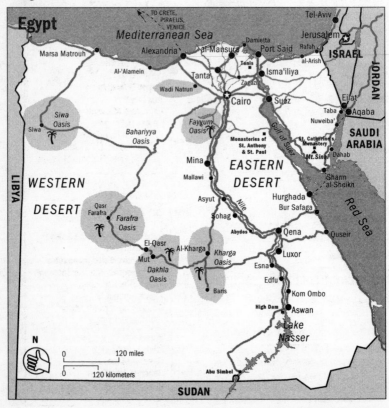

ACKNOWLEDGMENTS

The Let's Go 2002 series is dedicated to the memory of Haley Surti

TEAM EGY THANKS: Thank you to all the girls we've loved before, including: Sharmilicious; Prodass Melissa; and her cohorts; Noah, Anna and their mapland sidekicks; Batman; and you.

JOEY THANKS: Umm Kulthoum and Sharmi for hours of diversion and wonderful smoky voices; Eli, Rachel, Gautam, Ankur, Tal and Alex for a beautiful, lazy summer after all; Betsy for your smiling face; Dave for good humor and music; the Coöp, for alternativist thinking that makes it easier to say goodbye to this place; Lauren Grünsfeld and Paula for welcoming me back with open arms. Thank you Abba, Imma, Toby, Kathy, Ezra and Dina for your love and support.

DAVE THANKS: Mayo, Puja, Mike, Jen, DPM, MMI, KGS, VVG, and JML for distracting me from this job. Lauren, Mike, Chris, Phil, and Danielle for visiting. ABG and DMD for a great week off. PRC for being such a quiet roommate. Joey, Betsy, and Sharmi for your perpetual good spirits. Mom and Dad for your love and support.

BETSY THANKS: My family for raising me and for letting me come and go as I please, Mikey and Michelle for never-ending good times, and Tania for her over-the-top proofing skills. Also Salah al-Din for his antics, and my little sister Laura for being such an inspiring cream puff. And of course, the team: Dave, Sharmi, Joey.

Editor
Joey Shabot
Associate Editors
Dave Newman
Elizabeth Ogburn
Managing Editor
Ankur N. Ghosh
Map Editors
Noah Askin
Anna Malsberger

Publishing Director
Sarah P. Rotman
Editor-in-Chief
Ankur N. Ghosh
Production Manager
Jen Taylor
Cartography Manager
Dan Barnes
Design & Photo Manager
Vanessa Bertozzi
Editorial Managers
Amélie Cherlin, Naz F. Firoz, Matthew Gibson, Sharmi Surianarain, Brian R. Walsh
Financial Manager
Rebecca L. Schoff
Marketing & Publicity Managers
Brady R. Dewar, Katharine Douglas, Marly Ohlsson
New Media Manager
Kevin H. Yip
Online Manager
Alex Lloyd
Personnel Manager
Nathaniel Popper
Production Associates
Steven Aponte, Chris Clayton, Caleb S. Epps, Eduardo Montoya, Melissa Rudolph
Some Design
Melissa Rudolph
Office Coordinators
Efrat Kussell, Peter Richards

Director of Advertising Sales
Adam M. Grant
Senior Advertising Associates
Ariel Shwayder, Kennedy Thorwarth
Advertising Associate
Jennie Timoney
Advertising Artwork Editor
Peter Henderson

President
Cindy L. Rodriguez
General Manager
Robert B. Rombauer
Assistant General Manager
Anne E. Chisholm

RESEARCHER-WRITERS

▓ Christiaan Highsmith
Alexandria, Nile Valley, Desert Oases

Determined to take our coverage to a new level, Cantabrigian Christiaan battled devilish heat, reluctant diving schools, and befuddling maps with the shrewdness of a true outdoorsman and experienced traveler. His unfaltering drive, wide-eyed appreciation for his surroundings, and ever-smiling dedication paid off in the end, as he finally learned how to spell Eygpt. He even remembered to let his mom know how he was doing—what a guy.

▓ Adam Kampff
Jordan

We couldn't have found a chiller dude to cover this laid-back kingdom. From the moment a skinhead hit him in the head with a *Let's Go* recycling bin, it was clear that Adam and this job were meant for each other. The budding astronomer and Albany native brought a relaxed attitude and fresh eye to every archaeological site and toilet stall he visited. Though his personal hygiene may have left something to be desired, his copy was impeccably clean. Whether cruising through the desert (Christina Aguilera blaring) with an Iraqi hitchhiker or sucking down 50 cups of tea out of respect for Hashemite hospitality, Adam was a pleasure to work with.

▓ Ebon Lee
Cairo, Nile Delta, Sinai

With nerves of steel, Ebon braved the 120°F heat, fleas, incapacitating sickness found only in 3rd-class train cars, Cairene bureaucrats who treated bus schedules like matters of national security, and detainment by tourist police—all without even batting an eyelash (or complaining to his editors). Instead, this Kansas native who had never before crossed the Atlantic consistently sent in reliable, opinionated copy from the vantage point of the ultimate budget traveler. Proof that good things come to those who wait: Ebon's luck finally turned around, as he watched the sunrise from the top of Mt. Sinai and landed a date with Jasmine, one of Egypt's top belly dancers.

DISCOVER EGYPT

Gertrude Bell, one of the most famous travelers to the Middle East, said, "Few such moments of exhilaration can come as that which stands at the threshold of wild travel." Egypt is, without a doubt, adventure country *par excellence*. Wide expanses of desert dotted with lush green oases, colorful underwater seascapes, and labyrinthian tombs inspire exploration in the grand tradition of Lawrence of Arabia and Indiana Jones. Egypt brings many images to mind: colossal pyramids and gilded tombs, opulent pharoahs and omnipotent gods, the mighty Nile River and its dams. It is a country with an astoundingly rich past, so much so that most visitors probably know more about what Egypt was like 3000 years ago than about the modern-day state. But it is the Egypt hidden behind these national treasures and universal wonders that travelers come to know and love: the urban sprawl of Cairo and Alexandria, the unspoilt culture of the Bedouin, the unparalleled relaxation of a *felucca* ride down the Nile, and, above all, the astounding hospitality of Egyptians everywhere—from the oasis villages to the heart of Cairo. Egypt is a budget traveler's paradise. The sights are stunning, the culture fascinating, and bargains a way of life. However, travel here requires plenty of time, stamina, and patience. Most find that with a relaxed attitude, the hassles of traveling are surpassed by the intensity and beauty of the Egyptian experience.

FACTS AND FIGURES

NUMBER OF BEAUTY PRODUCTS INVENTED BY ANCIENT EGYPTIANS: 75: anti-wrinkle creams, depilatories, exfoliants, breath fresheners, and hair growth stimulators for balding men.

PERCENTAGE OF SURVIVING WONDERS OF THE ANCIENT WORLD: 100.

NUMBER OF MUMMIFIED CATS FOUND IN EGYPT AND SOLD TO ENGLAND TO BE USED AS FERTILIZER: 300,000.

LARGEST BURIAL GROUND IN THE WORLD: Valley of the Mummies, spanning six miles and holding about 10,000 corpses.

WHEN TO GO

Take into account **holidays** when arranging your itinerary (for a list of religious and national holidays, see **Holidays and Festivals,** p. 85). As in all Muslim countries, businesses close on Fridays. They may close during the afternoon on holidays, but are generally open in the morning. The most important event and the one most likely to complicate travel is **Ramadan** (Nov. 17-Dec. 15 in 2001; Nov. 6-Dec. 5 in 2002), the annual month-long fast during which Muslims abstain from food and drink from dawn to dusk. During this time, most restaurants are closed until sundown; shops may be open for a few hours in the morning and a short time after *iftar*, the breaking of the fast. Government services are either closed entirely or open only in the morning. It would be rude to smoke or eat in public at this time.

Also think about when everyone else is vacationing. Egypt's high and low seasons depend partly on the region: Cairo is a year-round mob scene, while summertime is partytime in Alexandria and on the Mediterranean and Red Sea beaches. In the Sinai, Oases, and Upper Egypt, reasonable temperatures make winter the high season, but younger travelers revel in summertime bargains despite the extreme heat. In southern Egypt, summer temperatures often reach 49°C (120°F) and can push 55°C (131°F). Fortunately, it's dry—your body's cooling system should know what to do. Winter brings perfect weather across the country. In arid Cairo, pollution makes summer afternoons hellish. Alexandria is temperate year-round, though quite humid. The Red Sea coast is comfortably warm in winter and hot but dry in summer; higher elevations in the Sinai can be freezing in winter and on summer nights.

THINGS TO DO

Egypt gets a lot of mileage for its historical sites. But while Egypt's ancient ruins, religious traditions, and *souqs* are delectable slices of the past on a backpacker's silver platter, the country offers more than just history. Cairo and Na'ama Bay feature hopping club scenes, while the sandy shores of the Sinai Peninsula will be sure to satisfy the most discriminating beach bunnies. For more specific regional attractions, see **Highlights of the Region,** at the beginning of each chapter.

SUN OF A BEACH

Northern Egypt embraces the Mediterranean Sea, and the Sinai Penninsula is cradled by the Red Sea. This prime location furnishes Egypt with enviable seascapes. Savor the lazy, marijuana-hazy daze of summer at **Dahab** (p. 289), one of the many beachside treasures along the coasts of the **Sinai Peninsula** (p. 270), known the world over as a scuba paradise. The beach-side towns **Na'ama Bay** (p. 285) and **al-'Arish** (p. 273) await those who dream of sun-bathing. Tired of jam-packed sands and jammin' discos? Weary travelers can create their own resort and hire a **felucca** to troll down the Nile (p. 206). Countless stretches of emerald coast drape Egypt's northern border. In particular, **Marsa Matrouh** (p. 175) offers spectacular Mediterranean serenity without the Mediterranean crowds.

SHOP 'TIL YOU DROP

Bargaining is a fact of life in Egypt. Almost every city has a *souq,* an outdoor bazaar that sells everything from spices to stilettos. Grab silver and spice and everything nice in market-ridden **Cairo** (p. 130), which is the best place in the Middle East to buy tapestries and *sheeshas*. If upscale beach-front shopping is more your speed check out stylish **Alexandria** (p. 156) or the duty-free shoppers' haven of **Port Said** (p. 254). For less luxurious goods, trek out to the camel markets in **Birqash** (p. 139) or **Daraw** (p. 238).

BLAST FROM THE PAST

Unless you plan to lock yourself in hotel rooms the whole time you're in Egypt, there is no escaping the countless ruins that testify to the country's illustrious past. The **Great Pyramid of Cheops** (p. 136) at Giza is the only wonder of the ancient world still standing, and it is a must-see on any itinerary. Crouching nearby, the **Sphinx** has been smiling down on travelers for millennia. Ancient architects, not wanting to discriminate too heavily in favor of the triangle, constructed many rectangular temples scattered throughout the country. It would take the lifetimes of a cat to see them all, but the cream of the crop, the temples at **Luxor** and **Karnak** (p. 213), can easily be incorporated into one lifespan.

Harder to get to is the temple of **Abu Simbel** (p. 251), but with its four massive statues of Ramses II, it is the icing on the cake. Narcissist extraordinaire, Ramses II left his image on every monument he saw, even going so far as to rub out the faces on statues of his predecessors to replace them with his own. The ruins of his funerary temple, the **Ramesseum** at Karnak (p. 228), are on the scale of his ego: ginormous. Dying was quite an affair in ancient Egypt, and it is unlikely that you will make it through Egypt without coming across some mummies—in the mummy room at the **Egyptian Museum** in Cairo (p. 125) for example, not far from the treasures of King Tut's tomb. Even if you are not a fan of Indiana Jones, the somber sepluchres of the **Valleys of the Kings, Queens, Nobles,** and **Artisans** (p. 225-p. 232) are sure to capture your imagination.

YOU, YOURSELF, AND YOU

Egypt has plenty of spots that can still rightly be called "off the beaten path." First and foremost, the wide expanses of desert offer quiet isolation perfect for bonding with your inner self. (Day-long and overnight desert tours are launched from all of the desert oases.) The oases at **Siwa** (p. 179) and **Fayyum** (p. 145) are peaceful and idyllic. For spiritual solitude, check out the monastery at **Wadi Natrun** (p. 152), an arcadia of cooing doves, flowing trees, and enlightened monks. To get wet but still keep your distance from the tourist masses, make like a local and vacation at **Marsa Matrouh** (p. 175) or **al-'Arish** (p. 273) on the Mediterranean coast.

■ LET'S GO PICKS

BEST PLACE TO LOOK, NOT TOUCH: Find your inner fish in the legions of brilliantly colored creatures as you flit through coral in the Red Sea in **Dahab** (p. 289), which ranks among the world's best places for fish-scoping.

BEST WONDER OF THE WORLD: head over to the **Pyramids at Giza** in Egypt (p. 136), the only one of the Seven Wonders of the Ancient World still standing.

BEST CAFE FREQUENTED BY A NOBEL LAUREATE: Smoke *sheesha* and read *Palace Walk* amidst the bustle of Khan al-Khalili at **Fishawi's** in Cairo (p. 133), the famous teahouse where Naguib Mahfouz spent endless *Arabian Nights and Days*.

BEST WAY TO TAN: Float down the Nile aboard a *felucca*, taking the time to cook in the sun while wiling away the hours.

BEST MAN-MADE LAKE: The imposing Aswan High Dam doubled Egypt's electrical output. It also created the 200m-deep **Lake Nasser** (p. 250), the world's largest artificial lake.

BEST REASON TO FINISH YOUR SPINACH: For the sweet tooth in you, dream your way into **al-'Abd** in Cairo (p. 106) for the creamiest whopping three scoops of ice cream you've ever had.

DIRECT LINES TO GOD: Learn the art of peaceful worship from the monks of **Wadi Natrun** (p. 152) or study the Qu'ran at **al-Azhar University** (p. 114), the world's oldest university and leading Islamic theological center. The more adventurous might want to look for the 11th commandment atop **Mt. Sinai** (p. 278).

SUGGESTED ITINERARIES

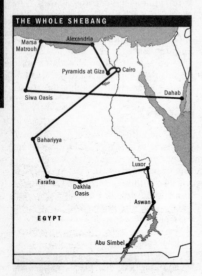

THE WHOLE SHEBANG

tling **Cairo** (p. 86), the largest city in the Middle East and Africa. The labyrinthine streets of the city are filled with beautiful mosques and churches, frenzied *souqs* where bargains abound, and a mile-a-minute nightlife unlike anything else in Egypt. The majestic pyramids at **Giza** (p. 135) are an easy daytrip from the city. The cosmopolitan calm of **Alexandria** (p. 156) to the north may seem a shock after Cairo, but you'll fall easily enough into the beachside city's evening-strolling, *sheesha*-smoking pace. Head west from Alexandria and discover the dazzling Mediterranean gem that is **Marsa Matrouh** (p. 175), a resort town rarely visited by tourists except as a base to the verdant **Siwa Oasis** (p. 179). Return to Cairo and catch a bus to the **Sinai Peninsula** (p. 270). Find your inner fish by diving and snorkeling through world-famous coral reefs, and kick back with the nomadic Bedouin near **Dahab** (p. 289).

1. THE WHOLE SHEBANG (4 WEEKS)

This is your chance to take part in a timeless adventure through the past and present. Hop on a train from Cairo to **Aswan** (p. 239), a city famous for its alabaster. You will love Aswan's unique Nubian flavor, which plays a large part in the surrounding villages and the comprehensive Nubian Museum, as well as its proximity to the ruins at Philae. Once you've had enough of Aswan, book a flight down to **Abu Simbel** (p. 251) to see some of the most awe-inspiring colossal remains in the world. Next on the ruins list is **Luxor** (p. 213), once the capital of ancient Egypt. Make sure to see the Valley of the Kings and the tomb of Queen Nefertari; though pricey, the latter attraction is Egypt's prized possession. Take a break from all the ruins by taking a leisurely *felucca* cruise up the Nile. Once you reach the town of Asyut, go west, pardner, and trek through the unforgettable desert oases. Start in the White Desert outside lush **Dakhla** (p. 194), then pause in **Farafra** (p. 193) before exploring the hot springs of **Bahariya** (p. 189). Emerge from the vast expanses of the western desert into bus-

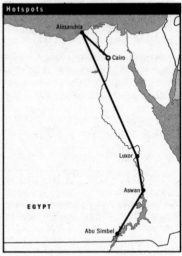

Hotspots

2. EGYPT FOR DUMMIES (1-2 WEEKS)

If you have limited time and want to see all those sites you've heard so much about, this itinerary's for you. Gobble up the highlights of **Cairo** (p. 86): the Egyptian Museum, bustling neighborhoods bursting with history and culture, unforgettable nightlife, and of course a quick daytrip to the pyramids at **Giza** (p. 135). Hop on a bus to the vibrant Mediterranean hub that is **Alexandria** (p. 156), boasting some of the best shopping and luxurious living around. Get yourself south to **Luxor** (p. 213)—if you have the time and feel self-indulgent, try floating up the Nile on a *felucca* (sounds like bazooka). Ogle the tombs and temples of ancient Thebes, then move on to more of the same at **Abu Simbel** (p. 251), where some of the most breath-taking ancient ruins in the world will leave you in awe.

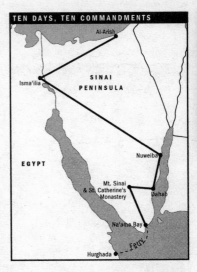

TEN DAYS, TEN COMMANDMENTS

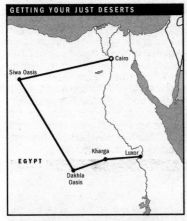

GETTING YOUR JUST DESERTS

3. GETTING YOUR JUST DESERTS (1-2 WEEKS)
Play "stranded in the desert" with plenty of bottled water at your side as you soak up the distinctive flavor of Egypt's many desert oases. Take a bus from Cairo to the picturesque **Siwa Oasis** (p. 179), where the people still cling to their unique Siwan culture and language. Get yourself from Siwa to **Dakhla Oasis** (p. 194), the diamond of Egypt's emerald necklace of oases. The oasis capital of Mut is a perfect springboard for exploration of the "pink oasis," so called because of the pink cliffs that surround the lush green farmland. Take a bus to **Kharga Oasis** (p. 199), the boomtown of the oasis circuit. From Kharga, take a few days to venture out to the astounding sites and quaint villages that surround the oasis capital. End your trip with a bang at the mind-boggling mecca of ancient relics that is **Luxor** (p. 213).

4. TEN DAYS, TEN COMMANDMENTS (BEST OF THE SINAI)
The Sinai peninsula is to the young and budget-conscious what the Riviera is to the rich and famous: a place to sleep, eat, swim, and sleep. Bus or fly from Cairo to **Hurghada** (p. 264) for divers' delights. Perched on the shore of the Red Sea, just inland from magnificent coral reefs, Hurghada is home to some of the best scuba diving and beaches around. But it gets even better in **Na'ama Bay** (p. 285), on the tip of the peninsula, where world-class dive centers and nightlife abound. To dry off, head inland to **St. Catherine's Monastery** (p. 280) at the foot of **Mt. Sinai** (p. 278). Bask in the serenity of this 1700-year-old monastery, then break a sweat climbing to the top of Mt. Sinai. Don't work yourself too hard; after the climb, head to **Dahab** (p. 289) for the quintessential Sinai experience. Great meals and happy hippies are a dime-a-dozen here. **Nuweiba** (p. 294) offers more of the same in a beautiful oasis setting. Rest and relax some more while admiring the engineering feat that is the Suez canal in luxurious, under-touristed **Isma'ilia** (p. 257). End your taxing trip with some quality beach time in beautiful **al-'Arish** (p. 273), yet undiscovered by Western beach-bums.

Mooooore Room.

Real American Airlines deals for students and faculty, online at StudentUniverse. Earn AAdvantage miles and enjoy *more room throughout Coach only on American*.

ESSENTIALS

FACTS FOR THE TRAVELER

ENTRANCE REQUIREMENTS.
Passport (p. 8): Required for all travelers.
Visa (p. 9): Required for citizens of non-Arab countries, except South Africa.
Letter of Invitation: Not required.
Inoculations (p. 19): Polio, hepatitis A, immune globulin (IG), typhoid, cholera.
Work Permit (p. 10): Required for all countries.
Driving Permit (p. 41): Required for all countries.

EMBASSIES & CONSULATES

EGYPTIAN CONSULAR SERVICES ABROAD

Australia: Embassy: 1 Darwin Ave., Yarralumla, Canberra, ACT 2600 (☎02 62 73 44 37; fax 62 73 42 79). **Consulates:** 124 Exhibition St., 9th fl., Melbourne, Victoria 3000 (☎03 96 54 86 34 or 96 54 88 69; fax 96 50 83 62). 112 Glen More Rd., Paddington, NSW 2021 (☎02 93 32 33 88; fax 93 32 32 88).

Canada: Embassy: 454 Laurier Ave. E., Ottawa, ON K1N 6R3 (☎613 234-4931; fax 234-6347). **Consulate:** 630 Rene-Levesque, Suite 2302, Montreal, PQ H3B 1S6 (☎514 861-6340; fax 861-6343).

Ireland: Embassy: 12 Clyde Rd., Dublin 4 (☎01 660 65 66 or 660 67 18; fax 668 37 45; embegypt@Indigo.ie).

UK: Embassy: 26 South St., London, W1Y 6DD (☎020 7499 3304; fax 7491 1542). **Consulate:** 2 Lowndes St., London, SW1 X9ET (☎020 7235 9777; fax 7235 5684).

US: Embassy: 3521 International Court NW, Washington, D.C. 20008 (☎202-895-5400; fax 244-4319). **Consulate:** 1110 2nd Ave., New York, NY 10022 (☎212-759-7120; fax 308-7643).

CONSULAR SERVICES IN EGYPT

Australian Embassy: World Trade Center, 11th fl., Corniche al-Nil, Bulaq, Cairo (☎02 575 04 44; fax 578 16 38; cairo.austremb@dfat.gov.au).

Canadian Embassy: 5 al-Sarayah al-Cobrah Sq., Garden City, Cairo (☎02 794 31 10; fax 796 35 48).

Irish Embassy: 3 Abu al-Feda St., Zamalek, Cairo (☎02 340 82 64; fax 341 28 63).

South African Embassy: 21/23 Giza St., 18th fl., Giza, Cairo (☎02 571 72 34; fax 571 72 41; saembcai@gega.net).

UK Embassy: 7 Ahmed Ragheb St., Garden City, Cairo (☎02 794 0850, fax 794 08 59). **Consulate:** 1 Nile St., Luxor (☎95 382 838).

US Embassy: 5 Latin America St., Garden City, Cairo (☎02 795 73 71, fax 797 32 00; www.usis.egnet.net).

TOURIST OFFICES

Wherever you find yourself in Egypt, tourist offices will not be hard to find. More than 30 offices are spread throughout cities like Alexandria, Port Said, Fayyum, Luxor, Aswan, and in the Sinai. In general, English is spoken well and maps are available. For information on history, religions, and tourist attractions in Egypt, see the Egyptian Tourist Ministry's thorough website, **www.egypttourism.org**. The central offices in **Cairo** can provide information for most cities (see **Tourist and Financial Services,** p. 96). Locations abroad include:

Canada: 1253 McGill College Ave., Suite 250, Montreal, PQ H3B 2Y5 (☎514-861-4420; fax 514-861-8071; eta@total.net).

South Africa: Regent Place Bldg. 1st fl., Mutual Gardens, Crabock Ave., Johannesburg, P.O. Box 3298 (☎11 880 96 02; fax 11 880 96 04).

UK: 170 Piccadilly, London W1V 9DD (☎171 493 52 82; fax 408 02 95).

US: 645 N. Michigan Ave., Suite 829, Chicago, IL 60611 (☎312-280-4666; fax 280-4788; egyptmdwst@aol.com). 8383 Wilshire Blvd., Suite 215, Beverly Hills, CA 90211 (☎323-653-8815; fax 323-653-8961; egypt@etala.com). 630 5th Ave., Suite 1706, New York, NY 10111 (☎212-332-2570; fax 212-956-6439; info@egypttourism.org).

DOCUMENTS AND FORMALITIES

PASSPORTS

REQUIREMENTS

Citizens of Australia, Canada, Ireland, New Zealand, South Africa, the UK, and the US need valid passports to enter Egypt and to re-enter their home countries. Egypt does not allow entrance if the holder's passport expires in under six months; returning home with an expired passport is illegal, and may result in a fine. Travelers with an Israeli stamp in their passports are allowed to enter the country.

PHOTOCOPIES

Be sure to photocopy the page of your passport with your photo, passport number, and other identifying information, as well as any visas, travel insurance policies, plane tickets, or traveler's check serial numbers. Carry one set of copies in a safe place, apart from the originals, and leave another set at home. Consulates also recommend that you carry an expired passport or an official copy of your birth certificate in a part of your baggage separate from other documents.

LOST PASSPORTS

If you lose your passport, immediately notify the local police and the nearest embassy or consulate of your home government. To expedite its replacement, you will need to know all information previously recorded and show ID and proof of citizenship. In some cases, a replacement may take weeks to process, and it may be valid only for a limited time. Any visas stamped in your old passport will be irretrievably lost. In an emergency, ask for immediate temporary traveling papers that will permit you to reenter your home country. Your passport is a public document belonging to your nation's government. You may have to surrender it to a foreign government official, but if you don't get it back in a reasonable amount of time, inform the nearest mission of your home country.

NEW PASSPORTS

Citizens of Australia, Canada, Ireland, New Zealand, the United Kingdom, and the United States can apply for a passport at the nearest post office, passport office, or court of law. Citizens of South Africa can apply for a passport at the nearest office of Foreign Affairs. Any new passport or renewal applications must be filed well in advance of the departure date, although most passport offices offer rush services for a very steep fee. Citizens living abroad who need a passport or renewal services should contact the nearest consular service of their home country:

Australia: Info ☎ 131 232; www.dfat.gov.au/passports. Apply for a passport at a post office, passport office, or overseas diplomatic mission. Passports AUS$132 (32-page), valid for 10 years. Children AUS$66 (32-page), valid for five years.

Canada: Canadian Passport Office, Department of Foreign Affairs and International Trade, Ottawa, ON K1A 0G3 (☎ 613-994-3500 or 800-567-6868; www.dfait-maeci.gc.ca/passport). Applications available online, at post offices, passport offices, and Canadian missions. Passports CDN$60; valid for 5 years (non-renewable).

Ireland: Pick up an application at a Garda station or post office, or request one from a passport office. Apply by mail to the Department of Foreign Affairs, Passport Office, Molesworth St., Dublin 2 (☎ 01 671 1633; fax 671 1092; www.irlgov.ie/iveagh), or the Passport Office, 1A South Mall, Cork (☎ 021 272 525). Passports IR£45; valid for 10 years. Under 18 or over 65 IR£10; valid for 3 years.

New Zealand: Send applications to the Passport Office, Department of International Affairs, P.O. Box 10526, Wellington, New Zealand (☎ 0800 22 50 50 or 4 474 81 00; fax 4 474 80 10; www.passports.govt.nz). Standard processing time is 10 working days. Passports NZ$80; valid for 10 years. Children NZ$40; valid for five years.

South Africa: Department of Home Affairs. Passports are issued only in Pretoria, but all applications must still be submitted or forwarded to the nearest South African consulate. Processing time is 3 months or more. Passports around SAR110; valid for 10 years. Under 16 around SAR85; valid for five years. For more information, http://home-affairs.pwv.gov.za.

UK: Info ☎ 0870 521 04 10; www.open.gov.uk/ukpass/ukpass.htm. Request application from passport office, main post office, travel agent, or online. Apply by mail, in person at a passport office, or complete the online form. Passports UK£28; valid for 10 years. Children UK£14.80; valid for five years.

US: Info ☎ 900-225-5674 (US$0.35 per min.); www.travel.state.gov/passport_services.html. Must apply in person at any federal or state courthouse, authorized post office, or Passport Agency (in most major cities); see "US Government, State Department" in the telephone book for addresses. Processing takes 6 weeks. New passports US$60; valid for 10 years. Under 16 US$40; valid for 5 years. May be renewed by mail or in person for US$40. Add US$35 for 2-week expedited service.

VISAS AND WORK PERMITS

VISAS. As of August 2001, citizens of Australia, Canada, Ireland, New Zealand, the UK, and the US need a visa—a stamp, sticker, or insert in your passport specifying the purpose of your travel and the permitted duration of your stay—in addition to a valid passport for entrance to Egypt. Citizens of **South Africa** do not need a visa to enter Egypt. It is better to get your visa in advance; however, in case of emergency, visas can be obtained at the airport in Cairo or at the Port of Alexandria, with some restrictions. Visas cost US$15 and can be easily obtained by submitting an application to the nearest Egyptian embassy or consulate. Applications may be printed from www.traveldocs.com/eg/visa.htm. Processing normally takes five business days, though sometimes may take significantly longer. These are good for one month, but renewable at police stations or at passport offices in major towns if you provide one photograph, E£12, and receipts showing that at least US$200 has been changed into Egyptian currency (reports vary on the strictness of this last rule). There is a 13-day grace period after the 30-day visa expires; if you still fail to renew your visa during this time, you will face (at least) a E£100 penalty upon departure. If your visa has been expired for more than a couple weeks, you will be treated to an all-expenses paid trip to the interrogation rooms of the Egyptian immigration office in **Cairo**. Visits to the Sinai from Israel or Jordan can be made on a two-week Sinai-only visa, available at borders. For more information, see **Border Crossings**, p. 38.

US and UK citizens residing in the US can take advantage of the **Center for International Business and Travel** (**CIBT**; ☎ 800-925-2428), one of several agencies which secures visas to almost all countries for a variable service charge. Be sure to double-check on entrance requirements at the nearest embassy or consulate for up-to-date information before departure. US citizens may also consult www.pueblo.gsa.gov/cic_text/travel/foreign/foreignentryreqs.html.

WORK AND STUDY VISAS. Admission as a visitor to Egypt does not include the right to work, which is authorized only by a special business visa. Entering Egypt to study also requires a special permit, which may be obtained after you have entered on a tourist visa. For more information, see **Alternatives to Tourism**, p. 47.

IDENTIFICATION

When you travel, carry two or more forms of identification on your person, including at least one photo ID; a passport combined with a driver's license or birth certificate is usually adequate. Many establishments, especially banks, may require several IDs in order to cash traveler's checks. Never carry all your forms of ID together; split them up in case of theft or loss. It is useful to bring extra passport-size photos to affix to the various IDs or passes you may acquire along the way.

For more information on the forms of identification listed below, contact the organization that provides the service, the **International Student Travel Confederation (ISTC)**, Herengracht 479, 1017 BS Amsterdam, Netherlands (☎ +31 20 421 28 00; fax 421 28 10; istcinfo@istc.org; www.istc.org).

TEACHER & STUDENT IDENTIFICATION. The **International Student Identity Card (ISIC)**, the most widely accepted form of student ID, provides discounts on sights, accommodations, food, and transport. The ISIC is preferable to an institution-specific card (such as a university ID) because it is more likely to be recognized and honored abroad. All cardholders have access to a 24hr. emergency helpline for medical, legal, and financial emergencies (in North America call 877-370-ISIC; elsewhere call US collect +1 715-345-0505, UK collect +44 20 8762 8110, or France collect +33 155 633 144), and holders of US-issued cards are also eligible for insurance benefits (see **Insurance**, p. 24). Many student travel agencies issue ISICs, including STA Travel in Australia and New Zealand; Travel CUTS in Canada; usit in the Republic of Ireland and Northern Ireland; SASTS in South Africa; Campus Travel and STA Travel in the UK; Council Travel (www.counciltravel.com/idcards/default.asp) and STA Travel in the US (see p. 32).

The card is valid from September of one year to December of the following year and costs US$22. Applicants must be degree-seeking students of a secondary or post-secondary school and must be of at least 12 years of age. Because of the proliferation of fake ISICs, some services (particularly airlines) require additional proof of student identity, such as a school ID or a letter attesting to your student status, signed by your registrar and stamped with your school seal. The **International Teacher Identity Card (ITIC)** offers the same insurance coverage as well as similar but limited discounts. The fee is AUS$13, UK£5, or US$22.

YOUTH IDENTIFICATION. The International Student Travel Confederation also issues a discount card to travelers who are 26 years old or under, but are not students. This one-year **International Youth Travel Card** (**IYTC**; formerly the **GO 25** Card) offers many of the same benefits as the ISIC. Most organizations that sell the ISIC also sell the IYTC (US$22).

CUSTOMS

Generally, items brought into Egypt are exempt from taxes. There is no formal declaration for personal items, but passengers may be asked to open their bags for customs officials when leaving the airport. When returning to your home country, you must declare valuable items purchased abroad and pay a duty on the value of those articles that exceeds the allowance established by the customs service. Keeping receipts for purchases made on your trip will help establish values when you return home. Make a list, including serial numbers, of carried valuables from home; if you register this list with customs before your departure and have an official stamp it, you will avoid import duty charges and ensure an easy passage upon your return. Goods and gifts purchased at **duty-free** shops abroad are not exempt from duty or sales tax at your point of return; you must declare these items as well. For more specific information on customs requirements, contact the customs information center in your country.

MONEY

CURRENCY AND EXCHANGE

The **Egyptian Pound** (E£), pronounced gin-EH in Arabic, is divided into 100 **piasters** (pt), also called *irsh* (plural oo-ROOSH). Coins come in denominations of 5pt (o), 10pt (١٠), and 20pt (٢٠); the last two look similar, so check the Arabic numbering. **Save exchange receipts** in case authorities ask for them when you are leaving the country. You are not allowed to carry more than E£1000 into or out of Egypt.

The currency chart below is based on August 2001 exchange rates between the Egpytian pound (E£) and Australian dollars (AUS$), Canadian dollars (CDN$), Irish pounds (IR£), New Zealand dollars (NZ$), South African Rand (ZAR), British pounds (UK£), US dollars (US$), European Union euros (EUR€), and Jordanian dinars (JD). Check the currency converter on the Let's Go Homepage (www.letsgo.com/Thumb) or large newspapers for the latest exchange rates.

EGYPTIAN POUND (E£)		
US$1 = E£4.00	E£1 = US$0.25
CDN$1 = E£2.60	E£1 = CDN$0.40
UK£1 = E£5.63	E£1 = UK£0.17
IR£1 = E£4.40	E£1 = IR£0.22
AUS$1 = E£2.00	E£1 = AUS$0.50
NZ$1 = E£1.60	E£1 = NZ$0.60
ZAR1 = E£0.50	E£1 = ZAR2.00
EUR€1 = E£3.50	E£1 = EUR€0.30
JD1 (JORDANIAN DINAR) = E£6.00	E£1 = JD0.17

As a rule, it's cheaper to convert money at your destination than at home. You should bring enough foreign currency, however, to last for the first 48hr. of a trip to avoid being penniless should you arrive after bank hours or on a holiday. Travelers from the US can get foreign currency from the comfort of home: **International Currency Express** (☎888-278-6628; www.foreignmoney.com) delivers Egyptian currency second-day (US$12) at competitive exchange rates.

When changing money abroad, try banks that have at most a 5% margin between their buy and sell prices. You lose money with every transaction, so convert large sums, but no more than you'll need.

If you use traveler's checks, carry some in small denominations (the equivalent of US$50 or less) for times when you are forced to exchange money at disadvantageous rates, but bring a range of denominations since charges may be levied per check cashed. Store your money in a variety of forms; ideally, you should carry some cash, traveler's checks, and an ATM and credit card. Travelers should also consider carrying Western currency such as US dollars (about US$50 worth). In the Middle East, foreign currency is often preferred to local, but avoid using Western money when you can. Throwing dollars around for preferential treatment may be offensive, and it can attract thieves. It also marks you as a stranger and can invite locals to jack up prices.

TRAVELER'S CHECKS

Traveler's checks are not widely accepted in Egypt, except at ritzy hotels. They are, however, exchangeable for cash at many banks or at any American Express office. **American Express** is the most widely recognized traveler's check in Egypt, and in some cities it is the only type accepted by businesses and banks. The most readily accepted checks are in US dollars or British pounds; checks in other currencies won't get you very far—if a place will exchange it, you'll get a terrible rate.

While traveling, leave a list of check numbers with someone at home. Also, keep check receipts and records of which checks you've cashed separate from the checks themselves. Never countersign checks until you're ready to cash them, and always bring your passport with you to do so. If your checks are lost or stolen, immediately contact a refund center (of the company that issued your checks) to be reimbursed; they may require a police report verifying the loss or theft. AmEx has offices in most major Egyptian cities (for a comprehensive list see **American Express** in the index), but if there is no office in the city you're in, you might have to wait to be reimbursed. Ask about toll-free refund hotlines and the location of refund centers when purchasing checks, and always carry emergency cash.

American Express: In Australia call 800 25 19 02; in New Zealand 0800 441 068; in the UK 0800 521 313; in the US and Canada 800-221-7282. Elsewhere call US collect +1 801-964-6665; www.aexp.com. Traveler's checks are available at 1-4% commission at AmEx offices and banks, commission-free to Gold Card holders and AAA members.

Thomas Cook MasterCard: In the US and Canada call 800-223-7373; in the UK call 0800 62 21 01; elsewhere call UK collect +44 1733 31 89 50. Checks available in 13 currencies at 2% commission. Thomas Cook offices cash checks commission-free.

Visa: In the US call 800-227-6811; in the UK call 0800 89 50 78; elsewhere call UK collect +44 20 7937 8091. Call for the location of their nearest office.

CREDIT CARDS

Where they are accepted, credit cards often offer superior exchange rates—up to 5% better than the retail rate used by banks and other currency exchange establishments. Credit cards may also offer services such as insurance or emergency help, and are sometimes required to reserve hotel rooms or rental cars. **MasterCard** and **Visa** are the most welcome; **American Express** cards work at some ATMs and at AmEx offices and major airports. Budget travelers will find that few of the establishments they frequent accept credit cards; aside from the occasional splurge, you will probably reserve use of your credit card for financial emergencies.

Credit cards can be useful for **cash advances,** which allow you to withdraw currency from associated banks and ATMs throughout Egypt instantly. Hefty transaction fees and beefy interest rates for cash advances make credit cards a more costly way of withdrawing cash than ATMs or traveler's checks. In an emergency, however, the transaction fee may prove worth the cost. To be eligible for an advance, you'll need to get a **Personal Identification Number (PIN)** from your credit card company (see **Cash Cards,** below). Be sure to check before you leave home about foreign transaction fees and interest rates.

CREDIT CARD COMPANIES. Visa (US ☎ 800-336-8472) and **MasterCard** (US ☎ 800-307-7309) are issued in cooperation with banks and other organizations. **American Express** (US ☎ 800-843-2273) has an annual fee of up to US$55. AmEx cardholders may cash personal checks at AmEx offices abroad, access an emergency medical and legal assistance hotline (24hr.; in North America call 800-554-2639, elsewhere call US collect +1 715-343-7977), and enjoy American Express Travel Service benefits (including plane, hotel, and car rental reservation changes; baggage loss and flight insurance; mailgram and international cable services; and held mail).

CASH CARDS (ATM CARDS)

Cash cards—popularly called ATM cards—are fairly widespread in Egypt. Depending on the system that your home bank uses, you can most likely access your personal bank account from abroad. ATMs get the same wholesale exchange rate as credit cards, but there is often a limit on the amount of money you can withdraw per day (around US$500), and imperfect computer networks sometimes fail. There is typically also a surcharge of US$1-5 per withdrawal. Be sure to memorize your PIN code in numeric form since machines elsewhere often don't have letters on their keys. Also, if your PIN is longer than four digits, ask your bank whether you need a new number.

The two major international money networks are **Cirrus** (US ☎ 800-424-7787) and **PLUS** (US ☎ 800-843-7587). To locate ATMs around the world, call the above numbers, or consult www.visa.com/pd/atm or www.mastercard.com/atm.

Thomas Cook Road Cash (US ☎ 877-762-3227; www.roadcash.com) is a Visa travel money system allowing you to access money from any ATM with the Visa logo, common in many Egyptian cities. You deposit an amount before you travel (minimum US$300 plus a US$15 administration fee), and you can withdraw up to that sum. The cards, which give you a favorable exchange rate for withdrawals, are especially useful if you plan to travel to many countries.

GETTING MONEY FROM HOME

AMERICAN EXPRESS. Cardholders can withdraw cash from their checking accounts at any major AmEx office and many representative offices (up to US$1000 every 21 days; no service charge; no interest). Withdrawals from any AmEx ATM are automatically debited from the cardholder's checking account or line of credit. Green card holders may withdraw up to US$1000 in any seven-day period (2% transaction fee; minimum US$2.50; maximum US$20). To enroll in Express Cash, cardmembers may call ☎ 800-227-4669 in the US; elsewhere call the US collect ☎ +1 336–668-5041. AmEx national numbers are the AmEx office numbers in each country. Consult the country-specific sections for those listings.

WESTERN UNION. Travelers from the US, Canada, and the UK can wire money abroad through Western Union's international money transfer services. In Egypt ☎ 02 355 50 23 to send and 02 594 07 41 to receive; in the US, call 800-325-6000; in Canada, ☎ 800-235-0000; in the UK, ☎ 0800 833 833. To wire money within the US using a credit card (D/MC/V), call 800-CALL-CASH (225-5227). The rates for sending cash are generally US$10-11 cheaper than with a credit card, and the money is usually available at the place you're sending it to within 1hr. To locate the nearest Western Union location, consult www.westernunion.com.

FEDERAL EXPRESS. Some people choose to send money abroad in cash via FedEx to avoid transmission fees and taxes. While FedEx is reasonably reliable, note that this method is illegal. In the US and Canada, FedEx can be reached by calling 800-463-3339; in the UK, 0800 12 38 00; in Ireland, 800 535 800; in Australia, 13 26 10; in New Zealand, 0800 733 339; and in South Africa, 011 923 8000.

US STATE DEPARTMENT (US CITIZENS ONLY). In dire emergencies, the US State Department forwards money within hours to the nearest consular office, which will then disburse it according to instructions for a US$15 fee. Contact the Overseas Citizens Service, American Citizens Services, Consular Affairs, Room 4811, US Department of State, Washington, D.C. 20520 (☎ 202-647-5225; nights, Sundays, and holidays 647-4000; http://travel.state.gov).

COSTS

The cost of your trip will vary considerably, depending on where you go, how you travel, and where you stay. The single biggest cost of your trip will probably be the round-trip (return) **airfare** to Cairo International Airport (see **Getting to Egypt: By Plane**, p. 32). Before you go, calculate a reasonable per-day **budget** that will meet your needs.

INFLATION SUCKS. Admission costs to major archaeological sights in Egypt are going up. Ticket prices for hot spots like the Pyramids at Giza and the temples at Luxor, set by Egyptian authorities, are scheduled to gradually increase up to 50% by October 2002. Sight listings in this book were researched in August 2001, and reflect prices current at that time. In planning your budget, allow for variations of 25-50% for sight admissions.

STAYING ON A BUDGET. Prices depend upon competition: in towns with heavier tourist traffic, you may spend as little as E£8 per night for clean, comfortable surroundings, while lower-quality accommodations in a town with few hotels and even fewer visitors can cost E£10-25. Prices also vary between high and low season. The high season in Alexandria is June to August, in the Nile Valley October to April. There is a hotel tax which varies by location, averaging around 20%. Unless otherwise noted, prices include tax but exclude breakfast. To give you a general idea, a bare-bones day in Cairo (sleeping in a hostel, buying food at a market) would cost about US$8 (E£30), while a slightly more comfortable day (sleeping in the occasional budget hotel, eating one meal a day at a restaurant, going out at night) would run US$24 (E£95). Don't forget to factor in emergency reserve funds (at least US$200) when planning how much money you'll need.

TIPS FOR SAVING MONEY. Considering that saving just a few dollars a day over the course of your trip might pay for days or weeks of additional travel, the art of penny-pinching is well worth learning. Do your laundry in the sink (unless you're explicitly prohibited from doing so). You can split **accommodations** costs (in hotels and some hostels) with trustworthy fellow travelers; multi-bed rooms almost always work out cheaper per person than singles. The same principle will also work for cutting down on the cost of restaurant meals. You can also buy food in **markets** instead of eating out. With that said, don't go overboard with your budget obsession. Though staying within your budget is important, don't do so at the expense of your sanity or health.

Carry cash with you, and have small bills on hand while visiting sights or wandering the streets of a town. Most officials like *bakhsheesh* (see below) and most stores, *service* drivers, and the like cannot (or will refuse to) make change. **No one** to whom you are giving *bakhsheesh* will give you change. Keep small bills separate from larger bills, so that people cannot point to your stash and demand more.

BUSINESS HOURS. On **Friday,** the Muslim day of communal prayer, most government offices, banks, and post offices are closed. Bank hours are ordinarily Sunday to Thursday 8:30am-2pm (although some banks in big cities are open daily), with money exchange available daily 8:30am-noon and 4-8pm. Foreign banks keep longer hours, usually Sunday to Thursday 8am-3pm. Other establishments, such as restaurants, remain open seven days a week. Store hours are ordinarily Saturday to Thursday 9am-9pm, with many also open Friday. Government offices are open 9am-2pm, though workers often leave before official closing times. Archaeological sites and other points of interest are typically open 8am-5pm, and will close an hour or two earlier in winter.

During the month-long holiday of **Ramadan** (running from early November to early December in 2002), some restaurants close entirely. Others open only after sundown, when the streets empty and everyone sits down to *iftar,* the breaking of the daily fast. Most shops close at about 3:30pm during Ramadan and re-open from 8pm to 11pm. Egyptians sit down for the second meal of Ramadan (*suhur,* pronounced su-HOOR) in the middle of the night, at around 3am.

THE ART OF THE DEAL

Bargaining in Egypt is a given: no price is set in stone, while vendors and drivers will automatically quote you a price that is several times too high; it's up to you to get them down to a reasonable rate. Successful merchants enjoy the haggling (just remember that the shopkeepers do this for a living and have the benefit of experience). With the following tips and some finesse, you might be able to impress even the most hardened hawkers:

1. Bargaining needn't be a fierce struggle laced with barbs. Quite the opposite: good-natured wrangling with a cheerful smiling face may prove your biggest weapon.

2. Use your poker face. The less your face betrays your interest in the item the better. If you touch an item to inspect it, the vendor will be sure to "encourage" you to name a price or make a purchase. Coming back again and again to admire a trinket is a good way of ensuring that you pay a ridiculously high price. Never get too enthusiastic about the object in question; point out flaws in workmanship and design. Be cool.

3. Know when to bargain. In most cases, it's quite clear when it's appropriate to bargain. Most private transportation fares and things for sale in outdoor markets are all fair game. Don't bargain on prepared or pre-packaged foods on the street or in restaurants. In some stores, signs will indicate whether "fixed prices" prevail. When in doubt, ask tactfully, "Is that your lowest price?" or whether discounts are given.

4. Never underestimate the power of peer pressure. Bargaining with more than one person at a time always leads to higher prices. Alternately, try having a friend discourage you from your purchase—if you seem to be reluctant, the merchant will want to drop the price to interest you again.

5. Know when to turn away. Feel free to refuse any vendor who bargains rudely, and don't hesitate to move on to another vendor if one will not be reasonable about the final price he offers. However, to start bargaining without an intention to buy is a major *faux pas*. Agreeing on a price and declining it is also poor form. Turn away slowly with a smile and "thank you" upon hearing a ridiculous price—the price may plummet.

6. Start low. Never feel guilty offering what seems to be a ridiculously low price. Your starting price should be no more than one-third to one-half the asking price.

TIPPING AND BARGAINING

Tipping and especially bargaining in Egypt is quite different and much more commonplace practice than you may be accustomed to; there are many unspoken rules to which tourists must adhere. Tipping (called *bakhsheesh* in Arabic) will be encouraged, and at times expected, almost everywhere you go. *Bakhsheesh* is your key to happiness in Egypt; it becomes most useful when used to procure special favors. The standard tip in a restaurant is usually included in the bill as a 10-15% service charge. Anything more on top of the bill is not expected. Taxi or *service* drivers do not expect tips. *Bakhsheesh* is also useful when sightseeing, as many places don't have tour guides. The alternative is to find a local to show you around for some cash. Egypt is *the* place to bargain; use your skills in the bazaars.

There are three kinds of *bakhsheesh*. The most common is similar to tipping—a small reward for a small service. The second kind of *bakhsheesh* is the giving of alms. There are beggars everywhere in Egypt who are willing to bestow rhetorical blessings in return for a little charity. There are also those who insist on opening a door before you can get to it or snatch your baggage from your hands and then demand *bakhsheesh;* don't feel obligated to give money in this situation. Another form of *bakhsheesh* is simply a bribe—a bad idea. Don't bribe government offiials.

TAXES

There is no sales tax in Egypt, nor is there a departure tax—though unscrupulous merchants and travel agents will sometimes try to collect them. Sometimes, extra money is already included in the bill. Other times, taxes may be added on to a bill at the last minute. It is best to ask all hotels (and even restaurants) about the taxes they may charge in advance.

ESSENTIALS

> **ARABIC FOR DUMMIES** A brief lesson in Egyptian Arabic:
> After *min fadlak* (please) and *shukran* (thank you), the most important word to know is
> **khawaga** (kha-WA-ga), because you are one. *Khawaga* loosely means "tourist," and
> implies "clueless, idiotic, and rich." Aside from those in hotels and restaurants, most
> prices are not posted, which means that *khawagas* may be charged more than any Egyp-
> tians. Avoid souvenir shops and kiosks near tourist attractions at all costs. When shop-
> ping, the key concept is **bargain,** and the key words are *ana mish khawaga* ("I am not
> an idiot"). Another word to remember is **bakhsheesh,** the art of tipping: baggage han-
> dlers, guards, and bathroom and parking attendants expect to receive a tip of 50pt-
> E£1. For a detailed breakdown of the different types of *bakhsheesh* and the attitudes
> toward it in Egypt, see **Tipping and Bargaining** (p. 15).

SAFETY AND SECURITY

PERSONAL SAFETY

The number one concern for most travelers planning a trip to the Middle East is
physical safety. While Egypt has remained mostly immune to recent disturbances
in the region, the most important thing to do is keep updated on current events.
Good sources for information are newspapers, television, and websites run by
your home country (www.state.gov for the US, www.dfait-maeci.gc.ca for Canada, www.fco.gov.uk for the UK, and www.dfat.gov.au for Australia).

BLENDING IN. To avoid unwanted attention, try to blend in as much as possible.
Tourists are particularly vulnerable to crime because they often carry large
amounts of cash and are not as street savvy as locals. Keep your money on your
person, preferably in a money belt concealed from sticky fingers. Respecting local
customs by dressing more conservatively may placate would-be hecklers. The
gawking camera-toter is a more obvious target than the low-profile traveler. This
is particularly tricky in the Middle East because the dress code and attitudes often
differ drastically from Western norms. Read over the **Customs and Etiquette** section
(p. 42) as well as **Women Travelers** (p. 42) before getting off the plane.

Familiarize yourself with your surroundings before setting out for the day; if you
must check a map on the street, duck into a cafe or shop. Carry yourself with confidence; an obviously bewildered bodybuilder is more likely to be harassed than a
stern and confident 98-pound weakling. If you are traveling alone, be sure that
someone at home knows your itinerary, and **never admit that you're traveling alone.**

> **FURTHER INFORMATION: SAFETY AND SECURITY**
> *Fielding's The World's Most Dangerous Places,* edited by Kathy Knoles (US$22),
> gives detailed descriptions of dangerous destinations around the world. *Don't
> Go!: 51 Reasons Not to Travel Abroad, But If You Must...176 Tactics for Coping
> With Discomforts, Distress and Danger,* by Hannah Blank (US$11), provides
> great tips for taking care of oneself on the road. For the lighter side of coping,
> see *Worst Case Scenario Survival Handbook: Travel* by Joshua Piven (US$15).
> For specific safety and travel warnings, consult your home country's department
> of State web page (see **Personal Safety,** above).

PROTECTING YOURSELF. Find out about unsafe areas from tourist offices, the
manager of your hotel or hostel, or a local whom you trust. You may want to
carry a **whistle** to scare off attackers or attract attention; also memorize emergency numbers for the city or area. Whenever possible, *Let's Go* warns of
unsafe neighborhoods and areas, but there are some good general tips to follow. When walking at night, stick to busy, well-lit streets and avoid dark alley-

ways. Do not attempt to cross through parks, parking lots or other large, deserted areas. The distribution of people can reveal a great deal about the relative safety of the area; look for children playing, women walking in the open, and other signs of an active community. Keep in mind that a district can change drastically from block to block. There are very few regions in the Egypt where violent crime against foreigners is a serious threat, and there are several simple precautions travelers can take (see **Protecting Your Valuables,** below). While many places have **pickpockets,** the most common thievery is simple **scamming.** Trust your instincts: if you feel you are getting something for nothing, be wary. On the other hand, if you feel that something is reasonably priced by Western standards, know that you may very well be paying too much for it. Labor and materials cost much less in Egypt than they do in the developed world, and prices should reflect that.

TRANSPORTATION. *Let's Go* does not recommend driving a **car** in crowded urban areas in Egypt. If you are using a car, learn local driving signals and wear a seatbelt. Children under 40 pounds should ride only in a specially designed carseat, available for a small fee from most car rental agencies. Study route maps before you hit the road, and if you plan on spending a lot of time on the road, you may want to bring a spare tire. If your car breaks down, wait for the police to assist you. For long drives in desolate areas, invest in a cell phone and jerry can to carry extra gasoline. Be sure to park your vehicle in a garage or well-traveled area. **Sleeping in your car** is one of the most dangerous—and often illegal—ways to get your rest. For info on the perils of **hitchhiking,** see p. 42.

SELF DEFENSE. There is no sure-fire way to avoid all the threatening situations you might encounter when you travel, but a good self-defense course will give you concrete ways to react to unwanted advances. **Impact, Prepare, and Model Mugging** can refer you to local self-defense courses in the US (☎ 800-345-5425). Visit the website at www.impactsafety.org/chapters for a list of nearby chapters. Workshops (2-3hr.) start at US$50; full courses run US$350-500.

FINANCIAL SECURITY

PROTECTING YOUR VALUABLES. Street crime is not common in Egypt, but there are a few steps you can take to minimize the financial risk associated with traveling. First, bring as little with you as possible. Leave expensive watches, jewelry, cameras, and electronic equipment (like your Discman) at home; chances are you'd break them, lose them, or get sick of lugging them around anyway. Second, buy a few combination padlocks to secure your belongings either in your pack—which you should never leave unattended—or in a hostel or train station locker. Third, carry as little cash as possible; instead, use traveler's checks and credit cards, keeping them in a concealed money belt (not a "fanny pack") along with your passport and ID cards. Fourth, keep a small cash reserve separate from your primary stash. This should entail about US$50 (US dollars are best) sewn into or stored in the depths of your pack, along with your traveler's check numbers and important photocopies.

CON ARTISTS AND PICKPOCKETS. Among the more financially threatening aspects of large cities are **con artists.** Especially in Egypt, where thriving tourism has existed for years and is often the only source of income, hustlers have finetuned the con into an art form. Possessing an innumerable range of ruses, they often work in groups, and children are the most effective. Beware of certain classics: sob stories that require money, rolls of bills "found" on the street, mustard spilled or saliva spit onto your shoulder to distract you while they snatch your bag. For some less obvious tricks of the trade, see **Scam Wars, Episode I,** p. 99.

Don't ever hand your passport to someone whose authority is questionable (ask to accompany them to a police station if they insist), and don't ever let your passport out of your sight. Similarly, don't let your bag out of sight; never trust a "station-porter" who offers to carry your bag or stow it in the baggage compartment or a "new friend" who wants to guard your bag while you buy a train ticket or use the restroom. Beware of **pickpockets** in crowds, especially on public transportation. Also, be alert in public telephone booths and around ATM machines. If you say your calling card number, do so very quietly; if you punch in a PIN, make sure no one can look over your shoulder.

ACCOMMODATIONS AND TRANSPORTATION. Never leave your belongings unattended; crime occurs in even the most demure-looking hostel or hotel. Bring your own **padlock** for hostel lockers, and don't ever store valuables in a locker.

Be particularly careful on **buses** and **trains;** horror stories abound about determined thieves who wait for travelers to fall asleep. Carry your backpack in front of you where you can see it. When traveling with others, sleep in alternate shifts. When alone, use good judgement in selecting a train compartment: never stay in an empty one and use a lock to secure your pack to the luggage rack. Try to sleep on top bunks with your luggage stored above you (if not in bed with you), and keep important documents and other valuables on your person.

If traveling by **car,** don't leave valuables (such as radios or luggage) in it while you are away. If your tape deck or radio is removable, hide it in the trunk or take it with you. If it isn't, at least conceal it. Similarly, hide baggage in the trunk, even though savvy thieves can tell if a car is heavily loaded by the way it sits on its tires.

TERRORISM

Travel in Egypt is safe except in **Middle Egypt** and the **Egyptian frontiers.** Since the summer of 1998, the US government has warned against traveling in Middle Egypt (especially near the governates of Minya, Asyut, Sohag, and just north of Qena), where terrorist attacks by extremist groups have occurred since the mid-1990s. Although there have been no attacks on foreign tourists since 1998, these areas should be considered slightly risky. Those wishing to visit areas near Egypt's frontiers should also be aware of the dangers of off-road travel and the possible threat of **landmines** (marked by barbed wire) from previous conflicts. The dangerous areas of Egypt's "frontier" include: the oases near the Libyan border (except for the Siwa Oasis); off-road areas in the Sinai; and sights south of Aswan near the Sudanese border (a disputed area known as the "Ha'ib Triangle"). Travel to the first two regions cannot be completed without permission from the Travel Permits Department of the Ministry of the Interior in Cairo. Those planning to visit Egypt for a long period of time should register with their home country's embassy.

DRUGS AND ALCOHOL

You are subject to the laws of the country in which you travel, not to those of your home country. **Illegal drugs** (including marijuana) are best avoided. Penalties for possession of, use of, or trafficking in illegal drugs are severe throughout the Middle East and include severe fines and jail time. Egypt may impose the **death penalty** on anyone convicted of smuggling or selling. Consulates can do no more than bring floral arrangements to prisoners, provide a list of attorneys, and inform family and friends. If you carry **prescription drugs** while you travel, it is vital to have a copy of the prescriptions themselves readily accessible at country borders.

Although there is an Islamic law forbidding **alcohol,** many people drink anyway. You may be asked to purchase alcohol for not-so-devout Muslims; unless they are underage, it is legal to do so if you are of age. The drinking age in **Egypt** is 21. It is strictly enforced in areas like Islamic Cairo, but may be quite lenient in other areas. In general, keep such practices to yourself and be careful. Since Islam prohibits the consumption of alcohol, it is improper to drink in the more traditional towns of Egypt, and anywhere at all during the holy month of Ramadan (see **Holidays and Festivals**, p. 310, for dates). In all areas, **public drunkenness** can jeopardize your safety and earn the disdain of locals.

HEALTH

Common sense is the simplest prescription for good health while traveling. Travelers complain most often about their feet and their gut, so take precautionary measures: drink lots of fluids to prevent dehydration and constipation, wear sturdy, broken-in shoes and clean socks, and use talcum powder to keep your feet dry.

BEFORE YOU GO

Preparation can help minimize the likelihood of contracting a disease and maximize the chances of receiving effective health care in the event of an emergency. For tips on packing a basic **first-aid kit** and other health essentials, see p. 24.

In your **passport,** write the names of any people you wish to be contacted in case of a medical emergency, and also list any allergies or medical conditions of which you would want doctors to be aware. Matching a prescription to a foreign equivalent is not always easy, safe, or possible. Carry up-to-date, legible prescriptions or a statement from your doctor stating the medication's trade name, manufacturer, chemical name, and dosage. While traveling, be sure to keep all medication with you in your carry-on, not your checked, luggage.

IMMUNIZATIONS AND PRECAUTIONS

Take a look at your **immunization** records before you go; if you are coming from a tropical area with a risk of yellow fever or cholera, such as Sub-Saharan Africa, you may be required to show certificates of up-to-date vaccinations to enter some countries. Travelers over two years old should be sure that the following **vaccines** are up to date: Measles, Mumps, and Rubella (MMR); Diptheria, Tetanus, and Pertussis (DTP or DTap); Polio (OPV); Haemophilus Influenza B (HbCV); and Hepatitis B (HBV). A booster of Tetanus-diptheria (Td) is recommended once every 10 years, and adults should consider an additional dose of Polio vaccine if they have not already had one during their adult years. Hepatitis A vaccine and/or Immune Globulin (IG) is recommended for travelers to Egypt, as well. If you will be spending more than four weeks in the Middle East, you should consider the typhoid vaccine. For more recommendations on immunizations and prophylaxis, consult the CDC (see p. 19) in the US or the equivalent in your home country, and be sure to check with a doctor for guidance.

USEFUL ORGANIZATIONS AND PUBLICATIONS

The US **Centers for Disease Control and Prevention (CDC; ☎** 877-FYI-TRIP; www.cdc.gov/travel) maintains an international fax information service and an international travelers hotline (☎ 404-332-4559). The CDC's comprehensive booklet *Health Information for International Travel,* an annual rundown of disease, immunization, and general health advice, is free online or US$25 via the Public Health Foundation (☎ 877-252-1200). Consult the appropriate government agency of your home country for consular information sheets on health, entry requirements, and other pertinent issues. For quick information on health and other travel warnings, call the **Overseas Citizens Services** (☎ 202-647-5225; after-hours 202-647-4000), contact a passport agency or an embassy or consulate abroad. US citizens can send a self-addressed, stamped envelope to the Overseas Citizens Services, Bureau of Consular Affairs, #4811, US Department of State, Washington, D.C. 20520. For information on medical evacuation services and travel insurance firms, see the US government's website at http://travel.state.gov/medical.html or the **British Foreign and Commonwealth Office** (www.fco.gov.uk).

FURTHER READING: USEFUL ORGANIZATIONS. For a detailed, country by-country overview of diseases, try the **International Travel Health Guide,** Stuart Rose, MD (Travel Medicine, $24.95). Information is also available at Travel Medicine's website (www.travmed.com). For general health information, contact the **American Red Cross,** which publishes *First-Aid and Safety Handbook* (US$5) available for purchase by calling or writing to the American Red Cross, 285 Columbus Ave., Boston, MA 02116-5114 (☎800-564-1234, M-F 8:30am-4:30pm). Useful **web pages** include CDC Travel Information's *Health Information for Travelers to the Middle East* (www.cdc.gov/travel/mideast.htm) and the United States State Department's *Tips for Travelers to the Middle East and North Africa* (travel.state.gov/tips_mid-east%26nafrica.html).

MEDICAL ASSISTANCE ON THE ROAD

Most Egyptian hospitals do not have the high quality of medical treatment found in North America, Europe, or Australia, and few doctors speak English. Luxury hotels may have resident doctors, and other hotels can usually get someone dependable in an emergency. You can also ask your embassy for a list of recommended physicians and pharmacists. Even big-city **pharmacies** do not carry Western brand-name drugs, but most Egyptian brands are equally effective and cheaper. Pharmacists in Egypt are authorized to write prescriptions (and are more lax about refills than most Western countries) and also able to give injections. There should be at least one pharmacy in each town, although finding a 24hr. store will prove difficult in small towns.

If you are concerned about being able to access medical support while traveling, there are special support services you may employ. The *MedPass* from **GlobalCare, Inc.,** 2001 Westside Pkwy., #120, Alpharetta, GA 30004, USA (☎800-860-1111; fax 770-475-0058; www.globalems.com), provides 24hr. international medical assistance, support, and medical evacuation resources. The **International Association for Medical Assistance to Travelers** (**IAMAT;** US ☎716-754-4883, Canada ☎416-652-0137, New Zealand ☎03 352 20 53; www.sentex.net/~iamat) has free membership, lists English-speaking doctors worldwide, and offers detailed info on immunization requirements and sanitation. If your regular **insurance** policy does not cover travel abroad, you may wish to purchase additional coverage (see p. 24).

Those with medical conditions (diabetes, allergies to antibiotics, epilepsy, heart conditions) may want to obtain a stainless-steel **Medic Alert** ID tag (first year US$35, annually thereafter US$20), which identifies the condition and gives a 24hr. collect-call number. Contact the Medic Alert Foundation, 2323 Colorado Ave, Turlock, CA 95382, USA (☎888-633-4298; www.medicalert.org).

ONCE IN EGYPT

Called **Pharaoh's Revenge** in Egypt, an upset stomach can spoil any vacation. A change in water and diet can result in diarrhea and nausea. Stay away from raw fruit and vegetables (many are injected with unsafe water to improve their color), and drink plenty of liquids, especially bottled water, which is inexpensive and readily available. This will help you avoid **amebic dysentery,** ingested with unclean food or drink. Though malaria is not common to Egypt, **rabies** is endemic. Stay away from stray dogs around monuments. Rabies can be contracted not only from a bite, but also from saliva of the sick animal contacting an open wound. It is fatal if not treated in time. Medical treatment or help is available wherever you see a **red crescent,** the symbol of medical services in Egypt (equivalent to the red cross seen elsewhere); it designates hospitals, ambulances, and other medical services.

EMERGENCIES Police: ☎122. **Ambulance:** ☎123. **Fire:** ☎124.

ENVIRONMENTAL HAZARDS

Heat exhaustion and dehydration: Heat exhaustion, characterized by dehydration and salt deficiency, can lead to fatigue, headaches, and wooziness. Avoid it by drinking plenty of fluids, eating salty foods, and avoiding dehydrating beverages (e.g. alcohol- and caffeine). Continuous heat stress can eventually lead to heatstroke, characterized by a rising temperature, severe headache, and cessation of sweating. Victims should be cooled off with wet towels and taken to a doctor.

Sunburn: If you're prone to sunburn, bring sunscreen with you (it's often more expensive and hard to find when traveling), and apply it liberally and often to avoid burns and risk of skin cancer. If you are planning on spending time near water, in the desert, or in the snow, you are at risk of getting burned, even through clouds. If you get sunburned, drink more fluids than usual and apply Calamine or an aloe-based lotion.

INSECT-BORNE DISEASES

Be aware of insects in wet or forested areas, while hiking, and especially while camping. Mosquitoes are most active from dusk to dawn. Use insect repellents, such as DEET. Wear long pants and long sleeves and buy a mosquito net. Wear shoes and socks, and tuck long pants into socks. Soak or spray your gear with per-methrin, which is licensed in the US for use on clothing. Natural repellents can be useful supplements: taking vitamin B-12 pills regularly can eventually make you smelly to insects, as can garlic pills.

Malaria: Transmitted by *Anopheles* mosquitoes that bite at night. Risk to travelers in Egypt is low. The incubation period varies from 6-8 days to as long as months. Early symptoms include fever, chills, aches, and fatigue, followed by high fever and sweating, sometimes with vomiting and diarrhea. See a doctor for any flu-like sickness that occurs after travel in a risk area. Left untreated, malaria can cause anemia, kidney failure, coma, and death. It is an especially serious threat to pregnant women. To reduce the risk of contracting malaria, use mosquito repellent, particularly in the evenings and when visiting forested areas, and take oral prophylactics, like **mefloquine** (sold under the name Lariam) or **doxycycline** (ask your doctor for a prescription). Be aware that these drugs can have serious side effects, including slowed heart rate and nightmares.

Dengue fever: An "urban viral infection" transmitted by *Aedes* mosquitoes, which bite during the day rather than at night. Risk to travelers in Egypt is low. Dengue has flu-like symptoms and is often indicated by a rash 3-4 days after the onset of fever. Symptoms for the 1st 2-4 days include chills, high fever, headaches, swollen lymph nodes, muscle aches, and in some instances, a pink rash on the face. If you experience these symptoms, see a doctor, drink plenty of liquids, and take fever-reducing medication such as acetaminophen (Tylenol). *Never take aspirin to treat dengue fever.*

Leishmaniasis, a parasite transmitted by sand flies, can occur in Egypt. Symptoms include fever, weakness, swelling of the spleen. There is a treatment, but no vaccine.

FOOD- AND WATER-BORNE DISEASES

Everything you eat should be cooked properly. In Egypt, where the risk of con-tracting traveler's diarrhea or forms of food poisoning is very high, never drink unbottled water that you have not treated. To purify your own water, bring it to a rolling boil or treat it with iodine tablets, available at any camping goods store. In risk areas, don't rinse your toothbrush under the faucet, and keep your mouth closed in the shower. Salads and uncooked vegetables are also full of untreated water. Other culprits are raw shellfish, unpasteurized milk, and sauces containing raw eggs. Insist on having any lukewarm meats or meat-sauces reheated and any-thing slightly undercooked put back on the grill. Peel all fruits and vegetables yourself, and beware of watermelon, which is often injected with impure water. Watch out for food, fruit, or juices from markets or street vendors that may have been washed in dirty water or fried in rancid cooking oil. Always wash hands before eating and after using the restroom to minimize the risk of Hepatitis A; bring a quick-drying antibacterial hand cleaner. Your bowels will thank you.

ESSENTIALS

■ **Traveler's diarrhea** results from drinking untreated water or eating uncooked foods, and can last 3 to 7 days. Symptoms include nausea, bloating, urgency, and malaise. If the nasties hit you, eat quick-energy, non-sugary foods with protein and carbohydrates to keep your strength up. Over-the-counter remedies may counteract the problems, but they can complicate serious infections. **Avoid anti-diarrheals** if you suspect that you are at risk for other diseases. If possible, avoid taking such medication unless strictly necessary (i.e., before embarking on an overnight bus trip), as how long your stools remain loose is an important diagnostic clue that remains unclear for those using anti-diarrheals. The most dangerous side effect of diarrhea is **dehydration.** The simplest and most effective anti-dehydration formula is 8oz. of (clean) water with ½ tsp. of sugar or honey and a pinch of salt. Soft drinks without caffeine or salted crackers are also good. Down several of these remedies a day, rest, and wait for the disease to run its course. If you develop a fever or if your symptoms don't go away after 4 or 5 days, consult a doctor. If children develop traveler's diarrhea, see a doctor, as treatment is different.

Dysentery results from a serious intestinal infection caused by certain bacteria. The most common type is bacillary dysentery, also called shigellosis. Symptoms include bloody diarrhea or bloody stools mixed with mucus, fever, and abdominal pain and tenderness. Bacillary dysentery generally only lasts a week, but it is highly contagious. Amoebic dysentery develops more slowly, with no fever or vomiting. However, it is a more serious disease, and may cause long-term damage if left untreated. A stool test can determine which kind you have, so you should seek medical help immediately. If you are traveling in high-risk regions (especially rural areas) obtain a prescription before you leave home.

Hepatitis A (distinct from B and C, see below) is a **high risk** in Egypt. Hep A is a viral infection of the liver acquired primarily through contaminated water, ice, shellfish, or unpeeled fruits and vegetables, and also from sexual contact. Symptoms include fatigue, fever, loss of appetite, nausea, dark urine, jaundice, vomiting, aches and pains, and light stools. Ask your doctor about the vaccine (Havrix or Vaqta), or ask to get an injection of immune globulin (IG).

Parasites such as microbes and tapeworms also often hide in unsafe water and food. For example, **Giardiasis** is acquired by drinking untreated water from streams or lakes all over the world. Symptoms of parasitic infections include swollen glands or lymph nodes, fever, rashes or itchiness, digestive problems, eye problems, anal itching and anemia. Boil your water, wear shoes, avoid bugs, and eat only cooked food.

Schistosomiasis (also called **bilharzia**) is a parasitic disease caused by a flatworm. The larvae mature inside freshwater snails and escape back into the water, where they can infect humans by penetrating unbroken skin. Avoid swimming in fresh water areas, particularly in Egypt, where the disease is most prevalent. If your skin is exposed to untreated water, rub it immediately and vigorously with a towel and/or rubbing alcohol. You may notice an itchy localized rash; later symptoms include fever, painful urination, diarrhea, loss of appetite, night sweats, and a hive-like rash on the body. Schistosomiasis can be treated with prescription drugs.

Typhoid fever is common in villages and rural areas in Egypt. While mostly transmitted through contaminated food and water, it may also be acquired by direct contact with another person. Symptoms include fever, headaches, fatigue, loss of appetite, constipation, and a rash on the abdomen or chest. Antibiotics can treat typhoid, but the CDC recommends vaccinations (70-90% effective) if you will be hiking, camping, or staying in small cities or rural areas.

OTHER INFECTIOUS DISEASES

Rabies is transmitted through the saliva of infected animals and is fatal if untreated. Avoid contact with animals, especially strays. If you are bitten, wash the wound thoroughly and seek immediate medical care. By the time symptoms appear (thirst and muscle spasms), the disease is in its terminal stage. A rabies vaccine, which consists of 3 shots given over a 21-day period, is available but is only semi-effective.

Hepatitis B is a viral infection of the liver transmitted through the transfer of bodily fluids, by sharing needles, or by having unprotected sex. Its incubation period varies, and symptoms may not show until many years after infection. The CDC recommends the Hep B vaccination for health-care workers, sexually active travelers, and anyone planning to seek medical treatment abroad. Vaccination consists of a three-shot series given over a period of time and should begin 6 months before traveling.

Hepatitis C is like Hep B, but transmission is different. Intravenous drug users, those with occupational exposure to blood, hemodialysis patients, and recipients of blood transfusions are at the highest risk, but the disease can also be spread through sex or sharing of items like razors and toothbrushes that may have traces of blood on them.

AIDS, HIV, AND STDS

Acquired Immune Deficiency Syndrome (AIDS) is a growing problem around the world. The World Health Organization estimates that at the end of 1999, there were almost 34 million people infected with the HIV virus, 27 million of whom were unaware of their HIV-positive status. The easiest mode of HIV transmission is through direct blood-to-blood contact with an HIV-positive person; never share intravenous drug, tattooing, or other needles. The most common mode of transmission is sexual intercourse. Health professionals recommend the use of latex condoms—take a supply with you before you depart for your trip. For detailed information on AIDS in Egypt, call the US Centers for Disease Control's 24hr. hotline at 800-342-2437, or contact the Joint United Nations Programme on HIV/AIDS (UNAIDS), 20, av. Appia, CH-1211 Geneva 27, Switzerland (☎41 22 791 36 66; fax 22 791 41 87). The Council on International Educational Exchange's pamphlet, Travel Safe: AIDS and International Travel, is posted on their website (www.ciee.org/Isp/safety/travelsafe.htm), along with links to other online and phone resources. Note that Egypt screens incoming travelers for AIDS and may deny entrance to those who test HIV-positive. This is particularly true for travelers who plan to spend an extended period of time in the country. Contact the nearest consulate of Egypt for up-to-date information.

Sexually transmitted diseases (STDs) such as gonorrhea, chlamydia, genital warts, syphilis, and herpes are easier to catch than HIV, and some can be just as deadly. **Hepatitis B** and **C** are also serious sexually-transmitted diseases (see **Other Infectious Diseases,** p. 22). Warning signs for STDs include: swelling, sores, bumps, or blisters on sex organs, rectum, or mouth; burning and pain during urination and bowel movements; itching around sex organs; swelling or redness in the throat; and flu-like symptoms with fever, chills, and aches. If these symptoms develop, see a doctor immediately. When having sex, condoms may protect you from certain STDs, but oral or even tactile contact can lead to transmission.

WOMEN'S HEALTH

Women traveling in unsanitary conditions are vulnerable to **urinary tract** and **bladder infections,** common and severely uncomfortable bacterial diseases that cause a burning sensation and painful and sometimes frequent urination. To try to avoid these infections, drink plenty of vitamin-C-rich juice and plenty of clean water, and urinate frequently, especially right after intercourse. See a doctor if symptoms persist: untreated, these infections can lead to kidney infections, sterility, and death.

Vaginal yeast infections are treatable but uncomfortable illnesses likely to flare up in hot and humid climates. Wearing loosely fitting trousers or a skirt and cotton underwear helps. Bring supplies from home if you are prone to infection, as they may be difficult to find on the road. In a pinch, some travelers use a natural alternative such as plain yogurt and lemon juice douche.

Tampons, pads, and **reliable contraceptive devices** are sometimes hard to find when traveling, so take supplies along. Women on the pill should bring enough to allow for possible loss or extended stays. In case you need to get more, bring a prescription, since forms of the pill vary a good deal.

Women considering an **abortion** abroad should contact the **International Planned Parenthood Federation (IPPF),** Regent's College, Inner Circle, Regent's Park, London NW1 4NS (☎0207 487 79 00; fax 74 87 79 50; www.ippf.org), for more information. Abortion is illegal in Egypt, but it is permitted on limited health grounds.

INSURANCE

Travel insurance generally covers four basic areas: medical/health problems, property loss, trip cancellation/interruption, and emergency evacuation. Although your regular insurance policies may well extend to travel-related accidents, you may consider purchasing travel insurance if the cost of potential trip cancellation/interruption or emergency medical evacuation is greater than you can absorb. Prices for travel insurance purchased separately generally run about US$50 per week for full coverage, while trip cancellation/interruption may be purchased separately at a rate of about US$5.50 per US$100 of coverage. **Medical insurance** (especially university policies) often covers costs incurred abroad; check with your provider. **US Medicare** does not cover foreign travel. **Canadians** are protected by their home province's health insurance plan for up to 90 days after leaving the country; check with the provincial Ministry of Health or Health Plan Headquarters for details. **Homeowners' insurance** (or your family's coverage) often covers theft during travel and loss of travel documents (passport, plane ticket, etc.) up to US$500. **ISIC** and **ITIC** provide basic insurance benefits, including US$100 per day of in-hospital sickness for a maximum of 60 days, US$3000 of accident-related medical reimbursement, and US$25,000 for emergency medical transport (see **Identification,** p. 10). Cardholders have access to a toll-free 24hr. helpline (run by the insurance provider TravelGuard) for medical, legal, and financial emergencies overseas (US and Canada ☎877-370-4742, elsewhere call US collect +1 715-345-0505). **American Express** (US ☎800-528-4800) grants most cardholders automatic car rental insurance (collision and theft, but not liability) and ground travel accident coverage of US$100,000 on flight purchases made with the card.

INSURANCE PROVIDERS. Council and **STA** (see p. 32) offer a range of plans that can supplement your basic coverage. Other private insurance providers in the **US and Canada** include: **Access America** (☎800-284-8300); **Berkely Group/Carefree Travel Insurance** (☎800-323-3149; www.berkely.com); **Globalcare Travel Insurance** (☎800-821-2488; www.globalcare-cocco.com); and **Travel Assistance International** (☎800-821-2828; www.worldwide-assistance.com). Providers in the **UK** include **Campus Travel** (☎01865 25 80 00) and **Columbus Travel Insurance** (☎020 7375 0011). In **Australia,** try **CIC Insurance** (☎9202 8000).

PACKING

Pack light. Lay out only what you absolutely need, then take half the clothes and twice the money. The less you have, the less you have to lose (or store, or carry on your back). Any extra space will be useful for any souvenirs or items you might pick up along the way. If you plan to do a lot of hiking, also see the section on **Camping & the Outdoors,** p. 27.

LUGGAGE. If you plan to cover most of your itinerary by foot, a sturdy **frame backpack** is indispensable. **Internal-frame packs** mold better to your back, keep a lower center of gravity, and can flex adequately on difficult hikes that require a lot of bending and maneuvering. **External-frame packs** are more comfortable for long hikes over even terrain (like city streets) since they keep the weight higher and distribute it more evenly. In addition to your main vessel, a small backpack, rucksack, or courier bag is useful as a **daypack** for sightseeing expeditions.

CLOTHING. No matter when you're traveling, it's always a good idea to bring a **warm jacket** or wool sweater, a **rain jacket** (Gore-Tex® is both waterproof and breathable), sturdy shoes or **hiking boots,** and **thick socks.** Flip-flops or waterproof sandals are must-haves for grubby hostel showers. Natural fibers are better than synthetics in the heat. Dark colors hide dirt, but light colors deflect sun. If you plan to visit any religious or cultural sites, remember that you'll need something besides tank tops and shorts to be respectful. In many areas—especially holy sites—both men and women should cover their knees and upper arms to avoid offending local rules of modesty. Leave jeans at home: bring along khakis or light cotton trousers. Well-cushioned sneakers are good for walking. Lace-up leather shoes with firm grips provide better support and social acceptability than athletic shoes. A double pair of socks—light absorbent cotton inside and thick wool outside—will cushion feet, keep them dry, and help prevent blisters. If you only want to bring one pair, the best all-around footwear are sneakers-*cum*-hiking boots. Talcum powder in your shoes and on your feet can prevent sores, and moleskin is great for blisters. You should also bring a comfortable pair of waterproof sandals, as sneakers get very hot and uncomfortable when the temperature skyrockets.

CONVERTERS & ADAPTERS. In Egypt, electricity is 220 volts AC, enough to fry any 110V North American appliance. 220/240V electrical appliances don't like 110V current, either. Americans and **Canadians** should buy an **adapter** (which changes the shape of the plug) and a **converter** (which changes the voltage; US$20). Don't make the mistake of using only an adapter (unless appliance instructions explicitly state otherwise). **New Zealanders** and **South Africans** (who both use 220V at home) as well as **Australians** (who use 240/250V) won't need a converter, but will need a set of adapters to use anything electrical.

TOILETRIES. Toothbrushes, towels, cold-water soap, talcum powder (to keep feet dry), deodorant, razors, tampons, and condoms are often available, but may be difficult to find, so bring extras along. **Contact lenses** and contact lens paraphernalia, on the other hand, are expensive and difficult to find, so bring enough extra pairs and solution for your entire trip. Also bring your glasses and a copy of your prescription in case you need emergency replacements. If you use heat-disinfection, either switch temporarily to a chemical disinfection system (check first to make sure it's safe with your brand of lenses), or buy a converter to 220/240V.

FIRST-AID KIT. For a basic first-aid kit, pack: bandages, pain reliever, antibiotic cream, a thermometer, a Swiss Army knife, tweezers, moleskin, decongestant, motion-sickness remedy, diarrhea or upset-stomach medication (Pepto Bismol or Imodium), an antihistamine, sunscreen, insect repellent, burn ointment, and a syringe for emergencies (get an explanatory letter from your doctor).

FILM. Film and developing in Egypt are expensive, so consider bringing along enough film for your entire trip and developing it at home. Less serious photographers may want to bring a disposable camera or two rather than an expensive permanent one. Despite disclaimers, airport security X-rays *can* fog film; buy a lead-lined pouch or ask security to hand-inspect it. Always pack film in your carry-on luggage, since higher-intensity X-rays are used on checked luggage.

OTHER USEFUL ITEMS. For safety purposes, you should bring a **money belt** and small **padlocks.** Basic **outdoors equipment** (plastic water bottle, compass, waterproof matches, pocketknife, sunglasses, sunscreen, hat) may also prove useful. **Quick repairs** of torn garments can be done on the road with a needle and thread; also consider bringing electrical tape for patching tears. Doing your **laundry** by hand (where it is allowed) is both cheaper and more convenient than doing it at a laundromat— bring detergent, a small rubber ball to stop up the sink, and string for a makeshift clothes line. **Other things** you're liable to forget: an umbrella; sealable **plastic bags** (for damp clothes, soap, food, shampoo, and other spillables); an **alarm clock;** safety pins; rubber bands; a flashlight; earplugs; garbage bags; and a small **calculator.**

ESSENTIALS

IMPORTANT DOCUMENTS. Don't forget your passport, traveler's checks, ATM and/or credit cards, and adequate ID (see p. 10). Also check that you have any of the following that might apply to you: a hosteling membership card (see p. 26); driver's license (see p. 41); and travel insurance forms.

ACCOMMODATIONS AND CAMPING

HOSTELS

Hostels are generally dorm-style accommodations in single-sex large rooms with bunk beds, although some hostels do offer private rooms for families and couples. The downside to traveling in the Middle East is that there aren't very many hostels. Those that do exist sometimes have kitchens and utensils for your use, bike or moped rentals, storage areas, and laundry services (but not facilities). In Egypt, a bed in a hostel will average around US$6-12. Some **colleges and universities** also open their residence halls to travelers when school is not in session, or even during term-time. These dorms are often close to student areas—good sources for information on things to do—and are usually very clean. Getting a room may take a couple of phone calls and require advanced planning, but rates tend to be low, and many offer free local calls. You can access university lodging worldwide by checking out *Campus Lodging Guide (19th Ed.)*, B&J Publications (US$15).

HOSTELLING INTERNATIONAL

Joining the youth hostel association in your own country (listed below) automatically grants you membership privileges in **Hostelling International (HI),** a federation of national hosteling associations. Many hostels in Egypt accept reservations via the **International Booking Network** (Australia ☎ 02 9261 1111; Canada ☎ 800-663-5777; England and Wales ☎ 1629 58 14 18; Northern Ireland ☎ 1232 32 47 33; Republic of Ireland ☎ 01 830 1766; NZ ☎ 03 379 9808; Scotland ☎ 8701 55 32 55; US ☎ 800-909-4776; www.hostelbooking.com). HI's umbrella organization's web page (www.iyhf.org), which lists the web addresses and phone numbers of all national associations, can be a great place to research hostelling in a specific region.

Some HI hostels also honor **guest memberships**—you'll get a blank card with space for six validation stamps. Each night you'll pay a nonmember supplement (one-sixth the membership fee) and earn one guest stamp; get six stamps, and you're a member. Most student travel agencies (see p. 32) sell HI cards, as do all of the national hosteling organizations listed below. All prices listed below are valid for **one-year memberships** unless otherwise noted.

Australian Youth Hostels Association (AYHA), Level 3, 10 Mallett St., Camperdown NSW 2050 (☎ 02 9565 1699; fax 9565 1325; www.yha.org.au). AUS$52, under 18 AUS$16.

Hostelling International-Canada (HI-C), 400-205 Catherine St., Ottawa, ON K2P 1C3 (☎ 800-663-5777 or 613-237-7884; fax 237-7868; info@hostellingintl.ca; www.hostellingintl.ca). CDN$35, under 18 free.

An Óige (Irish Youth Hostel Association), 61 Mountjoy St., Dublin 7 (☎ 01 830 4555; fax 830 5808; anoige@iol.ie; www.irelandyha.org). IR£10, under 18 IR£4.

Youth Hostels Association of New Zealand (YHANZ), P.O. Box 436, 193 Cashel St., 3rd Floor Union House, Christchurch 1 (☎ 03 379 9970; fax 365 4476; info@yha.org.nz; www.yha.org.nz). NZ$40, under 17 free.

Hostels Association of South Africa, 3rd fl. 73 St. George's St. Mall, P.O. Box 4402, Cape Town 8000 (☎ 021 424 2511; fax 424 4119; info@hisa.org.za; www.hisa.org.za). SAR45.

Scottish Youth Hostels Association (SYHA), 7 Glebe Crescent, Stirling FK8 2JA (☎01786 89 14 00; fax 89 13 33; www.syha.org.uk). UK£6.

Youth Hostels Association (England and Wales) Ltd., Trevelyan House, 8 St. Stephen's Hill, St. Albans, Hertfordshire AL1 2DY, UK (☎0870 870 8808; fax 01727 84 41 26; www.yha.org.uk). UK£12.50, under 18 UK£6.25, families UK£25.

Hostelling International Northern Ireland (HINI), 22-32 Donegall Rd., Belfast BT12 5JN, Northern Ireland (☎02890 31 54 35; fax 43 96 99; info@hini.org.uk; www.hini.org.uk). UK£10, under 18 UK£6.

Hostelling International-American Youth Hostels (HI-AYH), 733 15th St. NW, #840, Washington, D.C. 20005 (☎202-783-6161; fax 783-6171; hiayhserv@hiayh.org; www.hiayh.org). US$25, under 18 free.

HOTELS

Some Egyptian "hotels" charge as little as US$2 for the privilege of sleeping on the roof. With a little searching, a comfortable, safe (indoor) bed could be yours for US$10. Egypt also proudly offers **five-star** hotels. If the sun gets too hot or the post offices too crowded, stop by these air-conditioned palaces, relax in their chandelieried lobbies and send some letters home, or even treat yourself to some nice clothes from their self-contained malls. A service charge of 12% applies to hotels as well as a 5-7% sales tax. A further 1-4% tax is sometimes added to upper-end accommodations, so it is possible to find that a 23% tax has been added to the price of mid-range or top-end hotel rooms.

CAMPING AND THE OUTDOORS

Egypt's desert oases are unspoiled refuges from the modern world. Endless sand and sky make the oases perfect for exploration. Wade through date-laden palms and golden-white sand during the day, then savor Bedouin-style meals around a campfire and enjoy the tranquility of bedding down in a desert tent at night. Camping in Egypt is generally free or nearly free, but typically it will not be organized by a central camping agency, meaning that it is almost entirely unregulated. Always check with the local tourist agency, police, and other travelers before setting up camp to find out if there are certain places where camping is illegal. For information on hiking and camping, contact these companies for a free catalog: **Sierra Club Books,** 85 2nd St. 2nd fl., San Francisco, CA 94105-3441, USA (☎415-977-5500; www.sierraclub.org/books); **The Mountaineers Books,** 1001 SW Klickitat Way, #201, Seattle, WA 98134, USA (☎800-553-4453; www.mountaineersbooks.org).

DESERT SAFETY

The vast majority of life-threatening desert situations can be avoided by heeding the following advice: **stay hydrated.** Prepare yourself for an emergency, however, by always packing a first-aid kit, a reflector, a whistle, high energy food, and extra water for any hike. Dress in light, natural fibers. If spending the night in the desert, remember that temperatures drop dramatically at night.

Spring and fall are the most temperate season for hikes. In summer, most of the day will be in the shade with the Bedouin until the sun calms down, and in winter you'll freeze. The nights are frigid year-round. You may be able to rent blankets from the Bedouin, but don't count on it; bring a sweater and a warm sleeping bag.

Check **weather forecasts** and pay attention to the skies when hiking, since weather patterns can change suddenly. Whenever possible, let someone know when and where you are going hiking, either a friend, your hostel, a park ranger, or a local hiking organization. Do not attempt a hike beyond your ability—you may be endangering your life. See **Health,** p. 19, for information about outdoor ailments and basic medical concerns.

CAMPING AND HIKING EQUIPMENT

WHAT TO BUY...

Good camping equipment is both sturdy and light. Camping equipment is generally more expensive in Australia, New Zealand, and the UK than in North America.

Sleeping Bag: Most sleeping bags are rated by season ("summer" means 30-40°F at night; "four-season" or "winter" often means below 0°F). They are made either of **down** (warmer and lighter, but more expensive, and miserable when wet) or of **synthetic** material (heavier, more durable, and warmer when wet). Prices range US$80-210 for a summer synthetic to US$250-300 for a good down winter bag. **Sleeping bag pads** include foam pads (US$10-20), air mattresses (US$15-50), and Therm-A-Rest self-inflating pads (US$45-80). Bring a **stuff sack** to store your bag and keep it dry.

Tent: The best tents are free-standing (with their own frames and suspension systems), set up quickly, and only require staking in high winds. Low-profile dome tents are the best all-around. Good 2-person tents start at US$90, 4-person at US$300. Seal the seams of your tent with waterproofer, and make sure it has a rain fly. Other tent accessories include a **battery-operated lantern,** a **plastic groundcloth,** and a **nylon tarp.**

Backpack: Internal-frame packs mold better to your back, keep a lower center of gravity, and flex adequately to allow you to hike difficult trails. **External-frame packs** are more comfortable for long hikes over even terrain, as they keep weight higher and distribute it more evenly. Make sure your pack has a strong, padded hip-belt to transfer weight to your legs. Any serious backpacking requires a pack of at least 4000 in^3 (16,000cc), plus 500 in^3 for sleeping bags in internal-frame packs. Sturdy backpacks cost anywhere from US$125-420—this is one area in which it doesn't pay to economize. Fill up any pack with something heavy and walk around the store with it to get a sense of how it distributes weight before buying it. Either buy a **waterproof backpack cover,** or store all of your belongings in plastic bags inside your pack.

Boots: Be sure to wear hiking boots with good **ankle support.** They should fit snugly and comfortably over 1-2 pairs of wool socks and thin liner socks. Break in boots over several weeks first in order to spare yourself painful and debilitating blisters.

Other Necessities: Synthetic layers, like those made of polypropylene, and a **pile jacket** will keep you warm even when wet. A **"space blanket"** will help you to retain your body heat and doubles as a groundcloth (US$5-15). Plastic **water bottles** are virtually shatter- and leak-proof. Bring **water-purification tablets** for when you can't boil water. Although most campgrounds provide campfire sites, you may want to bring a small **metal grate** or **grill** of your own. For those places that forbid fires or the gathering of firewood, you'll need a **camp stove** (the classic Coleman starts at US$40) and a propane-filled **fuel bottle** to operate it. Also don't forget a **first-aid kit, pocketknife, insect repellent, calamine lotion,** and **waterproof matches** or a **lighter.**

...AND WHERE TO BUY IT

The mail-order/online companies listed below offer lower prices than many retail stores, but a visit to a local camping or outdoors store will give you a good sense of the look and weight of certain items.

Campmor, 28 Parkway, P.O. Box 700, Upper Saddle River, NJ 07458 (US ☎888-226-7667; elsewhere US ☎+1 201-825-8300; www.campmor.com).

Discount Camping, 880 Main North Rd., Pooraka, South Australia 5095, Australia (☎08 8262 3399; www.discountcamping.com.au).

Eastern Mountain Sports (EMS), 327 Jaffrey Rd., Peterborough, NH 03458, USA (☎888-463-6367 or 603-924-7231; www.shopems.com)

L.L. Bean, Freeport, ME 04033 (US and Canada ☎800-441-5713; UK ☎0800 891 297; elsewhere, call US +1 207-552-3028; www.llbean.com).

Mountain Designs, P.O. Box 1472, Fortitude Valley, Queensland 4006, Australia (☎07 3252 8894; www.mountaindesign.com.au).

Recreational Equipment, Inc. (REI), Sumner, WA 98352, USA (☎800 426-4840 or 253-891-2500; www.rei.com).

YHA Adventure Shop, 14 Southampton St., London, WC2E 7HA, UK (☎020 7836 8541). The main branch of one of Britain's largest outdoor equipment suppliers.

 ENVIRONMENTALLY RESPONSIBLE TOURISM. The idea behind responsible tourism is to leave no trace of human presence behind. A campstove is the safer (and more efficient) way to cook than using vegetation, but if you must make a fire, keep it small and use only dead branches or brush rather than cutting vegetation. Make sure your campsite is at least 150 ft. (50m) from water supplies or bodies of water. If there are no toilet facilities, bury human waste (but not paper) at least four inches (10cm) deep and above the high-water line, and 150 ft. or more from any water supplies and campsites. Always pack your trash in a plastic bag and carry it with you until you reach the next trash receptacle. For more information on these issues, contact one of the organizations listed below.

Earthwatch, 3 Clock Tower Place #100, Box 75, Maynard, MA 01754, USA (☎800-776-0188 or 978-461-0081; info@earthwatch.org; www.earthwatch.org).

Ecotourism Society, P.O. Box 668, Burlington, VT 05402, USA (☎802-651-9818; ecomail@ecotourism.org; www.ecotourism.org).

National Audobon Society, Nature Odysseys, 700 Broadway, New York, NY 10003 (☎212-979-3066; travel@audobon.org; www.audobon.org).

Tourism Concern, Stapleton House, 277-281 Holloway Rd., London N7 8HN, UK (☎020 7753 3330; www.tourismconcern.org.uk).

KEEPING IN TOUCH

BY MAIL

SENDING MAIL HOME FROM EGYPT

Standard **airmail** is the best way to send mail home from Egypt; be sure to write "**par avion**" in clear letters on the front. Airmailing postcards and letters weighing under 15g costs E£1.25 and normally takes 4-5 days to get to the UK and Ireland and 7-10 days to get to North America, Australia, or New Zealand, although delivery time can vary drastically for no apparent reason. If using post boxes, **blue** is for international airmail, while red and green boxes are for mail to other parts of Egypt. If your package is not time sensitive, **surface mail** is by far the cheapest alternative to send mail. It takes one to three months to cross the Atlantic and two to four to cross the Pacific—good for items you won't need to see for a while, such as souvenirs or books you've acquired along the way that are weighing down your pack. To speedily send packages by **Federal Express,** contact their office at 1079 Corniche al-Nil, Garden City, Cairo (☎02 357 13 00 or 355 10 63; fax 357 13 18).

SENDING MAIL TO EGYPT

Airmail letters under 1 oz. between North America and Egypt take four to seven days and typically cost US$1.55, or CDN$1.05. Allow at least seven business days from Australia (postage AUS$1.50 up to 50 grams) and 4-10 days from the UK (£0.65 up to 20g). Mark envelopes "airmail" or "par avion," or your letter or postcard may never arrive. If airmail is too slow, **Federal Express, DHL,** or **EMS (Express**

Mail Service) can deliver to Egypt quickly but will charge exorbitantly for their services. For example, FedEx (Australia ☎ 13 26 10; US and Canada ☎ 800-247-4747; New Zealand ☎ 0800 73 33 39; UK ☎ 0800 12 38 00) can get a letter from New York to Cairo in two days for US$32, and from London to Cairo in two days for UK£31.

RECEIVING MAIL IN EGYPT

There are several ways to arrange pick-up of letters sent to you by friends and relatives while you are abroad. Mail can be sent via **Poste Restante** to almost any city or town in Egypt with a post office, and it is usually quite reliable. Address *Poste Restante* letters like so:

Abraham ZAAFRANI

Poste Restante

City, EGYPT (مصر)

The mail will go to a special desk in the central post office, unless you specify a post office by street address. It's best to use the largest post office, since mail may be sent there regardless. It is usually safer and quicker, though more expensive, to send mail express or registered. When picking up your mail, bring a photo ID, preferably a passport. There is generally no surcharge; if there is, it should not exceed the cost of domestic postage. If the clerks insists that there is nothing for you, have them check under your first name or under "Mr." or "Ms.". *Let's Go* lists post offices in the **Practical Information** section for each city and most towns.

American Express travel offices throughout the world offer a free **Client Letter Service** (mail held up to 30 days and forwarded upon request) for cardholders who contact them in advance; address letters in the same way shown above. Many offices will offer these services to non-cardholders (especially AmEx Travelers Cheque holders), but call ahead to make sure. *Let's Go* lists AmEx office locations for most major Egyptian cities in **Practical Information** sections; for a comprehensive list see **American Express** in the index.

BY TELEPHONE

CALLING BETWEEN EGYPT AND HOME

A **calling card** is probably your cheapest bet. Calls are billed collect or to your account. You can frequently call collect without even possessing a company's calling card just by calling their access number and following the instructions. **To obtain a calling card** from your national telecommunications service before leaving home, contact the appropriate company listed below (using the numbers in the first column). To **call home with a calling card,** contact the operator for your service provider in Egypt by dialing the appropriate toll-free access number (listed below in the second column).

COMPANY	TO OBTAIN A CARD, DIAL	TO CALL FROM EGYPT, DIAL
AT&T (US)	888-222-0300	02 510 02 00
British Telecom Direct	800 34 51 44	02 365 36 44
Canada Direct	800-668-6878	02 365 36 43
Ireland Direct	800 40 00 00	N/A
MCI (US)	800 444-3333	02 355 57 70
New Zealand Direct	0800 00 00 00	02 365 37 64
Sprint (US)	800 877-4646	02 356 477
Telkom South Africa	10 219	N/A
Telstra Australia	13 22 00	N/A

You can usually make **direct international calls** from coin-operated pay phones in Egypt, but if you aren't using a calling card, you may need to drop your coins as quickly as your words. **Local calls** cost 10pt per 3min. from public phones, 50pt per 3min. from private phones in establishments.

Look for pay phones in public areas, especially train stations, as private pay phones are often more expensive. In-room hotel calls invariably include an arbitrary and sky-high surcharge than can run as much as US$0.75 per minute, or a flat fee of around US$10. If you do dial direct, first insert the appropriate amount of money or a prepaid phone card, then dial the international access code for the target country, and then dial the country code and number of your home. Prepaid phone cards (see below) and occasionally major credit cards can be used for direct international calls, but they are still less cost-efficient. (See the box on Placing International Calls (p. 31) for directions on how to place a direct international call.)

Placing a **collect call** through an international operator is even more expensive, but may be necessary in case of emergency. You can place collect calls through the service providers listed above even if you don't have one of their phone cards.

PLACING INTERNATIONAL CALLS. To call Egypt from home or to call home from Egypt, dial:

1. The **international dialing prefix.** To dial out of **Australia,** dial 0011; **Canada** or the **US,** 011; the **Republic of Ireland, New Zealand,** or the **UK,** 00; **South Africa,** 09; out of **Egypt,** 00.
2. The **country code** of the country you want to call. To call **Australia,** dial 61; **Canada** or the **US,** 1; the **Republic of Ireland,** 353; **New Zealand,** 64; **South Africa,** 27; the **UK,** 44; **Egypt,** 20.
3. The **city/area code.** Let's Go lists the city/area codes for cities and towns in Egypt opposite the city or town name, next to a ☎. If the first digit is a zero (e.g., 02 for Cairo), omit the zero when calling from abroad.
4. The **local number.**

CALLING WITHIN EGYPT

In addition to coin-operated public phones, you can also buy **prepaid phone cards,** which carry a certain amount of phone time depending on the card's denomination. Phone rates tend to be highest in the morning, lower in the evening, and lowest late at night.

TIME DIFFERENCES

Egypt is 2hr. ahead of Greenwich Mean Time (GMT). It is also 7hr. ahead of New York; 10hr. ahead of Vancouver & San Francisco; 1hr. ahead of Johannesburg; 7hr. behind Sydney; and 9hr. behind Auckland (NZ). Egypt observes Daylight Saving Time in summer.

2AM	5AM	10AM	11AM	NOON	7PM	9PM
Los Angeles Seattle San Francisco Vancouver	Boston New York Ottawa Toronto	London (GMT)	Johannesburg	All Egypt	Canberra Melbourne Sydney	Auckland

BY EMAIL AND INTERNET

In Egypt, there should be no trouble finding Internet access. **Internet cafes** and the occasional free Internet terminal at a public library or university are listed in the **Practical Information** sections of major cities. For lists of additional cybercafes in Egypt, check out the **Cybercafe Search Engine** (www.cybercaptive.com). Although the site is updated daily, don't despair if it doesn't list cafes in your target town: they are cropping up so quickly that no index is current. One money-saving strategy is to befriend college students and ask if you can use their campus terminals. Though in some places it's possible to forge a remote link with your home server, in most cases this is a much slower (and thus more expensive) option than taking advantage of free **web-based email accounts** (e.g., www.hotmail.com, www.yahoo.com, www.operamail.com). One hour usually costs between US$2 and US$5. Travelers with laptops can call an Internet service provider via a **modem.** Long-distance phone cards specifically intended for such calls can defray normally high phone charges; check with your long-distance phone provider to see if it offers this option.

GETTING TO EGYPT

BY PLANE

When it comes to airfare, a little effort can save you a bundle. If your plans are flexible enough to deal with the restrictions, courier fares are the cheapest. Tickets bought from consolidators and standby seating are also good deals, but last-minute specials, airfare wars, and charter flights often beat these fares. The key is to hunt around, to be flexible, and to ask persistently about discounts. Students, seniors, and those under 26 should never pay full price for a ticket.

AIRFARES

Airfares to Egypt peak between mid-June and late September; holidays are also expensive. The cheapest times to travel are early November to mid-December and early January. Midweek (M-Th morning) round-trip flights run US$40-50 cheaper than weekend flights, but they are generally more crowded and less likely to permit frequent-flier upgrades. Traveling with an "open-return" ticket can be pricier than fixing a return date when buying the ticket. Round-trip flights are by far the cheapest; "open-jaw" (arriving in and departing from different cities, e.g. New York-Cairo and Tel Aviv-New York) tickets tend to be pricier. Patching one-way flights together is the most expensive way to travel. Flying from hub to hub (e.g. London to Cairo) will win a more competitive fare than flying to or from smaller cities. While some European airlines fly to Alexandria, it is not considered a hub and tends to be more expensive. The cheapest gateway cities in the Middle East are typically Cairo, Istanbul and Tel Aviv.

If Egypt is only one stop on a more extensive globe-hop, consider a round-the-world (RTW) ticket. Tickets usually include at least five stops and are valid for about a year; prices range US$1200-5000. Try **Northwest Airlines/KLM** (US ☎ 800-447-4747; www.nwa.com) or **Star Alliance,** a consortium of 22 airlines including United Airlines (US ☎ 800-241-6522; www.star-alliance.com).

Fares will vary drastically from month to month. A round-trip student fare from the US or Canadian east coast will range US$700-1200; from the UK, UK£345-600; from Australia AUS$2600-3300; from South Africa ZAR7000-12,000.

Confirm international flights by phone within 72hr. of departure. Most airlines require that passengers arrive at the airport at least 2hr. before departure. One carry-on item and two checked bags is the norm for non-courier flights.

BUDGET AND STUDENT TRAVEL AGENCIES

While knowledgeable agents specializing in flights to the Middle East can make your life easy and help you save, they may not spend the time to find you the lowest possible fare—they get paid on commission. Students and under-27ers holding **ISIC and IYTC cards,** respectively, qualify for big discounts from student travel agencies. Most flights from budget agencies are on major airlines, but in peak season some may sell seats on less reliable chartered aircraft.

usit world (www.usitworld.com). Over 50 **usit campus** branches in the UK (www.usitcampus.co.uk), including 52 Grosvenor Gardens, **London** SW1W 0AG (☎0870 240 10 10); **Manchester** (☎0161 273 18 80); and **Edinburgh** (☎0131 668 33 03). Nearly 20 **usit NOW** offices in Ireland, including 19-21 Aston Quay, O'Connell Bridge, **Dublin** 2 (☎01 602 16 00; www.usitnow.ie), and **Belfast** (☎02890 32 71 11; www.usit-now.com). Offices also in Athens, Auckland, Brussels, Frankfurt, Johannesburg, Lisbon, Luxembourg, Madrid, Paris, Sofia, and Warsaw.

Council Travel (www.counciltravel.com). Countless US offices, including branches in Atlanta, Boston, Chicago, L.A., New York, San Francisco, Seattle, and Washington, D.C. Check the website or call 800-2-COUNCIL (226-8624) for the office nearest you.

CTS Travel, 44 Goodge St., **London** W1T 2AD (☎020 7636 0031; fax 020 7637 5328; ctsinfo@ctstravel.co.uk).

STA Travel, 7890 S. Hardy Dr., Ste. 110, Tempe AZ 85284 (24hr. reservations and info ☎800-777-0112; fax 480-592-0876; www.statravel.com). A student and youth travel organization with countless offices worldwide (check their website for a listing of all their offices), including US offices in Boston, Chicago, L.A., New York, San Francisco, Seattle, and Washington, D.C. Ticket booking, travel insurance, railpasses, and more. In the UK, walk-in office 11 Goodge St., **London** W1T 2PF (☎087 0160 6070). In New Zealand, 10 High St., **Auckland** (☎09 309 0458). In Australia, 366 Lygon St., **Melbourne** Vic 3053 (☎03 9349 4344).

StudentUniverse, 545 5th Ave., Suite 640, New York, NY 10017 (toll-free customer service ☎800-272-9676, outside the US 212-986-8420; help@studentuniverse.com; www.studentuniverse.com), is an online student travel service offering discount ticket booking, travel insurance, railpasses, destination guides, and much more. Customer service line open M-F 9am-8pm and Sa noon-5pm EST.

Travel CUTS (Canadian Universities Travel Services Limited), 187 College St., **Toronto,** ON M5T 1P7 (☎416-979-2406; fax 979-8167; www.travelcuts.com). 60 offices across Canada. Also in the UK, 295-A Regent St., **London** W1R 7YA (☎0207-255-1944).

FLIGHT PLANNING ON THE INTERNET. The Web is a great place to look for travel bargains—it's fast, it's convenient, and you can spend as long as you like exploring options without driving your travel agent insane.

Many airline sites offer special last-minute deals on the Web. Try **Cape to Cairo** (www.capecairo.com), **Cheap Tickets** (www.cheaptickets.com), **NOW Voyager** (www.nowvoyagertravel.com), **Travac** (www.travac.com), or **Travel Avenue** (www.travelavenue.com) for low fares to the Middle East. Other sites do the legwork and compile the deals for you—try www.bestfares.com, www.onetravel.com, www.lowestfare.com, and www.travelzoo.com.

STA (www.sta-travel.com), **Council Travel** (www.counciltravel.com), and ▨ **StudentUniverse** (www.studentuniverse.com) provide quotes on student tickets, while **Expedia** (msn.expedia.com) and **Travelocity** (www.travelocity.com) offer full travel services. **Priceline** (www.priceline.com) allows you to specify a price, and obligates you to buy any ticket that meets or beats it; be prepared for antisocial hours and odd routes. **Skyauction** (www.skyauction.com) allows you to bid on both last-minute and advance-purchase tickets.

Just one last note—to protect yourself, make sure that the site uses a secure server before handing over any credit card details. Happy hunting!

The commercial airlines' lowest regular offer is the **APEX** (Advance Purchase Excursion) fare, which provides confirmed reservations and allows "open-jaw" tickets. Generally, reservations must be made seven to 21 days ahead of departure, with seven- to 14-day minimum-stay and up to 90-day maximum-stay restrictions. These fares carry hefty cancellation and change penalties (fees rise in summer). Book peak-season APEX fares early; by May you will have a hard time getting your desired departure date. Use **Microsoft Expedia** (www.expedia.com) or **Travelocity** (www.travelocity.com) to get an idea of the lowest published fares, then use the resources outlined here to try and beat those fares. Low-season fares should be appreciably cheaper than the high-season (mid-June to Sept.) ones listed here. However, the fares listed here are also from "discount" airlines, which have fewer departure points and are less convenient than standard commercial centers like American and United, but probably offer better deals, unless you manage to grab a special promotion or airfare war ticket from one of the big boys.

TRAVELING FROM NORTH AMERICA

Lufthansa (☎ 800-399-5838; www.lufthansa-usa.com) has a wide variety of routes covering all major hubs of the Middle East, including Cairo and Alexandria, via Frankfurt.

Air France (☎ 800-237-2747; www.airfrance.com) serves Cairo mainly through Paris.

TWA (☎ 800-892-4141; www.twa.com) flies to Cairo.

EgyptAir (☎ 800-334-6787; www.egyptair.com.eg) has the most routes within the country, and also serves major cities like New York and Los Angeles.

Royal Jordanian (☎ 800-755-6732; www.rja.com.jo) flies to Cairo and many other, smaller airports.

TRAVELING FROM THE UK AND IRELAND

British Airways (☎ 845 773 33 77; www.british-airways.com) has daily flights to Cairo. Virtually all flights originate from London.

Austrian Airways (☎ 171 434 73 80; www.aua.com) connects to Cairo via Vienna.

EgyptAir (☎ 171 734 94 90; www.egyptair.com.eg) offers flights from the United Kingdom to the Middle East on a daily basis.

Royal Jordanian (☎ 207 878 63 00; www.rja.com.jo) provides connections between many cities in Europe and the Middle East through Amman.

TRAVELING FROM AUSTRALIA AND NEW ZEALAND

Qantas Air (☎ 13 13 13; www.qantas.com.au) flies from a variety of departure cities in Australia and New Zealand to London, from which connecting flights to the Middle East are easy to find.

Air New Zealand (☎ 02 92 23 46 66; www.airnz.com) has reasonable fares from Auckland to London, and often special sales at much lower prices. Again, it is necessary to find connecting flights to the Middle East.

EgyptAir (☎ 612 232 66 77; www.egyptair.com.eg) is one of the few airlines serving Cairo from Australia and New Zealand.

TRAVELING FROM SOUTH AFRICA

South African (☎ 11 978 10 00; www.saa.co.za) serves mostly Africa, including Cairo.

Lufthansa (☎ 011 484 47 11; www.lufthansa.com) reliably offers direct flights to Cairo from South Africa, and provides connecting flights to the rest of the Middle East through Eastern Europe.

British Airways (☎ 011 441 86 00; www.british-airways.com/regional/sa) has flights from Johannesburg and Cape Town to places in Europe with easy connections to the Middle East.

KLM (☎ 11 881 96 96; www.klm.com) serves South Africa to Cairo through Europe.

AIR COURIER FLIGHTS

Those who travel light should consider courier flights. Couriers help transport cargo on international flights by using their checked luggage space for freight. Generally, couriers must travel with carry-ons only and deal with complex flight restrictions. Most flights are round-trip only, with short fixed-length stays (usually one week) and a limit of a one ticket per issue. Most also operate only out of major gateway cities, mostly in North America. When available, round-trip courier fares from the US to Cairo run about US$400-750. Most flights leave from New York, Los Angeles, San Francisco, or Miami in the US; and from Montreal, Toronto, or Vancouver in Canada. Generally, you must be over 21 (in some cases 18). In summer, the most popular destinations usually require an advance reservation of about two weeks (you can usually book up to two months ahead). Super-discounted fares are common for "last-minute" flights (three to 14 days ahead).

Air Courier Association, 15,000 W. 6th Ave. #203, Golden, CO 80401 (☎800-282-1202; www.aircourier.org) provides their members with a list of opportunities and courier brokers worldwide for an annual fee.

International Association of Air Travel Couriers, 20 South Dixie Hwy., PO Box 1349, Lake Worth, FL 33460 (☎561-582-8320; courier@iaatc.com; www.courier.org) is another group that provides information on courier flights.

Now Voyager Travel, 74 Varick St., Suite 307, New York, NY 10013 (☎212-431-1616; www.nowvoyagertravel.com), offers both discount courier and non-courier fares.

TICKET CONSOLIDATORS

Ticket consolidators, or **"bucket shops,"** buy unsold tickets in bulk from commercial airlines and sell them at discounted rates. The best place to look is in the Sunday travel section of any major newspaper (such as *The New York Times*), where many bucket shops place tiny ads. Call quickly, as availability is typically extremely limited. Not all bucket shops are reliable, so insist on a receipt that gives full details of restrictions, refunds, and tickets, and pay by credit card (in spite of the 2-5% fee) so you can stop payment if you never receive your tickets. For more info, see www.travel-library.com/air-travel/consolidators.html or pick up Kelly Monaghan's *Air Travel's Bargain Basement* (Intrepid Traveler, US$8).

TRAVELING FROM THE US AND CANADA

Travel Avenue (☎800-333-3335; www.travelavenue.com) searches for best available published fares and then uses several consolidators to attempt to beat that fare. Other consolidators worth trying are **Interworld** (☎305-443-4929; fax 305-443-0351), **Pennsylvania Travel** (☎800-331-0947), **Rebel** (☎800-227-3235; travel@rebeltours.com; www.rebeltours.com), **Cheap Tickets** (☎800-377-1000; www.cheaptickets.com), and **Travac** (☎800-872-8800; fax 212-714-9063; www.travac.com), **Internet Travel Network** (www.itn.com), **Travel Information Services** (www.tiss.com), **TravelHUB** (www.travelhub.com), and **The Travel Site** (www.thetravelsite.com). Keep in mind that these are just suggestions to get you started in your research; *Let's Go* does not endorse any of these agencies. As always, be cautious, and research companies before you hand over your credit card number.

TRAVELING FROM THE UK, AUSTRALIA, AND NEW ZEALAND

In London, the **Air Travel Advisory Bureau** (☎020 76 36 50 00; www.atab.co.uk) can provide names of reliable consolidators and discount flight specialists. From Australia and New Zealand, look for consolidator ads in the travel section of the *Sydney Morning Herald* and other papers.

CHARTER FLIGHTS

Charters are flights a tour operator contracts with an airline to fly extra loads of passengers during peak season. Charter flights fly less frequently than major airlines, make refunds particularly difficult, and are almost always fully booked. Schedules and itineraries may also change or be cancelled at the last moment (as late as 48hr. before the trip, and without a full refund), and check-in, boarding, and baggage claim are often much slower. However, they can also be cheaper.

Discount clubs and **fare brokers** offer members savings on last-minute charter and tour deals. Study contracts closely; you don't want to end up with an unwanted overnight layover. **Travelers Advantage,** Trumbull, CT, USA (☎203-365-2000; www.travelersadvantage.com; US$60 annual fee includes discounts and cheap flight directories) serves larger cities in the Middle East, including Cairo.

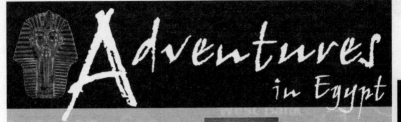

BY BUS

Bus routes connect Cairo with cities throughout the Middle East, with direct routes between several capitals. The following table summarizes distances between major cities in the Middle East and Cairo. Note that only **bold** distances represent direct routes.

DISTANCE BETWEEN CITIES (HOURS BY BUS)

	Alexandria	Ankara	Amman	Beirut	Cairo	Damascus	Istanbul
Alexandria		57	26	28½	**3**	25	51
Ankara	57		32	32½	54	29	**6**
Amman	25	32		**6**	**22**	4½	26
Beirut	28½	32½	**6**		25½	3½	26½
Cairo	**3**	54	**22**	25½		22	**48**
Damascus	25	29	4½	3½	22		23
Istanbul	51	**6**	26	26½	**48**	23	

BORDER CROSSINGS

TO JORDAN

A **ferry** shuttles between the port at **Nuweiba** and **Aqaba.** Nobody really knows what time the ferries leave, but the latest schedule had them both leaving daily at 3pm. **Taxis** from Nuweiba or Tarabin to the port cost E£5. The ticket office for the ferries is in a small white building 100m south of the port, past a bakery. The slow ferry takes 3hr. barring technical difficulties and costs US$33, payable in dollars or Egyptian pounds; a faster, less crowded, and more punctual **speedboat** takes 1hr. and runs at US$43. Show up a few hours before the earliest possible departure time to deal with customs and ticketing. For general ferry information, call 52 00 52 or 52 03 60. Jordanian **visas** can be obtained on board (Australia JD16, Canada JD36, Ireland JD11, New Zealand JD16, South Africa free, UK JD23, US JD33). There is no departure tax from Egypt.

TO ISRAEL

The most convenient option is **Taba** to **Eilat** (border open 24hr.). *Service* drop you right at the border, but the East Delta bus stop leaves a 200m walk north to the Promised Land. See the **Transportation** sections of towns in the Sinai for information on transportation to Taba. On the Israeli side, **bus** #15 runs daily every 15 minutes from the border checkpoint to Eilat until about 11pm except on Fridays, when the last bus is at 5:30pm (NIS3.20). **Taxis** (US$6 to downtown) also go to Eilat. Rented **cars** are not allowed to cross in either direction.

At the border you will be issued a free visa, the length of which is entirely determined by the border guards' mood and your appearance (min. one week, max. three months). You will have to pay a E£2 exit tax if you have traveled beyond the Sinai. The walk through the stations shouldn't take more than 1hr. Keep your Israeli entrance card—you'll need it to leave the country. Israeli customs will often let you walk right through their station, but make sure to stop there because you can't pass the final checkpoint without the customs stamp on your gate pass.

 POINTER FOR ENTERING ISRAEL. If you plan on traveling to Syria or Lebanon, have Israeli authorities stamp your visa on a separate piece of paper—you will not be allowed to enter these countries if there is an Israeli stamp in your passport. Israeli border authorities will often not let you leave Egypt without stamping your passport, so make trips to Syria or Lebanon beforehand.

Change money at decent rates at either the Taba Hilton or a bank in Eilat. **Al-Arish** is also a convenient crossing point. There is an E£18 Egyptian exit fee and E£10 charge for transfer into Israel. To enter Egypt at Rafah, you need a full Egyptian visa (not a Sinai-only), which cannot be obtained at the border.

GETTING AROUND EGYPT

Public transportation in Egypt is more prevalent and more pervasive than that of other Arab countries, but transportation to obscure sights may still be difficult to find (particularly in the summer, the off-season for tourism). Before that camel, Peugeot, or minibus spirits you off to the Nilometer or a distant praying baboon statue, make sure it's also up for the ride back.

BY PLANE

Egypt is served by **EgyptAir** (☎ 02 76 52 00); see **Cairo: Flights** (p. 86) for locations, prices, and destinations. EgyptAir's main office in the US is at 720 5th Ave., Suite 505, New York, NY 10019 (☎ 800-334-6787). **Air Sinai** (☎ 02 76 09 48; 77 29 49), in the courtyard of the Nile Hilton in Cairo, serves the Sinai and Israel.

 AIRCRAFT SAFETY. The airlines of developing world nations do not always meet safety standards. The *Official Airline Guide* (www.oag.com) and many travel agencies can tell you the type and age of aircraft on a particular route. This can be especially useful in the Middle East, where less reliable equipment is often used for inter-city travel. The **International Airline Passengers Association** (US ☎ 800-821-4272, UK ☎ 020 8681 6555) provides region-specific safety information. The **Federal Aviation Administration** (www.faa.gov) reviews the airline authorities for countries whose airlines enter the US. The **US State Department** travel advisories (☎ 202-647-5225; travel.state.gov/ travel_warnings.html) sometimes involve foreign carriers, especially when terrorist bombings may be a threat.

BY BUS

Though inexpensive, buses in Egypt can be slow, crowded, and hot. Companies include **Superjet,** West Delta Bus Company, and East Delta Bus Company. **West Delta** has a deluxe branch called **Golden Arrow** with vehicles sporting air-conditioning, refreshments, and bathrooms; unfortunately, they often show Egyptian soap operas with women shrieking at unsustainable volumes. Air-conditioned **East Delta** buses serve locales throughout the Sinai.

BY TRAIN

Egypt's railway system was the first established in both the Arab world and in Africa, and it shows. Trains in Egypt tend to take longer than buses. Schedules and signs in the train stations are rarely in English, but can be obtained from the tourist office or from ticket windows; fellow passengers can also help you. If lines are long and you're in a hurry, try boarding the train without a ticket—the conductor will usually sell one on board for an additional fee, even if the train is full.

Trains offer student discounts (ISIC card required) of up to 50%, with an average discount of about 30%. **Air-conditioned third-class** cars are comfortably small with reclining seats; shelling out more for first-class means only slightly larger seats and loud, braying Egyptian movies. Avoid the dangerous **third class. Second-class sleeper cars,** available on some regular trains, might be more comfortable for trips of 10hr. or more, but are overpriced. Reserve space in a sleeper at the wagon-lit offices in Cairo, Luxor, Aswan, and Alexandria. Seats for Cairo-Alexandria and Cairo-Upper Egypt trips should be reserved a day or two in advance. Reserve a week in advance around the time of the two major Islamic holidays: 'Eid al-Fitr, occuring during the last week of Ramadan, and 'Eid al-Adha (Feast of the Sacrifice), which takes place about three months later (see **Holidays and Festivals,** p. 85).

BY SERVICE AND TAXI

A cross between buses and taxis, The flexibly-scheduled *service* (pronounced "ser-VEES," also known as *taxi bin-nafar* in Middle and Upper Egypt and *taxi ugra* in Lower Egypt) are a ubiquitous, uniquely Middle Eastern, and surprisingly efficient method of getting around. *Service* are shared intercity taxis that run a specific route, and they depart when full or when passengers have agreed to split the price of a full carload. The local version of *service* is referred to as **minibus.**

Private taxis are inexpensive and convenient only in Cairo (black and white) and Alexandria (black and yellow or orange). Hail private taxis on the street instead of in front of a tourist trap, train station, or large hotel, and don't take a taxi if the driver approaches you. Discussing the price in advance only invites disagreement. *Never* ask the driver for the fare: open the door as you are paying with folded bills and leave the taxi without looking to the driver for approval. Have exact change and small bills ready, since change will never be made for you. "Special" means "rip-off": if this word is mentioned in your presence, firmly repeat *La* ("No").

BY CAR

Driving is extremely dangerous in the Middle East. You should be prepared as a pedestrian, passenger, or driver for unorthodox and aggressive moves. Egypt has one of the highest rates of car accidents in the world. **Wear a seatbelt.** Child safety seats are usually not available: strap on children's seatbelts and don't let kids sit in the front seat, if possible. In many regions, road conditions necessitate driving more slowly and cautiously than you would at home. For long drives in desolate areas, invest in a cellular phone and jerry can to carry extra gasoline. **Sleeping in your car** is one of the most dangerous—and often illegal—ways to get your rest. If your car breaks down, wait for the police to assist you.

 DRIVING PRECAUTIONS. When traveling in the summer or in the desert, bring substantial amounts of water (a suggested 5L of **water** per person per day) for drinking and for the radiator. For long drives to unpopulated areas, register with police before beginning the trek, and again upon arrival at the destination. Check with the local automobile club for details. When traveling for long distances, make sure tires are in good repair and have enough air, and get good maps. A **compass** and a **car manual** can also be very useful. You should always carry a **spare tire** and **jack, jumper cables, extra oil, flares, a torch (flashlight),** and **heavy blankets** (in case your car breaks down at night or in the winter). If you don't know how to **change a tire,** learn before heading out, especially if you are planning on traveling in deserted areas. Blowouts on dirt roads are exceedingly common. If you do have a breakdown, **stay with your car;** if you wander off, there's less likelihood trackers will find you.

RENTING

Renting a car is a useful option only for getting around the Sinai and the Western Desert Oases. Cheaper cars tend to be less reliable and harder to handle on difficult terrain. Less expensive 4WD vehicles in particular tend to be more top heavy, and are more dangerous when navigating particularly bumpy roads.

RENTAL AGENCIES. You can generally make reservations before you leave by calling major international offices in your home country. However, occasionally the price and availability information they give doesn't jive with what the local offices in your country will tell you. Try checking with both numbers to make sure you get the best price and accurate information. Local desk numbers are included in town listings; for home-country numbers, call your toll-free directory.

To rent a car from most establishments in Egypt, you need to be at least 18 years old. Some agencies require renters to be 25, and most charge those aged 21-24 an additional insurance fee. Policies and prices vary from agency to agency. Small local operations occasionally rent to people under 21 and tend to be cheaper, but be sure to ask about the insurance coverage, and always check the fine print.

COSTS & INSURANCE. Rentals in Egypt run about US$35 per day without a driver from the company, and US$50 with one. Expect to pay more for larger cars and for four-wheel-drives. Cars with **automatic transmission** can cost more than standard manuals (stick shift), and in some places, automatic is hard to find in the first place. It is virtually impossible, no matter where you are, to find an automatic four-wheel-drive.

Many rental packages offer unlimited kilometers, while others offer about 100km per day with a surcharge per 100km after that. Return the car with a full tank of gas to avoid high fuel charges at the end. Be sure to ask whether the price includes **insurance** against theft and collision. Remember that if you are driving a conventional vehicle on an **unpaved road** in a rental car, you are almost never covered by insurance; ask about this before leaving the rental agency. Beware that cars rented on an **American Express** or **Visa/Mastercard Gold or Platinum** credit cards in Egypt might *not* carry the automatic insurance that they would in some other countries; check with your credit card company. Insurance plans almost always come with an **excess** (or deductible), usually higher for younger drivers and for 4WD. This means you pay for all damages up to that sum, unless they are the fault of another vehicle. The excess you will be quoted applies to collisions with other vehicles; collisions with non-vehicles, such as trees ("single-vehicle collisions"), will cost you even more. The excess can often be reduced or waived entirely if you pay an additional charge.

National chains often allow one-way rentals, picking up in one city and dropping off in another. There is usually a minimum hire period and sometimes an extra drop-off charge of several hundred dollars.

DRIVING PERMITS AND CAR INSURANCE

INTERNATIONAL DRIVING PERMIT (IDP). If you plan to drive a car while in Egypt, you must be over 18 and have an International Driving Permit (IDP), though many places are pretty lax about these rules. It is a good idea to get an IDP anyway, in case you're in a situation (e.g. an accident or stranded in a small town) where the police do not know English; information on the IDP is printed in ten languages, including Arabic.

Your IDP, valid for one year, must be issued in your own country before you depart. An application for an IDP usually needs to include one or two photos, a current local license, an additional form of identification, and a fee. To apply, contact the national or local branch of your home country's Automobile Association.

CAR INSURANCE. Most credit cards cover standard insurance. If you rent, lease, or borrow a car, you will need a **green card,** or **International Insurance Certificate,** to certify that you have liability insurance and that it applies abroad. Green cards can be obtained at car rental agencies, car dealers (for those leasing cars), some travel agents, and some border crossings. Rental agencies may require you to purchase theft insurance in countries that they consider to have a high risk of auto theft.

ROAD TRAVEL ADVISORY. Highway travel in Egypt is incredibly danger-ous: Egypt has one of the highest road casualty rates in the world. **Intracity travel** is just as scary: at night, cars race by at 100kmph (60mph) without head-lights. Avoid *service* after sundown. Check with local tourism authorities or the Ministry of the Interior before venturing in private transport off main roads, partic-ularly in the following areas: the Western Desert (especially near the Libyan and Sudanese borders), along the Suez Canal and Red Sea Coast, and in the Sinai. If you need a permit, apply at the Ministry of the Interior in Cairo at 110 Qasr al-'Aini St. (☎354 83 00).

BY THUMB

Egypt is mostly untraveled desert; never count on getting a ride—you'll die of **dehydration** first. *Let's Go* strongly urges you to consider the risks before you choose to hitchhike. We do not recommend hitchhiking as a safe means of transportation. Hitching is not common in urban parts of Egypt. In recent years, the newspapers have been full of crimes perpetrated by hitchhikers along the roads between Cairo and Alexandria, making most drivers reluctant to pick you up anyway. Rides are reportedly easy to obtain in isolated areas (such as along the Great Desert Road) or for short jaunts in remote parts of the Nile Valley (where public transportation is difficult to find). Many drivers who pick up hitchhikers expect money anyway, so public transportation should be used wherever it is available.

 Let's Go strongly urges you to consider the risks before you choose to hitchhike. We do not recommend hitchhiking as a safe means of transportation.

SPECIFIC CONCERNS

CUSTOMS AND ETIQUETTE

Keep your soles out of sight—in or out of you shoes. Bottoms of **feet** resting any-where but on the ground is disrespectful. Before entering **mosques,** remove shoes and have socks ready to wear. Women must **cover** their heads and arms, and stand behind men. Outside of mosques, women usually congregate with other females, lining up with other women to buy tickets and sitting at the front of buses and trains. For men, speaking to unknown Egyptian women is a breach of etiquette and should be avoided.

It is customary for Egyptians to refuse the first **invitation** of an offering; tourists should do the same, as a genuine invitation will be repeated at least twice. If ever invited to a home but unable to attend, the householder will often press for a promise from you to visit in the future, usually for a meal. If you make such a promise, keep it. Failing to arrive will humiliate your host. It is also offensive to offer *bakhsheesh* to professionals, businessmen, or others who would consider themselves your equals.

Egypt prohibits drugs, and in many places, alcohol and pork. If you need to drink in the presence of others, ask first. Explicit sexual material, like magazines, photographs, tapes, or records is illegal and subject to confiscation.

WOMEN TRAVELERS

Women exploring on their own inevitably face some additional safety concerns, but it's easy to be adventurous without taking undue risks. Foreign women travel-ing alone will be **harassed** by Egyptian men—and so will foreign men. Egypt is not a place to visit if you want to be left alone, but harassment has more to do with socioeconomic exasperation and cultural misunderstanding than gender-based hostility. Harassment can take many forms, from overzealous salesmanship to touchy-feely *service* drivers, and from mildly sinister "hellos" to frightening and potentially harmful physical contact. The media has not helped the situation: movies and television tend to depict Western women as free and easy, and the racy nature of much Egyptian cinema has drastically altered expectations about how men and women should interact. If you are concerned, consider staying in hostels that offer single rooms that **lock** from the inside, or in religious organizations with rooms for **women only.** Communal showers in some hostels are safer than others; check them out before hopping in. Stick to centrally located accommodations and avoid solitary late-night treks or metro rides.

When traveling, always carry extra money for a phone call, bus, or taxi. **Hitchhiking** is never safe for lone women, or even for two women traveling together. Choose train compartments occupied by other women or couples; ask the conductor to put together a women-only compartment if he or she doesn't offer to do so first. Look as if you know where you're going (even when you don't) and approach older women or couples for directions if you're lost or feel uncomfortable.

 DRESS LIKE AN EGYPTIAN. Foreign women in the Egypt are guaranteed to attract a great deal of attention. While it is not necessary for women to dress in traditional Arab clothing, they should cover their bodies as much as possible, especially their legs and upper arms. Stay away from the following items of clothing: short skirts, shorts, athletic gear such as biking shorts, midriff-baring halter tops, V-neck blouses that descend more than an inch or two from the neck, tank tops, visible bra straps, and tight shirts. Except in the heavily touristed parts of the Sinai, these restrictions hold true even at the **beach.** Generally, the less you look like a tourist, the better off you'll be.

Wearing a conspicuous **wedding band** may help prevent unwanted overtures. Some travelers report that carrying pictures of a "husband" or "children" is extremely useful to help document marriage status. Even a mention of a **husband or brother** waiting back at your hotel may be enough of an antidote to your potentially vulnerable, unattached appearance. Women will find themselves approached much less frequently when escorted by a male over the age of 14, but should be wary of claiming to be "friends" with someone: the concept of friendship between men and women in the Arab world differs greatly from its counterpart in the West. Many Arabs see male-female relationships as euphemisms for something more ("friends with benefits," so to speak), and men often think that a woman's speaking to them implies a sexual advance. Some hotels frown upon unmarried couples sharing a room and some have been known not to allow it, especially if one of the people is a native.

Your best answer to verbal harassment is no answer at all; feigning deafness, sitting motionless, and staring straight ahead at nothing in particular will do a world of good. The extremely persistent can sometimes be dissuaded by a firm, loud, and very public "Go away!" or "Shame on you!" in the appropriate language (for useful phrases to use, see the inside back cover of this guide, or the box **Kiss My As(wan),** p. 245). Nothing reminds an Arab man of common manners better than public embarrassment. If this doesn't work, don't hesitate to seek out a police officer or a passerby if you are being harassed. Memorize the emergency numbers in places you visit and consider carrying a whistle or airhorn on your keychain. A self-defense course will not only prepare you for a potential attack, but will also raise your level of awareness of your surroundings and your confidence (see **Self Defense,** p. 17). Also be sure you are aware of the specific **health concerns** that women face when traveling (see p. 23).

TRAVELING ALONE

There are many benefits to traveling alone, including independence and greater interaction with locals. On the other hand, any solo traveler is a more vulnerable target of harassment and street theft. Lone travelers need to be well-organized and look confident at all times. Try not to stand out as a tourist, and be especially careful in deserted or very crowded areas. If questioned, never admit that you are traveling alone. Maintain regular contact with someone at home who knows your itinerary. For more tips, pick up *Traveling Solo* by Eleanor Berman (Globe Pequot Press, US$17) or subscribe to **Connecting: Solo Travel Network,** 689 Park Road, Unit 6, Gibsons, BC V0N 1V7 (☎604-886-9099; www.cstn.org; membership US$28).

Alternatively, several services link solo travelers with companions who have similar travel habits and interests; for a bi-monthly newsletter for single travelers seeking a travel partner (subscription US$48), contact the **Travel Companion Exchange,** P.O. Box 833, Amityville, NY 11701 (☎631-454-0880 or 800-392-1256; www.whytravelalone.com; US$48).

OLDER TRAVELERS

Discounts for senior citizens in Egypt are almost nonexistent. That being said, if you don't see a senior citizen price listed, ask, and you may be delightfully surprised. The books *No Problem! Worldwise Tips for Mature Adventurers,* by Janice Kenyon (Orca Book Publishers; US$16) and *Unbelievably Good Deals and Great Adventures That You Absolutely Can't Get Unless You're Over 50,* by Joan Rattner Heilman (NTC/Contemporary Publishing; US$13) are both excellent resources. For more information, contact one of the following organizations:

ElderTreks, 597 Markham St., Toronto, ON M6G 2L7 (☎800-741-7956; www.eldertreks.com). Adventure travel programs for the 50+ traveler in the Middle East.

Elderhostel, 11 Ave. de Lafayette, Boston, MA 02111 (☎877-426-8056; www.elderhostel.org). Organizes 1- to 4-week "educational adventures" in Egypt on varied subjects for those 55+.

The Mature Traveler, P.O. Box 15791, Sacramento, CA 95852 (☎800-460-6676). Deals, discounts, and travel packages for the 50+ traveler. Subscription US$30.

BISEXUAL, GAY, & LESBIAN TRAVELERS

Egypt is not a particularly rainbow-friendly locale—even though men hold hands in the street, this reflects a different cultural attitude about male physicality, not homosexuality (see **I Wanna Hold Your Hand,** below). As a country populated mainly by traditional Muslims, Egypt does not condone homosexual behavior. No one is openly gay in any public fashion, and homosexuality is technically **illegal** in Egypt. Be careful how you act in public—save displays of affection for somewhere safe.

Listed below are contact organizations, mail-order bookstores, and publishers that offer materials addressing some specific concerns. **Out and About** (www.planetout.com) offers a bi-weekly newsletter addressing travel concerns and a comprehensive site addressing gay travel concerns.

Gay's the Word, 66 Marchmont St., London WC1N 1AB (☎+44 20 7278 7654; www.gaystheword.co.uk). The largest gay and lesbian bookshop in the UK, with both fiction and non-fiction titles. Mail-order service available.

Giovanni's Room, 1145 Pine St., Philadelphia, PA 19107 (☎215-923-2960; www.queerbooks.com). An international lesbian/feminist and gay bookstore with mail-order service (carries many of the publications listed below).

International Gay and Lesbian Travel Association, 52 W. Oakland Park Blvd., #237 Wilton Manors, FL 33311, USA (☎800-448-8550; fax 776-3303; www.iglta.com). An organization of over 1200 companies serving gay and lesbian travelers worldwide.

International Lesbian and Gay Association (ILGA), 81 rue Marché-au-Charbon, B-1000 Brussels, Belgium (☎+32 2 502 2471; www.ilga.org). Provides political information, such as homosexuality laws of individual countries.

> **FURTHER READING: BISEXUAL, GAY AND LESBIAN.**
> *Spartacus International Gay Guide 2001-2002.* Bruno Gmunder Verlag (US$33).
>
> *Ferrari Guides' Gay Travel A to Z, Ferrari Guides' Men's Travel in Your Pocket,* and *Ferrari Guides' Inn Places.* Ferrari Publications (US$16-20). Purchase the guides online at www.ferrariguides.com.
>
> *The Gay Vacation Guide: The Best Trips and How to Plan Them,* Mark Chesnut. Citadel Press (US$15).

TRAVELERS WITH DISABILITIES

Unkempt roads, local ignorance, and lack of access ramps can make travel in Egypt prohibitively difficult for travelers with disabilities. Those with disabilities should inform airlines and hotels of their disabilities when making arrangements for travel; some time may be needed to prepare special accommodations. Call ahead to restaurants, hotels, parks, and other facilities to find out about the existence of ramps, the widths of doors, the dimensions of elevators, etc. **Guide dog owners** should inquire as to the specific quarantine policies of each destination country. At the very least, they will need to provide a certificate of immunization against rabies. The **Green Book** (http://members.nbci.com/thegreenbook/home.html) has a partial listing of accessible accommodations and sights in Egypt.

USEFUL ORGANIZATIONS

Mobility International USA (MIUSA), P.O. Box 10767, Eugene, OR 97440 (☎541–343-1284, voice and TDD; www.miusa.org). Sells *A World of Options: A Guide to International Educational Exchange, Community Service, and Travel for Persons with Disabilities* (US$35).

Society for the Advancement of Travel for the Handicapped (SATH), 347 5th Ave., #610, New York, NY 10016 (☎212-447-7284; www.sath.org). An advocacy group that publishes free online travel information and the travel magazine *OPEN WORLD* (US$18, free for members). Annual membership US$45, students and seniors US$30.

Directions Unlimited, 123 Green Ln., Bedford Hills, NY 10507 (☎800-533-5343). Books individual and group vacations for the physically disabled; not an info service.

I WANNA HOLD YOUR HAND Egyptian men may seem particularly affectionate to many travelers: they kiss each other on the cheeks, hold hands when strolling through bazaars, and even sit on each other's laps. Soldiers walk with a man on one arm and an AK-47 on the other. These amorous displays are merely manifestations of friendship and brotherhood in Egypt, as is evidenced by the very reserved manner in which Egyptian men treat their women. Women are considered very clean and chaste, and marriage is preceded by a strict courtship of two to three years.

MINORITY TRAVELERS

People of all skin colors will encounter less active racism in Egypt than they will **ignorance** about different ethnicities. **Ethnic Asians** may attract stares, especially in untouristed areas, and will usually be assumed Japanese. In some regions of Egypt, **black** travelers may find that they encounter some negative attention. This response arises largely from the fact that Africans, especially Sudanese, have sometimes been seen as interlopers in Egyptian society. **Blondes** attract particular curiosity in Egypt, since native blondes are virtually nonexistent (as are, therefore, dumb blonde jokes—so you can stop desperately trying to think of comebacks).

All over the Middle East, the highly explosive ethnic and religious tensions mean that people will likely be curious about your origins. Natives you befriend will often ask where your father comes from and which religion you were raised to practice. In particular, travelers with Biblical names or German-sounding surnames may be asked if they are **Jewish.** While non-Israeli Jews aren't necessarily viewed with hostility, Jewish travelers should avoid revealing their religion, as it could result in tension or even confrontation.

TRAVELERS WITH CHILDREN

Family vacations often require that you slow your pace, and always require that you plan ahead. When deciding where to stay, remember the special needs of young children; if you pick a small hotel, call ahead and make sure it's child-friendly. If you rent a car, make sure the rental company provides a car seat for younger children. **Be sure that your child is always carrying some sort of ID** in case of an emergency or in case he or she gets lost.

Children under two generally fly for 10% of the adult airfare on international flights (this does not necessarily include a seat). International fares are usually discounted 25% for children from two to 11. Finding a private place for **breast feeding** is often a problem while traveling, so plan accordingly. For more information, consult one of the following books:

> *Backpacking with Babies and Small Children,* Goldie Silverman. Wilderness Press (US$10).

> *How to take Great Trips with Your Kids,* Sanford and Jane Portnoy. Harvard Common Press (US $10).

> *Have Kid, Will Travel: 101 Survival Strategies for Vacationing With Babies and Young Children,* Claire and Lucille Tristram. Andrews McMeel Publishing (US$9).

> *Adventuring with Children: An Inspirational Guide to World Travel and the Outdoors,* Nan Jeffrey. Avalon House Publishing (US$15).

> *Trouble Free Travel with Children,* Vicki Lansky. Book Peddlers (US$9).

DIETARY CONCERNS

Egypt is definitely a meat-munching place, but there's always falafel, hummus, or one of other common vegetarian dishes (see **Food,** p. 84). Eggs are sold scrambled or hard-boiled in all the local markets. You won't find tofu or soybeans anywhere. To address dietary concerns at restaurants (e.g. "I am a vegetarian"), see the **Phrasebook,** p. 311.

The **North American Vegetarian Society,** P.O. Box 72, Dolgeville, NY 13329 (☎518-568-7970; www.navs-online.org), has information about vegetarian travel, including *Transformative Adventures, a Guide to Vacations and Retreats* (US$15).

Travelers who keep kosher should contact synagogues in Cairo and Alexandria by writing ahead (see p. 121 and p. 167) to inquire about hospitality. If you are strict in your observance, you may have to prepare your own food on the road or subsist on vegetables and bread alone. A good general resource is the *Jewish Travel Guide*, by Michael Zaidner (Vallentine Mitchell; US$17).

For more information, visit your local bookstore, health food store, or library, and consult *The Vegetarian Traveler: Where to Stay if You're Vegetarian*, by Jed and Susan Civic (Larson Publications; US$16).

ALTERNATIVES TO TOURISM

For an extensive listing of "off-the-beaten-track" and specialty travel opportunities, try the **Specialty Travel Index,** 305 San Anselmo Ave., #313, San Anselmo, CA 94960, USA (☎888-624-4030 or 415-455-1643; www.specialtytravel.com; US$6). **Transitions Abroad** (www.transabroad.com) publishes a bi-monthly on-line newsletter for work, study, and specialized travel abroad.

STUDYING ABROAD

Whether spending a summer, semester, or year abroad, Egypt is a good place to learn a new language, boasting a rich culture and history to boot. Most programs for foreigners in Egypt focus on intensive Arabic **language** instruction, while others offer classes in subjects like literature, history, and international affairs. Entering Egypt to study requires a special **visa,** which may be obtained once you have entered on a tourist visa. For more information, see **Work and Study Visas,** p. 10.

FURTHER READING & RESOURCES: STUDYING ABROAD.
StudyAbroad.Com Program Search (www.studyabroad.com)
Academic Year Abroad 2001-2002. Institute of International Education Books (US$47).
Vacation Study Abroad 2000-2001. Institute of International Education Books (US$43).
Peterson's Study Abroad 2001. Peterson's (US$30).
Peterson's Summer Study Abroad 2001. Peterson's (US$30).

UNIVERSITIES

Most American undergraduates enroll in programs sponsored by US universities. Those relatively fluent in Arabic may find it cheaper to enroll directly in a local university (though getting credit may be more difficult). Some schools that offer study abroad programs to foreign students are listed below.

American University in Cairo (AUC), 420 5th Ave., 3rd fl., New York, NY 10018, USA (☎212-730-8800; www.aucegypt,edu). **In Cairo:** 113 Qasr al-Aini St. Administers a full range of summer-, semester- and year-long programs in Cairo.

Cairo University, (www.cairo.eun.eg).

Amideast Study Abroad, 1730 M Street NW, Suite 1100, Washington, DC 20036, USA (☎202-776-9600). Supplies information and administers a range of programs.

Eastern Michigan University, 103 Boone Hall, Ypsilanti, MI 48197, USA (☎800-777-3541; fax ; www.emich.edu/abroad). Program called the European Cultural History tour combines tourism with academic instruction in Egypt.

Southern Illinois University at Carbondale, Study Abroad Programs, Carbondale, IL 62901, USA (☎618-453-7670; www.siu.edu/departments/study_abroad/main.htm).

Antioch Education Abroad, 795 Livermore, Yellow Springs, OH 45387 USA, (☎800-874-7986). Offers summer programs in the Middle East and North Africa.

UMass-American University in Cairo, William S. Clark International Center, University of Massachusetts Amherst, Amherst, MA 01003, USA (☎413-545-2710).

School for International Training, College Semester Abroad, Admissions, Kipling Rd., P.O. Box 676, Brattleboro, VT 05302, USA (☎800-336-1616 or 802-258-3267; www.sit.edu). Semester- and year-long programs in Egypt run US$10,600-13,700.

International Association for the Exchange of Students for Technical Experience (IAESTE), 10400 Little Patuxent Pkwy. #250, Columbia, MD 21044-3510, USA (☎410-997-2200; www.aipt.org). 8- to 12-week programs in Egypt for college students who have completed 2 years of technical study. US$25 application fee.

LANGUAGE SCHOOLS

These programs are run by foreign universities, independent international or local organizations, and divisions of Egyptian universities. They generally cost anywhere from US$1000-4000 and include lodging, food and side trips.

Center for Arabic Study Abroad (CASA), 1619 Mass. Ave. N.W., Washington, D.C. 20036, USA (☎202-663-5751; wwwwww.sais-jhu.edu/languages/Arabic). A consortium of 21 universities administered through Johns Hopkins University at AUC. See Emory University's site for extensive information (www.emory.edu/COLLEGE/CASA/).

Languages Abroad, 317 Adelaide St. West, Suite 900, Toronto, ON M5V 1P9 (☎416-925-2112; www.languagesabroad.com).

WORKING AND VOLUNTEERING

A special **work permit** is required in order to work as a foreigner in Egypt, which you can arrange after your arrival. Friends in Egypt can often help expedite work permits or arrange work-for-accommodations swaps.

Few foreigners work in the Middle East because acquiring a work visa or permit is often a bureaucratic nightmare. Being an **English speaker** does wonders for your marketability (tutoring, teaching, or translating English is your best bet). Some travelers in the Sinai work for hotels or dive centers in **Na'ama Bay** (see p. 285). A note on **archaeological digs:** although they abound in this area, most sites offer hard work, menial labor, and no pay (the Archaeological Institute of America listed below is an excellent source for finding more rewarding digs). **Volunteer** jobs for speakers of English are readily available almost everywhere.

American Field Service (AFS) runs the Egyptian Society for Intercultural Exchange, (ESIE), which sponsors summer-, semester-, and year-long homestay exchange programs in Egypt for current students and short-term service projects for adults. Has programs for nearly every country of origin; financial aid available. Contact ESIE at 10 al-Thawra St., Apt. 5, Mohandiseen, Giza, Egypt (☎2 360 61 42; fax 337 60 01; info-egypt@afs.org; www.afs.org/partners/egyhome.htm).

TEACHING ENGLISH

International Schools Services, Educational Staffing Program, P.O. Box 5910, Princeton, NJ 08543, USA (☎609-452-0990; www.iss.edu). Recruits teachers and administrators for American and English schools in the Middle East. US$150 program fee.

Office of Overseas Schools, US Department of State, Room H328, SA-1, Washington, D.C. 20522 (☎202-261-8200; fax 261-8224; www.state.gov/www/about_state/schools/). Keeps a comprehensive list of schools abroad and agencies that arrange placement for Americans to teach abroad.

ELS Language Centers/Middle East employs many English as a First Language (EFL) teachers in full- and part-time work in Egypt and Jordan. Contact them at their main office, P.O. Box 3079, Abu Dhabi, UAE (www.elsme.com; elsme@emirates.net.ae).

ARCHAEOLOGICAL DIGS

Archaeological Institute of America, 656 Beacon St., Boston, MA 02215, USA (☎617-353-9361; www.archaeological.org). The *Archaeological Fieldwork Opportunities Bulletin* (US$16 for non-members) lists field sites throughout the Middle East. Purchase the bulletin from Kendall/Hunt Publishing, 4050 Westmark Dr., Dubuque, IA 52004, USA (☎800-228-0810).

VOLUNTEERING

Volunteer jobs are readily available, and many provide room and board in exchange for labor. You can sometimes avoid high application fees by contacting the individual workcamps directly. A good place to contact is **Habitat for Humanity International,** 121 Habitat St., Americus, GA 31709, USA (☎800-422-4828; www.habitat.org). They offer international opportunities in Egypt to live with and build houses in a host community. Costs range from US$1200 to US$3500.

OTHER RESOURCES

Let's Go tries to cover all aspects of budget travel, but we can't put *everything* in our guides. Listed below are books and websites that can serve as jumping off points for your own research.

Hippocrene Books, Inc., 171 Madison Ave., New York, NY 10016 (☎212-685-4371; orders 718-454-2366; www.netcom.com/~hippocre). Free catalog. Publishes Arabic language dictionaries and learning guides.

Hunter Publishing, 130 Campus Dr., Edison, NJ 08818, USA (☎800-255-0343; www.hunterpublishing.com). Has an extensive catalog of travel guides and diving and adventure travel books.

Rand McNally, 150 S. Wacker Dr., Chicago, IL 60606, USA (☎800-234-0679 or 312-332-2009; www.randmcnally.com), publishes road atlases (each US$10).

Adventurous Traveler Bookstore, 245 S. Champlain St., Burlington, VT 05401, USA (☎800-282-3963 or 802-860-6776; www.adventuroustraveler.com).

Travel Books & Language Center, Inc., 4437 Wisconsin Ave. NW, Washington, D.C. 20016 (☎800-220-2665 or 202-237-1322; www.travelbks.com). Over 60,000 titles from around the world.

WORLD WIDE WEB

Almost every aspect of budget travel is accessible via the web. Within 10min. at the keyboard, you can make a reservation at a hostel, get advice on travel hotspots from other travelers who have just returned from the Middle East, or find out exactly how much a train from Luxor to Alexandria costs.

Listed here are some budget travel sites to start off your surfing; other relevant web sites are listed throughout the book. Because website turnover is high, use search engines (such as www.google.com) to strike out on your own.

THE ART OF BUDGET TRAVEL

How to See the World: www.artoftravel.com. A compendium of great travel tips, from cheap flights to self defense to interacting with local culture.

Rec. Travel Library: www.travel-library.com. A fantastic set of links for general information and personal travelogues.

Lycos: cityguide.lycos.com. General introductions to cities and regions throughout Egypt, accompanied by links to applicable histories, news, and local tourism sites.

INFORMATION ON EGYPT

Egyptian Tourist Authority (ETA): www.touregypt.net; www.egypttourism.org. Two sites with extensive coverage of major toursit destinations, hotels, and practical information.

Arabnet: www.arab.net. A one-stop guide to the Middle East, with extensive country-specific resources on geographic, political, and historical elements. Though the page is not strongly political, it regularly features inflammatory pro-Arab statements.

CIA World Factbook: www.odci.gov/cia/publications/factbook/index.html. Tons of vital statistics on Egypt's geography, government, economy, and people.

Foreign Language for Travelers: www.travlang.com. Provides free online translating dictionaries and lists of phrases in Arabic.

MyTravelGuide: www.mytravelguide.com. Country overviews, with everything from history to transportation to live web cam coverage of Egypt.

Geographia: www.geographia.com. Highlights, culture, and people of Egypt.

Atevo Travel: www.atevo.com/guides/destinations. Detailed introductions, travel tips, and suggested itineraries.

World Travel Guide: www.travel-guides.com/navigate/world.asp. Helpful practical info.

TravelPage: www.travelpage.com. Links to official tourist office sites in Egypt.

PlanetRider: www.planetrider.com. A subjective list of links to the "best" websites covering the culture and tourist attractions of Egypt.

AND OUR PERSONAL FAVORITE...

Let's Go: www.letsgo.com. Our constantly expanding site features photos and streaming video, online ordering of all our titles, info about our books, a travel forum buzzing with stories and tips, and links that will help you find everything you ever wanted to know about Egypt.

HISTORY & CULTURE

The Arab Republic of Egypt (*Gomhoriyyat Misr al-'Arabiyya*, or simply *Misr*) is home to natural and man-made wonders that are rivaled only by its 5000 years of rich recorded history. A quarter of the Arab world lives in Egypt, despite the fact that the driest desert in the world, the Western Desert, makes up almost all (97%) of the country's land mass. The Nile, the longest and most fertile river in the world, stretches its arms across this region full of ancient temple ruins and glittering desert oases, welcoming the Mediterranean with the open hands of its Delta. The Nile Delta cradles several jewels in its palm: the breathtaking Pyramids at Giza (and their predecessor at Saqqara, the oldest monument in the world); the dizzying streets and dazzling mosques of Cairo, the largest city in the Middle East and Africa; and cosmopolitan Alexandria, once home to the greatest library in the world. The mainland of Egypt is divided into Upper Egypt in the south (including Aswan, Luxor, and Nubia, the region where African and Egyptian culture merge); Middle Egypt; and Lower Egypt in the north (including Cairo). This orientation comes from the fact that the Nile flows from the south northward toward the Mediterranean. The Sinai Peninsula, to the east of mainland Egypt, is its own rugged wonderland: at its heart, hikers trudge through desert containing some of the oldest and most sacred religious sites in the world; along the coast, scuba divers plunge into the azure depths of the Red Sea, known as one of the planet's premiere underwater sightseeing spots.

HISTORY

Egypt is home to one of the most important civilizations of the ancient Middle East and one of the earliest urban and literate societies in the world. Egyptian culture had an important influence on both ancient Israel and ancient Greece, which in turn hugely influenced the development of modern Western civilization.

ANCIENT HISTORY

IN THE BEGINNING

Around 7000 BCE, the Sahara—until then a far more hospitable place to live—was in the process of becoming the arid desert that we know today. Thus began the migration of Saharan nomads to the Nile Valley, where many settled down permanently with the wife and kids and abandoned their old itinerant ways. These early Egyptians, living in small, autonomous chiefdoms, learned to use the Nile River for agriculture in the 4th millenium BCE. The annual flooding of the river was effectively the only source of the land's fertility, and various techniques of irrigation that were developed from this point on would play a huge role in determining the future of Egypt. A more organized society began to emerge around the river, as cities grew in importance and strength.

According to the famous **Narmer Palette** (an ancient mascara holder discovered along the Nile in 1898 CE), **King Menes** was the first true pharaoh of Egypt, uniting Upper (southern) and Lower (northern) Egypt in 2925 BCE. His kingdom, centered at Hierakonpolis, was one of the longest-lasting and most powerful in all of history, enduring 62 years until Menes was fatally mauled by a hippopotamus. However, the history of the **pre-dynastic period** in Egypt is pretty sketchy, and all the great stuff that legend attributes to Menes has been inconclusively identified by modern scholars with other archaic Egyptian kings—Scorpion, Aha, and Narmer himself.

2575-2130
Old Kingdom

OLD KINGDOM

The pharaohs of the **Old Kingdom** built a new capital at **Memphis** (now a pile of ruins) as Imhotep, history's 1st recorded architect, began constructing King Zoser's step pyramid at Saqqara, the forerunner of the later pharoahs' self-indulgent mausolea at **Giza** (p. 135). Most view this era as the pinnacle of ancient Egyptian civilization: at a time when even China had scarcely emerged from the Stone Age, Egyptians had invented writing and papyrus, developed increasingly sophisticated methods of irrigation, forged a national economy, recorded the history of eight dynasties of pharaohs, and built the most ridiculous of the Seven Ancient Wonders of the World.

26th century BCE
Great Pyramids
built at Giza

This achievement, of course, came at the expense of tens of thousands of Egyptian peasants, whose labor was brutally exploited to build the classical pyramids (such as those at Giza, built by the pharaohs of the 4th dynasty), as the pharaohs and other elites enjoyed lives of leisure. Believed to be earthly manifestations of the falcon-god **Horus,** the all-powerful pharaohs feared only death; their most magnificent monuments represent attempts to defeat this ultimate enemy. The Old Kingdom also saw Egypt begin to look outward, as Snofru—the 1st pharaoh of the 4th dynasty, ruling in the 26th century BCE—led military campaigns into Libya and Nubia and opened up trade in the Mediterranean and Lebanon.

The pyramids of the later pharaohs of the Old Kingdom decreased in size over time, reflecting the fact that the power of the pharaohs—once absolute—had dissipated, giving way to the growth of a powerful provincial nobility. With the end of the 8th dynasty, the Old Kingdom collapsed, ushering in a century of internal fighting, famine, and other troubles known as the **First Intermediate Period** (c. 2130-1938 BCE). After this period of strife, the princes of Thebes conquered Egypt and recentralized political authority, founding the Middle Kingdom under **King Mentuhotep II,** the 1st pharaoh of the 11th dynasty.

c. 2130-1938
First Intermediate
Period

1938-1600
Middle Kingdom

MIDDLE KINGDOM

During the **Middle Kingdom,** the can-do princes of Thebes reformed the government administration, led invasions into Palestine and Nubia, and built a number of important fortresses in these regions, not to mention most of the tombs in the **Valley of the Kings** (p. 225). Contact with the kingdoms of the south, particularly with Nubia, created in these far-off areas virtual satellites of pharaonic culture.

In Egypt itself, conservatism and order reigned. The predominant ideology of the era presented the Old Kingdom as a golden age of Egyptian civilization, while the First Intermediate Period had been a terrible interruption of the pharaohs' eternal rule. The catastrophe had been due, thought Middle Kingdom leaders, to innovations that had been made; to avoid a relapse of the chaos, no further societal change could be tolerated.

Nevertheless, internal political rivalries began to weaken the Egyptian dynasties in the 18th century BCE, at the same time that the **Hyksos,** a Semitic people of Syrian-Palestinian origin, rode in from Asia on chariots and settled in north Egypt. In about 1630 BCE, the Hyksos (whose name was probably an Egyptian word for "rulers of foreign lands") penetrated the desert citadels at **Thebes** (modern-day **Luxor,** p. 213) and ravished the Egyptian countryside, ruling Egypt as the 15th dynasty, and beginning another century-long interregnum, known as the **Second Intermediate Period.**

Though the Hyksos adopted Egyptian customs and introduced cool new ideas like fighting with horses, they never quite consolidated their power in Upper Egypt, where the Theban princes continued to exert influence. While the Thebans recognized the Hyksos' authority in principle, Thebes remained the religious capital of Egypt—and when the princes thought themselves sufficiently strong to revolt, they wasted no time in expelling the Hyksos and establishing the **New Kingdom.**

NEW KINGDOM

Upon the expulsion of the Hyksos, Thebes became the center of a theocratic police state. The high priests of the sun (now embodied in the god **Amun**) wielded unimaginable power, illustrated by the colossal temples built during this period. The increased power of the clergy would become problematic; sometimes they controlled even the pharaoh himself, and power struggles between the priesthood and the monarchy would plague the New Kingdom.

Egypt "modernized" its formerly primitive army by adapting the bronze weapons and horse-drawn chariots of the Hyksos they had just booted out. **Ahmose**—who founded the 18th dynasty around 1554 BCE—began a series of military campaigns, which were meant both as attempts to pillage the wealth and resources of far-off lands and as preemptive strikes against any would-be Hyksos that might ostensibly threaten Egypt in the future. Ahmose's successors invaded the Sudan, Palestine, and Syria, up to the Euphrates River. Now an empire ruled by warrior-kings, Egypt established control over most of the eastern Mediterranean. Trade in wood, olive oil, gold, ivory, and slaves brought stability and prosperity.

Despite the overwhelming power of the priests, the New Kingdom had its share of notable royalty. Among these was the cross-dressing 15th-century Queen **Hatshepsut,** who posed for a while as the regent of the young **Thutmose III,** but soon usurped his power, adopting a Horus name (limited to kings) and the complete trappings of pharaoh-ness, including the traditional false beard. Thutmose III ultimately gained power upon Hapshetsut's (mysterious) death, and he proceeded to establish himself as one of the great pharaohs of all time. His rule brought ancient Egypt to the peak of its power, as he conquered all of Syria, crossed the Euphrates to defeat the Mitannians, and pushed farther south into the Sudan.

Then, in the middle of the 14th century BCE, a renegade pharaoh named **Amenhotep IV** led a series of radical religious reforms that scared the behorus out of the established clergy. For a brief period, Amenhotep introduced a monotheistic cult to Egypt (the first such experiment in human history) centered around the new sun-god Aton. Changing his name to **Akhenaton** ("one who is helpful to Aton"), the pharaoh abandoned the old Theban temples and founded a new capital, Akhetaton, dedicated to the deity that the pharaoh and his wife **Nefertiti** considered to be the only true god. The **Hittites,** an increasingly powerful nation from the Anatolian (Turkish) plateau, chose this moment to begin their conquest of the Middle East, seri-

c. 1630
Hyksos invade Egypt, beginning Second Intermediate Period

1539-1075
New Kingdom

1554
Ahmose founds 18th dynasty

c. 1472
Queen Hatshepsut becomes pharaoh

1353-36
Akhenaton introduces monotheistic cult to Egypt

1333-23
Tutankhamen rees-
tablishes orthodox
Egyptian religion

ously threatening the already destabilized Egyptian kingdom. Under pressure from the still-powerful priests of Amun, Akhenaton's successor **Tutankhamun** (he of the famous intact tomb, discovered in 1922) restored the orthodox polytheistic religion and the capital at Thebes.

1279-13
Reign of Ramses II

Ramses II, who reigned from 1279-13 BCE, succeeded to a large degree in reconquering the Levant, winning great fame as a warrior during his long pharaoh-ship (the 2nd-longest in Egyptian history), despite a famous loss to the Hittites at the Battle of Kadesh; the truce signed after this battle is the oldest surviving peace treaty. Ramses II is probably best known, though, in the shiny-headed guise of Yul Brenner; historians believe that the Exodus of the Hebrews from Egypt (recounted in the Old Testament and the Charlton Heston film *The Ten Commandments*) probably took place during Ramses's reign.

1075
Kingdom splinters;
north controlled by
Tanites, south by
Theban priests

Despite the achievements and booming voices (et cetera, et cetera, et cetera!) of pharaohs like Ramses II, the New Kingdom slipped into a slow military and political decline. Egypt was definitively kicked out of the Middle East by European barbarians who had defeated the Hittites in 1200 BCE, and the ongoing struggles between the pharaohs and the clergy turned to the priests' advantage. In 1075 BCE, the kingdom finally fell apart, with the north ruled by the **Tanite** 21st dynasty, and the south controlled by the Theban priests. After the **Cushite** (Sudanese) pharaohs of the 25th dynasty reunified Egypt between in 650 BCE, the Assyrians, followed by the Persians, came like vultures to swallow up their already-decaying prey.

PERSIAN AND GREEK DOMINATION

The 6th century BCE saw the rise of the Persians (people from what is now Iran) in the Middle East, as Emperor Cyrus II incorporated all of the old Babylonian empire by 539. In 526 BCE, the last of Egyptian king of the Saite (26th) dynasty, **Ahmose II,** died. Six months later, Cyrus's son **Cambyses II** had

525
Persian king Cam-
byses II becomes
pharaoh

penetrated Egypt, reaching Nubia in 525. Cambyses, who ruled as pharaoh from 525-522, imposed a strict rule on the new Persian territory, but his successor **Darius I** restored Egyptian temples, maintained only a light tax burden, and pitched in on efforts to improve irrigation and the Egyptian economy. A revolt broke out in the Nile Delta upon Darius's death in 486

486
Revolt in the west-
ern Delta

BCE, perhaps instigated by Libyans in the western Delta. As payback, new Persian king **Xerxes** reduced Egypt to the status of a conquered province. Turmoil in the Delta continued, and after a number of rebellions, Egypt finally regained its independence after the death of Darius II in 404 BCE. Persia reestab-

404
Egypt regains its
independence

lished control of Egypt in 335 BCE, but it was to be short-lived, thanks to a certain young man from Macedonia.

332
Alexander the
Great liberates
Egypt from Persian
rule

When the young **Alexander the Great** arrived in 332 BCE, ruler of Greece and pretty much everything else, he freed the Egyptians from Persian rule and was hailed as a liberator. Declared the son of Amun and the legitimate pharaoh of Egypt by the Oracle of Amun in the Siwa Oasis (see **Reversal of Fortunes,** p. 182), Alex founded a new capital city and named it after himself: **Alexandria.** The big guy probably could have lived out the rest of his days as a local hero in the Egyptian sun, but he soon skipped town in search of new adventures and died in Babylonia, leaving Egypt to his successor **Ptolemy** (who also reigned as a legit pharaoh). Ptolemy's descendants (cleverly known as the **Ptolemies**) ruled Egypt for three centuries, building Alexandria into a cosmopolitan city and a major center of international trade, thanks to its position on the Mediterranean Sea at the crossroads of Asia, Africa, and Europe. Alexandria also became a hotbed of scientific research, attracting such luminous scholars as the geometer **Euclid** and the astronomer **Ptolemy.** With 500,000 volumes, Alexandria's **Biblioteka**, built in the 3rd century BCE, gathered in a single place the entire body of ancient Greek knowledge.

3rd century BCE
Library built at Alexandria

WHEN IN EGYPT, DO AS THE ROMANS DO

In 48 BCE, more than a century after Rome made its first overtures to the ever-feuding Ptolemies, **Julius Caesar** came to Egypt and made similar advances toward **Cleopatra VII,** queen of Egypt. She accepted an alliance with Caesar (in the greatest sense of the word, as Caesar allegedly fathered her son Caesarion) that left her secure until his assassination by Brutus et al. four years later. (Doh!) Unshaken, Cleopatra also formed a politico-sexual alliance with **Mark Antony** (not the crossover pop star), one of the three men vying to succeed Caesar. While Antony was otherwise occupied, 3rd wheel **Octavian** grabbed the empire for himself in 30 BCE, ruthlessly crushing the affair and the Ptolemaic dynasty at the **Battle of Actium.** At the height of the battle, both Cleopatra and Antony withdrew. The not-so-happy couple fled to Alexandria, but could do little more than await the arrival of the victorious Octavian (and undergo an unending series of costume changes). Alexandria was captured and Antony and Cleopatra committed suicide—he by falling on his sword, she by the bite of an asp (or so the Shakespearean legend goes).

48
Julius Caesar comes to Egypt to pay overdue fines

30
Octavian takes power, ending Ptolemaic dynasty

The Egypt of Imperial Rome and Byzantium was characterized by political stability and an increasingly entrenched bureaucracy (two traditions that modern Egypt has wholeheartedly embraced). During this period, Egypt was also the breadbasket of the Mediterranean, supplying most of the grain needed to support the empire's growing urban population. Accordingly, the Roman period was one of great difficulty for the rural peasant population, on whom the pressures of feeding the empire chiefly fell. Despite Roman rule, Egypt kept its Hellenic culture—Greek remained the preferred language of communication both for Egyptian elites and foreign populations, and Alexandria maintained its status as an intellectual center for philosophical and religious study and debate, even after the introduction of **Christianity.** Christianity arrived in Egypt around 40 CE with **St. Mark** and helped maintain relative social tranquility. Ultimately, the Roman Empire split in two, and in 395 CE, Egypt was attached to the eastern empire, based in Constantinople, which would become the **Byzantine Empire.** But religious divisions would soon undermine Egypt's place in the empire. The **Copts** worshiped Christ only as a divine figure, while the church at Constantinople believed he was both divine and human. This long-festering argument exploded in 451 CE when the Copts were excommunicated and forced to set up their own church in Alexandria. The modern-day Coptic minority in Egypt is descended from these original dissidents (see **Religion and Culture,** p. 74).

40 CE
Christianity arrives in Egypt

395
Egypt attaches to eastern half of Roman empire

451
Coptic Christians excommunicated

FROM ARABS TO BRITS

THE BIRTH OF ISLAM: NO SHI'ITE

Islam appeared in the Arabian city of **Mecca** (in modern-day Saudi Arabia) at the beginning of the 7th century. According to tradition, this new religion was revealed to **Muhammad** in 610, but the Muslim era is generally considered to have begun in 622, when the Prophet Muhammad and his followers were forced to flee Mecca and take refuge in nearby Medina, where they set up Islam's headquarters and built the world's 1st mosque. In 630, Mecca—which until then had been the home of an important polytheistic temple—became the first Holy City of Islam, with Medina second and Jerusalem third.

Muhammad's death in 632, beyond its theological implications, caused a serious political crisis for Islam. The Prophet had neglected to pick a successor, and no Muslim claimed the power of messengership possessed by Muhammad. Two factions appeared with different views on who should fill the void: one group thought it crucial that the successor be a member of Muhammad's family, while another argued that the new leader should be a close and trusted follower of Muhammad. The latter group threw its weight behind **Abu Bakr,** a close advisor to the Prophet and father of his favorite wife. With its support, Abu Bakr managed to consolidate power, taking the title **khalifah** (caliph), meaning deputy or successor. Abu Bakr reigned until 634, when he was succeeded as caliph by Omar and then Othman—all of whom established Medina as the seat of power. Othman was assassinated (by the brother of one of Muhammad's wives), and **Ali** came to power in 656. The rise of Ali, who was both nephew and son-in-law to the Prophet, caused a civil war, and thus a deep schism in Islam, between the **Sunnis** (the "orthodox"), who thought the caliph was to be chosen by the community of the faithful and accepted the legitimacy of the 1st four caliphs, and the **Shi'ites,** who supported Ali and his offspring. Despite this division, the first four caliphs are known by the majority of Muslims as the *Rashidun* (rightly-guided).

The spread of Islam began under the reign of Omar. In 636, the Muslims won a decisive victory against the Byzantine army in present-day Jordan, signaling the end of Byzantine power in the Middle East. The once-mighty Byzantine Empire had begun to face increased internal challenges to its power, and religious quarrels within Christianity were splintering the Church more and more—and so it was not surprising that the conquering Muslims met little resistance among the peoples of the Middle East. After overrunning the key cities of Palestine and Syria, General **'Amir ibn al-'As** was restrained from invading Egypt by a hesitant Caliph Omar. The intrepid general, however, had visited Alexandria as a youth and recognized the righteous amount of sweet booty that could be reaped through a conquest of the city. With or without the permission of the caliph, 'Amir marched a relatively small army (4000 men) into Egypt in 639 and defeated the Byzantines with staggering ease, kicking them entirely out of Egypt by 642. Historians do not agree on why the Arabs met by so little resistance, but it seems to be generally true that Egyptians were pretty tired of Byzantine rule. Even the Coptic Christians may have preferred the rule of the Muslims to the harsh persecution of their (supposed) co-

622
Muhammad and his followers flee to Medina

632
Muhammad dies; Abu Bakr becomes 1st caliph

656
Ali becomes caliph; Sunnis and Shi'ites split

636
Muslims defeat Byzantine army in Jordan

642
Muslims expel Byzantines from Egypt

religionists from Constantinople. Rather than adopting Alexandria as their capital, the invaders built Egypt's first Arabo-Muslim city, **al-Fustat** (p. 122), a garrison town roughly corresponding to the location of Cairo. Although not many Egyptians converted to Islam immediately, they welcomed Muslims' expulsion of the Byzantines.

To the dismay of his Shi'ite supporters, the ineffective Ali was assassinated by Syrian Governor **Mu'awiyah,** who took power in 661 and silenced the Shi'ite minority, establishing the **Umayyad** dynasty based in **Damascus.** This marked the true beginning of Arabo-Muslim civilization, as the Umayyad caliphs built magnificent mosques and phat palaces throughout the desert, even as they embarked on ambitious projects of military expansion. Some Muslims, however, felt that the Umayyads were a bit too secular in their outlook and goals, and in 750, a new group took over, establishing the more religious **Abbasid** dynasty—despite the fact that most Egyptian peasants had already been converted to Islam under the Umayyads. The Abbasids moved their capital from Damascus to the new city of **Baghdad,** where they developed a brilliant society where art and science flourished and a well-oiled bureaucratic machine full of tax collectors, judges, and scribes kept all the trains running on time from one end of the empire to the other (which by this time stretched from Morocco to India). To facilitate the slow process of Arabization, both the Umayyad and Abbasid caliphates adopted policies of tolerance toward Copts and other non-Muslims as long as they paid their taxes, which seemed like a pretty good deal to everyone.

DO THESE PANTS MAKE ME LOOK FATIMID?

But things would not be all hunky-dory for long. In 868, **Ahmad ibn Tulun,** appointed by the caliph as governor of Egypt, came to power. By this point the Abbasid empire was so vast that it was difficult for the caliph to keep tabs on goings-on far from Baghdad. So when ibn Tulun rounded up an army of loyalists and declared himself absolute ruler of Egypt, there wasn't a whole lot the caliph could do about it. The **Tulunid dynasty** the rogue governor founded was brilliant but brief, lasting only until 905. Good luck telling a Egyptian that death and taxes are the two certainties in life—pharonic Egypt managed to evade the former, and Tulunid Egypt dodged the latter. Under ibn Tulun, the flow of tribute to Baghdad stopped and living standards improved noticeably. In 905, though, the Abbasid caliph decided he had seen enough and dispatched an army to Egypt to lay the smack down, and Baghdad quickly reasserted its control over Egypt.

The death of the Tulunid dynasty in 905 left Egypt in chaos, a state of affairs that was unresolved by the **Ikhshidid dynasty.** In 969, the **Fatimids** arrived from Tunisia and booted the Abbasids out of Egypt for good. These new rulers were Shi'ites from what is now Iran who had established themselves across North Africa, founding a new dynasty in Tunisia. They were to be one of the most influential families in the history of Egypt, setting up their capital at **Cairo** and—with their control of Jerusalem— quickly asserting their status as the dominant power in the Middle East. The Fatimids improved trade by means of low tariffs

661
Mu'awiyah establishes Umayyad dynasty

750
Abbasid dynasty founded

868
Ahmad ibn Tulun begins Tulunid dynasty

905
Abbasids reassert control over Egypt

969
Fatimids take over Egypt

HISTORY & CULTURE

and good relations with merchants, and Egypt prospered under their rule. Most dramatically, though, the new rulers dared to proclaim themselves legitimate caliphs, considering the caliphs in Baghdad to have usurped the authority they believed rightfully belonged only to descendants of Muhammad. The severing of Egypt's ties with Baghdad—first initiated when the Tulunid dynasty stopped paying taxes—was now a complete political and religious split.

Thanks to trade all over the Mediterranean and stretching into Europe, Lebanon, Yemen, Africa, and India, the new caliphs' influence was wide-reaching. Trade expansion triggered a generally open culture within Egypt itself, particularly in the new capital of Cairo, a city that the Fatimids can probably take credit for founding. At first the city that would be known as *Misr* (the Arabic name for all of Egypt) was more or less just the seat of the powerful new caliphate, but little by little the Fatimids attracted the era's top artists and artisans to their capital. Yet the Fatimids were somewhat isolated from the Egyptians they ruled: not only were they foreigners, they were Shi'ite Muslims at a time when many Egyptians (particularly in the Nile Valley) were still Christians—except in sunny Sunni Cairo, where there was also a significant community of Jews.

At the beginning, the Fatimids made absolutely no efforts to win converts to Shi'ite Islam. However, at the beginning of the 11th century, Caliph **al-Hakim,** justifiably known as the "Mad Caliph," brought the policy of toleration to an abrupt (though temporary) end. His harsh, arbitrary, and probably mad orders included the sacking of al-Fustat, the destruction of the Church of the Holy Sepulcher (the site of Jesus's crucifixion) in Jerusalem, the murder of all dogs in Cairo (their barking annoyed him), and the banning of various types of vegetables and shellfish. His persecutions affected Jews and Christians (as well as Sunni Muslims) until he mysteriously disappeared while taking a walk (killed by vengeful mutts?) on February 13, 1021. Al-Hakim's not-so-mad successors reversed his religious policies and reinstated a policy of toleration, but the damage had been done: Christian Europe would use the Mad Caliph's intolerance (as well as the policies taken toward Christian pilgrims by the **Seljuk Turks** who booted the Fatimids out of Jerusalem in 1070) as a pretext for launching their own holy war against the Muslims—a series of attacks on the Middle East that would become known as the **Crusades.** Under the pressure of Crusader attacks, Muslim rivals, and—above all—internal political intrigue, the Fatimid dynasty fell apart in 1171.

996-1021
Rule of Mad Caliph
al-Hakim

GOODBYE CAESAR, HELLO SALADIN

1171
Fatimid dynasty
collapses; Salah
al-Din takes power

The fall of Fatimid rule in 1171 came with the rise in power of **Salah al-Din,** a Kurdish general from Syria who distinguished himself in the Crusades. Al-Din took the reins of power in Cairo, assuming the title of sultan. He restored Egypt's allegiance to the Sunni Abbasids (though the Abbasids' authority was by this time solely religious) and inaugurated the brief but popular **Ayyubid dynasty.** The dynasty's reign was plagued by internal and external strife. The new sultans took the concept of "domestic policy" very literally: the orthodox nepotism practiced by the Ayyubids was meant to solidify their power, but instead, the delegation of family members to pro-

1171-1250
Ayyubid dynasty

vincial posts led to unneccessary struggle. Additionally, the dynasty's rule was marked by constant war all over the Middle East with the incorrigible European Crusaders. Cairo, where al-Din built the **Citadel,** remained the capital of a huge territory, including all the old Abbasid holdings not under the control of the Crusaders or the Seljuk Turks (who would control Baghdad from this point on).

After al-Din's death in 1193, his offspring were largely unable to keep it together in the face of the Crusader onslaught, and the dynasty was weakened by interminable palace intrigue. The only real security for Ayyubid Egypt lay in its independent military strength. In order to maintain this advantage in the face of deteriorating control, Sultan **al-Malik al-Salih Ayyub** was forced to purchase Turkish slaves known as **Mamluks** to man his armies. This was not the brightest move. These mercenaries, originally from the Caucasus and the coast of the Black Sea, were not incompetent drunks falling asleep in their tents like the Hessians employed by Britain to fight George Washington's Continental Army. Rather, they were savvy soldiers who quickly rose to the top of the Ayyubid military ranks, and after the death of al-Salih Ayyub in 1250 CE, they managed to exploit a palace feud and elevate a member of their own ranks to the sultanate. The Mamluk rule lasted for two and a half centuries and brought Egypt to the peak of its evolution in the medieval period.

MAMLUK WHO'S TALKING

The Mamluks, who ruled Egypt from 1250 to 1517, were an interesting bunch. They were not Muslims or Arabs by origin, and some of them knew little if any Arabic. Yet they made Arabic the official language of Egypt and the rest of their empire, and they established Egypt as the unrivaled center of the Arab and Muslim world and effectively saved Egypt and a substantial portion of the Middle East from pagan domination. **Mongol invaders** had abolished the feeble Abbasid caliphate when they invaded and sacked Baghdad in 1258, but the Mamluks reinstated it in Cairo in 1261.

1193
Salah al-Din dies

HISTORY & CULTURE

1250
Mamluks seize control of the sultanate

1250-1517
Rule of Mamluks

1261
Mamluks reinstate Abbasid caliphate in Cairo

FRANKINCENSE, MY DEAR... I *do*

give a damn. For more than five millennia, frankincense was one of the most highly valued substances to the great cultures of the Middle East, Mediterranean, and even the Far East. This "pearl of the desert" was once worth as much as gold. Best known today as one of the gifts given to the baby Jesus by the three kings, frankincense had many aromatic, medicinal, and spiritual uses. The ancient Egyptians used it when embalming their pharaohs, and when the tomb of King Tut was opened in 1922, the fragrance could still be detected from a sealed flask after 3300 years. Believing that frankincense had protective qualities, Arab doctors scented their clothing with the fragrance before visiting ailing patients to avoid contracting contagious diseases. Though this may seem like specious medicine, during the time of the Black Plague in Europe (1603-66), perfumers were immune presumably because they were constantly surrounded by this essential oil. This prized scent had spiritual purposes as well: many ancient cultures believed that the smoke from burning frankincense carried their prayers to their god(s) above.

Under the Mamluks, mosques, colleges, hospitals, and monasteries were built and encyclopedias, chronicles, and dictionaries written. Art and architecture flourished under the 45 Mamluk sultans (that's an average reign of a paltry six years—who ever said it's good to be the king?), who magnified their prestige through a series of victories against the pesky Crusaders, whom they were finally able to expel from the Middle East once and for all. In addition, the Crusades did not stop the Mamluks from opening up a lucrative trade with Europe (and perhaps they facilitated it). The Mamluks understood the important role Egypt played in connecting the Indian Ocean and Africa with the Mediterranean, and under Mamluk rule Alexandria regained its previous importance, establishing contacts with Genoa, Venice, Catalunya, and the south of France.

Unfortunately for Egypt, the discovery of the route to India via the Cape of Good Hope signaled the end of Egyptian importance in trade (and, by extension, the country's prosperity). At the same time, in Istanbul (formerly Constantinople), the **Ottoman Turks** had put the Byzantine Empire out of its misery and was looking to expand their power. The Mamluks resisted the Ottoman invaders, but after a terrible defeat near Aleppo (in Syria) in which the Mamluk sultan was killed, the takeover of the Ottomans seemed inevitable. They effectively became the rulers of Egypt in 1517. The three centuries of Ottoman rule that followed were not a happy time for Egypt. Turkish **pashas** appointed by Ottoman bigwigs in Istanbul administered the region and didn't do such a great job of it. Egypt suffered several famines, and the country—weakened by the impositions of the pashas—grew poor. At the heart of the problem was that the Egyptian economy, which had been largely based for two centuries on the trade of Arab and Yemenite coffee, had run out of luck. Europeans had started to grow their own coffee on the appropriately named Indonesian island of Java and sold the stuff—somewhat ironically—to Cairene merchants. To make matters worse, Columbus's famous 1492 discovery of the New World moved Europe's economic focus away from the Mediterranean and the east, as European imperialists faced the prospect of seemingly limitless westward expansion. The Ottoman Empire, once all-powerful, was now the poor man of Europe.

1517
Ottomans conquer
Egypt

The hapless Ottomans even allowed the Mamluks to get their foot back into the door of power. By the 17th century, a distinct elite known by the title **bey** had emerged in Ottoman Egypt. This class was mainly comprised of Mamluk emirs, who had somehow managed to penetrate the top ranks of the imperial army and bureaucracy. By the early 18th century, Mamluk chiefs recognized by subordinate Mamluk beys were basically running the show in Egypt. Two of these emirs actually secured the Ottomans' de facto recognition of their autonomy in Egypt beginning in 1768. Ultimately, the powers-that-be in Istanbul decided to rein in the Mamluks and sent an army to Egypt to subdue them in 1786. The operation failed, and the Mamluks ruled Egypt until Napoleon's invasion in 1798.

1768
Ottomans recognize Mamluk emir's autonomy in Egypt

THROW ME A BONAPARTE

The idea of a French occupation of Egypt was floated around during the 17th and 18th centuries, but nobody quite got around to it until **Napoleon Bonaparte** sailed in from Toulon in 1798. The invasion was directly connected to the French war with Britain:

Napoleon hoped to disrupt British trade, threaten India, and perhaps gain a pawn to leverage in later negotiations with his enemy. Under the progressive rule of revolutionary France, it was argued, Egypt could emerge from the Ottoman dark age and return to its past glory. Along with guns and warships, Napoleon brought 167 specialists—engineers, architects, mathematicians, chemists, naturalists, artists, musicians, and writers—to Egypt, with all intentions of the invasion giving way to a full-fledged cultural "expedition."

1798
Napoleon
Bonaparte invades
Egypt

Napoleon landed in Egypt on July 1, 1798, and took control of Alexandria the next day. With assurances that the French supported Islam and the Ottoman government and meant only to free Egypt from the Mamluk usurpers, the French advanced on Cairo, winning a key victory over the Mamluk beys in the **Battle of the Pyramids** on July 21. Napoleon entered Cairo days later, where he met with religious leaders and set up councils meant to help the imperialists govern more democratically. But on August 1, British Admiral Horatio Nelson destroyed the French fleet in the **Battle of the Nile,** cutting off Napoleon's communication lines and making it impossible for him to consolidate his conquests. Napoleon moved on to Syria, besieging the city of Acre, but was turned away and headed back to France in 1801.

The expedition, however, did have some lasting effects. The invasion was the 1st European conquest of an Arab country in the history of Islam, the beginning of a colonial trend that lasted into the 20th century. After centuries of isolation from Europe under the Mamluks and Ottomans, Egypt was no longer safe from a Europe that had finally finished carving up the New World and had come back to work on the Old. In bringing a ridiculous number of specialists to Egypt along with his expeditionary force, Napoleon had invented modern **Egyptology,** the study of the culture and artifacts of ancient Egypt. The new discipline made its first big discovery very quickly, uncovering the **Rosetta Stone** in 1799, with which linguists were able to crack the code of ancient Egyptian hieroglyphs (see **It's All Hieroglyphs to Me,** p. 173). Mostly, though, the Napoleonic occupation had permanently weakened the Mamluks and inspired the Ottomans to redouble their attempts to keep control of Egypt.

1801
Napoleon retreats
to France

FLOAT LIKE A VICEROY, STING LIKE A BEY

1799
Rosetta Stone discovered

But the Ottomans just refused to learn their lesson. In order to subdue Egypt, they installed a **viceroy** and sent an occupying army into the region. The **Albanians,** who made up the most effective fighting force in this army, predictably grew into a unit to be reckoned with on the political battlefield as well, and in 1803 they mutinied against the Ottoman viceroy and replaced him with one of their own generals, who in turn was promptly assassinated. To replace the fallen leader, the Albanians chose his lieutenant: a general named **Muhammad 'Ali.** 'Ali (a.k.a. Cassius Clay) proceeded cautiously, sapping power from the Ottomans and Mamluks until 1805, when he took power into his own hands. After weeks of streetfighting in Cairo, Ottoman Sultan Selim III confirmed 'Ali as the viceroy. He stuck around for almost 45 years.

One of 'Ali's first orders of business was getting rid of the Mamluks who had been running Egypt in one way or another for over half a millennium. In his first decade as viceroy, 'Ali dismantled the

HISTORY & CULTURE

1805
Muhammad 'Ali
becomes viceroy

system of tax farming that diverted revenues to Mamluk elites, ultimately making himself the sole landowner in Egypt (and pissing off the free-trading British, who resented 'Ali's monopoly and ability to disregard the terms of Ottoman-British treaties). In 1811, 'Ali took his project of administrative reorganization perhaps a bit too far, inviting around 500 important Mamluks to dinner in the Citadel, where he had them all savagely murdered.

In other ways, though, 'Ali was a pioneer, setting the stage for creation of the modern Egyptian state. He overhauled the army (though he had to put down a mutiny when he tried to introduce Western training techniques too quickly), drafting peasants rather than purchasing the sort of mercenary-slaves that had proven all too eager to rebel against the Ottomans in the past centuries. Those who escaped conscription were employed by the state as workers, building up the region's infrastructure. While 'Ali's dream of an industrialized Egypt was not realized, he took many steps in that direction, modernizing public services, improving irrigation, building roads and bridges, promoting education, and introducing a certain amount of Western culture to Egypt. 'Ali was a despot, but an enlightened one.

1811
Muhammad 'Ali
massacres 500
Mamluk leaders

Egypt under 'Ali expanded militarily as well. The Ottomans, embarassed that the holy cities of Mecca and Medina were controlled by conservative **Wahhabi** Muslims, gave 'Ali carte blanche to invade the Arabian Peninsula. Between 1811-13, the Wahhabis were expelled from the Hijaz, and a later expedition led by 'Ali's son **Ibrahim Pasha** brought central Arabia under Egyptian control. 'Ali also moved up the Nile, pushing Egypt's borders southward into what is now the northern Sudan, taking control of a main route of the lucrative slave trade and beginning an African empire on which later rulers would expand. In 1831, 'Ali—concerned about the Ottoman sultan's growing power and eager to exploit Syria's timber trade—invaded Syria.

1811-13
Wahhabis expelled
from the Hijaz

After a rumble in the desert, the sultan ceded the Syrian provinces to 'Ali's Egypt in 1833. But in 1840, everything turned bad. His son Ibrahim was forced to evacuate Syria, and Egypt's empire in Arabia fell apart as well. The 1840s saw 'Ali a punch-drunk fighter past his prime, and going senile to boot. Ibrahim officially took over as viceroy in 1848, and 'Ali died a year later.

FROM ZEUS TO SUEZ

1833
Sultan cedes Syria
to Muhammad 'Ali

Ibrahim was not long for this world, either, and so the leadership of Egypt (now invested in a *khedive,* essentially a hereditary viceroy) passed to 'Ali's grandson **'Abbas.** 'Abbas was by nature something of a reactionary, distrustful of all things European and modern. He opposed French proposals to begin construction of a canal linking the Mediterranean and Red Sea (to be known forevermore as the **Suez Canal**), though he did permit Britain to build the **Alexandria-Cairo Railway.** The spread of European influence to Egypt, set in motion with the Napoleonic expedition of 1798, was beginning to resemble a runaway train. On the whole, though, 'Abbas rolled back many of his grandfather's reforms, though his cuts in spending actually made him popular among the lower classes, who were less burdened with forced labor and military service than under 'Ali. ('Abbas must not have been universally loved by the working man, however: two of his servants strangled him to death in 1854.)

1849
Muhammad 'Ali
dies

Next in line was **Sa'id Pasha,** 'Ali's fourth son. Sa'id wasn't quite a chip off the old block, but while he lacked his father's greatness he generally shared his reformist tendencies. In 1854, the Western-educated Sa'id made a deal with **Ferdinand de Lesseps,** a French buddy of his (and his dad's), known as the **Act of Concession,** allowing Lesseps to build a canal across the Suez isthmus. Two years later, Sa'id signed off on a follow-up agreement granting the aptly named Suez Canal Company the right to operate the canal for 99 years—a full life sentence—after its completion. Construction started in 1859, by which point Sa'id and the Ottoman sultan already opposed the project, but it was too late. Sa'id died in 1863, just as the Egyptian cotton industry was beginning to benefit from the price increases caused by the American Civil War, and another grandson of 'Ali's took over.

Isma'il, the first viceroy to be officially recognized as *khedive* (though the title had been used unofficially since 'Ali), accelerated the pace of modernization. He supported the Suez Canal construction, and after renegotiating with the French and drawing certain concessions (for instance, Isma'il refused to provide the Suez Canal Company with unlimited Egyptian peasant labor), he presided over the ceremonial opening of the canal in 1869. This engineering triumph, however, would prove to be the brief, shining moment in Isma'il's rule, which was increasingly characterized by a pattern of Egypt going into deeper and deeper **debt** to the European powers. To be fair, it was not a pattern that Isma'il began; rather it began with the champ's costly reforms and worsened during the viceroyships of 'Abbas and Sa'id. The problem was not helped by Isma'il's move to expand Egyptian control farther south and southwest, egged on by the increasingly involved Europeans (who were appalled by the slave trade that had built up in these regions). The beleagured *khedive* tried anything he could think of to stave off Egypt's bankruptcy, including selling his shares of the Suez Canal to Britain in 1875. The European lenders established the **Commission on the Public Debt** in 1876, and Isma'il was forced to accept British and French control over Egyptian revenue and expenditure: the slippery slope toward loss of autonomy was fully in place. Isma'il tried to resist the international control of his country, attempting to curry favor at home, but he had already lost a great deal of domestic support. Subversives and nationalists in Egyptian society (including the army) had begun to question the status quo, which was increasingly characterized by the influence of the Europeans, the emergence of ethnic Turks and Circassians as elites, and the dictatorial power of the *khedive*. Spurred by Isma'il's intransigence (and by the British and French), the Ottoman sultan fired Isma'il (like a rocket) in 1879, replacing him with his son—Muhammad 'Ali's great-grandson **Tawfiq.**

Predictably, the handpicked Tawfiq turned out to be a pretty big wuss. Britain and France moved quickly to crack down on the nationalist sentiment that Isma'il had begun to encourage, reinstating the joint British-French power over Egypt (known as **Dual Control**). The British controller, a man named **Evelyn Baring** (later to become **Lord Cromer**), was as much of a hardass as Tawfiq was a pawn. Perhaps trying to make up for his girly first name (in the same way that Napoleon had overcompensated for his diminutive stature), Baring essentially ruled Egypt's finances with an iron fist as the French gradually

HISTORY & CULTURE

1854
'Abbas murdered; Sa'id Pasha agrees to let French build Suez Canal

1859
Construction on Suez Canal begins

1869
Isma'il presides over opening of the Suex Canal

1876
European creditors establish Commission on the Public Debt

1879
Isma'il removed; Tawfiq becomes *khedive*

retreated from the scene. British and French financial control would not be enough, however, to keep Egypt in line. Concerned by the growing nationalist forces in both the **Assembly of Delegates** (led by one-time Prime Minister **Sharif Pasha**) and the army (led by **'Urabi Pasha**), the Europeans shut down the Assembly. Unrest continued, and rioting broke out after British and French naval forces showed up at Alexandria. However, France refused to go along with a July 11, 1882 bombardment of Alexandria, and from this point on Britain was in control. The Brits sent an expedition to the Suez Canal, defeated the 'Urabists in a battle near Cairo on September 13, and occupied Cairo the next day.

MODERN HISTORY

THE VEILED PROTECTORATE

1882
Britain begins occupation of Egypt

The British occupation of Egypt that ensued was to last 74 years. Initially, the new Liberal government of **William Gladstone** was hesitant to maintain a heavy presence in the country. For one thing, Egypt was technically part of the Ottoman Empire, and Britain didn't want to piss off the sultan any more than necessary. For another, the other European powers—especially France—would obviously resent British imperial advances into the hugely important region. But Britain had made a commitment to preserving its economic interests in Egypt (i.e. keeping the Suez Canal open, getting Egypt to repay its debts), and ultimately they were unable to protect their wallets without guns. With Baring playing puppetmaster and Tawfiq marionette, the British exercised increasing authority as time went on.

In 1892, however, Tawfiq died, and much to the Brits' dismay, his 17-year-old son, **'Abbas Hilmi II,** had no interest in listening to the crusty middle-aged Baring (now Lord Cromer). From the start, the teen *khedive* was intent on stirring things up. He canned the prime minister in 1893 and appointed a new one of his own choice, though he was stopped short by the British, who forced him to unfire the old P.M. In 1894, 'Abbas provoked the British once again, running his mouth with derogatory remarks about **Lord Horatio Kitchener,** the commander-in-chief of the limey imperial forces in Egypt. Once again, Cromer stepped in and made the hot-headed young *khedive* apologize. 'Abbas soon enlisted the help of **Mustafa Kamil,** a young Western-educated contemporary who shared his hatred of the British and endeavored—through speeches and his nationalist newspaper—to create an Egyptian nationalism based on anti-imperialism and support for the *khedive*. This movement was helped along by the 1896-98 effort to reconquer the Sudan, of which the British effectively took direct control. 'Abbas and Kamil's efforts were stymied by Britain and France signing the **Entente Cordiale** in 1904. The nationalists had looked to France as a liberal ally against the British imperialists; with the treaty between the two Western European powers, Kamil was forced to turn to the increasingly feeble Ottomans for support. (The Ottoman Empire, once the sick man of Europe, was now more or less on life support.) To make matters worse, Kamil died in 1908, just months after founding the **National Party.**

1892
Tawfiq dies; 'Abbas Hilmi becomes *khedive*

1896-98
Britain reconquers the Sudan

After the Entente with France, Britain's position in Egypt seemed extremely secure, but times were a-changing. In the aftermath of a nasty clash between British officers and Egyptian peasants that ended in a dead Brit, Cromer finally called it quits in 1907. His successor, **Sir Eldon Gorst,** was much less of an autocratic egomaniac. Gorst actually tried to understand the new generation exemplified by 'Abbas and Kamil, and he worked toward the goal of empowering Egyptians with governmental responsibilities and diminishing British control. Sadly, Gorst kicked the bucket in 1911, having not really had the chance to see whether his initiatives could have worked. At the very least, he had succeeded in pissing off the British colonial officers (though not quite appeasing the nationalists). Nationalists in the General Assembly voted down a proposal to prolong the Suez Canal's life sentence by 40 years, and the prime minister who supported the plan, **Boutros Ghali Pasha** (of the same prominent Coptic family that spawned former UN Secretary-General Boutros Boutros-Ghali) was assassinated days later. Kitchener, chosen as the new proconsul, promptly ended the experiment of working with the *khedive*.

WAR AND INDEPENDENCE

The days of the veiled protectorate were numbered—it was time for Britain to put up or shut up. Nobody, however, could have guessed the impetus for the next move: **World War I.** When Britain declared war with Germany and its allies (among them the Ottoman Empire), there was no more use in pretending that Britain was not really governing Egypt. In December 1914, Egypt was officially declared a British protectorate, and 'Abbas II—the last *khedive*—was removed from office. ('Abbas's uncle **Hussein Kamil** was appointed sultan in his place, though he soon died, and power shifted to his brother **Ahmad Fouad.**) Britain did not force Egypt to marshal troops for the war effort, but Egyptians—especially peasants—were profoundly affected by the war. Particularly during World War I, the Egyptian economy was so completely focused on the exportation of cotton to England's rheumatic textile mills that grain actually had to be imported to feed the rural population. The imposition of martial law and the closing of the Legislative Assembly hampered the efforts of the nationalists.

Immediately after World War I ended, however, the nationalists saw their chance. Just days after the armistice, three Egyptian politicians, led by **Sa'ad Zaghloul,** paid a visit to the British high commissioner and announced their intention to send a *wafd* (delegation) to Britain to argue the case for Egyptian autonomy in front of the powers-that-be from whom the colonial powers-that-be took their orders. The Brits didn't take the news very well, refusing to accept a delegation and throwing Zaghloul into jail for good measure—a move that provoked outrage among Egyptian nationalists on the ground. British war hero and resident smart guy **Lord Edmund Allenby** was quickly dispatched to Egypt, where he persuaded the imperial administrators to make some concessions to the nationalists. Zaghloul was released, free to build up his political organization, which became known as the **Wafd Party.** After some more machinations by Zaghloul and Allenby, Britain recognized Egypt's independence on February 28, 1922, ending the protectorate but maintaining British control over four crucial areas: the security of imperial communications, defense, the protection of minorities and foreigners, and the Sudan. The sultan was crowned **King Fouad I** of the new **Kingdom of Egypt.**

1908
Mustafa Kamil dies

1907
Lord Cromer quits; Sir Eldon Gorst named proconsul

1911
Gorst dies; Lord Kitchener named proconsul

1914
World War II breaks out; Egypt declared British protectorate; 'Abbas II removed from office

1918
War ends; Sa'ad Zaghloul announces intention to send a delegation *(wafd)* to Britain

The Kingdom of Egypt was formally a constitutional monarchy, with universal male suffrage and a bicameral legislature limiting the power of the king, but it never quite turned out that way in practice. In some senses, Fouad's domain was merely a puppet kingdom with Britain pulling the important strings. On the other hand, Fouad turned out to be more ambitious than anyone had thought, trying to assert his power both over the British and over the Wafdists, who—as Egypt's only real national party—were extremely popular throughout the country. The result was a decidedly undemocratic three-way power struggle between these competing actors. The Wafd, ideologically committed to independence from Britain and government by constitutional law rather than by royal dictatorship, was the only one of these groups that even professed anything approaching liberal democracy, and even they were willing to compromise and play Fouad and the British off one another to win concessions. For a while, they did a pretty good job of it: with a strong nationwide organization, monopoly on Egyptian populism, and charismatic leader in Zaghloul (until his death in 1927), the Wafd consistently dominated legislative elections. Increasingly, though, the Wafd began to splinter and quarrel internally, beginning with the defection of many Wafdists to the **Liberal Constitutionalist Party** in 1922. By 1936, when Fouad died (and was succeeded by his son **Farouk**) and the **Anglo-Egyptian Treaty of 1936** moved Egypt a step closer to true independence—though Britain continued to hold the Suez Canal—it was unclear whether the Wafdists would ultimately be capable of leading Egypt to complete autonomy. King Farouk came of age in 1937 and was eager to rule and very popular. His quest for power was aided by another split in the Wafd, and by clashes between the Wafdist youth **Greenshirts** and the fascist Blueshirts of Young Egypt. The Wafd won only 12 seats in the 1938 elections.

Egypt again came to center stage as an Allied base of operations during **World War II**. The decisive Allied victory at the **Battle of al-'Alamein** (just outside Alexandria, see p. 174) allowed the Allies to sweep into North Africa and halt the advances of Nazi General **Edwin Rommel's Afrika Korps** once and for all. Resentment toward the British reached a fever pitch during and after World War II as Egyptians—many of whom sympathized with Germany's oddly anti-imperialist rhetoric when it came to the Middle East (and Zionism)—rioted against the war. The Wafd, however, cooperated with Britain throughout the war and was rewarded when Britain forced Farouk to reinstate Wafd standard-bearer **Mustafa al-Nahhas** as prime minister in 1942 (it was Nahhas's fourth of five stints in the office). After they won an overwhelming victory at the polls in 1942, it looked as if Wafdists had played their cards right. However, the intervention had its costs: Farouk's distaste for al-Nahhas and the British had become obvious, and the Wafdist complicity with the British damaged its status as a legitimate nationalist party.

The end of the war brought no stability. The Wafd declined further, as political opponents called for the revision of the 1936 treaty and complete independence for Egypt. The **Muslim Brotherhood** grew from a reformist Islamic group into a huge, militant organization. Continued rioting and striking led the British—who were more than a bit preoccupied with the Palestine question—to finally leave Alexandria in 1947. Nationalism,

1922
Britain recognizes independence of Kingdom of Egypt; Sultan Fouad crowned king

1927
Sa'ad Zaghloul dies

1936
Anglo-Egyptian Treaty signed

1937
King Farouk comes of age

1942
World War II Battle of al-Alamein

both of the Egyptian and Arab varieties, had been picking up steam since the 1930s, with Egypt taking a lead role in the founding of the **Arab League** in 1943-44 and an increasing interest in the Palestinian struggle for a nation-state since 1936. Egypt hoped to regain some semblance of stability with its invasion of the newly declared state of Israel in 1948, but when the tiny Israeli army easily defeated a coalition of Arab states (Egypt, Jordan, Syria, and Iraq), the nation was completely humiliated and demoralized. Political and social instability reigned, as both the prime minister and the leader of the Muslim Brotherhood were assassinated within a two-month span. Nahhas returned to power in 1950 for the fifth and final time, and in 1951 he abrogated the 1936 treaty. But even the old Wafdist pro could not put an end to the national chaos. Guerrilla warfare against the British led to action in Isma'ilia, which in turn resulted in the city of Cairo being burned by demonstrators in January 1952. Nahhas was forced out, followed by a prime minister gong show—four new premiers in six months.

THE NASSER REVOLUTION(S)

Egypt was ripe for a revolution. There was much with which to be disenchanted—the corruption of King Farouk, the economic crisis and deep inequality in the country, the continued British control of the Suez Canal—and radicals on both the right and left had polarized political debates. The revolution, however, would come from the inside. Several young military officers, outraged at the incompetence of their elder leaders in the **Arab-Israeli War of 1948-49** and generally disenchanted with the state of things, formed the **Free Officers** coalition and staged a bloodless coup d'etat in July 1952. King Farouk was forced to abdicate, all political parties and the Constitution were abolished, and General **Muhammad Naguib** was elected prime minister (although the government was really controlled by a nine-member **Revolutionary Command Council** led by Colonel **Gamal 'Abd al-Nasser**). The aims of the Free Officers were fairly vague. The coup leaders were a motley crew of military men, united by a nationalist sentiment and a desire to restore Egypt's dignity after the disastrous invasion of Israel. The Free Officers certainly did not agree on any substantive policy program—some flirted with the Muslim Brotherhood, while others were essentially socialists. In a sense, then, the coup destroyed the prospects of a true left-wing or right-wing social revolution. Under Nasser's command, however, it would give way to a revolution from above. In any event, the monarchy was abolished and the king's property confiscated, and the **Egyptian Arab Republic** was declared on January 16, 1953.

Nasser wasted no time in cleaning up the unresolved issues that plagued the old regime. Negotiations with Britain secured an agreement on the question of the Sudan, which until now had been nominally attached to British-controlled Egypt. Britain agreed to put in place a process of self-determination that would result in **Sudanese independence** on January 1, 1956. In October 1954, Britain and Egypt reached an agreement (the **Anglo-Egyptian Treaty of 1954**) that provided for the removal of British troops still left in the Suez Canal zone. Meanwhile, Nasser—who had concealed his power so brilliantly that foreign correspondents didn't know who he was for over a

1945
World War II ends

1947
British leave Alexandria

1943-44
Egypt takes lead in founding of Arab League

1948-49
War of Israeli Independence (al-Naqba)

1951
Al-Nahhas abrogates 1936 Anglo-Egyptian Treaty

1952
Free Officers overthrow government

1953
Egyptian Arab Republic declared

year—moved to make his leadership official. He faced a challenge in 1954 from Naguib, the Free Officers' figurehead and a moderate who advocated the establishment of a parliamentary system. Nasser, younger and more radical, wanted to pursue more revolutionary objectives. Naguib won the support of the (miniscule) Egyptian middle class, the Muslim Brotherhood, and the leaders of the old political parties. Nasser, who was already strong within the military, turned toward the working class and the police for backing. Nasser's victory in the power struggle ensured that the new form of government would be somewhat leftist and at the same time highly reliant on the police and security apparatus as well as the military: a one-party, populist, (somewhat) socialist, corporatist regime that would engage in significant surveillance and manipulation of the civilian population. The first step would be Nasser's move to crush the Muslim Brotherhood after one of its members attempted to assassinate him in October 1954.

For all of his revolutionary flair, Nasser—who officially became president of Egypt in 1956—was initially interested chiefly in domestic reform and was rather sympathetic to the West. Equal parts brilliant strategist and power-obsessed dictator, he gained popularity because of his dedication to the plight of the **fellaheen** (peasant) majority in Egypt. On the international front, he was not originally the revolutionary that everyone remembers today. His agreements with the British regarding the Sudan and the Suez Canal were criticized domestically by the nationalists as too soft on the West. Furthermore, Nasser was not very interested in the Palestinian plight and saw little use in fighting Israel. (It is possible that the president, who lived as a child with his uncle in a building occupied by nine Jewish families, didn't hate the Jews as much as his ever-escalating rhetoric would suggest.) He was tragically drawn into the melee by events out of his control: Palestinian guerrillas were using Egypt-controlled Gaza as a base for attacks on Israel, and the Israeli policy of full-scale retaliation that was adopted in 1953 resulted in the death of 38 Egyptians in Gaza after a 1955 counterattack. As time went on, Nasser abandoned his hesitations about fighting Israel—a decision that would ultimately lead to his downfall.

Increasingly, Nasser turned toward the Soviet Union and the Arab world. He refused to join the **Baghdad Pact (Middle East Treaty Organzination,** a.k.a. the Central Treaty Organization), in which Iran, Iraq, Turkey, and Pakistan aligned themselves with Britain and the United States in the Cold War. This endeared Nasser to Moscow, and in 1955, Egypt and Soviet satellite Czechoslovakia signed an arms agreement—the first Soviet step into the Middle East, a region where it would become increasingly prominent. Egypt's official recognition of the People's Republic of China in 1956 was to be the straw that broke the camel's back. US Secretary of State **John Foster Dulles** then made his fatal miscalculation, withdrawing America's pledge to finance the building of a dam at Aswan.

This insult triggered the chain of events that would lead to the **Suez Crisis.** Nasser **nationalized the Suez Canal,** arguing that if America (and Britain) would not provide the funding for the dam, Egypt had to raise revenue somehow. Britain was outraged, as were the French (who were also irked by Nasser's support of the Algerian struggle for independence

1954
Anglo-Egyptian
Treaty signed

1956
Gamal 'abd al-
Nasser officially
becomes president, nationalizes
the Suez Canal

1955
Nasser signs arms
agreement with
Czechoslovakia

HISTORY & CULTURE

from France). The two erstwhile colonial powers enlisted the help of Israel in retaking the canal. On October 29, 1956, the Israeli army attacked Egyptian positions in the Sinai. Two days later, Israelis had secured the canal. Egypt refused a Franco-British ultimatum, and the two nations swiftly moved their troops into the canal zone. This time, though, the Europeans had miscalculated. A chorus of world opinion, led by *both* the US and the USSR, denounced the invasion, which smacked of old-school imperialism—and Britain and France were forced to withdraw. The United Nations moved into the canal zone with an international peacekeeping force to enforce the ceasefire, the Suez Canal left firmly in Egyptian control. Nasser had gambled, and although he had been crushed on the battlefield, he had won a huge political victory. (And the Soviet Union ultimately agreed to help finance the **Aswan High Dam** (p. 250), which opened in 1968.)

GROWTH OF PAN-ARABISM

Having defied the old colonial powers, Nasser was now a rock star in the Arab world, and he took the momentum and ran with it in a decidedly radical direction. Professing a new nationalist doctrine of **pan-Arabism,** Nasser—the first true Egyptian to rule Egypt in millennia—saw himself not only as the leader of Egypt, but of the entire Arab world, of Africa, and even of the entire Muslim world. The first (and last) step toward an united Arab world was taken in 1958, when Egypt and Syria merged to form the **United Arab Republic.** This experiment was to be short-lived: Syria backed out of the union in 1961, though Egypt continued to call itself the UAR. In the Cold War, although Nasser made gestures toward the USSR, Egypt officially maintained a policy of **positive neutrality** (in Nasser's one-party Egypt, the communists were enemies of the state)—a position of non-alignment also advocated by **Jawaharlal Nehru** of India and **Josip Broz Tito** of Yugoslavia.

The failure of the UAR was a major setback, but Nasser was determined to remain on the offensive, pumping up his anti-Israel rhetoric to maintain his standing in the Arab world and intervening on the republican side of the Yemeni civil war in 1962. The ensuing events would only confirm the impossibility of a united Arab front, however, as the intervention provoked a conflict with conservative Saudi Arabia, which supported the Yemeni royalists. America, a Saudi ally, cut off economic aid to Egypt in retaliation. Nasser reacted to the secession of Syria by moving to the left domestically as well, announcing that a doctrine of **scientific socialism** would be Egypt's road to modernization and industrialization; the **Arab Socialist Union** was created to replace Nasser's old corporatist organization, known as the **National Union.** In fact, the Nasser years were marked by the introduction of 20th-century innovations into rural villages, the rise of a new Egyptian middle class (once a bourgeoisie largely filled with foreigners), the improvement in the status of women, and the growth of industry. However, improvements in industry were never quite matched by improvements in agriculture, and the country's birth rate remained too high for the increases in output to translate into higher standards of living. Further, Nasser's Egypt was a police state where phones were tapped, mail opened, dissidents imprisoned, newspapers nationalized, and media censored.

1958
Egypt and Syria merge to form United Arab Republic

1962
Egypt intervenes on republican side of Yemeni civil war

HISTORY & CULTURE

Nasser's inflated rhetoric and grandiose plans eventually caught up with him. As the 1960s went on, terrorist raids on Israel carried out by Palestinian guerrillas increased in frequency, and a radical government in Syria pledged open support for these attacks in 1966. After an Israeli counterstrike on Jordan, Nasser was taken to task by ally-turned-rival Syria for hiding behind the **United Nations Emergency Force (UNEF)** that kept the peace along the Egypt-Israel border. Baited into abandoning his earlier policy of restraint (known euphemistically as "militant inaction"), Nasser finally called for the withdrawal of the UNEF from the Sinai border. The UN interpreted this as a demand for the removal of peacekeeping troops from Sharm al-Sheikh at the head of the **Gulf of Aqaba**—ostensibly to be replaced by the posting of Egyptian soldiers there and the closing of the gulf to Israelis.

1966
Syria pledges support for Palestine guerrilla attacks

Israel had made it clear that it would consider the closing of the gulf to be a declaration of war, and on July 5, 1967, Israel launched a preemptive strike on all Egyptian airfields, destroying most Egyptian planes while they were still on the ground and killing an estimated 10,000 Egyptians. The **Six Day War** that followed was a complete disaster for Egypt. In only six days, Israel took control of the Sinai Peninsula and other strategic locations, penetrating all the way to the Suez Canal on July 9. Nasser stepped down in disgrace, though a still-adoring public refused to accept his resignation. The Nasser era was truly over, though, and the leader had a heart attack and died on September 28, 1970—to be honored with the largest funeral ever held in Egypt.

1967
Six Day War

SADAT AND PEACE WITH ISRAEL

After the 1967 disaster, Nasser began a move to the right that was accelerated by his successor, Vice President **Anwar al-Sadat.** The seamless transition to Sadat, also a Free Officer, indicated that the election-legitimated authoritarian regime Nasser had created was quite stable (indeed, it remains intact to this day). The rules of the game were as follows: The president served a six-year term and was almost inevitably reelected for additional terms. The legislative branch of government consisted of the 444-member **People's Assembly,** half of whom had to be workers or peasants and a whopping 30 of whom had to be women.

1970
Nasser dies; Anwar al-Sadat becomes president

The three main bases of power in Egypt at the time—the security apparatus, the Arab Socialist Union (the country's sole legal political party), and the resurgent Muslim Brotherhood—expected Sadat to be a temporary leader. Sadat turned out, however, to be smarter than most observers had believed, outmaneuvering a plethora of rivals in 1971 and consolidating his power. Furthermore, Sadat (perhaps understanding that the days of the Soviet Union were numbered) recognized that Egypt's true interests lay with recognition of and peace with Israel—and, by extension, good relations with the United States. But Sadat knew that such a radical step would not be easy, particularly given the ferocity of the anti-Israeli sentiment that Nasser had stirred up throughout his tenure, and that it would be impossible to rush right to the bargaining table with Egypt's sworn enemies.

So Sadat made a calculated tactical move. On October 6, 1973—Yom Kippur, the holiest day of the Jewish calendar—Egypt and Syria launched a surprise attack on Israeli forces in the Sinai. Sadat knew that Israel could not be defeated (especially after America stopped waffling and committed itself to supporting Israel), but the **October War** (also known as the **Yom Kippur War**) was instrumental in strengthening Egypt's hand in negotiations. The stalemate—a far cry from the Israeli routs in 1948 and 1967—boosted Arab morale and weakened Egypt's ties with the USSR, whose military advisers were expelled by Sadat in 1972 because of their supposed reluctance to fight Israel. Declaring the war an Arab victory, Sadat was able to forge ahead with the **Sinai I** and **Sinai II** agreements in 1974 and 1975, which returned large parts of the Sinai to Egypt and secured commitments to foreign aid.

After these early successes, negotiations inevitably stagnated in the face of Israeli intransigence and Arab impatience, so Sadat decided to play another trump card. In a dramatic visit reminiscent of US President Richard Nixon's visit to China, Sadat traveled to Jerusalem and addressed the Israeli Parliament on November 17, 1977. Soon after, Sadat and Israeli Prime Minister **Menaḥem Begin** began secret peace negotiations at Camp David in America. With the help of US President **Jimmy Carter,** Begin and Sadat reached an agreement in 1978, known as the **Camp David Accords.** In exchange for control of the Sinai, the two countries normalized their political and economic relations, with Egypt officially recognizing Israel's right to exist. Nasser's pan-Arabist dream of the Muslim world rising up in unison to destroy Israel was dead.

Everything seemed to be going as planned for Sadat, who shared the 1978 Nobel Peace Prize with Begin and was hailed by the West for his steps toward economic liberalization and democratization of Egypt's political system. No longer committed to the Soviet Union or socialism in any substantive way, Sadat opened Egypt to market reforms, and with them, tons of foreign aid and investment. By the 1980s, America was forking over more than US$1 billion per year. At the same time, Sadat returned Egypt (at least somewhat) to a multi-party political system and dismantled the most repressive features of Nasser's nearly totalitarian rule.

But while Sadat was hailed in the West as a peacemaker and democrat, his support at home was crumbling. As the **Palestinian Liberation Organization** grew increasingly discouraged by the slow pace of progress on the Palestinian question, Sadat found it difficult to make the case to the Arab world that the peace treaty he signed with Israel would adequately protect Palestinian interests. Many thought that he had sold out Palestine to the West and the almighty American dollar. Shortly after Camp David, Egypt was expelled from the Arab League it had played such an integral role in founding 30 years before. Meanwhile, foreign aid did not prove to be a panacea for the ailing Egyptian economy. Neoliberal reforms resulted in widening gaps between rich and poor, and the persistent social problems that Nasser's scientific socialism had failed to fix only grew worse. In 1977, demonstrations in Egypt's cities led to an estimated 79 deaths and hundreds of Egyptians injured or thrown in jail. In September 1981, Sadat arrested 1300 political elites—a clear sign that his position was tenuous. The peasants (who had

1973
Sadat attacks Israel on Yom Kippur, beginning October War

1974-75
Sinai I and II agreements signed

1977
Sadat addresses Israeli Parliament

1978
Sadat signs Camp David Accords with Israel

HISTORY & CULTURE

never taken to Sadat the way they loved the heartthrob Nasser) were suffering dire economic hardship, leftists detested Sadat's liberal reforms and abandonment of the one-party socialist state, the old security apparatus resented Sadat's scaling back of the police state, and right-wing nationalists and Islamic fundamentalists—once Sadat's dependable supporters—turned against him after the peace treaty with Israel. This last group, the fundamentalists, would write the final chapter of Sadat's rule, as members of a Muslim fringe group assassinated Sadat at a military parade on October 6, 1981. Egypt did not mourn.

1977
79 die in urban demonstrations

IF IT AIN'T MUBARAK, DON'T MUFIX IT

Current President **Hosni Mubarak,** elected in 1981, continued his predecessor's policies with less derring-do and more domestic sensitivity. Mubarak—a former air force commander and October War hero—was responsible for developing Egypt's growing tourism industry, resuming diplomatic and trade relations with moderate Arab countries, and bandaging the wounds made by the flamboyant swathe Sadat cut through Arab politics. While Mubarak affirmed the Camp David Accords, he also cooled relations with Israel (while simultaneously keeping up ties with America, now Egypt's most important financial benefactor). Mubarak also attempted to address the domestic economic problems that led to Sadat's downfall, pledging early in his first term to relieve the inequality between the common people and the privileged elites who took home most of the benefits of foreign aid under Sadat. However, Egypt's economic problems worsened, and Mubarak was criticized for Egypt's policy of disengagement when Israel invaded Lebanon in 1982. Mubarak's caution paid off, though: although official relations with Israel remained intact, they were extremely tense until Israel's partial withdrawal in 1985—which was enough time for Egypt to mend its differences with the rest of the Arab world. In 1984, Egypt restored relations with the USSR and was readmitted to the Islamic Conference. In 1988, the Arab League invited Egypt to rejoin, dropping demands that Mubarak sever ties with Israel.

1981
Islamic fundamentalists assassinate Sadat; Hosni Mubarak becomes president

Mubarak's support of Saudi Arabia and Kuwait in the 1990-91 crisis that led to the **Persian Gulf War** was important in revitalizing Egypt's position at the center of Middle Eastern politics, as Egypt played a lead role in rallying other Arab countries against **Saddam Hussein's** Iraq. Additionally, Mubarak played a part in facilitating the Israeli-Palestinian peace agreement, known as the **Oslo Accords,** reached in 1993. Domestic obstacles for Mubarak in the 1990s included demands by opposition parties for more open democracy, as Egypt has not held free elections since 1950. The most significant political threat, however, continued to be internal Arab dissidents, in the form of the Islamist parties who remain intent on destabilizing the government and installing an Islamic theocracy. Mubarak has consistently appeased Islamic moderates (who are in the majority, anyway) in order to isolate militants: alcohol was banned on EgyptAir flights, the American TV show *Dallas* was taken off the air, and an Islamic newspaper, *al-Liwa' al-Islami,* was initiated. The past several years have seen a rise in Islamist-generated violence, with militants based in **Middle Egypt** striking at the status quo via attacks on government figures and assassinations of secularist intellectuals. The deadli-

1982
Israel invades Lebanon; Egyptian-Israeli relations cool

1988
Egypt rejoins Arab League

1991
Egypt supports Kuwait and Saudi Arabia in the Gulf War

HISTORY & CULTURE

est attack by Islamist militants involved the death of 58 tourists at **Luxor** on November 17, 1997, leading the government to drastically tighten security throughout the country. Mubarak himself escaped an assassination attempt in Ethiopia in 1995, and was slightly wounded in 1999 by a knife-wielding attacker. Still, modern Egypt's longest-serving president keeps on trucking, having been "elected" to his 4th term in 1999.

IN THE NEWS

Egypt's tourism industry, which was electrified by the shocking 1997 terrorist attack at Luxor, appeared to have made a brilliant recovery; but since the Israeli-Palestinian violence that broke out in September 2000, tourism in Egypt has gone back into a slump (though it remains safe to travel in the country). Relations with Israel, not surprisingly, have taken a similar turn. When Israeli troops bombarded the Gaza Strip in November 2000 in response to Palestinian terrorist attacks, Egyptians considered the reprisal to be an overreaction, and Mubarak recalled the Egyptian ambassador from Tel Aviv in protest. On the other hand, Egypt and Israel were able to reach a very different sort of agreement in January 2001, when the two nations inked a US$3 billion deal under which Egypt will supply its neighbor with natural gas until 2012. Despite regional conflict, it seems that business-as-usual is the order of the day in Egypt. In April 2001, US Secretary of Defense **Donald Rumsfeld** announced the Bush Administration's intention to remove American peacekeeping troops from the Sinai.

Meanwhile, Mubarak has come under increased fire for the persistent authoritarianism of his rule. Although reforms have been made, Egypt is still worlds away from being a legitimate democracy. No opposition candidates are permitted to stand in presidential "elections," which are really no more than referenda to rubber stamp Mubarak's continued rule. In the last four of these yea-or-nay propositions, Mubarak has won—on average—96 percent of the vote. In May 2001, Mubarak drew major heat when **Sa'ad Eddin Ibrahim**—a prominent Egyptian-American sociologist and advocate of civil rights and increased democracy in Egypt—was sent to prison for seven years. The trumped-up charges: accepting money from abroad without the government's permission, embezzling funds, and "defaming Egypt." Even after the conviction drew the outrage of human rights organizations, the United Nations, the European Union, and the Western media, Mubarak refused to override the verdict (which was reached by a panel of three Cairo judges even before the defense team had finished turning over its evidence). The trial has led many to question just how far Egypt has moved toward political liberalization—and whether the pressure of dealing with Egypt's substantial radical right (Muslim and otherwise) has gotten to the aging Mubarak. To make matters worse, 52 men were charged in July 2001 with engaging in immoral acts—the largest **anti-gay** trial in Egyptian history—leading Egypt's increasingly vocal gay community to claim that the government has stepped up harassment of gays in recent months.

In less contentious cultural news, the **Library at Alexandria** was supposed to reopen in 2001, nearly five millennia after Ptolemy I first commissioned the construction of the building. As is to

1997
Islamist attack at Luxor kills 58 tourists

1999
Mubarak elected to 4th term

HISTORY & CULTURE

be expected with a project on such a grand scale, the construction is running a little late, but is close to completion. As of August 2001, UNESCO projects the inauguration date at April 23, 2002. The original Library at Alexandria was mysteriously burned down near the end of the Roman Empire. The purpose of the new edifice is almost as unclear as the cause of the fire so many years ago. Egyptian authorities say that the library is being built to foster the research of scholars in the Middle East, and consequently, Arab countries have helped pick up a third of the library's US$150 million cost. These funds will be used to collect over 8 million books and manuscripts, and to construct a science museum, a planetarium, and a school for library studies. Many scholars and diplomats have criticized the project as a governmental propaganda machine, a library offering a multitude of resources to the public but not really fostering or even tolerating the sort of radical intellectual inquiry that the original library had. Press censorship in Egypt is quite widespread: books and news articles are frequently banned, and many scholars doubt that the government will allow them to research or publish works criticizing Middle Eastern and Arabic policies. For another look at the controversy, see **A Library Long Overdue,** p. 168.

RELIGION AND ETHNICITY

ANCIENT EGYPT

Much like other religions of the ancient world, ancient Egyptian religion sought to provide its adherents with an explanation for the natural phenomena surrounding them, including the agricultural cycles and the cycle of life and death. Egyptian religion was unique, however, in the degree to which it focused on death and afterlife as matters of concern in this world. Priests, pharaohs, and nobles spent virtually their entire lives preparing for death, from funerary arrangements to gathering the stuff they wanted to take with them on the road. The centrality of the gods in this venture was also a distinguishing feature, where the cult of a particular god would act as the focal point of preparation for death. Gods would also have changing qualities or functions, depending on the region of Egypt or the time period. For an introduction to the pantheon's cast of characters, see **Meet the Gods,** (p. 75).

ISLAM

The Arabic word *islam* translates, in its general sense, as "submission," and the basic tenet of Islam is submission to the will of God, **Allah.** Islam has its roots in revelations received from 610 to 622 CE by **Muhammad,** who was informed of his prophetic calling by the angel Gabriel. These revelations, the **Qur'an** (Arabic for "recitation"), form the core text of Islam. Muslims believe the Arabic text is perfect, immutable, and untranslatable—the words of God embodied in human language. Consequently, the Qur'an appears throughout the Muslim world (the majority of which is non-Arabic speaking) in Arabic. Muhammad is seen as the "seal of the prophets," the last and greatest in a chain of God's messengers that includes Jewish and Christian figures such as Abraham, Moses, and Jesus.

Islam is constitutionally established as the official religion of Egypt, with over 90% of the population belonging to the **Sunni Muslim** sect (see p. 76 for more information on the Sunnis). Western mores do not apply, especially in matters of family and sex. The visibility and freedom of most Egyptian women is limited. Egypt is one of the most important centers of Islamic theological study in the world, with Cairo's **al-Azhar University** (p. 114) at its heart. Al-Azhar is the oldest continuously operating university in the world and has graduated Islamic scholars from every Muslim country on earth since it was first founded in 972 CE.

MEET THE GODS The ancient Egyptians didn't play that monotheism game. Here's a brief rundown of their many deities:

AMUN "The Hidden One." Amun is typically portrayed as a ram-horned man with blue-colored flesh. In the New Kingdom he became associated with the sun-god Ra, and "Amun-Ra" became the king of the gods and a father figure to the pharaohs.

ANUBIS The jackal-headed god of cemeteries and embalming, whose black skin represents either the silt of the Nile or mummy flesh treated with chemicals. He is usually depicted weighing the hearts of the dead (the heart was considered the center of intellect and emotions) against Maat, the feather of truth.

ATON The sun at noon, usually depicted as a disk from which rays extend ending in outstretched hands holding *ankhs* (a Coptic cross). The heretical 18th dynasty pharaoh Akhenaton worshiped Aton as the one and only god, with the pharaoh as his one and only priest.

GEB The earth god, usually depicted as a reclining man holding up his sister-wife Nut (the sky goddess). He divided Egypt in two, giving Lower Egypt to his son Osiris and Upper Egypt to his son Seth.

HAPY The symbol of the Nile's annual flooding. He is depicted as a seaweed-tressed man with breasts and a rounded abdomen (representing fertility).

HATHOR The daughter of Ra, the goddess of joy and love, and the protectoress of women and travelers. She usually hangs out on tomb walls sporting cow horns with a sun disk between them.

HORUS The hawk-headed sky god and son of Isis and Osiris. When Seth cut out his eyes (they were later glued back on with divine saliva), they came to represent perfection and were known as a guard against evil (the *wedjat* eye).

ISIS Another sister-wife (to Osiris), usually depicted with a throne on her head. She is the protectoress and healer of children.

KHNUM Ram-headed potter god who sculpted both gods and men out of clay. He is known for controlling the Nile's annual flood.

KHONSU As the moon god, this young man holds the posture of a mummy wearing a moon disk on his shoulders. He is the son of Mut and Amun, thus completing the Theban triad. Also revered as the god of time and known as a lover of games.

MAAT The personification of cosmic order, usually depicted as a woman wearing an ostrich feather on her head.

MUT Symbolic mother of the pharaoh and Thebes' principal goddess (wife of Amun), who often appears as a lion-headed woman wearing a vulture-shaped headdress.

NUT Cow-shaped goddess of the sky and another sister-wife (Geb's), usually depicted stretched across the ceiling of a tomb, swallowing the sun and making the night. She is the mother of Osiris, Isis, Seth, and Nephthys, and sometimes identified as Mut.

OSIRIS The mummified god of the underworld and fertility and brother of Isis. Seth was so bitter when Geb divided up Egypt that he dismembered his brother Osiris and buried his body parts across Egypt. Isis collected the pieces and bandaged them together, making the first mummy; as a thank-you gift, Osiris fathered Horus by Isis before he headed for Duat (the underworld) to rule as lord and judge of the dead.

RA Don't step to Ra, the falcon-headed sun god with a sun disc upon his head who is so powerful that other gods often merge with him to enhance their own powers (Amun-Ra). He rides across the sky in his solar boat, rising from Duat (the underworld) in the east and reentering the land of the dead in the west.

SETH God of chaotic forces, synonymous with evil in much of Egyptian mythology. He performs his one good deed when he spears the evil snake Apophis as the boat of Ra begins its entry into the underworld every evening.

THOTH The ibis-headed scribe god, inventor of writing, and divine reckoner of time. Thoth sometimes took the form of a great white baboon with a giant penis.

HISTORY OF ISLAM

Muhammad rapidly gathered followers to his evolving faith. Staunchly monotheistic Islam met with ample opposition in polytheistic Arabia, leading to persecution in Muhammad's native city of **Mecca**. In 622, he and his followers fled to the nearby city of **Medina**, where he was asked to mediate a long-standing blood feud. This *hijra* (migration) marks the starting point of the Islamic calendar. In 630, Mecca surrendered to the Muslims, who had organized themselves into an army, thus making Muhammad the most powerful man in Arabia and leading numerous Meccans to convert to his new faith. This established the foundation for the concept of *jihad* ("struggle"), which refers first to the spiritual struggle against one's own desires, then to the struggle to make one's own Muslim community as righteous as possible, and lastly to the struggle against outsiders wishing to harm Islam.

Muhammad is not believed to be divine, but rather a human messenger of God's words. Several verses of the Qur'an demand obedience to the Prophet; his actions are sanctified because God chose him to be the recipient of revelation. The stories and traditions surrounding the Prophet's life and personal behavior have been passed on as *sunna* ("rules"), and those who follow the *sunna* (from which the term "Sunni" is derived) in addition to the teachings of the Qur'an are considered especially devout. The primary source for *sunna* are the *hadith*, a collection of sayings and deeds attributed to Muhammad. *Hadith* narratives had to go through a rigorous verification process before they were accepted as true; the tale had to be confirmed, preferably by those who saw the action, and the greatest weight was given to testimony by Muhammad's closest followers and relatives.

SUNNIS, SHI'ITES, AND SUFIS

Muhammad's nephew and son-in-law 'Ali was the catalyst for the major split in the Muslim world. When 'Ali was murdered in 661, the *Shi'at 'Ali* ("Partisans of 'Ali" or **Shi'ites**) believed he was the only legitimate successor to Muhammad, thus separating themselves from **Sunni** Muslims, who accepted the leadership of a appointed Caliph. A minority sect within Islam, Shi'ism is a faith with a sharp focus on divinely chosen leaders (or *imams*) who are blood descendants of 'Ali and his wife, the Prophet's daughter Fatima. Today, Shi'ite Muslims are the majority in Iran, and a significant minority in Syria, Lebanon, and Iraq.

In the 10th century, Sunni Muslim scholars *(ulama)* proclaimed the gates of *ijtihad* (individual judgment) closed; new concepts and interpretations could no longer stand on their own but had to be legitimized by tradition. There have been numerous reform movements throughout the Islamic world, including the conservative Wahhabi movement on the Arabian Peninsula, which rejects any religious innovations that occurred after the 3rd century of Islam. The movement of the thinker **Jamal al-Din al-Afghani** in the Middle East reacted to Western colonial activity in the Arab world and urged Muslims to reform themselves as the first step in rising to meet this challenge from an alien, more powerful culture. Another important figure in political Islam was **Muhammad Iqbal** in South Asia. An advocate of Pakistani independence, his poetry and philosophy stressed the rebirth of Islamic and spiritual redemption through self-development, moral integrity and individual freedom. There are four main schools of thought in the Islamic legal system, and the applicability of *sharia*, or Islamic law, is a subject of much strife in a number of Muslim countries, which have seen challenges to secular government institutions by movements carrying the banner of Islam.

Sufism is an ancient mystical movement within Islam, and Sufis stress the goal of unity with God. They are organized in hierarchical orders that prescribe different ways to reach God; some preach total asceticism, while others seem almost hedonistic in their pursuit of pleasure. Sufi *sheikhs* (masters) and saints are reputed to perform miracles, and their tombs are popular pilgrimage destinations. Jalal al-Din Rumi in the thirteenth century founded the famous order of the "whirling dervishes" (see **Twist and Shout, p. 77**), who wear long skirts, dance, and sing to produce a state of mind conducive to unity with God.

TWIST AND SHOUT Known to Westerners as **whirling dervishes,** the **Sufi** sect of Islam began in Konya, Turkey, during the mid-13th century. The origin of the word Sufi is a mystery. Some think that it derives from the root *suf* (wool), used to describe the woolen garments worn by the first members of the sect. Another theory is that Sufi came from the Greek *sophos,* meaning wisdom. The Persian word *darwish* literally means the "sill of the door"—hence, *dervish* would refer to the Sufi who is at the doorstep of paradise or enlightenment. The dervishes hope to cast off mundane worries and reach a higher spiritual plane through their perpetually whirling dance. The ritual is an entrancing display of color and devotion, a dizzying spin during which the dervish throws off cloak after cloak of earthly possession, eventually left with the soaring white fabric of his inner robe. Their spiritual dance likely inspired the "spinners" made famous at **Grateful Dead** concerts.

FIVE PILLARS OF ISLAM

Allahu akbar. Allahu akbar. Al-hadu an la ilaha illa Allah. Al-hadu anna Muhammadan rasul Allah. "God is greatest. God is greatest. I testify that there is no god but God. I testify that Muhammad is God's Messenger." These words are the **testimony of faith,** or *shahadah,* which is the first of the **five pillars** of Islam, which all Muslims must abide by and participate in. They are also the first lines of the Islamic call to prayer, which is broadcast five times a day from live or recorded *muezzins* perched atop the minarets of mosques. These words reflect the unity of God *(tawhid)* and the special place of Muhammad as God's ultimate messenger. Any person who wishes to convert to Islam may do so simply by repeating these lines three times. Enemies of Islam often memorized the lines before going into battle as an emergency survival tactic.

The second pillar is **prayer** *(salat)*, performed five times each day while facing the holy city of Mecca. Each prayer is preceded by ablution (ritual cleansing), begins with a declaration of intent, and consists of a set cycle of recitation and prostration. The Arabic word for Friday *(yom al-jum'a)* means "the day of gathering," and communal prayer is performed on this day.

The third pillar is **alms** *(zakat)*. Because all belongs to God, wealth is merely held in trust by human beings, and alms represent the bond between members of a community. Through required charity to those less fortunate, the contributor is purified from selfishness. *Zakat* has been historically administered as a tax, the level of giving is a percentage of the wealth and earnings of the individual.

The fourth pillar of Islam is **fasting** *(sawm)*, required during the entire month of Ramadan, the most holy month of the Islamic calendar. It is believed that the Prophet Muhammad received the Qur'an during the month of **Ramadan.** Between dawn and sunset, Muslims are not permitted to smoke, have sexual intercourse, or let any food or water pass their lips; exceptions are made for pregnant or menstruating women, the sick, and travelers—they must make up the fast at a later date. Fasting is meant for reflection; to teach Muslims to resist temptation and thereby control all their unchaste urges, better understand the plight of the poor, and be more thankful for the food with which God has provided them. As soon as the evening *adhan* is heard, Muslims break the fast and begin a night of feasting, visits to friends and relatives, and revelry. In busy metropolises like Cairo, the city stays up until just before dawn, but in quieter areas, a neighbor may circulate to houses, banging a drum and waking people for the *suhoor*, a meal eaten just before the crack of dawn in an attempt to avoid extreme hunger upon waking. The holy month ends with 'Eid al-Fitr, a day of intense celebration and vigorous feasting.

The last pillar is **pilgrimage** *(hajj)*, required once per lifetime for those who are financially and physically able to journey to the holy cities of Mecca and Medina (located in what is now Saudi Arabia) during the last month of the Muslim calendar. Worship is focused around the **Ka'aba,** which devout Muslims believe to be the first site of worship built by the first man, Adam, under instruction from God. The

HISTORY & CULTURE

> **WHO'S THAT GIRL?** *Hijabs* are the traditional garments that most Westerners think of when they think of Muslim women. *Hijabs* come in different colors, shapes, and sizes, but the must-own basic is a two-piece veil covering the head and hanging down over the collar, and comes in basic black or off-white. The outer portion is the facial veil, which snaps in place above the ears and consists of an opaque bottom layer with a narrow slit for the eyes and a sheer, slit-less outer layer that more conservative women pull down to cover the eyes. The second piece of the *hijab* is a scarf that covers the top of the veil, pinning it in place and hiding the hair. The scarf is tied in a variety of knots, depending on the woman's personal style. Today, *souqs* sell such modern adaptations as zip-front and nifty velcro facial veils. Many religious women choose to wear funky socks (some have even been seen wearing "Merry Christmas" stockings) as signs of individuality.

hajj unites Muslims and stresses the equal status of all who submit to God. Every worshiper, from the Gulf oil prince to the Cairene street-sweeper, must dress in simple white cloth, remove all accessories, and perform the same rituals. If you travel during the month of *hajj* (see **Holidays and Festivals,** p. 85), expect delays and pandemonium in airports.

CHRISTIANITY

Orthodox Christians, who belong to the **Coptic Church,** make up Egypt's largest and most significant religious minority, with population estimates somewhere between five and seven million. The relationship between the Copts and the Muslim government has always been strained, but with the rise of Muslim fundamentalism, tensions between the Muslim majority and the Coptic minority have erupted in acts of vandalism. Another one million or so members of the Egyptian population are Roman Catholics, Greek and Armenian Orthodox Christians, Protestants, and Jews. These groups thrived in colonial times but have dwindled in number due to emigration.

HISTORY OF CHRISTIANITY

Christianity began in Judaea among the Jewish followers of **Jesus.** The most significant sources on the life of Jesus are the **Gospels.** Scholars agree that the "synoptic gospels" of Mark, Matthew, and Luke were written in that order some time after 70 CE, drawing on an oral tradition that recorded the words of Jesus. The Gospel of John was written about 100 CE but has roots as old as the others. These sources provide a history influenced by the experiences of the church fathers and the belief that Jesus was the **Messiah** ("anointed one").

Various historical events date the birth of Jesus between 7 and 4 BCE. The Bible says that Jesus was spontaneously conceived and brought forth by Mary, a virgin, making him a product of God's creative power and free from humanity's original sin. According to Matthew, **Bethlehem** was the birthplace of Jesus, and Mary and Joseph moved to **Nazareth** to protect him. Jesus was baptized in the Jordan River by **John the Baptist,** a popular evangelist later hailed as the reincarnation of the 9th-century BCE Israelite prophet Elijah, herald of the Messiah (whose cave can still be seen in the Sinai, p. 280). Jesus later preached in the Galilee, speaking for the poor and the righteous, most notably in the Sermon on the Mount (Matthew 5-7). After about three years of preaching, Jesus went to Jerusalem, where the **Passion,** the events leading up to his death, took place. On Good Friday, he carried his cross down the **Via Dolorosa** until he reached the hill of Golgotha (or Calvary), now marked by the Church of the Holy Sepulchre, where he was crucified. According to the Gospels, three days after Jesus' crucifixion, on what is now celebrated as Easter, Mary and two other women went to Jesus' tomb to anoint his body and discovered the tomb empty. An angel announced that Jesus had been resurrected;

Jesus subsequently appeared to the Apostles and performed miracles. The **Resurrection** is the point of departure for the Christian faith, the beginning of an age when the faithful await Christ's *parousia*, or second coming.

At first, Christianity was a sect of Judaism, accepting the Hebrew Bible. However, the sect's defining tenet—that Jesus was the Messiah—severed it from mainstream Judaism. **St. Paul** (originally Saul of Tarsus) successfully adapted the faith of Christianity to meet the spiritual needs of the largest body of converts: former pagans. The incorporation of ancient festivals, such as the winter solstice, helped draw the common people to the new religion, and the usage of Platonic doctrines converted many intellectuals. The Christian faith was officially legitimized by the Edict of Milan, issued by Emperor Licinius in 313 CE. In 325 CE, **Emperor Constantine** made Christianity the official religion of the struggling Roman Empire. Constantine also summoned the first of seven Ecumenical Councils, held in Nicea, to elaborate and unify the content of the faith. The Council of Nicea came up with an explicit creed, declaring that Jesus Christ was of the same essence as the Father and that there were three equal parts to God. This crucial doctrine of the **Trinity**, which is implicitly supported in the Gospels, maintains that the Father, Son, and Holy Spirit are distinct persons, yet represent one God.

Despite these unifying dicta, the Christian community suffered many schisms through the centuries. The **Coptic Church** broke off in the 3rd century (see below), when other eastern branches began to drift away from western Christianity. In 1054, the **Great Schism** split Christendom into the Roman Catholic Church and the Eastern Orthodox Church. Whereas Rome upheld the universal jurisdiction and infallibility of the Pope, Orthodoxy stressed the infallibility of the church as a whole. In 1517, German monk **Martin Luther** sparked the **Reformation,** which split northern Europe from Roman Catholicism and led to the development of **Protestantism.** Protestantism is itself composed of many sects, which generally believe in salvation through faith rather than good works. Eastern Orthodoxy, too, is divided into multiple national traditions (Greek, Russian, Armenian).

THE COPTIC CHURCH

The term "Copt" is derived from the Greek word for Egyptian, *Ægyptos*, shortened in its Egyptian pronunciation to *qibt*. Copts in Egypt usually have tattoos of a domed cathedral or a tiny cross on their wrists. Of 58 million Egyptians, five to seven million are Copts, most of whom live in Cairo or Middle Egypt. Portions of the liturgy are still in Coptic, though most of the service is in Arabic.

St. Mark introduced Christianity to Egypt in 62 CE. Mass conversions transformed Alexandria into a Christian spiritual center, but Roman persecution also increased. The bloodiest days passed under **Diocletian,** who murdered so many Christians that the Copts date their Martyr's Calendar from 284 CE, the beginning of his reign. The situation changed drastically when **Constantine** made Christianity the official religion of the Roman Empire in 312 CE. Alexandria was recognized as a theological center and monasticism developed, while Christianity spread in Middle and Upper Egypt, becoming the majority religion by the 5th century. But controversies and religious quarrels would shape the power wars between Constantinople, capital of the eastern Roman Empire, and Alexandria. The patriarch of Constantinople contested the preeminence of the pope in Rome, while those from Alexandria and Antioch were jealous of the Byzantine clergy.

The heresy of **Arianism** began in Alexandria, when Egyptian theologians supported **Eutyches,** who preached monophysism (from the Greek *monos:* unique, and *phusis:* nature), or the unity of the nature of Christ incarnate. Causing further divides, **St. Cyril**, patriarch of Alexandria, contributed to the condemnation in 431 CE of the doctrine of Nestorius, the patriarch of Constantinople. Nestorius defended the radical separation of the divine and the human two natures of Christ. It was then that the Coptic church as it exists today was founded, when in 451 CE, the Alexandrian branch of the Church declared independence from Constantinople and formed the **Coptic Orthodox Church.**

Byzantine Emperor **Justinian** sought to restore Christian unity by exiling Coptic clergy to isolated monasteries. Copts welcomed the Persians as liberators from persecution when they captured Egypt in 619, as they did the Muslims conquerors in 641 CE. Since the Arab conquest, Copts in Egypt have lived as a religious minority in an Islamic state. In time, Coptic Christians adopted the Arabic and considered themselves an Arab community. Nevertheless, relations between Copts and Muslims have vacillated throughout history. In 1879, the equality of all Egyptians was declared, and was later confirmed in the constitution of 1922. In 1955 their confessional courts were suppressed and replaced by civil courts that applied Islamic law to all Egyptians, regardless of religious persuasion. Copts have shown themselves to be active in the nationalistic movements, defending a strictly Egyptian patriotism instead of a pan-Arab or pan-Islamic sentiment. As a result, they have periodically been victims of acts of violence on the part of Islamic extremists since the end of the 1970s.

The Coptic language, which belongs to the Semitic family, remains an important liturgical language, but for the most part, Arabic is used. The festival of Easter is a particularly solemn one and, in Cairo for example, the Coptic Christians all go to the new St. Mark Cathedral in the 'Abbasiyya district. Christmas, and the baptism of Christ, are also widely celebrated. (See **Holidays and Festivals,** p. 85, for a comprehensive list). Coptic Christians are farmers, professionals, businessmen and civil administrators, sometimes reaching high government positions. Boutros Boutros-Ghali, former minister of Egyptian foreign affairs and secretary general of the UN, is an example.

COPTIC ART AND ARCHITECTURE

Coptic art incorporates the influences of pharaonic and Hellenistic cultures. The Coptic cross borrows from the *ankh,* the hieroglyphic sign for "life" (vaguely resembling the human form), as well as from the crucifix on Golgotha. Embroidered tapestries and curtains displaying nymphs and centaurs descend from Greco-Roman mythology. Islamic art often borrows from the Coptic style. Many of Cairo's mosques were engineered by Coptic architects, and some are even converted Coptic churches. A visit to the Coptic Museum in Cairo (p. 127) offers a good glimpse of Coptic art.

Coptic churches usually have one of three shapes: cruciform, circular (to represent the globe, the spread of Christianity, and the eternal nature of the Word), or ark-shaped (the Ark of the Covenant and Noah's Ark are symbols of salvation). The sanctuary, or *haikal,* faces east, while the altar is hidden from worshipers by a curtain and panel of wood decorated with icons. The choir area is reserved for the priests. Behind the choir is the nave, made up of two parts. During the services, the men are separated from the women, just as the worshipers are separate from the priests: this explains the separation of the church into various compartments with partitions made of wood screens. Above Coptic altars hang ostrich eggs, symbolizing Resurrection (life out of lifelessness) and thus God's eternal love and care. Several churches constructed between the 5th and 7th centuries still stand, though most are in ruins. Even after the Arabian conquest, the number of Coptic churches and monasteries continued to increase. The large, new St. Mark Cathedral was built in 1965, and the first stone was placed by heartthrob and president Gamal 'Abd al-Nasser himself.

LANGUAGE

ANCIENT EGYPTIAN LANGUAGE

One of the earliest forms of writing was Egyptian **hieroglyphs** (sacred carvings). Alongside this pictorial system developed the **hieratic,** an abbreviated cursive script that retained only the vital characteristics of the pictures. After the 22nd Dynasty, scribes began using the sacred hieratic writing in a secular context, leading to the rise of a form known as Enchorial or **Demotic.** Eventually, even the sacred *Book of the Dead* (a compilation of spells and cult rituals) was translated into this script. Modern scholars owe much of their knowledge of ancient Egyptian linguistics to the **Rosetta Stone,** a stone tablet found in present-day Rashid dating from around 200 BCE that contains the same passage celebrating the crowning of King Ptolemy V recorded in hieroglyphic, Demotic, and Greek script. **Coptic,** today used only in liturgy, is a derivation of ancient Egyptian that uses the Greek alphabet plus six additional letters.

For more on the discovery and deciphering of ancient Egyptian inscriptions, see **It's All Hieroglyphs to Me,** p. 173.

ARABIC

The Arabic language belongs to the Semitic family, along with ancient Egyptian, Hebrew and Aramaic. The first written Arabic characters date from the 4th century CE. Pre-Qur'anic Arabic included an ensemble of dialects used all around the Arabian Peninsula. Before Islam (*al-Jahiliyya*), poetry held an especially privileged place; by the time of the writing of the **Qur'an,** literary language had already been used with a high level of aesthetic mastery. The language of the Qur'an became the model for the classical language, and the Qur'an has since been considered the most perfect embodiment of the Arabic language. Philologists have long debated the origin of the Qur'anic language. According to some, it is the language of the tribe of the Prophet Mohammed, (the Quraysh tribe), while others believe it was a poetic language common to all of Arabia. Other texts have enriched the body that serves to establish the literary models of classical Arabic, especially the compilations of the Muslim tradition (*hadith*).

Arabic superimposed itself on local languages everywhere the Arab conquerors went (Aramaic in the Near East, Persian and Turkish in central Asia, and Berber in North Africa), acquiring its status as an official language of exchange and culture (*adab*). This process did not exclude the progressive appearance of numerous dialects. From the year 1250 CE, with the end of the Abbasid Dynasty, the literary world slowed down. It wasn't until the 19th century before the language was reborn: first with the Arabic renaissance (*al-nahdda*) and then around the idea of an Arabic revolution (*al-thawra*). Egypt played a key role in these two movements. It is also from this period that a certain number of scientific and technical terms of European origin would influence modern Arabic.

Today, there are three distinct levels of the Arabic language. The first level corresponds to the Arabic of the Qur'an, also called **Classical Arabic.** Classical Arabic is primarily a written language, but it is also used in religious teaching and prayer. The second level is referred to as **Modern Standard Arabic,** which is a journalistic register used on television, on the radio, in the papers, and in some discourse. Arabic **dialects,** essentially oral, constitute the third level. This level divides into three regional groups: North African, Levantine, and Egyptian. Egyptian Arabic is not perfectly homogenous and numerous differences are perceived throughout the regions of Egypt (the language of the Sinai and desert Bedouins is incomprehensible for an Alexandrian). Despite these differences, which are essentially differences of vocabulary and pronunciation, rather than grammar, any speaker of Arabic usually refer to the literary language or to standard Arabic to communicate with an Arab from a different region.

In the Near East and, to a lesser extent, in the larger Arab-Islamic world, Egyptian Arabic holds a privileged position. The influence and quality of its cinema and the reputation of its singers and its soap operas have granted the Egyptian language a certain cultural status recognized by all (especially those with a television). The main phonetic difference between the Egyptian and Levantine pronounciation (includes the dialects of Jordan, Syria, Lebanon, the West Bank and Gaza) is that in Egypt the Levantine *j* sound (as in Julia) becomes a hard *g* (as in gulf, so Egyptians would say "Gulia"). In Upper (south) Egypt, the Nubians, or Sa'idis, replace the Classical Arabic *q* with a hard *g*. For a phrasebook of useful terms, see p. 311. For a glossary of Arabic words and common Middle Easter foods, see p. 314.

HISTORY & CULTURE

THE ARTS

LITERATURE

Most of the writings of the ancient Egyptians, such as the *Book of the Dead*, deal with magic and religion. The ancients dabbled in poetic love songs as well. Modern Egyptian literature dates back to the beginning of the 20th century; it was in 1914 that **Muhammad Hussein Haykal** wrote *Zaynab*, a work considered by some to be the first modern Arabic novel. Modern literature in Egypt is synonymous with the name of Cairene novelist **Naguib Mahfouz.** In 1988, Mahfouz became the first Arab to win the Nobel Prize for literature. Mahfouz's major work in the 1950s was *The Cairo Trilogy (Palace Walk, Palace of Desire,* and *Sugar Street)*, which seamlessly depicts the life of three generations in Cairo from World War I to the 1950s. His classic allegory *Children of Gebelawi* (1959), banned throughout the Arab world except in Lebanon, retells the stories of the Qur'an in a modern-day Cairo setting. **Tawfiq al-Hakim** wrote about his expereinces as an Arab attending university in Paris in his celebrated *A Bird from the East.* After World War II, writers took greater liberties in their use of the Arabic language, allowing elements of simpler, more light-hearted dialogue in their writings. **Yusuf Idris** is famous for putting the language of the common Egyptian dialect in his short stories, in such collections as *The Cheapest Nights.* By contrast, the work of **Taha Husayn** expressed gravity and distress, retelling his experiences as a student at al-Azhar in his famous *Stream of Days.* Notable among more contemporary authors is Alexandrene novelist and essayist **Edward al-Kharrat,** who is considered the father of modernism in Egyptian literature. His popular novels *City of Saffron* (1989) and *Girls of Alexandria* (1993) are both available in translation. The military disaster against Israel in 1967 brought an end to the humor of even the most independent artists.

Censorship has been a problem for Egyptian writers. *The Smell of It*, a semi-autobiographical work by **Sunallah Ibrahim** about life after prison, was published in Egypt only in a censored version. Doctor, feminist, and novelist **Nawal al-Sa'adawi,** who was also Egypt's Minister of Health from 1965 to 1972, stands out among women authors with her extensive writings (including the notable works *The Circling Song* and *The Naked Face of Arab Women*) on the psychological, sexual, and legal liberation of the Arab woman. Her works were once considered so controversial they were banned in her native country, and she herself was imprisoned in 1981 and forbidden from practicing medicine in Egypt, because of the perceived danger she posed to society.

Many non-Egyptians have written accounts of their travels and experiences within the country. In *The Innocents Abroad*, Mark Twain describes his misadventures in Egypt and other countries. For an engrossing—if oversexed—account of Alexandrene life, don't miss Lawrence Durrell's multi-narrator epic, *The Alexandria Quartet.* For an eye-opening account of early Western explorers roaming the Nile, read Alan Moorehead's *The White Nile* and its companion volume, *The Blue Nile*, which include hair-raising chapters on the French invasion of Egypt and the rise of Muhammad 'Ali. Michael Ondaatje's award-winning *The English Patient* contains sensual and incredibly accurate descriptions of early desert expeditions in the area.

MUSIC

With what is undoubtedly the richest and most varied musical tradition in the Near East, Egypt is the high place of the Eastern music industry, and the banks of the Nile attract the most inspired artists of the Arab world. Egyptian music began in the first three centuries of the Muslim era (between the 7th and 10th centuries

CE), which allowed it to develop independent of all Western influence. Traditional Egyptian folk music incorporates nasal horns churning out repetitive melodies to the incessant beat of drums. **Nubian music** (called *musiqa nubiyya* in Aswan) is equally enthralling. In general, it eliminates the horns and focuses on slow drumbeats and chanting choruses.

The music blaring from taxis, *ahwas,* and homes throughout Egypt is a slightly updated version of this traditional classical music. Egypt is the capital of the Arab music industry and the promised land for aspiring artists from all over the Arab world. Sayyid Darwish and the legendary **Muhammad 'Abd al-Wahhab** began as early as the 1910s and '20s to integrate Western instrumentation and techniques into Arabic song. Like Egyptian cinema, this type of music had its heyday in the '50s and '60s but shows no signs of waning in popularity today. In the '60s, the emphasis fell on strong, beautiful voices to unite Arabic music's disparate elements, and several "greats" of Egyptian music emerged. The greatest of these was the unmistakable and unforgettable **Umm Kulthum.** Her rags-to-riches story begins in the provinces, where her father dressed her up as a boy to sing with him at religious festivals; it ends in 1975 with a funeral that was bigger than President Nasser's five years earlier. In the interim, Umm Kulthum gave speeches, starred in musical films, and sang everything from post-revolutionary propaganda songs to love ballads. You will not leave Egypt without hearing Umm Kulthum's voice and seeing her sunglasses-clad face on a television screen or wall mural.

Music in the '80s and '90s saw a wholesale incorporation of Western influences. Modern Egyptian pop is totally danceable, mostly pre-packaged, and rarely long-lived. Among these transitory teen dreams, **Amr Diab** has endured as the best-selling Arab recording artist of all time. His upbeat songs provide singalong material at weddings, parties, and discos.

CINEMA

Egypt has had a near monopoly on the Arabic entertainment industry for most of the second half of the 20th century, ranking behind only Hollywood (United States) and Bollywood (India) in its prolific output. Egyptian films range from skillfully made modern dramas to comedies that pit down-and-out students against evil capitalists and bumbling police officers, with a smattering of southern Egyptians (portrayed as idiots) thrown in for comic relief.

The '50s and '60s were the golden age of Egyptian cinema. Alexandrene **Omar Sharif** *(Doctor Zhivago, Funny Girl)* ruled as an international film superstar and his former wife Fatin Hamama presided as queen of Arab cinema. The musicals of that period are still very popular, and feature well-dressed hipsters knitting their brows in consternation over the cruelty of love, the generation gap, and the difficulty of college examinations. Controversial auteur **Yusef Chahine** (credited with discovering Omar Sharif in a Cairo cafe and catapulting him to fame with 1954's *Blazing Sun*) has gained international acclaim for his lushly filmed, genre-bending masterpieces that tackle everything from sexual discovery to the hypocrisy of Western society. *The Emigrant* (1994) was initially banned in Egypt for depicting images of the Prophet Muhammad (a practice forbidden in the Muslim religion), but became a box office hit once the ban was lifted. His recent work includes *Destiny* (1997), which attacks modern Islamic fundamentalism by recounting the persecution of the Islamic philosopher Averroes.

The levying of heavy entertainment taxes in the '70s and the general atmosphere of profiteering in the '80s served to lower drastically the standards of modern Egyptian cinema to somewhere below chintzy tragicomedy. A new guard of young directors has begun to revitalize the industry by tackling such once-taboo topics as social conditions, terrorism, and the country's volatile relationship with Israel.

PUFF THE MAGIC SHEESHA In Egypt, relaxation has become synonymous with gurgling and puffing noises accompanied by the smell of sugary honey, apple, or rose tobacco. The instrument of pleasure is a popular smoking apparatus known in Egypt as a *sheesha* (elsewhere as an *argileh* or *nargilah*), which can be plain or ornately colored and decorated with feathers. It consists of a snake-like tube and a small bowl filled with burning coals, tobacco, and spices. Water vapor carries the tobacco smoke through the one-meter tube and into the mouth, making each puff smooth and sweet. The *sheesha* is thought to have been introduced in Egypt by the Turks, and became fashionable among the elite during the late 17th century. For a long time *sheesha* smoking remained an upper-class pleasure, but as of late the apple and honey puffs of smoke have become a veritable national pastime.

FOOD AND DRINK

The Egyptian breakfast of choice is **fuul** ("fool")—cooked, mashed fava beans blended with garlic, lemon, olive oil, and salt that are eaten with bread and vegetables. What's known as falafel elsewhere—chick peas and/or fava beans mashed, shaped into balls, and fried—is called **ta'amiyya** in Egypt, and both *ta'amiyya* and *fuul* are sold at street stands everywhere. Street vendors also sell *kibdeh* (liver) sandwiches, which don't score high on the smell test but go down quite scrumptiously. **Shawarma** made its way from the Levant to Egypt only recently; it is supposed to be sinfully fatty lamb rolled into a pita with vegetables and *tahina*, but Egyptians will slap any sort of meat into bogus French bread and call it *shawarma*. Popular **kushari** is a cheap, filling meal of pasta, lentils, and dried onions in tomato sauce.

At times you might feel that all you will ever get to eat will be *kofta*, kebab, and chicken. These carnivore's wet dreams are almost always served with salads, bread or rice, and *tahina*, a sesame-based sauce. *Kofta* is spiced ground beef grilled on skewers; kebab is chunks of lamb cooked the same way. Chicken is either fried (without batter), roasted on a rotisserie, or skewered, grilled, and called *shish tawouq*. Fried and stuffed pigeon *(hamam)* is a source of national pride, particularly in Alexandria, but most travelers are content to leave the dish, served whole, for the birds. *Biftek* (sometimes called *veal panné* on restaurant menus) is a thinly sliced veal, breaded and fried. You can get feta cheese with a year-long shelf life in no-refrigeration-needed packs—great for long road trips or cheap breakfasts. The brand *La Vache Qui Rit* (The Laughing Cow) is so popular that it has been adopted as a disparaging nickname for President Hosni Mubarak.

Fatir are flaky, chewy, doughy delights, filled with anything and everything and eaten either as a meal or for dessert. Other desserts include *ba'laweh* and rice pudding flavored with rosewater *(roz bel laban)*. Egypt's ruby-red watermelons *(butteekh)*, though sometimes known to be color-enhanced with non-potable water, make a juicy, hydrating communal snack. Also try the unbelievable **figs** *(teen)* and, in late summer, the papaya-like *teen shoki* (cactus fruit).

A popular drink among travelers is **'asab,** sugar cane juice, said to increase sexual prowess. Egyptians themselves are coffee and tea fiends. Egyptian tea is taken without milk but with enough sugar to make it syrupy. Egyptians prefer ahwa (Arabic coffee). Especially when you are in Upper Egypt, try *karkadeh*, a red drink made by brewing hibiscus flowers that is served hot or cold. Egypt brews its own beer, Stella, which costs between E£5 and E£8 in restaurants and bars, as well as the surprisingly good Sakara, which usually costs a pound or two more.

HOLIDAYS AND FESTIVALS

Government offices and banks close for Islamic holidays, but most tourist facilities remain open. The month of Ramadan can be a wonderful (if occasionally inconvenient) time to visit, especially in festive Cairo and Alexandria. Along with the regular Islamic festivals, the two Sufi rituals of **Zikr** and **Zar** are not to be missed (both rituals are practiced on Fridays in populous areas). In the former, a group of dancers whirl themselves into a frenzy; in the latter, women dance in a group, primarily as an exorcism rite. The Coptic celebrations of Easter and Christmas are tranquil affairs marked by special church services. The festival known as **Sham al-Nissim** falls on the first Monday after Coptic Easter, but has developed into a secular celebration. Sham al-Nissim was originally an outdoor spring festival in which ancient Egyptians and enslaved Jews feasted on pungent *fisikh* (dried and salted fish) as equals; the highlight of the festival was the ritual casting of a young woman into the Nile. *Fisikh* is still eaten at modern celebrations, but the young women stay dry; even the ritual of throwing a doll into the Nile has all but disappeared from the present-day festivities.

Islamic holidays are timed to local sightings of the moon, so dates are not set until the last minute and differ from country to country. The **holy day** in the Muslim world is Friday *(Yom al-Juma'a)*, when many business are closed. Businesses typically close on national holidays (listed below) as well. **Christian** holidays listed are those of the Eastern Orthodox or Maronite Church.

DATE	FESTIVAL	AFFILIATION
Nov. 1, 2001	All Saints' Day	**Christian**
Nov. 15	First Day of Ramadan (approximation)	**Islamic**
Dec. 12	Laylat al-Qadr	**Islamic**
Dec. 16	'Eid al-Fitr (end of Ramadan)	**Islamic**
Dec. 25	Christmas	**Christian**
Jan. 7, 2002	Epiphany	**Christian**
Feb. 23	'Eid al-Adha (Feast of the Sacrifice)	**Islamic**
Mar. 16	Muharram (Islamic New Year)	**Islamic**
Mar. 25	Ashoura	**Islamic**
Apr. 13	Good Friday	**Christian**
Apr. 15	Easter	**Christian**
May 25	'Eid Mawlid al-Nabi (Birth of the Prophet)	**Islamic**
June 3	Pentecost	**Christian**
June 18	Evacuation Day (Liberation Day)	**Egyptian**
July 23	Revolution Day	**Egyptian**
Aug. 15	Assumption of the Virgin Mary	**Christian**
Oct. 4	Isra' and Miraj	**Islamic**
Oct. 6	National Day (Armed Forces Day)	**Egyptian**
Oct. 24	Suez and National Liberation Day	**Egyptian**
Nov. 1	All Saints' Day	**Christian**
Nov. 6	First Day of Ramadan	**Islamic**
Dec. 6	'Eid al-Fitr (end of Ramadan)	**Islamic**
Dec. 23	Victory Day	**Egyptian**
Dec. 25	Christmas	**Christian**

HISTORY & CULTURE

CAIRO القاهرة ☎ 02

I arrived at length at Cairo, mother of cities and seat of Pharaoh the tyrant,
boundless in multitude of buildings, peerless in beauty and splendor, the meeting-
place of comer and goer, the halting-place of feeble and mighty, whose throngs
surge as waves of the sea.
    —Ibn Battuta, 14th-century globetrotter

Cairo has been the jewel of the Middle East and Africa for nearly the past millennium.
In 2600 BCE, the pharaohs of the Old Kingdom chose the sandy plateau just above the
Nile Delta for their ancient capital of Memphis—one of the world's earliest urban settlements and Egypt's capital until the beginning of the first century CE, when St. Mark
introduced Christianity to Egypt. For the next 600 years, the Coptic Church that grew
out of St. Mark's teaching marked the wrists of its faithful with tattoos and left even
more enduring marks in the architectural landscape of Old Cairo. The early decades
of the 7th century CE found Cairo in the throes of a power struggle between the Persian and Byzantine empires. Memphis and Babylon (the glitzy settlement across the
Nile) changed hands many times, while warfare near Babylon drove urban dwellers
to the villages. The city thus lay bereft and deserted at the time of the Arab conquest
in 641 CE. The leader of the Arab invaders, 'Amr ibn al-'As, set up camp at Fustat, the
precursor of modern Cairo. The Arabs were responsible for giving the city its name:
Fatimid leader Gawhar al-Sikelli dubbed it *al-Qahira*, or "the Conqueror."

The city swelled so much in size and grandeur under the Fatimids and their descendants that it soon became known simply as *Misr*, the Arabic name for all of Egypt.
During the next three centuries—Cairo's Golden Age—it became the most advanced
cultural center west of China. Although various conquerors throughout the Middle
Ages managed to carry off pieces of Cairo's glory, it remained far more populous than
any city in Europe. The Ottomans, however, reduced Cairo to the status of a provincial center in 1516. After a brief affair with Napoleon in the late 1700s, Cairo made a
grand entrance onto the 19th-century scene after a face-lift by its modern political
patron, Muhammad 'Ali. An Albanian emigré, 'Ali drove away Egypt's European conquerors and reinstalled Cairo at the forefront of the Arab world. His penchant for the
extravagant resulted in the numerous Cairene streets dotted with lofty Turkish-style
mosques and glittering European-style palaces.

The social upheaval of the Middle East has affected Cairo in the 20th century. Modern political and economic centralization in the capital is driving thousands of rural
Egyptians into the arms of the "Mother of the World" (*Umm al-Dunya*, as the medieval Arabs called Cairo), and she is struggling to cope with the needs of her growing
brood. Expansion has led to severely overcrowded neighborhoods, clogged thoroughfares, and urban pollution. Places where pharaohs and kings once lounged now
teem with barking street merchants and silver-tongued con artists. Amid tangled
webs of unlabeled streets and the dizzying calls of hawkers, Cairenes frequent their
favorite *sheesha* halls, navigate labyrinthine bazaars, and worship in hundreds of
ancient mosques and churches (and some synagogues). Cairo intimidates most of
those who pay the city only a perfunctory visit. But beyond the Pyramids and the
Egyptian Museum, patience and a sense of adventure will help you enjoy the apparent insanity of a city that seems always on the verge of some great event—or disaster.

✈ INTERCITY TRANSPORTATION

FLIGHTS

Flights leave from **Cairo International Airport** (š291 42 55 or 291 42 66), in Heliopolis.
EgyptAir has offices at 6 'Adly St. (š392 7649), at 9 Tala'at Harb (š393 28 36 or 393 03
81), and in the Nile Hilton (š579 30 49 or 579 94 43 for the sales office, š579 30 46 or
575 97 03 for the travel agent office). Round-trip flights to: **Aswan** (US$368),

Got ISIC?

SIC is your passport to the world.

Accepted at over 17,000 locations worldwide.
Great benefits at home and abroad!

o apply for your International Student, Teacher or Youth Identity Card
CALL 1-800-2COUNCIL
CLICK www.counciltravel.com
VISIT your local Council Travel office

Bring this ad into your local Council Travel office and receive
a free Council Travel/ISIC t-shirt! *(while supplies last)*

FALL/WINTER 2001 • FREE

student Travels

WORK, STUDY, TRAVEL ABROAD

CZECH IT OUT!
Exploring Prague and Other Pleasures in the Czech Republic

BOSTON
Weekend Wandering in Beantown

INSIDE
Your International Student Identity Card (ISIC) Application

PLUS
-Cuba
-Australia

Bedazzled By BRAZIL

Boundless Attractions From Beautiful Beaches to Spectacular Festivals to Lush Jungles

STOP IN FOR YOUR FREE COPY TODAY

STUDENT TRAVELS MAGAZINE

is now available at all Council Travel offices.

This FREE magazine is the student guide to getting around the world - on a student's budget!

council travel

America's Leader In Student Travel

Find your local office at
www.counciltravel.com

1-800-2COUNCIL

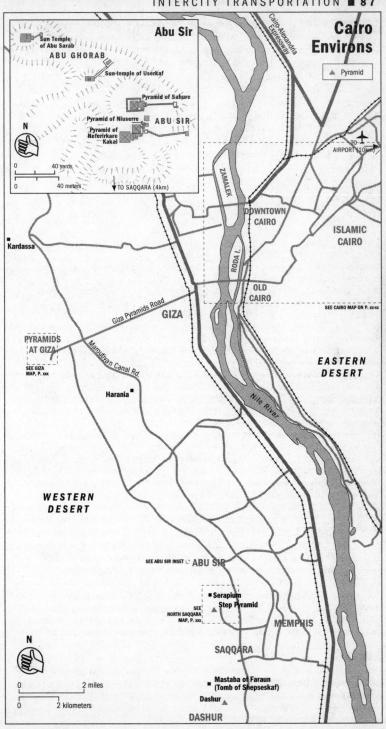

Cairo Environs

▲ Pyramid

Cairo-Alexandria Expressway

Abu Sir

Sun Temple of Abu Sarab
ABU GHORAB
Sun-temple of Userkaf
Pyramid of Sahure
Pyramid of Niuserre
ABU SIR
Pyramid of Neferirkare Kakai

N

0   40 yards
0   40 meters

▼ TO SAQQARA (4km)

ZAMALEK

DOWNTOWN CAIRO

ISLAMIC CAIRO

RODA I.

OLD CAIRO

TO AIRPORT (10km)

SEE CAIRO MAP ON P. xx-xx

CAIRO

Kardassa

Giza Pyramids Road   GIZA

PYRAMIDS AT GIZA

SEE GIZA MAP, P. xxx

Maroutiyan Canal Rd

Harania

EASTERN DESERT

Nile River

WESTERN DESERT

SEE ABU SIR INSET   ABU SIR

Serapium
Step Pyramid

SEE NORTH SAQQARA MAP, P. xxx

MEMPHIS

SAQQARA

N

0   2 miles
0   2 kilometers

Mastaba of Faraun (Tomb of Shepseskaf)

Dashur ▲

DASHUR

▓ HIGHLIGHTS OF CAIRO AND ENVIRONS

Don't miss the glorious complex of **Sultan Hassan** (p. 111), the **Mausoleum and Mosque of Qaytbay** (p. 118), and the immense **Citadel** (p. 111).

The **Egyptian Museum** (p. 125) showcases an unsurpassed collection of ancient treasures, including the famous loot from **Tutankhamun's tomb.**

A riddle from the **Sphinx** (p. 137): how can you visit Egypt without seeing the **Pyramids at Giza** (p. 135)? The answer: you can't. See where the whole pyramid fad got started by checking out Imhotep's **Step Pyramid** of Zoser-Netcherikhe at Saqqara (p. 140).

Hurghada (US$240), **Luxor** (US$232), **Marsa Matrouh** (US$110), **Sharm al-Sheikh** (US$240), **Suez** (US$170), and **Wadi Gadid** (US$235). **Air Sinai,** in the Nile Hilton (š577 29 49; open daily 9am-5pm), has round-trip flights to **Tel Aviv** (for trips less than 30 days US$238, longer trips US$320). Note that these are sample prices and individual flights will vary in cost. It is difficult and expensive to get flights out of Cairo to international destinations on short notice, so be sure to reserve in advance. For information on traveling to and from Cairo International Airport, see **Requirements, p. 8**.

TRAINS

Ramses Station is the main train station. (š575 35 55. Take the Metro to Mubarak. Ticket windows open daily 8am-10pm.) The **tourist office,** past the entrance on the left, can write out your destination and other details in Arabic to avoid confusion. (Open daily 8am-8pm.) The **information desk,** straight past the entrance, can also point you in the right direction. Which line you stand in at the ticket window depends upon whether you are reserving a seat in advance or trying to buy a ticket for the same day (often impossible). Women (and men traveling with women) should take advantage of the special **women's line** that may form at crowded times, which is much shorter and faster than the corresponding men's line. In addition, women are permitted and expected to push to the front of any line, head held high. Students receive a **30% discount** on almost all fares with an **ISIC card.** The trains enter their berths at least 30min. before departure time. None of the train numbers or destinations are in English, but other travelers, tourist police, or the information desk may lend a hand.

Trains leave for **Alexandria** every hour 6am-10pm. There are two types of trains, both air-conditioned—the **French line** (3hr.; every 1½-2hr. 10 per day; 1st-class E£20, 2nd-class E£12) and the faster **Spanish line** (2hr.; 8, 9am, noon, 2, 3, 6, 7pm; 1st-class E£22, 2nd-class E£17). Trains also run to: **Aswan** (13-16hr.; 7:30 and 10am; 1st-class E£73, 2nd-class E£43) and **Luxor** (9-12hr.; 7:30 and 10am; 1st-class E£63, 2nd-class E£36). Trains to Luxor and Aswan via Minya, Sohag, Asyut, and Qena.

Travel agents in the downtown area have been known to add airport taxes (there is no departure tax from Cairo) and other phantom fees to tickets. You should demand receipts for every pound you hand over and have them give you written estimates, including all taxes, for every flight you purchase. Once you have purchased a ticket, call the airline to make sure a seat is indeed reserved.

The area just outside the train station is chaotic, despite the numerous traffic police and traffic lights. Avoid crossing the treacherous roads by using the convenient tunnels of the Mubarak Metro station. But before heading underground, catch a glimpse of the massive **Statue of Ramses II,** standing calm amidst the storm.

BUSES

The bus system in Egypt is a four-wheeled embodiment of the government bureaucracy—things are always changing, no one can explain what is going on, yet somehow it all works out. Taking a bus can be quite a fuss in Cairo (as in much of the Middle East), as schedules shift daily, prices fluctuate, and drop-off points change without warning. Check a day or two before you need to take a bus to make sure it's going where you want for a price you're willing to pay. The buses themselves are quite nice—they are frequently air-conditioned and always equipped with large, comfortable seats, and many even serve food. Make reservations in person a day or two in advance for popular destinations.

Cairo's intercity bus terminal has shifted locations frequently in the past years (even recent schedules can be out of date). Unless otherwise noted, buses leave from **Turgoman Station (Mahattat Turgoman)** near Ramses Sq. Buses go to:

Alexandria and the Mediterranean Coast: Superjet (☎579 81 81) goes to **Alexandria** (3hr., every 30min. 5:30am-11pm, E£55) and **Marsa Matrouh** (5hr., 8am, E£37). Connections to **Siwa** from both destinations.

The Canal Zone: The **East Delta Bus Co.** (☎576 22 93) travels to: **Isma'ilia** (2hr., every hr. 7:30am-6:30pm, E£6.50); **Port Said** (2hr., every hr. 7:30am-6:30pm, E£15); and **Suez** (2hr., every 30min. 7:30am-6:30pm, E£6).

Hurghada: Superjet (8:30am and 2:30pm, E£47; 11pm, E£52) and the **Upper Egypt Bus Co.** (9am, 12:30, 3, 9:40, 11:30pm, midnight; E£45.50).

The Sinai: The **East Delta Bus Co.** (☎576 22 93) runs buses to: **Dahab** (8hr.; 7:30am, 1, 4:30, 11:30pm; E£55); **Nuweiba** (8hr., 7:30am and 10pm, E£50-55); and **Taba** (9hr.; 7:30am, E£50; 10pm, E£70). **Superjet** (☎579 81 81) runs buses to **Sharm al-Sheikh** (7hr., 11pm, E£55).

Upper Egypt: The **Upper Egypt Bus Co.** sends buses to: **Aswan** (13hr., 5:30pm, E£55); **Bahariya** (4-5hr.; 7 and 8am, E£12.50; 6pm, E£15); **Farafra** (7½hr., 10am and noon, E£40); **Kharga** (12hr., 8am, E£40); **Luxor** (9hr., 9pm, E£50).

International Buses:

The Levant: The **East Delta Bus Co.** sends buses to **Jordan** and **Syria** (22hr., 8pm, E£114) and **Turkey** (50hr., 8pm, E£310.50). **Superjet** leaves from al-Maza Sq. to **Jordan** (M, Tu, Th, Sa 6am; E£231) and **Syria** (Sa 10pm, E£310.50).

Tel Aviv and **Jerusalem:** Buses leave daily from the **Cairo Sheraton** (10hr., about E£150). Make reservations the day before at the Sheraton or at **Misr Travel,** on the 1st block of Tala'at Harb St.

SERVICE

Service leaving from Ramses Station travel to: **Alexandria** (E£10-12), **al-Arish** (E£15), **Isma'ilia** (E£6), **Port Said** (E£9), and **Suez** (E£5-7). *Service* from Giza Sq. travel to: **Alexandria** (E£11), **Fayyum** (E£5), **Mansoura** (E£9), **Tanta** (E£6), **Wadi Natrun** (about E£10), and **Zagazig** (E£5). *Service* to the rest of the Delta leave from Ahmed Hilmi Sq. Station. Prices are approximate, so watch what other passengers are paying. Unlike taxis, relatively few foreigners use *service*, so those that do can "get away" with paying the same as everyone else.

CAR RENTAL

If you're a daredevil or a maniac (or both), driving in Cairo is for you. **Avis** (š794 74 00) has branches throughout the city. The branch at Cairo International Airport (š265 24 29) is open 24hr. Join the millions of middle-class Egyptians driving Suzuki Swifts for US$50 per day, including insurance, taxes, and the first 100km. Most branches are open daily 8am-3:30pm. **Hertz** (š347 41 72) has branches at Cairo International Airport (š265 24 30), Ramses Hilton (š574 44 00 or 575 80 00), Semiramis Intercontinental Hotel (š354 32 39), and Meridien Hotel (š383 03 83). They offer Toyota Corollas for US$60 per day with unlimited mileage and air-conditioning. All branches open daily 9am-5pm. Keep in mind that Cairene traffic barely manages to avoid catastrophe even with experienced drivers at the helm. Those who are not familiar with the conventions of driving in Cairo are a danger to themselves and other motorists.

CAIRO

UPON ARRIVAL. Upon arrival at the **Cairo International Airport,** there are several options for getting downtown. Taxis are the simplest, but the most expensive (at most E£25); only take those that leave from the official stand, as they are monitored 24hr. by tourist police. Taxis will most likely drop you off at Tahrir Sq. (center of Cairo), and you can get anywhere from there. **Minibus** #27 (٢٧) and **bus** #400 (٤٠٠) go to Tahrir Sq. from the Airport's old terminal for 50pt (piasters). Gem Travel also runs a 24hr. **shuttle bus** to downtown (US$4).

All **trains** into Cairo stop at Ramses Station. **Bus** #160 (١٦٠) runs from there to Tahrir Sq. Black and white **taxis** to Tahrir Sq. cost E£2. The **Metro,** opposite the station, runs to Tahrir Sq. for 50pt. To walk (30min.), climb the pedestrian overpass and walk south on Ramses St., away from the Ramses II statue.

Buses from Israel usually drop passengers off at 'Abbasiyya Station. To reach Tahrir Sq. from 'Abbasiyya Station, hop into a southbound black and white cab (E£4-5) or walk left down Ramses St. as you leave the station; go beyond the overpass, and to the first bus stop on the right. From here many buses travel to Tahrir Sq. Buses from Jordan usually drop you off at **'Abd al-Munem Riad Station.** To reach Tahrir Sq. from here, walk right onto Gala'a St. as you exit, until you come to the Corniche al-Nil. At the corniche take a left onto Tahrir St.

Some hotels, as well as a tour guide by the name of ğMr. Salah Muhammad (š/fax 298 06 50; samoşintouch.com), offer free 24hr. shuttle service (reserve ahead of time by email) from the airport to downtown Cairo for visitors who will stay at their establishments or take Muhammad's tour of the Pyramids at Giza, Memphis, Saqqara, and the carpet school at Harania (E£40, not including entrance fees to sights, E£5 *Let's Go* discount if you book with him). For more information on the package, see **Pyramids at Giza,** p. 135.

❋ ORIENTATION

DOWNTOWN

At the center of it all is **Tahrir Sq.** *(Midan Tahrir)*, one of the many central districts planned by British and French colonialists. Local buses depart here for every metropolitan destination. Facing the square to the north is the monumental sandstone **Egyptian Museum;** adjacent to it on the west side of the square is the **Nile Hilton.** Entrances to the Sadat Metro station ring the square. At the southern end of the square is the hulking, concave **Mugamm'a Building,** headquarters of the Egyptian bureaucracy. The placid gardens and excellent bookstore of the **American University in Cairo (AUC)** are directly to the east of the Mugamm'a Building across Qasr al-'Aini St. A few blocks east on Tahrir St. is the Bab al-Luq public bus depot.

> The area in the immediate vicinity of Tahrir Sq. has been the scene of some **pickpocketing** by youngsters who may barely reach waist-level. Be wary of large, playful groups of local kids in and around the Square, as it is easy to get distracted. Most of the rest of Cairo is theft-free at any time of day.

The three most important streets coming out of Tahrir Sq. are Qasr al-'Aini St., Qasr al-Nil St., and Tala'at Harb St. **Qasr al-'Aini St.** runs south from Tahrir Sq. and ends at **Old Cairo** (also known as Coptic Cairo), the historic and spiritual center of the Copts, Egypt's Eastern Orthodox Christians. The American University in Cairo (AUC), Parliament, and some of the city's most beautifully preserved 19th-century colonial mansions line Qasr al-'Aini St. Just south of Tahrir Sq., sandwiched between Qasr al-'Aini St. and the **Nile River,** foreign embassies and banks cluster along the streets of the serene **Garden City** residential area. Farther south, the exclusive district of **Ma'adi** serves as home for many of Cairo's American expatriates. **Qasr al-Nil St.** begins in front of the Nile Hilton, cuts through Tala'at Harb Sq., and continues on to **Mustafa Kamal Sq.** In between lie many of Cairo's Western-style stores, banks, travel agents, and the AmEx office. **Tala'at Harb St.** runs from

A TRIP DOWN MEMORY LANE Many street names in Cairo have historical significance (for details, see **Modern History**, p. 64).

26 July Street: Commemorates the 1953 non-violent coup in which General Naguib and his Free Officers overthrew the king.

6 October Street: The date in 1973 when President Anwar Sadat staged a surprise attack on Israeli forces in the Sinai, earning him incredible popular support.

Sa'ad Zaghloul Street: Its namesake was the leader of the nationalist movement during World War I.

Salah al-Din Street: Salah al-Din al-Ayyubi (a.k.a. Saladin) assumed control of Egypt in 1171, fortified Cairo, and built its Citadel. His reign was a golden age for Egypt, and he is revered as one of the great heroes of Islamic history.

Tala'at Harb Street: Egypt's most famous economist, Muhammad Tala'at Harb, founded the country's first national bank (now the ubiquitous Banque Misr), which was the first bank in the world to conduct business in Arabic (as it still does).

the northeast side of Tahrir Sq. through **Tala'at Harb Sq.** toward Orabi Sq. and 26 July St. **Ramses Sq.** to the north (west of Orabi Sq.) and **'Ataba Sq.** (east of Orabi Sq., at the end of 26 July St.) form a rough triangle with Tala'at Harb Sq. enclosing the main business and shopping district, which is crammed with travel agents, banks, restaurants, clothing stores, and budget hotels. Due north of Tahrir Sq. lies **'Abd al-Munem Riad Sq.,** the starting point of **Ramses St.** and the city's main public bus depot. Heading northeast away from the Nile, Ramses St. runs up to **Ramses Sq.,** the Cairo train station (called **Ramses Station**), and the Mubarak Metro station. South of Ramses Sq. off Ramses St. is the Mahattat Turgoman **(Turgoman Bus Station),** where intercity buses come and go. Farther out on Ramses St. are **Cairo Stadium** and **Heliopolis,** a fashionable suburb where President Mubarak lives. Heading east from 'Ataba Sq., al-Azhar St. and al-Muski St. (a long shopping strip) both lead to the northern end of Islamic Cairo and the Northern Cemetery.

ISLAMIC CAIRO

Islamic Cairo was the heart of the city in the Middle Ages and continues to be the center of its religious life. It occupies the area southeast of downtown Cairo, marked by the **Citadel** and **Mosque of Ibn Tulun** in the south and **al-Azhar Mosque** and **University** in the north. Although this district has never benefited from a coherent urban plan, there are a few key streets and areas, the first of which is **Salah al-Din Sq.** *(Midan Salah al-Din).* Both the **Sultan Hassan Mosque** and **Rifa'i Mosque** border this square, as does the gargantuan Citadel. **Salah al-Din St.** runs south to the Southern Cemetery, while **al-Qala'a St.** is a main north-south thoroughfare. Branching off of al-Qala'a and heading toward **al-Azhar** and the market of **Khan al-Khalili** is **al-Mu'izz St.,** once the main avenue of the city. Finally, al-Azhar St. connects Islamic Cairo to 'Ataba Sq. and circumnavigates Khan al-Khalili and al-Azhar.

OTHER NEIGHBORHOODS

The main bridge crossing the Nile from the downtown area is **Tahrir Bridge,** connecting Tahrir Sq. to the southern tip of Gezira Island. The northern half of the island (connected to downtown by the 26 July Bridge) is **Zamalek,** Cairo's ritziest residential area and home to European expats and expensive restaurants. South of Zamalek is **Roda Island,** site of the Nilometer. Past Tahrir Bridge on the western bank of the Nile, the Cairo Sheraton Hotel presides over the residential neighborhood of **Doqqi,** home to a handful of embassies. North of Doqqi lies **Mohandiseen** (Engineer's City), built in the late 1950s by Nasser as a neighborhood for engineers. South of Doqqi, past the Cairo Zoo and across the Giza Bridge, is **Giza Sq.** Southwest is **Pyramids Rd.,** where overpriced and disreputable bars run from the square all the way to the **Pyramids of Giza.**

The major streets in Cairo are sometimes labeled in both English and Arabic, but a good map is helpful (most find they need maps more detailed than the one given out by the Egyptian Tourist Authority). Maps cost E£10-30 and are available

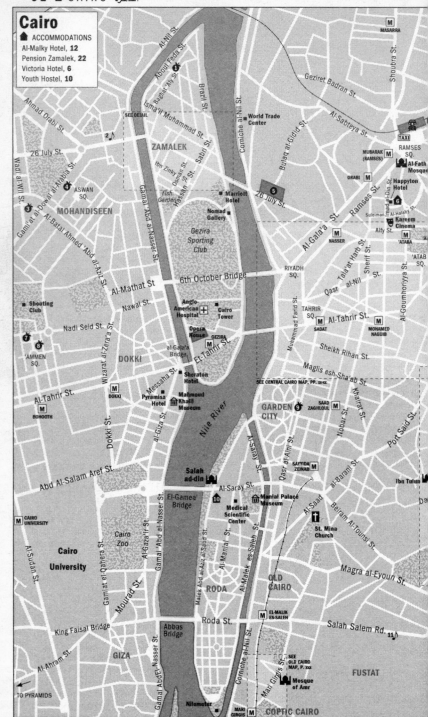

Cairo

🏠 ACCOMMODATIONS
Al-Malky Hotel, **12**
Pension Zamalek, **22**
Victoria Hotel, **6**
Youth Hostel, **10**

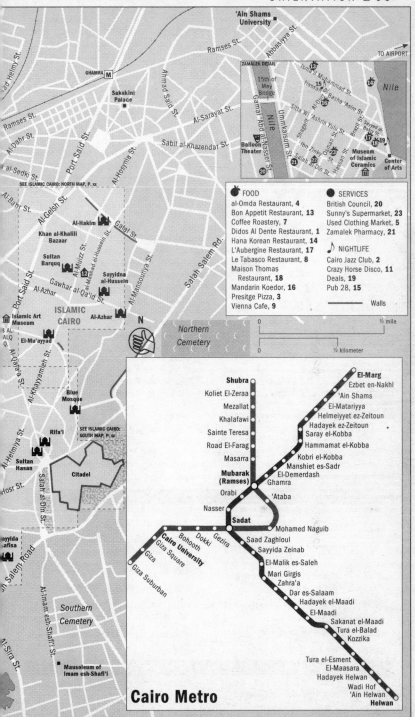

'Ain Shams University

TO AIRPORT

GHAMRA M

Sakakini Palace

ZAMALEK DETAIL

15th of May Bridge

Balloon Theater

Nile

Museum of Islamic Ceramics

Center of Arts

SEE ISLAMIC CAIRO: NORTH MAP, P. xx

Al-Hakim

Khan al-Khalili Bazaar

Sultan Barquq

Sayyidna al-Hussein

Islamic Art Museum

ISLAMIC CAIRO

Al-Azhar

El-Mu'ayyad

Northern Cemetery

Blue Mosque

Rifa'i

SEE ISLAMIC CAIRO: SOUTH MAP, P. xx

Sultan Hasan

Citadel

Sayyida afisa

Southern Cemetery

Mausoleum of Imam esh-Shafi'i

FOOD
al-Omda Restaurant, **4**
Bon Appetit Restaurant, **13**
Coffee Roastery, **7**
Didos Al Dente Restaurant, **1**
Hana Korean Restaurant, **14**
L'Aubergine Restaurant, **17**
Le Tabasco Restaurant, **8**
Maison Thomas
    Restaurant, **18**
Mandarin Koedor, **16**
Presitge Pizza, **3**
Vienna Cafe, **9**

SERVICES
British Council, **20**
Sunny's Supermarket, **23**
Used Clothing Market, **5**
Zamalek Pharmacy, **21**

♪ **NIGHTLIFE**
Cairo Jazz Club, **2**
Crazy Horse Disco, **11**
Deals, **19**
Pub 28, **15**

Walls

0   ½ mile
0   ½ kilometer

Cairo Metro

Shubra
Koliet El-Zeraa
Mezallat
Khalafawi
Sainte Teresa
Road El-Farag
Masarra
Mubarak (Ramses)
Orabi
Nasser
Sadat

El-Marg
Ezbet en-Nakhl
'Ain Shams
El-Matariyya
Helmeiyyet ez-Zeitoun
Hadayek ez-Zeitoun
Saray el-Kobba
Hammamat el-Kobba
Kobri el-Kobba
Manshiet es-Sadr
El-Demerdash
Ghamra
'Ataba

Bohooth
Dokki
Gezira
Cairo University
Giza Square
Giza
Giza Suburban

Mohamed Naguib
Saad Zaghloul
Sayyida Zeinab
El-Malik es-Saleh
Mari Girgis
Zahra'a
Dar es-Salaam
Hadayek el-Maadi
El-Maadi
Sakanat el-Maadi
Tura el-Balad
Kozzika
Tura el-Esment
El-Maasara
Hadayek Helwan
Wadi Hof
'Ain Helwan
Helwan

at most bookstores (p. 96). *The Complete Cairo Street-Finder: A-Z* is an authoritative map in book form. *Egypt Today* (E£10) publishes up-to-date street listings. Also, look for their *Dining Guide* and *Travel & Recreation Guide* (E£15 each).

E LOCAL TRANSPORTATION

METRO

The Cairo Metro is the fastest and cleanest ticket in town—worlds away from the rest of Cairo's bumpy and grumpy public transport. It was completed in 1987 as a joint project with France and Japan, and is the best (and only) subway system in all of Africa. Trains run along the main line, a 40km route linking the southern industrial district of Helwan to al-Marj in Heliopolis, with a number of stops downtown (look for the giant red "M" signs). An additional line connecting Giza was recently added; another line to Imbaba and al-Azhar via Zamalek is still under construction. Trains run about every 6min. (6am-midnight; 50pt-E£1.50). Save the ticket for exiting through the turnstiles or pay a fine of E£5. The stations downtown are **Mubarak** (Ramses Sq. and Railway Station), **Orabi** (Orabi St. and Ramses St.), **'Ataba** ('Ataba Sq.), **Nasser** (26 July St. and Ramses St.), **Sadat** (Tahrir Sq.), **Sa'ad Zaghloul** (Mansour St. and Isma'il Abaza St.), **Sayyida Zeinab** (Mansour St. and 'Ali Ibrahim St.), **al-Malik al-Saleh** (Salah Salem Rd.), and **Mari Girgis** (Old Cairo). Rush hour is before 9am and from 2-5pm. Although women can ride in any compartment, the first is exclusively for women and the second is reserved for women until 4pm.

MICROBUSES

Microbuses follow set routes to certain destinations, but tend to be flexible as long as all passengers are going to the same area. Stops are sometimes marked by a wooden shelter. If you don't have a basic command of Arabic, stick to the numbered, fixed routes. Microbuses go from **'Ataba Sq.** to Ramses Sq., Tahrir Sq., Northern Cemetery, Zamalek, Islamic Cairo, and Heliopolis. From **Tahrir Sq.**, microbuses leave for Heliopolis, Giza Sq., Doqqi, Mohandiseen, the Pyramids, and the airport terminals. Fares (25pt-E£1.50) depend on the length of the route.

MINIBUSES

Minibuses operate along many of the same routes as city buses. Although more expensive (50pt-E£1.50), minibuses are far more comfortable, and the orange-and-white buses operate on natural gas instead of unleaded. Minibus numbers appear in Arabic only. Numbers with a strike through them travel different routes from their ordinary counterparts (e.g. 39 goes to 'Abd al-Munem Riad, ~~39~~ goes to AUC).

FROM THE NILE HILTON:

#16 (١٦): al-Gala'a Bridge—Agouza

#27 (٢٧): Masr al-Gadida—Airport

#30 (٣٠): Nasser City—'Abbasiyya Sq.—Ramses Sq.—Abd al-Munem Riad 2

#32 (٣٢): Hai al-Tamin—Mugamm'a—Ramses Sq.—'Abbasiyya

#35 (٣٥): 'Abbasiyya—'Abd al-Munem Riad 2—Roxy—al-Hijaz Sq.

#49 (٤٩): Falaki Sq.—Tahrir Sq.—Zamalek

#50 (٥٠): Ramses Sq.—'Ataba Sq.—Citadel

#52 (٥٢), **56** (٥٦): Bab al-Luq—Tahrir Sq.—Ma'adi—Old Cairo

#54 (٥٤): Bab al-Luq—Rifa'i Mosque—Ibn Tulun Mosque—Citadel—S. Cemetery

#55 (٥٥): Ma'adi—Bab al-Luq

#58 (٥٨): Ramses Sq.—Manial

#77 (٧٧): Bulaq al-Dakrur—Khan al-Khalili—al-Darasa

#84 (٨٤): 'Ataba/Tahrir Sq.—Doqqi—Giza

FROM TAHRIR SQUARE:

#77 (٧٧), **102** (١٠٢), **103** (١٠٣): Bulaq al-Dakrur—Khan al-Khalili—al-Darasa

#183 (١٨٣): Giza

FROM 'ATABA SQUARE:

#26 (٢٦): Roxy—Tahrir Sq.—Doqqi—Giza

#48 (٤٨): Zamalek

#93 (٩٣): Mazalat—'Ataba Sq.—Basatin

BUSES

Few foreigners use the bus system, and with good reason: although very cheap (25-50pt), the buses are hot and cramped, and since they never come to a full stop, passengers must jump out the back to exit. Numbers and destinations are always in Arabic. Buses run 5:30am-12:30am (during Ramadan 6:30am-6:30pm and 7:30pm-2am), except for buses **#400** (٤٠٠) and **#400** (٤٠٠), which have 24hr. service to both **airport terminals** from Tahrir Sq. and Ramses Sq., respectively. Cairo's local bus depot is **'Abd al-Munem Riad Station,** north of the Egyptian Museum just below the towering, triangular Ramses Hilton. Several buses depart from the front of the old **Arab League Building,** to the west of the Mugamm'a along Tahrir St., adjacent to the bridge. Other bus stations are at **'Ataba Sq.** (to the Citadel, the Manial Palace, Giza, and Tahrir Sq.), and at **Giza Sq.** (to the Pyramids, airport, and Citadel).

FROM 'ABD AL-MUNEM RIAD STATION:

#8 (٨): Tahrir Sq.—Qasr al-'Aini—Manial—Giza—Mena House Hotel (Pyramids)

#63 (٦٣), **66** (٦٦): al-Azhar—Khan al-Khalili

#72 (٧٢): Sayyida Zeinab—Citadel—Imam al-Shafi'i Mausoleum

#82 (٨٢), **182** (١٨٢): Imam al-Shafi'i Mausoleum—S. Cemetery—Citadel

#99 (٩٩): Agouza—Sudan St.—Lebanon Sq. (Midan Lubnan)

#128 (١٢٨): 'Abbasiyya Sq.—'Ain Shams

#173 (١٧٣), **194** (١٩٤), **609** (٦٠٩): Tahrir Sq.—Citadel

#174 (١٧٤): Ramses—Sayyida Zeinab—Ibn Tulun—Sultan Hassan—Citadel

#400 (٤٠٠): Old Cairo Airport via Heliopolis (Roxy Sq.)

#403 (٤٠٣): Citadel—Sultan Hassan

#666 (٦٦٦): al-Gaili Museum

#900 (٩٠٠): Tahrir Sq.—Qasr al-'Aini—Manial (Youth Hostel)—Cairo University—Giza—Pyramids—Holiday Inn Hotel

#923 (٩٢٣): Basatin—Giza Sq.

#949 (٩٤٩): New Cairo Airport

FROM THE ARAB LEAGUE BUILDING:

#13 (١٣): Zamalek—Bab al-Luq

#19 (١٩), **203** (٢٠٣): Doqqi

#102 (١٠٢): Mazalat—Doqqi

#166 (١٦٦): 'Ataba Sq.—Doqqi

#815-173 (٨١٥-١٧٣): Medinat al-Talaba

FROM 'ATABA SQUARE:

#214 (٢١٤): Qanatir

#404 (٤٠٤): Citadel—Tahrir Sq.—Medinat al-Talaba

#801 (٨٠١), **951** (٩٥١): Citadel—'Abd al-Munem Riad

#904 (٩٠٤): Mugamm'a—Pyramids

FROM GIZA SQUARE:

#3 (٣): Pyramids

#30 (٣٠): Ramses Station

#949 (٩٤٩): Airport (both terminals)

FROM RAMSES STATION:

#30 (٣٠): Pyramids

#160 (١٦٠): Citadel—Tahrir Sq.

TAXIS

Never let a taxi hail you. Major hotels, sights, and transportation centers are crowded with drivers who will offer you rides at several times the actual price. Stick to the **black-and-white taxis** that collect passengers along the way. Meters have been installed in all taxis, but drivers rarely use them due to outdated gas costs and the prohibitive price of getting them fixed. However, any driver that mentions money before you arrive at your destination is trying to rip you off. Passengers are expected to know the price, so have the fare in hand and pay with folded bills as you exit the vehicle, without discussion or glancing back for approval. Drivers who do not speak English tend to inflate prices less than their polyglot colleagues; so use landmarks and either say or show a written copy of your destination in Arabic. Showing a map to the driver never works. (For more information, see **Essentials: By Taxi,** p. 40). Rides in the downtown area (Ramses Sq., Tahrir Sq., Zamalek, and Islamic Cairo) should cost about E£3-5. Trips to the pyramids are about E£15; those to Ma'adi and Heliopolis run around E£8-10. A taxi to or from the airport should cost no more than E£20-25. These estimates are very generous, so be prepared to brush off taxi drivers who demand more.

FRIEND OR TOUT? Downtown Cairo is the scene of Egypt's most aggressive street hustling. A walk from Tahrir Sq. to Orabi Sq. along Tala'at Harb is almost certain to gain you multiple "Egyptian friends," eager to help you get the best (for them) deals on perfume, papyrus, *felucca* rides, and hotel rooms. But you will also be approached by people who genuinely want to befriend you. Too often, jaded tourists treat everyone they meet with suspicion. There are a few ways to identify touts. First, be aware of your location. Anyone who approaches you downtown probably doesn't have your best interest in mind, while elsewhere the odds reverse. People who declare themselves your friend and ask you to go somewhere with them after 10 seconds are probably selling something (10min. is a different matter). One of the most certain giveaways is the phrase "Egyptian hospitality." Respectable Egyptians would never call attention to their own generosity.

🛂 PRACTICAL INFORMATION

TOURIST AND FINANCIAL SERVICES

Tourist Office: The **Egyptian Tourist Authority (ETA)** has offices scattered throughout the city. All provide free maps and info, and can make reservations or write out destinations in Arabic. The accuracy and utility of their information varies according to who is on duty. Some staff members tend to tell you what they think you should know rather than what you actually want to know. Locations include: **Cairo International Airport** (☎291 42 77; open 24hr.), at the entrance and next to the duty-free shops; **Giza** (☎385 02 59; open 24hr.), in front of Mena House Hotel; **Railway Station** (☎579 07 67; open daily 8am-8pm), on the left at the station's main entrance; **5 'Adly St.** (☎391 34 54; 8:30am-8pm), a 20min. walk from Tahrir Sq. If you want someone who speaks English well, your best bet is the 'Adly location. Follow Tala'at Harb St. and turn right on 'Adly St. The office is 3 blocks down on your left, just past the Tourist Police.

Student Cards: Medical Scientific Center, 103 Mathaf al-Manial St. (☎531 03 30), on Roda Island. South of the Manial Palace across the street from Kentucky Fried Chicken (look for the ISIC sign). Great source of information for travelers. Provides ISIC and Go25 cards (E£25; bring a photo and proof of student status). Student volunteer staff speaks excellent English and will quote prices for sights and entertainment. The center gives out free maps and pamphlets and organizes excursions to see the Pyramids and whirling dervish dancing.

Passport Office, Mugamm'a Building, 2nd fl. (☎792 69 00). This gray edifice at the southern side of Tahrir Sq. was constructed during Nasser's flirtation with the USSR, and the spirit of the Cold War lives on in its Soviet-style inefficiency. To navigate the visa extension process, first stop at the information desk on the 2nd fl. Having what you want written down in Arabic beforehand helps. Registration open Sa-Th 8am-8pm, visa extensions 8am-1pm. For smaller crowds, check the 2nd fl. of the **Ministry of Economy and Foreign Trade Building,** 8 'Adly St. (☎390 43 63), next to the EgyptAir office. Bring a passport photo for visa extensions (2-6 months E£10, 1 year E£40). Open Sa-Th 8am-1:30pm.

Currency Exchange: Banks and exchange services litter the downtown area. **Banque Misr** (☎391 75 71) has branches at major hotels, with a main office downtown at 151 Muhammad Farid St. All open Sa-Th 8:30am-2pm and 6-9pm. **Cairo Barclay's International Bank,** 12 Sheikh Yusef Sq., Garden City (☎794 94 15 or 794 94 22), 3 blocks south of Tahrir Sq. along Qasr al-'Aini St., accepts traveler's checks and has worldwide money transfer services. Open Su-Th 8:30am-2pm; Ramadan 10am-1pm. Foreign banks closed F-Sa, but most Egyptian banks open Sa. Money wired to Egypt through **Citibank,** 4 Ahmed Basha St., Garden City (☎795 18 73 or 795 18 74; open Su-Th 8:30am-2pm) or **Western Union,** 1081 Corniche al-Nil, Garden City (☎797 13 00 or 797 13 74; open Su-Th 9am-8:30pm), in the FedEx office.

ATM: Egyptian British Banks have machines that accept Express Net, Global Access, PLUS, and V cards. Locations in Semiramis Intercontinental, Zamalek Marriott, Cairo Sheraton, and Ramses and Nile Hiltons.

Thomas Cook, 17 Mahmoud Bassouni St. (☎574 37 76, 574 39 55, or 574 39 67; fax 576 27 50). Half a block west of Tala'at Harb Sq. Other offices throughout the city. Travel agency, money transfers, currency exchange, and cash advances on MC and V. Cashes traveler's checks. Open daily 8am-5pm.

American Express, 15 Qasr al-Nil (☎574 79 91, 574 79 92, or 574 79 96). Off Tala'at Harb Sq., opposite EgyptAir toward Ramses St. Members can have money sent to the office and have mail held there. Cashes traveler's checks. Open Su-Th 9am-4pm; Ramadan 9am-3:30pm. Other locations at the Nile Hilton (☎578 50 02 or 578 50 03), Marriott Hotel (☎736 01 36), Pullman Ma'adi (☎790 78 51), and 4 Syria St. (☎570 79 08 or 570 79 14) in Mohandiseen.

EMBASSIES AND CONSULATES

Australia, World Trade Center 11-12th floors, 1191 Corniche al-Nil (☎575 04 44), in Bulaq. Past the 26 July Bridge. Passports generally replaced in 5 working days (32-page passports AUS\$132, 64-page AUS\$198, payable in E£ only). Immediate replacement in case of emergency. Open Su-W 8am-4:15pm, Th 8:30am-1:45pm.

Canada, 3rd fl. of Arab-African Bank Building, 5 Midan al-Saraya al-Kobr (☎794 31 10 or 794 31 19, emergencies ☎796 36 44), in Garden City. Passports replaced within one week for E£115. Open Su-Th 9am-2pm.

Israel, 6 Ibn al-Malik St. (☎761 03 80 or 761 04 58), in Doqqi. Cross over to Doqqi from Roda Island on University Bridge (al-Gam'a). The street to the right of and parallel to the bridge is Ibn al-Malik. Security guards by the entrance will ask to see your passport. Visas E£60. Open Su-Th 10am-12:30pm.

Jordan, 6 al-Goheina St. (☎748 55 66 or 749 99 12), in Doqqi. 2 blocks west of the Cairo Sheraton. Visas (photograph required) free for Australians, E£28 for New Zealanders, E£63 for Brits, E£231 for Americans, E£91 for Canadians. Same-day service. Open Sa-Th 9am-2pm; arrive early to avoid the crowd.

Lebanon, 22 al-Mansour Muhammad St. (☎738 28 23, 738 28 24, or 738 28 25), in Zamalek. Photograph required for passports. Visas E£123. Any evidence of having been to Israel prohibits obtaining a Lebanese visa. Consular services open M-Th and Sa 9:30am-12:30pm.

South Africa, 21 and 23 Giza St., 18th fl. of the Nile Tower (☎571 72 38 or 571 72 39), in Giza. File applications for new passports here; they're sent to South Africa for processing. Entire process takes 8 weeks. In the meantime, you are issued a one-page Emergency Passport good for 3 months (E£50). Open Su-Th 8am-5pm; consular services Su-Th 9am-noon.

Syria, 18 'Abd al-Rahim Sabri St. (☎337 70 20), in Doqqi. Bring 2 photographs for a visa. Visas free for Australians and New Zealanders, E£182 for Brits, E£195 for Canadians, and E£211 for Americans. Anywhere from 1 day to 1 week for processing, depending on nationality. You are advised to apply for visas in your home country. Americans are sometimes denied visas at Syrian embassies in other Arab countries. Evidence of travel to Israel prohibits obtaining a Syrian visa. Open Sa-Th 9am-2pm.

UK, 7 Ahmed Ragheb St. (☎794 08 50), in Garden City. Also handles **New Zealand** affairs. Will replace passports within 4 days and only accepts E£ (32-page passports E£270, 48-page E£330). Open Su-Th 9am-1pm.

US, 5 Latin America St. (☎794 82 11, emergencies ☎795 73 71), in Garden City. 2 blocks south of Tahrir Sq. For the consulate, enter on Lazoughli St. around the block. Lost or stolen passports replaced overnight for US\$60 or E£ equivalent (US\$40 for renewal). Open Su-Th 8am-noon.

LOCAL SERVICES

Luggage Storage: Avoid the unreliable Ramses Station lockers. Get bilingual written proof of having stored anything at a hotel. Make sure that "storage" in budget hotels is a safe at the front desk and not just a hallway.

CAIRO

English-Language Bookstores: Lehnert and Landrock, 44 Sherif St. (☎393 53 24), between 'Adly St. and 26 July St. "L&L" offers a superb, wide-ranging selection of guidebooks, maps, histories, and postcards. Open M-F 10am-2pm and 4-9pm, Sa 9am-11pm. MC/V. **Used Books,** left of the statue by the Cairo Puppet Theater near 'Ataba Sq. Metro: 'Ataba. Among tracts on dialectical materialism and US Boy Scout manuals are titles for as low as E£4. **AUC Bookstore,** 113 Qasr al-'Aini St. (☎797 53 77), in the Hill House at the American University in Cairo. University texts, classic novels, Arab literature in translation, maps, and guide books. ID needed to enter the campus. Open Su-Th 8:30am-5pm. MC/V.

Newspapers and Magazines: The *Egyptian Gazette, al-Ahram Weekly,* and *Middle East Times* are Egypt's English newspapers. *Egypt Today,* a monthly magazine (E£10), is handy for current restaurant and entertainment listings. All are sold at **The Reader's Corner,** 33 'Abd al-Khaleq Sarwat St., downtown. Open M-Sa 10am-7pm. Many hotels and street stands from Tahrir Sq. to Tala'at Harb Sq. sell foreign language publications.

American Cultural Center, 5 Latin America St., Garden City (☎794 96 01 or 576 27 04; library ☎795 05 32 or 797 34 12), inside the US Embassy, across from the British Embassy. Tourists in Egypt for at least 12 months are eligible to join no matter what their nationality (bring 2 photographs and a passport). Members can borrow books and watch videos. All American citizens have access to the A/C library's collection of popular magazines and books on America. Occasional free films and lectures. Call for a schedule. Open Su-F 10am-4pm; in winter M-F 10am-4pm.

Supermarkets: Seoudi Market, 25 Midan al-Missaha St., Doqqi (☎748 84 40 or 748 84 41); 20 Hijaz St., Mohandiseen (☎346 03 91); and 15 Ahmad Hishmat St., Zamalek (☎736 35 86 or 735 03 70). A fully stocked supermarket with low prices. All open daily 9am-2am. **Sunny Supermarket,** 11 al-'Aziz 'Osman St., Zamalek (☎342 11 21), up the road from the Pension Zamalek south of 26 July St. A more expensive option offering an impressive array of Egyptian and Western products. Sunny's also has a bulletin board where you can find information on anything from Arabic lessons to apartments for rent. Open daily 8am-10pm.

Laundromat: Circle Cleaning, 24 26 July St. (☎576 08 55), near the Supreme Court and the intersection with Tala'at Harb St. Open daily 9am-9pm. The place is a madhouse—be prepared to fight your way to a machine—so you're better off doing your laundry yourself or paying a maid in your hotel. 50pt per piece is reasonable.

Swimming Pools: Fontana Hotel (☎592 21 45 or 592 23 21), in Ramses Sq. has a teal-tiled pool on its 7th fl. patio (E£15 per day). Cairo's sporting clubs also sell day passes for E£20: the **Gezira Sporting Club** (☎735 60 00), in front of the Marriott Hotel in Zamalek; the **Ma'adi Sporting Club,** 8 al-Nadi Sq. (☎790 54 55); and the **Heliopolis Sporting Club,** 17 al-Merghany St. (☎291 00 65). Day passes at 5-star hotels up to E£30, though at some large, busy hotels, no one will notice if you jump in.

EMERGENCY AND COMMUNICATIONS

Emergency: Police: ☎122, 126, or 303 41 22. **Fire:** ☎125 or 391 01 15.

Tourist Police, 5 'Adly St. (☎390 19 44 or 390 60 28, emergencies ☎126). In the same building as the Tourist Office. Also at Cairo International Airport (☎637 25 84), the Manial Palace Hotel in Giza (☎385 02 59), and Ramses Station.

24-Hour Pharmacies: Victoria Pharmacy, 90 Qasr al-'Aini St. (☎794 86 04). **Isaaf Pharmacy** (☎574 33 69) on Ramses St. and 26 July St. **Seif Pharmacy,** 76 Qasr al-'Aini (☎794 26 78). **Zamalek Pharmacy,** 3 Shagarat al-Durr (☎735 24 06).

Hospitals: The best-equipped is **Al-Salaam International Hospital** (☎524 02 50), Ma'adi, Corniche al-Nil. Other options: **Anglo-American Hospital** (☎735 61 62 or 735 61 65), Zamalek, on Botanical Garden St. below the Cairo Tower; and **Cairo Medical Center** (☎258 05 66, 258 02 17, or 258 10 03), in Heliopolis at Roxy Sq.

Fax Office: You can send and receive faxes at the business office of the **Ramses Hilton** (fax 575 71 52 or 578 22 21). Sending prices vary by destination; receiving costs E£4 per page. Most telephone offices can also send faxes.

SCAM WARS, EPISODE I

Never underestimate the power of the con side. The most notorious con, the **hotel scam,** begins the moment you step off the plane. Have two or three hotels in mind and avoid taking a taxi or otherwise making verbal contact (besides a firm, polite "no") with anyone who offers you anything at the airport. Do not believe anyone who claims your chosen hotels are closed, whether they are taxi drivers, "tour guides," or even (underpaid) tourist police. Simply find another driver, get dropped off at a nearby landmark, or refuse payment. When in Cairo (or any other city) do not let yourself be a taken to a hotel by a taxi driver or "hotel manager." This only succeeds in inflating the price due to hefty commissions and in bringing you to a dishonest establishment that may have further designs on your wallet. The second con is the dreaded **tour con.** Even at reputable hotels, the management may push tours of high cost and low quality. Always check with the tourist office for a list of fair prices. Day excursions to the Pyramids and Saqqara may be an excuse to take you to perfume and papyrus shops along the way. Several hotels in Cairo offer *felucca* and Nile cruise trips between Aswan and Luxor: these are the most serious **rip-offs.** Skip the middleman and contact **Amigo Tours,** in the Isis Hotel in Aswan (☎097 31 68 43). Inclusive multi-day trips (excluding train fare) cost US$65 for a *felucca* and US$145 for a Nile cruise. As with any tour, seek to pay the balance directly to the tour company and only after you arrive at your destination—whether it be Alexandria or Alderon.

Telephones: Main Telephone Office, on Ramses St., one block north of 26 July St. Other offices in Zamalek, Airport, Ma'adi, Tahrir Sq., 'Adly St., and Alfy St. (under the Windsor Hotel). All open 24hr. You can make **collect calls** and **credit card calls** with the USA-Direct, UKDirect, CanadaDirect, and JapanDirect phones in the lobbies of the Ramses Hilton, Marriott, and Semiramis Hotels (for access numbers, see **Keeping in Touch,** p. 29). Yellow Menatel and red NilePhones can make international calls. For a 25% surcharge, you can also place international calls at the business service offices in the Meridien, Sheraton, and Nile Hilton hotels. Open 24hr. **Directory Assistance:** ☎140.

Internet Access: Internet access has recently become cheaper and more widespread. A growing number of hotels offer access to their guests, usually for about E£10 per hr. The **Internet Egypt Cafe** (☎578 04 44) in the Nile Hilton Mall has fierce A/C and several banks of computers. 15min. minimum E£3; 30min. E£6; 1hr. E£12. Open daily 7am-midnight. The **Hany Internet Cafe,** 16 Sarwat St., 1 block north of the Berlin Hotel, offers a small but serviceable place to get online. 30min. E£3; 1hr. E£6.

Post Office, 55 Sarwat St. (☎391 26 14), in 'Ataba Sq. under the dome. Often crowded, but blissfully empty shortly before closing. Packages require export license, available from airport, hotels, and tourist shops. Open Sa-Th 8am-7pm; Ramadan 9am-3pm. Most post offices in Cairo sell stamps and have EMS. **24hr. EMS** on Bidek St. One convenient branch is at 13 Metitte Bash St. in Tahrir Sq. (☎575 43 13), opposite the Egyptian Museum. Open Sa-Th 9am-9pm. Stamps sold and letters mailed at major hotels.

Federal Express, 1081 Corniche al-Nil, 8th fl., Garden City (☎792 33 01), opposite the Meridien Hotel on the east bank of the Nile. Open daily 8am-8pm.

▟ ACCOMMODATIONS

Downtown Cairo, on and around **Tala'at Harb St.,** is littered with dozens of budget hotels and dorms occupying the upper floors of colonial buildings. All hotels listed below accept reservations, include breakfast in their prices, and have fans and 24hr. hot water in all rooms unless otherwise noted. "Hotels" and "hostels" are close cousins in Egypt. Many hotels have dorm beds available and many hostels have single or double rooms. Most maids will do your laundry (usually about 50pt per article). If you're in Cairo for a while or during low season, bargain for a reduced rate. Single-sex groups should have no problem renting **a flat** (E£500-2000 per month), but landlords often frown upon renting to coed groups. The billboards at the AUC entrance and the Sunny Market in Zamalek list available apartments.

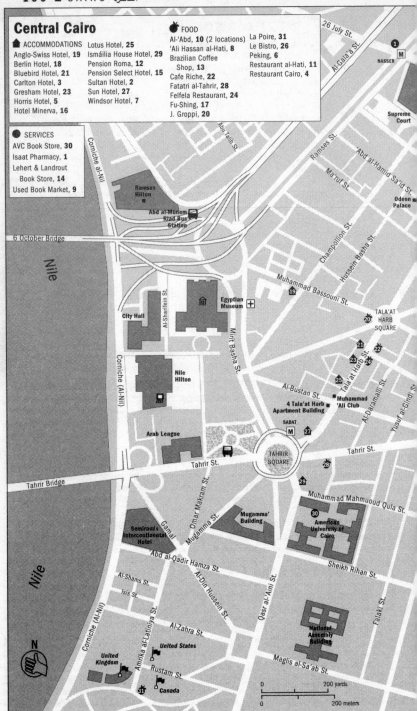

Central Cairo

🏠 **ACCOMMODATIONS**
Anglo-Swiss Hotel, **19**
Berlin Hotel, **18**
Bluebird Hotel, **21**
Carlton Hotel, **3**
Gresham Hotel, **23**
Horris Hotel, **5**
Hotel Minerva, **16**

Lotus Hotel, **25**
Ismáilia House Hotel, **29**
Pension Roma, **12**
Pension Select Hotel, **15**
Sultan Hotel, **2**
Sun Hotel, **27**
Windsor Hotel, **7**

🍎 **FOOD**
Al-'Abd, **10** (2 locations)
'Ali Hassan al-Hati, **8**
Brazilian Coffee
  Shop, **13**
Cafe Riche, **22**
Fatatri al-Tahrir, **28**
Felfela Restaurant, **24**
Fu-Shing, **17**
J. Groppi, **20**

La Poire, **31**
Le Bistro, **26**
Peking, **6**
Restaurant al-Hati, **11**
Restaurant Cairo, **4**

⬤ **SERVICES**
AVC Book Store, **30**
Isaat Pharmacy, **1**
Lehert & Landrout
  Book Store, **14**
Used Book Market, **9**

26 July St.

Al-Gala'a St.

NASSER

Supreme
Court

Corniche al-Nil

Ramses
Hilton

Abd al-Muriem
Riad Bus
Station

Abu Talib St.

Ramses St.

Abd al-Hamid Sa'id St.

Ma'ruf St.

Odeon
Palace

6 October Bridge

Nile

Champollion St.

Hussein Basha St.

Muhammad Bassouni St.

Al-Sharifein St.

City Hall

Egyptian
Museum

Corniche (Al-Nil)

Nile
Hilton

Miri Basha St.

TALA'AT
HARB
SQUARE

Tala'at Harb St.

Al-Bustan St.

Muhammad
'Ali Club

Al-Daranhalli St.

Yusuf al-Gindi St.

Arab League

SADAT
M

4 Tala'at Harb
Apartment Building

Tahrir St.

Tahrir Bridge

Tahrir St.

TAHRIR
SQUARE

Muhammad Mahmuoud Qula St.

Omar Makram St.

Ganal

Mugamma St.

Mugamma'
Building

American
University of
Cairo

Sheikh Rihan St.

Semiramis
Intercontinental
Hotel

Abd al-Qadir Hamza St.

Nile

Al-Shams St.

Al-Din Hussein St.

Isis St.

Qasr al-Aini St.

National
Assembly
Building

Falaki St.

Corniche (Al-Nil)

Amrika al-Latiniya St.

Al-Zahra St.

United
Kingdom

United States

Rustam St.

Canada

Maglis al-Sa'ab St.

N

0   200 yards

0   200 meters

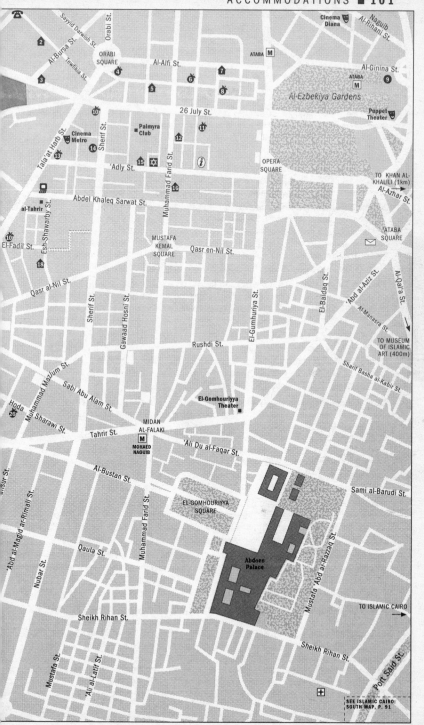

BUDGET

Pension Roma, 169 Muhammad Farid St. (☎391 10 88 or 391 13 40), 1 block south of 26 July St. and two blocks east of Tala'at Harb St. Turn right on 'Adly St. and left after the synagogue, and look for the hotel's green sign above the Gattegno department store, between 'Ataba and Nasser Metro stations. Owner Madam Cressaty keeps her beautifully designed *pensione* immaculately clean and perfectly maintained. Well-furnished rooms may have a breezy balcony, but no fans. Towels, toilet paper, and soap provided. Fan rental E£2.50. Free storage. Singles E£29.50; doubles E£40, with shower E£55; triples E£73.50, with shower E£82. Reservations recommended.

Hotel Minerva, 39 Tala'at Harb St. (☎392 06 00, 392 06 01, or 392 06 02), one block toward Tala'at Harb Sq. from 26 July St. Entrance is on Mamar El Central St. between Tala'at Harb St. and Sherif St. Beautifully renovated bathrooms, vast balconies, and hardwood floors add a touch of elegance. Rooms come with sinks. Often full, so reservations are recommended. Singles E£23; doubles E£35; triples E£48. Fan rental E£2.

Sultan Hotel, Venice Hotel, and Safari Hotel, 4 Souq al-Tawfiqia St. (☎577 22 58, 574 32 69, and 575 07 52). These 3 hotels collectively occupy the 1st 5 floors of one address. All are extremely cheap, with friendly, honest management. **Venice** has Internet access for E£8 per hr. Japanese backpackers seem to find **Safari** particularly attractive. Breakfast not included, but a fruit market thrives just outside the entrance. Dorms E£6-8; the ones at **Sultan** are the most comfortable. Singles and doubles E£25.

Pension Select Hotel, 19 'Adly St., 8th fl. (☎393 37 07), next to a synagogue. High above the street noise, the Select offers rooms that are quiet and off the beaten path. Many rooms have access to a shared balcony with a sweeping view of the city. Singles E£25; doubles E£40; triples E£60.

Sun Hotel, 2 Tala'at Harb St., 9th fl. (☎578 17 86 or 773 00 87). Worshiped by budget travelers for its convenient location—less than a block from the Metro, on the left as you leave Tahrir Sq. Features satellite TV, a kitchen, and a lively lobby area with crammed couches. Comfortable beds in compact rooms. Bargain for longer stays. Dorm beds E£15; singles E£30; doubles E£40; triples E£51.

Youth Hostel (HI), 135 Malik 'Abd al-'Aziz al-Sa'ud St., Roda Island (☎364 07 29; fax 98 41 07). Metro: Sayyida Zeinab. Exit to the right and walk straight to the Nile. Cross the Sayala Bridge and continue straight across Roda Island to the Nile's main channel. Turn left just before the University (al-Gam'a) bridge (with Salah al-Din Mosque to your right); the hostel is 10m away on the left. The hostel is clean and quiet, a nice island retreat from downtown. A bit isolated from tourist sights (but not the Nilometer!). No lockout. Curfew 11pm. Call ahead for reservations. Single-sex 8- and 3-bed dorms E£15 and E£20; nonmembers E£1 extra.

Isma'ilia House Hotel, 1 Tahrir Sq., 8th fl. (☎796 31 22), by the exit of the Sadat Metro station in the direction of AUC. A warm, convenient hotel with diligent management. The rooms are fairly standard, but have stupendous views of Tahrir Sq. Singles E£20, with shower E£25; doubles E£40, with shower E£50; triples E£51, with shower E£60.

Bluebird Hotel, 42 Tala'at Harb St., 6th fl. (☎575 63 77), opposite 'Adly St. heading toward Ramses St. A fairly clean and well-maintained option, though some of the walls are rather thin. Separate baths for men and women, satellite TV, and common kitchen. Singles E£20; doubles E£40; triples E£60.

Anglo-Swiss Hotel, 14 Champollion St., 6th fl. (☎575 14 97), 2 blocks west of Tala'at Harb Sq. From Tahrir Sq., turn right on Champollion in the northwestern end of the square before the museum, by the parking lot. The hotel will be to your left at the intersection with Mahmoud Bassouni St. Play the piano in the sunny dining hall or watch some TV in a pleasant living room before retiring to quiet, if sometimes drab, rooms with shared baths, most with balcony. Friendly management, but not the most reputable around. Avoid the touts that hang around the hotel. French spoken. Singles E£20; doubles E£30. Student discount.

Gresham Hotel, 20 Tala'at Harb St. (☎576 20 94), just off Tala'at Harb Sq. Not all rooms come with fans. Travelers may have better deals on tours elsewhere. Singles E£25, with bath and A/C E£35; doubles E£40, with bath and A/C E£45; triples E£55, with bath and A/C E£65; quads E£70, with bath and A/C E£80.

A BIT SWANKIER

⦿ Berlin Hotel, 2 al-Shawarby St. (☎/fax 395 75 02; berlinhotelcairo@hotmail.com). From Tala'at Harb Sq., walk up Qasr al-Nil toward Mustafa Kamal Sq. The entrance to this new hotel is on a pedestrian-only street. Friendly proprietor Hisham is generous with his wealth of information and advice and makes sure all are well cared for. Elegant rooms boast private showers, full-length velvet curtains, and quite possibly the most comfortable beds available for any price in Cairo. All rooms have A/C. Internet access E£10 per hr., MediaRing Internet phone calls to anywhere in the world available at E£2 per min. Hotel can arrange transportation from airport—a good idea, since Berlin's policy against paying commissions has earned some enemies among unscrupulous taxi drivers. Reservations recommended. Singles US$20; doubles US$25; triples US$30.

⦿ Victoria Hotel, 66 Goumhoriyya St. (☎589 22 90 or 589 22 91; fax 591 30 08). From the 'Ataba Metro station, walk north along Goumhoriyya to reach this 3-star hotel. Professional service and amenities beyond the dreams of most budget travelers, including a bank, Internet cafe, and hairdresser. Restaurant and posh bar with satellite TV. Rooms with polished wood floors, A/C, bath, and TV. Full breakfast buffet included. Reservations recommended. Singles US$19; doubles US$25; triples US$30. AmEx/MC/V.

Windsor Hotel, 19 Alfy St. (☎591 58 10 or 591 52 77; fax 592 16 21; windsorcairo@link.com; www.windsorcairo.com). Clean facilities with excellent service in an atmosphere of old-time grandeur make this a character-ful place to spend a night in Cairo. The hotel's gem is the Barrel Bar (named for the barrel furniture), which once served as the British Officers' Club and retains nostalgic artifacts from the old days. Monty Python's Michael Palin hung out here while filming *Around the World in Eighty Days.* Rooms have A/C, towels, crisp sheets, and comfy beds. Reservations recommended. Singles with shower US$29.50, with bath US$37- 46.50; doubles with shower US$38.50, with bath US$47-56.50. Prices include tax. 25% *Let's Go* discount, 15% during peak seasons. 5% credit card service charge may be added. AmEx/MC/V.

Happyton Hotel, 10 Aly al-Kassar St. (☎592 86 00). With your back to Tala'at Harb St., turn left on Emad al-Dein St. from Alfy St. at Cinema Diana. Turn right on Kassar St. to reach the entrance. This hotel has the distinction of offering the cheapest rooms with A/C and private bath in the city. Includes a small bar in the lobby, as well as a restaurant. Singles E£46; doubles E£66; triples E£84.

Lotus Hotel, 12 Tala'at Harb St. (☎575 627; fax 575 47 20; www.lotushotel.com). The sister hotel of the Windsor offers upscale accommodations close to Tahrir Sq. Restaurant and bar 2 floors up. Singles E£60, with shower and A/C E£90; doubles E£90, with shower and A/C E£120; triples with shower and A/C E£160. MC/V.

Carlton Hotel, 21 26 July St. (☎575 50 22; fax 575 53 23), beside the Cinema Rivoli and near the vegetable market and intersection of Tala'at Harb St. and 26 July St. Friendly management succeeds in maintaining the 1930s glory of this aging institution, though rooms often remain vacant. Each room comes with satellite TV, A/C, and furnished balconies. Dinner is served nightly on the rooftop garden, complete with stunning views. Breakfast not included. Singles E£65; doubles E£90.

Pension Zamalek, 6 Salah al-Din St. (☎735 93 18) in Zamalek. Turn south on Osman St. from 26 July St., then right on Salah al-Din. Pleasant rooms with a quiet residential atmosphere lead to furnished balconies. Breakfast served in a relaxing cafe. Reservations recommended. Singles E£50; doubles E£80; triples E£120.

Horris Hotel, 5 26 July St. (☎591 04 78, 591 05 47, or 591 08 55). Enter from Alfy St. behind Cinema Diana. Modern building with a sparsely-stocked bar. Rooms with bath, A/C, and TV. Some rooms upstairs have balconies with views reaching to the Citadel. Singles E£64; doubles E£105; triples E£127; tax and service charge not included.

Al-Malky Hotel, 4 al-Mashhad al-Hussein St. (☎592 88 04; fax 589 67 00), next to al-Hussein Mosque and Khan al-Khalili Market. In the heart of Islamic Cairo, away from the downtown bustle, but in the thick of the shopping bustle. You'll get used to the call of the *muezzin* to prayer 5 times a day. Singles E£45, with A/C and bath E£55; doubles E£50, with A/C and bath E£70.

▐ FOOD

Sticking with the same old *fuul* and *ta'amiyya* will require only 50pt to amply fill your stomach. A good place for *kushari* (E£1.50-3) is **al-Tahrir,** on Tahrir St. near Bab al-Luq or on Abdel Khalek Sarwat St. near Tala'at Harb St. **Lux,** on 26 July St., is another tasty choice. Fresh **fruit juice,** on sale anywhere you see bags of fruit hanging around a storefront, is one of the highlights of the Egyptian culinary experience. As long as the place looks clean and has running water behind the counter, it is probably safe to drink, though you should know that glasses are merely rinsed between customers. At places without waiters, pay first and then exchange your receipt for food.

EATING OUT IN CAIRO

AMERICAN		Cafe Curnovsky (p. 106)	ZA
Kentucky Fried Chicken (p. 105)	DT	▨ Didos Al Dente (p. 106)	ZA
McDonald's (p. 105)	DT	L'Aubergine (p. 106)	ZA
Pizza Hut (p. 105)	DT	Le Bistro (p. 105)	DT
		Le Tabasco (p. 107)	MO
CAFES		Maison Thomas (p. 106)	ZA
▨ Al-'Abd (p. 106)	DT	Prestige Pizza (p. 107)	MO
Brazilian Coffee Shop (p. 106)	DT		
Coffee Roastery (p. 107)	ZA	**MIDDLE EASTERN**	
Coffee Shop Naguib Mahfouz (p. 107)	IC	Al-Gamhorya (p. 107)	IC
J. Groppi (p. 106)	DT	'Ali Hassan al-Hati (p. 106)	ZA
Khan al-Khalili Coffee Shop (p. 138)	GI	Al-Omda (p. 107)	MO
La Poire (p. 106)	DT	Al-Tabei (p. 105)	DT
Mandarin Koedar (p. 107)	ZA	Al-Tahrir (p. 104)	DT
▨ Simonds (p. 107)	ZA	Cafe Riche (p. 105)	DT
		Egyptian Pancakes (p. 107)	IC
CHINESE AND KOREAN		Fatatri al-Tahrir (p. 105)	DT
Fu-Shing (p. 105)	DT	Felfela (p. 105)	DT
Hana Korean Restaurant (p. 106)	ZA	Lux (p. 104)	DT
Peking (p. 105)	DT	Pyramids Shishkebab Restaurant (p. 138)	GI
		Restaurant al-Hati (p. 105)	DT
FRENCH AND ITALIAN		Restaurant Cairo (p. 105)	DT
Bon Appetit (p. 106)	ZA		

DT downtown **GI** giza **IC** islamic cairo **MO** mohandiseen **ZA** zamalek

Sit-down meals are often relatively cheap by Western standards and are usually worth the small investment, as long as you choose wisely from the menu. Even at more expensive restaurants, you can create a handsome meal out of hummus, *baba ghanoush* (grilled eggplant dip), and salad for under E£10. *Fatir*—a filo dough-like bread stuffed and topped with vegetables, meats, or sweets—is far tastier than the imitations of Italian pizza in town, and usually cheaper (E£5-10). A 5% **sales tax** on food and a 10-12% **service charge** at sit-down restaurants are added to the bill. A **minimum charge** of about E£2 is common among more expensive restaurants. Additionally, a small **tip** (E£1) is usually in order.

Vegetarians have an advantage, as Cairo's veggie fare is cheaper and better-tasting than the poor-to-mediocre meat dishes found in most restaurants. Since cheap restaurants and street vendors often advertise vaguely labeled "meat" that could very well have been pulling a cart a few days before, even militant carnivores may discover a sudden empathy for animals.

While eating local food is an essential component of the Egyptian experience, you might also want to try the cleaner, faster, air-conditioned Western fast-food chains lined up across from AUC on Mahmoud St. **Pizza Hut** offers slices for E£2 each. (☎356 26 28. Open daily 9am-4am, delivery until 3am.) Next door, **Kentucky Fried Chicken** is a bit cheaper but serves buns in place of the biscuits so treasured by the Colonel and his cohorts. **McDonald's,** near AUC, offers combos for about E£9. (☎355 81 31. Open daily 10am-2am.) All have free delivery up to 2km away.

DOWNTOWN

RESTAURANTS

Al-Tabei, 31 Orabi St. (☎575 42 11), north of Orabi Sq., 100m south of Ramses St. The menu is primarily veg., though there are some meat dishes. A sprawling meal of *ta'amiyya, fuul,* oven-roasted eggplant, and a large plate of salads (choose 4 for E£3) will amount to only a few pounds. The interior is clean and bright, the service professional and blue-vested. Open daily 9am-1am.

Fatatri al-Tahrir, 166 Tahrir St., 1 block east of Tahrir Sq. If the decor is minimal, it's to keep your attention focused on the food, which includes the best *fatir* downtown. Get your filo topped with meat, vegetables, or sweets (E£6-10). A medium-sized *fatir* makes a large meal (E£8); small (E£6) and large (E£10) also available. Finish it off with a tall glass of fruit juice from the excellent stand next door. Open 24hr.

Felfela, 15 Hoda Sha'rawi St. (☎392 27 51 or 392 28 33), off Tala'at Harb St., one block south of Tala'at Harb Sq. The cool rainforest ambiance attracts a crowd of both tourists and locals, who sit at tables made of huge tree stumps, with vines hanging overhead. Full meal of *waraq 'einab* (stuffed grape leaves) E£12; stuffed pigeon E£17. Also delicious is *om 'ali,* a pastry baked with milk, honey, and raisins (E£6). Of more interest to the budget traveler is Felfela Take-Away, around the corner at 15 Tala'at Harb St. which excels at simple foods like *fuul* (50pt), *ta'amiyya* (50pt), and lentil soup (E£2). Both open daily 6am-midnight.

Restaurant al-Hati, 8A 26 July St. (☎391 88 29). The glitzier younger sibling of 'Ali Hassan al-Hati (see below), complete with marble tiles, mirrors, and far better food. Standard Egyptian entrees E£25-30. Take-out. Open daily noon-midnight. AmEx/MC/V.

Peking, 14 Saraya al-Azbakia St. (☎591 23 81), behind Cinema Diana between Alfy St. and 26 July St. Cairo's most popular Chinese restaurant. Pamper yourself with the complimentary steaming hand towels before a full meal with appetizer, 3 dishes, and dessert—don't miss the honey-walnut Tarte Lee (E£40-60). Alcohol served. Free delivery. Open daily noon-midnight. AmEx/MC/V. **Other branches:** Mohandiseen (☎349 98 60), New Ma'adi (☎516 42 18), and Heliopolis (☎270 56 78).

Le Bistro, 8 Hoda Sha'rawi St. (☎392 76 94), down the street from Felfela. Walk down the stairs, pick up a French newpaper, and sit down to a French menu that you can study as you listen to soft French music. By the time the bill comes (*en français, bien sûr*), you will have enjoyed a decent imitation of Gallic cuisine. Entrees E£20-30. Open daily noon-midnight. AmEx.

Fu-Shing, 28 Tala'at Harb St. (☎576 61 84), in an alley running west from the street. Walk up the stairs past the Arabic and Chinese calligraphy. Exotic items (purple seaweed soup E£4) and diverse veg. options make this Chinese restaurant a delicious escape from ho-hum(mus) street vendor fare. Entrees E£15-25. Open daily noon-10pm.

Cafe Riche, 17 Tala'at Harb St. (☎392 97 93). This storied cafe-restaurant, once a favorite of radicals and revolutionaries, may intimidate budget travelers from the outside, but step inside for a diverse selection of foods ranging from traditional Middle Eastern to modern Western. Pasta E£10. Rib eye steak E£32. Stuffed quail E£30. Open daily 10am-midnight. AmEx/MC/V.

Restaurant Cairo, the 2nd restaurant on the left side of the street that forks to the right from Orabi Sq, 1 block south of Alfy St. A good place to pick up cheap meat dishes: the half chicken (E£5.5), soup (E£1.5), and stuffed pigeon or lamb kebab with salad and bread (E£10) are delicious. Open 24hr.

'Ali Hassan al-Hati, 3 Midan Halim Basha (☎591 60 55), between Alfy St. and 26 July St., 1 block south of the Windsor Hotel. High ceilings, crystal chandeliers, and a name recognized by the average person on the street; nevertheless, the food and service fall short. Entrees E£15-20. Open daily noon-midnight.

CAFES

⚑**Al-'Abd,** 25 Tala'at Harb St. (☎392 44 07), opposite the Arab Bank building. This upscale bakery-cafe provides the perfect antidote to Cairo's heat: a whopping 3-scoop mango ice cream cone (E£1.50). Ask to sample any of the tempting pastries. Open daily 8:30am-12:30am. **Another branch:** 26 July St., 1 block east of Tala'at Harb St.

J. Groppi, on the west side of Tala'at Harb Sq. This confectionery opened its doors to Europeans and Europeanized Egyptians in 1891 and hasn't changed its decor since. Make your purchases in the bakery or linger in the A/C coffee shop. A great place for a date (chocolate-covered or not). The mango and apricot jams make for a tart retort to the excellent Turkish coffee. A snack will cost about E£5. Open daily 7am-midnight.

La Poire, 18 Latin America St. (☎355 15 09), across the street from the British Embassy in Garden City. Come for the extensive selection of ice cream flavors (E£1.75 per scoop) but stay for the croissants, eclairs, and sticky-sweet *ba'laweh* (about E£1.50 per serving)—and don't leave until you're *poire*-shaped. Open daily 7am-midnight.

Brazilian Coffee Shop, 38 Tala'at Harb St., at the intersection with 'Adly St. This A/C restaurant upstairs from the Miami Cinema serves cappuccino and espresso (E£2.50 each). A great place to read the morning paper with your favorite middle management chums. Chicken sandwich E£6. Open daily 6am-midnight.

ZAMALEK

RESTAURANTS

⚑**L'Aubergine,** 5 Sayyed al-Bakry St. (☎735 65 50). From 26 July St., turn right at Brazil St.; turn right again at the 1st opportunity and the restaurant is a few meters ahead. The atmosphere is Louis Armstrong covering Edith Piaf. Spinach lasagna (E£19), *l'aubergine moussaka* (E£18), and a refreshing gazpacho (E£8) typify the exclusively veg. selection. **Cafe Curnovsky,** the Eggplant's sister restaurant upstairs, serves meat (E£25-30). Both open daily noon-1am. Reservations accepted. V.

⚑**Didos Al Dente,** 26 Bahgat Basha 'Ali St. (☎735 91 17). Walking north along the western corniche, take a right onto Muhammad Anis St.; Didos Al Dente is two blocks ahead on your left. Fashionable young Egyptians come for the wide selection of pastas with 18 different sauces (E£5-15), plus side dishes such as the excellent *insalata al-funghi* (E£11). Open daily noon-1am. Reservations a good idea for groups during the evening.

Maison Thomas, 157 26 July St. (☎735 70 57), on the right near the base of the bridge as you come into Zamalek from Cairo. Hip French/Italian bistro filled with hanging salamis and wheels of cheese that evoke the Mediterranean's other coast. A wide range of salads and baguette sandwiches at a wide range of prices, but it's the Italian-style pizza that brings the crowds (E£15-20). Gorge yourself like a pig on any of numerous pork options. Free delivery. Open 24hr.

Hana Korean Restaurant, 21 Ma'had al-Swissry St. (☎735 18 46), in al-Nil Zamalek Hotel. Take a right off 26 July St. onto Brazil St. and the restaurant is to the right after a bend in the road. This A/C haven, popular among tourists and expats, serves up shark-fin soup (E£9) and *bulgogi* (tender slices of beef they barbecue right at the table; E£23). Entrees come with a complimentary assortment of 7 side dishes, including two kinds of *kimchi* (cabbage or vegetables that have been spiced and fermented). Stella (E£7) is everyone's favorite gal. Open daily 11:30am-11pm.

Bon Appetit, 3 Isma'il Muhammad St. (☎735 43 82 or 735 91 08), one block from the Flamenco Hotel on the west side of Zamalek. The cleanest place in town to try tongue sandwiches (E£4.75). Main courses E£10-30. Open daily 9am-1am. AmEx/MC/V.

CAFES

⊠ Simonds, 112 26 July St. (☎ 735 94 36), just east of the intersection where Hassan Sabri St. becomes Brazil St. The New York chic feel lures an eclectic mix of locals and foreign emissaries who sip *café au lait* (E£2.75) and fresh-squeezed orange juice (E£2.50) while munching on pastries (E£1-2). A huge selection of savory desserts. Open daily 7am-9pm.

Mandarin Koedar, 17 Shagarat al-Durr St. (☎ 735 50 10). Take a right off 26 July St. at the Misr Gas Station onto Shagarat al-Durr St. and follow the crooked lane for 200m. Cool to the core: a wide selection of ice cream (E£1.50 per scoop) and pastries served up in an arctic A/C setting. Open daily 9am-11pm.

MOHANDISEEN

Le Tabasco, 8 'Ammen Sq. (☎ 336 55 83). From the Dokki Metro station, follow Tahrir St. west for 600m, then take a right at Babel St. and continue for another 600m. One of the best restaurants in Cairo, this perpetually trendy establishment stays en vogue by constantly shaking up the menu. Dim candlelight and soft jazz accompany the Mediterranean-centered cuisine. Appetizers E£10-24. Pasta E£10-20. Main dishes E£20-40. Open daily 1pm-midnight. Reservations required. AmEx/MC/V.

Al-Omda, 6 al-Gaza'ir St. (☎ 346 22 47), a few doors from the Atlas Hotel on Gam'at al-Duwal St. Grape leaves E£8-15. Full meals E£10-25. Dine-in (A/C) or delivery. Open daily noon-3am.

Prestige Pizza, 43 Geziret al-'Arab St. (☎ 347 03 83), just east of Wadi al-Nil St. Coming from Gam'at al-Duwal St., turn right before al-Ahli Bank. Inexpensive pizza served in a laid-back atmosphere. The "normal" size pizzas (E£12) are quite enough to satisfy most appetites. "Prestige" size E£17. Open daily noon-1am. AmEx/MC/V.

Coffee Roastery, 46 Nadi Seid St. (☎ 749 88 82). An Egyptian expat in San Francisco exported this cafe to Cairo. Sip a caffe latte (E£4) while reading through *Time* or your choice of Egyptian teenybopper magazines. Open daily 8am-midnight. AmEx/MC/V.

ISLAMIC CAIRO (KHAN AL-KHALILI)

Egyptian Pancakes, 7 al-Azhar Sq. (☎ 590 86 23), half a block from the intersection of al-Azhar St. and Gohar al-Qa'it St. Tired of the same old *kushari* and kebab? Small (E£10), medium (E£12), or large (E£15) *fatir* topped with sweets (honey, coconut, or raisins) or meats. Open 24hr.

Coffee Shop Naguib Mahfouz, 5 al-Badistante Ln. (☎ 590 37 88), two blocks west of al-Hussein Mosque. Not on *Sugar St.*, as those familiar with Nobel laureate Mahfouz's work might hope. This pricey restaurant is a calm oasis of delectable food in the maddening bustle of Khan al-Khalili. Engage in *Small Talk on the Nile* as you sip on fresh fruit juices (said to be the favorites of Mahfouz, who was once a regular here). No doubt he also appreciated the clean restrooms and nightly live music. No *Autumn Quail,* but you can try a Lebanese kebab (E£39) or *tabbouleh* (E£6.50). Minimum charge E£10 per person, E£2 music charge. Open daily 10am-2am. AmEx/MC/V.

Al-Gamhorya, on al-Azhar St., 1 block east of the green pedestrian overpass at al-Ghouri Mosque and Mausoleum. A perfect *kushari* stop-off (E£1.50). Single women may feel out of place among the mostly male clientele. Open daily 9am-11pm.

◎ SIGHTS

Centuries of history come together in the streets of Egypt's capital, where the dusty ghosts of dynasties past fight to be remembered amid the emerging spirit of a metropolitan future. In **Islamic Cairo** (p. 109), the devout prostrate themselves before some of the Muslim world's most revered sites while small-time capitalists haggle in **Khan al-Khalili** (p. 115), the ancient bazaar nearby. In the **Cities of the Dead** (p. 117), mausolea and tombs coexist with a poor but vibrant community. Christian and Jewish minority communities are centered in the **Coptic** district of **Old Cairo** (p. 120), and the remains of **al-Fustat** (p. 122) house the earliest Egyptian mosque. **Modern Cairo** (p. 123) rushes to embrace the future, while the city's **muse-**

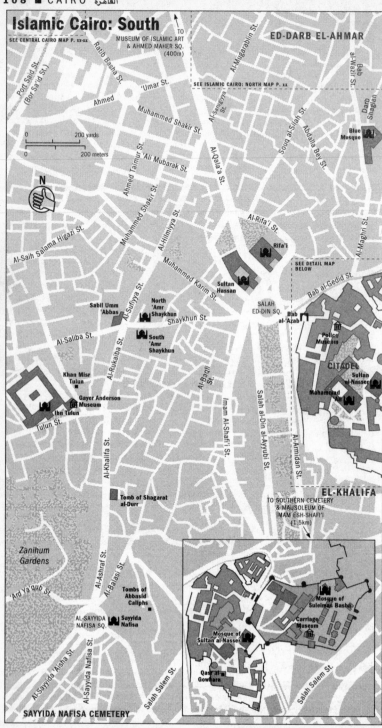

Islamic Cairo: South

SEE CENTRAL CAIRO MAP P. xx-xx

ED-DARB EL-AHMAR

TO
MUSEUM OF ISLAMIC ART
& AHMED MAHER SQ.
(400m)

SEE ISLAMIC CAIRO: NORTH MAP P. xx

Port Said St.
(Bor Sa'id St.)

Ratib Basha St.

'Umar St.

Ahmed

Muhammed Shakir St.

Al-Sarugiyya St.

Al-Migarablin St.

Bab al-Wazir St.

Darb Shaglan

Blue Mosque

Ahmed Taimur St.

'Ali Mubarak St.

Al-Qala'a St.

Muhammed Shakir St.

Al-Himiyya St.

Souq al-Silah St.

Abdalla Bei St.

Al-Maghri St.

Al-Saih Salama Higazi St.

Al-Rifa'i St.

Muhammed Karim St.

Rifa'i

SEE DETAIL MAP BELOW

Bab al-Gedid St.

Sabil Umm 'Abbas

Al-Sufiyya St.

North 'Amr Shaykhun

Shaykhun St.

Sultan Hassan

SALAH ED-DIN SQ.

Bab al-'Azab

Police Museum

CITADEL

Al-Saliba St.

Al-Rukaiba St.

South 'Amr Shaykhun

Sultan al-Nasser

Khan Misr Tulun

Al-Baqfi St.

Gayer Anderson Museum

Ibn Tulun

Muhammad Ali

Tulun St.

Al-Khalifa St.

Imam Al-Shafi'i St.

Salah al-Din al-Ayyubi St.

Al-Amidan St.

EL-KHALIFA

Tomb of Shagarat al-Durr

TO SOUTHERN CEMETERY
& MAUSOLEUM OF
IMAM ESH-SHAFI'I
(1.5km)

Zanihum Gardens

Al-Ashraf St.

Al-Balasi St.

'Ard Ya'qub St.

Tombs of Abbasid Caliphs

AL-SAYYIDA NAFISA SQ.

Sayyida Nafisa

Mosque of Suleiman Basha

Carriage Museum

Mosque of Sultan al-Nasser

Al-Sayyida 'Aisha St.

Al-Sayyida Nafisa St.

Salah Salem St.

Salah Salem St.

Qasr al-Gowhara

SAYYIDA NAFISA CEMETERY

0   200 yards
0   200 meters

N

CAIRO

ums (p. 125) strain to weave together its four millennia of history. Note that **price hikes** of 25-50% on admission tickets to major sights are scheduled for the coming year; see **Inflation Sucks,** p. 14, for more information.

ISLAMIC CAIRO

The great 14th-century historian Ibn Khaldun once said, "He who has not seen Cairo cannot know the grandeur of Islam." The resplendent mosques and monuments of Cairo's medieval district rank among the world's finest examples of Islamic architecture. Unlike Damascus and Baghdad (the other capitals of the medieval Islamic world), Cairo was spared the devastation of Mongol invasions. Make sure to see the historical sights the area has to offer, but spare some time to wander through today's living Islamic Cairo and catch a glimpse at ancient way of life whose customs, like the domes and minarets above, have endured through the centuries.

GENERAL ADVICE

It takes at least two days to explore Islamic Cairo, and the area holds riches enough to fill many more. **William Lyster** and **SPARE (Society for the Preservation of Architectural Resources in Egypt)** publish a superb set of four 3-D maps of Islamic Cairo (E£10 per map). The *City Map of Cairo* (E£10) has an indexed map of Islamic Cairo. For in-depth descriptions and history, try *Islamic Monuments in Cairo: A Practical Guide*, by Caroline Williams (E£60). That book and most maps are available at the AUC Bookstore (p. 98).

Many of the important monuments charge entrance fees (E£6-12, half-price with ISIC). At free sights (mosques in particular), you will be expected to give *bakhsheesh* to the gatekeeper (E£1 should be adequate). At the biggest mosques, the man who "guards" your shoes while you are inside usually expects compensation of some kind. Students purchasing discounted tickets should pay 50pt-E£1 in *bakhsheesh*. Where permitted, climbing the minaret is included in the ticket price. Opening hours are estimates at best, so declare your interest to whomever is around and someone will let you in; a tour of Islamic Cairo confined to already-unlocked doors will miss many of the city's treasures.

Most "ornamental" mosques—those no longer used for regular prayer—are open daily from 8am to 5pm. Other mosques are open from dawn until dusk, but visitors are not welcome during prayer times. Wait a few minutes after the congregation has finished before entering. There are usually separate entrances for men and women. Night visitors are often not permitted, although some travelers rave about watching the sunset paint Cairo dusty pink from atop a minaret. Avoid visiting noon-2pm on Fridays, when the Muslim community gathers for afternoon prayer. Certain highly venerated mosques—namely, Sayyida Hussein, Sayyida Zeinab, and Sayyida Nafisa—are believed to contain the remains of descendants of Muhammad and are officially closed to non-Muslims.

Even more so than in the rest of Cairo, visitors must dress modestly in Islamic Cairo: revealing clothing will attract a great deal of unsolicited and unfriendly attention and will prevent admission to many mosques. Residents consider shorts, miniskirts, and exposed shoulders disrespectful. Women are encouraged to cover their hair with a hat or scarf in the mosques; when head coverings are required, they can usually be rented for a few piasters. In some mosques (such as Muhammad 'Ali) an entire *galabiyya* is provided for free. It is important to avoid sandals and wear clothes that you don't mind getting dirty: just as Islamic Cairo is full of charm, so are its streets full of trash and dust. Since you will often be asked to remove your shoes, socks are a good idea. Bring a plastic bag for your shoes to avoid the 50pt charged by custodians to watch them while you are touring. Never let the soles of your shoes touch a mosque floor.

SOUTHERN ISLAMIC CAIRO

MOSQUE OF IBN TULUN. Built in 879 CE, the fortress-like Mosque of Ibn Tulun is the largest and third-oldest of Cairo's Islamic monuments. If you stand on Qadri St., the entrance is around the left side. Once inside the gate, the **Gayer-Anderson**

SIGHTSEEING STRATEGY. Although each of the following sights can be visited individually, *Let's Go* has divided Islamic Cairo into four easily navigable regions (each of which can be visited in a leisurely **half-day** walking tour): **Southern Islamic Cairo** and the **Mosque of Ibn Tulun** (p. 109), the **Citadel** (p. 111), **Central Islamic Cairo** (p. 113), and **North al-Mu'izz St. and the Walls** (p. 115). A stopover at al-Azhar University (p. 114) and the bazaar at Khan al-Khalili (p. 115), both centrally located, can easily be tacked on to any of these trips.

Museum (p. 127) is to your left and the mosque's courtyard is straight ahead. The serene courtyard covers almost seven acres and has six *mihrabs* indicating the direction to Mecca. In the center of the courtyard, an ablution fountain *(mayda'a)*, added in 1296 CE by a Mamluk sultan, is still used for washing before prayer time. The mosque, like many other early Islamic monuments, has pared-down decorative elements and an arcade-encompassed courtyard design modeled after the house of the Prophet Muhammad.

The mosque is named after Ahmed ibn Tulun, who served as the Abbasid governor of Egypt until he broke with the sultanate and established an independent city-state, Qatai'i, with its capital around this building. The minaret and its unusual external staircase (a harrowing climb culminating in a great view) were probably modeled after the Great Mosque of Samarra in Iraq. A less substantiated theory explains that after the mosque was built, it became clear that the *muezzin* could see impure things during his ascent to the top of the minaret. His glimpses of unveiled women relaxing in their homes led architects to build inner stairwells with hopes that the *muezzin* would stay more focused on prayer. *(Take minibus #54 (٥٤) or bus #72 (٧٢) from Tahrir Sq., or take the Metro to Sayyida Zeinab and then bus #501 (٥٠١) (35pt) to Qadri St., which leads to Ibn Tulun. Open daily 8am-6pm; Oct.-Mar. 8am-5pm; Ramadan 8am-4pm. E£6, students E£3.)*

TOMB OF SHAGARAT AL-DURR. Heading east on Tulun St., turn right onto al-Khalifa St. to find the small Tomb of Shagarat al-Durr on your left. Built in 1250 CE, the tomb is the burial place of a politically prominent Muslim woman (one of only a dozen women to have ruled in the Muslim world) and the last Ayyubid building constructed in Cairo. Shagarat al-Durr (Tree of Pearls) was a slave who rose to power after marrying al-Salih Ayyub, the final ruling member of Salah al-Din's Ayyubid Dynasty. After having her son murdered, Shagarat al-Durr declared herself queen and governed Egypt alone for 80 days before marrying the leader of the Mamluk forces and engineering the succession of the Mamluk Dynasty. The renegade couple managed to rule happily until the queen discovered that her new husband was considering a second marriage and had him murdered as well. Not to be outdone, the prospective second wife avenged the death of her lover by beating Shagarat al-Durr to death with a pair of wooden clogs and then hurling her body from the top of the nearby Citadel, leaving her corpse to the jackals and dogs. The remains were put together in this small, rather unremarkable tomb. Even so, the wall mosaics are worth the *bakhsheesh* (E£1).

If you continue on al-Ashraf Khalifa St. you will find the Mosque of Sayyida Nafisa (see p. 119). Retrace your steps to the left to return to the Mosque of Ibn Tulun. From the main entrance of Ibn Tulun, head left and take a right at the intersection with Khodairi St., which eventually turns into al-Saliba St.

SABIL UMM 'ABBAS. On the left side of Saliba St. is Sabil Umm 'Abbas, an Islamic endowment that became the home of the **Life and Culture Center** in 1990. Tucked away in Islamic Cairo, the artists rarely get visitors and are anxious to share their passions with interested travelers. The medieval exterior inscribed with Islamic calligraphy contrasts with the contemporary Egyptian art found inside, which includes paintings, textile designs, silk screens, and remarkable lamp shades. *(Open Sa-Th 9am-2pm. Free.)*

MOSQUE AND KHANQAH OF 'AMR SHAYKHUN. Walk north on al-Saliba St. past the intersection with al-Siyuqiyya St. to find these two buildings facing each other on opposite sides of the street, complete with matching facades, doors, and minarets. The entrance to the mosque (the building on the right as you walk north on al-Saliba St.) is up an alley—pop in to check out the amazing stained glass windows installed to keep out evil *djinns*. General Shaykhun is buried in the *khanqah*, a Sufic monastery, parts of which are undergoing renovations. Slip up the stairway near the door to explore the long hallways of cells where Sufi mystics once lived.

▨SULTAN HASSAN COMPLEX. Compared with the mosque of Muhammad 'Ali which it faces, this masterpiece from the Mamluk era seems more genuine, striking for both its sheer bulk and intricate detail. Unlike the Pyramids at Giza, which convey the mighty power of the pharaohs with their own might and size, the majesty of Sultan Hassan's complex stands in complete contradiction of his weak rule. The only time Sultan Hassan ever slipped out from under the thumb of the Mamluk generals who controlled him was in 1356 CE, when he built this majestic *madrasa* and mausoleum; unfortunately, the tightwad generals murdered him when they got the bill. The spacious interior courtyard is surrounded by four vaulted arcades known as *irwans*, which once housed the four major schools of judicial thought in Sunni Islam. On either side of the easternmost *mihrab*, bronze doors open onto the beautifully decorated mausoleum—the inlaid marblework is the finest in Cairo. *(To reach Sultan Hassan and the Rifa'i Mosque (as well as the Citadel), continue down Saliba St. to Salah al-Din Sq. From Tahrir Sq., take bus #173 (١٧٣) or minibus #54 (٥٤). From the southern edge of 'Ataba Sq., take Muhammad 'Ali St., which becomes al-Qala'a (Citadel) St. To get back to Tahrir Sq., take bus #194 (١٩٤) or #609 (٦٠٩). Open Sa-Th 8am-6pm, F 9-11am and 2-5pm; Oct.-Mar. Sa-Th 8am-5pm, F 9-11am and 2-5pm; Ramadan Sa-Th 8am-4pm, F 9-11am and 2-4pm. E£12, students E£6.)*

RIFA'I MOSQUE. Next door to the Sultan Hassan complex stands the enormous Rifa'i Mosque, built by the mother of Khedive Isma'il, who is buried here with her son King Fouad and grandson King Farouk (Egypt's last monarch). In the room next to Farouk lies the tomb of Muhammad Reza Pahlavi, the last Shah of Iran, who was exiled in 1979 after the Islamic Revolution. Rifa'i's stupendous size and polished interior will make your neck sore. Near the ticket window is a pleasant lawn—a great place to catch your breath before moving on to other sights. *(Same directions, hours, and prices as Sultan Hassan Complex.)*

THE CITADEL (AL-QALA'A) القلعة

From Tahrir Sq., take bus #82 (٨٢), 83 (٨٣), or 609 (٦٠٩). From 'Ataba Sq., take bus #401 (٤٠١) or minibus #50 (٥٠) or 55 (٥٥). A taxi from downtown costs E£5. Enter from either the northern or southern gate. From Hassan and Rifa'i, head right (south) along the wall and circle the Citadel. The entrance is on Salah Salem St. Open daily 8am-6pm; Oct.-Mar. 8am-5pm; Ramadan 8am-4pm; closed Friday during prayer; entrance locked 1hr. before closing. E£20, students E£10, including all museums and mosques.

Crowned by the dome and tall minarets of the Muhammad 'Ali mosque, the enormous Citadel *(al-Qala'a)* watches over Islamic Cairo's tangled alleys. Salah al-Din began construction in 1176 CE, and the building has been continually expanded and modified since then (most notably by the Mamluks and Muhammad 'Ali). Almost all the rulers of Egypt from the 13th century until 1874 lived here. The complex contains three large mosques and four operating museums: as you walk around the curved road from the Citadel gate, the tin-helmeted **Mosque of Muhammad 'Ali** will be on your left and the **Mosque of Sultan al-Nasser** on your right; several courtyards away is the third mosque, the **Mosque of Suleiman Basha.** To the south of the Mosque of Muhammad 'Ali is **Qasr al-Gowhara** (Diamond Palace).

MOSQUE OF MUHAMMAD 'ALI. The mosque of Muhammad 'Ali is easy to spot from anywhere in the Citadel. Those flying into Cairo can see its metallic domes glistening in the sun. In 1830, 'Ali leveled the western surface of the Citadel, filled in the famous 13th-century Mamluk palace Qasr al-Ablaq, and built

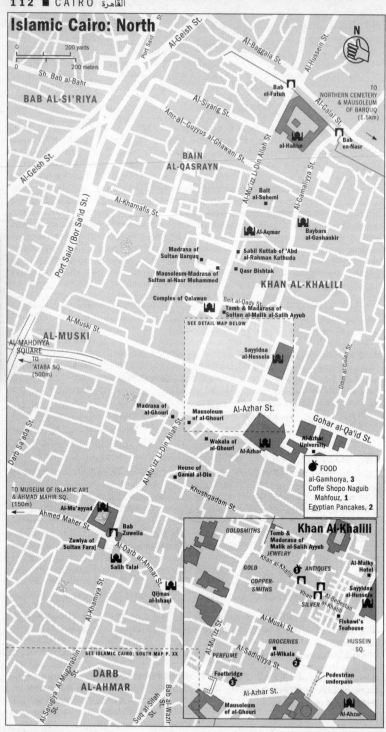

Islamic Cairo: North

0 | 200 yards
0 | 200 meters

Sh. Bab al-Bahr

Al-Geish St.

Port Said St.

Al-Baggala St.

Al-Hussein St.

BAB AL-SI'RIYA

Al-Siyarig St.

Bab
el-Futuh

TO
NORTHERN CEMETERY
& MAUSOLEUM
OF BARQUQ
(1.5km)

Al-Galal St.

Amr-al-Guyyus al-Ghawani St.

BAIN
AL-QASRAYN

al-Hakim

Bab
en-Nasr

Al-Geish St.

Al-Kharnafis St.

Port Said (Bor Said St.)

Al-Mu'izz Li-Din Allah St.

Ac-Gamaliyya St.

Bait
al-Suhemi

Al-Aqmar

Baybars
al-Gashankir

Madrasa of
Sultan Barquq

Sabil Kuttab of 'Abd
al-Rahman Kathuda

Mausoleum-Madrasa of
Sultan al-Nasr Muhammed

Qasr Bishtak

KHAN AL-KHALILI

Comples of Qalawun

Beit al-Qady St.

Tomb & Madarasa of
Sultan al-Malik al-Salih Ayyub

Al-Muski St.

AL-MUSKI

AL-MAHDIYYA
SQUARE

TO
'ATABA SQ.
(500m)

SEE DETAIL MAP BELOW

Sayyidna
al-Hussein

Umm al-Gulan St.

Darb sa'ada St.

Madrasa of
al-Ghouri

Mausoleum
of al-Ghouri

Al-Azhar St.

Gohar al-Qa'id St.

Al-Mu'izz Li-Din Allah St.

Wakala of
al-Ghouri

Al-Azhar

Al-Azhar
University

🍏 FOOD
al-Gamhorya, 3
Coffe Shopo Naguib
Mahfouz, 1
Egyptian Pancakes, 2

House of
Gamal al-Din

Khushqdam St.

TO MUSEUM OF ISLAMIC ART
& AHMAD MAHIR SQ.
(150m)

Al-Mu'ayyad

Ahmed Maher St.

Bab
Zuwella

Tomb &
Madarasa of
Malik al-Salih Ayyub

GOLDSMITHS

Khan Al-Khalili

Zawiya of
Sultan Faraj

Al-Darb al-Ahmar St.

GOLD

JEWELRY

Khan al-Khalili

ANTIQUES

Al-Malky
Hotel

Salih Talai

COPPER-
SMITHS

Al-Khamiya St.

Qijmas
al-Ishaqi

Khan
SILVER

Al-Bedestan
al-Khalili

Sayyidna
al-Hussein

Al-Muski St.

Fishawi's
Teahouse

Al-Muizz St.

GROCERIES

HUSSEIN
SQ.

Al-Sadiqiyya St.

al-Wikala

PERFUME

Al-Saueya Al-Mugarabim St.

SEE ISLAMIC CAIRO: SOUTH MAP P. XX

DARB
AL-AHMAR

Footbridge

Pedestrian
underpass

Bab al Wazir
Suq al Silah

Al-Azhar St.

Mausoleum
of al-Ghouri

Al-Ahzar

CAIRO

his mosque on the ruins as a reminder of Turkish domination. Modeled after the Aya Sophia in Istanbul, the mosque is a favorite of postcard-makers and tourists, but art historians disparage it as a third-rate copy of the great Ottoman mosques in Turkey. The edifice is also known as the Alabaster Mosque because it is covered inside and out with clear alabaster, hauled over from Beni Suef. Only one outer face remains bare: when sugar daddy Muhammad 'Ali died, so did the mosque's funding.

Visitors enter the mosque through a courtyard presided over by an ornate (and never-functional) gingerbread-house-like clock of French design. In 1845, when Muhammad 'Ali presented France with the obelisk from Luxor Temple (which now stands in Place de la Concorde in Paris), King Louis Philippe thanked the ruler by presenting him with this clock. Egyptians have always been somewhat ticked off about getting a dud of a clock in return for a first-rate obelisk—and perhaps have wondered why they didn't bring the obelisk next door to Switzerland—but this didn't stop Muhammad 'Ali from decorating the interior of his mosque in a 19th-century French-salon-inspired style, complete with lavish Parisian architectural details (visible mostly on the five main domes and 15 mini-domes), a chandelier, and 365 tiny lanterns. Any architectural shortcomings are redeemed by the view from the terrace by the exit, where you can see all of Cairo and the Pyramids. At prayer time, you can hear a thousand simultaneous *muezzin* calls to prayer, a haunting chorus that seems projected from the belly of the city itself.

MOSQUE OF SULEIMAN BASHA. The Turkish-inspired Mosque of Suleiman Basha was the first Ottoman mosque in Cairo, built in 1527 by one of the Ottoman governors who headed the Janissary Army. The small-domed mosque, also known as **Sariat al-Gabal** (Mountain Palace), has a cozy prayer hall decorated with different calligraphic styles and a courtyard consisting of four *irwans*. Only punch-drunk Muhammad 'Ali fans should walk south to the **Carriage (Hantour) Museum,** which houses carriages used by the champ's family, and little else of interest.

MOSQUE OF SULTAN AL-NASSER. This is one of the few major buildings in the Citadel to escape the hand of architectural busybody Muhammad 'Ali (although the interior was stripped by Sultan Selin several hundred years before 'Ali arrived). The mosque is well known for the tile decoration on its minarets, constructed by Iranian craftsmen. Go through the gate with two flags on your left to enter another courtyard with superb views of Cairo and the mosques below.

QASR AL-GOWHARA (THE DIAMOND PALACE). This half-palace was built in 1811 by Muhammad 'Ali and named after one of his wives. In 1974, a burglary attempt resulted in a fire that destroyed half of the palace. The surviving half consists of a large reception room (in the excessive French style 'Ali loved), where 'Ali once received 500 of his closest Mamluk allies before having them murdered on their way out. Also on display are a few of the gold- and silver-adorned tapestries from the Ka'aba in Mecca; Mecca presented Cairo with one of these tapestries every year until 1961.

CENTRAL ISLAMIC CAIRO

From Salah al-Din Sq., walk north along the Citadel for 100m until Bab al-Wazir St.

BLUE MOSQUE (MOSQUE OF AQSUNQUR). This 14th-century edifice owes its name not to the words scrawled in blue marker on the main door, but to the colored Syrian tiles that line the interior, added in 1652 by a Turkish governor homesick for Istanbul's grand tiled mosques. The prayer hall to the right has one of the oldest marble *minbars* (pulpits) in the Islamic world. The top of the minaret is a great vantage point for viewing the Citadel to the south, Khan al-Khalili to the north, and the southern end of the City of the Dead to the east. *(On Bab al-Wazir St., several blocks down and on the right. Open daily 8am-6pm; in winter 8am-5pm; Ramadan 8am-4pm. E£6, students E£3.)*

MOSQUE OF QIJMAS AL-ISHAQI. This mosque, dedicated to the Chief of the Royal Stable and Chargé d'Affaires for the pilgrimage to Mecca, is on al-Darb al-Ahmar (Red Way), which commemorates Muhammad 'Ali's bloody massacre of the Mamluks. Its unremarkable exterior gives no inkling of the serene, colorfully lit interior of marble and wood inlaid with complicated ivory patterns. Under the prayer mats in the east *irwan* lies an ornate marble floor, an example of geometric Mamluk design. Tip the custodian to uncover it for you. *(Head 2 blocks north of Bab al-Wazir St. where it becomes al-Darb al-Ahmar. To get into the mosque, gesture to locals, and they will retrieve the custodian. Open daily 8am-4pm. Free, but bakhsheesh is appropriate.)*

BAB ZUWEILA. Bab Zuweila is the most imposing of the three remaining gates into Fatimid Cairo, named after the Berber tribe that once guarded it. Egyptians also call it *Bawwabat al-Metwali* (Gate of the Tax Collector) after the civil servant who used to wait for victims there. It is topped by two minarets from the Mosque of al-Mu'ayyad, an interesting juxtaposition of military might and Islamic culture. *(The gate is at the intersection of al-Darb al-Ahmar and al-Mu'izz St.)*

MOSQUE OF AL-MU'AYYAD. The Mamluk ruler al-Mu'ayyad was once imprisoned on the site of this mosque. Upon becoming sultan, he tore down the prison and built this house of worship over it between 1415 and 1420. The huge door may look familiar to you; it was taken from the Sultan Hassan Mosque. The arcaded building has a lovely garden and excellent inlaid marblework in the prayer hall. Give the guard *bakhsheesh* and he will let you climb the minaret for a spectacular view of Islamic Cairo. *(Go north through Bab Zuweila. The mosque is on the left. Open daily 8:30am-7pm. E£6, students E£3.)*

AL-AZHAR UNIVERSITY الازهر

Al-Azhar University is the oldest continuously operating university in the world and the foremost Islamic theological center. Established in 972 CE by the Fatimids (who belonged to the Shi'ite Muslim sect), it rose to pre-eminence in the 15th century as a center for the study of Qur'anic law and doctrine. It is still considered to be the final arbiter on all doctrinal issues related to Sunni Islam, the sect to which the focus of study at al-Azhar was shifted once the Ayyubids came to power (and today the majority sect of Islam). Both the University and the Mosque of al-Azhar stand just a few steps from the midpoint of al-Mu'izz St. at the end of al-Azhar St., facing the square.

AL-AZHAR MOSQUE. To reach the central courtyard of this arcaded mosque, enter through the double-arched gate and pass under the **Minaret of Qaytbay** (built in 1469). Although the stucco decoration of the courtyard's facade is a reconstruction, the *mihrab* in the central aisle is original. The **library**, just left of the main entrance, holds over 80,000 manuscripts. For about E£1, the caretaker will allow you to climb one of the locked **minarets** for a fantastic view of Cairo and Khan al-Khalili below you. *(Open Sa-Th 7:30am-9pm, F 9am-noon and 2-7pm. E£12, students E£6. Women must cover their heads at the entrance.)*

UNIVERSITY. Around the corner from the mosque is where al-Azhar's 8000 students take classes from October to May. Students sit on the plush red carpets of the mosque's *riwaq* (the arcaded aisle around the central courtyard), cramming for exams. The theological curriculum has remained virtually unchanged since the Mamluk era, though more recent secular arrivals include physics and medicine. Women, though allowed in the mosque, may not study at al-Azhar; they attend a sister school near 'Abbasiyya Sq. The university uses the Socratic method of teaching, with a professor seated in the center of a circle of students, guiding the dialogue through questions. Give a small consideration to the caretaker and he'll show you the **tomb** of the university's founder.

SAYYIDNA AL-HUSSEIN MOSQUE. The Sayyidna al-Hussein Mosque was built in the Turkish style (note the pencil minarets) by Khedive Isma'il in the 1870s. It is highly revered throughout the Islamic world as the resting place of the skull of

Hussein, grandson of the Prophet Muhammad. The head is rumored to have been transported to Cairo in a green silk bag in 1153, almost 500 years after its owner died in the Battle of Karbala in modern-day Iraq. On *'Eid Mawlid al-Nabi* (Birthday of the Prophet), the President of Egypt traditionally comes to pray at Sayyidna al-Hussein while boisterous festivities take place in the square. During Ramadan, this square is the best place to witness the breaking of the fast after evening prayers (at sundown). Restaurants display their fare a half-hour before prayers begin, and famished patrons stampede to the tables afterward. After blood-sugar levels return to normal, the square erupts in celebration. *(Across al-Hussein Sq., 100m north of al-Azhar Mosque. Closed to non-Muslims.)*

KHAN AL-KHALILI AND ENVIRONS

▨KHAN AL-KHALILI BAZAAR. Khan al-Khalili, just west of al-Hussein Sq., is the largest and most notorious bazaar in Egypt. The Mamluk prince Gharkas al-Khalili established the market in the 1380s. Today it is still a requisite stop for countless tour buses, whose occupants pour forth to find that perfect little *tchotchke* for friends and family back home. As usual, however, the package tourists rarely stray far from the comfort of their air-conditioned buses and miss most of the good stuff. Revel in the free-market frenzy as you pass through the copperware, perfume, spice, gold, silver, and *sheesha* sections of this vast bazaar. Though the tacky souvenirs are often overpriced, the time-honored institution of bargaining still thrives. Be ferocious if you intend to strike a good deal (often one-fifth to one-third of the starting price, if not less); pretending to walk away usually elicits a discount. The farther you go from the heart of the market, the more authentic the wares become. A word of warning: Khan al-Khalili is a **thief's** paradise. Many a hard-won bargain has been rendered moot by a wallet disappearance. Also, be sure **not** to enter shops with any hustlers you meet in the street; the store will inflate the prices to include the hustler's commission. After a hard day of bargaining, Cairenes stay up late into the night at one of the Khan's many sidewalk cafes. The most renowned of these is **Fishawi's,** which offers respite from the market bustle with flavored *sheesha* and exotic juices (see **Ahwas,** p. 133). Although women traveling alone are safe, they should be prepared to deal with men who come close enough to whisper unsolicited "compliments."

AL-MUSKI ST. Considerably less tourist-ridden, but more crowded and dirtier than Khan's bazaar, this long avenue is where Egyptians come to shop for everyday items like cologne, shoes, cloth, furniture, pillowcases, and food. This is the place to come if you want to see Egyptians haggling over the price of underwear. Al-Muski stretches from al-Mu'izz St. all the way to Port Said St., running parallel to and one block north of al-Azhar St. It is also a convenient route between downtown and Islamic Cairo. For more places to shop in Cairo, see **Shopping,** p. 130.

AL-GHOURI COMPLEX. This al-Mu'izz St. complex consists of a *madrasa* and mosque (closed for renovations as of August 2001) across the street from a **mausoleum,** where whirling dervishes enchant visitors (W and Sa 9pm; see **Performing Arts,** p. 128). Al-Ghouri also hosts plays every once in a while; stop by and ask the guards about the calendar. From the *madrasa*, mausoleum, and mosque, head east on al-Azhar St., then right onto Sheikh Muhammad Abduh St. At No. 3 (on your right), you'll see the magnificently preserved *wikala* (inn for merchants; built in 1505), now transformed into a center for handicrafts and folk arts. *(Mausoleum and wikala open Sa-Th 9am-9pm. E£6, students E£3.)*

NORTHERN AL-MU'IZZ STREET AND THE WALLS

To minimize mileage in this area, walk from al-Azhar up al-Mu'izz St., through both Bab al-Futuh and Bab al-Nasser. Return by way of al-Gamaliyya St., which runs roughly parallel to al-Mu'izz St. from Bab al-Nasser past the Mosque of al-Hussein to the square in front of al-Azhar. Expect to shell out about E£15 at each of the sites below.

The section of al-Mu'izz St. between al-Azhar Mosque and Bab al-Futuh was once known as *Bayn al-Qasrayn* ("between the two palaces"—also the title of one of Naguib Mahfouz's novels) after the two Fatimid palaces that once stood here. Although those palaces were destroyed by the rulers of later dynasties, the area is still lined with many Fatimid and early Mamluk architectural attractions. A brisk walk through this part of al-Mu'izz St. is a wonderful way to see stunning Islamic architecture from the outside. This area is also home to a **bazaar** for restaurant supplies that is locally known as the best place to buy reasonably priced *sheesha* pipes. Forget that gaudy and overpriced tourist junk in the heart of Khan al-Khalili—and that second-rate bong you had your eye on back in your hometown's seedy record store—and shop here alongside Egyptian *ahwa* owners for the most authentic smoking equipment (E£15-45).

COMPLEX OF SULTAN AL-MALIK AL-SALIH AYYUB. The last ruler of Salah al-Din's Ayyubid Dynasty and the unfortunate husband of super-paranoid queen Shagarat al-Durr (see p. 110), Sultan Ayyub built this tomb, *madrasa*, and mosque in the 13th century. You'll recognize it by its square minaret pointing resolutely heavenward. The *madrasa* has ornate arched windows in the shape of boat keels. The custodian has keys to the adjacent domed mosque. *(Proceed north on al-Mu'izz St. from the intersection with Gohar al-Qa'id St. After passing 4 small side streets, you can see the tomb and madrasa on your right. The entrance is off a small alley on the right.)*

COMPLEX OF SULTAN QALAWUN. The Mamluk Sultan Qalawun sponsored the construction of this impressive mausoleum, *madrasa*, and hospital in 1284 (prior to his death en route to attack a Crusader fortress in Palestine). Although the Mamluks and the Crusaders didn't get along very well, their architectural styles did—note the Romanesque windows borrowed from the Crusaders' Levantine castles. Only the three high *irwans* of the original *muristan* (mental hospital) remain. The ornate stucco work inside is original, though the undersides of the arches have been restored. The exquisite wood screen separating the tomb from the rectangular forecourt also remains untouched. Before the 14th century, Egypt was the world's center for glasswork, and the Qalawun mausoleum offers especially dazzling glass mosaic work. *(On al-Mu'izz St. Complex open daily 8am-6pm, though in practice hours vary. To gain access to the mausoleum, hunt down the guard, purchase a ticket, and have the guard unlock the door. E£6, students E£3. Video cameras not allowed without written permission from a tourist office; the nearest one is on al-Darb al-Asfar, next to Beit al-Suheimi.)*

COMPLEX OF SULTAN BARQUQ. Barquq, the first of the Circassian Mamluk sultans, led the wildly popular Circassian Invasion in the 14th century, rising to power with bandmates Paul, George, and Ringo through a series of assassinations. His **mosque** was erected in 1386—a century after Qalawun's complex—and the difference in style is striking. The inner courtyard has four *irwans*, the largest and most elaborate of which doubles as a prayer hall. Its beautiful timber roof has been restored and painted in rich hues of blue and gold. Four porphyry columns (quarried in pharaonic times from mountains near the Red Sea) support the ceiling, while the floor is decorated with disks of marble that are actually slices of Greek and Roman columns (Egypt has no marble). *Bakhsheesh* gets you into the Sultan's **tomb,** constructed of high-quality inlaid marble with an elegant green and gold vine motif decorating the drum of the dome. *(On al-Mu'izz St., next door to the complex of Sultan al-Nasser Muhammad. Open daily 10am-7pm. E£6, students E£3.)*

MOSQUE OF AL-AQMAAR. This small but architecturally important Fatimid-era mosque was built in 1125 CE, the first Cairene mosque to have the stone-facade-and-shell motif (found within its keel-arched niche) that became popular during that era. Al-Aqmaar means "the moons," and refers to the way the stone facade sparkles in the moonlight. The northern corner is typical of later Cairene architecture; the height of the niche is just about equal to that of a loaded camel, and it was intended to make the turn onto the side street easier for the hump-backed creatures to negotiate. *(Bear left at the fork in al-Mu'izz St. and continue north along al-Mu'izz to the next right-hand side street. Mosque of al-Aqmar is on the corner.)*

BEIT AL-SUHEIMI AND ENVIRONS. The 16th-century Beit al-Suheimi was built by Suheimi, the *sheikh* of al-Azhar Mosque, for himself and his various wives. The house, Cairo's finest old building, has just reopened after undergoing renovations. Artisans have restored the finely carved wood ceilings and colorful stained-glass windows. The *khanqah* (Sufi monastery) known as **Baybars al-Gashankir** is nearby. Erected in 1310, it is the oldest surviving example of a *khanqah* in Cairo. *(Proceeding north from al-Aqmar Mosque, turn right onto al-Darb al-Asfar and follow the winding alley about 50m. The doorway on the left marked with a small, green plaque is the entrance to Beit al-Suheimi. Walk along al-Darb al-Asfar away from al-Mu'izz St. and you'll eventually come to al-Gamaliyya St. Across the street is Baybars al-Gashankir.)*

NORTHERN WALLS. Islamic Cairo is bordered on the north by the remains of the Fatimid walls. Built in 1087, these colossal fortifications are the best surviving example of pre-Crusader Islamic military architecture. Three of the rampart's original gates still stand: **Bab al-Nasser** ("Victory Gate"—at the top of al-Gamaliyya St.) and **Bab al-Futuh** ("Conquest Gate," literally "Opening Gate"—at the north end of al-Mu'izz St. in front of al-Hakim Mosque) are connected by a stretch of wall so thick it has a tunnel; these walls once wrapped around the Fatimid city to **Bab Zuweila.** Look for graffiti left behind by French soldiers at the end of the 18th century during the Napoleonic invasion, and then check out the spiffed-up sections of the walls restored by more French folks at the end of the 20th century.

AL-HAKIM MOSQUE. The Fatimid-era al-Hakim Mosque was built between 990 and 1010 and remains the second-largest mosque in Cairo. The grandson of thoroughfare namesake al-Mu'izz, al-Hakim is often referred to as the "Mad Caliph" and was actually the inspiration for the crazy Ali-Hakim in Rodgers and Hammerstein's famous musical *Oklahoma!* Al-Hakim's unpredictable rages meant death to Christians, Jews, his enemies, his friends, and—on one occasion—all the dogs in Cairo. He ensured the confinement of women by forbidding cobblers to make shoes for them. He even banned the cooking of *mulukhiga* (a green vegetable eaten throughout Egypt), renaming it *mulukhiyya* (meaning "royal") and restricting its consumption to his family. He was assassinated soon after he announced that he was an incarnation of God. His chief theologian, al-Darazi, fled to Syria and founded the Druze sect there. The mosque was recently restored (amid great controversy) by the Aga Khan Foundation, which chose not to restore the mosque to its original glory but instead jazzed it up with chandeliers and a neon *mihrab*, making it suitable not only for prayer, but also for ballroom and disco dancing. *(Just inside the walls between Bab al-Nasser and Bab al-Futuh. Entrance off al-Mu'izz St. Open daily 9am-6pm. E£6, students E£3. Climbing minaret permitted.)*

CITIES OF THE DEAD مدن الموت

The Cities of the Dead teem with life, serving as home to some of Cairo's finest Islamic architecture along with several hundred thousand living, breathing Cairenes. The areas to the northeast and south of the Citadel contain hundreds of spectacular tombs and mausolea; unlike their more pious predecessors, Mamluk sultans spared no expense in the construction of their final resting places, perhaps knowing their dynasties would not survive for long. During the late 1960s, a serious housing shortage for lower-income Egyptians, combined with the perennial issue of migration from the countryside to the city, sparked the trend of transforming burial chambers into homes. Unlike most graveyards, the Cities of the Dead have streets, house numbers (not even found in Cairo's city center), and even a regular bus system and postal service. The modern residents of the medieval necropoles dwell amid the funerary architecture, and many families have even incorporated the grave markers into their houses and yards. Tombs frequently serve as clotheslines and soccer goals. On Fridays, the gravesites swarm with visitors arriving to pay respects to the deceased. Many of the plots are enclosed by walls, encompassing an adjoining chamber and small house where families pray for their ancestors on holy days. The Egyptian custom of picnicking at the family tomb on feast days may be an ancient holdover from pharaonic times, when the corpse was believed to require nourishment for good health in the afterlife. Visitors are not permitted in the mosques on Fridays or during prayer times.

NORTHERN CEMETERY

Go east along al-Azhar St. from al-Azhar Mosque, hugging the wall on your left. When the road forks, turn left under the overpass; this leads to the southern section of the northern necropolis. Bus #176 (١٧٦) from 'Ataba Sq. stops in front of the Mausoleum of Barquq. Bus #77 (٧٧) or 904 (٩٠٤) from Tahrir Sq. stops in the cemetery.

The Northern Cemetery, northeast of al-Azhar, has broad avenues and courtyards containing the finest monuments in the Cities of the Dead. Posh modern mausolea sit alongside structures dating from the late (14th-16th century) Mamluk period.

TOMBS OF TULBAY AND TUGHAY. These tombs were erected to honor two wives of Sultan al-Nasser Muhammad. **Tughay** was renowned for her beauty and piety, and her grieving husband constructed an appropriately fine tomb for her. The base of the dome is decorated with tiles in the Iranian style, fashionable after a peace was reached with Iran two decades prior to the tombs' construction. Egypt's penchant for the cosmopolitan during that era is evidenced by the use of arabesques and Chinese peony designs on the central *mihrab*. Although the harems of the Mamluk sultans were frequently hotbeds of intrigue and jealousy (and even more frequently simply hot beds), Sultana **Tulbay** was quite close to Sultana Tughay and built her tomb next to that of her deceased co-wife and friend. *(From al-Azhar St., turn right at the 1st long street, and walk 1 block south. Facing the tombs with your back to the long street, Tughay's tomb is on the right; Tulbay's is on the left.)*

▨MAUSOLEUM AND MOSQUE OF QAYTBAY. Enter the complex through the marble northern doorway, passing through a rectangular sanctuary that affords the best views of the polychromatic striped brickwork of the complex, whose likeness graces the Egyptian one-pound note. Qaytbay was a Mamluk slave who rose through the ranks of the army to become leader of Egypt near the end of the 15th century, ruling for 28 years. Qaytbay was not without enemies, so he watched his back, designing his **mausoleum** with three secret doors for quick escapes. Apparently his efforts paid off—Qaytbay was the only Mamluk ruler who was not assassinated. Qaytbay designed the prayer niche such that it requires devotees to pray over the ruler's remains in order to face Mecca. The mausoleum also contains two black stones bearing footprints said to be those of the Prophet Muhammad. The **mosque** itself has a remarkable dome (with an unusual echo effect that the caretaker will demonstrate) that uses geometric and arabesque designs. Ask to climb the minaret to see the intricate workings on the outside of the dome. *(Upon leaving the alley, turn left and walk 2 blocks, then turn right at the 1st major street; there will be a small domed tomb on the left opposite the start of the street. Follow this street for 3 blocks; turn left up the lane with a stone arch, around 40m down the lane. This is the gate of Qaytbay's complex. Open daily 9am-9:30pm. E£6, students E£3. Bakhsheesh required to climb the minaret.)*

COMPLEX OF SULTAN ASHRAF BARSBAY. Originally intended as a *khanqah*, the 15th-century **mosque** of Sultan Ashraf Barsbay has meticulously fashioned marble mosaic floors; lift the prayer mats to see the colorful tilework. Barsbay pulled out all the stops to construct his combined mosque, *khanqah*, and mausoleum complex in 1432. Adjoining the mosque to the north is Barsbay's **mausoleum** (a domed chamber containing his remains and those of his slaves), an elaborately decorated *mihrab*, and gleaming mother-of-pearl and marble mosaics. The dome decorations are complex geometric designs, which replace the chevrons used in earlier tombs (such as that of Barquq, below). The wooden *minbar* is one of the best in Cairo. *(3 blocks north of the Qaytbay complex and 50m south of the Mausoleum of Barquq, along the cemetery's main thoroughfare. Open daily 9am-7pm. Free.)*

MAUSOLEUM OF BARQUQ. Like the mausoleum of Sultan Barsbay, this mausoleum (identified by its twin domes and minarets) was built in 1411 as a *khanqah*. There is limited decoration in the mausoleum, as excessive ornamentation was seen as a distraction from contemplating the full glory of Allah. This asceticism did not apply to Barquq's mausoleum in the northern corner, which has the largest stone domes in Cairo, though it is not as intricate as those of Barsbay and Qaytbay. Behind the mosque is a contemporary military cemetery. *(North of the Barsbay complex. Open daily 8am-6pm; Oct.-Apr. 8am-5pm. E£6, students E£3.)*

TOMBS. Built in 1456 CE, the **Tomb of Barsbay al-Bagasi** is decorated with an intricate geometrical design resembling a tulip, a variation on the Moroccan motif of *dari w ktaf* (cheek and shoulder). The nearby **Tomb of Emir Suleiman** was built about 90 years later; its dome is decorated with a series of zig-zag stripes. *(In front of the Mausoleum of Barquq. To get back to 'Ataba or Tahrir Sq., either take bus #167 (١٦٧) from the bus stop in the square to the west of Barquq's complex or ask locals for help and they'll tell you which bus goes downtown. Free, but caretaker will expect E£1-2 of bakhsheesh.)*

SOUTHERN CEMETERY

The Southern Cemetery is a sprawling expanse of tombs dating from the Fatimid period to the present. The silence in the cemetery is disturbed only by occasional noise from the squatters who inhabit the area (and make it unsafe for women to come here at night). The area is easily accessible by foot from the Mosque of Ibn Tulun, Sultan Hassan, or the Citadel. From Ibn Tulun or Sultan Hassan, proceed east to Salah al-Din Sq., just southeast of the Citadel, then head directly south following the southern slope of the Citadel. When you reach the traffic circle, walk under the overpass and take the right-hand fork, al-Qadiriyya St., which becomes **Imam al-Shafi'i St.**, the main thoroughfare in the cemetery. You can also take bus #82 (٨٢) or minibus #54 (٥٤) from Tahrir Sq.

MAUSOLEUM OF IMAM AL-SHAFI'I. The Southern Cemetery's most impressive edifice is the celebrated Mausoleum of Imam al-Shafi'i. The largest Islamic mortuary chamber in Egypt, the mausoleum was erected in 1211 by Salah al-Din's brother and successor in honor of the great Imam al-Shafi'i, founder of one of the four schools of judicial thought of Sunni Islam. *Shafi'i* is still the dominant judicial system in Egypt and much of East Africa. In 1178, Salah al-Din first built a large monument over the grave of Imam al-Shafi'i, which is currently housed within the 13th-century mausoleum and often crowded with Muslims offering prayers. The teak memorial depicts the Imam himself, and is one of the finest surviving pieces of Ayyubid wood-carving. Two mosques adjoin the tomb chamber. The 1190 mosque is closed to non-Muslims. The 1763 mosque, open to all, remains a center of worship and has a distinctive boat that holds grain for birds on its dome. *(Bus #72 (٧٢) from 'Abd al-Munem Riad Station goes to the mausoleum. Open daily 6am-7pm. Free, but E£1 bakhsheesh appropriate.)*

TOMB OF THE FAMILY OF MUHAMMAD 'ALI. Just as Muhammad 'Ali spent plenty of time and money on his country, he put an equal amount of effort into providing for his family and their remains. His favorite wife Tulun, her sons, and their families are all buried in these marble tombs, directly behind the tomb of the Imam Shafi'i. Like 'Ali's mosque, which is criticized by art historians for cheesily imitating the mosques of Istanbul, the tombs fail stylistically, decorated in gaudy colors and outlandish designs. The headpieces on each tomb indicate the gender and rank of the deceased. *(Known to most public transportation drivers by its Arabic name, Haush al-Basha. Open daily 9am-9pm. E£6, students E£3.)*

MOSQUE OF SAYYIDA NAFISA. Those approaching the Southern Cemetery can't miss Sayyida Nafisa's tall, single minaret and ornate dome on the western edge. The mosque is Egypt's third-holiest Islamic shrine and one of Cairo's three congregational mosques. It honors the great-great-great-granddaughter of the Prophet, who died in 824 CE and began attracting droves of pilgrims to her tomb soon thereafter. So many mausolea were erected in the immediate vicinity of her tomb that historians suspect that it was this shrine that sparked the development of the Southern Cemetery. Although the mosque is closed to non-Muslims, the beautiful white dome, well-kept exterior, and nearby grassy lawns merit a visit.

CAIRO

TOMBS OF THE ABBASID CALIPHS. Adjoining the Mosque of Sayyida Nafisa on the eastern side are the less-than-impressive Tombs of the Abbasid Caliphs. At the peak of their authority, the Abbasid caliphs ruled the entire Muslim world (except Spain) from their capital, Baghdad. The last reigning caliph fled Baghdad in 1258 after invading Mongols toppled the regime. The Mamluk sultan welcomed the caliph upon his arrival in Egypt, and went so far as to praise the deposed ruler in an effort to legitimize his own rule. Subsequent Mamluk rulers continued to harbor a succession of caliphs, all the while preventing them from gaining any real power. Finally, the sultan in Istanbul declared himself caliph in 1517, thereby consolidating the authority of the Ottoman Sultanate. The Abbasid caliphs have since been deposed, but members of the family are still buried within the 13th-century mausoleum. (Caretaker will unlock the gates for E£1 bakhsheesh.)

OLD CAIRO قاهرة القديمة

Old Cairo is a remarkable testament to the religious diversity of Egypt: mosques, Coptic churches, and a synagogue coexist here peacefully. The region known as Old Cairo consists of Christian **Coptic Cairo** (below) and Islamic **al-Fustat** (p. 122), also serving as the center of Jewish Cairo. Although most of the Jewish population left in 1949 and 1956, 42 families still inhabit this quarter and worship at the ancient **Ben-Ezra Synagogue** (p. 121). The easiest way to reach Old Cairo is to take the **Metro** from Tahrir Sq. toward Helwan to Mari Girgis station (50pt).

As you face the Church of St. George, a staircase to the left on Mari Girgis St. descends into an alley leading into the heart of Old Cairo. The churches here have their own quiet beauty, but the real charm of the neighborhood is in its twisting alleys. These narrow passages, barely marred by souvenir vendors, are cool and quiet. The sun bakes the ancient brick as the occasional Cairene ducks around the corner or underneath an arch to enjoy a smoke or visit a friend.

COPTIC CAIRO

Ancient Egypt inspires images of towering pyramids, hieroglyphs, and mummy cases dripping with jewels. Many mistakenly assume that this ancient pharaonic era shifted directly into the Islamic age of mosques and medieval fortifications. However, the interim period between Cleopatra and the caliphs was the time of the Roman conquest, which led to the spread of Christianity and the conversion of the Emperor Constantine in 324 CE. Indeed, Christianity was the dominant faith in Egypt for 300 years—from the fall of the pagan Romans until the arrival of Islam—and about 6 million Christian Copts currently live in Egypt, mostly in Old Cairo or Middle Egypt (see **Religion and Ethnicity,** p. 74).

Most of Cairo's Coptic churches are tucked away from the street, and the older ones have simple entrances. Though the churches do not charge admission and do not usually require *bakhsheesh* (this neighborhood is pleasantly free of the hustlers that infest other sections of Cairo), all have donation boxes. A few congregations have programs in which their younger members take turns offering tours of their respective churches. No money is expected, and you'll see much more than you would on your own. Those seeking serenity should avoid churches on Sundays or on church saint's day, when hundreds of Coptic Cairenes and their children migrate from church to church, receiving blessings and pronouncing their faith. Ongoing renovations of the churches and other buildings in Coptic Cairo began in the summer of 2000; entrance to these buildings, however, is still allowed.

■ **CHURCH OF MARI GIRGIS (CHURCH OF ST. GEORGE).** This Greek Orthodox church, built in the 6th century over one of the towers of the Fortress of Babylon, is dedicated to the Roman soldier George, whose famed tussle with a dragon is shown in a large relief in the courtyard. The current building was renovated in 1909, and its steps spiraling into the air represent the infinity of God. Inside are some of the most vivid and best-preserved icons in Old Cairo. The church and the nunnery of St. George nearby (where a chain-wrapping ceremony commemorating the torture of St. George is sometimes performed) both claim to house the chains used to torture the famous saint. The small doorway to the right of the staircase leads to a room where you can try on the chains for yourself. *(From the Mari Girgis Metro station, take a left. The entrance is along the wall on the right. Open daily 8am-5pm. Free.)*

CHURCH OF THE VIRGIN (AL-MU'ALLAQA CHURCH). This beautiful Coptic church is referred to as *Mu'allaqa* ("Hanging One") because it was suspended 13m above the ground between two bastions of the fortress of Babylon; look for the trap door under the carpet alongside the wall to the right of the entrance to see the distance to the ground below. The building itself is ark-shaped, its roof held up by eight pillars on each side (one for every member of Noah's family). Pointed arches and colorful geometric patterns decorate the main nave; in the center, an elegant pulpit (used only on Palm Sunday) rests on 13 slender columns—one each for Christ and his disciples. The conspicuous black and gray marble columns symbolize Judas Iscariot (who famously betrayed Jesus for 30 pieces of silver) and Doubting Thomas (who didn't believe Jesus had been resurrected until actually having seen him). Though most of the icons have been removed for the duration of the renovation, some of the most famous remain, including one of the Holy Mother with an infant Jesus and John the Baptist.

This church holds a special place in the annals of Coptic history, thanks to its involvement in the miracle of **Mokattam Mountain.** A doubtful caliph issued an ultimatum to Pope Ibrahim ibn al-Zar'a and the Coptic population—prove that the faithful can move mountains, or die. The Copts in the area prayed for three days and three nights in the Church of the Virgin until, on the third night, their bowing and wailing of *Kyrie eleison* (Greek for "Lord, have mercy") supposedly shook the earth and moved Mokattam a few inches. *(On your left as you face the Mari Girgis Metro station. Coptic orthodox masses W 7-9am, F 8-11am, Su 6-8:30am and 9-11am.)*

COPTIC MUSEUM. Directly across from the Mari Girgis Metro station is the Coptic Museum, home to the world's largest and finest collection of Coptic art, texts, textiles, metalwork, and iconographic materials (see p. 127).

BEN-EZRA SYNAGOGUE. Named for the great Spanish poet and scholar Abraham ibn Ezra, this synagogue is the oldest in Egypt and a house of worship for the country's few remaining Jews. The synagogue was built in the 7th century BCE on a site Moses supposedly used for prayer before the Exodus. The Copts eventually took over the building (which explains why its design resembles that of the nearby churches), but in 1115 CE, the caliph returned it to the Jewish community. The temple is beautifully decorated, combining Islamic geometric patterns with the Star of David. The exquisite arabesque ceiling dates from the Coptic occupation of the site. Directly in front of the entrance is a cenotaph (empty tomb) commemorating Ben-Ezra. The staircase behind it is the pulpit where the rabbi stands. Jewish history buffs can check out the collection of Hebrew books in the adjacent library. *(With your back to the Church of St. Barbara, the synagogue is approximately 25m to the left. The library is directly behind the synagogue, at the end of the path to the right of the main entrance. ☎354 26 95. No photography.)*

CHURCHES OF ST. BARBARA, ST. CYRUS, AND ST. JOHN. St. Cyrus and St. John were torn apart by wild beasts during the notorious persecution of Christians by Roman Emperor Diocletian, but the only wild beast in the church now is an occasional wandering cat. Legend holds that when the caliph discovered that both churches were being restored, he ordered the architect to destroy one of them. Unable to choose, the architect paced back and forth between the two buildings until he died of exhaustion; the caliph was so moved he allowed both to stand.

The eponymous saint of the **Church of St. Barbara** was killed by her pagan father when she attempted to convert him. Her bones rest in the tiny chapel accessible through a door to the right as you enter her church. The bones of St. Catherine supposedly lie here as well (see **St. Catherine's,** p. 276). A 13th-century wooden iconostasis graces the church's ornate interior of carved wood and metalwork. The Coptic Museum (p. 127) now holds most of the church's furniture. *(To the left, at the end of the alley that starts at the stairs next to Mari Girgis Church. Open Su-Th 11am-5pm)*

TRAJAN'S GATE AND BATTLEMENTS. Cairo's only substantial classical ruins are the **Iron Gate** of Roman Emperor Trajan's fortress of Babylon (built during the first century CE) and parts of the battlements that accompanied it. This fortress once covered 60 acres, and the Muslims could only capture it when Coptic Patriarch Cyrus ordered the defenders to surrender. *(In front of the Coptic Museum, directly across from the Mari Girgis Metro station.)*

AL-FUSTAT الفستات

*To reach al-Fustat, take the **Metro** to Mari Girgis (50pt). With your back to the station, head north along Mari Girgis St. until you see the minarets of the Mosque of Amir on your right. If you take a **taxi** from downtown (E£4), ask to go to Misr al-Qadima or Gami' Amir.*

Adjoining Coptic Cairo to the north are the partially excavated remains of al-Fustat, one of the oldest Islamic settlements and the seat of the Egyptian caliphate for 250 years. Al-Fustat was the name of a garrison town that some historians say comes from *fossatum*, Latin for "entrenchment." A different account of al-Fustat's founding holds that the conquering General 'Amir ibn al-'As sent word to the caliph in Medina that the magnificent Roman port of Alexandria would be the perfect place for the capital of Egypt. To 'Amir's dismay, the caliph preferred to establish his outposts along desert trade routes, which were invulnerable to the naval attacks of seafaring Christians. The disappointed general returned to the area (a Roman town called Babylon) to find that a white dove had nested in his tent during his absence. Interpreting this as a divine omen, 'Amir founded the new capital of Egypt there and dubbed it al-Fustat (City of the Tent). The military camp soon grew into a prosperous city with large houses, running water, and a sophisticated sewer system. Al-Fustat remained the capital of Egypt until the Fatimids established the neighboring city of al-Qahira ("the Conqueror") in 969 CE (see **Cairo**, p. 86). In 1168, Crusader King Amalric of Jerusalem invaded al-Qahira, and the resident Fatimids preferred to burn al-Fustat to the ground to prevent it from falling into the hands of the Crusaders. The ruins were quickly scavenged for building materials, and al-Fustat's days of importance ended ignominiously as the city garbage dump.

As a result, the present-day architectural remains of al-Fustat are insubstantial, and a stroll through the site reveals little more than traces of cisterns, drains, cesspools, and rubbish. The main reasons to visit al-Fustat (aside from a few interesting churches) are the **Mosque of 'Amir**—Egypt's oldest mosque—and the pottery district. Al-Fustat sprawls over the large area behind the mosque. If you venture out to this district in the heat of summer, bring plenty of water. It is best to avoid the area at night, since it is isolated and lacks police protection.

MOSQUE OF 'AMIR. The present-day Mosque of 'Amir ibn al-'As, Egypt's first mosque, occupies the site of the original building of 642 CE, and is four times the size of its predecessor. The oldest portion of the current mosque is its crumbling southeast minaret, added during the Ottoman period. The mosque has been rebuilt countless times over the centuries, most recently in 1983. There is little of historical or architectural interest about the current building, especially in comparison with the nearby Coptic churches. Architectural fragments, thousands of pieces of Islamic pottery, and imported Chinese porcelain have all been discovered here, but most pieces are currently displayed at the Islamic Museum and in the new Islamic Ceramics Museum (p. 128). Behind the Mosque of 'Amir is the **pottery district,** which provides the clay pots and pipes used to store water and transport sewage throughout Cairo. Watch modern-day artisans at work feeding smoke-belching kilns with leather scraps and garbage, but ask before you take their picture, or you may be slapped with a E£5 fee. *(Open daily 9am-5pm. E£6, students E£3.)*

OTHER SIGHTS. Walk straight down the street opposite the entrance to the Mosque of 'Amir to **Deir Abu Seiffein,** a complex of three 8th-century Coptic churches. The wooden entrance to the churches is about 500m ahead on the right. (*Odass,* or liturgy, read in Coptic Su 6-10am, W 8am-noon, and F 7-11am. Open daily 8am-5pm.) The oldest church with the finest icons in Deir Abu Seiffein is the **Church of St. Mercurius**

Felopatir (also called the Church of Abu Seiffein), dating from the 4th century but restored during the Middle Ages. Mercurius Felopatir, a Roman soldier, was beheaded because of his Christian beliefs, even after he helped fend off Berber attacks. The martyr is also called Abu Seiffein ("the dude with two swords") because an angel gave him a heavenly sword to go with his military saber.

The church's ebony, ivory, and cedar **iconostasis** separates the front vestibule from the nave. The elaborate, gabled roof is evidence of masterful Coptic carpentry, as pieces are fitted together without screws or nails. You can peer into the **Chamber of St. Barsoum,** where the saint supposedly lived with a cobra (not his wife) for 25 years. Upstairs are the ancient and miniscule churches of St. George of Rome, St. John the Baptist, and the 144,000 Martyrs, all of which were rediscovered when the plaster was accidentally chipped away from multiple layers of icons. As of August 2001, the chapels were closed for renovation.

Down the street is the 4th-century **Church of St. Shenouda,** dedicated to one of the most famous Coptic saints. This chapel contains seven altars and two fine iconostases of red cedar and ebony. The smallest of the three main churches at Deir Abu Seiffein is the early 8th-century **Church of the Holy Virgin,** a one-room chapel crammed with rare icons, paintings, and three altars. Across the Nile on Roda Island is a particularly interesting variation on the ubiquitous Cairene **Nilometer** (a glorified stairwell built to measure the depth of the Nile). The Abbasids built it around 850 CE and carved Qur'anic verses about water on its interior walls. The Ottomans lent a hand by adding a dome in the 19th century. If both entrances to the Nilometer are locked, use *bakhsheesh* or ask one of the many children playing nearby to pester the custodian.

MODERN CAIRO

The heart of Cairo beats in **Tahrir Sq.** (Liberation Sq.), with the **Egyptian Museum** on the north side and the **Mugamm'a** to the south, and cars speeding suicidally in between. However, the city's "downtown" also includes the many squares surrounding Tahrir Sq., particularly **Tala'at Harb Sq., Ramses Sq.,** and **'Ataba Sq.** You'll find yourself in an architectural wonderland whose cosmopolitan, French-influenced flavor may come as a welcome relief from the dusty ancient quarters and shantytowns of much of the rest of the city. Even if you think you have seen everything downtown, a walk down the deserted streets by the first light of dawn will surely reveal a new side of the city. For a couple of hours, downtown Cairo pauses to catch its breath before the frenzy of a new day, leaving its dozens of old colonial buildings momentarily undisturbed. To truly escape the hubbub, head to the quieter corners just outside downtown: posh **Zamalek** beckons from the middle of the Nile, and the small suburbs of **Heliopolis** and **Garden City** are only a few steps away.

TAHRIR SQ.

One block up from Tahrir Sq. at the intersection with Bustan St. are two particularly fine old buildings. On the south side of the intersection is the **4 Tala'at Harb St.** apartment building, elaborately decked out from its foundation to its richly decorated dome. Across the street, the more restrained and renovated **Muhammad 'Ali Club** glistens in the Cairo sun; look for the carved faces in the moldings.

TALA'AT HARB SQ.

Just north of Tahrir Sq. is Tala'at Harb Sq., named after the founder of the Egyptian National Bank and ringed with buildings in a variety of European styles. On the west side of the square is **J. Groppi's** (see p. 106), once *the* place to see and be seen (although the only things to see there now are the fabulous Italian mosaics at the entrance). The cafe's lip-smacking pastries used to be exported to Europe's elite, and its frequent concerts and dances during the colonial period were the hottest ticket in Cairo and always a top priority on Victorian social calendars. Although the July Revolution brought that world to an abrupt end, Groppi's remains a stodgy reminder of Cairo's colonial heyday.

Further up Tala'at Harb St. is the **Cinema Metro,** a beautiful movie palace from the 1930s that often shows English-language films as well as Arabic flicks. Farther north, Tala'at Harb St. intersects with 26 July St. West of Tala'at Harb St. is the **Sha'ar Ha-Shamaim Synagogue.** The temple's name is Hebrew for "Gate to the Sky," and its 1920s architecture is indeed heavenly. (Open Sa. Free.) Three blocks east of the square on Qasr al-Nil St. is the beginning of al-Sherifein St., home to the Egyptian **stock exchange.** In a bid to impress foreign investors, al-Sherifein and surrounding side streets are adorned with Old World-style street lamps and carefully manicured landscaping. One block north of 'Adly St. on Tala'at Harb St. is the faux leaf-encrusted brick of the **Davins Bryan Building,** which once outfitted explorers. To the south is **St. Joseph's Church,** the center of the city's Catholic community.

'ATABA SQ.

To the west of downtown is 'Ataba Sq. and the **Ezbekiya Gardens.** Although they are now fenced in and look like little more than a lawn with a few small palm trees, the Gardens were for many centuries the magnificent, verdant center of the city's social life. A patch of thick trees remains in the south corner to hint at the gardens' old glory, first under the Mamluks and then during the colonial period (when it was redesigned by the landscape architects of the Bois de Boulogne in Paris). In the northeast corner of 'Ataba Sq., just past the skyscraper with an antenna, are the double brass domes of the **Sedanoui Department Store.** Although it was built to rival the *prêt-à-porter* extravaganza Au Printemps in Paris, nationalization has left the store with shoddily constructed and hideously ugly *prêt-à-jeter* fashions. The building's interior is still worth a stop, with a huge open center and two staggeringly large cut-glass chandeliers.

SAKAKINI SQ.

The **Sakakini Palace,** in the middle of Sakakini Sq. east of the Ghamra Metro stop, is like nothing else in the city. The merchant Sakakini struck it rich when he sent a caravan of camels to the rat-infested Suez Canal; to celebrate his luck, he built this ornate palace and festooned it with a bizarre assortment of statuary depicting ferocious beasts and frolicking maidens. The carving above the main entrance represents Sakakini himself. You can get a good view from the outside, but the caretaker will show you around the interior for a few pounds of *bakhsheesh* if you arrive midday. Though the palace is currently used as storage space for tables and anatomical models, you can still see the beautiful rococco paintings on the ceilings. (Open daily 10am-2pm. Free.)

ZAMALEK

The quiet, tree-lined streets of the island-suburb of Zamalek are a great place to take a breather from the noisy hustle-and-bustle of the city. Zamalek was first settled in the colonial era, when the **Gezira Club** in the north (which still owns much of the island) was a second home to the British elite. A walking tour of the sights in and around Zamalek is a cosmopolitan change of pace from the ancient sites and medieval architecture that characterize the rest of Cairo. Spend an afternoon browsing the galleries and exhibitions at the opera complex at the south end of the island (particularly those at the **Egyptian Modern Art Museum,** p. 127). When the sun sets, head for the scattered restaurants for some of Cairo's best food (see p. 106).

CAIRO MARRIOTT. The building that now houses the Cairo Marriott, along the east bank of Zamalek, was built in 1869 for Empress Eugenie (wife of Napoleon III) during the grand opening of the Suez Canal. Around the same time, it hosted the world premiere of Verdi's opera *Aida*, long regarded as the seminal work in the grand tradition of Egyptian fetishization (rivaled by Lawrence Durrell's *The Alexandria Quartet*). If the slings and arrows of budget travel have you down, the Marriott has good restaurants, cafes, shops, and a swimming pool. Across the river to the west are **houseboats** that housed cabarets and nightclubs during World War II. One was owned by a belly dancer, employed by the Germans, who used her charms to acquire secrets from British agents.

CAIRO TOWER. The tower dominates the city's skyline and has an excellent (if pricey) view of the city. Commissioned by Nasser and completed in 1961, it was built to commemorate the rise of industry in Egypt. At 187m (60 stories) high, the tower is 50m taller that the Great Pyramid. A rotating restaurant on the top floor sells expensive drinks and meals. *(Open daily 9am-midnight; lines form at sunset. E£30.)*

HELIOPOLIS

This suburb of Cairo was founded in 1906 by Belgian industrialist Edouard Empain as a community for foreigners. Its broad avenues and odd Euro-Islamic fusion architecture make it an interesting trip out of central Cairo. The highlight of Heliopolis is **Empain's Palace.** To get there, head south on Shahid Tayyar Nazih Khalifa. The estate is a strange riot of carved elephants and Cambodian motifs that you can explore on your own (with a little *bakhsheesh* to the caretaker). The huge building behind the high wall in Heliopolis is the **President's Palace.** Down Cleopatra St., across from Mubarak's pad, are the beautifully decorated offices of the **Heliopolis Company** (the suburb's planners). Al-Ahram St. is home to several cheap **cafeterias** that were once major hangouts for Allied troops during World War II, as well as a **basilica** just past the cafeterias. At night, Heliopolis comes alive, as residents flood the shops, malls, and cafes on Roxy St.

GARDEN CITY

Just southwest of Tahrir, historic Garden City has fine examples of British colonial architecture, housing a large part of Cairo's expat population. French-built, recently renovated **Qasr al-'Aini Hospital,** the first hospital in Cairo, lies in west Garden City on the north end of Roda Island. In northeast Garden City is **Maglis al-Sha'ab** (Parliament), close to the **Mugamm'a** building. Along the Nile are a plethora of **embassies,** including those of the US and UK, as well as five-star hotels like **Shephards** and the **Semiramis.**

MOHANDISEEN

Built in the 1960s to house Egypt's *mohandiseen* (engineers), this district is now home to many expats and well-to-do Egyptians and has some of the best bars and restaurants in Cairo. Its main boulevard, **Gam'at al-Duwal al-Arabiya,** is lined with palm trees, fast food joints, and duty-free shops. (Note that to purchase duty-free products you must bring your **passport.**)

🏛 MUSEUMS

EGYPTIAN MUSEUM متحف مصر

In Tahrir Sq. Open daily 9am-4:45pm. E£20, students E£10. Camera privileges E£10, video E£100. Mummy Room E£40, students E£20.

Of the world's great museums, this behemoth may very well have the single most amazing collection. More certainly, it's housed in one of the worst facilities. Priceless artifacts—any one of which would be the *pièce de resistance* at an ordinary museum—are stacked on top of each other and crammed into dusty corners. Though the museum is filled with mummies and pharaonic treasure, it manages to retain the atmosphere of a warehouse. The heavily touristed areas (such as the Tutankhamun and Akhenaton rooms) are very well-labeled, but many descriptions are unhelpfully banal ("Pot," "Clay"), and others are just plain wrong ("Woman," reads the desciption of a portrait of a bearded man). Other items have no explanation at all. The crowded rooms deserve their popularity, but some of the smaller, infrequently visited side rooms are equally fascinating and far away from the maddening tourist hordes. Unless you choose to buy the E£100 catalog, the first item to check out should be the wall map to the left of the entrance. Flash photography is not permitted, but most of the museum is fairly well-lit (though, amazingly, not air-conditioned), so bring along a camera.

TUTANKHAMUN ROOM. Of all the collections in the museum, the treasures from **Tutankhamun's tomb** are the best-displayed and most popular. Originally squeezed into less than 100 cu. m, the booty now occupies a quarter of the second floor. The eastern corridor contains decorated furniture, golden statues, delicate alabaster lamps, weapons, amulets, fossilized undergarments, and other bare necessities for a King of the Underworld. **Room #4** displays King Tut's famous gold, glittering all over coffins and funeral masks, as well as an astounding collection of amulets, scarabs, and jewelry. The mask made to fit over the head of Tut's mummy contains more than 4kg of solid gold inlaid with quartz and lapis lazuli. In the hallway sit the king's internal organs, each in its own gilded coffin. The countless souvenir versions of these items, sold in tacky *souqs* and found on gaudy T-shirts and fake papyri, only make the originals look more amazing.

NARMER PALETTE. In the small glass case opposite the entrance (and surrounded by mobs of tourists with their guides) is the Narmer Palette, a stone slab commemorating the unification of Upper and Lower Egypt in about 3100 BCE by the mythical founder of pharaonic dynasties, King Narmer (a.k.a. Menes, see **Ancient History**, p. 51). From here, navigate the first floor in a clockwise direction around the central courtyard to get a sampling of pharaonic art from the Old Kingdom to the Greco-Roman period. Walking down the west corridor, you can visit the three rooms off to the right for a few minutes each. The first two rooms feature the best of the Old Kingdom, including a diarite statue of Chephren and a wooden statue named "Sheikh al-Balad" by workers who thought that it resembled their boss. The third room displays limestone artifacts from the Middle Kingdom.

AKHENATON ROOM. In the Akhenaton room (at the rear of the first floor) are statues of the heretical pharaoh who introduced Egypt to a monotheistic cult centered around the sun god Aton. Aton was represented as a disk with rays ending in hands that sometimes held *ankhs*, the Egyptian symbol for life. Artwork from this period is recognizable for its realistic portraits (versus the stiff and stylized portraits of other periods) and feminine body shapes. Read more about Akhenaton-era hijinks by sticking your head between the legs of the king's shapely statue to get a view of the informational plaque. Past the Akhenaton room are a collection of **statues** from the New Kingdom. In the room in the northeast corner, look for a painting of **Ramses II** clutching the cowering enemies of Egypt by their hair.

GREEK AND ROMAN ROOMS. Down the hall from the painting of Ramses II are the Greek and Roman rooms, where Classical art sits side-by-side with such oddities as a statue of a nude woman with the legs and tail of a chicken. Around the corner toward the entrance is a remarkable statue of **Alexander the Great.** His body is stiff and pharaonic, while his head is carved in the style of Greek naturalism.

FAYYUM PORTRAITS. Room #14, in the inner northwest corner of the second floor, exhibits the realistic portraits found on Ptolemaic-era mummies, mostly from the Fayyum region. The portraits depict their subjects as they looked just before death, in contrast to the statues and *stelae* of earlier Egyptians, who preferred a more timeless look. The result is haunting, with the long-dead expressively gazing back at their viewers.

MUMMY ROOM. The controversial mummy room is in the southeast corner of the second floor. Former President Anwar al-Sadat closed the famed room in 1981 because the display offended some Islamist groups who felt it was disrespectful toward the dead. (Unfortunately for Sadat, the gesture did little to appease the fundamentalists who assassinated him a few months later.) The reopening of the room was delayed by the mummies' continued decomposition, which left them offensive to just about everyone. Now restored and lodged in a dimly lit, air-conditioned room, the mummies require a separate ticket purchased outside the room (E£40, students E£20). Don't expect to learn how the mummification process worked, as there are no descriptions except identifications of each mummy. Nevertheless, the room does not lack in visceral impact: the well-preserved corpses (Seti I looks like he's sleeping) laid out in climate-controlled glass cases were once the most powerful people in the world. For more on mummies, see **Mummy Dearest,** p. 220.

OTHER ROOMS. The west corridor has unlabeled, oblong **mummy cases** in layers, and room #37 has square mummy cases used in the Middle Kingdom. The **papyri** in the middle of the second floor put those sold in the streets today to shame, while the fine gold jewelry collection in the room to the left of Tut's room #4 will make you think the stylish necklace you bought at Khan al-Khalili is tacky. At the opposite end of Level II from the gold of Tutankhamun is the modest **Tomb of Yuya and Thuyu,** more typical of the tombs in which most Egyptians rested for eternity. Animal-rights activists may cringe in nearby **room #53,** where mummified remains of cats, birds, monkeys, and a huge fish are slowly rotting to dust in their non-humidity-controlled surroundings.

OTHER MUSEUMS

Though one could spend an entire vacation with the mummies, Cairo has a number of other interesting museums housing everything from calligraphy to collage.

Islamic Art Museum (☎390 99 30), in Bab al-Khalaq Sq. at the intersection of Port Said, Muhammad 'Ali, and Ahmed Maher St. The hiding place of many of the artifacts missing from the mosques, mausolea, and *madrasas* of Cairo. Also contains Islamic art from the rest of the Middle East. Don't miss the miniature paintings and gold-leaf Qur'ans in the calligraphy room at the back, or the room that gleams with gilded swords and armor. Open Sa-Th 9am-4pm, F 9-11:30am and 1-4pm; in winter F 9-am12:30pm and 2-4pm. E£16, students E£8.

Coptic Museum (☎363 97 42), directly opposite the Mari Girgis Metro station. The world's finest collection of Coptic art. 14,000 textiles, paintings, icons, and other pieces. 2nd fl. icons include many superb paintings in a variety of styles; compare an icon of the Virgin Mary suckling baby Jesus with a carving of the Egyptian goddess Isis feeding her son Horus. The Nag Hammadi Library, next to the textiles, houses 12 Coptic Gnostic codices from the 4th century. Unlike most museums in Cairo, this collection is well labeled in French and English. Open daily 9am-5pm. E£16, students E£8. Camera privileges E£10, video E£100.

Egyptian Modern Art Museum (☎736 66 55), in the Opera Complex in Zamalek. Cross the bridge from Tahrir Sq. or take the Metro to the Opera. Work by Egyptian artists in a variety of media and 20th-century styles, exhibited in a modern, A/C gallery. A welcome reminder that Cairo's art is not confined to tombs and sarcophagi. Open Sa-Th 10am-1pm and 5-9pm. Free.

Gayer-Anderson Museum, 4 Ibn Tulun St. (☎364 78 22), in front of Ibn Tulun Mosque. Originally two separate buildings, these 16th- and 18th-century mansions were joined when Major Gayer-Anderson, an English art collector, arrived in the 1930s and proceeded to fill his home with eclectic artifacts and furniture. When he left Egypt in the '40s, he gave the mansion and its contents to the government. Ask the caretaker to show you the secret door behind a cabinet leading to a balcony overlooking the ballroom. To Egyptians, the museum is enigmatically known as "The House of the Cretan Woman." You may recognize some rooms from the James Bond flick *The Spy Who Loved Me.* Open daily 9am-4pm. E£16, students E£8. Camera privileges E£10, video E£100.

Mahmoud Khalil Museum, 1 Kafour St., Doqqi (☎336 23 76), 200m from the Cairo Sheraton. A fantastic collection, housed in an A/C mansion, consisting almost exclusively of paintings by such 19th-century European greats as Monet, Van Gogh, Degas, and Toulouse-Lautrec. Open Tu-Su 10am-6pm. E£25, students E£10.

Manial Palace Museum (☎388 74 95), on the north half of Roda Island. The complex was built in the 19th century by the prolific Muhammad 'Ali and, like many of his other buildings, reflects Ottoman influence (particularly the must-see residential palace). The macabre hunting museum is filled with animal heads. Open Sa-Th 9am-4pm, F 9am-12:30pm and 2-4pm. E£10, students E£5. Camera privileges E£10, video E£100.

Museum of Islamic Ceramics, al-Gezira Arts Center, 1 Sheikh Marsafy St., Zamalek (☎737 32 98), next to the southwest corner of the Marriott Hotel. Proof that less is more, this superb new museum houses an exquisite collection of well-labeled ancient Islamic and contemporary ceramics in the well-organized, A/C rooms of a converted Ottoman palace. Open Sa-Th 10am-3pm and 5pm-9pm. Free.

Mugamm'a al-Funun Center of Arts (☎340 82 11), on the corner of Ma'had al-Swissry St. and 26 July Bridge, in Zamalek. Rotates exhibitions of works by contemporary Egyptian and foreign artists, many of which are on sale (E£800+). Also screens free films; consult *Egypt Today* or *al-Ahram Weekly* for a schedule. Nile-side serenity doesn't get any better than the garden here. Open Sa-Th 10am-1:30pm. Free.

🎵 ENTERTAINMENT

CINEMA

A few cinemas run English-language films four to six months behind their release in the US; *al-Ahram Weekly* (75pt) has listings in English. All of these air-conditioned theaters are packed with Egyptian teenagers on Thursday nights. Films usually show at 10:30am, 1:30, 3:30, 6:30, and 9:30pm, with a midnight showing on Thursdays (E£10, in winter E£20). The cinema in the **Ramses Hilton Hotel Annex** has two screens, one of which always shows a film in English. (š574 74 35). **Metro Cinema,** 35 Tala'at Harb St. (š393 75 66), near Tala'at Harb Sq., and **Kareem Cinema,** 15 Imad al-Din St. (š592 48 30), alternate English and Arabic movies.

DANCE

▣ **Mausoleum al-Ghouri** (š510 08 23), on al-Mu'izz St., just south of the pedestrian overpass near al-Azhar University in Islamic Cairo. Renovated 500-year-old palace hosts free Sufi music and whirling dervishes (spinning at over 100rpm) on W and Sa nights (9pm, in winter 8pm). Arrive early to the 1hr. show, as seats fill up fast.

Balloon Theater (☎347 17 18), on al-Nil St. at the Zamalek Bridge, Agouza. Regular performances of Rida's Troupe, one of the best Egyptian folk dance companies. Tickets E£10-30. Shows daily 9:30pm.

Falafel Restaurant (☎577 74 44), at the Ramses Hilton (behind the Egyptian Museum). Prix-fixe dinner (US$31) includes a fabulous folk dancing show by the Hassan Troupe. Dinner 8pm-10pm. Show 10:30pm. Open Sa-Th 9pm-midnight. Reservations required.

Coquillage (☎735 61 26), at the foot of Tahrir Bridge in Zamalek, connected to Qasr al-Nil Casino. Coffee shop by day, lavish hall of stained glass with Arabic dancing and singing by night. Fettuccine with chicken (E£35) dazzles the taste buds; variety show dazzles the eyes and ears 10pm-4am. Open 24hr. Reservations recommended. MC/V.

MUSIC AND THEATER

Cairo Opera Complex (☎737 06 01), outside the Opera Metro station in Gezira, south of Zamalek. Hosts the Cairo Symphony Orchestra, outdoor jazz performances, and visiting operas. Jacket and tie required for men attending main hall performances (travelers have been known to borrow snazzy clothing from kind hostel workers). Season runs Sept.-June; casual open-air performances held July-Aug. daily at 9pm. Main hall and small hall E£15-50, outdoors E£15-25. Student discount usually 30%. Check *al-Ahram Weekly* or *Egypt Today* for details. Box office open daily 10am-3pm and 4-9pm.

Al-Gomhoriyya Theater, 12 al-Gomhoriyya St. (☎390 77 07), at the intersection of al-Gomhoriyya with 'Abd al-'Aziz St. Performances by the Arabic Music Troupe and the Cairo Symphony Orchestra, usually F evenings.

Wallace Theater (☎797 63 73), in the AUC New Campus, on Muhammad Mahmoud St. near McDonald's. Features 2 plays in English per year. AUC also hosts a variety of concerts, from jazz to chamber music, and free movie festivals at the library. Open fall-spring. Call or check bulletin boards around the Old Campus (near the AUC bookstore).

Cairo Puppet Theater (☎591 09 54 or 591 83 67), outside the easternmost Metro entrance in Ezbekiya Gardens near 'Ataba Sq. World-famous shadow puppets perform in Arabic, but are universally comprehensible. W-M 7:30pm, F and Su 10:30am. E£5.

British Council, 192 al-Nil St., Agouza (☎303 15 14), 1 block south of 26 July St., next to Balloon Theater. Free performances by visiting British and Egyptian artists and the occasional free film. Call for information on upcoming events. Large library (open M-Sa 10am-8pm) has CD and video equipment and a traveler-oriented teaching center. Office open Su-Th 9am-3pm.

Egyptian Center for International Cultural Cooperation, 11 Shagarat al-Durr St., Zamalek (☎736 54 19). Free art exhibitions, Arabic language courses, lectures, tours, and shows. See *al-Ahram Weekly* or *Egypt Today*. Open Sa-Th 10am-3pm and 4-9pm.

FELUCCA RIDES

Consider hiring a swallow-winged **felucca** and lazing on the river during the day or night. Most *feluccas* can accommodate up to eight people comfortably. The more passengers, the cheaper; bargain for a good rate. *Feluccas* for hire dock just south of the Qasr al-Nil (Tahrir) Bridge on the east bank. Across the corniche (on the water) from the Meridian Hotel, shrewd negotiators can snag a boat for E£10 for a 1hr. ride. A nominal tip (E£1-2) is expected at the cruise's end. Travelers seeking multi-day cruises (especially popular in Upper Egypt, near Luxor and Aswan) should see **Tips on Traveling by Felucca,** p. 208, and **Rolling on the River,** p. 209. **Hantours** (horse carriages) are also enjoyable, especially on a breezy evening. Avoid the *hantours* in front of major hotels; catch one downtown, on the corniche under Tahrir Bridge. Don't pay more than E£10 for a 30min. ride.

OUTDOOR ACTIVITIES

GIZA ZOO. With wide walkways, picnicking families, and children playing soccer, the Giza Zoo doubles as a park. Nevertheless, for less than E£1 you can take pictures with the animals, feed them (20pt a pop), and get close enough to the lions to get goose bumps on the back of your neck. *(Right in front of you as you cross the University Bridge—al-Gama'a—west into Giza. Open daily 9am-4pm. 25pt. Camera privileges 20pt.)*

PHARAONIC VILLAGE (AL-QARIA AL-FARA'ONIYA). This Disney-fied village was founded by former Egyptian ambassador and self-proclaimed papyrus king Dr. Hassan Ragab. Visitors board motorboats and chug through canals past statues of the gods and historically reconstructed scenes of ancient papyrus-making, temple wall-painting, and mummification. All this is described in detail by a guide speaking the language of your choice. Disembark to view a temple, houses, and King Tut's tomb reconstructed to appear as it did when Howard Carter discovered it in 1922. The price is steep, but the village is high on information and low on hassle. It's definitely worth it if (and only if) you're not going to see the real thing in Luxor. *(5km south of downtown, on Jacob's Island in Giza. ☎571 86 76. Open daily 9am-9pm; in winter 9am-5pm. E£55, students E£40, groups of 10 or more E£30 per person. Lunch E£17.)*

FUTBOL. You can catch a *futbol* (soccer) game at the stadium on Ramses St. in Nasser, toward the airport. September through May, local rivals **Zamalek** and **Ahly** take on teams from farther afield. Be cautious of the people next to you; if their team scores, they may set off a firecracker. First- and second-class seats are E£25 and E£10, respectively, but if you're interested in seeing ballistic fans and are willing to accept the small risk of a riot, grab a bleacher seat for E£5. *(Check al-Ahram or ask around for schedule information. Get tickets at the teams' box offices—Zamalek's is south of 26 July St. in Mohandiseen; Ahly's is in Gezira next to the Cairo Tower.)*

FOURTH OF JULY. On American Independence Day (or the closest weekend to it), homesick Americans come together at the Cairo American Primary and Secondary School in Ma'adi. Drop by if you miss hearing pure, unbroken American English

CAIRO

and want to collect your two free soft drinks and slice of watermelon. Each attendee of the event also receives a free ticket to the raffles held throughout the evening (last year's prizes included return tickets to any destination in the US). Bring your US passport—your taxes have already footed the bill—and a pair of swimming trunks. Call the American Embassy (š794 82 11) for hours and directions. Be persistent even if your inquiries are met with confusion.

⌐ SHOPPING

OUTDOOR MARKETS

Cairo's biggest and most famous market is **Khan al-Khalili** (see p. 115). Navigating the maze of alleyways that lie within the *khan* may seem like madness, but there is a method to it. Most gold, copper, and antique dealers lie along Khan al-Khalili St., which changes to al-Badestani St. as it heads east. Perfumes, spices, and cloth can be found a few blocks south, between al-Azhar and al-Muski St.

In the market south of **Sayyida Zeinab,** each alley offers different wares. Take the Metro to Sayyida Zeinab, then walk 5min. toward the minarets of the Sayyida Mosque. Other major markets are northeast of **'Ataba Sq.** To get to 'Ataba Sq. from Tahrir Sq., go east along Tahrir St., then up 'Abd al-'Aziz St. **Souq al-Tawfiqia** runs between Ramses and Tala'at Harb St., one block north of 26 July St. Produce stalls stand beside kitchen-equipment booths, all laid out in brilliant displays. On summer days, hose-wielding shopkeepers water the shop entrances to reduce heat and settle the dust.

DEPARTMENT STORES

If hard-core bargaining doesn't appeal to you, you can head to one of Cairo's upscale department stores. **Omar Effendi** has several branches downtown. Be forewarned that ever since the Egyptian government nationalized the department stores, the shops have had little to offer beyond outlandishly tacky, out-of-date clothes in various brown-and-orange combinations. More expensive shopping centers lure foreigners and wealthy Egyptians with higher-quality goods. The **World Trade Center** on the corniche, north of the Ramses Hilton, is the biggest. A bit less expensive is **al-Yamama Center** (affectionately called the "Yo Mama Center" by expats), at 3 Dr. Taha Hussein St. in Zamalek, where you can watch music videos or sporting events on the large-screen TV in the ground-floor cafe. For assuredly high-quality versions of wares found in the *khan* (copper, antiques, papyrus) and a minimum of bargaining, try Ma'adi's tree-lined **Road Nine** (Metro: Ma'adi).

VENI, VIDI, VENDI Buying and selling in the Egyptian capital transcends mundane business—it's an intricate give-and-take that has evolved over centuries. Think of it as a game to be relished, not a battle to be won. Bargaining is a given: no price is set in stone, and shopkeepers enjoy the haggling (just remember that they do it for a living and have the benefit of experience). If you play hardball, the vendors will not lower the price; chatting will bring you more success. Theatrics, rather than stubbornness, get results. Walk away in disbelief several times. Do a brief Mexican hat dance while you weigh the pros and cons of the purchase. Never get too enthusiastic about the object in question. Instead, point out flaws in workmanship and design. Have a friend discourage you from your purchase—if you seem reluctant, the merchant will want to drop the price to interest you again. Ideally, you should know the approximate worth of the item, then make an offer sufficiently below that to gain leverage. A good deal could be anywhere from one-tenth to three-quarters of the starting price. For more advice on driving a hard bargain, see **Tipping and Bargaining,** p. 15.

CLOTHING AND TEXTILES

At the **Tent-Makers' Bazaar,** south of Bab Zuweila in Islamic Cairo, you can commission the making of a Bedouin tent (far out of a budget traveler's league) or buy appliqué pillowcases (E£20) and bedcovers (E£300). The **Nomad Gallery,** 14 Saraya al-Gezira, Zamalek, near the Marriott, is known for its top-quality jewelry, textiles, and crafts. They're not big bargainers, but their prices are as low as they go at the Tent-Makers' Bazaar. (š736 19 17. Open M-Sa 10am-3pm. AmEx/MC/V.) Across from the Ibn Tulun Mosque, **Khan Misr Tulun** sells quality handicrafts from all parts of Egypt and Africa. (š365 22 27. Open M-F 9am-5pm.) The best places to shop for woven **rugs** are the stores along **Saqqara Rd.** near the Pyramids, where Harania artists weave up a storm (see p. 139). On Friday mornings there's a **junk market** at the Mausoleum of Imam al-Shafi'i, where many bizarre items are bought and sold.

 HOW TO GET RIPPED OFF. The touts in the street of Khan al-Khalili who try to get you into stores also get a commission. To make up for the commission, the store owner raises the price. You'll never get a good price at a store to which a hustler has brought you.

There's a colorful **used clothing market** daily at the east end of 26 July Bridge. The stands hawk modern and vintage Western clothing as well as some traditional Egyptian garb, much of it for less than E£10. If you're looking for something comfortable to wear while lounging around the house, you can pick up a used *galabiyya* here or splurge on a new one (E£15-30) at the **market** south of al-Ghouri Mosque and Khan al-Khalili on al-Mu'izz St. Casual clothing for several well-known Western brands is made in Egypt, and you may want to take advantage of the slightly lower (but fixed) prices. Most of these goods are available in boutiques on the main streets and in department stores. For more exotic attire, **al-Wikala** (š589 74 43), 73 Gawhar al-Qayid St., in the alley south of the Egyptian Pancake House, is considered one of the best places to buy bellydancing costumes.

BOOKS AND MUSIC

There's a huge **used book market** daily at the fringe of Ezbekiya Gardens, next to the puppet theater, with volumes in Arabic, English, French, and German. Most stalls also stock one- or two-year-old Western magazines bought as surplus from overseas vendors. Titles are not organized very well, so it's best to come for browsing. (For bookstores, see p. 98.) If you develop a taste for Arab pop music, the best place to pick up a few tapes is Shawarby St., a left turn off Abdel Khaleq Sarwat St. at the Misr gas station one block east of Tala'at Harb St. Look for **Inter-sound,** at the north end of the street. They have a wide selection of Arab classical and pop, and some Western music.

JEWELRY AND METALWARE

Cairo is a center of the jewel trade, and prices here tend to be markedly lower than in the West. Often, gold or silver jewelry can be made to order for barely more than the cost of the metal itself. Never ask for the price first. Look at a piece of jewelry carefully and then ask the shopkeeper to weigh it in front of you. Inquire about the grade of gold or silver; gold content under 18 karat is rare in Egypt. Always make sure you see the stamp indicating level of purity on both gold and silver items. One of the best shopping areas is in the **Khan al-Khalili Souq al-Fida** (silver market), where you can find Turkish, pharaonic, and Nubian designs in addition to more modern creations. Ceramic plates and trays of varying sizes and designs are available throughout the *khan* for E£15-20, while an average-sized *sheesha* should cost about E£30-35. For the best *sheeshas* in Cairo, however, bypass the junk sold at the khan and head to the **restaurant supply bazaar** on al-Mu'izz St. (see p. 116). Copper or brass mugs, coffeepots, and ashtrays are also available.

CAIRO

PAPYRUS

The "papyrus" sold throughout Cairo is usually banana leaf, a cheap look-alike. Real papyrus can be scrunched up and will not retain any wrinkles, while banana leaf crackles and stays crunched. Handpainted papyrus is even rarer; if anything even vaguely looks like a print, it is. A smudged artist's signature is the usual tip-off. To see the real stuff at correspondingly higher prices, head to **Dr. Ragab's Papyrus Factory,** a right turn off al-Gala'a Bridge heading west from Tahrir Sq. Another authentic option is the **Sa'id Delta Papyrus Center,** 21 al-Ghouria St., 3rd fl. (š512 07 47), by Darb al-Ahmar near the Umayyad Mosque. The bazaars are full of fake but colorful artwork for those who think a neon pink Osiris would look great next to a velvet Elvis portrait.

BACKGAMMON

Tawila boards cost E£60-120, depending on the quality and your bargaining skills. Make sure the board is absolutely flat when it's opened and laid on a table, as they are occasionally warped or wobbly. Pieces are often made (and sold) separately from the board. Check to see that they fit on the triangles, and that there are 15 of each color. You should pay less if the pieces are plastic. **Maka al-Mokarama,** 7 'Adly St. (š393 89 80), next to the tourist office, has quality boards but lacks the hassle and fun of Khan al-Khalili, where scads of stores sell them.

SPICES AND PERFUME

Thousands of perfume and spice shops give some sections of Cairo a happily fragrant air. Excellent Middle Eastern spices like *za'tar* are difficult or impossible to find in the West; here, they are sold by the kilo for a few pounds. The quality of perfumes ranges dramatically. Rub some on the back of your hand: if it's oily or shiny, oil has been added to the perfume to stretch the liquid weight. Vendors of perfume will often misquote the size of a container; they know most tourists (especially Americans) can't tell a milliliter from a millipede. A 60ml jar should be about the length of a middle finger. A gram costs 50pt-E£1 (far cheaper than the dope you will be offered in the market near 'Ataba Sq.). Besides simple essences like lotus, rose, and musk, many shops have a "menu" of renowned perfumes they can imitate. **Harraz Agricultural Seeds, Medicinal, and Medical Plants Co.,** east of Bab al-Khalq Sq. on Ahmed Mahir St., sells every imaginable spice and folk remedy at reasonable prices. They have an herbalist-in-residence upstairs if you're wondering what the dehydrated seahorses are good for. (Open Sa-Th 9am-9pm.) If the self-proclaimed "sheikh of spice" won't cut you a good deal, **Khodr,** next door, has similar wares, as do many vendors in Khan al-Khalili.

THAT WHICH WE CALL A ROSÉ... by any other name could be disgusting and potentially fatal. Although many tourists are familiar with **Stella** and **Sakkara,** Egypt's decent stabs at beer-brewing greatness, few encounter the rest of Egypt's potent potables. Egypt produces wines such as *Reine Cléopatre* and *Cru des Ptolemées* in an attempt to evoke the wine expertise of the French and the bacchanalian ancient Greeks, but the concoctions are barely drinkable, no matter how evocative their names. The vaguely suggestive wine *Obelisque* is a little kinder to the palate, but not to the wallet. *Omar Khaggam* also produces a drinkable but expensive red wine. Egypt's hard liquors have names that will make you tipsy just hearing them. Egyptian teetotalers must combat the harmful effects (and puns) of **Johnny Wadi's Brown Label, Gordoon's Gin, Gardan's Gin,** and **Gordon's Kin.** Before you sit down to a cool kin and tonic, be warned that these hack liquors are sometimes distilled from wood and have been linked to blindness and even death.

🔒 NIGHTLIFE

As the sun sets on the Egyptian capital, *sheesha* smoke fills the air, strolling locals mill about the markets, and decked-out scenesters dance 'til (almost) dawn at the discotheques dotting the side streets of the city. The free publication *Croc*, available at most bars, is an up-to-date guide to the Cairene scene. During **Ramadan** (see **Holidays and Festivals**, p. 85), Cairenes take to the streets around al-Azhar and Hussein Sq., along the corniche, and all over the bridges spanning the Nile. Starting around 10pm, there are street performances, magic shows, and general shenanigans and tomfoolery. Most cinemas also have midnight screenings during this month. The following listings are as easy to navigate as A-B-C-D—**Ahwas, Bars, Clubs,** (belly) **Dancing**.

AHWAS (COFFEEHOUSES)

Although you'd never guess it from the incessant honking, Cairenes love to relax, meet with friends, and contemplate the sweet mysteries of life. Much of this ruminating occurs in the *ahwas* (coffeehouses) that dot many street corners and alleys east of the Nile. A typical *ahwa* has gossipers in one corner, *tawila* (backgammon) players in another, and *sheesha* smoke and Turkish coffee steam winding throughout. *Sheesha* tobacco is smoother and more delicious than cigarette shag and comes plain or flavored (apple is ubiquitous). Foreigners and women are welcomed at all the *ahwas* listed below. Several others downtown welcome foreigners, but with the intention of cheating them. Tactics include trying to charge for bottled water whether customers ask for it or not, telling them that their *sheesha* is "finished" after 5min. and needs to be replaced (a good *sheesha* withstands at least 20min. of dedicated smoking), and just plain overcharging. Specifically, **avoid** the *ahwa* on Tahrir St. just east of Tahrir Sq. Elsewhere, staff is usually honest and prices cheaper (E£1.50 for tea and *sheesha*), but women may feel decidedly uncomfortable in these houses of male bonding. Nevertheless, anyone in Cairo for more than a few days should seek out the more traditional establishments. Just try to determine the mood of the place before you sit down. For other options, try the **Cafes** listings under each region of the **Food** section (p. 104). For further info on *sheesha*-smoking, see **Puff the Magic Sheesha**, p. 84.

🔒 **Fishawi's Khan al-Khalili** (☎590 67 55), 4 doors down from al-Hussein Hotel, just off al-Hussein Sq. The oldest of Cairo's teahouses, Fishawi's is also the least typical, with table after table of tourist families and nary a *galabiyya* in sight. The decor, however, is stunning. Nicknamed "Café des Miroirs," Fishawi's is furnished in a 19th-century Turkish style with panels of mirrors and woodwork, chandeliers, and brass tables. Customers spill onto the walkway, sipping their mint tea (E£2) and *karkadeh* (E£3) and smoking aromatic cappuccino, banana, apple, or cantaloupe *sheesha* (E£3). Open 24hr.

Vienna Cafe, on Qasr al-Aini St. south of Tahrir Sq., 70m past the Misr gas station. Frequented by middle-class Egyptians, this well-tended cafe in Garden City has great *sheesha* and friendly service. Tea E£1.50. *Sheesha* E£2.50. Open daily 7am-2am.

Maroush, 64 Lubnan St., Mohandiseen (☎346 68 91), a E£5 taxi ride from downtown. A ritzy *ahwa* for a ritzy neighborhood, but relaxed, even by coffeehouse standards. Outdoor patio makes for a great escape with a *sheesha* (E£5). Open daily 8am-2am.

BARS

Cairo isn't known for beer guzzling, but considering the strict Islamic prohibition against alcohol, it has a good number of bars. These fall into two categories: cheap places serving only Stella and catering to middle-aged Egyptian males, and livelier establishments filled with a combination of the young, the rich, and the expatriated. All of the bars listed below fall into the latter category. Several examples of the first kind can be found around the north end of Tala'at Harb St., especially on Alfy St. Women should avoid those places.

🦶 **Barrel Bar,** at the Windsor Hotel, 19 Alfy St., 2nd fl. (☎591 58 10 or 591 52 77). No music or dancing, but the period atmosphere ensures a constant stream of AUC students and tourists, and the occasional movie star. The lounge resembles a museum documenting Cairo's days under British rule, but this museum serves Stella (E£8.50) and has a well-stocked bar. Open daily 10am-1am.

Cairo Jazz Club, 197 26 July St. (☎345 99 39). Groove nightly with a crowd of international scat cats who come here to grab some Ella and a Stella (E£12) or to jump, jive, and cocktail (E£20) around the clock. The best live music scene in Cairo. Restaurant serves up decent entrees (E£15-25). Shows start at 10:30pm. Open daily 8pm-2am.

Deals, 2 al-Sa'id al-Bakry St., Zamalek (☎736 05 02), a right turn off 26 July St. at the base of the bridge to downtown. Cairo's younger set mingles and tingles in this tiny joint. Drink prices (including French wine by the glass) belie the name, but the A/C and rock music ensure that this hangout fills up quickly. Stella E£8. Open daily 4pm-2am.

El Gato Negro, 32 Jeddah St., Mohandiseen (☎361 68 88). Stylish hepcats scope the Mohandiscene from this classy lair while sipping on anything from water (E£3) to top-notch scotch and whiskey (E£18). The adjacent restaurant serves up a variety of delicious foods (pizza, pasta, Middle Eastern fare). Cover-less dance floor opens at 10pm. Open daily 1pm-2am. AmEx/MC/V.

Pub 28, 28 Shagarat al-Durr St., Zamalek (☎340 92 00), kitty-corner to the Mandarin Koedar ice cream store (p. 107). Take a right off 26 July St. at the Misr gas station; the pub's brick facade will be on your left. The closest you'll come to Dublin in Cairo, this dimly lit pub serves a wide selection of spirits (E£9+). Next thing you know, it'll be raining outside. Open daily noon-2am. AmEx/V.

Odeon Palace, 6 Dr. 'Abd al-Hamid Sa'id St. (☎576 79 71), off Tala'at Harb St., just northwest of Tala'at Harb Sq. A relaxing rooftop spot for insomniacs in the mood for food, *sheesha,* or a colorful nighttime view. Stella E£9. Open 24hr.

CLUBS

The Cairene club scene is smaller, tamer, and less crowded than that of Beirut and Istanbul. The clubs on **Pyramids Road** in Giza overflow with Gulf Arabs, but are extremely expensive—a night out can cost over E£200. Elsewhere clubs are more affordable, but depending on the place, night, and mood of the bouncer, single men may have a hard time getting in. Always call to check on the latest rules, and wear something sleek, black, and non-denim to improve your chances. The summer of 2001 found Cairo in the middle of a salsa rage, and as of August 2001, most clubs featured a weekly salsa night. Otherwise, the playlist is a mixture of Arabic pop and American Top 40.

Jackie's Joint, Nile Hilton, Tahrir Sq. (☎578 04 44 or 578 06 66, ext. 285 or 214). One of Cairo's hotspots, with lines out the door most nights. Features themed nights 2 or 3 times a week—call to check what's on. Minimum charge E£35 (includes a drink). Happy hour Sa-Su 10pm-midnight. Open daily 9pm-4am.

Crazy House Disco, Cairoland Entertainment Center, 1 Salah Salem (☎366 10 82 or 366 10 83). Careen into dancing Cairenes at this local favorite, which features a hyperactive fog machine. E£25 cover includes 2 beers. Open daily 11pm-5am.

Hard Rock Cafe, in the Meridien Hotel. Brand new and hugely popular with pop-culture crazed Egyptian youth, this branch of the international chain looks and acts precisely like all the others around the world. Disco open daily midnight-4am.

BELLY DANCING

Authentic belly dancing is a popular evening diversion for those who can afford it. Like bars, dancing establishments divide into two completely separate categories, neither of which resembles the eroticized version popular in the Western imagination. For a E£2-5 cover charge, you can watch a show at one of several inexpensive venues downtown. However, these are good only as a form of ironic entertainment and have more in common with a comedy club than anything else. A dancer will typically wander around the floor (sort of) in time with the blaring orchestra, and occasionally throw in one of the two or three moves in her repertoire. To divert attention from their ineptitude, dancers often drag spectators onto the floor, so sit away from the center if you'd rather watch the entertainment than become it. Avoid any appetizers placed at the table; these are not free and can add a zero to your bill if you're not careful. The real entertainment comes after a couple rounds of Stellas, when the customers jump onto the stage to show off their own moves. These joints have little in common with clubs operated by five-star hotels. A five-star dancer has complete creative control over her performance and employs her own orchestra. Women will have no problem attending shows alone, and the Gulf Arabs who form most of the audiences regularly bring their familes. Such convenience has a price—up to E£200, including dinner. Keep in mind that the quality of the performance depends most on the skill of the dancer; call ahead to check who is scheduled for a particular night. Names to look for include the Egyptian dancers Dina and Lucy, and the Argentine Asahan.

Palmyra Club, in an alley off 26 July St. west of Sherif St. The cleanest, largest, and most reputable of the downtown joints. Stella E£12. Shows run 1-4am. Cover E£5.

Nile Maxim Cruise (☎342 48 33), at the Marriott Hotel in Zamalek. Glitzy Nile cruiser with chandeliers, mirrors, enormous windows, and jacked-up A/C. Floating show features top-level dancer and whirling dervish for E£70, including salad and dessert. Add at least E£50 for dinner. Daily 8 and 11pm. Call for reservations. MC/V.

Other clubs: Respected venues include **Semiramis Intercontinental Hotel** (☎795 71 71), on the corniche and visible from Tahrir Sq., and **Pyramisa Hotel Cairo,** 60 Giza St. (☎336 70 00 or 336 80 00). Shows usually start at 1am. Dinner begins around 10pm. Call for reservations.

OTHER NIGHTLIFE

In the evenings, middle-class Egyptian couples swarm to the boat cafes (misleadingly called **casinos**) lining the Nile on Gezira Island. Some boats anchor permanently at the edge of the water. The **Casino al-Nil** and **Pasha 1901,** on the west side of Tahrir Bridge, are among the best (E£10 min.). Ranging from simple to swanky, these places are packed on Thursday nights. For real **gambling,** head to the Nile Hilton, Marriott, or Sheraton Hotel. Gamblers must be at least 21; show your **passport** to enter. You are not permitted to game with Egyptian currency, but worry not: casinos can change pounds to US dollars faster than you can lose them (min. bet US$5). Drinks are free if you gamble.

🗺 DAYTRIPS FROM CAIRO

PYRAMIDS AT GIZA (AL-AHRAM) الاهرام

For the best combination of speed and economy, take the Metro to Giza Square (60pt), then a microbus from the east side of the Metro station (left as you exit the station; 30pt). **Minibus** *#183 (١٨٣; 40pt) from Tahrir Sq. and #26 (٢٦) from 'Ataba Sq. are slower. The last stop is often 1km from the Pyramids; cross the street and follow the main road to get there. A taxi from downtown should cost less than E£20, though drivers often ask for more. The easiest and most comfortable way back is on a special tour bus that leaves outside the tourist office every 10-15min. (E£2.50). Hotel managers in Cairo can arrange* **tours,** *but be sure to compare prices.* **Mr. Salah Muhammad** *(š/fax 298 06 50; mobile 012 313 84 46; samoṣintouch.com) offers chauffeur-driven tours of Memphis, Saqqara, the carpet school at Harania, and the Pyramids at Giza for E£40 each (E£35 for Let's Go users who book directly), including a guide. Entrance fees not included (leave at 9am, return at 5pm). Book at least the night before. Although sunrise at the Pyramids is impressive, guards won't let you in until regular hours of operation. Site open daily 8:30am-5pm; Nov.-Apr. 9am-4pm. Pyramids and Sphinx complex E£20, students E£10. 2 smaller pyramids E£10, students E£5. Great Pyramid limited to the 1st 100 visitors who appear at 8:30am and 1pm. E£20, students E£10.*

A 12th-century Arab historian once said, "All things fear time, but time fears the Pyramids." Centuries later, these great stone monoliths inspire mixed reactions from their visitors. For some, the Pyramids are the highlight of a trip to Egypt; others come away disappointed. Since everyone wants to see these stirring testaments to human achievement, nowhere else is Egypt's ravenous tourism industry so persistent. For a solid mile leading up to the pyramids, souvenir shops, alabaster factories, and papyrus museums conspire to pawn off "ancient" artifacts that are manufactured while-u-wait. At the foot of the pyramids, an army of hustlers not unlike a biblical swarm of locusts hounds you: Bedouin imposters rent camels and Arabian "race" horses, children peddle tourist dreck at inflated prices, and self-appointed guides approach at every turn. A firm *"la, shukran"* ("no, thanks") can prove useful at the Pyramids, even with the man who claims to be the mayor of Giza (he isn't). That said, if you can blot out the racket below and forget your expectations, you will be able to see this wonder of the ancient world as generations of awe-struck travelers have before you.

The three main pyramids at Giza were built for three pharaohs from the 4th dynasty: **Cheops** (Khufu), **Chephren** (Khafre), and **Mycerinus** (Menkaure), a father-son-grandson trio that reigned during the 26th century BCE. The pyramids are lined up in order of size and age, from Cheops to Mycerinus. All three entrances face north, and the bases are aligned with the four cardinal directions. The smaller, surrounding pyramids belonged to the pharaohs' wives and children. Each of the pyramids was once attached to its own funerary complex, which included a riverside pavilion and a mortuary temple where the pharaoh's cult could continue for eternity. A long, narrow causeway linked the mortuary temple with the neighboring waters of the Nile. Attendants brought the mummy of the deceased ruler across the Nile by boat and up the causeway in a solemn procession, depositing it in its sacred resting place at the heart of the pyramid.

 SIGHTSEEING STRATEGY. The best time to visit the Pyramids is Friday, when some of the more pious hagglers take the day off, and most other attractions are closed anyway. Be wary of going before 9:30am from November to March, when fog shrouds the Pyramids in the morning, but crowds tend to pick up as the day progresses. Be warned that you can't get inside the Pyramids or boat museum after 5pm. Good shoes are key for those who plan on internal exploration. External climbing is not permitted.

GREAT PYRAMID OF CHEOPS. Built around 2550 BCE, the Pyramid of Cheops is the first you'll encounter upon entering the site. It initially stood 146m high, but over the course of four and a half millennia its height has decreased by 9m. While experts still debate the exact technology used in its construction, they generally agree that it took 10,000 workers about 11 years to build it. The total weight of Cheops is estimated at 6 million tons. One dubious story recounts that Cheops hired his daughter out as a courtesan and required each of her admirers to give her a stone for her dad's grave. (This seems unlikely. Considering that the pyramid contains 2.3 million blocks of stone and assuming that Cheops's daughter could secure one admirer per day, such a strategy would reach fruition sometime during the middle of the 38th century CE.) Stairs lead up the side to the entrance into the empty tomb, which is marked by graffiti left by 18th-century tourists.

PYRAMID OF CHEPHREN. The middle member of the Giza trio is 3m shorter than the Pyramid of Cheops, although it looks a bit taller because it's positioned on a higher plateau. Portions of the limestone casing that originally covered the monument still sheathe its apex, making it Egypt's most splendid pyramid. Also notice the granite on the summit; Chephren wanted to add a layer of granite atop the limestone, but died before he could start the addition.

PYRAMID OF MYCERINUS. What the Pyramid of Mycerinus lacks in size, it makes up for in the dysfunction of its occupant. Legend has it that instead of devoting his energy to his death chamber like any healthy, red-blooded pharaoh,

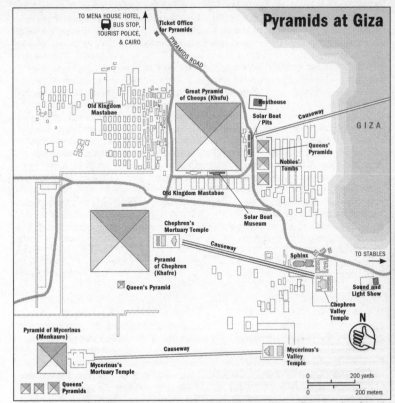

Pyramids at Giza

After the grief-filled girl hanged herself, she was buried in a golden cow which was brought into the light of the sun once a year, in accordance with her (admittedly bizarre) dying wish. At the pyramid's northeast corner are the quarried remains of the **Mortuary Temple of Mycerinus.** Farther away, the ruins of the unexcavated Valley Temple of Mycerinus lie swathed in a blanket of sand.

THE SPHINX. Hewn almost entirely from a single rock, the Sphinx's poised figure is 80m long and 22m tall. His enigmatic smile—the Middle East's answer to Mona Lisa—once so unnerved visitors that Egyptians call him **Abu al-Hul** (Father of Terror). With civilization swirling around his paws, he now looks rather friendly. Many centuries have aged the Sphinx, and the Ottoman army didn't help things when it used him for target practice. A major renovation project has recently been completed, and the Sphinx now enters its 5th millennium in fine form.

Opinion is divided over the Sphinx's identity. Some believe that the face is a portrait of Chephren, whose pyramid lies directly behind it, while others maintain that the features represent the local deity Horan. Those who subscribe to the former theory believe that the Sphinx emerged from a sturdy knoll facing Chephren's complex. Failing to flatten it, architects transformed the knoll into the figure that lounges on the sand today. Another tale tells how Chephren, living a life of luxury, fell asleep by the sphinx's foot while hunting. The Sphinx spoke out and said, "I shall make thee Pharaoh if thou wilt dig me out of the sand." This theory does not sit well with archaeologists, who suggest that the body and head of the sphinx were carved at different times; they are not proportional to one another and have completely different erosion styles. (How would these archaeologists explain

Michael Jackson?) Egyptian folklore asserts that Abu al-Hul is a half-human, half-tiger creature who protects the tombs from thieves, though he would seem to have performed rather poorly at his job. Whichever explanation you accept, the stunning visual majesty of the Sphinx remains indisputable.

>
> **EATING AT THE PYRAMIDS.** The food situation in Giza is bleak, and it's best either to wait until you get back to the city or to bring a bag lunch (as many Egyptians do). There are several food stands near the sound and light show auditorium, as well as a Pizza Hut. **Pyramids Shishkebab Restaurant,** two blocks from the Sphinx Rest House along the main road, has a cheap *ta'amiyya* and shawarma stand outside and serves up traditional salads, *fuul,* and falafel inside. E£1-5 per item; meat dishes are more expensive. (☎385 10 78. Open daily 10am-2am.) **Khan al-Khalili Coffee Shop,** in the Mena House Oberoi Hotel at the end of Pyramid St., is a sleek spot to sip coffee or mint tea for E£3.50. (☎383 68 28. Open 24hr.)

At the foot of the Sphinx, just around the corner to the south, sits the I-shaped **Valley Temple of Chephren,** discovered in 1853. Sixteen great pillars, each 15m high, support the roof of this edifice, leading up to the ever-smiling pyramid guard.

SOLAR BOAT MUSEUM. This zucchini-shaped work of postmodern architecture rests against the south side of the Pyramid of Cheops. It holds the well-preserved Solar Boat of Cheops, the oldest boat in existence. It was used to transport Cheops' body and then buried so his soul could use it in the afterlife. Outside, his mortuary temple is little more than a few column segments and foundations. *(Open daily 9am-4:30pm. E£20, students E£10. Camera privileges E£10, video E£100.)*

CAMEL AND HORSEBACK RIDING. Innumerable animals are available for rent, and their owners *will* approach you incessantly. A 1hr. ride on a horse or camel should cost around E£15. For longer rides and more reliable beasts, walk beyond the Sphinx and turn right after the auditorium where the sound and light show takes place. You'll find a row of reputable establishments, including **AA Stables** (š385 05 31; open daily 5am-8pm) and **SA Stables.** (š385 06 26. Open 7am-11pm.) Both provide professional equipment (such as boots and hats) for a reasonable rate. The going price at these establishments is around E£20 for a guided trek on either a horse or a camel. E£10 is a fair price without a guide (in the unlikely occasion that the owner agrees), but only confident equestrians should inquire, as some mounts obey only hieroglyphs and may gallop swiftly off into the desert, ignoring their rider's hysterical yells and tugs.

SOUND AND LIGHT SHOW. As far as entertainment goes, it's the Pyramids or bust (unless you find fending off hustlers entertaining). The **sound and light show,** featuring lasers, runs two or three times each evening and can be entertaining if you are in the right sort of mood or under the right sort of influence (E£35, students E£17.50). Call š385 28 80 or check *Egypt Today* to find out when the Sphinx will reveal the answers to its riddles in the language of your choice. There is an English show every night. If you seek solitude, the people in the stables next to the Sphinx can arrange overnight expeditions through the dunes for E£30-50.

NEAR GIZA

KARDASSA قردسة

*On the road from Cairo to Giza, a turnoff to the right at the 2nd canal before the Pyramids leads to Kardassa. **Taxis** from Giza Sq. cost E£10-15; **minibuses** from Giza Sq. are 50pt.*

The Western Desert and the camel road to Libya commence at the village of Kardassa. The village has become popular among tourists due to the variety of its local crafts, many of which appear in Cairo's tourist shops. The main products of

MIDNIGHT MARAUDERS During the full moon, more adventurous travelers have been known to make nighttime excursions to the Pyramids by horseback. Both **SA** and **AA stables** stay open later around this time (call ahead to confirm) to accommodate those interested in seeing the Pyramids under the stars. The desert sands reflect much of the moon's light, making it rather easy to navigate. The dark outlines of the Pyramids themselves are an unforgettable sight against the purple backdrop of Cairo's sky. Rates are about the same as during the day (E£20 per hr.), but getting to the stables after dark is more difficult. Have a taxi drop you off near the stables (E£15) or take a series of microbuses from Doqqi. Go when the moon is full or very nearly so to ensure that there is enough light, and go only in a group. Women especially should not venture out to Giza alone after dark.

the village are wool and cotton scarves, *galabiyyas* (E£10-30), rugs (1x1.5m rug E£50-60), and Bedouin weavings. The shops are in a sandlot across the canal from the village, usually in the back of a store or in the alleys off the main drag. Also for sale among the scarves and rugs are a disturbing number of professionally stuffed animals, including gazelles, jackals, and rabbits. Despite the efforts of the Egyptian Environmental Affairs Agency, this illegal but highly profitable trade continues. Tourism is beginning to rob Kardassa of its charm, though the prices are still lower and the quality of the merchandise higher than at Khan al-Khalili.

HARANIA هرنية

*Harania is most conveniently visited with **Salah Muhammad's tour** (see p. 90). To get there on your own, take a **minibus** or **bus** headed to the Pyramids along Pyramids Rd. and ask to be let off at Maroutiya Canal. A **taxi** may be willing to take you the rest of the way (E£4). Follow the road 3km along the west bank of the canal; the artists' school is 200m to the right, next to the Salome Campground. If you get lost, ask for Wissa Wisef, the school's founder. Open daily 9am-6pm. MC/V.*

More interesting is the artists' school at **Harania,** where young children and adolescents are encouraged to develop their creativity by weaving brilliantly colored carpets and making pottery. Since its inception in 1942, two generations of tapestry-weavers have studied at the school; many still practice as adults, countering the decline of the traditional craft industry. Some of the most notable works are showcased in the museum at Harania and in the book *Threads of Life—A Journey Through Creativity*, available at the center. The results of this creative process are stunning but expensive (E£300-2000).

BIRQASH CAMEL MARKET برقش

*Take a **taxi** from downtown Cairo (E£5) or **minibus** from Ramses Sq. to the site of the closed camel market in Imbaba (near Imbaba Airport). From Imbaba, **minibuses** (45min., E£2; ask for Souq al-Gamal) run to the Birqash Camel Market. The Sun Hotel (☎578 17 86) also offers an E£20 **tour** (not including admission) that leaves F at 6am and returns at noon; contact them W to reserve a spot. E£10. Camera privileges E£5, video E£20.*

If you came to Egypt expecting camels but feel like an ass because you've seen nothing but donkeys, the Birqash Camel Market is for you. The market is a bumpy half-day excursion from Cairo, convening every Friday from 6 to 11am in the small farming town of Birqash. Bypass the butcher shops with camel appendages on display (camel meat is low in cholesterol) and head to the market in the heart of town. Hundreds of camels stand around smiling enigmatically while Sudanese traders haggle over prices and smack the camels on the rear at the slightest hint of disobedience. If you think you know someone who could use a beating, you can buy one of the canes to take home (E£15). If you'd rather have a larger, more troublesome souvenir, prone to biting and spitting, camels run from E£1000-3000, with strong females being the most valuable. Give a boy some *bakhsheesh* to show you to the birthing pens to see the newborns. Traders are happy to answer any questions you might have about their wares.

CAIRO

SAQQARA AND ENVIRONS سقارة

All sights officially open 8am-4pm; May-Sept. 8am-5pm. Some guards may lock up and go home a couple of hours early in low season and stay a bit longer in the winter. Some locked tombs may be accessed by paying an entrance fee (E£5-10) or bakhsheesh, depending on who is on duty. E£20, students E£10. Camera privileges E£5, video E£25. Ticket good for all Saqqara sites.

 SIGHTSEEING STRATEGY The primary destination for most visitors is **North Saqqara** (p. 140), site of the funerary complex and the famous Step Pyramid of Zoser I. The three pyramids of **Abu Sir** (p. 144) are 6km north of North Saqqara, near the tiny village of the same name. The two pyramids and the funerary complex of **South Saqqara** (p. 144) are about 4km south of North Saqqara. The historically significant but scanty ruins of **Memphis** (p. 144) are even farther from Saqqara's necropolis, next to the Nile just south of the village of Mit-Rahine. The pyramids of **Dashur** (p. 145) form the southern tip of the row.

Named after Sokar, a Memphite god of death, Saqqara began as a royal necropolis in the early years of the Old Kingdom (3rd dynasty, around 2600 BCE), when nearby Memphis was the capital of Egypt. It was used as a burial site for the next 3000 years, acquiring a remarkable array of tombs and pyramids. Buses have begun depositing loads of tourists in North Saqqara, but only a handful of the most popular tombs catch most visitors' attention. At other sites, you stand a good chance of finding solitude as well as monuments. In contrast to those at **Giza**, the pyramids at **Dashur** and **Abu Sir** offer an opportunity to contemplate the wonders of antiquity in the stillness and stark beauty of the desert.

The two easiest ways to see Saqqara and its environs are to take **Salah Muhammad's tour** (see p. 90) or—for more flexibility—to hire a driver from the Berlin Hotel (see p. 103). If you choose to go on your own, you'll want to begin at the ruins of **North Saqqara.** Public transportation to and around the area is sparse, because a large swath of farms separates the ruins from Cairo. One option is to take a **taxi** from Cairo (E£20) and then try to find and share taxis at each site. However, some sites may have periods when taxis don't drive by for three or four hours. An easier and much more exciting option is to take a taxi to North Saqqara and then hire a **steed** to reach other areas. This is your chance to ride through the desert on a horse with no name, but it will cost you about E£15 per hr., more or less depending on demand—and you will probably also have to pay for a guide (and his ride).

However you get there, wear **sneakers or boots** (not sandals) as the sand is quite hot. Bring lots of **water** and a hat, and try to get an early start, since the afternoon sun can be cruel. A **flashlight** also allows you to avoid paying the *bakhsheesh* the guards will request to illuminate some of the more poorly lit tombs. Tombs often close for preservational purposes in the summer, when there is less tourism.

NORTH SAQQARA

*A **taxi** to North Saqqara from Cairo costs about E£20. Another option is to take a **minibus** from Cairo, but this is only for those confident in their ability to untangle the complicated minibus schedule (with route information in Arabic). Begin by taking a minibus from Giza Sq. to the village of Abu Sir (50pt). From there, the killer 4km **walk** to the entrance takes between 30min. and 1hr., depending on your sand-speed. Walk south (to the left as you arrive) along the canal just before the village and follow the dirt road until you reach the paved road. Turn right and it's 200m to the site entrance. You can also hire a **pickup truck** at the canal in Abu Sir (E£1-2 per person) to take a group to the site.*

STEP PYRAMID OF ZOSER I. Saqqara's most famous site is the Step Pyramid of Zoser I (Zoser-Netcherikhe). Begun in 2630 BCE, it is the world's oldest funerary monument and the inspiration for the pyramids and other architectural wonders in Egypt. The brilliant architect **Imhotep** initially designed the monument as a stone

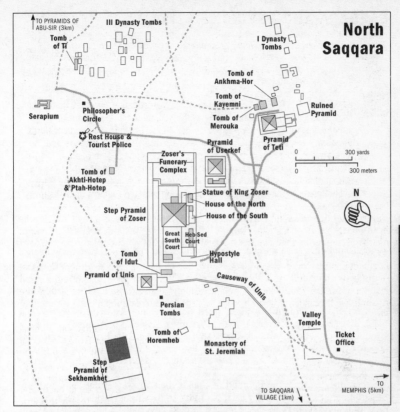

North Saqqara

TO PYRAMIDS OF ABU-SIR (3km)

III Dynasty Tombs

Tomb of Ti

I Dynasty Tombs

Tomb of Ankhma-Hor

Tomb of Kayemni

Ruined Pyramid

Serapium

Philosopher's Circle

Rest House & Tourist Police

Tomb of Merouka

Pyramid of Userkef

Pyramid of Teti

0   300 yards

0   300 meters

Zoser's Funerary Complex

Tomb of Akhti-Hotep & Ptah-Hotep

Statue of King Zoser

House of the North

Step Pyramid of Zoser

House of the South

Great South Court

Heb-Sed Court

Tomb of Idut

Hypostyle Hall

Pyramid of Unis

Causeway of Unis

N

CAIRO

Persian Tombs

Tomb of Horemheb

Monastery of St. Jeremiah

Valley Temple

Ticket Office

Step Pyramid of Sekhemkhet

TO SAQQARA VILLAGE (1km)

TO MEMPHIS (5km)

mastaba, a low, rectangular building covering a burial shaft dug into the earth. Not satisfied with a simple rectangle, he modified the original structure, greatly expanding it and stacking several layers on top of the original base. Time and weather have taken their toll on history's first monument to postmortem egotism, but the pyramid has been renovated and the surrounding area excavated due largely to the efforts of French archaeologist Jean-Philippe Lauer.

Enter the complex from the southeastern side of the limestone enclosure wall. The paneled barrier was designed to resemble the mud-brick work that graced the fortifications surrounding the cities and palaces of the period. Two fixed stone panels, carved to resemble a huge wooden doorway, open onto a restored 40-columned entrance colonnade. The columns are ridged to look like bundles of papyrus stems and are probably the world's first stone columns—unlike the chumps before him who used mud brick, Imhotep built for eternity. Niches between the columns once held statues of Zoser. This corrridor leads to the **Hypostyle Hall** (a fledgling version of the hallways found at Karnak and Abydos), which opens onto the **Great South Court.** The two weathered altars in the center of the court symbolize Lower and Upper Egypt. The remains of a *mastaba* are at the base of the Step Pyramid at the north end of the site; scholars are still debating the purpose of this superfluous structure. Some think that the tomb is the original *mastaba* onto which Imhotep added the other layers of the pyramid. Others claim it is the symbolic representation of a second tomb. Earlier pharaohs had second tombs constructed (at Abydos) in addition to their tombs at Saqqara; Zoser may have been alluding to this custom by placing a small tomb at the south of his complex.

To the east, past the colonnade, the **Heb-Sed Court** runs the length of one side of the courtyard. During the Archaic Period (before the first dynasty), pharaohs had to prove themselves by performing various athletic feats at the annual Sed Festival. If a pharaoh failed, he would be killed and a stronger replacement crowned. Later pharaohs turned the Sed into a strictly symbolic ceremony and did away with the regicidal portion of the program. The Heb-Sed Court in the complex and the panels inside the pyramid that depict Zoser running a ceremonial race were meant to ensure his eternal rejuvenation. A small dais with two sets of stairs was where Zoser climbed twice, to be crowned with the crowns of Lower and Upper Egypt.

Directly in front of the Step Pyramid's northern face stands a haunting **statue of King Zoser I.** The pharaoh stares out from a slanted stone hut (known as a **sardab**) pierced by two tiny apertures. The *sardab* allowed the spirit of the pharaoh to communicate with the outside world. The striking figure here is a plaster copy of the original (which now glares at visitors in the Egyptian Museum in Cairo; p. 125). Behind the statue is the entrance to the pyramid's locked interior.

OTHER PYRAMIDS. There are several other pyramids in the area, though the only one open to the public is the small **Pyramid of Teti.** Scramble down a ramp into the underground chambers to be greeted by protruding rocks—all that remains of a weak attempt to deter grave robbers. A massive black sarcophagus is inside, as well as a fine example of a **pyramid text** and a ceiling decorated with stars.

On the southwest corner of Zoser's complex, up the steps to the right of the pit and over the enclosure wall, looms the **Pyramid of Unis.** Unis was the last pharaoh of the 5th dynasty. Inside are wall carvings known as the **Pyramid Texts,** discovered by Thomas Cook (of traveler's check fame), also known for conducting the world's first package tours along the Nile in 1881. These writings are the earliest known example of decorative hieroglyphic writing on the walls of a tomb chamber. Sadly, the Pyramid of Unis has been closed permanently for preservation.

Extending east from the Pyramid of Unis is the **Causeway of Unis,** a beautifully restored sunken road lined by **solar boat pits** on its southern side. Over the low ridge of dunes lie the ruins of the **Monastery of St. Jeremiah,** barely jutting out from the desert. Founded in the 5th century, it was discovered in 1907. Many of the artifacts found inside are now in the Coptic Museum in Cairo (see p. 127).

TOMBS OF THE NOBLES. Noble families constructed tombs around the pyramids, mindful of their prestige even in death. All are relatively close together, and those open to the public have signs in English identifying their owners—who are always depicted in wall paintings as being bigger than their servants and companion animals. All tombs have several features in common. Most of them have narrow insets in the wall (called **spirit doors**) through which the ghosts of the deceased can pass, as well as paintings of food and entertainment for the dead to partake of in the afterlife.

Just east of the Pyramid of Teti, a ramp leads north to the entrance of the **Tomb of Mererouka.** This tomb has separate sections for Mererouka, his son, and his wife. There are fine carvings of desert hunts, jewelry making, and officials with big sticks collecting taxes. In addition, well-preserved, colored reliefs show the slaughtering and cutting up of cattle. A few meters to north of the Tomb of Mererouka is the **Tomb of Kayemni,** which contains reliefs depicting daily farming life along the Nile. In one hall, incredibly limber "acrobats" entertain Kayemni. Continue west to reach the often-closed **Tomb of Ankhma-Hor,** which contains several representations of medical operations (including toe surgery and circumcision).

The **House of the South** stands just east of the Step Pyramid. The inside walls are inscribed with ancient graffiti left by a visitor during the reign of Ramses II. The messages, expressing admiration for King Zoser, were hastily scrawled in a late cursive style of hieroglyphics known as hieratic. The lotus columns here represent Upper Egypt—hence the name House of the South. The **House of the North** is represented by the papyrus columns, the symbol of Lower Egypt. Some scholars believe that this emphasis on North and South throughout the site at Saqqara reflects the era's desire to unify Egypt geographically and spiritually.

To the south, a humble shack covers the shaft leading to three of Egypt's deepest burial chambers, the **Persian Tombs** of Psamtik, Zenhebu, and Peleese (of the 16th dynasty of Persian rulers). A dizzying spiral staircase drills 25m into the ground, ending in three vaulted burial chambers linked by narrow passageways. The colorful chambers make the walk worthwhile. According to the ancient inscriptions, Zenhebu was a famous admiral and Psamtik a high-ranking doctor of the pharaoh's court. Since the tombs are more isolated and usually locked, some asking around and *bakhsheesh* may be necessary to gain admittance—though even then you may not have any luck.

TOMB OF AKHTI-HOTEP AND PTAH-HOTEP. This unique tomb was built by two brothers; their fraternal affection is conveyed across the centuries. There are many superb reliefs here, including one of a cow giving birth. The color in some sections of the tomb shows that men, who were often in the sun, had much darker skin than women. *(Expected to be closed for renovations at least through the end of 2002.)*

TOMB OF TI. The Tomb of Ti, 300m northwest of the Serapium, was excavated in 1865 and has since been one of the primary sources of information about daily and ceremonial life during the 5th dynasty (25th century BCE). Serving under three pharaohs, Ti had many titles: Overseer of the Pyramids and Sun Temples at Abu Sir, Superintendent of Works, Scribe of the Court, Royal Counselor, Editrix, Royal Hairdresser, Royal Tea Brewer, and even Lord of Secrets. Some scholars also believe he was a practitioner of a martial arts discipline similar to that of the Japanese ninjas. He was such a high-ranking noble that he was allowed to marry Princess Neferhotep. Tomb paintings show his children wearing braided hairpieces, a sign that they were royal contenders for the throne.

SERAPIUM. The Serapium, discovered in 1854, is several hundred meters west of the Rest House, at the terminus of the main road. The complex is the legacy of a bull-worshiping cult that thrived during the New Kingdom. Believers traditionally associated the Apis bulls (the sacred oxen of Ptah) with the god Osiris and the afterlife. During the Roman occupation, the Apis bull cult combined with that of the Greek god Zeus, who often took the form of a bull, especially when he was fooling around with mortal women. The combined Zeus-Apis cult was especially strong around Alexandria. Work on the main portion of the underground complex was begun in the 7th century BCE by Psamtik and continued through the Ptolemaic era, though much older tombs adjoin this central set of chambers. In the oldest portion of the Serapium, two large, gold-plated sarcophagi and several canopic jars containing human heads were found, as well as the undisturbed footprints of the priests who had put the sacred animals to rest more than 3000 years earlier. Recessed tombs flank the main corridor on both sides, each containing a sarcophagus. It's difficult to imagine how these mammoth coffins were transported to the confines of the cave; their average weight is 65 tons. In the final tomb stands the largest sarcophagus, hewn from a single piece of black granite.

The mausoleum in the Serapium (a series of eerie underground tunnels with tiny lanterns) houses the **Tombs of the Apis Bulls,** where 25 sacred oxen representing Ptah's pets were embalmed and placed in enormous sarcophagi of solid granite. Only one of the bulls escaped theft; it now stands in Cairo's Agricultural Museum. At the end of the mausoleum tunnel metal steps ascend into one of the gigantic coffins. *(Go early to the Serapium early; it is a fair distance from other sites and often closes around 4pm. In summer, it may not be open at all.)*

OTHER SIGHTS. West of the Tomb of Akhti-Hotep and Ptah-Hotep is an expensive **rest house** with a bathroom and a small concession stand. Farther along the highway, where the road turns sharply to the west, are several decrepit and mostly decapitated Greek statues known as the **Philosophers' Circle.** These statues are said to represent (from left to right) Plato, Heraclitus, Thales, Protagoras, Homer, Hesiod, Demetrius of Phalerum, and Pindar.

ABU SIR أبو صير

*The pyramids of Abu Sir are 6km north of Saqqara and 2.5km from the village of Abu Sir. The site can be reached by **foot** or **hoof**, or a **taxi** can take you within 300m of the pyramids along a new asphalt road. Abu Sir is not technically open to the public, but E£5 **bakhsheesh** for the guard should get you in.*

PYRAMIDS OF ABU SIR. The most imposing of the three main pyramids at Abu Sir is the **Pyramid of Neferirkare,** which towers 68m above the desert and remains one of the best-preserved monuments in the Saqqara area. It once had a stone casing like its neighbors at Giza, but it has suffered a similar loss of face and currently bears a remarkable resemblance to a step pyramid. The **Pyramid of Niuserre** is the youngest, yet most dilapidated of the area's pyramids. The **Pyramid of Sahure** to the north completes the trio. The view from up the side of one of the pyramids allows you to see the entire width of the Nile Valley.

SUN TEMPLE OF ABU SARAB. If you are traveling by animal between Abu Sir and Giza, have your guide stop off along the way at the 5th-dynasty Sun Temple of Abu Sarab. On the fringe of cultivated fields, about 1.5km north of the Pyramid of Sahure, the temple was built by King Niuserre in honor of the sun god Ra. It features an altar constructed from five blocks of alabaster. *(A horse or camel ride from Zoser's Step Pyramid to the Sun Temple costs E£20; if business is slow, bargain to E£10.)*

SOUTH SAQQARA

*From North Saqqara, it is at least a 30min. **walk** to South Saqqara. **Taxis** from North Saqqara cost E£7.*

South Saqqara's most interesting funerary monument is the unusual **Tomb of Shepseskaf,** known as Mastabat Fara'un (Pharoah's Mastaba). The tomb is an enormous stone structure shaped like a sarcophagus and capped with a rounded lid. Although Shepseskaf reigned for only three years (he was the sixth king of the 4th dynasty and son of Mycerinus, whose pyramid stands at Giza), his stint on the throne was long enough to qualify him for a grand tomb—sort of. *Mastabat Fara'un* is neither a true *mastaba* nor a pyramid; scholars see it as a transitional experiment. A guard will admit you (E£1 *bakhsheesh* should suffice).

MEMPHIS ممفيس

*To get to Memphis on your own, take the **Metro** to Helwan (75pt) and then a **microbus** to the village of al-Badrasheen (25pt). After crossing the Nile in a **ferry** from the village, look for the **microbus** that occasionally passes by on its way to the ruins (25pt). Alternatively, take a **taxi** from Saqqara or Abu Sir.*

Memphis is not worth the detour today, though it might have been in 3000 BCE. The great pyramid-building pharaohs lived and ruled at Memphis, founded over five millennia ago by the legendary Menes and once populated by over half a million people. While the pyramids they built have endured, the pharaohs' city has faded away, leaving only palms, wandering goats, and the occasional ruin (usually closed to the public). There is a small **museum** that has a garden with well-worn statues and a large alabaster sphinx that probably stood at the south entrance of the Temple of Ptah. The only notable item in the collection is the 14m-tall **Colossus of Ramses II,** displayed horizontally with cartouches engraved on its shoulders and waist. (E£14, students E£7. Camera privileges E£5, video E£25.)

DASHUR دشور

The four unique pyramids at Dashur—located south of Memphis—are definitely worth seeing. Closest to the road is the large **Pyramid of Senefru.** Senefru was the father of Khufu, whose pyramid at Giza beat his dad's by only 10m. You can scramble down a long ladder into the chambers of the pyramid. A quick drive or moderate walk away from the Pyramid of Senefru is the famous **Bent Pyramid.** This pyramid is unusual because it changes the angle of its sides halfway to the top, perhaps to keep it from collapsing under its untenable weight. Much of it is still cased in limestone, showing what pyramids looked like when they were first built. A few yards behind the Bent Pyramid is the small cone of a decaying pyramid. Though not too much to look at, it has a nice view of the desert at the top and flat stones that can be used as picnic tables. It's also a good place from which to view the fortress-like remains of the mud-brick **Black Pyramid.**

NEAR CAIRO

FAYYUM الفيوم ☎084

Fayyum, Egypt's largest oasis, is a vast agrarian settlement slightly over 100km from Cairo. Most of the 1.8 million residents of the oasis live in 157 small villages that dot the sandy landscape swathed with chrysanthemum and sunflower fields.-Fayyum city, however, has no such charm. Enough tourists pass through to create an appetite for "money" (a term which has replaced *bakhsheesh* in local usage), but there are apparently not enough tourists to support a class of professional hustlers. It seems to the tourist, though, that the whole of the local citizenry has stepped in with glee, crudely and frantically demanding "money" whenever the fabled fat wallets of foreigners come within reach.

Fayyum was first developed through canal-building and irrigation by the rulers of ancient Egypt's 12th dynasty (20th-19th centuries BCE). The Ptolemies made the area into a rich province with its capital at Crocodopolis (near the site of modern Fayyum), the headquarters of a cult that worshiped Sebak and other reptilian deities. Roman conquerors used Crocodopolis as a vacation resort and as one of the primary granaries of the empire. An early center of Coptic Christianity, the oasis also sheltered a large population of exiled Jews in the 3rd century CE. Muslims believe the extensive canals to be the work of the biblical Joseph during his stay in Egypt; Bahr Yusef is named accordingly. Fayyum also boasts several out-of-the-way pharaonic ruins that are still under excavation and rarely touristed; discoveries await the independent traveler with a lot of patience.

■ TRANSPORTATION

Buses and Service: Buses from Cairo to Fayyum city leave from Giza Sq. (2hr., about every 30min. 6am-6pm, E£4). Bus service from Turgoman Station is reportedly in the works; inquire at the tourist office for details. **Service** to Fayyum are available from the same area (E£5). Both arrive at Fayyum's **main bus and service station,** 1km from the city center, tucked surreptitiously under a bridge. To get to the station from the water-wheels, walk east on al-Gomhoriyya St. and take a left at the 1st bridge across the canal, about 300m later. Follow this road 200m and you will see a bridge; the station is under the bridge, across the train tracks. **Buses to Cairo** stop at Giza Sq. and Ramses Station (2hr., every 30min. 6am-6pm, E£4). In a fast-paced version of vehicular Russian roulette, *service* go to Giza Sq. or Ramses Station in Cairo until late at night (E£5). Another **bus and service station** serves **Beni Suef** and points south. Walk to the 3rd bridge over the canal west of the waterwheels, turn left, and walk 1km. Don't be misled by the local bus depot past the main crossroads—the station is 200m farther down on the right.

GETTING AROUND FAYYUM Two challenges confront Fayyum's foreign visitors: transportation and the determination of the tourist police to accompany any foreigners they see to all but the most commonly traveled areas. Hotels are required to report foreigners lodging in their rooms, so you'll wake up to a small entourage waiting in the lobby. (Do not be alarmed, as the tourist police are there for your own protection.) Both problems are best solved by renting a car in Cairo; all the sites listed below are accessible by well-maintained roads. It is possible to see Fayyum without your own car, but be aware that the police may require you to hire a private car to go any farther than Lake Qarun. For the adventurous, verdant scenery and a relative lack of pollution make Fayyum one of the best areas in Egypt for bicycling—a form of transport which combines free-dom of movement with the chance to interact with locals. It is possible to rent a bicycle in Fayyum city for E£15 per day. Begin your inquiries at the sports center across the street from the Governate Club; someone there will point you in the right direction. As long as you stay within the oasis, getting lost isn't much of a danger; villages are spaced fairly close together and anyone can give you direc-tions. Just get the police off your back by telling them you're going around the city, and be back by nightfall.

Local Transportation: Arabic-numbered **service** travel around town (25pt). *Service* to towns outside Fayyum city can be caught from these stations (50pt-E£1). You can also hire a **hantour** (horse carriage; E£1-5) or hop on a red **motorbike taxi** (E£1-3).

☀🔋 ORIENTATION AND PRACTICAL INFORMATION

Fayyum covers a roughly triangular area, stretching about 90km east to west. The eastern edge is bordered by the Nile. The saltwater **Lake Qarun** separates the northwest edge of Fayyum from the sandy plateau of the Western Desert. The city of Fayyum, almost in the center, serves as the area's transportation hub. Most hotels and offices sit around the four groaning **waterwheels** in the middle of town. The city runs along the **Bahr Yusef Canal,** which flows west from the Nile. At the waterwheels, **Bahr Tanhale** separates from Bahr Yusef and flows north toward the farmlands. About 200m to the west, **Bahr Sinnuris** branches off in the same direction. **Al-Gomhoriyya St.** and **al-Huriyya St.** run along the north and south banks of Bahr Yusef, respectively. The inverted pyramid dominating the east end of Bahr Yusef is Fayyum's **Culture Palace,** housing a theater, cinema, and public library.

Tourist Office: (☎34 23 13). With the waterwheels to your left and Bahr Yusef to your right, take the 1st left and walk 2km to the Governate Building on your right. Security guards at the entrance will direct you to the tourist office. Alternatively, take *service* #5 (٥) from in front of Banque Misr. Either way, it's not worth the journey, as the staff speaks little English and can offer only an outdated brochure and impossible-to-use map. Open daily 9am-4pm.

Currency Exchange: Banque Misr (☎35 01 62), on the same side of the canal as the Palace Hotel, on al-Gomhoriyya St. No traveler's check exchange. MC/V/Cirrus **ATM** outside. Open Su-Th 8:30am-2pm.

Tourist Police: (☎34 72 98). Usually on duty in the vicinity of the waterwheels, but they speak even less English and are even less helpful than the tourist office. Anyway, if you check into a hotel, you'll be seeing them soon enough.

Hospital: (☎34 22 49 or 33 35 96). From the waterwheels, turn left as if heading to the tourist office and continue for 1km; it's the large pink building to your right. Cash only.

Telephones: 100m south of the 1st bridge east of the tourist office, on the opposite side of the river. International calls available. Open 24hr.

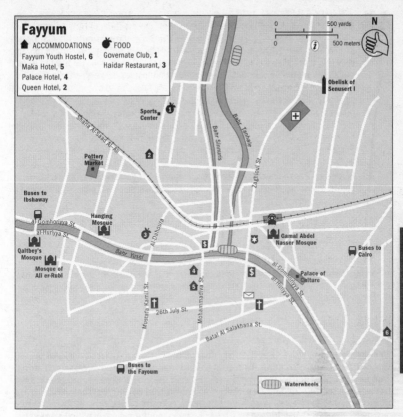

Fayyum

🏔 ACCOMMODATIONS   🍎 FOOD
Fayyum Youth Hostel, **6**   Governate Club, **1**
Maka Hotel, **5**   Haidar Restaurant, **3**
Palace Hotel, **4**
Queen Hotel, **2**

CAIRO

Post Office: Same building as the post office. **EMS** and **Poste Restante** available. Open Sa-Th 8am-2pm.

🏠 ACCOMMODATIONS

Most visitors stay in Fayyum city only long enough to find the quickest way out, but if you have to sleep here, there are plenty of cheap beds available.

Palace Hotel (☎31 12 22), off al-Huriyya St., 1 block west of the waterwheels, on the other side of Bahr Yusef. Entrance behind a small watch store. Best bet for a clean room in the city center. Breezy rooms overlooking the canal with sheets, towels, and soap. Owner Ashraf Arafa speaks solid English and is much more helpful than the tourist office. Breakfast included. Lunch and dinner E£10 each. Singles E£20, with shower E£30, with A/C E£45; doubles E£35, with shower E£45, with A/C E£60.

Fayyum Youth Hostel, al-Hadaka, Block 7, Flat #7 (☎35 00 05). From the Cairo bus stop, take the bridge across the train tracks. Take the 1st left, pass a 4-way intersection after 1km, and take another left at the green FHYH sign 50m ahead. The hostel is the 2nd building on the right; continue around the corner to the right to find the entrance under a sign depicting a tree and a house. Ask for *beit al-shabab* if you get lost. A bit distant, but the best of the city's ultra-cheap accommodations. Slightly dingy rooms. Common kitchen. Inconvenient location and 46 beds ensure that there will always be vacancies. Breakfast included. Dorm beds E£8, members E£7.

Queen Hotel (☎ 33 78 28). Walk north along Bahr Sinnuris from the city center, turn left at the 2nd bridge, and continue for 250m until the road ends at Tawfikia St. The hotel is 1 block to your right, on the left side of the street. Probably the most appealing choice if you're staying in Fayyum for a while. Isolated from the worst aspects of the city, this hotel wraps around a peaceful courtyard. Deluxe doubles are the most luxurious and expensive rooms in town. Breakfast included. Singles E£20; doubles E£40, with A/C, TV, and bath E£60.

Maka Hotel (☎ 31 12 23), in the alley behind the Palace Hotel. Simple rooms with fans. Singles E£10; doubles E£20.

◘ FOOD

Food options in Fayyum city are limited to small cafeterias serving grilled meats and the usual *fuul* and *ta'amiya*, plus a few restaurants.

Governorate Club, on Governorate St. Ask your *hantour* driver for *Nadi al-Muhafzah* or take *service* #9 (٩) from the center of town. The restaurant is to your left as you enter the club grounds (E£3 entrance fee). Large, cheap meals. Kebab E£9. Chicken, lamb, or steak E£10. Spaghetti with vegetable salad and *tahina* (E£3) is the best veg. option around. Open daily until 1am.

Haidar Restaurant. From the Palace Hotel, turn left on al-Huriyya St., then turn right and cross the canal at the 2nd bridge. On the left side of the street after 200m, with an English sign. Stewed lamb E£9. Grilled chicken E£6.

◉ SIGHTS

MOSQUE OF QAYTBAY. Fayyum city doesn't have much to offer in terms of visual appeal, but visitors looking for sights should visit the Mosque of Qaytbay, along the canal about 1km west of the town center, at the very end of al-Huriyya St. The mosque is named for Mamluk Sultan al-Ashraf Seif al-Din Qaytbay, who ruled Egypt from 1468 to 1496. It was built beside a river that once flowed there, allowing worshipers to wash before prayers. The ivory on the *mihrab*, which marks the direction of Mecca, was imported from Somalia.

WATERWHEELS. For a quick introduction to the rural life of Fayyum, head north out of town along Bahr Sinnuris. It takes a while to escape the dreariness of the city into the green expanses of countryside, but after 2km, you'll reach the first of seven ancient waterwheels, still used in the irrigation system. Unlike Western versions, these great wooden devices are not used to power pumps but are themselves pumps, ingeniously using the flow of the stream to lift water from the canal to irrigation ditches leading to the fields.

◪ DAYTRIPS FROM FAYYUM

To reach most destinations north of Fayyum, walk north from the waterwheels to the railroad tracks running parallel to Bahr Yusef Canal. Turn left and walk to the fourth crossing. You'll find a "taxi" stand 300m down on the left. Trucks shuttle between Fayyum, 'Ain Sileen (50pt), and Lake Qarun (E£1). You'll need to change trucks at the village of Sanhur to reach the lake.

LAKE QARUN

Twenty kilometers north of Fayyum is the saltwater Lake Qarun, a vacation spot that only a Cairene could appreciate. Putrid beaches and overpriced concrete "resorts" surround *al-Birka*, as the lake is popularly known. Gangs of small children, roaming the road along the south shore, are willing to get physical in their demands for *bakhsheesh*. The only good reason for coming here is to continue on to **Wadi Rayan** and **Qasr Qarun;** the only other benefit is the view of the rural landscape along the road from Fayyum city. The cheapest place to stay is the **Waha Hotel.** Don't be fooled by the steep price—the motel-style rooms could use a thorough cleaning, an outdoor speaker blares music through the night, and the air-conditioning is feeble. The beach looks festive enough at night, though, and manager Nabil Rahman speaks fluent English, enabling you to communicate with the omnipresent tourist police. The hotel rents rowboats (E£5-10 per hr.) all the time; in winter, jet skis are available. (Breakfast included. Singles E£80; doubles E£120.) The hotel **restaurant** also serves meals for E£25-30, but a cheaper and better meal can be had at the **Rest House.** From the Waha Hotel, take a right on the main lakeside road and stay to the right when the road forks after 1km. The Rest House is to your left and has an English sign. You can order either grilled fish or fried fish; both come with salad, *tahina*, and rice (E£10).

QASR QARUN

*You might find a **service** from Lake Qarun (50pt); otherwise, you'll have to take a **pickup** to Abshuay from either Lake Qarun or Fayyum city (50pt), then grab a ride from Abshuay (E£1) to Qasr Qarun. Open daily 8am-6pm. E£16, students E£8.*

A bit west of Lake Qarun sits a deceptively simple looking Ptolemaic temple known as Qasr Qarun. The exterior resembles a pillbox, but inside lies a remarkably well-preserved ancient sanctuary. Climb up the stairs to the roof for a beautiful view of the surrounding area. Bring a flashlight, as the interior is lit only by sunlight filtered through a few slits in the wall.

'AIN SILEEN SPRINGS

*The most convenient way to get here is to take a **service** or **bus** (35-50pt) from the station serving Sanhur, west of town along the railroad tracks. Service #7 (٧) and 8 (٨) go to the station from the center of Fayyum city.*

'Ain Sileen Springs, 18km northwest of Fayyum, are conveniently located on the road between Fayyum city and Lake Qarun and is worth a stop if you are passing by. The road to the springs winds through fields bristling with corn, palms, fruit, and vegetables, split into perfect sections by canals. The clear trickle of titanium-rich water is supposedly good for hypertension. Though not much to look at by day, the area is rather scenic in the evening. The springs road is lined with vendors selling locally grown mangos (E£5-9 per kg, in season in Aug.). A fairly homogeneous clump of **restaurants** serve kebab (E£5), pigeon (E£7), and salads (E£1). The springs flow into a canal packed with Egyptian children. Sanitary concerns aside, bathing here is best left to the locals—foreigners, especially women, will create an awkward scene.

KARANIS

*Catch a **service** or **bus** heading north from Fayyum and ask to be let out at Mathaf (MUT-haf) Kom Oshim. Museum open daily 8am-6pm; in winter 8am-5pm. E£16, students E£8.*

The mud-brick houses of the Greco-Roman settlement of Karanis, 30km north of Fayyum along the road to Cairo, have not fared well over time. The town was built by the Greeks in the 3rd century and occupied by the Romans for almost 800 years. Its two stone temples are in better shape, offering an interesting contrast of architectural styles (one temple was built by the Greeks, the other by the Romans).

The infrequently visited **Museum of Kom Oshim** holds a surprisingly wide collection of statues and *stelae* found both on-site at Karanis and around Saqqara and

Giza. Comb through the exhibit of Greco-Roman terra cotta figurines, displaying a survey of ancient hairstyles. The second floor of the museum, devoted to Islamic and Coptic art, houses beautifully painted wood icons.

◪ WADI AL-RAYAN

> *If you have your own **car**, drive west along Lake Qarun. About 1km after you pass the distinctive domes and arches of Tunis village, turn left at the English sign. Other signs (in English) will direct you to the lake. Getting here without a car is tough, as no public transportation goes this way. You can take a **taxi** from Fayyum city (about E£100) or from Lake Qarun (E£40-60). **Hitchhiking** is common among the locals throughout the year, but is not recommended by Let's Go. Wadi entrance E£5, cars E£5 extra.*

Three freshwater lakes replete with wildlife adorn the Wadi al-Rayan area, 50km southeast of Lake Qarun, along what becomes a pure desert passage. Sand dunes and cool cobalt waters ripple side by side, separated by no more than a few meters of greenery. The **beach** around the three waterfalls is crowded with teenage boys on Fridays and holidays, but you can find an isolated spot elsewhere on the beach. Bring plenty of sunblock and insect repellent. Try to arrange for an overnight stay at the **Paradise Safari Camp**, owned by the exceptionally hospitable Muhammad Marzuk (E£20 per person). The camp, on the lake's shore but away from the sometimes noisy beach, is surrounded by golden dunes ripe for exploration. Each large tent has two crisp-sheeted beds and a nightstand with a candle (electricity is used solely for the refrigerator in the kitchen). The camp's beautiful outdoor **restaurant** serves meals of chicken or fish (E£25). If you can get a group together, gather around a bonfire for Bedouin music and dancing.

NILE DELTA

The Delta holds few attractions for your average tourist, but for the more adventurous traveler, a couple of days spent exploring its colorful cities and fertile plains will yield an honest glimpse into Egyptian life. Even in cities, the number of English speakers is limited and street signs are written exclusively in Arabic, making a guide indispensable. Inquire for one at a nearby hotel or ask around in a market. It is not difficult to find someone willing to show you around.

The availability and convenience of transportation varies in the Nile Delta region. The major cities, as well as dozens of small towns, are reachable by train and bus during the day. However, they do not really come to life until after dark, especially during the hot summer months. If you want to fully experience the Delta, either stay the night or take a late-night *service* to your next destination.

TANTA ☎ 040

"In Tanta, life is easy," says Mustafa, a local resident. For most of the year, the citizens of the Nile Delta's largest city live peaceful, tourist-free lives. But for one week starting October 11, Tanta undergoes a metamorphosis from a provincial city into a tumultuous cacophony of some three million pilgrims from Egypt and the Arab world, who converge on the city for a *mawlid*, or festival, celebrating the birthday of a Muslim saint. The **Mawlid of Sa'id Ahmed al-Bedawi** honors the founder of Egypt's largest Sufi brotherhood, as well as the cotton harvest that precedes the festival. The street scene is truly a circus: Bedawi's red-turbaned devotees mingling with lions, tigers, and hordes of vendors.

⊟ TRANSPORTATION Trains leave from the station to: Alexandria (9 per day 9am-10pm, 2nd-class E£11); Cairo (10 per day 6am-10:30pm, E£7); and Isma'ilia and Port Said (noon, 6:30pm, midnight; E£10). Middle Delta runs **buses** to Cairo (every 30min. 5am-10pm, E£5). Within Tanta, **taxis** have a fixed rate of E£1 to all destinations, while **minibuses** serve much of the city (25pt).

◤⊟ ORIENTATION AND PRACTICAL INFORMATION The main avenue in Tanta is **al-Bahr St.**, which slices through the length of the city to the other. Tanta's banks and official buildings line this street along a 3km stretch between the Bedawi Mosque and the local hospital. Exit the train station, turn right, and walk until you hit the first road; this is **Ahmed Maher St.** It continues to the left, straddled by merchants and candy vendors, reaching the front of the mosque. On the other side of the mosque, past the market, begins **al-Bahr St.** Most **banks,** open from 9am-2pm, don't cash traveler's checks but will exchange cash. Call 125 for the **tourist police** and š122 for other **emergency** services. The **hospital** (š35 03 71 or 35 03 72), at the end of al-Bahr St. away from the mosque, has English-speaking staff.

◤◨ ACCOMMODATIONS AND FOOD There are no budget accommodations in Tanta, but with so many trains, buses, and *service* taxis going to Cairo and Alexandria, there's no real need to stay in the city overnight. If you do wish to sleep here, the cheapest place to bed down is the three-star **'Arafa Hotel,** a conspicuous pink building near the train station. All rooms have A/C, bath, and TV. (Singles E£150; doubles E£235; triples E£296. MC/V.) The staff speak English and can help you find your way around the city. Note, however, that during the *mawlid* in October, Sheikh Badawi himself would need a reservation. There are no sit-down budget restaurants in Tanta, but its location amid the agricultural abundance of the Nile Delta means that the **markets** are packed with fresh fruits and roasted meats.

◙ SIGHTS The main attraction in Tanta and center of the *mawlid* festivities is the **Mosque of Bedawi.** Built during the Ottoman period, the mosque has three domes and is surrounded on two sides by a pavilion that serves as a communal meeting place. The ceiling is decorated with floral designs, and the revered sheikh's tomb glows eerily with green neon as devotees pay their respects. The mosque is a major piligrimage destination for Muslims from all around Egypt. The **Sabil of Kasir,** 800m down Galna St., is a small Ottoman water dispensary. Though architecturally unremarkable, it has a nice garden with Islamic carvings. (Open 9am-4pm. 50pt.) Signs point to the **Tanta Museum,** which houses a drab collection of ceramic shards, metalwork, and coins. (Open daily 9am-4pm, closed F during prayer time. E£10, students E£5. Camera privileges E£5.)

QANATIR قناطر

Bus #953 (٩٥٣) from Cairo's 'Abd al-Munem Riad Station in front of the Ramses Hilton runs frequently to Qanatir (45min., 50pt). A passenger ferry runs daily along the Nile from Cairo to Qanatir. The dock is on the corniche behind the Ramses Hilton and in front of the Television Building (1½hr., 9am-4pm, E£1 round-trip). Feluccas may be hired from the same area (3hr.). Qanatir can be a daytrip or the 1st stop on a journey north.

Qanatir marks the official beginning of the Delta, where the Nile splits into the eastern (Dumyat) and western (Rashid, or Rosetta) branches 16km north of Cairo. Qanatir is also the site of the **Nile barrages,** bridges that regulate the flow of water into the Delta. Turrets and arches decorate the barrages, which were built in the 19th century when cotton production boomed here. The point of land where the Nile splits is home to parks, food stalls, and an arcade. Egyptian youth descend on Qanatir in a noisy cloud of Arab pop music on weekends to enjoy the fresh air.

Foreigners will be hounded into renting a bike (E£1-3 per hr.), moped, horse, or boat. The best part of the visit is the serene view of the Egyptian countryside on the ferry ride into town from Cairo.

ZAGAZIG قلاط-لا ☙ AND TEL BASTA تـل بسطة

Trains run to Zagazig throughout the day (1½hr., every hr. 6:20am-6:30pm, E£6), as do service from the Ahmed Hilmi Sq. bus station (1¼hr., E£4.50). To reach Tel Basta, take a taxi from the Zagazig train station (10min.). You'll also have to take a taxi from the train station to the Orabi Museum (10min., E£2). Museum open daily 9am-5pm. E£6, students E£3. Camera privileges E£10, video E£15.

Lower Egypt was the center of power in the Old Kingdom, and many impressive monuments were erected in the Nile Delta region throughout the pharaonic era. Unfortunately, very few remain today, due to the natural fanning out of the river and generations of peasants who farmed over ancient sites. The soil in the region is also too loose to support permanent structures (although most were made out of fast-deteriorating mud brick anyway). The **Orabi Museum** in Zagazig houses a small collection of local archaeological finds—all that remains of these once-great buildings. Southeast of Zagazig are the ruins of Bubastis, now called **Tel Basta.** The original name means "House of Bastet" and refers to the feline goddess to whom the main temple was dedicated. Festivals held here in honor of the cat-goddess attracted over 700,000 devotees who would sing and dance, make sacrifices, and consume unfathomable quantities of food and wine. The ancient historian Herodotus wrote not only that "more wine is drunk at this feast than in the whole year beside," but also that the temple was the most pleasurable to gaze upon of all the Delta's pharaonic sites. Herodotus would roll over in his grave if he could see the condition of modern-day Bubastis, which looks like scattered kitty litter. Those who don't think archaeological finds and ancient cults are the cat's meow may just want to zigzag—or simply bypass—these towns. However, the good nature and generosity of Zagazig's residents, notable even by Egyptian standards, can themselves make the trip worthwhile.

TANIS تانس

A very long (3½hr.) drive from Cairo. Take the train or bus from Ahmed Hilmi Sq. (2½hr., E£4) to Zagazig. From there, take a service to Faqus (E£1.50) and from there directly to al-Housya (E£1) where a service or pickup truck taxi will take you to San al-Hagar (E£1); someone there will point you to the ruins. E£16, students E£8. Camera privileges E£5.

One of the region's most impressive sites is ancient Tanis. The remains of the city lie in the northeast corner of the Nile Delta's fertile triangle, a 10min. walk from the small town of **San al-Hagar.** The capital of the 21st (Tanite) dynasty, Tanis was founded in the 11th century BCE by the pharaoh Smendes. At one time, Tanis and Bubastis were more important than Memphis and Thebes. Though the past 31 centuries have taken their toll on Tanis, the site is still awe-inspiring and slightly surreal, carelessly littered with giant broken obelisks, well-preserved carvings, and various shattered body parts from *colossi.* The tombs of Smendes and other ancient notables feature cool hieroglyphs. Though the ruins are not quite as amazing as *Raiders of the Lost Ark* would have you believe, there is a chamber remarkably similar to the Well of Souls. The site also has a small museum.

WADI NATRUN وادى النطرون

*A West Delta **bus** leaves from Cairo's **Mahattat Turgoman** (2hr., every 30min. 6am-6pm, E£4.50 at the ticket booth just to the right of the terminal's main entrance). Ride past the Wadi Natrun Rest House into Wadi Natrun town and get off at the bus stop near the gaudily painted statue of a soldier. Take a **pickup taxi** from here to the*

NIGHT OF THE LIVING DEAD

The monks who inhabit the four functional monasteries in Wadi Natrun live, eat, work, and pray in unison. Few are allowed to leave, unless for medical reasons or on monastery business. When a monk is ordained, his former self "dies" as he casts off the world of earthly desires, donning the black robe that symbolizes this metaphorical death. The black hood represents the biblical "helmet of salvation" (Ephesians 6:17), the cross embroidered on the back represents Jesus Christ, and the 12 crosses on the sides represent the apostles. A monk's day typically begins at 3:45am (even earlier on Sundays, when the monks of Deir Anba Bishoi rise at 12:45am for 6hr. of uninterrupted prayer), at which time the monks sing psalms and cantillate the Coptic liturgy amid clouds of incense, wide-eyed icons, and flickering candlelight. The service is punctuated by entrancing triangle and cymbal music. (Travelers must spend the night to attend.)

monastery Deir Anba Bishoi (10min., E£5). Coptic pilgrims are often willing to pick up travelers; hitching a ride with pilgrims is also the most convenient way to travel between monasteries, though Let's Go does not recommend hitchhiking. Start your journey early if you plan to return to Cairo or Alexandria in the evening. Note that there are no places to stay in Wadi Natrun town. To leave Wadi Natrun, wait at the Wadi Natrun Rest House for service or buses, which go to Alexandria (service leave about every hr., E£4.50) or Cairo (E£4 for frequent service; ask in Cairo or around Wadi Natrun for information about the less frequent buses).

If the chaos of Cairo has left you feeling slightly insane, Wadi Natrun's monasteries, flowering trees, cooing doves, and friendly monks are a wonderfully soothing antidote. For 1500 years, the 50 monasteries of Wadi Natrun were the backbone of the Coptic community in Egypt. The four that stand today (forming an ill-proportioned cross on the desert landscape) are more than relics; they are functional places of worship serving the spiritual needs of Egypt's Orthodox Christians, who flock here in tour buses all summer. The first Christian monastery in Egypt was established in the Eastern Desert by St. Anthony the Great (250-355 CE; see **St. Anthony's Monastery,** p. 262). In 330 CE, one of Anthony's disciples established the monastic lifestyle in Wadi Natrun. More than a millennium and a half later, during the 1980s, interest in Coptic monasticism was so great that new rooms were added to accommodate the many novice ascetics arriving in the Natrun Valley. Wadi Natrun is also home to the last surviving type of papyrus, which, due to the high salinity of the water (*wadi* = valley, *natrun* = salt), is a dwarf subspecies that never exceeds 2m (large papyrus, found in the Delta, was last seen in the mid-19th century).

 SIGHTSEEING STRATEGY. Deir Anba Bishoi is open every day of the year, while Deir al-Suryan, Deir Anba Baramus, and Deir Abu Maqar close for Lent. With the exception of those at Deir Abu Maqar, all monks happily receive foreign tourists and provide free tours of their monasteries. Some travelers try to arrange overnight stays, although this is primarily a privilege of religious pilgrims. For information on overnight stays, contact the Coptic Patriarch in Cairo at 22 Ramses St., Aboiyye (š02 282 53 74), and see the specific monastery descriptions below for details. Non-pilgrims are often allowed to camp near the monasteries. As at most religious sites in the Middle East, you should wear modest attire (no shorts or sleeveless shirts) and remember to remove your shoes before entering the church. No flash photography.

DEIR ANBA BISHOI. With seven churches, the Monastery of St. Bishoi is the largest and most accessible of the four monasteries. Dating from 381 CE, Deir Anba Bishoi's original limestone and silt construction is now covered in plaster. It was rebuilt in 444 after being sacked by barbarians and now contains the remains of St. Bishoi, who is still believed to perform miracles for the faithful. Monks used to sleep in the desert, coming to the church only for services, but attacks by nomads in the 9th century prompted the construction of sleeping chambers, a protective wall, and a tower connected to the wall by a draw-bridge. From atop the tower you can see a white swath in the distance—this is the salt that gives Wadi Natrun its name. The second floor's **Chapel of the Virgin Mary** exhibits 1500-year-old Gothic-style arches, an Egyptian innovation brought to Europe from Byzantium by the Crusaders. Don't leave without hearing the amplified echo in the old communal dining room, along with an amazingly well-preserved set of vestments from the Islamic conquests. *(15km from the Rest House. Ask for Father Sedrak or Teodoros, each of whom speaks excellent English and provides free tours. Open daily 8am-5pm.)*

DEIR AL-SURYAN. The "Monastery of the Syrians," named for the monks who once inhabited it, was established when a group of 4th-century monks left the Monastery of St. Bishoi following a theological dispute. With the resolution of the dispute in the 5th century, the Egyptian Copts no longer needed this alterna-monastery. In the beginning of the 8th century, a Syrian merchant purchased the monastery for use by monks from his homeland, the first of whom arrived at the beginning of the 9th century. The monastery was prominent throughout the 10th century, and by the 11th century it housed the largest community in Wadi Natrun. Today Deir Al-Suryan is home to 130 resident monks and 15 monks-in-training.

The monastery is best known for frescoes the Syrians painted over the original Egyptian work. The monks here will be quick to tell you that they have what is widely considered the world's most beautiful fresco, depicting the Annunciation (when the angel Gabriel told Mary that she was pregnant), on the **altar room** ceiling to the right as you enter. To the left the ceiling is decortated with a Dormition fresco, in which Jesus, surrounded by the twelve apostles, receives the soul of his dead mother into his arms. Also in this room is an enormous set of ebony doors known as the **Door of Symbols,** whose leaves form the screen to the sanctuary in the Chapel of the Virgin Mary. The panels depict the seven epochs of the Christian era.

At the back of the church is a low, dark passageway leading to the private **cell of St. Bishoi.** The monks will show you an iron staple and chain dangling from the ceiling and explain how St. Bishoi would fasten it to his hair, thereby maintaining a standing position lest he fall asleep during his all-night prayer vigils. Set in the floor at the western end of the church is the **lakan** (marble basin), which is used for washing the monks' feet on holy days. Outside in the courtyard sits the **miracle tree,** which supposedly sprang from the staff of a Syrian saint in the 4th century. From the main entrance, go left past the courtyard garden and then take another left. The age-old Tamarind tree sits inside the building's corner. *(Facing away from the entrance to Deir Anba Bishoi, turn left and walk 5min. along the paved road. Open Su-F 9am-7pm, Sa 9am-7pm; in winter Su-F 9am-6pm, Sa 9am-3pm. Monks give free tours. No overnight stays.)*

DEIR ANBA BARAMUS. Founded in 342, this monky house is known as the Monastery of the Virgin Mary, though "Baramus" derives from the Coptic word "Romeos" (or Romans), in honor of Roman Emperor Valentinus's two sons, monks Maximus and Domitius. Tradition says that a crypt under the altar holds the remains of these two holy men who worshiped here. Relics of St. Moses and St. Isadore are kept to the left of the altar in the old church. The corpse of St. Moses once shook hands with passersby through a small aperture in his casket, but for the past 200 years, he has not been quite as cordial, and the opening has been sealed. *(4km northwest of Deir Anba Bishoi. Take a taxi from Wadi Natrun town or catch a ride from Deir Anba Bishoi. Open daily 10am-5pm. Find the resident English speaking monk for a free tour. Talk to the bishop about overnight stays, but they are usually reserved for pilgrims.).*

DEIR ABU MAQAR. The Monastery of St. Maccarius was founded by St. Maccarius the Great (300-390 CE) and is the oldest of the Wadi Natrun monasteries. St. Maccarius remained a religious hermit throughout his life and lived in a cell connected by a tunnel to a small cave. (Virtually none of that original building remains.) At the start of the 11th century, the monastery became the refuge of monks fleeing Muslim persecution. During the Middle Ages, the monastery was famous for its library, which remained intact until Europeans discovered the treasures in the 17th century and removed them. *(8km southeast of Deir Anba Bishoi. Visitors not permitted without prior approval. Fax the monastery at 048 60 10 57 or send a letter to P.O. Box 2780, Cairo. State the date and time of your visit, how long you wish to stay (no longer than 2hr.), and whether you would like to eat there. Overnight visits are granted to religious groups and students of theology or history. Hire a car at the Wadi Natrun Guest House for the 15min. drive.)*

ALEXANDRIA ☏ 03

الاسكندرية

The population of Alexandria (al-Iskandariyya) swells to 12 million during the summer, as Gulf Arabs, Africans, and Egyptians flock to the city's gentle Mediterranean breezes. Outside the city center, apartment buildings dot the length of Alexandria's two harbors. Alexandria shares the dirt, crowds, and noise of Cairo, but a different spirit pervades Egypt's second-largest city. Only here can an evening meal combine Greek *souvlaki*, British ale, French pastries, and the serenade of a *muezzin*'s call to prayer. Western fashions are prevalent, alcohol flows freely, and French replaces English as the second language of choice.

Besides what can be found in an intriguing museum and a large catacomb complex, only bits and pieces of classical Alexandria remain to remind the visitor of its long and vibrant history as a Mediterranean seaport. It all started when a triumphant Alexander the Great stumbled upon this little fishing village (then called Rhakotis) en route to the Oracle of Amun at Siwa. The conquering hero became so enamored with the spot that he ordered a grand metropolis built upon it, then left for Siwa and never returned. Ptolemy was just as ptempted by the Mediterranean city as his predecessor and set about pampering Alexandria with the best ancient Greece had to offer. Alexandria's *Mouseion* (including the famous 500,000-volume library) soon became the greatest center of learning in the ancient world. Euclid invented his geometry there while Erastothenes estimated the circumference of the earth; later, Ptolemy devised a tremendously popular faith in which Zeus and the pharaonic bull-god Apis were fused into the new deity Serapis.

Ptolemy's creatively named successor, Ptolemy II, fostered trade in the city, which soon became the richest commercial center of its day. To help the traffic along, Ptolemy II constructed the Lighthouse of Pharos Island, one of the seven wonders of the ancient world (now collapsed). After all the back-stabbing and booty-snatching involving Cleopatra, Mark Antony, Octavian, and others with tetrasyllabic names, the Romans took control of the city. With the return of political stability, Alexandria continued to grow in size and intellectual importance. Schol-

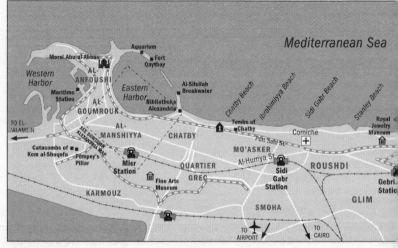

✴HIGHLIGHTS OF ALEXANDRIA AND THE MEDITERRANEAN COAST

The shores of **Marsa Matrouh** (p. 178) are the treasure of the coast, while the pristine waters of **Cleopatra's Beach** (p. 179) were a playground for pharaonic lovers.

The **Greco-Roman Museum** (p. 167) preserves a sense of Alexandria's glorious past, while the **Roman Amphitheater** (p. 166) and **Pompey's Pillar** (p. 169) embody it.

In the **Siwa Oasis** (p. 179), the unique Siwan language and culture still thrive. Follow Alexander's footsteps to the **Oracle of Amun** (p. 183), famous ancient fount of wisdom.

---

arly interests shifted to theology, and Alexandria was the site of the creation of the Septuagint (the first Greek translation of the Hebrew Bible) for the expatriate Jewish population after the destruction of the Temple in Jerusalem. Legend has it that the translation was named for the 72 scholars who each labored in isolation but produced exactly the same text. Legend also teaches that St. Mark introduced Christianity to the city in 64 CE, founding what would become the Coptic Church. With Emperor Constantine's conversion in 314 CE, the influence of the Christians grew, and they turned on their pagan neighbors with vengeful glee, burning the *Mouseion* in the process (see **A Library Long Overdue,** p. 168). It was all downhill from there: the new capital in Cairo soon eclipsed Alexandria's glory, and a series of 13th-century earthquakes finally reduced the immense lighthouse to rubble.

A rejuvenated modern city burst forth when Muhammad 'Ali made Alexandria a port for his navy and redug the canal to the Nile. During the 19th century, breezy Alexandria became a favorite holiday spot for expatriate Europeans, wealthy Turks, and Egyptian nationals, as well as the setting for several major works of literature (like *The Alexandria Quartet*). In the 20th century, Alexandria continued to occupy a privileged position as the cooler of Egypt's two major cities, and the setting of choice for Egyptian filmmakers's famous melodramas.

In recent years, Alexandria's popular Governor al-Mahgoub has initiated a series of modernization projects to make the city even more accessible to visitors. Construction of the great Bibliotheka is nearly complete and the coastal 6-lane corniche is in the final stages of expansion. Known throughout Egypt for their shopping, the downtown streets are crowded with visitors in search of bargains. Late into the evening, sounds of street vendors hawking their wares mix with lively conversation from cafes. Twenty-somethings abound, hailing from the city's many universities, and Alexandrians of all ages are proud of their popular city and warmly welcome visitors into their midst.

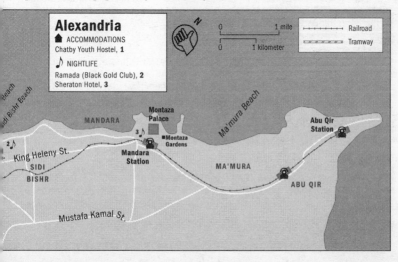

Alexandria

🔺 ACCOMMODATIONS
Chatby Youth Hostel, **1**

🎵 NIGHTLIFE
Ramada (Black Gold Club), **2**
Sheraton Hotel, **3**

Railroad · · · · · · ·
Tramway ┅┅┅┅┅

0 —————— 1 mile
0 —————— 1 kilometer

> # GIVING THEM THE FINGER
> When the Apostle St. Mark the Evangelist came to Alexandria to bring Christianity to Egypt in 64 CE, he quickly won many followers. Pagans and Gnostics, who made up the majority of the population, felt threatened by the new Bishopric of Alexandria. In 67 CE, they ambushed St. Mark while he was giving a Mass and dragged him behind some horses around the streets of the city until he was killed. Not content with his death, they tied the body to a stake and started a fire, but the corpse would not burn. Frustrated, they instead beheaded the dead saint and called it a day. His remains were gathered up by the local church, where they lay until the 9th century, when zealous visitors from Venice (a city notorious across the Eastern Orthodox world for its relic-snatching) stole the body to be reinterred at the Basilica di San Marco. Meanwhile, the head remained in Egypt after being transferred to the Church of St. George in Cairo, where it would be used, like other relics, during important religious celebrations. Fast forward to 1997, when at a summit of the Sees (the regional seats of church authority), Pope John Paul II returned one of St. Mark's fingers to the Coptic Pope Shnouda III. This gesture of papal reconciliation now rests at the Coptic Orthodox Patriarchate in Alexandria.

✈ INTERCITY TRANSPORTATION

Alexandria lies at the junction of lush Delta farmlands, the barren Western Desert, and the Mediterranean coast. Cairo is a 3hr. drive to the southeast on either of two roads. The scenic Delta road (231km) crosses both branches of the Nile and passes through the industrial city of Tanta, while the desert road (225km) nudges Wadi Natrun and passes through Giza.

FLIGHTS
Al-Nozha is Alexandria's new **airport,** located several kilometers southeast of downtown. Local bus #203 (٢٠٣) and minibus #703 (٧٠٣) run between Orabi Sq. and the airport. **EgyptAir,** 19 Sa'ad Zaghloul Sq. (☎486 59 37 or 486 59 38), is just east of Ramleh Station Sq. Open daily 8am-8pm. **Lufthansa,** 6 Tala'at Harb St. (☎487 70 31), flies nonstop to Frankfurt on Sa, M, W, and Th at 7:35am; one-way E£2575. **Olympic Airlines** (☎486 10 14 or 486 72 95; fax 482 89 01), in Sa'ad Zaghloul Sq. one block east of EgyptAir, flies to Athens Tu and F at 8:45am. One-way E£1035, youth E£730. Open M-F 8:30am-4:30pm, Sa 8:30am-12:30pm. **British Airways,** 15 Sa'ad Zaghloul Sq. (☎486 15 65 or 487 66 68.), flies to London Tu and F at 10:50am. One-way E£2800, student E£2300.

TRAINS
All trains leave from Misr Station, south of Sa'ad Zaghloul Sq., and arrive at Sidi Gabr Station, near May Sq., about seven minutes later. There are two options for trains to **Cairo:** the turbocharged **Turbini** trains (2hr.; 7, 8am, 2, 3pm, 7, 7:30; 1st-class E£30, 2nd-class E£22) or the slower **French** trains (3hr.; 6, 11am, 1, 3:30, 5, 8, 9:30pm; 1st-class E£23, 2nd-class E£14). The **3rd-class** trains run frequently (3:30am-11pm; E£6). A train also runs to Marsa Matrouh (5hr.; 6:45am; 2nd-class E£17, 3rd-class E£8.10). All trains offer student discounts.

BUSES
Find buses and tickets at the complex in 15 May Sq., behind Sidi Gabr Station. **Superjet** (☎429 85 66), offering A/C, snacks, bathrooms, and ever-endearing Egyptian movies, runs buses to: Cairo with stops at Giza, Tahrir Sq., al-Maza, and Cairo airport (3hr., 4hr. to the airport; every 30min. 5am-1pm; downtown E£20, airport E£25); Hurghada (8hr., 8pm, E£80); Port Said (4½hr., 6:45am,

E£22); and Sharm al-Sheikh (11½hr., 6:30pm, E£77). **West Delta** (☎428 90 92) runs buses daily to: Cairo via Giza Sq., Tahrir Sq., and usually the Cairo airport (3hr.; every 30min. 5am-1:30am; downtown E£20, airport E£25-28); Hurghada (11hr., 6:30pm, E£60); Marsa Matrouh (5hr.; 7, 7:30, 8, 8:30, 9, 10:30, 11am, noon, 1, 2:30, 3pm; E£15-23); Port Said (4½hr.; 6, 8am, 3:30, 4:30pm; E£17, with A/C E£22); Siwa (7½hr., 8:30, 11am, 2pm; E£27); Tanta (6:45am, noon, 1:15pm; E£6); and Zagazig (2hr.; 8, 10am, 2, 3, 4pm; E£13-15).

SERVICE

Service are cheap but packed (sometimes 20 people per minivan). Vans and station wagons depart from **Muharram Bey Station,** a 5min. drive out of town; *service* departing from Misr Station will take you there. Prices are approximate. *Service* go to: Abu Qir (30min., 80pt); Cairo (3hr. by the desert road, E£10); Marsa Matrouh (3hr., E£25); Port Said (4hr., E£10); Tanta (1½hr., E£4); and Zagazig (4hr., E£10).

CAR RENTAL

Avis, in the Cecil Hotel on Sa'ad Zaghloul Sq., rents Toyota Corollas to those over 25. (☎483 74 00; fax 483 64 01. Open daily 8am-10pm. US$50 per day, US$0.25 per km over 100, plus tax and insurance.)

◆ ORIENTATION

Alexandria stretches from Abu Qir Bay to the western harbor. The entire 28km of coastline, lined by the main road referred to as the **corniche,** is crowded with glistening skyscrapers and deteriorating hotels jockeying for a spot near the Mediterranean. Alexandria's architect, Dinocrates, planned the city with broad boulevards rigidly arranged in a grid to harness sea breezes. The breezes still waft, but the order is long gone. Ancient Alexandria was built around **Pharos Island** (now a peninsula separating the eastern and western harbors), and the area still serves as the heart of the city. The downtown commercial district—called **al-Manshiyya,** or Midan Ramleh—is the hub of Alexandria's nightlife and tourist trade. Along the curve of the eastern harbor, northeast of downtown, is **al-Goumrouk,** a grandiose residential neighborhood that holds many old mosques. The **Karmouz** district, which encompasses Alexandria's main train depot **Misr Station,** borders the southern edge of al-Manshiyya. Its streets of overflow with students, workers, and the rest of the proletariat. Pompey's Pillar and the Catacombs of Kom al-Shoqafa are also here. **Al-Anfoushi,** home to Fort Qaytbay, occupies the farthest tip of Pharos Island.

The best place to orient yourself downtown is **Sa'ad Zaghloul Sq.** on the waterfront, which showcases a mamouth statue of the man himself. Bordering the southeast corner of Sa'ad Zaghloul Sq. is **Ramleh Sq.** (Midan Ramleh), the main depot for the intracity tramway and a hub for intercity buses. Many municipal buses and minibuses service the busy stop in front of the square on the corniche or on the south side across from Trianon Cafe.

Heading west on the south side of Ramleh Sq. is **Sa'ad Zaghloul St.** (which does *not* border Sa'ad Zaghloul Sq.), a main shopping artery that runs to **Orabi Sq.** The two squares serve as transportation hubs. All yellow trams out of Ramleh Station pass through here, as do a number of minibuses. The southern end is also called **Tahrir Sq.,** and the larger area **al-Manshiyya Sq.**

The corniche starts at the northern tip of al-Anfoushi and winds the length of the city's coastline to reach the **Sidi Bishr** district, **Montaza Palace,** and **Ma'mura Beach,** which demarcates the city's far eastern border. Note that the corniche is also called **26 July Ave.**

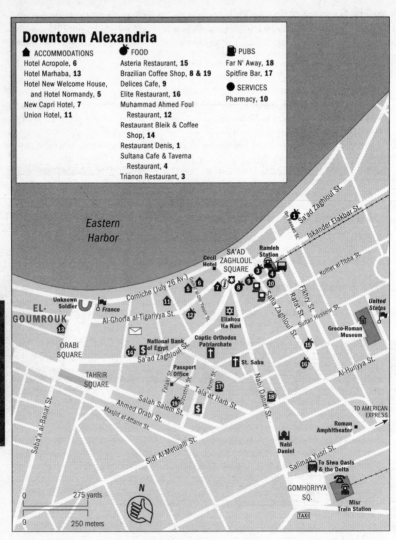

Downtown Alexandria

ACCOMMODATIONS
Hotel Acropole, **6**
Hotel Marhaba, **13**
Hotel New Welcome House,
   and Hotel Normandy, **5**
New Capri Hotel, **7**
Union Hotel, **11**

FOOD
Asteria Restaurant, **15**
Brazilian Coffee Shop, **8 & 19**
Delices Cafe, **9**
Elite Restaurant, **16**
Muhammad Ahmed Foul
   Restaurant, **12**
Restaurant Bleik & Coffee
   Shop, **14**
Restaurant Denis, **1**
Sultana Cafe & Taverna
   Restaurant, **4**
Trianon Restaurant, **3**

PUBS
Far N' Away, **18**
Spitfire Bar, **17**

SERVICES
Pharmacy, **10**

In addition to the corniche, two main arteries traverse the stretch from downtown to Ma'mura. **Alexander the Great (al-Iskandar al-Akbar) St.** lies several blocks inland. In Sidi Bishr, the street changes its name to Khalid ibn al-Walid St. to welcome you to *(bienvenidos a)* Miami Beach, where it ends. The second major artery is **al-Huriyya St.**, which runs all the way to Montaza. East of its intersection with **Nabi Daniel**, al-Huriyya becomes **Sidi Metwalli**.

☲ LOCAL TRANSPORTATION

All of Alexandria's main squares, transportation centers, and the corniche lie within walking distance of each other. A brisk half-hour walk will take you from Old Pharos Island to the Shooting Club along the corniche. The rest of the city is accessible by municipal tram, bus, minibus, and private microbus or taxi. Riding the **tram** is by far the easiest way to get around the city. Look above the car's middle door for the train route in English. Mini buses are fast, frequent, and cheap, but no mortal has yet unlocked the secret of their organization, since routes are at the whim of the driver.

BUSES

There are three terminals: in **Ramleh Station** (on the east side of Sa'ad Zaghloul Sq.), in **Misr Station.**, and in **Muharram Bey Station.** Buses run from approximately 5:30am to midnight or 1am (2am during Ramadan) and cost 25-35pt, or 50pt to outside beaches like al-'Agami or Montaza. Buses are marked in Arabic numerals.

FROM SA'AD ZAGHLOUL SQ.:	FROM ORABI SQ.:
#1 (١): Sidi Bishr & 15 May Station (A/C)	**#203** (٢٠٣): Airport
#2 (٢): al-'Agami (A/C)	**#220** (٢٢٠): Sidi Bishr
#3 (٣): al-'Agami via Montaza (A/C)	**#231** (٢٣١): Citadel
#214 (٢١٤), **#215** (٢١٥): Maritime Station	**#251** (٢٥١): Abu Qir via al-Huriyya St.
#221 (٢٢١): Ma'mura	**#260** (٢٦٠): Abu Qir via the corniche
#403 (٤٠٣): Dakhla	
#750 (٧٥٠), **#760** (٧٦٠): Hannoville	

MINIBUSES

A more appetizing alternative to the crowded city buses, minibuses run from 5:30am to 1am (2am and sometimes even later during Ramadan). They cost 50pt. Stand on the street and hold up the number of fingers equal to the number of passengers. Tell the driver or man in the passenger's seat where you are going, and he will motion for you to join them or stay put.

FROM SA'AD ZAGHLOUL SQ.:	FROM ORABI SQ.:
#700 (٧٠٠), **#705** (٧٠٥): Muharram Bey	**#703** (٧٠٣): Airport via Sa'ad Zaghloul
#703 (٧٠٣): Airport	**#704** (٧٠٤): Fishing club
#706 (٧٠٦): Citadel	**#724** (٧٢٤): 15 May Station
#725 (٧٢٥): Citadel via the corniche	**#736** (٧٣٦): Ma'mura
#735 (٧٣٥), **#736** (٧٣٦): Montaza	**#737** (٧٣٧): Abu Qir
#750 (٧٥٠): Bitash	**#779** (٧٧٩): Mandara
#760 (٧٦٠): Hannoville	
#781 (٧٨١): International Gardens	

FROM MISR STATION:	FROM MONTAZA:
#728 (٧٢٨): Montaza and Abu Qir	**#735** (٧٣٥): Sa'ad Zaghloul, Qaytbay
#729 (٧٢٩): Abu Qir	
#755 (٧٥٥), **#765** (٧٦٥): al-'Agami	FROM RAS AL-TIN:
#770 (٧٧٠): Ma'mura	**#735** (٧٣٥): Montaza via the corniche

TRAMS

Trams all start from **Ramleh Station** and come in two colors. **Blue** trams (25pt) head east and pass by the Sporting Club before ending at al-Nasser Station. **Yellow** trams (20pt) head west and pass Orabi Sq. before turning north or south. They run every few minutes until midnight, occasionally until 1am, and until 2am during Ramadan. The middle car of every three-car tram is for **women only;** on two-car trams, one is marked "ladies" and the other "gentlemen." Hop on at any stop or flag one down, and pay on board. Look for the route number on the front of the train, not the longer car numbers painted on the sides. When in doubt, call out your stop to the driver or passengers, and maybe they'll stop to help.

TAXIS

A local taxi ride in Alexandria is marginally less death-defying than one in Cairo, and it is an inexpensive way to avoid the slow grind of the tram and the sardine-can squalor of the city buses. Hail one going in your direction and shout your destination into the window. The meters never run. No matter how big your group (three is the maximum), you can get away with E£5 to most places in the downtown area. Longer trips (Montaza or Abu Qir) are E£15-20, and past midnight you'll have to bargain harder. There is an E£1 minimum.

PRACTICAL INFORMATION

TOURIST AND FINANCIAL SERVICES

Tourist Office: Main office (☎484 33 80 or 485 15 56) on Nabi Daniel St., at the southwest corner of Sa'ad Zaghloul Sq. Fluent English speakers. Open daily 8:30am-6pm, Ramadan 9am-4pm, holidays 8am-2pm. Branch offices at **Misr Station** (☎392 59 85; same hours), **Maritime Station** (☎480 34 94; open 8am-5pm and additional hours for boat arrivals), and the **airport** (☎427 87 64 or 427 10 36). Free copies of *Alexandria by Night and Day* and *Alexandria and the Beaches.*

Passport Office: 22 Tala'at Harb St. (☎484 78 73). Walk west on Sa'ad Zaghloul Sq. from Ramleh Station Sq. and bear left on Falaky St. by the blue sign when Sa'ad Zaghloul curves toward the sea. Tala'at Harb St. is the 1st left. Open Sa-Th 8am-3pm. Handle visa extensions in Cairo if at all possible.

Consulates: Israel, 15 Mena St., Loran (☎544 95 01). Open Su-Th 9:30am-3:30pm. **Lebanon,** 63 al-Huriyya St. (☎482 65 89). **UK,** 3 Mena St., Rushdi (☎546 70 01), off Kafr Abdou St. about 6km east of downtown, several blocks south of the corniche. Open Su-Th 8am-1pm. For **US,** contact the American Center (see **Cultural Centers,** below) or the US Embassy in Cairo (see p. 97).

Currency Exchange: Better rates than banks, but they only take cash. **National Bank of Egypt** in Cecil Hotel in Sa'ad Zaghloul Sq. is fast. Open daily 8:30am-noon and 5-8pm. **National Bank of Egypt** (☎484 09 53), a few blocks east of Sa'ad Zaghloul Sq. on al-Ghorfa al-Tigariayya St. on the corner of Nabi Daniel and Salah Salem, gives MC/V advances (no traveler's checks). Open Su-Th 8:30am-2pm, has ATM. **Banque Misr,** up the street and around the corner from the passport office on Tala'at Harb St., has ATMs.

American Express: 10 Patrice Lumumba St. (☎495 09 18; fax 495 09 17), near the Roman Amphitheater. Full service office, but doesn't hold mail. Open daily 9am-4pm.

Thomas Cook: 15 Sa'ad Zaghloul St. (☎484 78 30; fax 487 40 73; tcalex@attmail.com), just east of Ramleh Station Sq. Here you can arrange plane tickets, holidays, and tours, cash traveler's checks, make hotel reservations, and pick up train schedules. Open daily 8am-5pm.

LOCAL SERVICES

English-Language Bookstore: The best is the **Alex Center for Multimedia & Libraries**, 181-183 Ahmed Shawky St. (☎545 37 14; alexcntr@ritsec2.com.eg; www.acml-egypt.com), which has an impressive collection of English titles, including a wide variety of classiscs, works of Egyptian history, numerous textbooks, maps, and even the *Guinness Book of World Records*. **Al-Ma'aref,** 44 Sa'ad Zaghloul St. (☎487 33 03); another entrance is on the south side of Sa'ad Zaghloul Sq. Strange selection of textbooks, translations of Arabic works, and trashy paperbacks. Open M-Sa 10am-9:30pm. **General Egyptian Book Organization,** 49 Sa'ad Zaghloul St. (☎486 29 25), just down the street from al-Ma'aref. Medium-sized selection ranges from *Sweet Valley High* to *The Art of Pediatrics*, with an immense collection of Agatha Christie. Open M-Sa 10am-8pm.

The Used Book Market, at the southern end of Nabi Daniel St. near Misr Station, is an entire block of obscure, inexpensive English titles.

Cultural Centers: British Council, 9 Ptolemies (Batalsa) St. (☎ 486 01 99). Open Su-Th 8:30am-8pm; library open Su-W 10am-8pm, Sa and Th 10am-3pm. **American Cultural Center,** 3 Phara'ana St. (☎ 486 10 09). Turn left on al-Huriyya St. from Safia Zaghloul St., walk 1 block past the 1st sign for the Greco-Roman Museum, turn left, then take the 1st right. Book and video library. Inquire about **teaching jobs** at the English Teaching Program. Cultural events calendar posted outside. Open Su-Th 8:30am-6pm

EMERGENCY AND COMMUNICATIONS

Emergency: Ambulance: ☎ 123. **Police:** ☎ 122. **Tourist Police:** ☎ 483 33 78.

Tourist Police: Montaza Palace (☎ 547 33 95). Main office upstairs from tourist office in **Sa'ad Zaghloul Sq.** (☎ 487 33 78). Both open 24hr. Other branches in **amphitheater** (☎ 490 62 73), **Citadel** (☎ 480 91 44), and **Greco-Roman Museum** (☎ 482 89 12).

Pharmacy: Pharmacy Strand (☎ 486 51 36), opposite the tram at the intersection of Sa'ad Zaghloul St. and Safia Zaghloul St. Open 9am-1am.

Hospitals: Armed Forces (☎ 544 88 58 or 542 34 50), on the corniche in Sidi Gaber, take the blue tram to al-Shiekh Station. Open 24hr. **Al-Mowasah** (☎ 421 28 85 or 421 28 88), on al-Huriyya St. in al-Haddara is closer to the center of town but in shabbier condition. Open 24hr.

Telephones: Menatel phones scattered throughout downtown area. **Ramleh Station Sq.** office charges E£4 for 1min. to US. Open 24hr. Additional offices at **Misr Station,** at west end of Sa'ad Zaghloul St. on **Sultan Hussein St.** Open daily 8am-10pm. Lines are down for hours at a time, and you may be abruptly cut off. **Luxury hotels** (try the Cecil in Sa'ad Zaghloul Sq.) offer more reliable, but also more expensive, overseas connections. Rates to: US, Canada, and Europe E£4.85 per min., Australia E£6.25 per min.

Internet Access:

Al-Jaber CompuComm Services, 20 Mahmoud Azmi St. (☎ 483 27 95; aljaber@alexcomm.net), around the block from the Coptic Patriarchate heading south. Look for the sidewalk sign mentioning "Internet." Only has 1 terminal, but the owner serves tea while you're online. E£8 per 30min., E£15 per hr. Open daily 9am-11pm.

Zawia, 62 Safia Zagloul (☎ 484 80 14; zawia@iaa.com.eg; www.alex-cam.com). From Raml Station head south on Safia Zaghloul St. and take the 1st right onto Dr. Hassan Fadaly St.; Zawia is on the left. Look for the red and blue sign. Fast connection access the Internet on 8 computers, and there is a fax machine upstairs.

ICC Internet (☎ 487 44 59), on Safia Zaghloul St. just past Zawia. Look for a blue and red sign on the 2nd fl. Take a right into the alley before the pharmacy and follow the signs upstairs. Fast connections on 10 computers. A/C. E£5 per. hr. Open daily 10am-1am, 24hr. in summer.

Global Net (☎ 495 89 81 or 491 28 89; Ghada-mehany@globalnet.com.eg), on Nabi Daniel St. across from the French Cultural Center, after al-Huriyya St. when heading toward Misr Station. No English sign; 6th fl. A/C room with fast connections. E£6 for 30min., E£10 per hr. Open 24hr.

Post Office: All open Sa-Th 8am-3pm, and most have **EMS** (until 2pm). A branch at the tram stop at **Ramleh Station Sq.** (☎ 486 07 46) and one on **al-Ghorfa al-Tigariyya St.** (☎ 480 53 29) 3 blocks west of Sa'ad Zaghloul Sq. **Poste Restante** until 1pm. Packages are held at the office of **Misr Station** (☎ 393 29 53 or 393 29 54), 10m south of al-Huriyya St. An office in front of the **Sidi Gabr Railroad Station** has EMS.

⌂ ACCOMMODATIONS

E.M. Forster liked Alexandria so much that he wrote a guidebook for it and named a character in *A Room with a View* after the Cecil Hotel. Nowadays, visitors are paying more for location than quality, though bargaining is always an option at the cheaper hotels. Steer clear of the ultra-cheap (E£10 per night) dives that line the streets running south from the corniche near Ramleh Station

Sq. It's better to stay in one of the hotels listed below: all are clean, cheap, and within walking distance of the two main squares. None have fans, unless noted, as most Alexandrians depend on sea breezes for air-conditioning. In summer, look for corner rooms with cross ventilation.

Streets in **al-Manshiyya Sq.** teem with budget hotels. For a beachside retreat, head out to **Sidi Bishr** (14km) or **Montaza** (18km), where the posh amenities make up for the inconvenience of staying so far from the center of town. The only **camping** possibility is the beach at Abu Qir, but police generally only give permission to large groups. Interested travelers should inquire at the tourist office. Reservations are a good idea in summer, especially on weekends.

▨ **Hotel Union,** 6 Muhammad Noaman St. (☎480 73 12; fax 480 73 50), off the corniche on the 2nd block behind the Cecil Hotel. This popular hotel has large, classy rooms with balconies and great views of the harbor. The comfortable lounge with the picture window and Mel Tormé tunes can't be beat. On the pricier side, but the comfortable beds, towels, and spotless bathrooms are well worth it. Breakfast E£6. Singles E£37; doubles E£63; triples E£67.

Chatby Youth Hostel (HI), 32 Port Said St. (☎592 54 59; fax 591 47 59), next to the tombs of Chatby. Clean, classy, comfortable, *and* inexpensive, this 175 bed hostel fills up quickly. Each spotless double and triple has a desk and occasionally a refrigerator. Restaurant serves 3 meals per day; breakfast included. 8-bed dorms E£12.60; doubles E£22.60 per person; triples E£17.60 per person.

New Hotel Welcome House, 8 Gamal al-Din Yassin St., 5th fl. (☎480 64 02), on the 1st block off the corniche behind the Cecil Hotel. Oddly named but well-maintained hotel with old but clean rooms, great prices, and views to match. Popular with the backpacking crowd. Rooms come with tiny baths. Singles E£16-22; doubles E£22; triples E£30.

New Capri Hotel, 23 al-Mina al-Sharkia, 8th fl. (☎490 93 10), same building as tourist office off Sa'ad Zaghloul Sq. A bit inland, but the rooms are spacious and the blue bathrooms immaculate. Corner rooms offer panoramic views of the square. Breakfast included. Singles E£37; doubles E£52; triples E£65.

Hotel Acropole, 27 Gamal al-Din Yassin St., 4th fl. (☎480 59 80), at end of the block behind the Cecil Hotel. Aging rooms include desk, dresser, and beds with thin mattresses. Prices vary with views, which range from panoramas to brick walls. Breakfast included. Singles E£15-35; doubles E£40-45; triples E£55-65.

Hotel Normandy, 8 Gamal al-Din Yassin St., 4th fl. (☎480 68 30). This dubious establishment was mentioned in Australian phenom Ted Simon's landmark travel narrative *Jupiter's Travels.* All rooms have three old (and crotchety) beds, high ceilings (with peeling paint), and shared baths (with stained tubs). Some have a nice view of the water. Bathrooms are adequate. Prices negotiable, especially if you begin to walk out. Singles E£15; doubles E£25; triples E£30; room with a view E£5-10 extra.

Hotel Marhaba, 10 Ahmed Orabi Sq. (☎480 09 57 or 480 95 10), on the northwest side of Orabi Sq. These posh digs were the former summer residence of the King of Libya, and it shows: wallpapered rooms come with towels, soap, sinks, and Egyptian TV. Louis XIV sitting rooms on each floor, and the rooftop sports breakfast buffet, a pool table, and a lonely bar. Singles E£35; doubles E£49, with shower E£57.50; triples E£68, with shower E£76.50.

🖸 FOOD

Meat, fruit, seafood, and vegetables can be found in the **souqs** of al-Mo'asker (take any blue tram six or seven stops east and walk south) and Bahary (take yellow tram #16 along the corniche, get off before the Mosque of Morsi Abu al-Abbas and walk inland two blocks). The fishmongers will cook purchases on the spot for E£3-5. **Supermarkets** dot the area around Sa'ad Zaghloul Sq. Gastronomic voyeurs should sneak a peek into **Muhammad Ahmed's Falafel Workshop,** which dishes out insight into the falafel-making process; green Industrial Revolution-era falafel churners spin chickpeas into a heavenly mash. Go up 'Abd al-Fattah al-Hadari St. from Muhammad Ahmed Fuul Restaurant, listed below, and turn right down the first alley to the brick building on the left.

RESTAURANTS

The restaurants of Alexandria are a delicious reminder of the city's cosmopolitan heritage. The cheap falafel and *fuul* found throughout Egypt are readily available, but Alexandria also boasts fine Italian and Greek restaurants downtown, where French pastries vie with *ba'laweh* and *kinafeh* for the affections of the strolling crowds. And of course, this "Queen of the Mediterranean" naturally features excellent seafood. Roam the streets of **al-Manshiyya** for a variety of tasty and reasonably-priced meals. Southeast of Sa'ad Zaghloul Sq., the streets teem with possibilities. If some of the smaller establishments have only Arabic menus, don't let that worry you. Communicate the old-fashioned way: follow your nose and point.

■ **Muhammad Ahmed Fuul,** 17 'Abd al-Fattah al-Hadari St. (☎483 35 76). Walk away from Sa'ad Zaghloul Sq. on al-Ghorfa al-Tigariyya St. and take the 1st left, 10m up on the left. *Fuul*-lovers flock to this local family favorite. Scrumptious take-out for E£2 or less, a full sit-down meal nextdoor E£6. Open daily 6am-1am.

■ **Elite,** 43 Safia Zaghloul St. (☎486 35 92), 1 block north of al-Huriyya St. Breezy, stylin' artists' cafe and restaurant since 1900, run by a friendly Greek matriarch. Wrap-around glass windows, high-beamed ceilings, and 2 decks of tables give a maritime feel. Steak E£18-33, chicken E£16-19, filling pasta E£3.50-10, Stella beer E£6.25. Open daily 8am-midnight.

Kadoura Restaurant (☎480 09 67), on the corniche about a block before the Tikka Grill sign, 2½km west of Sa'ad Zaghloul Sq. toward Fort Qaytbay; look for the neon sign above the door. Locals rave about Kadoura's delicious seafood. Choose your prey downstairs from several varieties of fish, crab, and calamari (some still moving), then head up the slippery spiral stairs for a great view of the ocean and corniche crowd below. Waddle out after a massive meal of seafood, salad, bread, and drink (E£30). Fish prices seasonal. Open daily noon-midnight.

Restaurant Bleik, 18 Sa'ad Zaghloul St. (☎484 08 80). Walk west on Sa'ad Zaghloul until you're two blocks from Orabi Sq. A mixture of Lebanese and Egyptian cuisine. Enjoy such delicacies as quail and brain with rice (E£9) or sample from a range of Lebanese specials (E£4-14). Pastries E£2. Open daily 9am-10:30pm.

Restaurant Denis, 1 Ibn Bassam St. (☎486 17 09), located in the northeast corner of Sa'ad Zaghloul Sq. on a side street leading to the Corniche, adjacent to the corniche. Good seafood at fair prices. Waiter brings the day's catch to your table so you can sea food before eating it. Fish E£27-30 per kg. Calamari E£12. Shrimp E£40. Beer and wine served. Open daily 10am-midnight.

Taverna (☎487 85 91), on the southern side of Ramleh Station, across from the trams and next to KFC. A touristy crowd enjoys the "famous fish menu" (E£14-40), Italian specialties (E£4-14), and shawarma, pitched as "our nicest dish." Good prices and a convienent location. Branch at Montaza Gardens offers take-out only. Open daily 7:30am-3am (2am in winter).

Trianon (☎482 09 86), at the corner of Sa'ad Zaghloul and Ramleh Station Sq. A landmark from the city's *belle époque* and former hangout of illustrious literary types, this 80-year-old restaurant has both indoor and outdoor seating. Prices are reasonable (entrees E£13-26), with some great bargains: *mousaka* is E£13, and 3-course French breakfast with coffee is E£12. Open daily 7am-midnight; outdoor cafe open later.

Asteria, 40 Safia Zaghloul St. (☎462 22 93). Casual Italian bistro and cafe serving pizza (E£7-14) and pasta (E£3.50-14.30), with tasty granitas to wash it all down. Sandwiches, while cheap (E£3.50), are very small. Open daily 9am-midnight.

CAFES

Sa'ad Zaghloul Sq. is packed with coffee and pastry shops while ice cream parlors cool off the Ramleh Station Sq. Along the corniche you'll find ritzy cafes and *sheesha* joints; cheaper, more traditional cafes *(ahwas)* await farther inland. **Ma'mura** offers a lively waterfront scene, where a youthful crowd buzzes until after midnight. Popular places to grab grub and *sheesha* include: the **Antazza Cafe,** serving food after 7pm (off of Sa'ad Zaghloul St. and across from the mosque, no English sign), **Minouche** (Italian food E£10-20), and **Cafino** (above Antazza, open late).

▨ **Brazilian Coffee Store,** in 2 locations: 20 Salah Salem St. and a stand-up joint at 44 Sa'ad Zaghloul St. (☎486 50 59). Cozy up to the bar at the Salah Salem location to examine green coffee plant tiles. The wonderfully rich coffee (E£1.50) draws a loyal local following. Croissants E£1.60. Both stores open daily 7am-11pm.

Delices (☎486 14 32 or 486 54 60), opposite the corniche in Sa'ad Zaghloul Sq. French and Middle Eastern desserts. More posh for your nosh: the sea-view terrace is a great place to enjoy savory pastries (E£2-5), ice cream (E£2.50-10), or coffee (E£4.25). Open daily 7am-1am.

Sofianopoulo Coffee Shop (☎487 15 17), on Sa'ad Zaghloul St., next to Restaurant Bleik. Classic coffee shop with outstanding prices: capuccino (E£2), tasty croissants (E£1.25). Aspiring astronauts can enjoy Tang on tap (E£1.25). Open daily 9am-11pm.

Sultana (☎486 27 69), on the south side of Ramleh Station Sq., across from the trams. Offers a luscious array of sundaes and ice cream (E£1.75 per scoop), waffle cones made while you wait. Turns into an animal house at night. Open daily 9am-1am, and (boy, do) they deliver.

Cafe Baudrot, 23 Sa'ad Zaghloul St. (☎486 56 87). With its expansive vine-trellised garden straight out of a *Town and Country* magazine, this cafe is a fine retreat from the busy streets. Perfect for musing over beer (E£9), coffee (E£4.50), cake (E£3), or even dinner (chicken or fish E£20). Tax and service not included. Open daily 7am-midnight.

Samadi Patisserie (☎480 51 14), on a lush patio adjacent to Tikka Grill. It's no secret that Samadi doles out generous helpings of *ba'laweh, basbouseh, kinafeh,* and other sweet goodies (E£2-4 per piece). Fresh strawberry ice cream E£2 per scoop. Open daily 9am-2am. AmEx/MC/V.

◉ SIGHTS

The modern city of Alexandria was built atop the ruins of ancient Alexandria, leaving Classical remains eight meters underground. The scattered places where ancient foundations are visible offer fascinating glimpses of a city with a diverse cultural and religious history. That said, archaeological wonders are not the primary appeal of Alexandria as they are of other Egyptian destinations. This city's charm lies in its Mediterranean disposition—the people, the breezes, the beaches. Note that **price hikes** of 25-50% on admission tickets to major sights are scheduled for the coming year; see **Inflation Sucks,** p. 14, for more information. Also note that exorbitant camera privilege fees are not always enforced.

DOWNTOWN ALEXANDRIA

▨**ROMAN AMPHITHEATER.** This dazzling white marble structure is the only Roman amphitheater in all of Egypt. Stand on the round stone in the stage, whisper *Et tu, Brute?*, and your voice will be heard by conspirators all the way in the theater's back row. Archaeologists recently finished excavating a 100m-long Roman bath and villa behind the theater. The villa contains a stunning bird mosaic discovered in 1998. *(Just northwest of Misr Station and south of Cinema 'Amir. From Sa'ad Zaghloul Sq., walk up Nabi Daniel St. past al-Huriyya St. to the next big intersection. Turn left across from a gas station and go 200m; the entrance is on the left. ☎390 29 04. Open daily 9am-5pm; Ramadan 9am-3pm. E£6, students E£3. Camera privileges E£10; video E£150.)*

■**GRECO-ROMAN MUSEUM.** On display here are the most interesting and unusual relics of ancient Alexandria, including a mummified crocodile, exquisitely painted sarcophagi of Greco-Roman nobles (said to have provided inspiration for later Renaissance artists), and well-preserved statues of superstars like Caesar, Augustus, and Cleopatra. The pride of the museum is the beautiful mosaic of Alexandria as "Queen of the Ocean." *(5 al-Mathaf al-Roumani St. Walk south from the corniche along Safia Zaghloul St., turn left on al-Huriyya St., then left at the museum sign. ☎482 58 16. Open Sa-Th 9am-5pm, F 9am-noon and 2-5pm; Ramadan and holidays 9am-3pm. E£16, students E£8. Camera privileges without flash E£10, video E£150.)*

ELIYAHU HA-NAVI SYNAGOGUE. Guarded by a tall iron gate, this synagogue is still central for Alexandria's Jewish community and the greatest of the few Jewish sights still standing in the city. The gracious Joe Harari in the Communauté Israelite Grand Rabbinat office to the right as you enter the courtyard will show you around the building, let you look at old photographs, and tell you all about Alexandrian Jews. Although Alexandria once had more than 100,000 Jews and a synagogue in every neighborhood, this is the last one still in use for the 50 or so Jews who remain. The temple now holds an impressive collection of beautiful Torah scrolls from the closed synagogues. Built in 1885 by Baron Jacques L. de Menasce for the then-thriving community, the towering edifice sports five aisles, stained glass windows, pink Italian marble columns, dangling chandeliers, and wooden pews—check out the international assemblage of names on the brass seat markers. *(Walking away from Sa'ad Zaghloul Sq. on Nabi Daniel, take the 1st left after the intersection with Sa'ad Zagloul St. The iron gate is on the left. Open Su-F 10:30am-1pm.)*

COPTIC ORTHODOX PATRIARCHATE. The Patriarchate is in a beautiful church (founded in 67 CE and rebuilt in 1950) with mosaics, stained glass, hanging ostrich eggs, and a finely painted *iconostasis*. The first 47 patriarchs of the Alexandrian See (the regional seat of church authority), starting with St. Mark, some of whose remains are in a chapel to the left of the *iconostasis*, are buried within. Their names are listed in a niche on the right side of the church. *(Walking down Sa'ad Zaghloul St. from the square, take a left on Nabi Daniel continuing away from the square and then take the 1st right onto al-Akbat St. Open daily, services 6-8am and 8-10am.)*

MONASTERY OF ST. SABA. Sitting on the site of what was once a temple to Apollo, this 17th-century church in the Greek Orthodox Monastery of St. Saba is another testament to the historical importance of Christianity in Alexandria. Before 1965, there were 300,000 Greeks living in the city, though Nasser's assumption of power caused their numbers to dwindle, and the current population has settled around 1000. A giant bronze bell sits outside the church, while inside there are beautiful paintings, a spectacular collection of amulets, a giant bronze bell, and the marble table on which St. Catherine was beheaded. The church has recently been undergoing renovations; inquire at the tourist office about accessibility. *(Walk up Safia Zaghloul St. from Sa'ad Zaghloul Sq. to Sultan Hussein St. Turn right, then take the 2nd left. Open daily 7:30am-12:30pm and 3:30-6pm. Free.)*

WEST OF DOWNTOWN

MOSQUE OF MORSI ABU AL-'ABBAS. This is the city's largest mosque and Alexandria's most elaborate example of Islamic architecture. The holy Sidi Shehab al-Din Abu al-'Abbas ibn al-Khazragi came from Muslim Spain before the expulsion of the Moors to spread the teachings of the Qur'an in Egypt. His tomb rests underneath the mosque in the back, and legend has it that he rose from his tomb to catch

A LIBRARY LONG OVERDUE The great **Bibliotheka Alexandria** stood as an intellectual center of the ancient world for over 250 years. Alexander the Great's general Ptolemy I founded the library around 295 BCE, filling its shelves with scrolls from Athens. Unfortunately for academics, Julius Caesar caught up with Alexandria on his road to Rome in 48 BCE, allegedly destroying most of the ancient library and its collection of 500,000 scrolls. What remained was completely destroyed in 391 CE by crusading bibliophobe Bishop Theophilus, who led a pagan-hating mob to raze the building in the name of Christianity. Almost 2000 years later, Egypt has decided that it is time to try again. In 1987, UNESCO announced a project to resurrect the building that even Cleopatra could not save. A Norwegian firm designed the 45,000 sq. m behemoth in the shape of a circle. Built in the Royal Quarter where its predecessor is thought to have stood, the modern library's diameter stretches 160m, slanting down towards the ocean. Seven of the building's 11 floors have an ocean view, and the plan is for its shelves to hold an 8 million volume collection that will serve as the region's primary center for research and study. But opening day keeps getting pushed back as Alexandrians continue to wait for their US$200 million library. Not that waiting is anything new to a city in need of a library since the days of Julius Caesar. For information on the political obstacles facing the restoration team, see **In The News,** p. 73

bombs during World War II. Come nightfall, his coffin, like the exterior of the mosque, is bathed in a green neon glow. *(1km south of Fort Qaytbay along the corniche. Dress modestly. Women allowed in back room only. Open daily 5am-10pm, except during prayer times: 1, 4, 9:40pm, and sunset.)*

FORT QAYTBAY. The Islamic Fort Qaytbay was constructed on the ancient island of Pharos, on the foundations of the famous lighthouse. Fishermen and lovebirds alike congregate along the dramatic seaward walls, drawn by the waves and pleasant sunsets. Silt connected the island to the mainland, leaving the fort at the tip of a peninsula. Built in 1480 CE by Mamluk Sultan al-Ashraf Qaytbay, the citadel houses the remains of the French fleet sunk by Admiral Nelson in the battle of Abu Qir (see **Abu Qir,** p. 172). There is a small mosque in the center of the tower, and the entire fortress is aligned so that the mosque's *mihrab* faces Mecca. Unfortunately, the main tower and mosque are under rennovation (call ahead for updates), but the ramparts offer a sweeping view of the city. On the road to the tramway is the **aquarium,** which has more visiting school groups than schools of Red Sea fish. *(Take yellow tram #15 west from Ramleh Station and get off at the sharp left turn, or take any bus going to Ras al-Tin. You'll find yourself in the middle of a fish market. At the point where the tram turns left, make a right on the road between the Kuwait Airlines sign and the mosque. The fort is at the end of this road. Minibus #707 (٧٠٧) or 719 (٧١٩) from Ramleh Station Sq. takes you to the beginning of the street. ☎ 480 91 44. Fort open daily 9am-6pm summer; 9am-5pm winter. E£12, students E£6. Camera privileges E£10, video E£150. Aquarium open daily 8am-3pm. E£1. Camera privileges E£1, video E£5.)*

ANFUSHI TOMBS. The Anfushi tombs were built for Greek occupants who had adopted Egyptian customs in the first half of the 3rd century BCE. Cut into the limestone of what was once Pharos Island, they are placed in two groups around a staircase leading into an open court and may well extend farther under the palace gardens. Many of the tombs are decorated with colorful geometric designs or painted to look like marble. On the wall facing the stairs of tomb #2 is an interesting painting depicting the purification of the dead. *(On Ras al-Tin St. Take the yellow tram from Ramleh Station and ask for Ras al-Tin St. Get off just before the palace. Open daily 9am-5pm. E£12, students E£6. Camera privileges E£5.)*

SOUTH OF DOWNTOWN

CATACOMBS OF KOM AL-SHOQAFA. This enormous, three-tiered complex of Roman tombs (descending some 35m below ground) is one of the best Classical sites in the city. The gate is decorated with winged serpents, Medusa heads, a pine cone (symbolizing Dionysus), and a *caduceus* (symbolizing Mercury, the *psychopompos* or leader of the dead to the Underworld). The main tombs are on the second level and are richly decorated with sculptures and reliefs of Egyptian gods with virile Roman bodies (a blend of pharaonic and Roman art). A statue of jackal-headed Anubis stands near the entrance to the innermost burial chamber. Scenes above the sarcophagi show the Egyptian gods and a mummification, along with the worship of the Apis bull. The sarcophagi are decorated in a Roman style, with garlands and bull skulls. Try to lift the lids—it's impossible, because the bodies were placed inside from passages behind. As you exit, notice two statues of Anubis, one in which he is dressed as a Roman legionnaire and one in which he has the body of a serpent. *(Facing the entrance to Pompey's Pillar, turn left and walk straight. Pass a mosque on the left and continue for another block. The tombs are on the left. Open daily 8am-4:30pm; Ramadan 18am-3pm. E£12, students E£6. Camera privileges E£10, video E£150.)*

POMPEY'S PILLAR. This 25m pillar of pink granite from Aswan is all that remains of the Serapium (Temple of Serapis, the bull-god), which was leveled once the Roman Empire adopted Christianity. The best finds from the ruins have been moved to the Greco-Roman Museum, but the pillar stands proud atop a small hill guarded by two granite sphinxes. Named in the Middle Ages by ignorant Crusaders with a flair for the alliterative, Pompey's Pillar actually dates from the time of Diocletian, a Roman who came to power several centuries after Pompey. One story holds that Diocletian was so incensed by an Alexandrian revolt that he swore he would massacre the rebellious people until blood stained the knees of his horse. As he entered the already defeated but mostly un-massacred town, his mount stumbled into a pool of blood, prematurely fulfilling his oath. The emperor spared the life of the city's inhabitants, and the lone pillar (once the tallest structure in Alexandria) remains as a symbol of the people's gratitude to him and his klutzy horse. Another story says that the pillar commemorates the time Diocletian gave the city free grain during a famine. *(Southwest of Misr Station. Take bus #309 (٣٠٩) or tram #16 from Ramleh Station Sq. and get off on Karmouz St. Enter on the southern side of the complex. Open daily 8am-5pm; Ramadan and other holidays 10am-3pm. E£6, students E£3. Video privileges E£150.)*

EAST OF DOWNTOWN

TOMBS OF CHATBY. Discovered in 1904, the Tombs of Chatby date from the 3rd century BCE and are believed to be the oldest surviving tombs in Alexandria. Before being carted off the Greco-Roman Museum postmortem trinkets filled the underground chambers. The ground above the small tomb is cluttered with random columns and Greco-Roman artifacts deemed unworthy for the museum. *(On Port Said St., across from St. Mark's College in the Chatby beach area. Open daily 8am-5pm. E£6, students E£3. Camera privileges E£5.)*

MUSTAFA KEMAL NECROPOLIS. This necropolis consists of four tombs from the 2nd century BCE decorated in a Hellenic style. Tomb #1 has an airy courtyard and a faded fresco depicting a libation scene over the middle doorway, complete with doric columns and sphinxes. *(Take tram #2 to the Rushdi tram station and walk towards the corniche on al-Mo'asker al-Romani St. Open daily 9am-4pm. E£12, students E£6. Camera privileges E£5.)*

ROYAL JEWELRY MUSEUM. Behind the governor's residence in Glim sits the architecturally intriguing Royal Jewelry Museum. Originally the Palace of Muhammad Ali's Granddaughter Fatima al-Zahra'a, the museum contains gleaming baubles of Egypt's last royal families. The gold figurines of a Persian chess set contain some 425 Flemish diamonds. But wait, if you think that's a lot, the E£10 million crown of King Fouad's first wife contains 2159 diamonds, among them a centerpiece 250 carat wonder. *(27 Ahmed Yahya St. Take tram #2 to Zezenia. Look for the Roman chariotieer painted on the side of the Faculty of Arts building. Facing away from the ocean, walk left until reaching Adly Yakan St., then turn left, go to the end of the block, and take another left. ☎586 83 48. Open Sa-Th 9am-4pm; F 9-11am and 1:30-4pm. E£20, students E£10. Camera privileges E£10, video E£150.)*

🅲 BEACHES

Cairenes flood the Alexandrian waterfront during the summer months. For more peaceful surroundings, head to the **Sinai** (see p. 270) or the calm (but expensive) waters west of Alexandria (tram #1 or 2 from Ramleh Station Sq.). The 400 acres of flora at **Montaza Palace and Gardens** were once used as the summer retreat of King Farouk. Today, they are still the jewel of Alexandria's beaches. The palace and its museum have been closed to the public, but the beach is always busy despite its steep price (especially on weekends), and the gardens and groves are a favorite picnic spot for Alexandrians. Pizza Hut, Chicken Tikka, a supermarket, and juice and ice cream stands are all just outside the garden gates. (☎457 30 79. Beach E£10 via the Venesia Hotel; E£65 through the gates of the 5-star waterfront Helnan Palestine Hotel. Open daily 11am-1am. Gardens open 24hr.; E£4, holidays E£5.) Not far from Montaza, Ma'mura remains a favorite among vacationing Cairenes. Beach access E£5; chair and table E£3; umbrella E£7; changing station E£1; paddle boats E£30. Both beaches reachable by bus #221 (٢٢١), #250 (٢٥٠), or #260 (٢٦٠), or by minibus #770 (٧٧٠). **San Stefano's Beach**, between Montaza and Sa'ad Zaghloul Sq., is much closer to the city center, as its weekday crowds and rubbish attest. (E£8 admission includes a chair and an umbrella. Closes at 9pm.)

🅳 ENTERTAINMENT

CINEMAS

English-language films are shown at the **Renaissance Royal** (☎485 57 25), west of the intersection of Nabi Daniel St. and al-Huriyya St. Take a left after the intersection onto Fouad St. Showtimes daily at 12:30pm and 3:30 (E£7) and 6:30pm, 9:30, and midnight (E£10). The French Cultural Center at 30 Nabi Daniel St. (☎492 08 04) occasionally shows films, as does the American Cultural Center (see p. 163).

PERFORMING ARTS

Every August, the outdoor **Muhammad 'Abd al-Wahab Theater,** on the corniche at Ramleh Station Sq., showcases traditional dancing. Al-Fir'a Rida (Rida's Troupe) and al-Fir'a al-Qawmiya (the National Troupe) both feature belly dancers and high-energy choreography representative of various areas in Egypt—including the cane dance from Upper Egypt (performances nightly at 10:30pm; reserve tickets one or two days in advance; front-row E£12, cheap seats E£5; avoid the uncomfortable box seats). These troupes also perform regularly at the conference halls near the new library along the corniche. The **circus** sets up camp in Alexandria during the summer. Ask the tourist office for the location of the two daily shows (E£2-7). For more highbrow entertainment, check the **Conservatoire de Musique d'Alexandrie,** 90 al-Huriyya St. (☎487 50 86). In September, the **Alexandria World Festival** brings theater and dancing to the city. Inquire at the tourist office for details.

BILLIARDS AND SPECTATOR SPORTS

Billiard tables charge by the hour throughout the city. A friendly owner runs the local favorite **Free Ball** in the southwest corner of Ramleh Station on the second floor (E£15 per hr.; snooker E£20 per hr.; coffee but no alcohol). The **Marhaba Hotel** in Orabi Sq. has a pool table (E£10 per hr.; alcohol served; open nightly 10pm-2am). If the sound of thundering hooves makes your pulse race, head to the **Antoniadis Palace and Gardens** in Smouha, on the wide road bordering the zoo. For over 50 years, Alexandria's working classes have gathered here on summer Sundays to watch working horses, with carriages of all kinds, race at breakneck speed. (Arrive by 6pm. 75pt.) Ask at the tourist office for info on the various **sporting events** at the Alexandria Municipal Stadium.

■ NIGHTLIFE

CLUBS AND DISCOS

The cosmopolitan days of Alexandria's Hellenistic hedonism are long gone, replaced by the relaxed atmosphere of outdoor cafes. As the sun sets, *sheesha* cafes come alive with the sound of slapping dominos and the smell of fruity smoke. Evening strolls and waterfront cafes are some of the most attractive features of life in Alexandria. Arabic music eminates from the numerous storefronts in **al-Manshiyya,** as shoppers peruse the streets well past midnight. The action is concentrated downtown between Orabi Sq. and Sa'ad Zaghloul Sq., home to endless storefronts and the best bars, pastry shops, and coffee houses. Hopping between them is a great way to soak up liquor or wash down desserts.

Downtown, **Far 'N Away** is the best option for dancing on Thursday and Friday nights. A disco opens beside the bar, spinning a variety of American tunes. The **Lourantos** nightclub has drinks and Arabic dancing girls from 1am-6am (cover E£75). Dance the night away on Sidi Bishr's beachfront pavilions where weekends rock with late-night parties (cover E£5-10). **Nightclubs** can be found in most of the luxury hotels. There's no cover, but beware the stealthily levied **minimum charges.** Try the Ramada Renaissance on the corniche in Sidi Bishr, home to **Black Gold.** (Open daily 10pm-5am. Entrance on the corniche side. Min. E£30.) The ultrafab head to the **Sheraton** in Montaza to compare Rolexes. (Open daily Jul.-Sept., Th-Tu rest of the year; 10:30pm-4am. Minimum E£35.) Many discos don't allow single men or women, and some relegate lone males to the bar and forbid them from dancing. These rules are usually relaxed for foreigners, though, especially those willing to make a small donation.

BARS

Thursday and Friday are the big nights out in Alexandria, although "big" is relative in a town that places very little emphasis on drinking. During the week the bars are mostly empty. **Far 'N Away** the best pub in town is located at 14 al-Hurreyya past the intersection with Nabi Daniel St. Stylish American feel with a long wooden bar and hardwood floors (Stella E£15), also serves Tex-Mex and American fare. Just down al-Hurreyya, the upstairs bar at **L'Ossobuco** restaurant welcomes foreigners with soothing jazz and Stellas for E£10. Another cool option is **Spitfire,** 7 Rue Bourse al-Hadema, at the west side of a small square where Sa'ad Zaghloul St. and Hassan al-Sheiko St. meet. Decals and posters cover every inch of this expat favorite, and mellow '80s music calms rattled nerves (Stella E£7.50). A unique find is **Sheik 'Ali,** around the corner to the south from the Sofianopoulo Coffeeshop when heading toward Sa'ad Zaghloul Sq. The long marble bar is a great place to enjoy appetizers or a Stella (E£7.50). The Athineos Hotel, between Ramleh Station and the corniche, also has a bar (Stella E£8.50) with an ocean view, comfortable chairs to lounge in, and *sheesha* (E£4). To fully relive World War II memories, head to **Monty's Bar,** on the second floor of the Cecil Hotel. Prints of classic paintings are barely visible in the dim lighting. General Montgomery's former headquarters now charges five-star prices for cocktails. (Open daily 4pm-2am. Stella E£8.50.) If Monty's high prices have got you down, head up to the roof garden for a fantastic view of the square and the water, but be careful where you sit—the sharp, green objects are actually cacti (Stella E£8).

◪ DAYTRIPS FROM ALEXANDRIA

EAST OF ALEXANDRIA

ABU QIR ابو قير ☎ 03

*From Alexandria's Misr Station, take local **bus** #251 (٢٥١) or #260 (٢٦٠), or **minibus** #728 (٧٢٨) to Abu Qir (20min., every 30min. 7am-10pm, 50pt). 3rd-class **trains** also leave from Misr or Sidi Gabr Station (45min., every 10min. 5am-1am, 45pt), local **taxis** from downtown (15min., E£15-20), or **service** from Misr Station (40min., E£1). Within Abu Qir, horse-drawn carriages (**hantour**) start trotting from al-Bahr al-Mayyit St. (E£2-3).*

On a small peninsula 5km east of Alexandria, Abu Qir has yet to be absorbed by the relentless expansion of the "Queen of the Mediterranean." It was here in 1798 that British Admiral Horatio Nelson took the French fleet by surprise without any navigational charts to guide him. Today, all hints of a military history are gone, and Abu Qir's **beach** is a peaceful and convenient place to enjoy the blue sea and its bounty of edible denizens.

There are no accommodations in Abu Qir, necessarily making it a daytrip from Alexandria. As always, produce and the ubiquitous *ta'amiyya*, shawarma, and *fuul* stands are found in the *souq* near the train station. Only sharks get seafood fresher than that served in Abu Qir's two major sit-down restaurants, both with great views of the beach. The Greek-owned, colorfully muraled ▧**Zephyrion,** 41 Khalid ibn al-Walid St. (☎560 13 19), is the oldest restaurant in town, founded in 1929. Blow on in for a full fish meal (E£25-35) and wash it down with a Stella (E£5.50). Nearby is the similarly priced and appropriately named **Bella Vista.** Nobel Prize-winning President Anwar Sadat was a cook here before he joined the army. Sit at his spot in the far left corner. (☎560 06 28. Open daily noon-midnight.)

One of the cleanest **public beaches** in the area is a short walk down any side street on the left as you face away from the train station. Most Alexandrians go on the weekends, so weekdays are best if you want the beach to yourself. As always, women should be wary of swimming uncovered, though a T-shirt and shorts are sufficiently modest for lounging around this beach.

RASHID (ROSETTA) رشيد

*On the northern edge of the Nile Delta, about 1hr. east of Alexandria. A West Delta **bus** runs from Muharram Bay Station in Alexandria (2:30pm, E£4). **Microbuses** leave from the Tikka Grill in Alexandria, 1 block inland from the corniche (E£3). 3rd-class **trains** run from Misr Station (every hr. 7am-8pm, E£2) via Ma'mura and return to Alexandria (9 per day 5:50am-8pm). **Service** are easy to catch at Muharram Bay in Alexandria, but the returning ones depart infrequently (E£3-5).*

Rashid (Rosetta) is the western meeting point of the Nile and the Mediterranean (Dumyat is the eastern meeting point). Not many visitors besides aspiring Egyptologists and those with plenty of time on their hands venture here. It owes its fame to the **Rosetta Stone,** the key to unlocking the hieroglyphs discovered here in 1799 by Napoleon's army. The port is dotted with provincial Ottoman mosques and houses from the 17th and 18th centuries. Unfortunately, trash-lined streets detract from Rashid's historic homes, many of which have been recently restored. A cast of the stone is on display in the museum here (the Rosetta Stone is in London's British Museum). It describes the coronation and numerous titles of Pharaoh Ptolemy V in three tongues: Demotic (the common language), ancient Greek (the royal language), and hieroglyphs (the holy language). Although hieroglyphs had previously been indecipherable, ancient Greek certainly was not; by comparing the three translations, scholars finally created a basic dictionary of hieroglyphs.

FORT OF QAYTBAY. About 5km from Rosetta, the recently restored Fort of Qaytbay (not to be confused with one by the same name in Alexandria) guards a strategic entrance to the Nile. Built in 1479 by Sultan Ashraf Qaytbay to serve as a first line of defense against the Crusaders and Ottomans coming from the Delta, the fort used to overlook the surrounding land. Clay and silt deposits have built up around it so that today, the ground has risen to the level of the fort. A significant reconstruction took place in 1799, when the French strengthened the fortress's wall with stone imported from Upper Egypt. A soldier noticed carvings on one of the stones, and it is this **Rosetta Stone** that enabled Jean-François Champollion to unlock the mysteries of the hieroglyphic alphabet. *(The easiest way to get to the fort is by green-and-white local* taxi *(round-trip E£10). The romantic way is to find a willing fisherman and go by* **boat,** *observing the beautiful scenery on the way (20min., E£10 per person round-trip). Open daily 8am-4pm. E£12, students E£6.)*

ZAGHLOUL MOSQUE. The badly damaged 17th-century Zaghloul Mosque is at the end of the main street running south from the train station. For a more scenic approach, walk inland from the corniche, past the museum, and south through the *souq.* Past the rancid water and refuse are some Arabic inscriptions, archways, and decorated columns.

THE ROAD TO MARSA MATROUH

Microbuses and **service** *cruise the Alexandria-Marsa Matrouh road all day. Just flag one down (E£3.50 from Alexandria to the Atic Hotel, another E£5-8 to get to Marsa Matrouh).*

The coastline west of Alexandria stretches for several hundred kilometers along Egypt's Mediterranean coast, culminating in the beach resort **Marsa Matrouh.** The Mediterranean's natural beauty can do wonders for the tired body and soul. If you time your day right, you can bask and feast at the beach, stop to visit **al-'Alamein Memorials,** and make it to Marsa Matrouh by sunset. Though many coastline segments between Alexandria and Matrouh are depressingly devoid of budget hotels, opportunities for free and secluded **camping** are virtually unlimited (simply check in with the nearest police station or military office).

IT'S ALL HIEROGLYPHS TO ME Hieroglyphic writing

was used in instances of special religious significance, such as inscriptions on a temple wall or spells designed to speed a pharaoh to a happy afterlife. Since the inscriptions are in part decorative, they are often written in mirror-image pairs; in such cases, the writings are read from different directions. To tell which direction is the beginning, look for a human character; the direction the person or god is facing is usually the beginning. Before the discovery of the **Rosetta Stone,** the most popular theory was that each glyph represented an idea: elaborate, fanciful, and utterly incorrect translations were made from many papyri and inscriptions. The Rosetta Stone provided the revolutionary insight that each glyph stood for an individual sound, rather than a complex meaning. The stone became the key to the long-forgotten script because of its trilingual engraving—Greek, Demotic, and hieroglyphic. The hieroglyphic alphabet uses combinations of sounds to represent words, much like the English alphabet. To provide more exact syntax, the hieroglyphic alphabet also includes characters that clarify meaning and resolve the problem of homonyms.

A number of resorts along the coast let passersby use their facilities for a fee. The plush **'Aida Beach Hotel** (☎410 28 02), 80km west of Alexandria, offers a low rate (E£30), which pays for pool use and a soft drink, or a high rate (E£100), which includes lunch and use of a beach cabin. Day use at the **Atic Hotel** includes a splendid shoreline, two pools, and a playground (a domed gatehouse 90km west of Alexandria with red letters above it. ☎410 63 93. E£20; with lunch E£45). The cheapest sandy spot is the **Marina Beach Club,** 95km west of Alexandria. It'll cost you E£20 (including umbrella and chair) to use the beautiful beach populated by wealthy Alexandrians zipping around on jet skis (E£200 per hr.).

AL-'AGAMI العجمى

Upper-middle-class Alexandrian sun worshippers flock to al-'Agami to escape the bustle of the city, instead embracing a world of concrete villas, chain restaurants, and private beaches. During the peak summer months, crowds compete elbow-to-elbow for beach space and women grow courageous in the quest to bare more than a knee here or a nape there. In winter, hours shorten, prices descend, hemlines drop, and the town quiets down.

To get to al-'Agami, take bus #2 (٢), 3 (٣) or 12 (١٢) from Sa'ad Zaghloul Sq. in Alexandria (E£1-2). Al-'Agami is actually two towns—Bitash and Hannoville. In **Bitash,** villas and expensive hotels mingle with restaurants and Western-style boutiques. In **Hannoville,** the quieter, more spinsterly sister city, a few budget hotels are crammed in between rows of apartments. When Egyptians say "al-'Agami," they're generally referring only to Bitash. Each town is oriented around a 2km-long main street (**Bitash St.** and **Hannoville St.,** respectively) that extends from the highway to the beach and is lined with stores and groceries.

There is no reason to stay in al-'Agami; Alexandria is 30min. away and the hotels here are pricey. Most beaches, such as the belly-and-bicep baring **Fardous (Paradise) Beach,** are private and hard to use. **Abu Qir** and **Montaza** are better bets. The greatest concentration of restaurants is in Bitash, where the main road forks into Bitash St. and al-Asal St. Along with various chain restaurants, **al-Omda** serves up copious quantities of meat, and **La Dolce Vita** scoops up sweet Italian-style gelato.

AL-'ALAMEIN العلمين

Al-'Alamein is a sober interruption in the giddy spree of villa construction that dominates the Mediterranean coast. Here, in November 1942, Allied forces led by British Field Marshal Sir Bernard Montgomery halted the advance of the German Afrika Korps, saving Alexandria, Egypt, and the Suez Canal and oil fields of the Middle East from Nazi takeover. The Allied victory here marked the beginning of the end for the Axis Powers in North Africa and crushed the mystique surrounding the "Desert Fox," German Field Marshal Erwin Rommel, whose force of Panzer tanks had previously seemed invincible. Nearly 10,000 soldiers lost their lives at al-'Alamein, and 70,000 were wounded.

Non-A/C **West Delta buses** traveling between Marsa Matrouh and Alexandria or Cairo pass through al-'Alamein, though you can also go to a **service** depot and name your destination. Get off at the police checkpoint, right before the road to the British War Cemetery; the museum lies left of the main road connecting Alexandria to Marsa Matrouh. To leave town, flag down a *service* or **minibus** heading to Alexandria (1hr., E£5) or Marsa Matrouh (2hr., E£8-10) on the main road (the road leading to the museum and cemetery that merges with the main road Alexandria- Marsa Matrouh road. A hired **taxi** costs E£100, for either a round-trip from Alexandria or a cross-desert run.

WAR MUSEUM. The displays of weaponry and military garb are impressive but sterile. There are English descriptions of Rommel, Montgomery, and other participants in the battle. A map bedecked with hundreds of tiny red and green bulbs recreates the changing landscape of the North African campaign. *(On the west side of the village; near the bus stop and main square. Open daily 9am-5pm. E£5. Camera privileges E£5, video E£20.)*

BRITISH WAR CEMETERY. The British War Cemetery, about 250m east of the museum, is a more powerful testament to the cost of the battle. Here lie 7367 soldiers from all over the Commonwealth, 815 of whom have headstones bearing only the inscription "Known Unto God." Ringed by purple flowers and set against the seemingly interminable desert, the excruciatingly tidy rows maintained by the British War Graves Commission are made even more poignant by the personalized epitaphs. *(Open Sa-Th 7am-2:30pm. Free.)*

> **WARNING:** Do not wander unguided through the desert. While the grounds themselves have been cleared of **landmines,** strips of land between cemeteries remain dangerous.

GERMAN AND ITALIAN CEMETERIES. The less frequently visited German and Italian cemeteries (8km and 12km west of town, respectively) perch on a small peninsula overlooking the sea. It is difficult to get directly to these monuments without a private car or hired taxi. Microbuses along the Alexandria-Matrouh road will let off passengers 2km from the monuments—lucky travelers may be able to convince *service* drivers to give them a door-to-tomb ride. Whichever way you travel, make sure you're armed with lots of water.

MARSA MATROUH مرسى مطروح ☎046

Fanning out from a bay of pure cobalt blue, this resort city—home to the best beaches on Egypt's north coast—makes a pleasant stopover for travelers in no rush to get to Siwa. In summer, Egyptian families pack the mold-and-pour concrete villas and bathe along the 5km crescent of white sands and gentle waves. At night, the streets fill with horn-happy drivers, gaggles of mothers looking for bargains, and shouting vendors selling useless junk. Marsa Matrouh's natural harbor has served travelers, merchants, and soldiers from Alexander the Great to Rommel the Desert Fox. Now the majority of sea vessels in Marsa are rented by the hour, and the police patrolling the Libyan border comprise the only major military presence in the area.

TRANSPORTATION

Flights: EgyptAir (☎493 43 98), on Gala'a St., 3 blocks west of Alexandria St. Flights to **Cairo** (1hr.; W, F, Su 10:30am; US$55). Office open June-Sept. Tu-Su 9am-2pm and 6-9pm. No flights in off season.

Trains: Station (☎493 39 36) is 1 block east of the south end of Alexandria St., and about 1km from the corniche. Runs trains to **Alexandria** (6hr., 3rd-class 7am and 3:30pm, E£3.50. 2nd-class and sleeper cars S, Tu, and Th 11pm, E£26).

Buses: Station is 2km south of the corniche past the train tracks, to the left facing away from the ocean. Book ahead for Cairo buses, especially during summer. Arrive 30min. early to buy tickets and get a seat. Far fewer A/C buses Nov.-May. **Golden Arrow** (☎493 10 79) sends A/C buses to **Alexandria** (3hr.; 9, 11am, 2, 3, 4, 6pm, with additional buses in summer; E£20) and **Cairo** (5hr.; 8:30am, 10:30, noon, 2:30, 3:30, 4:30pm,

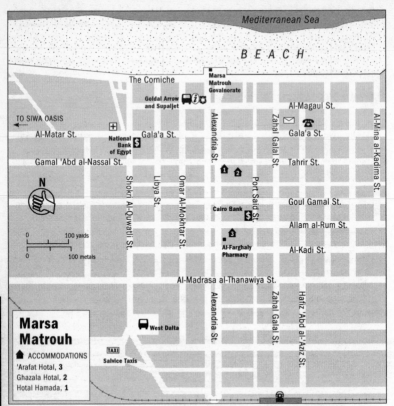

Marsa Matrouh map showing: Mediterranean Sea, BEACH, The Corniche, Marsa Matrouh Govalnorate, Goldal Arrow and Supaljet, TO SIWA OASIS, Al-Matar St., National Bank of Egypt, Gala'a St., Gamal 'Abd al-Nassal St., Al-Magaul St., Zahal Galal St., Gala'a St., Alexandria St., Al-Mina al-Kadima St., Tahrir St., Shokri Al-Ouwati St., Libya St., Omar Al-Mokhtar St., Port Said St., Cairo Bank, Goul Gamal St., Allam al-Rum St., Al-Farghaly Pharmacy, Al-Kadi St., Al-Madrasa al-Thanawiya St., Zahal Galal St., Hafiz 'Abd al-'Aziz St., West Delta, Salvice Taxis.

Marsa Matrouh

⬗ ACCOMMODATIONS
'Arafat Hotel, **3**
Ghazala Hotel, **2**
Hotal Hamada, **1**

with additional buses in summer; E£36). **Superjet** (☎ 493 48 98) offers A/C buses to **Alexandria** (3hr.; noon and 2:30pm; E£20) and **Cairo** (5hr.; 9, 11am, 1:30, 3, 4pm; E£37). Superjet buses do not always run in winter. **West Delta** (☎ 493 20 79) has non-A/C buses to: **Alexandria** (5hr.; 2 7, 11am, noon, 1, 5, 8pm, and additional buses in summer; E£20); **Cairo** (7hr.; 7:30am with additional buses in summer; E£28); and **Siwa Oasis** (5hr.; 7:30am, 1:30, 4, 7:30pm; E£12).

Minibuses: Leave for the surrounding beaches from where al-Matar splits into 2 streets behind the Omar Effendi store, 5 blocks west of Alexandria St.

Service: *Service* leave irregularly from the bus station to **Alexandria** (E£12); infrequently to **Siwa Oasis** (E£15) and nearby beaches.

Bike Rental: On Alexandria St., 2 blocks south of the corniche. E£2 per hr., E£10 per day; bargain for long-term rental.

✦ ORIENTATION

Your feet will serve you well in Marsa Matrouh—a cross-town stroll should take no more than 15min. You only need to know two streets to find your way around town: the **corniche,** which stretches the length of the bay, and **Alexandria St.,** which runs perpendicular to the corniche. Alexandria St. begins at the **Marsa Matrouh Governorate** and heads inland to the **train station** and hill 1km south of town. Most hotels and government offices cluster along the corniche and the streets running parallel to it. Heading inland from the corniche, the most important of these are

Gala'a St., Tahrir St. (also called Gamal 'Abd al-Nasser St.), **Goul Gamal St.,** and **Allam al-Rum St.** Parallel to Alexandria St. to the east are **Port Said St.** and **Zaher Galal St.**

While Marsa Matrouh is a resort town, it is also only 215km from Libya—hence the noticeable military presence in the surrounding areas. It is wise to carry your **passport** with you outside of town and at the more out-of-the-way beaches.

ⓘ PRACTICAL INFORMATION

Tourist Office: Egyptian Tourist Authority (☎ 493 18 41), on the corniche 1 block west of Alexandria St., behind the Governorate building. Friendly English-speaking staff. Ask for the map booklet *Alexandria and Marsa Matrouh,* which lists some hotels and restaurants. Open daily 9am-8pm; in winter 9am-7pm.

Passport Office (☎ 493 38 10), 1 block north and ½ block east of the train station, just off Alexandria St. Open for **visa extensions** Sa-Th 8am-3pm.

Currency Exchange: The National Bank of Egypt, on Shokri al-Quwatli St., 4 blocks west of Alexandria St. Changes traveler's checks and has an **ATM.** Open daily 8:30am-5pm.

Police (☎ 93 33 76), 1 block south of the corniche, 2 blocks east of Alexandria St. Little English spoken. Contact the police in case of a **medical emergency.** Open 24hr.

Tourist Police (☎ 493 55 75), next door to the tourist office. Little English spoken; tourist office or Superjet staff can help you communicate when they're open. Open 24hr.

Pharmacy: Al-Farghaly Pharmacy (☎ 493 93 93), at the corner of Alexandria St. and Allam al-Rum St., 3 blocks south of the corniche. Open daily 8am-2am.

Hospital: Military Hospital (☎ 493 52 86 or 493 43 70), on Gala'a St., 3 blocks west of Alexandria St. It is better to seek treatment in Alexandria or Cairo if possible.

Telephone Office: Opposite the post office. Crowded and unreliable for international calls. Sells phone cards. Open 24hr. **Hotel Riviera Palace,** on the north end of Alexandria St., has pricier but more dependable phone and fax service. Open 24hr. There are **Menatel** phones along Alexandria St.

Post Office (☎ 493 23 67), 2 blocks east of Alexandria St. and 1 block south of the corniche. No *Poste Restante.* Open Sa-Th 8:30am-2pm.

🏠 ACCOMMODATIONS

High season in Marsa Matrouh runs from June to October, with the bulk of its tourist action in July and August. There is also a spurt of Egyptian vacationers during Ramadan. In the off season, upscale hotels along the corniche offer surprisingly low rates. No matter what time of year, you are sure to find a room at one of the budget hotels on and near Alexandria St. Because few foreigners frequent these places, many have neither English signs nor English speakers—sign language or Arabic experimentation (see **Phrasebook,** p. 311) may be in order.

Groups of two or more can rent one of the many available flats in town. From June to September, **Awam Beach Flats** (☎ 493 51 74), west of Alexandria St. off the corniche behind the Mosque of Awam, offers two-bedroom flats for up to six people with living room, bath, and kitchen for E£100 per night.

If they don't mind sharing the beach during the day, couples can relax at **Marine Fouad** (☎ 493 85 55) on Rommel's Peninsula, where wonderful rooms with baths and three meals a day for two people cost E£110. (Open June-Sept.). **Camping** is permitted on the beach in front of the Semiramis Hotel free of charge, but you must check in with the **tourist police** first.

▨ **Hotel Lido** (☎ 493 22 48), on al-Galaa St., east of Alexandria St. Impeccable rooms with new beds, fans, TVs, and balconies. Private baths have towels and soap. Breakfast E£4. Singles E£44; doubles E£53.

Hotel Hamada (☎ 493 33 00), on the corner of Tahrir and Alexandria St. Bare-bones, reasonably clean rooms with shared baths. Avoid the din from the streets below by getting a room away from the corner. Singles, doubles, and triples E£10 per bed.

'Arafat Hotel (☎ 493 36 06), east of Alexandria St. on Tahrir St., down a side street 1 block past the Hotel Hamada. Dusty rooms with clean baths. A 3D picture of a (ra) fat cat watches over the reception area. Singles E£20; doubles E£30; triples E£45.

Ghazala Hotel (☎ 493 35 19), on Allam al-Rum St., in a 3-story white building just east of Alexandria St., 6 blocks from the corniche. Around the corner from al-Farghaly Pharmacy. Dark but well-kept rooms with firm beds and great sofas. Dank baths don't always have hot water. Dorms E£10; singles E£15; doubles E£20.

🍴🎭 FOOD AND ENTERTAINMENT

Strolling along the corniche and chilling out in *ahwas* are the major after-hours recreational sports in Marsa, just as they are in most of the towns along Egypt's Mediterranean coast. The Beau Site Hotel, on the corniche 1.5km west of Alexandria St., serves pricey drinks in its comfortable **bar** (Stella E£11). They also run a **disco** beside the bar and a **bowling alley** across the street. A raised outdoor patio 100m west of the end of the corniche (across from the Armed Services hotel compound) hosts energetic **live music** in a breezy, friendly setting in July and August.

🍕 **Pizza Gaby** (☎ 493 07 91), just past the Negresco Hotel at the west end of the corniche. A/C haven on the sea is a perfect spot to admire the sunset. Tasty pizzas E£9-14. Grilled meats E£18-23. Middle Eastern salad buffet E£5. Open daily noon-1:30am.

Hammo al-Temsah Fish (☎ 494 33 83), on the corner of Port Said and Tahrir St. Choose your fish from the market next door and enjoy a hearty and inexpensive dinner (E£18) at one of the outdoor tables. Open daily 9am-midnight.

Abu Aly Pizza (☎ 494 23 04), on Alexandria St., 3 blocks south of the corniche. This 2-story restaurant offers a wide selection of soups, sandwiches, and desserts. Fresh pizza E£10.50-18.50. Shawarma E£2.50-6. Open daily 9am-3am; 9am-2am in winter.

Panayotis Greek Restaurant (☎ 493 24 74), on the west side of Alexandria St., 2 blocks south of the corniche. Simple menu includs a fresh fish dinner (E£30), calamari (E£25), pizza (E£8.50-16), and Stella (E£7.50). Open daily 8am-2am.

🏖 BEACHES

Marsa Matrouh's glorious beaches are its *raison d'être*. However, just as in Alexandria, some women swim fully clothed, and only the most liberal beaches allow bikinis or revealing one-pieces. No matter how tolerant a beach may be, women should arrive well-covered and gauge the mood of the crowd once there, as the level of acceptance can vary from day to day. Since most Egyptian visitors prefer to relax on the sand, even crowded areas have lots of open water for swimming.

To reach these beaches, catch a *service*, minibus, or pickup truck (E£2-4 per person to 'Agiba or Cleopatra beaches) from the eastern side of Anwar Al-Sadat St., behind the Omar Effendi store. Drivers leave once there are enough passengers (usually every hr. 9am-4:30pm; summer only).

🏖 **'AGIBA BEACH.** Surely the most spectacular of the area's sights is 'Agiba ("miracle" in Arabic), about 25km from Marsa Matrouh. Golden limestone cliffs plunge down to meet azure waters, where waves crash over eroded rock formations and into sandy coves. Swimming is not always permitted, but a barefoot walk along the rocks is one of the best ways to spend a few hours around Marsa Matrouh. Bring **food**—there is only a soft-drink stand here. Archaeologists are currently excavating a tiny **Temple to Ramses II** 2km to the east, near Umm Araham village. The site is on the other side of the road, but as of August 2001, it was off-limits to visitors.

SIWI MADE SIMPLE
Most Siwan children's first language is Siwi, an unwritten Berber dialect. It is incomprehensible to the rest of Egypt and sounds almost Scandinavian at times. As children grow up, parents and schools make sure they learn Arabic as well. The possible permutations of the following words (the **bold** words are in Siwi) should keep you occupied until the donkeys come home:

mashi	yes	**oula**	no
gaf lahk	go	**shiek**	you
oushi	give me	**ehk sehk**	I want
aksoom	meat	**aman**	water
azumur	olives	**tene**	dates
ihkseikh teswi aman	I want water	**tanta elhal ineik**	How are you?
tanta wook	What is this?	**betin ismetinik**	What's your name?

BEAU SITE HOTEL BEACH. At the far west end of the corniche, the Beau Site Hotel has one of the most beautiful beaches around. Though somewhat overrun by frolicking Egyptian children, the beach is cleaner and more liberal than most others. There is no charge for non-guests, but they ask that you rent an umbrella (E£12 per day) or a chair (E£3 per day). During off season, umbrellas are free. Security guards on the hotel's private beach ensure that bathers can wear bikinis without being harassed.

ROMMEL'S ISLE. The eastern part of the harbor is called Rommel's Isle, but it actually isn't an isle at all, and can be reached by donkey cart (E£3), bike (E£10 per day), boat (E£1), or pickup truck taxi (50pt). Nestled in the peninsula is the **Rommel Museum,** housed in the caves that Rommel used as his headquarters during Germany's North African campaign. On display are his overcoat (size 41L) and various German and Italian maps showing the order of battle, yet the small faux cave is hardly worth the price. The **beach** outside, however, is a favorite destination of Egyptian tourists and fills up quickly. (*Museum open daily in summer 9am-4pm. E£5.*)

THE LOVE BEACHES. West of the main beach, the **Beach of Love (Shati' al-Gharaam)** fondles the western horn of the bay and can be easily reached by foot or kayak. Inconsiderate visitors have begun to spoil the sand while enjoying the sun, and heaps of litter float out to sea every day. You'll encounter more wind, less trash, and the tantalizing **Cleopatra's Beach** 14km farther west, on the far right-hand side of a small cove called **Cleopatra's Bath.** Legend has it that the queen and Mark Antony would come here to bathe, and as the waves crashed into the cove, the water would shoot toward the heavens and cascade back down on the lovers' entangled bodies. The peaceful but shallow **Obayyid Beach,** 18km west of Marsa Matrouh, draws Egyptian families staying at their company's tents on the shore, making it pretty boring unless you're there with your friends from the office.

SIWA OASIS واحة سيوة ☎046

Emerging from 300km of barren sand, the palm trees and freshwater springs that comprise Siwa seem like a desert mirage. A walk among the people of this small town and its surrounding villages only deepens the sense of disbelief. Instead of Arabic, the Berber language of Siwi is spoken, and the few married women who venture outside cover themselves from head to toe in blue *tarfudit* veils. Electricity only came to Siwa about 10 years ago, and the thousands of TVs in this town of mud-brick homes are only the most recent in a long history of outside invaders.

ALEXANDRIA

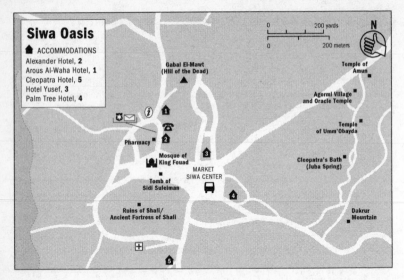

Siwa Oasis

⌂ ACCOMMODATIONS
Alexander Hotel, **2**
Arous Al-Waha Hotel, **1**
Cleopatra Hotel, **5**
Hotel Yusef, **3**
Palm Tree Hotel, **4**

Gabal El-Mawt
(Hill of the Dead)

Temple of Amun

Agormi Village
and Oracle Temple

Temple
of Umm'Obayda

Pharmacy

Mosque of
King Fouad

MARKET
SIWA CENTER

Cleopatra's Bath
(Juba Spring)

Tomb of
Sidi Suleiman

Ruins of Shali/
Ancient Fortress of Shali

Dakrur
Mountain

The Temple of Amun, east of the central town, housed one of the most famous oracles of the ancient world. After taking Egypt from the Persians in 331 BCE, Alexander the Great set out across the desert to learn Amun's prophecy and conquer Siwa. With the centuries that followed came more conquerors: Muhammad 'Ali brought the territory under Ottoman control in 1820, the British occupied it in the early 20th century, and Desert Fox trotted into town during World War II.

Even today, the people here are Siwans first, Egyptians second, and they look skeptically at the technological changes that are making their desert buffer just a short stretch of sand. In 1984, the Egyptian government completed the road connecting Siwa to Marsa Matrouh, turning a week-long camel trek into a quick 4hr. bus ride. Cairo has integrated the oasis into the national economy, and Arabic has replaced Siwi as the language of instruction in schools. Today, younger Siwan women don Egyptian fashions, and local folklore is losing ground to soap operas. These changes are not yet pervasive, and local tradition still regulates everyday life. Local festivals during fall and winter, especially the Feast of Siaha on the first full moon in October, are celebrated with relish and bring in droves of spectators. Older women still wear the traditional Siwan costume, with intricately braided hairdos and heavy silver jewelry around their arms, necks, and heads. Residents request that visiting women cover their arms and legs. Alcohol and open displays of affection are forbidden.

▐ TRANSPORTATION

The most practical way to reach Siwa is by **bus** from Marsa Matrouh or Alexandria, but courageous groups with a **car** can travel the 420km stretch of rough road from the Bahariya Oasis. **Pickup trucks** can be hired to take you the other way for about E£700 per load. One-way overnight **tours** to Bahariya can also be arranged through the tourist office for E£900 for up to seven people.

Buses: To **Alexandria** (E£27) via **Marsa Matrouh** (8hr., 7am, 10, 5pm, and 10, E£10).

Local Transport: *Service* pickup trucks will bring visitors around the oasis. Pick them up in front of the tourist office, but first check inside for times.

⚡🛈 ORIENTATION AND PRACTICAL INFORMATION

Siwa Oasis is in a desert hollow about 300km southwest of Marsa Matrouh. Its western edge comes within 50km of the Libyan border. The valley spans 82km east to west and 30km north to south. Most visitors concern themselves only with Siwa town and nearby villages. **Buses** stop in the **market center** in the shadows of the ancient fortress of **Shali.** The **tourist office** and **police** are back up the road to Marsa Matrouh, while the **King Fouad Mosque,** the town's largest building, is nearby.

Tourist Office: (☎460 23 38), from the bus stop, walk towards the mosque and take a right, following the road to the white building opposite the post office. An oracle unto himself with regard to all things Siwan, **Mahdi Muhammad 'Ali Hweity**—sociologist, fluent English-speaker, and native Siwan—arranges sightseeing expeditions and obtains camping permits. Open Sa-Th 8am-2:30pm and 6-10pm; in winter Sa-Th 4-10pm.

English-Language Bookstore: Hassan's Handicrafts and English Bookshop, between the mosque and the tourist office. A few English books on Egyptian history and culture and some novels. Run by the fab Mr. Hweity of the tourist office. Open Sa-Th 8-11pm; in winter 3-10pm.

Police: (☎460 20 08), in the same building as the post office. Open 24hr.

Pharmacy: Yusef's Pharmacy, on the road to the Cleopatra Hotel. Open daily 9am-2pm and 6pm-midnight; in winter 9am-noon.

Hospital (☎460 20 19). Go south 1km from the town square and take a right at the 1st 4-story building on the left. Open 24hr.

Telephone Office: Next to the Arous al-Waha Hotel.

Internet Access: Muhammad Ibrahem's Internet Service (☎460 20 49), next door to the Palm Trees Hotel. Siwa is, after all, the middle of the desert; connections are slow. Muhammad recommends composing on a word processor (E£8 per hr.) before going online (50pt per min.). Knock loudly if lights are out. Digital camera rental. Open 24hr.

Post Office: Across the street from Arous al-Waha Hotel. Open Sa-Th 8am-2pm.

🏠 ACCOMMODATIONS

Most crash pads in Siwa cluster around the main square. Slow business in the summer means it is fairly easy to find a good room, but in winter Siwa has more tourists than donkeys, so make reservations or consider an outlying hotel. Unless otherwise noted, all rooms have fans. **Camping** is available free on **Dakrur Mountain,** 4km southeast of town, or for E£5 at ▓**Bir Wahad,** 12km south of town. (see **South of Siwa,** p. 185). Bring a warm sleeping bag and insect repellent. Check in with Mr. Hweity at the tourist office before pitching your tent.

▓**Palm Trees Hotel** (☎460 23 04), 20m down a side road from the town square. Clean, comfortable rooms with fans and balconies, but the best part of this hotel is the idyllic grove filled with palm-leaf furniture out back. Laundry machine and bike rentals. Singles E£7.50-10; doubles E£15, with bath E£18; triples E£27.

▓**Hotel Yusef** (☎460 21 62), in the center of town. The name is painted across the top floor. Cleanest rooms in town. Friendly owner Salameh is committed to guest satisfaction. Balconies overlook Siwa and beyond. Women can sunbathe on the roof terrace in peace. Bike rentals. Dorms, singles, and doubles E£6 per person.

Alexander Hotel (☎460 05 12; fax 460 00 06), opposite the post office. Clean but old, with dim rooms and private baths. Dorms E£7; singles E£10; doubles E£15. Prices 30% higher in winter.

Cleopatra Hotel (☎ 460 21 48), south of the town square on the main road, past the Shali fortress. A newer and slightly pricier establishment with stuffy rooms, but great balcony views and immaculate private bathrooms. Antony and Cleo would have preferred the spacious "bungalow" doubles in the building next door (E£34). Breakfast E£5. Singles E£14; doubles E£18.

Arous al-Waha Hotel (☎ 460 21 00; fax 460 20 28), across from the tourist office in the northwest part of town. Huge, spotless rooms and private baths. Breakfast included. Singles E£30.50; doubles E£49. Prices up to 50% higher in winter.

⬛ FOOD

All Siwan restaurants are vegetarian-friendly, and many feature Indian-inspired meals. Local **stores** are well stocked with local produce (dates E£1.25 per kg). If you ask a local may offer you a taste of *lagbi*, a sweet palm-tree juice and local specialty served only before 10am—it ferments by noon. Because Siwans tend to be more reserved than most other Egyptians, only a few travelers receive **invitations** to eat or stay with a local family. Invitations are usually offered by children or adult men. At dinner, your hosts may try to sell you homemade crafts, or they may simply want to talk. Exercise caution before accepting hospitality—solo women should decline invitations from single Siwan men.

Restaurants line the two market squares and are generally open from 8 or 10am to midnight or 1am. In summer, the menus shrink. Siwan eateries are mainly indistinguishable from one another, but there are a few tried-and-true favorites.

'Abdou's Restaurant, on the street running along the north side of the square. Unusual quiche-style veg. pizza E£7-13. For breakfast, try the pancakes with banana, honey, and yogurt (E£3.50). Open daily 8am-midnight.

East-West, same street as 'Abdou's. Yummy grilled chicked E£10. Open daily 9am-1am.

Palm Trees Hotel, 20m down a side road from the town square, Marvelous garden restaurant with small but delicious portions. Breakfast E£1-4. Dinner E£2-10.

👁 SIGHTS

Ringed by multicolored desert mesas and waves of sand dunes, all under a piercing blue sky, Siwa is Egypt's most beautiful oasis. Most of Siwa's sights are easily accessible by bike trips down smooth dirt roads lined with palm trees. The more distant surrounding villages can be reached by local bus or through one of many tours offered by hotels and restaurants. *Carettas* (donkey-drawn taxis) always stand ready, making for a slow and bumpy (but thoroughly Siwan) trip. Mr. Hweity of the tourist office has posted new blue signs around town to mark Siwa's important buildings and roads. A **half-day tour** is a bargain at E£15 per person.

REVERSAL OF FORTUNES According to the ancient historian Herodotus, **King Cambyses** of Persia "detached a body of 50,000 men with orders to attack the Ammonites (a.k.a. the Siwans), reduce them to slavery, and burn the oracle of Zeus." No one is sure *why* he wanted to conquer Siwa, but it's an accepted fact that the Persian ruler turned his wrath on this desert oasis shortly after invading Egypt in 525 BCE. Some have theorized that Siwa's famed **Oracle of Amun** may have predicted a short reign for the new invaders, so a threatened Cambyses decided to demonstrate his power over prophecy. Predictably, things did not go according to plan. The troops made it to Kharga Oasis, then vanished without a trace. Legend holds that the whole army was buried in a sandstorm, but explorers and archaeologists have failed to find any sign of the troops in the dunes. The prophecy did ultimately come true; in 331 BCE **Alexander the Great** ousted the Persians and ended what was indeed a short reign.

SIWA TOWN

RUINS OF SHALI. From atop the ruins of the crumbling medieval fortress-town of Shali (which simply means "town" in Siwi), you can see the quiet streets of Siwa town wind through a cluster of mud houses and luxuriant palm gardens. The wall encircling Shali once protected Siwa from marauding Berbers and Bedouin. There was little room within the walls to build, so houses were cramped. Although the mud-brick structures were sturdy, torrential rains washed away most buildings about twice a century. After Muhammad 'Ali conquered Siwa in 1820, there was less need for fortification, so Siwans were quick to build more spacious homes outside the walls. Several days of fierce rain in 1985 severely damaged much of Shali, and what remains today is a surreal landscape of tangled walls and eroded mud-brick that may house a donkey here, a family there, or an abandoned gaggle of free-range chickens. The walls are quite secure, and it is safe to wander through the ruins. Every Thursday night after the last call to prayer (around 9pm, in winter 6pm), some local Muslims gather for religious ceremonies outside the mud-brick **Tomb of Sidi Suleiman,** who was the town's patron saint, beside the King Fouad Mosque. Visitors are invited to watch.

TRADITIONAL SIWAN HOUSE. The 1985 rains motivated a visiting Canadian ambassador to try to preserve Siwan culture, so he raised funds to construct the permanent Traditional Siwan House. The house serves as a museum of Siwan garb, silver jewelry, and children's toys. *(Down the road from the tourist office, opposite the King Fouad Mosque. Open Sa-Th 10am-noon; ask tourist office about other hours. E£1.50.)*

NORTHERN SIWA

GABAL AL-MAWT (HILL OF DEATH). The acropolis of Gabal al-Mawt rises 1km to the northeast of ancient Siwa. The hill is home to several Ptolemaic-era tombs that Romans robbed and reused. These tombs went undiscovered until World War II, when Siwan families crammed into caves to seek shelter from Italian bombs. The scattered human bones and mummy wrappings that litter the site belonged to the Romans, as did the niches that mar the ancient frescoes. The first sepulcher is the **Tomb of Si-Amun.** The intact decoration shows the bearded nobleman with Osiris, and the magnificent ceiling depicts the six stages of the sun's journey across the sky and a beautiful field of stars. The **Tomb of Mesu Isis,** 5m to the east, has damaged paintings of Osiris and Isis. The **Tomb of the Crocodile** features paintings of the scaly chomper once buried there, although his corpse has been removed. The **Tomb of Niperpathot,** the oldest in Siwa, housed the body of a nobleman of the 26th dynasty (around 662 BCE) and includes paintings of his Nubian and Greek wives and their multiracial sons. *(Tombs are to the left as you enter from the access road. A custodian unlocks tombs daily 9am-2:30pm. Free, but E£2-4 bakhsheesh is appropriate.)*

EASTERN SIWA

The Temple of Amun and the Temple of Umm 'Obayda lie 1km apart on the same road. A bike trip looping around the road might take in the two temples, followed by a dip at Cleopatra's Bath, then onto Dakrur Mountain, and from there back to town. Rent a bike from town or hail a *caretta* (E£10).

ORACLE OF AMUN. A 13th-century gate made of palm logs graces the entrance to the acropolis on which this oracle is perched. Some of the massive inner chambers (all that remains upright) are still adorned by extensive carvings. Follow the same path as Alexander the Great to reach the oracle: go through the stone temple's simple gateway into the outer court, then cross the inner court to reach the center. The Oracle of Amun is thought to date from the 26th dynasty (c. 660 BCE). It became widely celebrated in later dynasties and gained popularity even with the ancient Greeks, who constructed many shrines to Amun in their home city-states. Greek and Roman historians recorded the mystical rituals necessary to invoke an answer from the oracle: priests carried a sacred boat containing the image of

Amun, while women sang and danced in procession. Alexander did all of this to seek the answer to the million-dollar question: Was he a god, the son of Amun? He also supposedly asked the oracle another question in private, but what he queried will never be known. The secret died with him, less than 10 years after his visit.

TEMPLE OF UMM 'OBAYDA. Down the curving road 1km south of the Oracle of Amun, are the remains of the Temple of Umm 'Obayda, also dedicated to Amun. Surviving the ravages of time and an 1877 earthquake, the temple was reasonably well-preserved until 1897, when a local official demolished the remains to collect stone for the construction of new public buildings. One wall remains upright, with inscriptions dedicated to the Egyptian gods.

CLEOPATRA'S BATH. A pleasant 1km bike ride through the quiet, green palm groves around Siwa leads to **Juba Springs,** renamed Cleopatra's Bath by the tourist authority. A tiled basin 15m in diameter now encircles a deep blue pool, which bubbles lightly from the large spring below. Although the pool is mostly frequented by men, fully clothed women should also feel comfortable swimming here (as comfortable as one can be swimming fully clothed), and may enter via the enclosure next to the spring. If you visit at sunrise or in the late evening, you may be the only person there.

HAMMAM RAMAL (SAND BATH). On **Dakrur Mountain,** 1km south of Cleopatra's Bath, nearly 1000 rheumatics congregate each summer for 10-day stints in the Hammam Ramal. The procedure may sound like a Siwan torture method, but it's actually painless: under supervision of a specialist, the "bather" is buried in sand from the neck down while his head is protected from the sun's heat. After a stint in the sand, the patient stays indoors for the rest of the day, then repeats the procedure. *(E£30, including room and board.)*

ABU SHROUF AND ENVIRONS. Abu Shrouf, 27km east of Siwa toward Bahariya, is a beautifully clear and deep spring, and cleaner than any of Siwa's pools. Local legend has it that Abu Shrouf is the only place in the oasis with female donkeys. If a male donkey escapes from Siwa, the first place his owner looks is Abu Shrouf. This myth has even influenced local slang: if a Siwan man has a pleasant night with his wife, he tells his friends, "Last night I went to Abu Shrouf!" You too can go there, either with the tour arranged by Mr. Hweity from the Siwa tourist office (4 people, E£15 each) or by private taxi (about E£80 for a half-day round-trip). A large spring ca^{ll}ed **Qurayshat,** 7km west of Abu Shrouf, was a major farming area during Roman times. Although the spring is not very interesting in itself, the drive past desert shepherds and wild scenery is worthwhile. A small **Bedouin village** lies 5km to the east. Though the government built them houses, the Bedouin preferred to live in tents and keep their livestock in the new homes. Unamused that its projects were being used as barns, the government destroyed many of the tents and forced the Bedouin to live in houses. The ruins of **al-Zaitoun** lie between the Bedouin tents and their small village. The settlement wallows in the hot desert, where a circular olive press still stands among the crumbling buildings.

WESTERN SIWA

▓ **FATNAS.** Plan to spend at least one sunset in idyllic Fatnas, or Fantasy Island, 4km west of town. Accessible by a small causeway, Fatnas Pool is not to be missed. The sun sets over the glistening salt lake as you sit by a palm grove sipping mint tea (E£1.50) and relaxing in a hammock or wicker chair. Ride a bike through palm tree fields and local settlements, passing the occasional donkey cart. From the far western corner of an adjoining garden, observe a limitless sea of sand.

BILAD AL-RUM (CITY OF THE ROMANS). An unidentified stone structure and several tombs in the hillside are known collectively as Bilad al-Rum. Up the road behind barbed wire are the remains of a **Doric temple.** Greek archaeologist Liana Souvaltzi caused a stir in 1995 when she announced that she had discovered the

> **GREASED LIGHTNING** Not long ago, Siwans ran a smuggling operation to carry goods on the sly from Libya into Egypt on donkeys. The nighttime treks would proceed perfectly until the beasts (unaware of the clandestine nature of the mission) would bray and alert the Border Patrol officials, thereby spoiling the whole operation. Siwans wracked their brains to figure out a way to pacify the carriers until someone somehow discovered that if the asses' asses were greased, the brutes would be unable to create the force needed to let air out of their mouths. A team of French scientists is currently researching this exciting discovery.

tomb of Alexander the Great within the temple walls. A team of 12 archaeologists quickly flew in from Greece and determined that the tomb's inscriptions were not Alexander's, but those of another important Greek official. Although Alexander wanted to be buried in Siwa, his general, Ptolemy, purloined the corpse and buried it in his capital, Alexandria, where it lies today (somewhere underneath the modern roads and high-rises). **Campers** can ask the tourist office for special permission to sleep here, then take the bus back to Siwa the next morning.

SOUTHERN SIWA

■ **BIR WAHAD.** Bir Wahad ("Well #1"), lies 12km deep into the sand dunes south of Siwa. Riding a four-wheel-drive through the dunes is exhilarating, as your driver climbs high up and then races down the mountains of desert sand, until two small, lush oases rise from the nothingness. A cool pond sits on one side of a tall dune, while the other side boasts a hot spring with water clean enough for bathing. Nearby, a desert garden grows watermelon and cantaloupe. A number of Siwans offer **guided tours** for around E£60—inquire at the tourist office to find out who offers the best package. A **camp** is set up there where you can sleep under the stars (E£5; with dinner E£10). If you spend the night, bring insect repellent and a **blanket** from your hotel—it gets cold in the desert, even in July.

▐ SHOPPING

You can shop for exquisite **handicrafts,** including intricately embroidered clothing, veils, and *margunahs* (large, decorated woven baskets) in Siwa. Several stores have sprung up around the town square, including **Siwa Original Handicraft,** to the left of 'Abdou Restaurant, and **Hassan's Handicrafts,** next to the telephone office. Bargaining in craft shops can be difficult, since the (mainly female) artisans set the prices themselves and aren't around to haggle. Shawls can start at E£90 and baskets at E£30. The types of crafts sold are changing to accommodate tourist tastes. Siwa's silversmith died several decades ago without training an apprentice, so it is difficult to find jewelry here nowadays.

ALEXANDRIA

WESTERN DESERT OASES

"The call of the desert, for thinkers of the city, has always been irresistible. I do not think they find God there, but that they hear more distinctly in the solitude, the living verb they carry within themselves."
    —T.E. Lawrence

The Western Desert (known as the Libyan Desert until World War II) is the largest and driest in the world, covering two-thirds of Egypt's area but supporting only 1% of its population. It boasts some of the highest temperatures on record, despite the fact that its oases—**Bahariya, Farafra, Dakhla,** and **Kharga**—mark the trail of a prehistoric branch of the cool, wet Nile. Each oasis sits in a depression surrounded by an escarpment, the top of which marks the usual level of the desert floor. Subterranean water seeps through these depressions, which lie at or near sea level. The water flow begins as the rains of equatorial Africa replenish the wells and springs annually, and it takes thousands of years to journey north through underground fissures. The Romans were the first to irrigate the area by tapping deeper reserves with their water wheels and aqueducts, known as **'Ain Romani.** The Egyptian government is finally following suit by spending vast sums on its **New Valley Project** to use underground water to promote agriculture and the relocation of landless peasants from the Delta to the New Valley.

    The desert oases are still somewhat off the beaten tourist path. Though the popularity of the oases is rising and the number of visitors steadily increasing, sights remain uncrowded and prices low, especially during the summer. The best time for all but extreme penny-pinchers to visit the oases is between October and April, as it is not unusual for summer temperatures, especially at Dakhla or Kharga, to reach 52°C (126°F). Even at night, summer temperatures persist into the upper 20s (over 80°F). Air conditioning is making its way across the desert, but at present, only Dakhla and Kharga offer it. Similarly, traveler's checks can only be cashed in Dakhla and Kharga, so have plenty of money on hand before venturing westward. For important **desert safety** information, see **Essentials,** p. 27.

▓ HIGHLIGHTS OF THE WESTERN DESERT OASES

Ever wanted to walk on another planet? You can come imitate the experience in the other-wordly landscape of sand and chalk formations that is the **White Desert** (p. 194).

Sometimes a mirage is just a mirage: the oasis towns of **al-Qasr** and **Balaat** don't actually exist. See p. 194 to find out.

The legendary caravan trail, **Forty Days Road** (p. 203) traverses **Kharga Oasis** (p. 199).

OASIS ESSENTIALS

GETTING AROUND THE OASES

BY BUS

Inexpensive buses run from Asyut to Kharga and Dakhla. Bus travel between the oases requires even more flexibility and patience than in the rest of Egypt Published schedules are no more than rough guesses, so you should get to the

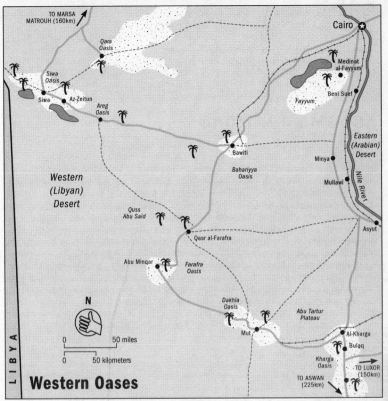

Western Oases

station at least 30min. before the scheduled departure time. When there is no published material available, ask as many people as possible, follow the consensus, and arrive early. The most accurate information will come from local tourist offices and bus officials.

BY TAXI OR SERVICE

Special taxis travel from Cairo to all of the oases, from Asyut to Kharga, and from Kharga to Luxor. They sometimes offer a faster and more comfortable journey—check out what the vehicle looks like and ask how many people will be crammed in. *Service* between all oases are affordable, and often quicker than buses.

CAR CAVEATS. First and foremost, it is always a long way between gas stations. While every oasis has at least one fuel pump, it is essential to buy jerry cans and fill them with enough gas to cover the vast distances between towns. A trailer guzzles huge quantities of fuel, so bring extra to fill an entire tank. Additionally, several containers of potable water are vital in case you get stranded. Try to drive in the cool morning or late afternoon, but never drive at night—the chances of getting lost on unlit roads increase dramatically, and hidden potholes are especially lethal. Note that foreigners are prohibited from leaving the main road. Don't pull an *English Patient*: never drive in a sandstorm. If you do get caught in one, stop, turn the car's rear to the wind, and wait.

BY CAR

Car rental is convenient and comfortable—albeit expensive—for desert travel. A giant loop along the Great Desert Road and the Lower Nile Valley in either direction beginning in Cairo is about 1700km. Any car must be in top condition and fully outfitted for intense desert travel in order to survive the long, hot, poorly maintained roads. **Four-wheel drive** is highly recommended. Another option is a **trailer** (caravan); renting one can solve a lot of problems, including those of transporting food, water, and extra gas, and finding a comfortable place to sleep.

ACCOMMODATIONS

The best alternative to staying in hotels is **camping**. Several budget campsites are run by hotels near Bahariya and Dakhla. Otherwise, most fertile land belongs to farmers who will usually permit you to pitch your tent. The ideal spot is just outside the main town of an oasis, where there is usually a small pool of water (ask the locals for the *'ain*, or spring) and nothing to keep you company but the sound of silence. Or trek out into the desert where cool temperatures and breezes carry away the mosquitoes, and the sand makes a soft mattress. Sleeping on the dunes has its own set of dangers—you might be sharing the desert expanse with ticks, wasps, scorpions, cheetahs, foxes, rats, amorous strangers, and tiny hedgehogs that roll into spiky balls when frightened. You might roll up yourself if you encounter one of the seven kinds of **poisonous snakes** in Egypt, among which is a family of lethal vipers. They rest under rocks and sand, coming out to drink at night. If you see snake tracks going in one direction, calmly go in the other. Common sense, a first aid kit, and a snake bite kit are recommended, even though snakes are rare and snake attacks rarer still. If you prefer mosquito bites to the threat of reptile venom, each of the oases has at least one cheap, clean hotel or rest house.

FOOD

Oasis groundwater tastes much better than that of the other Egyptian municipalities; however, while safer than water near the cities, it can still ruin a trip. The main towns of all the oases have restaurants and markets where you can fill up on food, but don't expect variety or refinement. The best meals are at locals' homes—with a winning smile and a little luck, you can taste for yourself.

SAFETY AND SECURITY

WOMEN TRAVELERS

Women should follow certain guidelines when swimming in springs. They are unlikely to be bothered in isolated springs not frequented by locals. The same goes for pools cordoned off and connected to tourist rest houses. Women should not, however, enter pools where men are already bathing. Sometimes women can bathe in a separate pool (local women bathe separately in the evening), provided they wear a *galabiyya* (loose-fitting robe). Women traveling without men should not embark on overnight desert excursions unless pre-arranged by a tourist official. Even then, care and common sense are key. Solo women heading for the oases should be prepared to deal with harassment. For more on what women can expect traveling in Egypt, see **Women Travelers**, p. 42.

TAXES, TOURISM, AND TRUST

Despite what out-of-date sources may tell you, you need only flash a **passport** at the numerous military checkpoints, and sometimes not even that. In Dakhla, Kharga, or Farafra, you will be asked to pay a one-time **tourism development tax** (E£5) by a tourist officer or by an employee of your hotel. Keep the receipt as proof or you may have to pay again.

> ## TOMB MUCH OF A GOOD THING
> In June 1999, a team of archaeologists led by Dr. Zahi Hawass announced the discovery of an enormous ancient burial ground in Bawiti, the main city in Bahariya. Fifty mummies were unearthed in four rooms of the six-mile cemetery, which probably dates back almost 2000 years. The site supposedly contains more than 10,000 mummies, making it the largest burial ever uncovered and earning it the title **"Valley of the Mummies."** Almost as remarkable as the quantity of the haul is its quality: some of the mummies (who were mostly wealthy aristocrats and rulers) wear gold masks and still have visible depictions of Egyptian deities on their chests. Others are buried in a more typically Roman style, with bodies coated in plaster or covered with linen and laid to rest in terra cotta sarcophagi marked with realistic representations of the deceased's face.

The Western Desert has been attracting an increasing number of visitors with its traditional village lifestyle, stunning landscapes, and low prices. Bahariya, in particular, is seeing an exponential increase in tourism thanks to the recently discovered Roman ruins and "Valley of the Mummies" (see **Tomb Much of a Good Thing,** p. 189), as well as overnight tours to the Black and White Deserts (see p. 192). With this sudden bumper crop of tourists comes the creeping influence of the smell of tourist money. Each oasis has people whose English is good, knowledge of the area fair, and sense of capitalism extraordinary. They are often friendly and helpful, but their assistance has a bloated price tag attached. For the best information, head for the New Valley's **tourist officials:** Muhammad 'Abd al-Qader in Bahariya, Umar Ahmed in Dakhla, and Ibrahim M. Hassan in Kharga. They will answer your questions in excellent English for free and can arrange for fairly priced **guides and transportation.** Without them, you are at the mercy of the wolves.

BAHARIYA OASIS الواحة البحرية ☎018

The land turns a deep shade of red as you approach Bahariya, thanks to the vast deposits of iron that are quarried in an immense mine just off the highway, 40km away from Bawiti. This small oasis, 330km south of Cairo, has been a stopover for caravans traveling between the Nile Valley and the rest of North Africa since pharaonic times, when merchants used to load their donkeys with wine from al-Qasr (the present-day town of Bawiti). In later centuries, Bahariya enthusiastically welcomed Mecca-bound pilgrims, who would often join the traders on their trans-desert trek. Today, the only "pilgrims" in Bahariya are the caravans of rip-roaring European adventurers gallivanting through the oasis in Land Rovers—because of its relatively close proximity to Cairo, Bahariya attracts visitors who crave a few days in the desert. Factor in the opening of several Roman-era sights in 1999, in addition to growing interest in the recently unearthed "Valley of the Mummies" (see **Tomb Much of a Good Thing,** p. 189), and it's easy to see why Bahariya has become far more commercial and cutthroat than the other oases. Unfortunately, Bahariya's ancient ruins are spread over several kilometers, so hire a car for the day or truck it on a bicycle. The nearby gardens, springs, and desert offer relief, but not enough to make anyone stay longer than necessary. Its food stores, market, coffee shops, and three gas stations make this oasis an unavoidable stop for those heading to Farafra.

▐ TRANSPORTATION

The Bahariya Oasis is linked to Cairo by a decently paved road that heads past the Pyramids of Giza, then turns southwest across the desert to the town of **Bawiti.**

Buses: Touts congregate by the bus ticket and reservation office in a blue shed across from the Paradise Hotel (open daily 7am-noon and 8-11pm). A 3pm bus also leaves from al-Monib in Giza. All 7am and 6pm buses continue to **Farafra** and **Dakhla.** Get there early to secure a seat. Daily buses to **Cairo** (5hr.; 7am, noon, 3pm, midnight; E£12.50).

Minibuses: Minibuses run daily between Bahariya and **Cairo's** Sayyidna Zeinab bus station (5hr., E£11). Infrequent service to **Farafra** (E£11). Look for groups gathering by pickup trucks and minibuses in Bawiti on the main street. Minibuses leave when full.

🔢 PRACTICAL INFORMATION

Tourist Office: (☎ 80 30 39 or 80 30 35; 80 26 00 in the evening), 1st fl. of the government compound, which is just before the post office. It is the largest building in town, surrounded by a metal fence, and counts among its staff city council member Muhammad 'Abd al-Qader, who is the best source of information in Bahariya (after 2pm, find him in the lobby of the Paradise Hotel). Open daily 8am-2pm.

Currency Exchange: The **National Bank for Development** is next to the post office. Exchanges cash only. Open Su-Th 8am-2pm.

Gas Stations: 2 on the main road, about 1km out of town towards Cairo.

Pharmacy: (☎ 80 36 55), on the left 50m past Bayoumi's Popular Restaurant as you head towards Cairo on the main road. Open daily 8am-1am.

Hospital: (☎ 80 23 90), on the road toward Cairo. Take the 1st left and walk to the end of the dirt road. The hospital is on the left. Open 24hr.

Telephone Office: Opposite the Paradise Hotel. No international service, but you may be able to get through using MCI, AT&T, or an Egyptian calling card, all of which use local access numbers to connect you with the rest of the world. Open daily 8am-10pm.

Post Office: 2 doors down from the government compound as you head toward Farafra. Limited services. Open Sa-Th 8:30am-2pm.

🏠 ACCOMMODATIONS

Ahmed's Safari Camp (☎ 80 33 99; ☎/fax 80 20 90; ahmed_safari@hotmail.com), 4km south of Bawiti. The massive grapevine-covered veranda, good food, free rides to and from town, and occasional live Bedouin music sweeten the bitter taste of isolation. Ahmed's friendly drivers meet each bus as it arrives in front of the Paradise Hotel. Numerous improvements and additions are in the works for winter 2001-02. Bare huts E£5 per person, breakfast an additional E£2.50. Concrete cabanas with breakfast included E£10-25 per person. Deluxe domed gazebos with shower and breakfast E£50.

Pyramid Mountain Safari Camp (African Camp) (☎ 80 21 84), 17km west of Bawiti. Turn off the main road near the northern end of town. Most visitors come through Hotel Alpenblick, but you can arrange your own transportation out to this clean, tranquil camp run by friendly Sudanese (E£30-35 round-trip per car). The nearby hot spring Bir Ghaba is the highlight of this camp. Breakfast E£15. Basic dinner E£5. Huts E£10 per person.

New Oasis Hotel (☎/fax 80 30 30), 300m down the road leading past Bayoumi's Restaurant and 'Ain Bishmu spring, behind the al-Bishmu Hotel. Resembling something out of a honeymoon package deal, clean and classy rooms sport new beds and baths, wall-to-wall carpeting, and colorful decor. Call ahead to reserve a room, especially during the winter, as large tour groups often claim rooms well in advance. Breakfast included. E£25 per person.

Hotel Alpenblick (☎ 80 21 84), a white-domed building 250m past the "cheapest shop in town" sign as you walk with your back to the city council building and the tourist office. Lodgings here are a bit nicer than other options in Bawiti, but they're not quite worth the added expense. Rooms have carpets, fans, and mediocre bathrooms. Mahmoud, the general manager, organizes trips to the hot springs. Restaurant serves dinner. Breakfast included. Singles E£20; budget doubles E£20; regular doubles E£40, with bath E£56; triples E£60, with bath E£84.

Paradise Hotel (☎ 80 26 00), in the main square, 50m west of the government compound. Shared rooms in this government-run establishment are dark and stuffy and common bathrooms are rather grimy, but the price is hard to beat. E£3.50 per person, with breakfast E£5. Basic rice and vegetable dinner E£6.

FOOD

Pickings are slim for restaurants in Bawiti. Most hotels serve three meals a day. **Bayoumi's Popular Restaurant,** across from the police station, sits next to the government compound just off the main road to Cairo. Ask in advance about prices. (Full meal around E£10. Stella E£7. Breakfast E£5. Open 5am-midnight.) **Restaurant Rashed,** about 200m out of town on the right side of the Cairo road heading east, serves breakfast (E£4), meat and rice (E£8), macaroni (E£4 with meat, E£2 without). Open 8am-midnight. **Al-Gahsh,** in the main square, also serves up morning *fuul* and falafel. Don't miss the **falafel stands** down the main road toward Farafra.

SIGHTS

Hotel managers run group tours of all the area's springs and sights, (E£60 per car accommodates 6 people or more). You can hire a taxi through the tourist office or on your own for E£30 for a 2-3hr. trip; E£80 for a full day.

HOT SPRINGS. Bahariya's hot springs give you the chance to get in touch with your inner lobster and are quite clean despite the faint scent of sulfur. **'Ain Bishmu,** down the road from Bayoumi's Popular Restaurant following the signs for al-Bishmu Hotel, holds steady at a lukewarm 30°C. The cold (25°C) and hot (44°C) springs at **Bir al-Mattar,** eight kilometers southeast of Bawiti, pour out of a viaduct into a small cement pool (taxi E£15-20 round-trip). Men bathe here by day, women by night. The bumpy "road" to Bir al-Mattar (really just a desert track—drivers beware) continues southeast through the desert to ■**Bir al-Ghaba,** 17km from Bawiti. This site has both a hot and cold spring in another sumptuous oasis landscape. Both men and women can swim here (taxi E£30-40 round-trip). Less appealing is **Bir al-Ghilis** (also known as Bir al-Dahkema), a steamy, pump-activated spring only a 10-minute walk out of town on the same road as 'Ain Bishmu; head to Bayoumi's Popular Restaurant and ask for directions (taxi E£5 round-trip).

MUSEUMS. The **Antiquities Museum** (or **Mummy Hall**) is where some of the finds from the surrounding ruins, including pottery shards and five mummies, are kept. Ask the Inspector of Antiquities to dig up the key to the painted subterranean tomb dating from the pharaonic era. Nature is Bahariya's real attraction, but the **Oasis Heritage Museum** in Bawiti is also worth a visit. Talented local artist Mahmoud Eed creates life-like clay figurines to populate dioramas depicting traditional oasis life. *(Antiquities is 500m out of town, on a dirt road that turns right off the road toward Cairo. Ask at the tourist office to arrange a visit. Open Sa-Th 8am-1:30pm. Free. Oasis Heritage is 900m out of town, on the left, heading toward Cairo. Drop E£5 in the box at the back.)*

AL-QASR. Explore the narrow streets and ancient squares of Bahariya's oldest town and ancient capital. A Zawian (as Libyan exiles under Italian rule were called) mosque, Bahariya's oldest town square—Midan Abusti—and traditional oasis homes on old, narrow streets are highlights of a trip through Bawiti's western sibling and the capital of Bahariya in pharaonic times. *(Head down the road past al-Bishmu Hotel and take a left at the square. Take the 1st left to reach Midan Abusti.)*

TOMBS AND TEMPLES

Head 500m out of Bawiti on the main road towards Cairo and turn right onto the 1st dirt road. Past the foodstands, take the 1st left to reach the grey stone ticket office. All sights open daily 9am-5pm. E£30, students E£15. Camera privileges E£25, video E£100.

In spring 2001, five newly excavated ancient ruins were opened to tourists. A single ticket gives admission to the Antiquities Museum plus the five sights listed below and can be purchased in a small grey hut across from the museum. The sights are spread over several kilometers in and around Bawiti. Rent a bicycle or arrange a taxi through the tourist office to see each sight.

▨ TOMB OF BANNENTOIU. Descend a small staircase and duck through the door to enter the main chamber of this 26th-dynasty tomb. Strikingly vivid and colorful pictures grace the walls. On the right-hand side, Bannentoiu stands between Anubis and his priest, who is introducing the golden-haired wonder to an erect Amun-Ra. The great god is pictured missing an arm and a leg—his punishment for impregnating all the women of Bannentoiu's town. The back right wall of the main chamber was damaged by a Cairene thief who removed the plaster and paintings (he was later caught and the paintings recovered, but they have not been returned to Bahariya). In the second chamber, the right wall shows gods Tehuti and Maat weighing Bannentoiu's life for admission into the afterlife. *(Cross the Cairo road and walk straight down a dirt path. Buildings give way to a barbed wire fence after 100m. Enter through the opening in the fence on the left.)*

TOMB OF ZED-AMUN EF ANKH. Bannetoiu's father is buried next door in a similarly styled 26th-dynasty tomb. In two different frescoes Zed-Amun Ef Ankh makes sacrifices to his gods. At the back of the chamber you can see the work of Romans who unsuccessfully dug away at a false door. Silly Romans, tombs are for kids!

TEMPLE OF 'AIN AL-MUFTELLA. The temple of the "mother of the spring on the sand dune" is composed of two separate buildings with faint inscriptions on the inside of the stone walls. At the back of larger building, behind a locked door, are the clearest inscriptions of this 18th-dynasty temple. Look for a troupe of 7 dancing girls performing in front of the god of happiness and love. The god's small body, large head, and lion's tail indicate that he may have been a foreign god from the East. *(4km outside of Bawiti in al-Qasr. Facing Ahmed's Safari Camp, travel towards Bawiti and turn left onto the well-paved asphalt road. Where the road branches, go straight onto the dirt road leading to the temple.)*

TOMB OF AMENHOTEP HUY. Most of the inscribed drawings on this late 18th-dynasty tomb have faded away, but some images can still be seen. On the wall to your right as you enter is a drawing of Amenhotep Huy's servants storing wine while he and his wife sit on mats. In the right corner of the far wall is a large image of Amenhotep seated with his wife, facing the goddess Hathor, who is pictured as a cow. This is one of the less impressive tombs around. *(1½km from Bawiti on the road toward Farafra. Take a right onto the dirt road 150m past the military compound.)*

TEMPLE OF ALEXANDER THE GREAT. There isn't much to see at the ruin of Alexander's only Egyptian temple. Discovered in 1938, the back wall of the temple shows a faint image of Alexander with Amun and other Egyptian gods. His official stamp was found there, but it has been removed and taken to Cairo. Behind the temple lie the ruins of the priests' housing. *(4km outside Bawiti. Take the dirt road behind Ahmed's Safari Camp and continue left behind the sheet metal building. Continue down the dirt road 50m until you reach the caretaker's hut.)*

NEAR BAHARIYA: THE ROAD TO FARAFRA

*The best way to ensure a reasonable price for a **tour** from Bahariya is to arrange one through Muhammad 'Abd al-Qader at the tourist office. Organizing overnight desert tours from Farafra may be cheaper, but call ahead to al-Badawiya Hotel if possible. If you can't round up a posse, you can see the area from a public **bus** (sit on the driver's side). Every site except al-Wadi Oasis can be reached by a regular car, but a 4x4 is more fun. Overnight tours including food, transportation, and sleeping arrangements for a desert camping experience should run E£350 per car (5 people can fit), E£450 for a 4x4, and E£750-800 for a 3-day, 2-night extended tour. Summer is the cheapest time to go but the hardest time to find riding partners. Drivers will begin by demanding E£800 for trips to Farafra, so bargain hard.*

The 183km road from Bawiti to the Farafra Oasis runs through spectacular canyons, wind-blown mesas, and rugged desert landscapes from which precious gemstones were exported during the reign of Ramses II. The eastern and western escarpments of the Bahariya depression meet at a point about 60km south of Bawiti; the road winds through this pass and onto a brief plateau before plummeting into the Farafra Oasis.

Leaving Bawiti, you'll first pass through the **Black Desert,** known for its dark mesas and crumbly flats peppered with sun-blasted rock and tufts of dry desert grass. Tours usually drop groups at the base of **Black Mountain,** where a short but steep 300m climb yields a striking view of the surrounding desert. The idyllic oasis village of **al-Hayiz** (E£60 per truckload as a daytrip from Bawiti) lies 5km off the main road to Farafra, 40km from Bawiti. Gardens and a spring make this simple village a nice spot to camp overnight and enjoy fresh watermelon or apricots for breakfast. **Crystal Mountain** (nothing more exciting than a roadside hill with quartz deposits) rises about 100km from Bawiti. Farther along is **al-Agabat,** which means "strange," "beautiful," or "difficult" in Arabic. Camel caravans that struggled to cross this desolate land of rugged plateaus rising sharply from the sandy desert floor gave the area its name. The palm trees and the small, desolate **Magic Spring** of the empty **al-Wadi Oasis** (the only location that requires a 4x4) are about 140km from Bawiti and usually included in 3-day trips. The oasis is striking amidst the towering dunes and grazing gazelles. About 40km outside Farafra, the black buttes suddenly give way to the **White Desert,** known for its breathtaking views and stunning chalk formations. For more on the White Desert, see p. 194.

FARAFRA OASIS واحة الفرافرة ☎010

Farafra claims an impressive 16% of Egypt's entire territory and borders both Libya and Sudan. Five years ago the area was home to a mere 5000 people, but immigration since then has brought that figure to over 14,000. Nonetheless, the oasis's main town, Qasr al-Farafra, still the smallest of the oasis capitals, attracts fewer tourists than its counterparts. The main road through this dusty, sleepy town hosts all three supermarkets, a handful of restaurants, and three small cafes. Farafra makes a good starting point for overnight desert tours, but not much else. However, recent increases in tourism have led to a bit of development, and province president Muhammad Ra'afat Amin has done much to redefine the region's image: hotels have been privatized, over 60,000 acres of land have been reclaimed through a large-scale irrigation effort, and an airport is in the works.

█ TRANSPORTATION Buses and **service** arrive and depart from Tamawy Cafe, under the bus station sign on the Bahariya-Dakhla road; ask around for the latest bus schedule quirks. Reception staff in al-Badawiya Hotel and Aiman in Hossin's Restaurant speak English and are helpful with bus information. **Buses** run daily to Dakhla (5hr., 2pm and 2am, E£12) and Bahariya (2½hr., 10am and 10pm, E£12), continuing on to Cairo (8hr., E£25). **Minibuses** and *service* are also a good way to get to Dakhla. Around 6am and 6pm are the best times to travel; ask around the night before to secure a seat (4hr., E£12-15). A **gas station and repair shop** is on the main road, 500m down from the bus stop. *Let's Go* never recommends **hitchhiking.**

⧉ PRACTICAL INFORMATION All services are on or just off the Bahariya-Dakhla road. As you head toward Bahariya, you'll pass the **police station** and **post office** (open Su-Th 8am-2pm) on your left, followed by the **telephone center,** which offers unreliable international service (open daily 8am-midnight). Next to the post office is the **city hall,** where government officials with spotty English may be of assistance planning desert excursions, but don't count on it. (Open Sa-Th 8am-2pm.) For better, honest assistance talk to chef Aiman at Hossin's Restaurant. The **hospital** sits 1.5km out of town on the main road toward Bahariya. (☎51 00 47. Open 24hr.)

▐▐ ACCOMMODATIONS AND FOOD. Al-Badawiya Hotel (☎51 00 60, fax 51 04 00, badawya@link.net), 750m from the bus stop in the direction of Bahariya, has beautifully decorated, painstakingly cleaned rooms and toilets, and stunning bedouin architecture. Don't miss the rooftop terrace. Breakfast E£2-15; lunch and dinner E£5-20. Laundry service E£1-2. (Dorms E£15; rooms E£20 per person, with bath E£40 per person.) **Camping** in the nearby desert or at **Bir Sitta** (6km from town) might make for a more organic experience, but bring plenty of insect repellent. Also check your shoes and pants before getting dressed—scorpions and huge biting ants thrive in these parts. Don't let them thrive in yours. The huts of several budding gourmands are clustered around the bus station. **Hossin's Restaurant,** opposite Tamawy Cafe and 30m toward Dakhla, offers traditional desert fare, outdoor seating, and a friendly English-speaking chef named Aiman who serves up tasty meals and good advice for E£6.

◙ SIGHTS. The **art museum,** conveniently situated across from the oxymoronic Military Intelligence Office, displays sculptures and paintings made of local materials (sand, mud, and sticks) by the talented local artist, Badr, depicting life in Farafra. (Open daily 9am-1pm and 4pm-sunset. Free.) The hot spring **Bir Sitta** (Well #6), 6km west of town, is an idyllic spot to swim and camp (transportation E£15-20 per carload). If you're fed up with the flatulent scent of the sulfur wells, head to **Birkat Abu Noss,** 15km outside of town, to cool off. This lake is 2km off the road to Bahariya; turn left just before the checkpoint (round-trip transportation E£30).

NEAR FARAFRA OASIS

WHITE DESERT صحراء بيضاء

*An average overnight trip in a **4x4** from Farafra should cost about E£250-500 per carload, depending on the type and length of trip. An average desert safari should cost about E£350 per carload. More establishments in Bahariya and Dakhla are beginning to offer reasonable White Desert tours (see **Dakhla: Accommodations and Food,** p. 197); inquire ahead to compare prices. The incorrigible Mr. Saat, manager of al-Badawiya Hotel often insists on outlandish prices. If you don't mind being stranded in the desert for several hours on the way back, take a **bus** to Bahariya (10am, E£12) and ask to be let out at the White Desert (make sure the driver will do this before you leave Farafra) and then catch the next bus back to Farafra, which may be after 6pm.*

The White Desert (about 40km from Farafra) has overnight camping and breathtaking views. Spooky fungoid chalk formations stand stark white in daytime, glow shades of bashful fuchsia by dusk, and turn orange by dawn. A typical tour of the desert from Farafra (the best starting point for a trip to the White Desert) passes through both verdant **Wadi Henis** and the village of **Karaween,** which has marvelous springs and gazelles. Visiting during or near a full moon can be a particularly otherworldly experience. As you leave the White Desert, you'll pass a **cold spring.** For information on traveling between the Bahariya and Farafra Oases, see p. 192.

DAKHLA OASIS واحات الداخلة ☎088

If traveling through some of the other desert oases seems like a challenge, Dakhla (also known as the "pink oasis" for the surrounding pink cliffs) is the reward. Affordable food, appealing lodgings, and picture-book Islamic sights and natural backdrops all come together in and around **Mut,** the oasis capital, unlike anywhere else in the Western Desert. The work of 75,000 Dakhlans has resulted in a widening wave of greenery, including peanuts, rice, and other crops. Yet this poster-child for the New Valley Project has not allowed itself to be urbanized in the manner of Kharga; a mix of Nubians, Sudanese, Libyans, and Berbers peacefully inhabit this laid-back oasis without abandoning their traditional way of life.

▐ TRANSPORTATION

Flights: The **airport,** 10km south of Mut, is served by **EgyptAir** (☎82 28 53 or 82 28 54), which has an office in the courtyard opposite the police station in town. Flights to **Cairo** (W 8:50am; E£615, US$160). Open Sa-Th 8:30am-2:30pm.

Buses and Service: Buses and *service* depart from **Mut Station** (☎82 15 38), in New Mosque Sq. Arrive early and don't expect to leave on time. Buses to **Cairo** (7pm and 9pm, E£35-40) via **Kharga** (2½hr., E£8) and **Cairo** (12hr., 6am and 6pm, E£30) via **Farafra** (5hr.). Local buses run to **Asyut** (6am, 8:30, 1pm, 5pm, 10pm; E£16) via **Kharga** (E£8) and **Balat** and **Bashendi** (E£1), leaving Tahrir Sq. across from the police station and stopping frequently along the way. Bus schedules change frequently so ask the tourist office for updates. *Service* are more reliable, especially early in the morning. *Service* and minibuses to: **Farafra** (5hr., 6am or when full, E£15), **Kharga** (3hr., 6am or when full, E£8), and **Asyut** (6hr., 6am or when full, E£16).

Taxis: Taxis offer sightseeing tours (one day E£50-60, shorter one-sight-only trips E£10-20); ask in New Mosque Sq. or at the tourist office. Covered pickup trucks shuttle frequently between Tahrir Sq. and Balaat, Bashendi, and al-Qasr (E£0.50-1). The early bird catches the truck: around 6am and early afternoon are the best times to try.

Bike Rental: In Abu Muhammad Restaurant on al-Thrawa al-Khadra St. E£10 per day.

▐ ORIENTATION AND PRACTICAL INFORMATION

The Dakhla Oasis, 320km from Farafra and 190km from Kharga, is bounded by **West Mawhub** (80km west of Mut) on one side and the fertile **Tineida** (40km east of Mut) on the other. Cultivated regions also dot the well-paved main highway. The most appealing of these are **al-Qasr** (30km west of Mut), **Balaat** (30km east of Mut), and **Bashendi** (35km east of Mut). The capital of the Dakhla Oasis is **Mut** (pronounced "moot"), named for the Egyptian mother goddess and wife of Amun (see **Meet the Gods,** p. 75). Mut has two focal points: **Tahrir Sq.,** at the intersection of New Valley St. and the southeast-northwest Kharga-Farafra Hwy., and **New Mosque Sq.,** one kilometer south on New Valley St.

Tourist Office: The **new office** (☎82 16 86 or 82 16 85) is 400m away from Tahrir Sq. on the road to Farafra, across the street from Abu Muhammad Restaurant. The **old office** (☎82 04 07) is across from the mosque in New Mosque Sq., in the same building as the Tourist Rest House. The knowledgeable Omar Ahmed (☎94 07 82) speaks English and helps arrange transportation. Both open Su-Th 8am-2pm and 8-10pm.

Currency Exchange: Misr Bank (☎82 00 63), in Tahrir Sq., on the road towards New Mosque Sq. Changes traveler's checks and cash. Open Su-Th 8:30am-2pm and 6-9pm, and sporadically Sa 8am-2pm for changing money.

Gas Station: On the outskirts of eastern Mut, on left side of the road to Kharga. Another station west of Mut, 1km from Tahrir Sq. Open 24hr.

Police: (☎82 15 00), in Tahrir Sq.

Pharmacy: There are 7 pharmacies in Mut. One is directly across the street from the new mosque in New Mosque Sq. Open daily 8am-2pm and 4-10pm.

Hospital: The **main hospital** (☎82 15 55 or 82 13 32) is 1km from Tahrir Sq., toward Kharga. Smaller hospitals are in each village. Open 24hr.

Telephones: From New Mosque Sq., walk east along 23 July St. to Anwar Restaurant, then veer left toward the red-and-white tower about 30m ahead on the left. Open 24hr. For **international service,** try the 2 private telephone offices by the Tourist Office on the road to al-Qasr or the office by New Mosque Sq.

Post Office: One in New Mosque Sq., another on al-Ganeim St., around the corner from the telephone office. Both open Su-Th 8am-2pm.

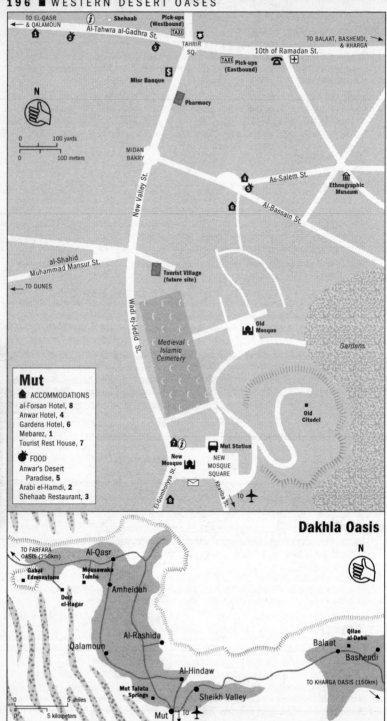

DESERT OASES

TO EL-QASR & QALAMOUN

Shehaab

Pick-ups (Westbound)

Al-Tahwra al-Gadhra St.

TAXI

TAHRIR SQ.

TAXI Pick-ups (Eastbound)

10th of Ramadan St.

TO BALAAT, BASHENDI, & KHARGA

Misr Banque

Pharmacy

N

0 — 100 yards
0 — 100 meters

MIDAN BAKRY

As-Salem St.

Ethnographic Museum

Al-Bassain St.

New Valley St.

al-Shahid Muhammad Mansur St.

TO DUNES

Tourist Village (future site)

Wadi el-Jedid St.

Medieval Islamic Cemetery

Old Mosque

Gardens

Old Citadel

Mut

ACCOMMODATIONS
al-Forsan Hotel, **8**
Anwar Hotel, **4**
Gardens Hotel, **6**
Mebarez, **1**
Tourist Rest House, **7**

FOOD
Anwar's Desert Paradise, **5**
Arabi el-Hamdi, **2**
Shehaab Restaurant, **3**

New Mosque

Mut Station

NEW MOSQUE SQUARE

El-Gamhonrya St.

Kharba St.

TO

Dakhla Oasis

N

TO FARFARA OASIS (250km)

Al-Qasr

Gabal Edmonstone

Mousawaka Tombs

Deir el-Hagar

Amheidah

Al-Rashida

Qalamoun

Qilae al-Daba

Balaat

Bashendi

Al-Hindaw

TO KHARGA OASIS (150km)

Mut Talata Springs

Sheikh Valley

Mut

TO

0 — 5 miles
0 — 5 kilometers

ACCOMMODATIONS

If you're not down with sleeping out in the dunes, Dakhla has the choicest lodgings of the oases, making it the place to stay should you need a couple of days' respite from the sand.

Al-Forsan Hotel (☎ 82 13 43; fax 82 13 47; elforsan@usa.net), close to New Mosque Sq. on the main road running to Tahrir Sq. wins the location and cleanliness awards. Pool table and a satellite TV on the covered patio. Spacious rooms are ideal for larger groups. Breakfast E£5. E£10 per person, E£15 with bath; E£25 with A/C and bath.

Gardens Hotel (☎ 82 15 77), 20m down a dirt road from Anwar's Desert Paradise Restaurant and Hotel, has a leafy garden and very polite management. Stick to the breezy rooms with fans unless you don't mind stuffy rooftop dorms. Breakfast included with rooms over E£20. A curious washing machine churns out clean clothes in small batches; E£1 per load. Dorm beds E£8; singles E£12, with bath E£15; doubles E£16, with bath E£20; triples E£18, with bath E£24.

Anwar Hotel (☎ 82 00 70, ☎/fax 82 15 66), at the intersection of al-Salem and al-Bassain St., boasts breezy rooms and balconies. Rooms and common baths are very clean and neat. Breakfast included with private rooms. Throw a mattress on the roof for E£7. Dorms E£15, some have A/C; singles E£10, with A/C E£20; doubles E£20, with A/C E£35; triples E£30, with A/C E£55.

Mebarez (☎ 82 15 24). A 4-story mustard-yellow building 800m from Tahrir Sq. on the road to Farafra, Mebarez tries with dubious success to be upscale. It specializes in housing large European tour groups during the winter. All rooms have fans and balconies. Breakfast E£5, lunch and dinner E£15. Singles E£28; doubles E£42. Bath, A/C, and breakfast add E£16.

Tourist Rest House (☎ 82 04 07), across from the mosque has a small doorway with a black sign over it. Dirty rooms with mediocre bathrooms; E£5 per person.

Bedouin Camp (☎ 85 08 05; ☎/fax 85 04 80), 7km northwest of Mut on the road to al-Qasr. If you came to the oasis for a break from the same old hotel scene, ditch Mut and head to this hilltop camp. Clean, wooden huts with concrete floors and well-kept shared baths. Breakfast included. Dinner E£10-15. Large common area used for impromptu bongo performances. Inquire about desert jeep and camel tours. E£15 per person.

FOOD

The desert oases are not known for their filling cuisine, but Dakhla's is the best around. Three brothers have restaurants on the road between Tahrir Sq. and al-Qasr. **Hamdy,** just before the Mebarez Hotel, serves large multi-course chicken and meat meals (E£10), **Arabi** offers the same fare as well as fresh duck, rabbit, and pigeon specialty meals from his farm out back (E£20). Both open 8am-11pm. Around the corner from the Garden Hotel is **Anwar's Desert Paradise Restaurant,** so named, perhaps, for the aging air-conditioning (full meal E£9). **Shehaab,** whose English sign reads "restaurant," is the first restaurant outside of Tahrir Sq. on the road to al-Qasr. This local favorite with sawdust under the tables offers traditional fare (full meal E£4). **Al-Forsan Hotel** has a classy outdoor restaurant offering meals at plebeian prices (kebab meal E£12-15).

SIGHTS

There's little of interest in **Mut,** but the oasis capital is a great starting point for **Western Dakhla,** which includes the village of al-Qasr and surrounding archaeological digs, and **Eastern Dakhla,** which includes the villages of Balaat and Bashendi (see **Dakhla: Practical Information,** p. 195, for more information). In the cooler months, biking to some spots is feasible, although you'll still need to bring plenty of water—and then some.

WESTERN DAKHLA

Hire a pickup for a day (E£50-70) or hop on the pickup truck taxis that circle the sites. Ask the Dakhla tourist office for help on tours, itineraries, and prices.

QALAMOUN. The distinctly medieval hilltop village of Qalamoun was the capital of Dakhla in Mamluk times. In the Islamic era, Qalamoun functioned as an administrative center. Its inhabitants today claim Turkish and Mamluk ancestry. The town's name has two possible translations: "Amun's pens" (*qalam* means pen), for the scribes who lived here, or "Amun's citadel" (*qala'a* means fortress), as Qalamoun's panoramic perch offers military defense. Near the center of town is an Ayyubid **mosque,** uphill through the maze of narrow passages and traditional mud-brick houses. *(5km west of Mut is the Bedouin village of al-Douhous, where the road splits for 25km before joining up again; the left fork takes you to Qalamoun.)*

AL-GEDIDA. Al-Gedida ("New Town," so named because it's only 300 years old) is known for its **arabesque factory.** In cooperation with 'Ain Shams University and the German Embassy, locals make decorated woodwork with palm tree branches. For more delicious handiwork, sample the town's sweet harvests: apricots in May, mangos in late July, and dates in October. *(5km past Qalamoun, on the road to al-Qasr. Factory open Sa-Th 8am-2pm. Free.)*

MOUSAWAKA TOMBS. These tombs are closed for renovations as of August 2001, though a worker may be present to show you around the jagged rock headstones dating from the first and 2nd centuries CE and the slightly newer domed tombs. Outside, small caves dug into the hill house skeletons and mummies; nowhere in Egypt can you get more up close and personal with a mummy than here. *(3km west of al-Gedida, on the left or 5km south of al-Qasr, take a right at the white Arabic sign leading to a dirt road.)*

DEIR AL-HAGAR. Half the fun of this Roman temple is the road leading up to it, which twists and turns around a small village and passes three Roman remains before leading up to a ridge which affords a striking view of Deir al-Hagar rising out of the desert dunes. Dedicated to the immortal Theban trio of Mut, Amun-Ra, and Khonsu, the temple was built during the reign of Nero and added to by his immediate successors. Roman emperors ruling in Egypt had no problem playing the role of pharaoh, and this temple combines Egyptian gods with the hieroglyphic names of Roman emperors. A long colonnade lines the path to a small temple and its vivid inscriptions. Ask to see the small exhibit by the entrance. *(8km from al-Qasr. Across the street from the Mawhoub building, follow the road to the village, where a dirt road takes you 1½km to the desert temple. Open daily 8am-5pm. E£20, students E£10.)*

AL-QASR القصر

The most edifying daytrip from Dakhla is al-Qasr, a twisty 32km from Mut on the northern fork. This charming contemporary town was built in and around the substantial remains of Dakhla's medieval Islamic capital. The older buildings, adorned with lively accounts of pilgrimages to Mecca, are a model of comfortable architecture, as their mud buildings remain cool in summer and warm in winter. The **old village** of al-Qasr lies 400m to the north of the main road through the new village. On the main road at the western edge of town, there is a large **map** of the village. Within the old village, arrows direct you to the sights. Still, sights are hard to find without a guide (E£5 tip expected). The number of old village residents is dwindling, replaced by children selling handicrafts. **Al-Qasr Rest House,** on the main road at the turnoff to the old village, serves up traditional desert fare as well as ice cream and cold drinks. (☎87 60 16. Breakfast E£2, lunch E£5, dinner E£7.) The hotel upstairs offers basic rooms (E£10 per person) and rooftop mattresses (E£2). There is also a market, 30m from the hotel on the same side of the road. A **medical clinic** is 50m toward Mut.

WorldPhone. Worldwide.

MCI℠ gives you the freedom of worldwide communications whenever you're away from home. It's easy to call to and from over 70 countries with your MCI Calling Card:

1. Dial the WorldPhone® access number of the country you're calling from.
2. Dial or give the operator your MCI Calling Card number.
3. Dial or give the number you're calling.

- Egypt   7955770

Sign up today!

Ask your local operator to place a collect call
(reverse charge) to MCI in the U.S. at:

1-712-943-6839

For additional access codes or to sign up, visit us at www.mci.com/worldphone.

www.mci.com/worldphone

It's Your World...

www.mci.com/worldphone

OLD VILLAGE SIGHTS. The **Minaret of Nasser al-Din** is the only extant part of an 11th-century Ayyubid mosque; a 19th-century mosque surrounds the old tower. Down the gnarled alleys north of the minaret stands **Qasr Madrasa,** an intact two-story mud-brick building thought to have been either an Ayyubid school-house or the entertainment hall of an Ottoman palace. Villagers later used the building as a courtroom and the nook on the left as you enter was a small prison. Also inside the maze of buildings are a grain mill and olive press. Many of the doorways of the old village are adorned with ornate wooden lintels that reveal the name of the owner, builder, and carpenter as well as the date of construction. Bits of a pharaonic arch and a Roman doorway hint at al-Qasr's pre-Islamic past. On the southern fringes of the old town you can see a waterwheel and a functioning **pottery works,** where villagers churn out everything from ashtrays to chamberpots.

EASTERN DAKHLA

BALAAT. In the crowded old section of Islamic Balaat (pop. 5000), long, dark passageways burst into a courtyard with palm fronds and grapevines. These pathways were built with ceilings as a defense tactic—during invasions, the enemies' camels and horses could not fit through the alleys. Ask to see the **mayor's house,** with its assembly courtyard, speech balcony, and Ottoman wrought iron lamps and bedframes. Outside the old village are several markets selling snacks and drinks.

QILAE AL-DABA. Dakhla's pharaonic governors were buried in these red-brick tombs during the 6th dynasty. A team of French archaeologists has uncovered three unusual inverted step pyramids as well as a mummified governor. *(Behind Balaat; walk past the bus stop toward Bashendi on the main road for 500m and then take a left before a row of trees onto the dirt road marked by twin sign poles. Follow the electric wires into the desert. One pyramid can be seen from the road. Follow the dirt road 1km into the desert and head for the brown tomb rising from the desert sand. Ask locals for al-Maqabr al-Fara'oniya. Open daily 8am-5pm. E£20, with ISIC E£10—but there is often nobody there to collect the toll.)*

BASHENDI. Though less picturesque than its younger brother Balaat, Bashendi sits atop a recently discovered temple and various Roman-era tombs that make a visit worthwhile. This isolated village has tiny, twisting streets and is more of a working town than the other old Islamic villages of Dakhla. The large stone **Tomb of Ketenus** contains six rooms, including one decorated with scenes of a 2nd-century Roman mingling with the gods Min and Seth. Before you can mingle with the ghosts of Romans past, you'll need to get the key from the tombkeeper. Next door to the Tomb of Ketenus is the prominent **Tomb of Bashendi,** which consists of a distinctly Bedouin domed roof atop a Roman foundation. The tomb commemorates the village's beloved namesake; you might join locals who decorate the inside of the holy man's tomb with henna. If the guard isn't around to open the tombs, another villager will do the honors. There are also a number of hot and cold springs to which residents can direct you, though local touts would rather lead you to the Bashendi **carpet works,** where youths weave beautiful rugs for E£100 and up. *(5km east of Qilae al-Daba, 40km from Mut. Ask locals for al-Maqabr al-Romaniya. Tomb of Ketenus E£16, students E£8.)*

KHARGA OASIS الواحة الخارجة ☎ 92

Kharga is the capital of the New Valley Province *(al-Wadi al-Gideed)* and Egypt's most effective attempt at a desert boomtown. Little is known about Kharga's early pharaonic history, although it must have been agriculturally productive—its hieroglyphic name is *hibis*, or "plow." Kharga became prosperous during Roman times due to its proximity to trade routes, including the Darb al-Arba'een (Forty Days Road), between Egypt and Sudan. Beginning in the 4th century, Kharga was a large Christian settlement and center for monasticism, to which sundry Christian figures (including Bishop Nestorius, founder of the heretical Nestorian sect) were exiled by religious and political rivals. The oasis's role as Egypt's Siberia continued into the 20th century, when Nasser banished Mustafa Amin, founder of *al-Akhbar* (Egypt's largest circulating daily), to Kharga after the 1952 revolution.

When the New Valley Project began in earnest in the early 1980s, the town again prospered. The streets of Kharga, filled with new cookie-cutter apartments, are largely lifeless and boring by Egyptian standards, but the ruins on its periphery astound. Welcome relief from Kharga's New Town can be found in the narrow alleyways of the Old Town, where locally made ceramics and carpets are available in the *souq*. The recent rise of tourism may be causing Kharga to rapidly modernize, but a side trip from one of the area temples to small oasis towns provides a glimpse of the friendly agricultural life that thrives there. Be aware of local customs; women are asked not to wear shorts or sleeveless tops. While Kharga is safe, visitors may encounter the local tourist police who trail tourists as they move throughout the oasis. Ditch them if you can, or use them to your advantage as a (free) personal taxi service.

Kharga is the closest oasis to the Nile Valley, a mere 240km from Asyut. A newly paved road heads south from the city, skirting dunes and small oases on the way to **Bulaq** (15km south), **Baris** (90km south), and **Luxor** (270km west).

⬛ TRANSPORTATION

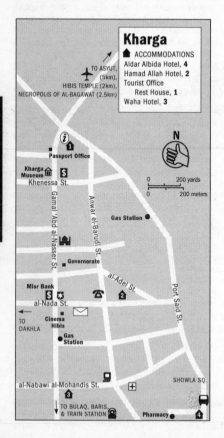

Kharga

▲ ACCOMMODATIONS
Aldar Albida Hotel, **4**
Hamad Allah Hotel, **2**
Tourist Office
   Rest House, **1**
Waha Hotel, **3**

TO ASYUT,
   (5km),
HIBIS TEMPLE (2km),
NECROPOLIS OF AL-BAGAWAT (2.5km)

Passport Office

Kharga Museum

Khenessa St.

Gamal Abd al-Nasser St.

Anwar el-Barudi St.

Gas Station

Governorate

al-Adel St.

Misr Bank

al-Nada St.

Port Said St.

TO DAKHLA

Cinema Hibis

Gas Station

al-Nabawi al-Mohandis St.

SHOWLA SQ.

TO BULAQ, BARIS,
& TRAIN STATION

Pharmacy

0   200 yards
0   200 meters

N

Flights: EgyptAir (☎92 16 95), in the Governorate, 2 blocks north of the Misr Bank intersection on Nasser St. Open Sa-Th 8am-2pm. **Airport** turnoff is 3km north of town on Asyut Rd., then another 2km southeast. Flights to **Cairo** (25 min., Su 7:50am, US$40) via **Asyut** (US$54) or via **Dakhla** (W 7:50am, E£450). Minibus or taxi to airport from Showla Sq. E£5.

Trains: 5km south of the intersection of al-Nabawi al-Mohandis and Nasser St. Take a taxi from town for E£5. Check with the tourist office for schedule updates; trains do not run every day. Trains go to **Luxor** and **Baris,** leaving Kharga at 6am and leaving Baris for Kharga at 2pm.

Buses: Intercity buses arrive and depart from Showla Sq. to: **Asyut** (3hr.; 6, 7, 8, 11am, noon, 2, 7:30, 10pm; E£7); **Cairo** (11hr.; 6am E£23, 9 and 11pm E£30); **Dakhla** (2½hr.; 1, 8, 11am, 2, 10pm; E£7). **Local buses** to **Baris** (3hr.; 1, 3, 7am, noon, 2:30pm; E£1.60) and **Dush** (1½hr., 6 and 11am, E£2). Schedules change, so see tourist office for updates.

Service and Minibuses: Catch *service* and minibuses in Showla Sq.

6-10am and 5-10pm are the best times to find *service,* as locals stay out of the midday sun. Service to **Asyut** (2½hr., E£8), **Dakhla** (2hr.; E£8, "special" unshared E£100), and occasionally **Baris** (E£3). With a group, a special taxi to Luxor may be feasible (4hr., E£300-350 per car). Hiring a *service* or minibus to Baris for the day costs E£50-75. For sights north of town, a roundtrip "special" pickup **taxi** should cost around E£10. Within town, **covered truck taxis** scurry along al-Nabawi St. from Showla Sq., turn up Nasser St., and head for the tourist office at the northern end (10pt).

✦ 🛈 ORIENTATION AND PRACTICAL INFORMATION

Gamal 'Abd al-Nasser St. runs north-south and is bisected by **al-Nada St.,** which heads west to Dakhla. At this intersection you'll find Cinema Hibis, the **Misr Bank** (traveler's check exchange, V cash advances; open Su-Th 8:30am-2pm), and the **police station** (☎ 122). The main branch of the **post office** is just off al-Nasser St., behind Cinema Hibis. (**EMS** service. Open Sa-Th 8am-2pm. Smaller branch in Showla Sq.) At the northernmost end of al-Nasser St., just before it heads off to the ruins and Asyut, stand the rest house and **tourist office,** where the resourceful Ibrahim Hassan, regional director of oasis tourism, will make your stay in the oases as pleasant as possible by smoothing over any bumps with his excellent English. (☎92 12 06; ☎/fax 92 12 05. Open daily 8:30am-8pm and occasionally until midnight. Mr. Hassan is in Kharga Su-Tu and in Dakhla Th-Sa.) The **passport office** (open Sa-Th 8am-2pm) faces the tourist office, and the **tourist police** is next door. (☎92 13 67. Open 24hr.) Grab a **pickup taxi** (10pt) to get to this part of town.

The southern end of al-Nasser St. intersects **al-Nabawi al-Mohandis St.,** which runs east-west. This street curves slightly northeast to **Showla Sq.,** where you'll find the intercity bus, *service,* and minibus stations. The main **hospital** is off al-Mohandis St. toward Showla Sq. (☎ 122 or 92 07 77. Open 24hr.) **Aleman Pharmacy** sits between Aldar Albiadaa Hotel and Showla Sq. (Open daily 9am-midnight.) Get online at **Computer Technology Center,** on al-Nabawi St. (Open Sa-Th 9am-midnight. E£10 per hr.) One block south of Showla Sq., on the left as you walk past Aldar Albiadaa Hotel, is a small blue Internet office without an English sign. (Open 24hr. E£30 per hr.) **Al-Dawati Telephone Central,** in Showla Sq., has the most reliable international service. (Open Sa-Th 8am-midnight.)

🏠 ACCOMMODATIONS

Rooms with fans are essential in the summer, and they don't hurt in the winter.

Waha Hotel (☎92 03 93), on al-Nabawi al-Mohandis St., close to the corner of Gamal 'Abd al-Nasser St. A 30min. walk from Showla Sq., near grocery stores and restaurants. Simple, tidy rooms with balconies and crisp linen. The common bathrooms are strictly cold water affairs. Dorm beds E£5-8; singles E£7, with hot water, bath, and fan E£16; doubles E£16, with bath E£22.

Aldar Albiadaa Hotel, only steps away from the bus station, is a favorite among travelers. The rooms and baths are well-cleaned but noisy due to the bustle below. Singles E£15, with bath E£20; doubles E£20, with bath E£28; triples E£24, with bath E£30.

Hamad Allah Hotel (☎92 50 17) on al-'Adel St., 1 block from the Telecom tower. Shady trees circle the building, which features posh and peaceful doubles with wall-to-wall carpeting, refrigerator, A/C, TV, bath, and towels. Breakfast included. Lunch E£15, dinner E£17. Singles E£38, with A/C E£63; doubles E£54, with A/C E£90.

Tourist Office Rest House, (☎92 12 05) directly behind the tourist office on Gamal 'Abd al-Nasser St.. Villas come with living rooms, TV, fully equipped kitchens, and A/C. Ideal for groups of 4 or more. E£22 per person.

DESERT OASES

FOOD

Cuisine in Kharga is adequate on a good day, and a decent rotisserie chicken seems to be the specialty (half of a bird with rice, vegetables, salad, and bread E£5-8). Clusters of budget eateries and coffee shops can be found on al-Nabawi al-Mohandis St. between Gamal 'Abd al-Nasser St. and Showla Sq. The greatest concentration of restaurants is around al-Basatin Sq. Vegetarians have to make do with beans and rice. A restaurant at the entrance to the *souq* street offers *fuul* and falafel (50pt) for breakfast.

◎ SIGHTS

MUSEUM AL-WADI AL-GADID (NEW VALLEY MUSEUM). This is the *pièce de resistance* of the New Valley's tourism drive, housing an extensive collection of artifacts from ruins throughout the New Valley oases, and a few pieces from the Egyptian Museum in Cairo. Displays include prehistoric stone tools, wooden sarcophagi, sandstone sphinxes, mascara jars, and Roman coins. *(Open Sa-Th 9am-5pm, F 9am-noon and 3-5pm. E£20, with ISIC E£10. Camera privileges E£10.)*

TEMPLES OF HIBIS AND NADURA. The **Temple of Hibis** was begun in 588 BCE (during the 26th dynasty) by Apnias and completed in 522 BCE by Darius I, making it one of only two Persian-built Egyptian temples. Although dedicated to the Theban trio of Amun, Mut, and Khonsu, the temple is distinguished by its depictions of Persians and of Seth, god of the Oases, with a blue body and a falcon head. First-century Roman inscriptions on display discuss legal issues, including women's rights. Crowning a knoll across the road from the Temple of Hibis is the **Temple of Nadura,** built in the 2nd century BCE during the reign of Roman Emperor Antonius. Little of it stands today, but the site offers an excellent view of the oasis and some faint hieroglyphic inscriptions. *(At the northern end of town, 2km north of Hotel al-Kharga and close to the road on the left. A shared covered taxi will take you to the tourist office (and possibly farther) for E£1. From there, walk or try to hop on an intertown taxi (E£2). The scaffold-covered Hibis will be closed for several years for renovation but you can walk around the outside. Nadura, closer to town on the right, is open to the public. Free.)*

NECROPOLIS OF AL-BAGAWAT. The 263 above-ground tombs (also called chapels) of the Christian Necropolis of al-Bagawat stand eerily at the desert's edge. From the 3rd through 8th centuries, a sizeable Christian community (including many hermits and some of the religion's first monks) inhabited Kharga. The necropolis is visible from the road, and an asphalt lane leads to the ticket booth. If you go up the hill along the marked path, you'll come to the **Chapel of Exodus,** with ceiling murals depicting the pharaoh's army chasing Jews as they flee from Egypt From the doorway, you can see Moses on the left, to the right of a tree. Adam and Eve stand below him next to a doorway with ankh-like crosses. On the other side of the tree, slightly underneath it, is Daniel. In front of the Chapel of Exodus are the interconnected frescoed chapels #23-35, the resting places of members of a wealthy local family. The interior frescoes of biblical scenes in the **Chapel of Peace (#80)** exemplifies Coptic painting in the early Alexandrian style. Greek inscriptions identify Adam and Eve, Noah's Ark, and the Virgin Mary. Atop the cemetery's central hill stands a ruined 4th-century mud-brick basilica. *(500m past the Temple of Hibis on the road to Asyut. Open daily 8am-6pm, in winter 8am-5pm. E£20, students E£10.)*

FACTORIES. A little more than 500m south of al-Nabawi St. down al-Nasser St. is a **pottery and carpet factory,** where young women make and sell handicrafts. Pottery runs 50pt-E£30, and carpets start at E£33. Next to the pottery showroom is a small museum displaying clay scenes of oasis life, fantastic photos of locals in action, and handmade baskets. Another 300m down al-Nasser St. is the **date factory,** where

200 women at conveyor belts take plucked, washed, steamed, blind, dried, hot, and double dates and stuff them with peanuts. *(Pottery and carpet factory open Su-Th 9am-2pm. Date factory open Sept-Jan. Sa-Th 8am-1:30pm. Both free.)*

NEAR KHARGA

For a full day of exploration, hire a pickup **taxi** for the day from Kharga (E£50-75). Plenty of shared taxis go from Kharga as far as **Bulaq** (50pt). Catch them at north end of Showla Sq. Each day, **buses** go to **Baris** (2hr., 7am and 2pm, E£1.50) and back (11am). *Service* run infrequently between Kharga and Baris (E£3). Morning is the best time to travel. **Hitchhiking** is difficult and dangerous in the extreme heat.

DARB AL-ARBA'EEN (FORTY DAYS ROAD) درب الاربعين

If you've come all the way to Kharga, don't miss the road along the old camel trail that leads south to the town of Baris, known as Darb al-Arba'een (the Forty Days Road). The road follows the floor of the valley east of Kharga. The temples of Ghwita, Nadura, and Dush were lighthouses of the desert, notifying weary traders that shelter, food, and rest were near. From any of those hilltop temples, look eastward for a view of this legendary caravan route. Extending from the western Sudan to the Egyptian Nile Valley, Darb al-Arba'een trafficked more slaves than any other land route in history.

GHWITA TEMPLE. Vast sandscapes are all that thrive between Kharga and Ghwita Temple, 17km to the south. The 10m-high walls of the temple-fortress dominate a hill 2km east of the road. The mud-brick exterior gives way to a multi-chambered stone temple dedicated to Amun, Mut, and Khonsu. Built by Darius I, the temple served as the center of a thriving, grape-producing community in pharaonic times. *(Take a pickup taxi from Showla Sq. (50pt) and get off after the big orange gas tanks. From the main road, it is 1km to the left. Open daily 8am-5pm; in winter 8am-6pm. E£16, students E£8.)*

ZAYAN TEMPLE AND WELLS. At the 25km mark you'll come across the village of **Nasser** and its shaded, dirty Nasser Wells. **Zayan Temple,** dedicated to Amun, sits 5km east of Nasser Wells, near the village of Araf, on a road that loops around from north of Ghwita Temple to a point north of Bulaq. Originally built in the Ptolemaic era, the Romans restored the site and built a fortress, of which there are still remnants. A colonnade leads to the small interior temple, where hieroglyphs decorate the doorways. *(To get to Zayan Temple, hop on a pickup or public bus headed for Baris and have the driver drop you off at Araf. A round-trip taxi should cost no more than E£20 for both Ghwita and Zayan. Zayan is 5km outside Ghwita Temple on the asphalt road. To return to Kharga or continue on to Baris, walk 1km to Bulaq and catch a pickup taxi, bring lots of water and wait by the road. Let's Go does not recommend hitchhiking. Open daily 8am-5pm, in winter 8am-6pm. E£16, students E£8.)*

BARIS بارس

The secluded desert outpost of Baris (the sign at the edge of the town ironically reads "Paris") est 90km au sud de Kharga et comme l'enfer en été (over 50°C), mais il fait beau en avril. Until 10 years ago, merchants made a 40-day camel trek from here to the border of Chad to purchase an ingredient used in local soap, each expedition reputedly bringing the merchant E£20,000. More recently, difficulties with the Sudan have closed the border, making the profitable journey impossible. Today Baris is quiet and dusty, but it offers beautiful views of the surrounding desert and a window into the typical agricultural oasis lifestyle, free from the tourist influences that have infiltrated Kharga. Since there is no place to spend the night, start your trip to Baris early. The nearby temple is worth a visit, and the friendly locals make this town a nice rest stop before heading back to Kharga.

DESERT OASES

Mr. Farkhat from the Kharga **tourist office** is available in Baris (Th-Sa). If you walk down the central street, perpendicular to the main road, old Baris will be on your right and the gardens straight ahead. The blue building resembling a doghouse sells kebab, *fuul*, and falafel every day except Friday. Numerous cafes line the street and a few markets offer snacks.

An abandoned **public housing complex** designed by Egyptian architect Hassan Fathy stands 300m northwest of the **rest house.** Construction was halted when war broke out in 1967 and never resumed, as the government correctly assumed that the villagers wouldn't want to live in buildings resembling tombs.

DUSH TEMPLE هيكل دوش

A paved road leads 23km southeast from Baris to the Dush Temple. Baris pickup taxi drivers will make a special round-trip to Dush for E£20, wait included, but are hard to find. Open daily 8:30am-5pm. E£20, students E£10.

The temple has an overabundance of heat and a shortage of visitors during the summer, but there's more to the deceptively large temple than meets the eye. Particularly thrilling are the decorated, seemingly endless inner chambers that lead you deeper and deeper into the heart of the temple. Originally built for the worship of Serapis and Isis, the building dates back to the rule of Roman emperors Trajan and Hadrian. The sand around the temple is slowly parting to reveal a church, pottery shards, and a well with clay pipes. These pipes tunnel down to an underground city, leading archaeologists to believe that Dush was a prosperous settlement that was abandoned when the wells ran dry.

NILE VALLEY وادي النيل

How doth the little crocodile
Improve his shining tail
And pour the waters of the Nile
On every Golden Scale.
    —Lewis Carroll

Originating at the equatorial high water marks of Lake Victoria and Lake Taru, the Nile winds north through Uganda, Ethiopia, and the Sudan, pouring into Lake Nasser and Egypt, where its banks are home to 95% of the country's population.

Before the construction of the Aswan High Dam in 1971, the Nile overflowed its banks every year, depositing the rich silt that made the valley the most fertile region in the world. This yearly inundation was the most important time of the year for ancient Egyptians and the reason for ancient religions to focus on the river's cycles. No major temple along the length of the Nile Valley was without a **nilometer,** a graded pit used to measure and predict the river's depth. For millions of ancient Egyptians, no oracle was more influential.

The region between Cairo and Luxor is known as **Middle Egypt,** home to the majority of the country's Coptic Christian population. Akhenaton built his capital at Tel al-Amarna; farther south stand the temples at Abydos and Dendera. Luxor marks the northern boundary of **Upper Egypt,** stretching upstream (south) to Lake Nasser and the Sudanese border. Tourists flock here to see the underground maze of ancient architecture on Luxor's west bank and the imposing temples at Edfu and Abu Simbel.

In summer, temperatures average over 45°C (113°F), frequently breaking 50°C (122°F). This is *a bit* warm, but the complete lack of humidity makes it possible to continue most essential biological processes, even as the sand slowly drips into beads of glass. Hotel managers, guides, and others of their ilk are desperate for business in the summer, so bargain hard. To avoid the heat, plan most of your touring for between 6 and 11am; to avoid the crowds, shoot for late afternoon. In November through May, temperatures drop and prices rise.

▨HIGHLIGHTS OF THE NILE VALLEY

Don't miss the stupendous **Luxor and Karnak Temples** (p. 219) in Luxor.

Tired of temples? Two bad: the cream of the crop are the twin **Temple of Hathor** at Dendera (p. 253) and **Temple of Horus** at Edfu (p. 235). A **felucca cruise** from Aswan lets you see them in style (for more information on *feluccas*, see p. 206).

Aswan is famous for its immense **High Dam** (p. 239), but the most stunning constructions lie south, at **Abu Simbel** (p. 251).

GETTING AROUND THE VALLEY

BY SERVICE, BUSES, AND TRAINS

Traveling by **service** is the cheapest and most convenient option for shuttling between the river towns at almost any time of day. Unfortunately, security throughout Upper and Middle Egypt prohibits *service* trips between more distant cities. "Special" (i.e. "ripoff") **taxis** are a possibility, but prices are high. Another option is to travel with the police escorted **convoy** (check with the local tourist office for schedule). As regulations regarding tourist travel in Egypt are constantly changing, inquire at a tourist office or *service* stop to determine the best way to go. Don't let yourself get too frustrated trying to find a ride; you'll need your nerves in top form to cope with drivers' recklessness. **Buses** are often slightly cheaper than *service*, and run more frequently, but they can be horribly slow, hot, and unreliable. Most stop running at 6pm. Buses are best for transport out of Luxor or Aswan, where you can reserve air-conditioned buses by going to the station a day or two in advance. In the smaller towns between, you may not find an empty seat, and schedule reliability plummets. **Trains** can be a hassle for short trips, but first- or second-class air-conditioned compartments are a great value for the long Luxor-Aswan haul or for more distant sights north of Luxor. Third-class travel is possible, but authorities discourage tourists from taking third-class trains and obtaining schedules may be difficult. See listings in **Luxor** (p. 213) and **Aswan** (p. 239) for more specific information.

BY NILE CRUISER

Tough times for tourism in Egypt have opened up an option for budget travelers on a binge: the **Nile Cruiser.** Book a cabin on a triple-decker, pool-topped cruise ship and slip from Luxor to Aswan or vice versa (one-way is 2 nights), hobnobbing with French tourists the whole way. Travel agents can book for you at a mark-up (US$45-80 per person per night) or you can go to the dock yourself and chat with the boat receptionist about open cabins (as low as US$35 per person per night). The air-conditioned, two-room suites come with TVs and showers. All meals are included, but drinks are extra pricey. A *kalish* will cart you to the temple and back at each stop. Several travel agents (including Eastmar and Misr Travel) dot the corniche south of the Winter Palace in Luxor. In Aswan, agencies can be found around the southern end of the corniche. If you find a bargain, you'll enjoy two days of pure bliss: sunning by the pool and watching the palms float by, interrupted only for daily feedings.

BY FELUCCA

For those who want to get up close and personal with the Nile while still sticking to a tight budget, a **felucca** (sounds like "bazooka") cruise is a slow-paced way to absorb the Egyptian countryside and regain sanity after days in overcrowded *service*. *Feluccas* (Nubian for "boats") have been sailing the Nile for thousands of years—and *felucca* scams have been going on for at least that long. The more careful you are in navigating the crowded docks, the more carefree you can be while your captain navigates down the river.

The typical Nile-cruising *felucca* sleeps up to eight people (though some can hold more), has a single tall mast with a characteristically angled boom, and is piloted by an English-speaking Arab or Nubian Egyptian. When traveling alone, gather a group of like-minded tourists (aim for six) in hotel lobbies, the many restaurants along the Nile, or on a tour to Abu Simbel. You can also ask at the tourist office. As a last resort, join a group already assembled by a captain. Be sure to meet these people beforehand, or you may find yourself stuck in a horrifying Middle Eastern version of MTV's *Road Rules.* Your bargaining position is strongest when a full group is assembled, so rounding up a posse may be worth the effort.

Members of a six-to-eight-person group leaving Aswan pay E£35-40 each to Kom Ombo (1 day, 1 night), E£50-90 to Edfu (3 days, 2 nights). These prices include a E£5 registration fee and all meals on board. For registration in Aswan, the captain will ask for your passport, and in some cases, a deposit or the E£5 registration fee. Have an assembled group ready, or the captain may try to hold your passports hostage until he can corral other passengers. Prices don't vary much from captain to captain, so the most important variable is the vibe you get. During the summer, prices may dip a bit due to the shortage of tourists, but it's harder to find a full group. Conversely, prices rise in winter, but finding a full group is easier. As of August 2001, *feluccas* are not allowed in Luxor—all stop in Edfu. The quick trip to Kom Ombo cuts the adventure short, but most find the voyage to Edfu just right.

Lower Nile Valley

MEDITERRANEAN SEA

Abu Qir
Rosetta (Rashid)
Alexandria
Damanhur
Tanta
Mansura
Rashid
Dumyat
Deir Anba Baramus
Deir al-Suryan
Zagazig
WADI
NATRUN
Benha
Bubastis
Qanatir
Deir Anba Bishoi
Deir Abu Maqar
Giza
Cairo
Pyramids of Giza
Helwan
Abu Sir
Memphis
Saqqara
Dashur
Lake Qara'un
Qara'un
Fayyum
Hawara
al-Lahun
WADI AL-RUWAYAN
Beni Suef
al-Fashn
Magagha
Nile River
Beni Mazar
Deir Gabal al-Teir
Tehna (Acoris)
Mina
Beni Hassan
Tuna al-Gabal
Ashminein (Hermopolis)
Mallawi
Tel al-Amarna
Dairut
Manfalut
Abnub
EASTERN DESERT
TO KHARGA
Asyut
Al-Badari
WESTERN DESERT
Tima
Akhmim
Deir Anba Shenouda (Deir al-Abayyad)
Sohag
al-Mansha
al-Balyana
Abydos
Qena
Dendera

N

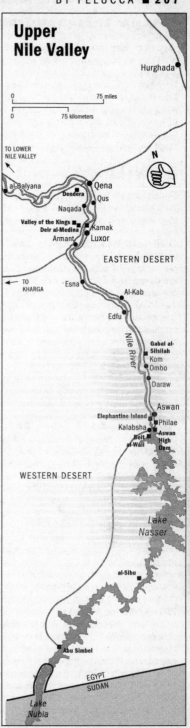

Upper Nile Valley

Hurghada

0 — 75 miles
0 — 75 kilometers

TO LOWER NILE VALLEY

al-Balyana
Qena
Dendera
Qus
Naqada
Valley of the Kings
Deir al-Medina
Karnak
Armant
Luxor
EASTERN DESERT

TO KHARGA

Esna
Al-Kab
Edfu
Nile River
Gabal al-Silsilah
Kom Ombo
Daraw
Aswan
Elephantine Island
Kalabsha
Philae
Beit al-Wali
Aswan High Dam
WESTERN DESERT
Lake Nasser
al-Sibu
Abu Simbel
EGYPT
SUDAN
Lake Nubia

N

TIPS ON TRAVELING BY FELUCCA

CHOOSE THE CAPTAIN ON YOUR OWN

From the moment you step off the train in Aswan, you will be constantly approached by *felucca* captains or—more often—middlemen sent out to round up suckers. Every hotel manager and every man in the local *ahwa* has his favorite *felucca* captain (from whom he receives a commission), so the word on the street is almost useless. Commission-charging hotels, even if they don't add to the price of the trip, will take money away from your captain who may then be inclined to cut corners on the trip to make up for his losses. From the northern local ferry terminus on Elephantine Island (p. 244) in Aswan, Captain Jamaica runs a polished, though somewhat pricey, *felucca* operation. The charismatic captain owns seven feluccas and runs by far the most popular trips. If you're in a pinch for time or are having a hard time rounding up fellow travelers, pay Jamaica a visit, as he is likely to have one of the seven *feluccas* sailing soon. Keep in mind that Captain Jamaica sells the trips but his relatives actually captain the boats, so make sure to meet your captain before sailing.

LOOK FOR EXPERIENCED CAPTAINS

Go down to the river yourself, meet and talk with several captains, inspect several boats, and take a list of potential candidates to the tourist office to make sure they aren't pirates or perverts. Ask to see comment books and talk to fellow travelers. Check for lifejackets. Be skeptical of any cute aliases the captain uses (the Most Inappropriate Boat Captain Nickname Award goes to Captain Titanic)—an honest captain will tell you his real name if asked. Also be wary of captains who speak little English: these typically younger captains often lack the experience necessary to handle sailing emergencies (several capsizings in recent years have been caused by high winds and inept sailors). You're better off with a gnarled, salty old man who speaks English well (if a bit colorfully) than with some wet-behind-the-ears pollywog who is just learning the ropes. If you decide to back out of a trip or switch captains, you should receive a full refund, minus E£10-15 if your captain has already bought food.

PRE-ARRANGE THE FINAL DESTINATION

Make sure that the captain clearly understands the final stop. For example, many *felucca* trips to Edfu actually stop at a way-station 40km from a town where prearranged microbuses take passengers the rest of the way. Captains are tempted to stay close to home to save themselves a time-consuming return against the current. Unscrupulous boatsmen have been known to drop their passengers off without mentioning such arrangements, claiming that it was "close enough."

CHECK YOUR PROVISIONS

Choose a captain who takes care of the cooking. An extra-special captain who cooks Nubian dishes in the *felucca* or stops at his village for a home-cooked meal is a godsend. A captain should also bring at least two cartons of bottled **water;** make sure it is aboard before you depart and check that the tabs are sealed, as they may be filled with tap water. In addition, bring at least three bottles of water per person per day for drinking, cooking, and brewing tea. You can also ask for a big jerry can of tap water to be brought along to be used instead of the Nile for washing dishes and faces. For those looking for more exciting libations, beer can be procured at the liquor store on the corniche.

SOHAG

Sitting on the west bank of the Nile 465km south of Cairo, Sohag sees a huge influx of Coptic pilgrims making their way to the famous White and Red Monastaries every July and August. But the real *raison d'être* as far as tourists are con-

ROLLIN' ON THE RIVER Top *felucca* captains to avoid:

10. *Captain Hook.* Good at fencing, not so good at dodging crocodiles.

9. *Captain Ahab.* Dude has to take his mind off that stupid white whale and watch where he's steering the boat.

8. *Captain Kangaroo.* Beloved TV personality has trouble navigating without the help of Mr. Green Jeans, Mr. Moose, and Grandfather Clock.

7. *Captain Morgan.* Rum pitchman unlikely to pass sobriety checkpoints on the Nile.

6. *O Captain! My Captain!* Famous Walt Whitman poem. Unfortunately, the skipper isn't much help after having "fallen cold and dead."

5. *Soy capitán.* Yo no soy marinero, soy capitan, soy capitan, soy capitan. If he crashed Ritchie Valens's plane, you shouldn't get on a boat with him.

4. *Cap'n Crunch.* Sugary breakfast cereal will rot your teeth.

3. *Captain Kirk.* Rule #17: Never trust a *felucca* captain with a bad toupee.

2. *Captain Marvel.* Nega-Bands give this superhero the power to fly faster than the speed of light, to breathe in space, and to shoot energy blasts. But he can't swim.

1. *George Clooney.* Star of *The Perfect Storm* drowned Marky Mark, lost all the fish, and wasted millions of moviegoers' money. Stay out of his *felucca* at all costs.

cerned is the spectacular temple of Abydos, 50km south of Sohag in the town of al-Balyana. Tourists are rare here, and locals are friendly and genuine. Security in Sohag is especially tight, and visitors should not be surprised to be accompanied by a group of armed guards for the duration of their stay.

TRANSPORTATION

The **train station** is 100m west of the Nile. Trains go to Luxor (3½ hr.; 6:30, 7:30am, 1:15, 2:30, 7pm; E£15) and Cairo (7½hr.; noon and 2pm; 1st-class E£40-55, students E£25; 2nd-class E£30-40, students E£20). The **bus station,** 1km south on the street in front of the train station, sends buses to Cairo and Luxor. A small **service** station is across from the bus station, but the main station is 2km farther south. Take a microbus (50pt) and ask the driver to drop you off at "*mahattat microbus.*" *Service* run frequently north and south along the Nile, but police limit tourist travel to within Middle Egypt

ORIENTATION AND PRACTICAL INFORMATION

Most shops and restaurants in Sohag lie between the Nile and the train station. Facing the train station, 500km to the right, is the traffic circle known as **Midan al-Arf,** home to the main mosque. Running west from the circle is the **souq.** The large corniche runs along the Nile. **National Bank of Egypt,** on the corniche to the right facing the river, exchanges currency. **Banque Misr,** between the corniche and Midan al-Arf, has a 24hr. **ATM.** (Both banks open Su-Th 8:30am-2pm.) The **post office,** with **EMS** service, is on the corniche north of the National Bank of Egypt (Open Su-Th 8am-2pm.)

ACCOMMODATIONS AND FOOD

The cleanest hotel in town—and the only one that welcomes tourist—is **Abou al-Wafa Hotel.** Look for the bright neon sign behind the train station. Cross the underpass and the hotel is on the left. Clean comfortable rooms come with air-conditioning, clean sheets, and fully tiled common bathrooms. (☎31 44 23. Breakfast E£5. Singles E£30; doubles E£55.) *Fuul,* falafel, and fruit stands line the street in front of the train station. **Port Said Restaurant** is behind the Abou al-Wafa Hotel; no English sign. This quintessential Egyptian restaurant serves traditional meat, rice, and salad dishes (E£5-10).

⚡ DAYTRIPS FROM SOHAG

THE WHITE AND RED MONASTERIES

Take a microbus from the train station or one of the service stations and ask for Deir al-Abyad (50pt-E£1). Deir al-Ahmar (the Red Monastery) is a short microbus ride away (50pt).

Where the southwest corner of Sohag meets the desert, two famous Coptic monasteries rise out of the sand. **Deir al-Abyad** (the **White Monastery**), was founded by St. Shenouda in the 4th century, and is the larger and more impressive of the two monasteries. Built by 5000 monks, using blocks from nearby pharaonic temples, the monastery's outside walls resemble an ancient Egyptian temple. The thick walls did not deter attacks by Libyans and Arabs in the 6th century, but the monks persevered; they still inhabit the monastery today. Most of the artwork inside the main chapel dates from the 9th century CE. Above the altar is a painting of Christ on his throne, surrounded by an eagle, an ox, a lamb, and a man. Four apostles—Luke, Matthew, John, and Mark—decorate the border. On a pillar to the left of the altar is a faint picture of the founding saint. In July and August, crowds of pilgrims flood the monastery in a four-week festival of baptisms, masses, and celebration. During these weeks, a market in the outer courtyard sells everything from food to toys. Eight monks and a supervisor live and perform services in the monastery during the rest of the year.

Deir al-Ahmar (the **Red Monastery**) lies 2km down the road from Deir al-Abyad. Smaller and quieter, the main chapel is constructed of stone and supported by several small pillars. Rough coloring and faded paintings decorate the inside.

ABYDOS ابيد وس

*Although Abydos is officially open to the public, security concerns in Middle Egypt mean that visitors to the temple will probably be transported by **police convoy**. The site is accessable from the town of al-Balyana, a 45min. **microbus** ride from Sohag (E£1.50-2). You can also get to al-Balyana from Luxor: take north-bound **train** #981 (٩٨١) to al-Balyana from Luxor (2hr., 8am, E£9-11). If you aren't able to catch a tourist bus back, you will be stranded at the train station until 1:15 or 2:30pm. From al-Balyana, you and a mandatory party of your closest armed friends will continue to the temple (E£7). Bring food and water; the nearby restaurant has inflated prices and may not have any food if business is slow. Open 6am-6pm. All sites E£12, students E£6.*

The ancient city of Abydos was the site of a necropolis and temple dedicated to the god Khenti-Amentiu. Pharaohs from the first dynasty onward chose to be buried at the site, which attracted corpses from all over Egypt **Osiris,** god of the dead, subtly co-opted Abydos and the worshipers of Khenti-Amentiu during the 3rd dynasty. Legend has it that the body of Osiris himself lies buried on these grounds. After his famed dismemberment at the hands of his brother, Seth (see **Meet the Gods,** p. 75), Osiris's head was said to have landed here. The cult of Osiris centered here ritually reenacted the battle between Osiris and Seth as a sacred annual custom. The city that was Abydos has all but vanished, but after a look at the magnificent white limestone **Temple of Seti I,** dedicated to a 19th-dynasty pharaoh, it is not hard to imagine the wonder that drew pilgrims from all over the Kingdom.

The Temple of Seti has been partially reconstructed. Three of the original seven doors remain on the **Portico of Twelve Pillars,** which guarded the entrance into the temple proper. The central doorway leads to the **First Hypostyle Hall,** lined with 24 colossal columns in the shape of papyrus plants. This grandiose entrance gives way to the **Second Hypostyle Hall,** which contains some of the finest bas-reliefs ever carved in Egypt At the far left corner of the Second Hypostyle Hall, a long narrow corridor known as the **Gallery of the Kings** leads southeast. This simple passage houses one of Egypt's most treasured finds, the **Kings' List,** which mentions the names of 76 Egyptian rulers from Menes of Memphis to Seti I, the temple's royal patron. Adding this list to previous knowledge, historians were able to map the sequence of Egyptian dynasties.

In the south wing of the temple, beside the entrance to the Gallery of the Kings, a doorway leads to a chamber with a tiny chapel to its right. The chapel contains a kinky relief showing the mummy of Osiris, in the form of a falcon, impregnating Isis. At the temple's rear is the elaborate **Inner Sanctuary of Osiris,** painted with scenes of Osiris's life. The sanctuary is flanked by three small shrines bedecked with the temple's best-preserved reliefs. Immediately behind the temple is the **Osirion,** a now partially submerged tomb that Seti built for himself in the style of the Old Kingdom. Ask a tomb guard to take you to the much less well-preserved **Temple of Ramses III** through a desert of broken ceramic to the north. The temple contains some interesting hieroglyphs and a mix of Coptic and pharaonic styles. Only the bottom of the temple remains, but the colors in the small antechambers are vivid. In one, Ramses II drinks the milk of cow goddess Hathor; in another, imprisioned Syrians are tied together by their necks.

QENA قـنـة ☎096

Sixty-five kilometers north of Luxor, Qena rests quietly by the Nile, oblivious to the hordes of tourists descending on her southerly neighbor. Tour buses pass through town in droves on their way to the spectacular Temple of Hathor, but few visitors stay beyond their temple tour. Those who do will be rewarded with Egypt's cleanest streets and the opportunity to be the sole traveler in town. The new governor has made modernization and cleanliness his priorities: apartment buildings have fresh coats of white paint, and a corps of orange-clad street cleaners keep the roads spotless (in marked contrast to the rest of Egypt). Agriculture dominates the the life and economy of Qena, but in the evenings, the streets come alive with strolling people and the sound of slapping dominoes.

▐ TRANSPORTATION. The train station lies at the center of town, 2km east of the Nile. **Trains** go to Luxor (45min.; 5:30, 8am, 2:30, 4, 5:30, 9pm; E£5) and Cairo (8½hr., 10 per day 4am-12:15am, E£36-46). The bus station is 1.5km west of the train station and 500m from the Nile on al-Manshiya St. (take a taxi for E£3-4). **Buses** go to: Luxor (1hr., 6 per day 7am-7pm, E£3-5); Cairo (10½hr., 5 per day 6:30am-10:30pm, E£50); Hurghada (3hr., every hr. 6am-10pm, E£15).

▄▟ ORIENTATION AND PRACTICAL INFORMATION. Qena has only a few main streets. Shops and cafes are concentrated in front of the train station along **Sidi 'Abd Rahima St.** Perpendicular to the main entrance of the train station is **al-Gamil St.,** which winds 2km to the Nile. A large **clock** marks the traffic circle 500m down al-Gamil St. from the train station. Take a right two blocks before the clock to reach the **police station** (emergency ☎122). Next to the police is the **post office** (open Su-Th 8am-2pm) and the **National Bank of Egypt** (exchange open Su-Th 8:30am-2pm). Another post office, with **EMS,** is 150m down the street on the left after the clock. The Telecom Egypt **phone office** is on a street to the right after you pass the clock. Qena's **hospital** (☎33 43 94) is by the Nile on the road to Dendera, past the bus station. Dr. Kamal Mahmoud Mustafa's **pharmacy** is to the right of the train station on Sidi 'Abd Rahima St. (open 24hr.).

▐▐ ACCOMMODATIONS AND FOOD. There is little incentive to remain in Qena beyond a temple visit, as the cleanest hotels are overpriced and often full. To get to **New Palace Hotel,** walk away from the train station on **al-Gamil St.;** the hotel is in an alley on the left. New Palace offers the best combination of cleanliness and economy, with clean sheets, balconies, and air-conditioning. The quality of rooms varies, so ask to look around. (☎32 25 09. Singles E£25; doubles E£50.) One block past the pharmacy on Sidi 'Abd Rahima St. is the substantially cheaper and much dirtier **al-Bait Hota Hotel.** Small rooms come with fans. (☎33 37 55. Singles E£10; doubles E£15.) The **souq,** past the pharmacy to the left, provides fruits, vegetables, *fuul,* and falafel.

THE LAST OF THE ANCIENT EGYPTIANS The

sacred symbols of the ancient Egyptian religion are the stuff of souvenir shops these days, but for one woman, they were much more. After falling down the stairs of her home in England in 1907, three-year-old Dorothy Eady was declared dead. When the town doctor returned an hour later to the room where he had laid the young girl's body, he was shocked to find her contentedly playing on her bed. Alive and well, the normal (if slightly rambunctious) British lass began insisting she was an ancient Egyptian and started begging to be taken "home." She was, she later said, a former priestess-in-training at the Temple of Seti in the holy city of Abydos. After a chance meeting on the temple grounds, she fell deeply in love with the Pharaoh Seti I and found herself in a rapturous affair that contravened all the rules of the priesthood. When the temple's high priest demanded a confession, ancient Egyptian Eady-as-priestess eventually took her own life rather than betray the name of her lover.

The real-life Eady devoted her life to "returning home," fulfilling her destiny at the temple, and taking her place at Seti's side in the afterlife. In 1956, after 20 years as a distinguished employee of the Egyptian Department of Antiquities (where she worked with and won the respect of some of the most distinguished Egyptologists there), Eady transferred to the ancient site of Abydos. There, known in the village as *Omm Seti* (mother of Seti), she helped to guide work at the temple, exhibiting an uncanny familiarity with the grounds. Eady treated the temple as the sacred sanctuary it once was, praying and making offerings to the gods until her actual death in 1981. She was buried in the desert to the northwest, at last ready to take her place at Seti's side.

▶ **DAYTRIP FROM QENA: DENDERA.** The Temple of Hathor at Dendera is one of the few sights in Middle Egypt that remained accessible throughout the fundamentalist uprising. While it is a bit out of the way, those who make the trip will find a structure unique in the options it offers the exploring tourist. Built of Nubian sandstone, the temple dates from the first century BCE. It is one of the most complete ancient temples in all of Egypt, second only to the temple at Edfu. The late Ptolemies and the Romans found it politically expedient to associate themselves with the benevolent goddess, and her temple thus escaped destruction. Hathor is depicted with a cow's head or ears, or wearing a crown of two horns cradling the sun disk. Because her specialty was love, Hathor was identified by the Greeks as Aphrodite. During an annual festival, a statue of Hathor was carried in a sacred procession down the Nile to meet Horus of Edfu (see p. 234).

Eighteen columns are topped by cow heads in the **Great Hypostyle Hall.** In the temple's inner sanctum, paintings depict the embalmer's art, while the ceiling is decorated with pictures of the goddess Nut. The second hypostyle hall, also called the **Hall of Appearances,** gives way to the **Hall of Offerings,** where daily rites were performed. In the artsy kiosk in the southwest corner of the roof, priests performed the ceremony of "touching the disk," in which the soul of the sun god Ra appeared in the form of light. To the right is a gently sloping staircase leading up to the roof. Turn your flashlight off for a moment as you make your way up the stairs. The lights are dim, the smell is strange, and it is hard not to feel that you are a part of the sacred religious procession chiseled on the wall to your right.

The **Hall of the Ennead** immediately precedes the inner sanctuary. The chamber on the left is the wardrobe; opposite it, a doorway leads through a small treasury into the **Court of the New Year,** where sacrifices were performed during the New Year festival. On the ceiling of the colorful portico, Nut gives birth to the sun, whose rays shine upon the head of Hathor. The so-called **Mysterious Corridor** surrounds the **Sanctuary** on three sides, and 11 chapels—each with a distinct religious function—open off it. A small chamber known as the **Throne of Ra** sits behind the northernmost of the three doorways behind the sanctuary. A miniscule opening in its floor leads to the crypt, a subterranean hallway embellished with reliefs. some of inlaid alabaster. Many rooms on the upper floors feature ceiling paintings of Nut swallowing the sun at sundown and giving birth to it at dawn. On the roof of the temple, near the edge, is graffiti left by French soldiers in 1799. *(Take a taxi from Qena to the temple (E£7). Temple open 7am-5pm. E£12, students E£6. In summer, bats inhabit the temple, so bring a flashlight.)*

LUXOR الاقصر ☎095

This ancient capital of Upper and Lower Egypt still humbles visitors three millennia after the height of its power. Luxor is built on the site of Ta Ipet (known by its Greek name, Thebes), which flexed its muscles during the rule of the New Kingdom (18th-20th dynasties, 1539-1075 BCE). Egypt's ancient history is more tangible here than anywhere else in the Nile Valley, and droves of tourists come to marvel at Luxor's sandstone temples and mysterious tombs. Unfortunately, the tourism industry has spawned a society of ruthless hoteliers, greedy guides, and cunning cab drivers: be wary of anyone who uses the word "free" in Luxor. With proper bargaining, however, a few pounds a day can net refreshing accommodations, satisfying cuisine, and access to unforgettable sights.

■ INTERCITY TRANSPORTATION

Flights: The airport, 8km northeast of town (no bus; taxi E£20), is served by **EgyptAir** (☎38 05 80), next to the Old Winter Palace Hotel. Flights to: **Aswan** (3 per day, E£203); **Cairo** (1hr., 4 per day, E£456); **Sharm al-Sheikh** (3 per week, E£401). While it is possible to purchase EgyptAir tickets at the airport (☎38 05 86 or 38 05 89), it is not recommended. Tickets to international destinations must be purchased in Luxor.

Trains: The train station (☎37 20 18) is at the head of al-Mahatta St., 750m inland from Luxor Temple. Lockers E£1.25 per day. Trains to **Aswan** are less comfortable than *service* or *feluccas* (3hr.; 7:30am and 5:30pm; 1st-class E£23-27, A/C 2nd-class E£14-18; students 1st-class E£16-20, 2nd-class E£11-15). Tourists are restricted to 2 crowded express trains to **Cairo** (8-10hr.; 8:20am and 8:50pm; 1st-class E£56-70, 2nd-class with A/C E£36-46; students 1st-class E£31-35, 2nd-class E£23-24). Reserve sleeper cars 1 day in advance. Walk on for a fee; reserve a seat to be safe.

Buses: The bus station is near the exit of Karnak Temple. Buses to: **Aswan** (4½hr., 6 per day 7:15am-8pm, E£8) via **Esna** (1hr., E£3), **Edfu** (1½hr., E£8), and **Kom Ombo** (3hr., E£10); **Cairo** (11½hr., 7pm, A/C E£50); **Dahab** (18hr., 5pm, E£95) via **Sharm al-Sheikh** (E£85); **Hurghada** (8 per day, 6:15am-8pm, E£15-20) via **Qena** (1hr., E£3-5) and **Suez** (E£31-40); **Port Said** (11½hr., 8pm, E£50). Hours and rates change often.

Service: Off al-Karnak St., 1 block inland from the Luxor Museum. Early morning and late afternoon *service* leave when full, usually about every 15min. Out-of-town trips must be made with police convoys. Daily convoys by expensive "special" taxi leave from a side street near the Antiquities Museum and go to **Aswan** (7, 11am, 3pm); **Abydos** and **Dendera** (8am and 2pm, full-day taxi E£250; 2pm departure is for Dendera only). Check with the tourist office for updates and changes.

■ ORIENTATION

You can easily get around Luxor on foot. The city lies on the east bank of the Nile, 670km upstream from Cairo and 220km downstream from Aswan. Surrounded by a heavily cultivated floodplain, the city is at the heart of an agricultural area, with a farmers' *souq* on Tuesdays. The metropolis can be divided into three sectors: the **city of Luxor** proper on the east bank, the village of **Karnak** a few kilometers north, and **Thebes** on the west bank. Finding your way around is easy as long as you know the main thoroughfares. **Al-Mahatta St.** (Station St.) runs perpendicular to the Nile. The **train station** is on this street, 750m inland, on the eastern edge of Luxor. Exit the train station at a 45-degree angle to the left and you will eventually reach **Television St.,** where signs advertising the many budget hotels and pensions in town appear. **Al-Nil St.** (**the corniche**) runs south along the river, turning into Khalid ibn al-Walid St. past the Novotel. **Al-Karnak St.** starts north of the temple and runs parallel to the corniche, just inland. **Luxor Temple** is on the corniche at the center of town, and **Karnak Temple** is 3km farther. The **bus station** is at the exit of Luxor Temple.

⊏ LOCAL TRANSPORTATION

Minibuses: The cheapest and quickest transportation in the city is (25pt). The most common route goes from al-Karnak St. to al-Mahatta St. to Television St.

Kalish: Riding to Karnak Temple on a **kalish** (carriage) can be pleasant (E£5). Kalishes are also good for baggage transport.

Bike Rental: You can rent a bike (E£5-7 per day) on al-Mahatta and Television St., or ask at a hotel. **Motorbikes** available at the Sherif Hotel and a small shop off Television St.

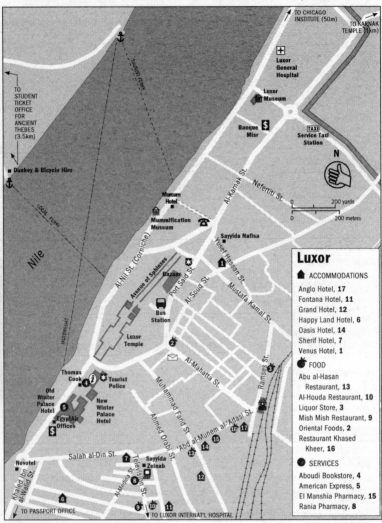

Luxor

⌂ ACCOMMODATIONS

Anglo Hotel, **17**
Fontana Hotel, **11**
Grand Hotel, **12**
Happy Land Hotel, **6**
Oasis Hotel, **14**
Sherif Hotel, **7**
Venus Hotel, **1**

🍎 FOOD

Abu al-Hasan
  Restaurant, **13**
Al-Houda Restaurant, **10**
Liquor Store, **3**
Mish Mish Restaurant, **9**
Oriental Foods, **2**
Restaurant Khased
  Kheer, **16**

● SERVICES

Aboudi Bookstore, **4**
American Express, **5**
El Manshia Pharmacy, **15**
Rania Pharmacy, **8**

Turn left after the Takia Cafe. (E£50-60 per day; no helmets). To visit the west bank sites on motorbike, catch a ferry in front of Luxor Temple.

Flying Pigs: On the corner of Television and Radio St. (50pt).

⑦ PRACTICAL INFORMATION

TOURIST AND FINANCIAL SERVICES

Tourist Office: (☎37 22 15 or 37 32 94), left of the New Winter Palace Hotel. Open daily 8am-8pm. Additional branches at the **train station** (☎37 02 59; open daily 8am-8pm) and **airport** (☎37 23 06). Low on free and useful literature, but the one in the bazaar has bus and train schedules with price listings.

Passport Office: (☎38 08 85), on the left of Khalid ibn al-Walid St., 1km south of the Novotel, on the left before the tan CIB Bank. Visas extended. Open Sa-Th 8:30am-2pm; Ramadan 9am-2pm.

Currency Exchange: Available in most hotels and numerous banks on the corniche. **National Bank of Egypt,** on the corniche 50m south of the Old Winter Palace Hotel, accept traveler's checks and offers cash advances on MC/V. Open daily 8:30am-10pm, in winter 8:30am-9pm.

ATM: Outside the two branches of **Banque Misr,** one at the north end of Television St. and another a block inland from the corniche, north of the Mercure Hotel. Also at **National Bank of Egypt.** All accept AmEx/MC/V, PLUS, and Cirrus.

American Express: (☎37 83 33; ☎/fax 37 28 62), on al-Nil St. in front of the Old Winter Palace Hotel, south of Luxor Temple. Holds mail, sells traveler's checks, wires and exchanges money and checks. Open Su-Th 8am-7pm, F-Sa 9am-3pm.

Thomas Cook: (☎37 24 02), on al-Nil St. in front of the Old Winter Palace Hotel. Cashes traveler's checks and organizes tours of Thebes (half-day E£135).

English-Language Bookstore: 'Aboudi Bookshop has 3 locations in the tourist bazaar complex on al-Nil St. Good but costly Egyptology books, countless sappy romances, and a few paperbacks in English, French, and German. Open daily 8am-10pm. Kiosks in front of tourist bazaar and in the train station sell foreign periodicals.

EMERGENCY AND COMMUNICATIONS

Emergency: ☎123.

Police: ☎122. The police station is off al-Karnak St., 200m north of Luxor Temple. **Tourist Police** (☎37 66 20), in the tourist bazaar on al-Nil St. Also in the train station (☎37 38 45). Both open 24hr.

Late-Night Pharmacy: 24hr. duty rotates—inquire at any hotel. **Rania Pharmacy** (☎37 12 86), at the north end of Television St., is well stocked with Egyptian drugs and basic toiletries. Open daily 8am-midnight. **Al-Manshia** (whose sign reads "nshia"), on 'Abd al-Munem al-Adasi St., carries mostly medicine. Open daily 7:30am-noon.

Hospitals: Luxor International Hospital (☎38 71 92), on the southern end of Television St., is a new, modern facility. Accept cash, credit cards, and medical insurance. **Luxor Public Hospital** (☎37 20 25 or 37 28 09), on al-Nil St. north of the museum, is a definite step down. Cash only.

Telephones: Central Telephone Office, west off al-Karnak St., just north of Luxor Temple. Open 24hr. Other less crowded offices are on **al-Nil St.** in front of the Old Winter Palace Hotel (the cheapest **fax** services in the city are here) and in the **train station.** Both offices open 8am-8pm. Hotels may charge twice as much as telephone offices.

Internet Access: 'Aboudi Internet Cafe (☎37 23 90; aboudishop@yahoo.com), on the 2nd fl. of the 'Aboudi Bookshop on al-Nil St. just south of the Luxor Temple. E£12 per hr. Refreshments E£2. Open daily 9am-10:30pm. **Abu Khaled Internet** (☎37 00 67), 50m from the intersection with Salah al-Din St. E£8 per hr. Open daily 10am-2am.

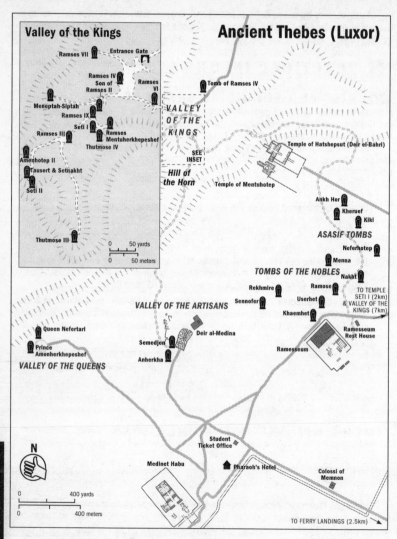

Ancient Thebes (Luxor)

Valley of the Kings

Ramses VII • Entrance Gate
Ramses IV • Son of Ramses II • Ramses VI • Tomb of Ramses IV
Meneptah-Siptah • Ramses IX
Seti I
Ramses III • Ramses Mentuherkhepeshef
Thutmose IV
Amenhotep II
Tausert & Setnakht
Seti II
Thutmose III

VALLEY OF THE KINGS

SEE INSET

Hill of the Horn

Temple of Hatshepsut (Deir el-Bahri)
Temple of Mentuhotep

Ankh Hor
Kheruef
Kiki
ASASIF TOMBS
Neferhotep
Menna
TOMBS OF THE NOBLES
Nakht
Rekhmire • Ramose
Sennofer • Userhet
Khaemhet
TO TEMPLE SETI I (2km) & VALLEY OF THE KINGS (7km)

VALLEY OF THE ARTISANS
Queen Nefertari
Prince Amonherkhepeshef
VALLEY OF THE QUEENS
Semedjen • Deir al-Medina
Anherkha
Ramesseum Rest House
Ramesseum

0   50 yards
0   50 meters

Student Ticket Office
Medinet Habu
Pharaoh's Hotel
Colossi of Memnon

N

0   400 yards
0   400 meters

TO FERRY LANDINGS (2.5km)

Post Office: On al-Mahatta St., 100m east of Luxor Temple. Offers **Poste Restante** (passport required for pickup) and **EMS.** Open Su-Th 8am-2pm; EMS 8am-noon. Other branches near the tourist office and in the train station. Open daily 8am-2pm.

ACCOMMODATIONS

EAST BANK (LUXOR CITY)

If you come to Luxor by train, you will disembark into a writhing mass of arms waving hotel cards. Decide where you want to go and stick to your guns. Many hawkers will quote incorrect prices or tell you the hotel you have in mind is full or shut down. *Kalish* drivers may take you to a different hotel from the one you request, assuming you don't know any better or are too tired to complain. Demand to be taken to your hotel or withhold payment. Women traveling alone should be prepared for sexual overtures from employees in some of the small hotels. If a firm refusal doesn't do the trick, complain to the manager or the tourist police.

For the most part, though, staying in Luxor is a treat. Air-conditioning comes quite cheap and there are ample opportunities for hard-core bargaining. Shop around and enjoy the wildly exaggerated accounts of just how much a breakfast costs the owner. Travelers with patience or those with groups of three or four will be rewarded: air-conditioned rooms can be had for as low as E£4-6 if you play your cards right, and roof or terrace mattresses for E£3-4. The majority of the budget hotels are clustered around Television St. and Yusuf Hassan St. Most hotels have laundry service (50pt-E£1 per piece) and bike rentals (E£5-7).

Hotel managers make their money from overpriced tours of the west bank, so count on being encouraged to take one. Happy Land offers guided air-conditioned bus tours (though they can be crowded) for E£45 and donkey tours for E£35. Never accept prices higher than these.

■ **Happy Land Hotel** (☎ 37 18 28; fax 37 11 40; happylandluxor@hotmail.com), 150m off al-Medina St., a few blocks past Television St. (look for the huge sign). The owner will go to great lengths to demonstrate his establishment's nearly obsessive cleanliness. Towels and toilet paper in each room. Comfortable rooftop restaurant with satellite TV serves hearty breakfast. Internet E£10 per hr. Trips to west bank (E£45) and Dahab (E£85). A/C dorms E£7.50. Singles with fan E£15; doubles E£18; add E£5-7 each for bath and A/C. Triples E£12.50 and quads E£9.50 per person; bath and A/C included.

■ **Fontana Hotel** (☎ 38 06 63), off Television St. Super-clean rooms (try to get one with a balcony) and incredible shared baths. Breakfast included. Ask the owner to use the laundry machines yourself for no fee. Fans in every room. Singles E£8, with A/C E£10; doubles E£10, with A/C E£15, A/C and bath E£20; small triples with bath and A/C E£25-30; prices a few pounds higher in winter.

Venus Hotel (☎ 37 26 25), on Yusef Hassan St. Convenient (if hectic) location, with fairly clean tiled rooms and large windows. As always, insist on the correct price for rooms and tours if at first you are quoted something that seems too high. Breakfast included. Singles E£10, with A/C and bath E£15; doubles E£20/E£25; triples E£22.50/E£30; quads E£30/E£40; prices E£5-10 higher in winter. **Mars Bar** on the 2nd fl. features pool table, foosball, satellite TV, and cheap drinks (Stella E£6).

Anglo Hotel (☎/fax 38 16 79), in the alley to the left of the train station. Some of the clean rooms have balconies. Pricey tours. Breakfast included. Singles E£15, with A/C E£20; doubles E£25-30/E£35; triples E£30/E£45.

Oasis Hotel (☎ 36 59 00), on Muhammad Farid St. Clean, spacious rooms, but the bathrooms could stand to be renovated. Prime location, with restaurants and fruit stands nearby. Can be pushy about tours. Breakfast included. Dorms have fans; all other rooms have bath and A/C. Dorm beds E£6; singles E£10; doubles E£15; triples E£18. Bargain with the manager for lower prices.

Sherif Hotel (☎ 37 07 57; khaeli@hotmail.com), on Badr St., the 1st right off Television St. Bob Marley's image, music, and habits thrive in this friendly establishment. Breakfast E£3. Rooms with fan E£7 per person; for A/C add E£5 per room.

Grand Hotel (☎ 38 29 05), on Muhammad Farid St. Less frequented by travelers, tucked into a quiet corner just past the Oasis on the right. The small, covered rooftop patio is pleasant. Sizeable rooms have seen better days. Travelers may find better deals on tours elsewhere. Breakfast E£3.50. Singles with fan E£6, with A/C E£7.50; doubles E£12, with A/C E£15; triples E£15, with A/C E£18.

WEST BANK (ANCIENT THEBES)

It is generally more convenient to sleep on the east bank in Luxor proper, but the west bank offers quiet surroundings and the chance to roll out of bed and into the Theban necropolis at the opening bell. A taxi from the ferry docks (E£5) is the only practical way to get to hotels unless you can manage to bike it with a pack. For information on crossing the Nile, see **West Bank**, p. 223.

Pharaoh's Hotel (☎31 07 02; fax 31 01 10), farther down the same unpaved road as the ticket office. This area's best hotel, with carpeted rooms and a garden restaurant (full lunch/dinner E£25). Rooms come with A/C, bath, and breakfast. Singles E£40, in winter E£60; doubles E£70/E£100; triples E£80/E£150.

🍴 FOOD

Luxor may be an archaeologist's paradise, but it's purgatory for the frugal gourmet. Two *kushari* houses stand out from the pack: **Sayyida Zeinab,** on Television St., and **Sayyida Nafisa,** on Yusef Hassan St. The **coffeeshop** in the New Winter Palace Hotel has a paltry but cheap all-you-can-eat dessert buffet (E£16). A **liquor store** on Ramses St. is on al-Mahatta St. to your right as you leave the train station. (Open daily 8am-2pm and 5-11pm.) Hotel managers can also procure beer for you.

The west bank in particular lacks decent budget restaurants. **Tutankhamun,** next to the ferry landing, offers the usual chicken and kebab dinners (E£15-20). Most hotels have restaurants, but they're often closed and the quality is inconsistent, especially in the summer when business is slow.

Mish Mish (☎38 17 56), on Television St., across from al-Houda. A big hit with travelers. Good prices, tasty food. Pasta E£3-5. Pizza E£4-12. Meat E£8-12. Free delivery and 9% student discount. Open daily 10am-midnight.

Amoun Restaurant (☎37 05 47), just north of the Luxor Temple and the bus station in the tourist bazaar. A tourist favorite, Amoun serves a variety of Western dishes in A/C comfort. Try the refreshing lime juice and delectable banana milkshakes. Pizza starts at E£7, entrees average E£10. 10% student discount wipes out service charge and tax. Open daily 7am-midnight.

Restaurant Khased Khear (☎38 45 80), on 'Abd al-Munem al-Adasi St. (al-Manshia St.), 1 block from the train station. Cozy and cool interior has a nautical feel, but Khased's specialty is kebab (E£6-10). Take-out available. Open daily 11am-1am.

Oriental Foods, next to Chicken Hut on the intersection of al-Mahatta St. and Port Said St. Unrivaled falafel or *fuul* sandwiches (50pt each). Open 11am-1am.

Abu al-Hasan al-Shazly (☎37 12 14), on the corner of 'Abd al-Munem al-Adasi St. and Muhammad Farid St., near the Oasis Hotel. Locals and tourists alike enjoy the Ottoman decor of this 2-story behemoth of a restaurant. Big portions of budget fare. Pizza E£8-12. Meat dishes E£8-20. Pasta E£3.50. 2-egg omelets (E£3.50) get the job done when hotel breakfasts fall short. Open daily 8:30am-3am.

Classic Restaurant (☎38 17 07), on Khalid ibn al-Walid St. in the St. Joseph Hotel; look for the yellow sign before the passport office. Classy establishment with excellent food. Perfect for a well-deserved meal after conquering Thebes (especially if mild heat stroke has loosened the grip on your wallet). 4-course meal E£24. Stella E£7. On Fridays when they have sufficient numbers the Classic offers a belly dancing buffet (9pm; in winter 7pm. E£50). Add 19% tax. Open daily 6-10:30pm. AmEx/MC/V.

Al-Houda (☎38 53 28), on Television St. Friendly staff and surprisingly diverse menu. 6-course value meals are a great bargain at E£15. Pizza, chicken, *shish tawouq* E£6-8. Student discount. Open daily 11am-11pm.

👁 SIGHTS

EAST BANK

Luxor has two major temples and two museums. **Luxor Temple** (p. 219) stands in the heart of the city, adjacent to the Nile. The temple's lighting and late hours make it perfect for a first date. Going north on al-Nil St., the **Mummification Museum** (p. 223) and the small but excellent **Luxor Museum of Ancient Egyptian Art** (p. 223) house sculptures and artifacts unearthed at Karnak and elsewhere. **Karnak Temple** (p. 221), the Leviathan of pharaonic architecture, sprawls just a few kilometers north. The entire 3km route between the temples of Luxor and Karnak was once connected by the sacred **Avenue of the Sphinxes,** built by

Queen Hatshepsut (Hat-*Cheap*-Suit). The ever-modest Ramses II took the liberty of adding a small statuette of himself to each sphinx. The final stretch of the avenue remains complete, with two rows of sphinxes near the **Temple of Khonsu,** to the right of the main entry to Karnak Temple. Karnak Temple is best seen early in the morning, while the museums are perfect for an afternoon cool-off, and Luxor Temple is best at night. Note that **price hikes** of 25-50% on admission tickets to major sights are scheduled for the coming year; see **Inflation Sucks,** p. 14, for more information.

LUXOR TEMPLE هيكل الاقصر

Enter on the al-Nil St. side, 400m north of the New Winter Palace. Evening is the best time to visit, as temperatures are comfortable and the temple looks cool in the dimmed light. Open daily 6am-10pm, in winter 6am-9pm. E£20, students E£10.

Although Karnak gets all the glory, Luxor Temple is grand in its own right and much more comprehensible to the visitor than its big brother. Most of the temple was built around 1380 BCE by Amenhotep III. Significant portions were also erected by famous pharaohs from Ramses II to Tutankhamun, each striving to make his mark. Luxor Temple was meant to serve as a **love nest for the gods.** Once a year, during the Opet festival, the statues of Amun and his consort Mut would be taken from Karnak Temple and loaded onto a sacred boat. Amidst much rejoicing and beer guzzling, priests carried the statues on their shoulders to Luxor Temple, where the happy couple spent 24 days and nights together in the sanctuary. During one of their retreats the moon god Khonsu was conceived, completing the Theban triad (see **Meet the Gods,** p. 75). Romans used the temple as a military camp in the 4th century CE. The Mosque of Abu al-Haggag, added by the Fatimids in 1077 CE and still in use today, prevents work on the gallery on the left, so only the end portions of the Avenue of the Sphinxes (the 3km road connecting the Luxor and Karnak Temples) have been unearthed and restored.

Ramses II built the enormous **First Pylon,** nearly 24m tall and 65m wide. The pylon is inscribed with images of Ramses II smiting the Hittites. In front of the pylon stand three of the six original **Colossi of Ramses II,** two seated and one standing. A red granite obelisk flanks the doorway; its twin was given to France in 1831 in exchange for a fake clock (see **Mosque of Muhammad 'Ali,** p. 111) and now graces the Place de la Concorde in Paris. The granite statues of the **Court of Ramses II,** past the pylon, originally portrayed Amenhotep, but were altered when ancient Egypt's favorite egomaniac assumed the throne. Seventy-four enormous columns and the **Mosque of Abu al-Haggag** occupy the temple's largest chamber. The right wall of this court shows the sons of Ramses II leading a funerary procession. On the right after entering through the first pylon is a small shrine built by Hatshepsut and Thutmose III, 100 years before Amenophis III began construction on the larger temple.

Continue through the court's papyrus columns to the **Colonnade of Amenhotep III,** where the 14 columns have open lotus crowns. Tutankhamun had the walls of the colonnade inscribed with scenes from the festival of Opet. From here, proceed into the **Court of Amenhotep III.** Beyond this court rises the hypostyle hall antechamber with its 22 columns. The back wall depicts Amenhotep III being coronated by the gods. The Egyptian government is spending E£9 million to restore these columns, whose foundations crumbled when the construction of the Aswan High Dam raised the water level in the area (see **Moving a Mountain,** p. 252).

Roman legionaires converted the next room into a chapel by covering the ancient inscriptions with plaster. A side room contains Latin inscriptions to Julius Caesar. The second antechamber, with pictures of the pharaoh making sacrifices to Amun, escaped the Romans' wrath. To the left is the **Birth Room,** displaying the divine birth of Amenhotep III. His mother Mutemuia delivers under the watchful eyes of Isis and Khnum (who sits at his potter's wheel molding the great pharaoh's soul). Alexander himself had the bas-reliefs (in which he appears in pharaonic attire before Amun and other deities) added

NILE VALLEY

> # MUMMY DEAREST
>
> The ancient Egyptians wanted to live forever, so they had to be certain their bodies were fit for the long haul of the afterlife. In predynastic times, people were buried in simple pits in the sand. The heat and arid conditions dried the bodies out and prevented decay. As civilization advanced, efforts were made to provide for a more comfortable afterlife. Elaborate tombs served to speed decay, separating corpses from the drying sands; the process of mummification was perfected during the New Kingdom era. Before a body was wrapped in white linen bandages, it was preserved in a number of different ways. The least effective and least expensive was a simple washing and cleansing of the corpse. The next level involved filling the body's orifices with a caustic, corrosive fluid, then plugging up the holes. Several days later, the plugs were removed and the putrid fluid drained. The super-deluxe preservation package required that an incision be made in the 'Abdomen. All of the viscera, save the heart and kidneys, were removed (including the brain, either through the base of the skull or through a nostril) and preserved in canopic jars. These jars were amphora-shaped alabaster containers with engravings on the sides and lid. The body was then packed with *natrun*, a natural salt found in Wadi Natrun. After 40 days, the salt was removed and ointments, spices, and oils such as frankincense were applied in combination with intricate patterns of wrappings. The essences reacted over time to form a black, pitch-like substance that gives mummies their names (*moumiya* is Arabic for pitch).

when he built the **Sanctuary of Alexander the Great,** in the third antechamber. Fertility god Min receives disproportionate attention in this sanctuary, complete with a shrine for the sacred barque of Amun. Storage rooms on either side are engraved with inventory lists.

MUMMIFICATION MUSEUM

100m north of Luxor Temple on the bank of the Nile. ☎38 15 02. Open daily 9am-1pm and 5-10pm; in winter 9am-2pm and 4-9pm. E£20, students E£10. Free monthly lectures are offered in English during the winter; call ahead for schedules.

This new riverside museum gives an insightful view into the meticulous and often misunderstood process of mummification (see **Mummy Dearest,** p. 220). English descriptions take the visitor through the entire process from purification of the body to the fields of the afterlife. A well-preserved mummy and elaborate wooden sarcophagi highlight the collection. Also on display are sophisticated surgical instruments and a mummified menagerie consisting of a monkey, goose, and crocodile—and a cat in a Pez dispenser-shaped coffin.

LUXOR MUSEUM OF ANCIENT EGYPTIAN ART

A 15min. walk north of Luxor Temple on al-Nil St. Open daily 9am-1pm and 5-10pm; in winter 9am-1pm and 4-9pm. E£30, students E£15. Wheelchair accessible.

The Luxor Museum contains a wonderfully edifying collection of antiquities—proof that less is sometimes more. Unlike the heaps of objects squeezed into Cairo's Egyptian Museum (see p. 125), the treasures here have multilingual descriptions, and the exhibits have been thoughtfully arranged with the help of the Brooklyn Museum of Art in New York. The recreated **mural** of 283 sandstone blocks on the second floor, found within Karnak Temple, depicts Akhenaton and Nefertiti in adoration of the sun god Aton, along with numerous artisans and peasants at work. The first floor contains several small statues, including one of Thutmose III that is considered one of the best ancient Egyptian statues in existence. The gallery also includes smaller artifacts such as drinking vessels, precious jewelry, bronze statuettes, and Alexandrian coins from the 2nd century CE. The **Cachette Hall** holds 16 marble and granite statues found in the 1980s beneath Luxor Temple. The most handsome statue is the red granite likeness of Amenhotep III (1405-1367 BCE).

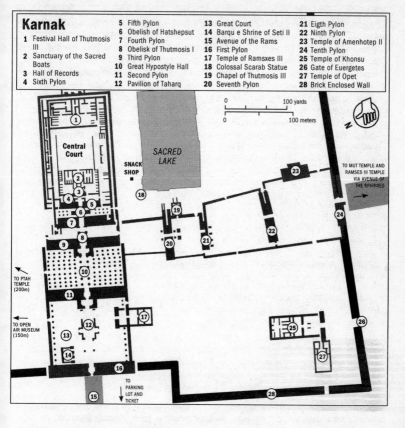

Karnak

1 Festival Hall of Thutmosis III
2 Sanctuary of the Sacred Boats
3 Hall of Records
4 Sixth Pylon
5 Fifth Pylon
6 Obelisk of Hatshepsut
7 Fourth Pylon
8 Obelisk of Thutmosis I
9 Third Pylon
10 Great Hypostyle Hall
11 Second Pylon
12 Pavilion of Taharq
13 Great Court
14 Barque Shrine of Seti II
15 Avenue of the Rams
16 First Pylon
17 Temple of Ramsxes III
18 Colossal Scarab Statue
19 Chapel of Thutmosis III
20 Seventh Pylon
21 Eigth Pylon
22 Ninth Pylon
23 Temple of Amenhotep II
24 Tenth Pylon
25 Temple of Khonsu
26 Gate of Euergetes
27 Temple of Opet
28 Brick Enclosed Wall

KARNAK TEMPLE هيكل كرنك

*Local **minibuses** run between Karnak Temple and the train station (25pt). Make sure the driver is going as far as the temple, and don't let him hike up the price at the end of the ride. You can also reach the temple by **bike, foot,** or **kalish** (E£3-5). The Karnak complex covers over 5 acres of land and is difficult to cover thoroughly, so bring water and come early in the day. Open daily 6am-6:30pm; in winter 6am-5:30pm. E£20, students E£10; use of a tripod E£20. If you seek more than a general impression of the place, a **guided tour** is useful, and latching onto one is easy. The **sound and light show** is a fascinating way to explore the temple for a 1st-time visit and pique your curiosity for a more in-depth visit the following morning. English shows M and Th 8pm, Tu-W and F-Su 9:15pm; in winter M 6pm, Tu 9pm, W-Su 7:30pm. Times may change, so check at your hotel or at the tourist office. E£33.*

Karnak Temple is overwhelming in its intricacy and proportions. Every major period in Egypt's ancient history since the collapse of the Middle Kingdom is represented in the additions to this complex of shrines dedicated to the sun god Amun and his family. Karnak Temple is the product of centuries of one-upmanship, as pharaoh after pharaoh added his mark to the temple in an effort to demonstrate the greatness of Amun (and himself). It was also the center of power for Amun's high priest, whose powers often exceeded even those of the pharaoh.

The temple is a hodgepodge of additions and alterations spanning millennia, but because of long-lasting pharaonic architectural traditions, the different pieces comprise a harmonious whole. As you push your way inside, think of each section as a layer of history built onto the original shrine at the core. The deeper you pro-

NILE VALLEY

ceed into the building, the farther back in time you go. The temple is oriented along two axes: a primary east-west axis following the path of the sun god Amun and a secondary axis proceeding north-south to Luxor Temple.

Enter the temple from the west, with the Nile behind you, and pass through the **Avenue of the Rams,** another double-rowed boulevard of creatures (this time, lions' bodies with rams' heads) dedicated to Ramses II. The curly-horned ram was one of Amun's sacred animals.

The first and largest pylon was never completed and probably dates from the 25th dynasty. Look for the ancient mud-brick scaffolding, on the right as you enter, used to erect the massive wall. The **Great Court,** the single largest element of the temple complex, dates from around the same time. Seti II built the chambers on the left to house the sacred barques of the Theban triad of Amun, Mut, and Khonsu. The largest room housed the barque of Amun, pictured on the wall. On the right is a temple built under Ramses III, consisting of a large open court and three inner chambers. Twenty 7m statues of the warrior-king line the open court, while its walls depict his conquests. An open papyrus column in the center of the Great Court is all that remains of the 25th-dynasty (689-664 BCE) Ethiopian King Taharq's pavilion. Constructed without a roof, the pavilion was used for a ceremony in which a statue of Amun-Ra was recharged by the sun's rays.

Pass through the recycled second pylon (Ramses II made it with blocks from one of Akhenaton's temples) into the **Great Hypostyle Hall.** With 12 central columns and 122 subsidiary columns, it's a pinnacle of pharaonic architecture. The central colonnade (from 1375 BCE) is the oldest part of the hall; Ramses II made other additions, and his royal cartouche is featured prominently on many of the columns. The walls are covered with images of Amun, who is often receiving offerings from the kings. A side door on the left allows visitors to view the hunting and battle scenes inscribed on the outside wall. A path here leads north to the small **Temple of Ptah.** Inside the temple a columned path leads to a small inner sanctuary with a headless statue of seated Ptah. The dark room on the right contains an eerie black stone statue of the lion-headed goddess Sekhmet.

Back in the main temple, emerge from the forest of sandstone to find the obelisk of Thutmose I on the right. This courtyard connects the two sections of Karnak temple; a turn to the right takes you south along the north-south axis. Continuing east, the 30m-high granite **Obelisk of Queen Hatshepsut,** the tallest obelisk in Egypt, towers in front of the fourth pylon. Hatshepsut, who considered herself a female king, brought the stones from Aswan and inlaid them with bushels of gold. Passing through the rubble of the fifth pylon and the granite sixth pylon, enter the **Hall of Records,** containing two elegant granite pillars, one decorated with carvings of the lotus of Upper Egypt and the other with the papyrus of Lower Egypt From the hall, enter the **Sanctuary of the Sacred Boats,** built by Alexander the Great's half-brother Philip around 300 BCE. A room to the north of the sanctuary contains colorful images of the gods, placed there by Hatshepsut. Her images were erased by her ungrateful son and successor Thutmose III, who had the wall completely covered, unknowingly preserving it until the present day.

Straight ahead across the open courtyard, the **Festival Hall of Thutmose III** dominates the eastern edge of the Karnak complex. Built to commemorate the pharaoh's victories in the mysterious north, it contains carvings of strange plants and animals brought back from his campaigns. The star-studded ceiling survives intact, supported by 52 tapered pillars. Some of the bases were actually whittled down to make room for large processions. In the 6th century CE, the hall was converted into a church; frescoes of haloed saints still adorn the interior walls and column shafts. Beyond a low wall to the east, the **Gate of Nectanebo** marks an early entrance to the complex. South of the Festival Hall, the limpid waters of the **Sacred Lake** sizzle in the heat. Priests purified themselves every morning in the holy waters of this rectangular pool before performing ceremonies in the temple. Note the large **scarab beetle** at the northwest corner of the lake. It is said that if a woman runs clockwise around the scarab three times, she will soon be pregnant.

Circle back to the junction of the two temple axes to explore the secondary north-south axis. The **Cache Court** in front of the seventh pylon is named for the thousands of statues uncovered during excavations, some of which can be seen in front of the pylon. The south face of the pylon is covered with images of Thutmose III battling enemies. Also in front of this face sit the bottom half of two large statues. The eighth pylon also depicts victorious Egyptian kings in the heat of battle while several statues guard its south face. In August 2001, the gate in front of the eighth pylon was closed for renovations.

KARNAK OPEN-AIR MUSEUM. The museum is north of the great court; look for a small sign and go back toward the entrance. The museum is comprised of three excavated chapels and a motley crew of well-labeled wall fragments. The **Red Chapel** of Queen Hatshepsut is displayed in rows of blocks, along with the Middle Kingdom **Alabaster Chapel.** The latter has flowing white walls streaked with brown, a welcome relief from the acres of sandstone. *(E£10, students E£5.)*

WEST BANK

*The cheapest way to get to the west bank is on the local tourist **ferry,** which docks directly in front of Luxor Temple (E£1; bicycles 25pt extra). Ferries run from 6am to 4pm. **Private motorboats** take passengers across for E£5 per boat. From the local ferry landing, it is a 1km walk north to the ticket kiosk, then 3km to the Colossi of Memnon. See **Sightseeing Strategy,** p. 223, for information on getting around once you are on the west bank.*

When they weren't preoccupied with empire-building and invader-expelling, the rulers of Thebes busied themselves preparing for eternity. As followers of the sun god Amun, the elite of the New Kingdom aspired to tombs on the west bank, where the sun sets and the afterlife supposedly begins. Pharaonic obsession with the afterlife made the necropolis of Thebes into the world's fanciest graveyard. Over millennia, robbers and archaeologists have nabbed much of the treasure, but the site still features an unparalleled collection of Egyptian funerary art.

New Kingdom rulers took no chances with the security of the afterlife. Earlier pharaohs had been too convinced of the mortality of their sacred tombs. Thieves had mastered the delicate art of pyramid pilfering at Memphis, making off with afterlife amenities of a grandeur that can now only be imagined. A radical change in burial practices was in order. The pharaohs of Thebes would not have their treasure rest anywhere but beside their mummified remains.

To conceal the location, contents, and design of the tombs, the work was done in secrecy by a team of laborers who dwelt within the necropolis. Perfecting techniques of tomb construction, decoration, and mummification, these 300 artisans devoted themselves to the City of the Dead over the course of generations, passing expertise down through familial lines. The remains of **Deir al-Medina** (Valley of the Artisans, see p. 230) have been thoroughly excavated and are among the most complete town remains in Egypt. Tomb design reflected the new emphasis on secrecy. Instead of one ostentatious pyramid, there were pairs of funerary monuments: an underground grave, lavishly outfitted with the articles demanded by the hectic afterlife and sequestered in an obscure recess of the desert; and a grandiose mortuary temple where the monarch could be worshiped for eternity. Architects incorporated dead-end passages, fake sarcophagi, hidden doorways, and deep shafts to foil the most cunning robbers. Once a pharaoh was safely stowed, workers immediately began to construct the tomb destined for his successor.

◙ **SIGHTSEEING STRATEGY: NILE WEST BANK** In **summer,** explore the necropolis in the early morning; in **winter,** afternoons are sometimes less crowded. Guards at the less-visited sites tend to lock up and head home a little early, especially in the summer. All sites open at 6am and officially close at 5pm (4pm in winter); stragglers won't be kicked out as long as they get in before closing. Bring plenty of **water** and a **flashlight.** Tomb guards have been known to turn off the lights to force you to rely on them for guidance. Here are some transportation options once you're at the west bank:

NILE VALLEY

On foot: If you have time and stamina, walking is the best and probably safest way to see the sights on the west bank. All of the sights (except for the Valley of the Kings) are within 3km of the Colossi of Memnon. Once on the main road (1km from the ticket office), catch a covered pickup truck to the Colossi of Memnon (25pt). Special taxis travel directly from the ticket office to the Colossi of Memnon for E£5 (more in summer). The Valley of the Kings is 8km by paved road, but the walk is worth it for the chance to follow the donkey trail up and over **Gabal al-Qurn** (Hill of the Horn). The peak was once sacred to the goddess of silence, Mirtseger, and with good reason—the serene quiet at the top of the hill is matched only by the view of the ruins. A simple geographic division is **North** (Valley of the Kings, Seti Temple, Hatshepsut, Ramesseum, the Tombs of the Nobles) and **South** (Valley of the Queens, Medinat Habu, the Valley of the Artisans); this division makes for a two-day exploration.

Guided tour: Tours in air-conditioned coaches with English-speaking guides are most popular. All budget hotels book tours, but many charge a hefty commission. Do not under any circumstances book tours for Luxor in Cairo, as travel agents are likely to slap a hefty commission onto an already inflated price. There's no need to pay more than E£45 for a tour; simply negotiate with your hotel manager or join the Happy Land tour. Some tours include up to 40 people, so check in advance with your hotel about numbers. A better option (with a better price) is to book a tour directly with noted guide and Egyptologist **Mahmoud 'Abd Allah** (☎37 28 21, or 01 22 15 71 45). Better known as Sunshine, he speaks English and has been giving good, cheap tours for 24 years.

By donkey: Mark Twain wrote that riding a donkey in Egypt "was a fresh, new, exhilarating sensation worth a hundred worn and threadbare pleasures." The novelty of donkey travel (which wears thin as quickly as the seat of your pants) and the fantastic views afforded by the trail as it climbs its way up to the Valley of the Kings have led to a burgeoning burro-borrow market. Arrange an excursion through your hotel that includes donkey and ferry ride (E£35) or hire your own animal in the village of Gezira (just inland from the ferry) or at the local dock. One suggested donkey route starts at the Valley of the Kings, circles to the Temple of Hatshepsut and the Ramesseum, then returns home.

By bike: A few serious hills are challenging, especially during the summer. Rent bikes in Luxor or by the local ferry landing (E£5). Many hotels, including the Sherif, rent motorbikes (E£50-60 per day).

By taxi: Taxis lack air-conditioning and are more expensive (E£25-35 per hr. is reasonable), but they allow you to cover the most ground. Hordes of drivers wait at both ferry landings. You can hire a taxi in Luxor, but a trip by the new bridge can drive up prices. When bargaining, ignore nonsense about government rates and per person charges.

One region in particular seemed ideal for entombment: a narrow, winding valley walled on three sides by jagged limestone cliffs and approachable by a single rocky footpath. This isolated canyon, known as the **Valley of the Kings** (p. 225), became the burial place of New Kingdom pharaohs. Although it looked promising on papyrus, it failed to deter hoodlums, and few of the tombs escaped pillage. Queens, favored consorts, and select offspring were accorded ceremonial burial with full honors and security precautions in a separate corner of the west bank, the **Valley of the Queens** (p. 232). Esteemed members of the Theban aristocracy also practiced elaborate burial customs, and several of the resulting **Tombs of the Nobles** (p. 230) rival royal burial chambers in craft and design. Last but not least, the **Valley of the Artisans** has two very impressive tombs of pharaonic artists. Over 400 tombs continue to decay in the necropolis, but only a handful are accessible. The most imposing of the west bank's massive **mortuary temples** (p. 227) are the **Colossi of Memnon,** the **Temple of Hatshepsut** (Deir al-Bahri), and the Temple of Ramses III (better known as **Medinat Habu**) near the Valley of the Queens. The ruins of the **Ramesseum** (the Temple of Ramses II), though shattered, also merit a visit.

NILE VALLEY

GET DOWN AND DIG IT An archaeologist's work is never done, especially in Luxor. Although it would appear that most of the treasures of the old tombs and temples have been whisked away, archaeologists are still concerned with what they can learn through excavation (and finding a little new treasure never hurt anyone, either). The Department of Antiquities oversees and conducts many ongoing projects, from the restoration of the Ramesseum to current digs at the Karnak Temple and Valley of the Kings. A recent promising find is the discovery of the largest tomb ever found in Egypt, a vast 107-room (and counting) complex being excavated by a team led by the American archaeologist Kent Weeks. The name of Ramses II has been identified four times, giving rise to speculation that this could be the final resting place of the great pharaoh's many sons. Entry into the tomb, designated **KV5,** has been hampered by falling rocks, and it is completely off-limits to the public. Other avenues of research include remote sensing, which detects irregularities beneath the surface without costly digging, and excavation within the city of Luxor itself.

VALLEY OF THE KINGS وادى الملوك

5km from the Nile, but there's no direct path. 2 possible routes to the beginning of the Valley road exist. You can go past the Colossi of Memnon, continuing straight toward the Valley of the Artisans; at the end of the road, hike 3km over the Hill of the Horn. Alternately, turn right at the ticket office (follow the signs), pass the Ramesseum, then turn left at the military checkpoint (after 2km) where the road gently winds for 5km through desolate mountain valleys. Tombs open daily 6am-5pm; in winter 6am-4pm. A single ticket provides access to 3 tombs. E£20, students E£10. The rest house near the entrance has overpriced water, warm juice, and public toilets.

The Valley of the Kings, no more than 400m long and 200m wide, can easily be toured on foot using the clearly marked, well-groomed gravel paths. Over 64 known tombs honeycomb the valley, numbered in the order they were discovered. Most are closed to the public, but the best-known tombs are almost always accessible. Every few months the open tombs are rotated to minimize wear and tear and to add a little variety—which, after all, is the spice of afterlife. Ask at the tourist office to find which are currently open.

TOMB OF RAMSES IV (#2). The second tomb on the right is the tomb of Ramses IV. The tomb was once used as a Byzantine church, and Coptic graffiti adorns the wall to the right of the entrance. Damaged decorations in the corridor give way to a bath of color and well-preserved adornments closer to the burial chamber. The tomb contains wall paintings excerpted from the *Book of the Dead* and the *Book of Gates* (look for the beautiful solar boat in the burial chamber). The 365 small statues in the tomb portray the pharaoh's guardian spirit and were believed to facilitate his resurrection each night of the year, when Amun-Ra crossed to the west bank. The figures on the left wall, facing the sun god, will be resurrected, while the upside down figures on the right wall represent doomed non-believers. A vividly colored ceiling and huge, cartouche-shaped sarcophagus make this one of the best tombs in the valley. Royal cartouches were thought to preserve the king's name forever inside their oval shape; Ramses figured that a cartouche-shaped sarcophagus ought to preserve his body forever.

TOMB OF RAMSES IX (#6). The intricately detailed ceiling of the 12th-century BCE tomb of Ramses IX (on your left when you enter the valley) features gold figures displaying their *joie de mort* against a deep blue background. To the right of the entrance, the pharaoh is shown offering a gazelle to Amun-Ra. Farther on the right, the reliefs show Ramses making offerings to the god of justice, who holds a balance, and to Osiris, god of resurrection, and making 136 negative confessions (I never lied, I never spent time in a Turkish prison, etc.). Directly opposite these reliefs, Ramses is playing the same game with Horus to gain safe passage through the two lakes of fire. A long corridor descends to an anteroom covered with protective demons, serpents, and wild beasts. A pit beyond the long corridor in the burial chamber holds Ramses IX's sarcophagus. The ceiling of the chamber was not smoothed and the text appears in shorthand because Ramses IX died before his tomb was ready. Most of the painting had to be completed during the 70 days needed for mummufucation.

TOMB OF RAMSES VI (#9). The third-largest tomb in the valley after those of Ramses II and Seti I, this crypt is known for its ceiling of winged cobras, decapitated enemies, and a spectacular 18m-long depiction of the sky god, Mut. The various red disks along Mut's body depict the daily path of the sun—she would give birth to it every morning and then swallow it in the evening. The vast sarcophagus in the burial chamber was split by tomb robbers who heated it and doused it in water, causing the stone to expand and crack—you can see the charred marks.

TOMB OF RAMSES III (#11). Nicknamed the "Tomb of the Harp Players" after the two plucky musicians depicted on one of its interior antechambers. The size and artistic skill of the decorations reflect Ramses III's successful 31-year reign. Left of the entrance, the pharaoh prays to Ra-Hurakhti (looking suspiciously like Horus in his hawk form). Colorful side rooms are decorated with paintings of their former contents. The penultimate chamber boasts a vivid portrayal of ancient chariot races on its left wall. Past the first chamber, the sacred barque of Ra is piled high with gods as it travels through the secret gates towards the afterlife. The pillared chamber is filled with pictures of the peoples of the world. On the right wall, non-believers are tied to plants. Luckless Ramses III was killed in a palace plot, burgled post-mortem, and—as a final insult—stolen and shipped in his magnificent sarcophagus to the Louvre in Paris.

TOMB OF RAMSES I (#16). The steep entrance next to the tomb of Seti I (#17, see **Other Tombs** below) descends into the tomb of Ramses I, a single burial chamber dominated by Ramses's pink granite sarcophagus. The tomb walls, some of the best in the valley, are painted with scenes of Ramses hobnobbing with the gods. The first corridor is the shortest in the valley, perhaps a reflection of Ramses's brief rule (1320-18 BCE).

TOMB OF TUTANKHAMUN (#62). The west bank's most renowned tourist attraction, the tomb of Tutankhamun, stands directly in front of the rest house in the middle of the valley and requires a special ticket (E£40, students E£20). The real treasures are at the Egyptian Museum in Cairo (see p. 125), and the interior of this small tomb may not be worth the extra cash. If you plan to see it, visit it first or you'll probably be disappointed after seeing the others.

The only pharaonic tomb to evade grave robbers, Tut's treasure box was discovered in 1922 by archaeologist Howard Carter and has toured the world several times before returning to its permanent home in the Egyptian Museum. Tutankhamun's mummy was encased in the innermost of four snugly nested, superbly decorated cases, three of which can be seen in Cairo. Fortunately, the raiding Egyptologists left behind the outermost case (a gilded wood extravagance covered in rich jewels) and Tut's exquisitely carved sarcophagus. The perfectly preserved interior walls of the burial chamber depict colorful scenes from the *Book of the Dead*, which were transcribed from the pyramid writings at Saqqara (see p. 140). Egyptologists had expected that the tomb would contain little of interest because Tut reigned only two years, but Carter ignored professional censure and toiled for six years in the Valley of the Kings. After more than 200,000 tons of rubble had been moved, Carter's patron reluctantly decided to abort the project. Before admitting failure, Carter explored one more possibility: a site in front of the tomb of Ramses VI, in an area covered with workers' huts. Confounding the critics, he chanced upon an ancient doorway beneath the shanties. The tomb had been opened by robbers, but the thieves had apparently been caught in the act by necropolis guards, because the treasures had been hastily stacked and the entrance resealed. Three mummies were found in the tomb, including that of the boy-king himself.

TOMB OF MERENPTAH (#8). Across from the rest house and down a short path, Merenptah's tomb descends past several pillared halls. On the left as you enter, a colorful painting depicts the pharaoh addressing Ra-Hurakhti. Further down in the first pillared hall, pictures of Nubians and Syrians from the *Book of Gates* adorn the walls to the left. A detailed scene of Merenptah making offerings to Osiris and an unfinished statue also decorate the room. A huge granite sarcophagus rests in the middle of the burial chamber with the pharoah's visage carved into the top. The top walls contain the only remaining images of what once must have been an intricately decorated burial room.

TOMB OF THUTMOSE III (#34). The most dramatically situated burial site in the necropolis is the cliffside Tomb of Thutmose III, reached by a long, steep staircase that ascends a precipitous ravine squeezed between towering limestone cliffs. To get to the tomb, follow the dirt road that begins next to the Tomb of Ramses III (#11) leading southeast up the hill. The tomb's location provides the ultimate example of the 18th-dynasty pharaohs' attempt to hide their tombs. Thutmose III's is built in a fault, where it became naturally concealed by debris left by flash floods, but the ingenious design did not deter grave robbers. Queen Hatshepsut appointed her freakishly short stepson Thutmose III as a military leader; he became her rival and eventually took the throne from her. His conquests reached as far as the fourth cataract of the Nile to the south, Crete and Cyprus to the north, and the Euphrates to the east. His grave is decorated with unusual hieratic text (shorthand hieroglyphics, see p. 80) and strangely beautiful stick-figure representations of Khnum and other gods. The first pillared hall holds 741 figures from the *Book of the Dead*. The novel cartouche-shaped burial chamber still contains his red granite sarcophagus (don't tip the guard for showing you that it's empty).

TOMB OF SIPTAH (#47). Past the turnoff to Thutmose III, Siptah lies to the left. A single corridor leads to a roped-off burial chamber and a distant view of Siptah's sarcophagus. The corridor itself is grand, with a large golden sun disk greeting visitors at the entrance. On the left, Siptah meets various gods, while farther down the corridor is covered in intricate hieroglyphics representing the *Book of the Dead*. In the second half of the corridor, 44 of Ra's 72 shapes are shown.

TOMB OF TAUSERT/SETNAKHT (#14). Across from Siptah, this large tomb escapes most tour groups. A corridor leads from the entrance past a chamber with a splendid painting of Horus and Anubis greeting Osiris, through a domed room with a winged ram on the right wall, and into a large burial room containing Tausert's huge sarcophagus and the remnants of a brilliant ceiling painting.

TOMB OF SETI II (#15). This tomb is south of Tausert/Setnakht. Instead of covering the tomb's walls with plaster frescoes, the artisans carved images directly into the mountain walls. Bizarre but true: the mummy of an unknown man rests in a chamber before the damaged burial room. Seti's remains are elsewhere, but his image is carved into the lid of his granite sarcophagus. Seti's ancestor lies in the **Tomb of Seti I (#17),** the valley's longest tomb.

MORTUARY TEMPLES

The pharaohs may have hidden their tombs, but they didn't want the living world to forget about them. In addition to its spectacular rock-hewn tombs, the west bank is peppered with **mortuary temples,** mammoth structures honoring the royal deceased. Though overshadowed by Luxor's Karnak Temple in scale and importance, the West Theban temples of Hatshepsut (Deir al-Bahri), Ramses III (Medinat Habu), Ramses II (Ramesseum), and Seti I are still fascinating. The following temples, all accessible from a road running parallel to the Nile, are listed from south to north. From the ferry docks, head inland 3km past the Colossi of Memnon until you come to an intersection. A road to the left leads to Medinat Habu, 500m to the southwest. Deir al-Bahri, Medinat Habu, and the Ramesseum all require individual tickets (E£12 each, students E£6); purchase them at the ticket office just past the Colossi of Memnon.

COLOSSI OF MEMNON. All that remains of the largest mortuary temple (dedicated to Amenhotep III) on the west bank is the pair of statues known as the **Colossi of Memnon,** towering in magnificent isolation on the north side of the entrance road to the necropolis. Looking over the plain from a height of 20m, these figures of Amenhotep were Thebes' greatest tourist attraction during the Roman era. At night, an eerie whistling sound emanated from the statues; as Memnon was the mythical son of Aurora, the goddess of the dawn, the Romans believed the sound was actually Memnon wailing in anticipation of his mother's rays. In fact, the sound was produced by a clever water device which emitted a sharp whistle when heated by the rising sun. Designed by the Alexandrian engineer Heron, the device fit neatly (and secretly) into the cracked knee of the earthquake-damaged statue, and was used by priests to attract hordes of (paying) devotees. When Emperor Septimius Severus decided to restore the monument in 196 CE, the priests withdrew the device to avoid exposing their secret. *(Free.)*

MEDINAT HABU (TEMPLE OF RAMSES III). This complex of well-preserved edifices stands to the left at the end of the road after the Colossi. Relatively few tourists visit this site; a tranquil hour is enough to take it in. The best part of the complex is the Mortuary Temple of Ramses III, decorated with reliefs of the pharaoh's many successful military campaigns, including his victories over the mysterious "Sea People" (who dangle by their hair from his fist). Enter the temple through its large fortified gate. Climbing the stairs on the gate's opposite side leads to a small open chamber where Ramses III is believed to have stayed while visiting the temple. (It was likely also the site of his assassination.) The temple is warrior-themed throughout: the main pylon, also known as the Royal Pavilion, resembles a military fortress rather than a temple. One relief explains the importance of securing houses of worship so that peace and order could then spread elsewhere, and several reliefs show prisoners being put to death. On the back of the main pylon are savory piles of conquered hands and tongues. Beyond the gate are two relief-rich courts. On the left side of the second court a window opening is supported by statues of human heads. Behind the second pylon are the remains of large statues of Osiris standing in front of eight papyrus-shaped columns. This "window of appearances," used for royal speeches, was meant to show the king standing on the heads of his vanquished enemies. *(Public bathrooms and a refreshment stand outside the gates.)*

RAMESSEUM (TEMPLE OF RAMSES II). Farther north, beyond the student ticket office, is the Mortuary Temple of Ramses II. A tour of the Ramesseum may not be worth a long side-trip and shouldn't exceed 30min. In most of the ravaged temples, visitors attempt to gather from the ruins an idea of the spectacle that once was, but at the Ramesseum, the ruins themselves are the grandest statement of all. The same pharaoh who had Abu Simbel tailor-made to his specifications built the Ramesseum to house another mammoth exercise in narcissism. The shattered remains of the 1000 ton, 17m **Colossus of Ramses II** (his fingers are over 1m long) were the inspiration for Percy Bysshe Shelley's famous poem: "My name is Ozymandias, king of kings: / Look on my works, ye Mighty, and despair!" Their broken enormity leads many to similar sentiments. The colossus, which was transported in one piece from the pharaoh's granite quarries in Aswan to Thebes, originally overlooked the passageway leading into the second court. Even shattered, the remnants (including head, upper arms, and one foot) are imposing.

DEIR AL-BAHRI (TEMPLE OF HATSHEPSUT). Just north of the Ramesseum, a paved road leaves the main north-south thoroughfare and heads northwest, winding around to the Temple of Hatshepsut. If on foot, you can save some time by cut-

MUMMIES IN THE NIGHT In the late 1870s, members of the Antiquities Service noticed many New Kingdom funerary objects appearing on the European black market. **Charles Wilbur**, a wealthy American antiquer, was enlisted to go undercover and identify the source of the treasures. After making clear that he would pay high prices for authentic pieces, Wilbur was eventually led to Luxor. Across the river in the town of Qurna, he was shown an item that had come from a recently opened royal burial. Wilbur secretly telegraphed Gaston Maspero, the Director General of the Antiquities Service, who rushed to Luxor and began intense questioning of all involved. Several weeks later, **Muhammad 'Abd al-Rasul**, the head of the most prominent antiquities-dealing family in Luxor, confessed that his family had found a tomb near the Mortuary Temple of Hatshepsut. Archaeologists were quickly summoned and found the deep shaft burial containing the mummies of the New Kingdom's greatest kings: Thutmose III, Ahmose (founder of the New Kingdom), and Ramses II, among many others. The 'Abd al-Rasul family had kept the shaft a secret for 10 years, quietly selling their stash. The Antiquities Service, aware of the security risk that a public disclosure would cause, employed hundreds of men to load the mummies onto ships. The bodies were hurried down the Nile and now reside in the Egyptian Museum in Cairo.

ting through the village on the left side of the road (before it splits). In the center of the necropolis, the temple is 500m north of the Tombs of the Nobles. The temple's ancient Egyptian name, *Djeser Djesern*, means "most splendid of all," and with good reason: Hatshepsut's masterpiece rises in three broad, columned terraces from the desert floor against a dramatic backdrop of sheer limestone cliffs.

After the death of her husband Thutmose II, Hatshepsut became the ruler of the kingdom, the only woman ever to assume the title of pharaoh (see **Ancient History,** p. 51). Her temple was excavated by French and Egyptian archaeologists and is currently being restored by a joint Polish-Egyptian team with support from the US and France. No images of Hatshepsut remain intact. After her death, her stepson Thutmose III—who had to wait 20 years before coming into his own as pharaoh because she refused to marry him—defaced virtually all of them, and placed his name on the statues of a bearded Hatshepsut that line the third level. Men: can't live with 'em, can't be reincarnated with 'em.

If you walk from the lower court up a wide ramp to the central court, you'll come upon a colonnaded back wall that contains, from left to right, the Shrine of Hathor, the Colonnade of the Expedition of Punt, the Birth Colonnade, and the Shrine to Anubis. Inside the shrine of Hathor lies the only remaining image of Queen Hatshepsut as she stands between Hathor and Amun-Ra. If you look hard enough it is possible to spot her through the bars at the end of the chapel. The Punt reliefs show Egyptian expeditions to modern-day Somalia, and the exchange of goods with the locals. The Birth Colonnade details Hatshepsut's birth and childhood. Another huge ramp leads to the upper court with a rock-cut sanctuary. This court is closed to the public because it was badly ruined and sadly defaced by 7th-century Copts who used the temple as a monastery.

TEMPLE OF SETI I. You'll have a fair amount of trouble getting to this place, and there's not that much to see once there. Go north on the main road and follow it to the military checkpoint. Turn right to visit what remains of the Mortuary Temple of Seti I, father of Ramses II, a warrior who enlarged the Egyptian empire to include the island of Cyprus and parts of Mesopotamia. Seti was also one of the first men to wear earrings—a fact archaeologists gleaned from his well-preserved mummy-lobes. Although the booty from his successful campaigns has been stolen, the relief work, ranked among the finest executed in ancient Egypt, still remains.

VALLEY OF THE ARTISANS

One ticket includes the Workers' Walled City, the Temple of Deir al-Medina, and the two tombs. E£12, students E£6.

NILE VALLEY

TOMBS OF THE ARTISANS. The accessible artisans' tombs are in such excellent condition that it is hard to believe they were painted so many centuries ago. Unlike the formal decorations on the walls of royal tombs, these tombs contain very creative drawings of the afterlife. Some artisans spent almost 30 years building their tombs, as they could only work on their own tombs on the single rest day of the ancient 10-day week. Two amazing tombs are open to the public: the **Tomb of Sennedjen**, artist for Ramses III, and the **Tomb of Anherkha**, "Deputy Master of the Two Egypts in Truth Square"—i.e. head artist for Ramses IV.

WORKERS' WALLED CITY. To reach the plentiful though visually uninspiring remains of the Workers' Walled City, go past the Colossi of Memnon and follow the small road west, past the ticket office. The Workers' Walled City was the only area of the west bank inhabited during the New Kingdom, and it is the best window archaeologists have found into the nature of urban life in ancient Egypt. Since the workers and artists knew the whereabouts of the tombs they were digging, their movements were strictly controlled, and they lived in isolation (the entire walled city was roofed over). To prevent any leaks, the priests had many of the workers' tongues cut off when construction was over. A typical house consisted of a kitchen, living room, and bedroom. Some had stairways for access to the rooftops, a welcome relief from the heat and smell below.

TEMPLE OF DEIR AL-MEDINA. About 60m down the road from the Workers' Walled City stands the Temple of Deir al-Medina (Monastery of the Town), an elegant shrine from the Ptolemaic era. Dedicated to Hathor, the goddess of love, and Maat, the representation of divine order (see **Meet the Gods**, p. 75), the temple was named when Christian monks constructed a monastery next door.

TOMBS OF THE NOBLES

A few hundred meters southeast of the Temple of Hatshepsut is the west bank's sardine-packed burial site for nobility, with more than 400 tombs. Tickets (E£12, students E£6) are usually good for two tombs. The 1st pair listed provides the most punch for your pound. Many villagers will volunteer their services, but a guide is unnecessary. Maps are available in bookstores on the east bank.

Throughout the New Kingdom, Theban aristocrats served as advisors and had de facto control over much of the pharaoh's empire. The pharaoh often remained ignorant of the most crucial political developments, while members of the elite fought each other for control of the kingdom. Some aristocrats affected pharaonic status by amply providing themselves with luxuries for the afterlife and devising well-hidden underground tombs. Unlike the pharaoh (who would assuredly live among the gods after his death), Theban aristocrats needed more assurance that a comfortable existence awaited them in the afterlife. Accordingly, every facet of their earthly lives was carefully recorded on the walls of their tombs, leaving the decoration more mundane than the reliefs found in pharaonic tombs. Because of the inferior limestone in this portion of the necropolis, artisans could not carve in relief. Instead, they painted murals on a whitewashed stone surface. These tombs are simpler than those of the pharaohs: they all start with a terrace leading to a decorated vestibule, followed by a corridor.

TOMBS OF REKHMIRE (#100) AND SENNOFER (#96). The westernmost tomb belongs to Rekhmire, a governor of Thebes who advised Thutmose III and prided himself on his administrative genius. A historian's delight and perhaps the most absorbing of the tombs in the Theban necropolis, the **Tomb of Rekhmire** contains biographical narratives depicting the range of activities Rekhmire oversaw.

In the first chamber, tax evaders are tried by Rekhmire, who sits with a set of rolled papyrus texts strewn at the foot of his judgment throne; the presence of the papyrus suggests that written law existed as early as 1500 BCE. On the inner, left-hand wall, processions of tribute-payers arrive from Crete (top), Syria (middle), and the African kingdoms of Punt (modern-day Somalia) and Nubia (bottom). Other scenes show Egyptians drinking themselves silly during what was known as the Festival of the Valley. The niche at the top of the rear wall was intended to contain a statue of Rekhmire himself.

Trek 50m up the hill west of Rekhmire's tomb to reach the **Tomb of Sennofer,** known as the "Tomb of the Vines." A delightful lattice of purple and green filigreed grapevine crawling all over the ceiling simulates a shady arbor for Sennofer, overseer of the royal gardens of Amun under Amenhotep II. The plan of the tomb is as unusual as its decor: a curving wall leads into the first room, which in turn leads straight back into the pillared burial chamber. The big, wet eyes of **the love-cow Hathor** follow you around the tomb from the tops of the columns. The superb condition and expressiveness of the paintings make this small tomb worth the detour.

TOMB OF RAMOSE (#55). The incomplete tomb of Ramose was built during the reign of the heretic king Akhenaton (Amenhotep IV). Ramose, one of the first converts to Akhenaton's monotheistic religion that worshiped Aton, was governor of Thebes and vizier under that same pharoah. The tomb displays the stylistic contrast between the art produced in the Old Kingdom and that produced under Akhenaton. In the columned first chamber, all of Egypt pays homage to Aton, a blood-red disk emitting shafts of light that end in small hands holding *ankhs* and other religious symbols. Around the doorway, images carved in unpainted relief reflect the traditional, stylized tastes of the Old Kingdom, with scenes of Ramose and his family making offerings and Egyptians cheering Ramose's conversion to the Aton cult. In contrast, the wall to the left as you enter displays the strangely distorted figures and realistic composition typical of Akhenaton's reign, with images of ambassadors from foreign lands learning about the new god. These images support the intriguing and rather popular theory that the heretical Akhenaton came from another planet: the sun-disc Aton looks startlingly like a flying saucer, and the oblong heads and elongated arms of the wall figures greatly resemble common representations of aliens.

TOMB OF USERHET (#56). Continue up from the tomb of Ramose to that of Userhet the Scribe, a few meters to the south. Although an ascetic Christian monk who made his home within the chamber destroyed most of the female figures adorning the walls, the tomb's decor retains a certain blithe spirit because of the unusual pink tones of the interior frescoes. Userhet, Amenhotep II's royal scribe (around 1408 BCE), had his resting place painted with daily pedestrian scenes: on the right-hand wall of the first chamber, men wait their turn in line for the local barber, while duck-offering scenes cover the wall of the entrance.

TOMB OF NAKHT (#52). Slightly north of Ramose's tomb is a trail that leads off the main road and winds east a short distance to the tomb of Nakht. The first chamber contains a reconstruction of an exquisite statue of Nakht, scribe of the royal granaries under Thutmose IV (the original was lost at sea on its way to the US during World War I). Also in the first chamber are photographs of some of the other removed contents and a series of well-labeled diagrams explaining the images within the second chamber. The most famous image from the Tombs of the Nobles—three musicians playing the flute, harp, and lute—is on the left wall, to remind Nakht in the afterlife that his wife was a singer.

ASASIF TOMBS. Southwest of the Temple of Hatshepsut lies Asasif, a current archaeological hotspot. Turn left onto a dirt road after the Ramesseum and make sure to bring a flashlight. Asasif became the most popular aristocratic burial area during the 25th and 26th dynasties (around the 7th century BCE), though the **Tomb of Hor-Ef (#192)** was constructed 700 years earlier. Enter the burial site through an outer courtyard containing other tombs, where a series of well-wrought reliefs stands against a protecting wall. Note the provocative ceremonial dance featuring a chorus line of women, a jumping bird, a noisy monkey, flautists, and drummers to the left of the doorway. On the right, 16 swooning princesses surround pharaonic heartthrob Amenhotep III.

The larger tomb of **Ankh Hor** dates to the 26th dynasty and descends deeply into a large underground tomb complex. Most walls are undecorated, but various antechambers house piles of bones and even a partially mummified man, so bring a flashlight. An open-air courtyard holds the tomb's only reliefs, scenes of Anch Hor and his family. In the middle of the courtyard, a sacrificial table is inscribed with pictures of offerings to the gods.

As you enter the **Tomb of Kiki (#409),** about 10m north of Hor-Ef, the gods Thoth and Anubis discuss the readings of a giant scale. The burial chamber remains unfinished, leaving a series of faceless figures outlined in red. To get to the **Tomb of Neferhotep (#48),** walk 100m east along the dirt path from Kiki, then turn right (south) and walk 20m to the tomb, immediately in front of a village house. Most of the seated stone figures within the tomb are fairly intact.

VALLEY OF THE QUEENS وادى الملكات

During the later years of the New Kingdom, a special burial area was chosen for the wives and children of the pharaohs. Traditionally, the pharaoh's closest relatives were buried beside the monarch, but this arrangement changed during the reign of Ramses I (14th century BCE), when princes, consorts, and wives were buried in the Valley of the Queens. Directly west of the Colossi of Memnon at the end of the main road, the Valley of the Queens contains fewer than 30 royal tombs. Check at the ticket kiosks to find out which are currently open.

TOMB OF TITI (#52). As the favorite wife of Ramses III, Titi's tomb is richly decorated—but small. Reliefs show Titi praying and presenting musical instruments to Ra. In Roman times her tomb was used as a house, so the decorations lack the well-preserved freshness of some of the other area tombs.

TOMB OF AMONHERKHEPESHEF (#55). The tomb of Amonherkhepeshef, the son of Ramses III, is richly adorned with bas-relief carvings. In one, Ramses III introduces his nine-year-old son (wearing the groomed topknot of a pharaonic prince) to each of the major deities. Colored scenes of deities and farmers fill entire walls—a rare sight in Theban tombs. The sarcophagus that held the prince's mummy stands in the rear burial chamber. A dessicated fetus lies curled in a small glass display next to the remains of a still-born younger brother of the prince. The lively paintings make this tomb a cheaper, welcome alternative to the much more famous tomb of Queen Nefertari.

TOMB OF QUEEN NEFERTARI (#66). Touted as Egypt's finest tomb, the pricey tomb of Queen Nefertari is open to the first 150 people who can afford a ticket (E£100, students E£50). Stay alert: the moisture on your breath damages the tomb's colors, so you'll only have 10min. to absorb what you can. The vivid tones of the tomb walls are breathtaking, and it's a good thing they are: it took seven winters, US$6 million, and the expertise of the Getty Institute to preserve and restore this masterpiece dedicated to the favorite wife of Ramses II. The reliefs in the first chamber include the cow-goddess Hathor leading Nefertari by the hand, thousands of hieroglyphs, and a scarab-faced goddess. A sea-green and starry ceiling canopies the stairs down to the queen's burial chamber. Columns in the burial chamber portray green-skinned Osiris and Hathor.

🎵 🎭 ENTERTAINMENT AND ACTIVITIES

FELUCCAS. For a truly Luxorious diversion, while away the hours aboard a *felucca* on the Nile. **Banana Island,** a small, palm and fruit tree-studded peninsula 2mi. upriver, is a popular destination (2hr.; E£35-40; E£5 entrance fee paid to the family living on the island). Overpriced souvenir stands detract from an otherwise rustic experience. Banana Island can also be reached by bicycle: follow the Nile 5km south past the Novotel and turn left onto a tiny dirt road before the turnoff for **Crocodile Island.** The Mövenpick luxury resort and tourists have replaced the thousands of crocs of yore on Crocodile Island. *Feluccas* are prohibited from sailing after sunset.

SWIMMING. For E£10 you can beat the heat by the pool at **Emilio Hotel** (down the street from the Venus Hotel), **St. Joseph Hotel** (on Khalid ibn al-Walid St.), **Shady Hotel** (on Television St.), or **Luxor Wena Hotel** (on the corniche, fee includes unlimited rounds of billiards and backgammon).

CAFES. The many **ahwas** on the streets of Luxor are filled with Egyptians smoking *sheesha*, drinking coffee, and playing dominoes and backgammon. Foreigners are usually welcome, but solo women may attract unwanted comments. **Tikia,** on Television St., is more comfortable and friendlier than the other shops. Locals enjoy meeting foreigners, so don't be surprised if you are invited to a **wedding party** while in Luxor (or at least asked to buy liquor from duty-free store "for my sister's wedding tomorrow"). Think twice before disrupting a wedding party—"guests" are often expected to pay admission.

⚑ NIGHTLIFE

The King's Head on Ibn Walik St. is a popular pub in the British tradition, with pizza (E£13) and a wide drink selection (Stella E£10; cocktails E£12). Play pool for E£20 per hr. **Mars Bar** in the Venus Hotel (Stella E£6) has a foosball table, billiards, and satellite TV. Most discos in Luxor are not hip, not cheap, and not worth it. Dance floors are about the size of a large table, and most DJs play songs you don't like and terrible remixes of the songs you do. If you're set on going anyway, try the popular disco at **Mercure Hotel** (also called the ETAP), on al-Nil St. At 12:30am, the music changes from Top 40 dance remixes to Arabic music, and the belly dancing starts. An older crowd joins the youngsters for the nightly display of undulating flesh. (E£30 minimum. Stella E£12. Open daily 10pm-2am.) Most popular among local swingers is the Disco on **Le Lotus** at the Novotel (at the intersection of Salah al-Din and al-Nil St.), on a boat docked beside the hotel. (No minimum. Stella E£14, cocktails E£19. Usually open W-Sa 10pm-3am, but schedule changes seasonally—inquire at the front desk.)

BETWEEN LUXOR AND ASWAN

The 228km stretch of the Nile between Luxor and Aswan meanders past three heavily-touristed rural towns in the south: **Esna, Edfu,** and **Kom Ombo.** These towns make excellent daytrips—Esna and Edfu from Luxor; Edfu, Kom Ombo, and the camel market at **Daraw** from Aswan—or you can live like a pharaoh by taking a *felucca* trip from Aswan to Edfu. By water, the entire route (including stops in Esna, Edfu, and Kom Ombo) takes three to five hedonistic, sun-drenched days.

ESNA اسنا ☎095

Esna (58km south of Luxor) is a study in ignorant bliss: the *doyennes* of Esna's local coffee shop calmly sip their tea and smoke their *sheeshas* as if the luxury cruiser rolling into dock were just another *felucca*. Inland, people trot through the streets of the *souq* oblivious to the extraordinary Greco-Roman temple at its center. While little here will capture the imagination for more than a few hours, the spectacle of Esna and the temple it surrounds are well worth a visit.

⬛ TRANSPORTATION. The most Egyptian way to get to Esna is by **felucca** or **Nile cruiser** from Luxor or Aswan. Trains, buses and *service* also reach Esna from the north and south. The highway and **train** station are on the east bank of the river, connected to town by a bridge. Cross the canal in front of the train station to catch pickup *service* traveling across the Nile bridge to Esna village and the temple (50pt). The **bus** and **service** stations are at the town's northwestern edge beside a small canal bridge (E£1 to the temple). Grab a pickup *service* to take you to the ticket office. In addition to *service*, you can take a **kalish** (cart) from either station to the temple (don't pay more than E£1.50-2 for a ride anywhere in town), or you can walk 2km toward the Nile from the bus station.

⁊ ORIENTATION AND PRACTICAL INFORMATION. Esna has only a few main streets important to tourists. The main drag, **Nile St.,** runs along the bank of the river. At the temple's **ticket booth,** which sits in a small kiosk on the river side of the street where the cruise boats dock, Nile St. meets **Souq St.,** a 200m stretch of tourist bazaars running up to the temple. Follow Nile St. 200m north as it branches left away from the river for the **Bank of Alexandria.** (☎40 05 26. Open Su-Th 8:30am-2pm; Ramadan 10am-1:30pm; additional exchange hours Su-Th 6-9pm; in winter 5-8pm.) To exchange traveler's checks and foreign currency, visit the convenient **bank kiosk** opposite the ticket booth. The non-English speaking **tourist police** (☎51 06 86) are on Souq St., and the slightly more helpful **police station** is about 250m north on Nile St. as it runs away from the river. **Pharmacy Confidence** sits confidently just north of the ticket office. (☎51 05 32. Open M-Sa 9am-2pm and 5-11pm; in winter 4-9pm.) The **post office** is south of the ticket booth on Souq St. (Open Su-Th 8am-2pm.) Numerous stores along the riverfront allow **international phone calls.**

▐▐ ACCOMMODATIONS AND FOOD. There is little incentive to remain in Esna longer than it takes to visit the temple, but **Hotel al-Haramein** will do in a pinch. The hotel is 1km south (through the *souq*) of the temple's eastern wall and about the same distance inland from the Nile. Pass to the right of the white wall enclosing a gray concrete building, then walk another 100m. There are no signs, but the police can help you find your way. (☎51 19 22. Singles E£12; doubles E£12, with bath E£25; triples E£20-30.) The **souq** provides *ta'amiyya* and produce.

◙ SIGHTS. Although the **Temple of Khnum** was begun in the 18th dynasty, it is largely a Roman creation and in many ways a feeble imitation of Egyptian technical and artistic achievements. The wall on the west side of the site suggests original temple remains from the Greek era, but excavations have yet to begin. **Khnum** was the ram-headed creator god (who reputedly molded the first human being on a potter's wheel; see **Meet the Gods,** p. 75) and was worshiped in this region around the First Cataract and at his sanctuary on Aswan's Elephantine Island (see p. 244). The cataract was an important economic and cultural center for the area south of Luxor, and the pharaohs of the 18th dynasty dedicated this temple to the local deity to garner regional support. Remains of a small Coptic church in front of the temple attest to the site's layered religious history.

The temple's elaborate hallway (all that remains of what was once a much larger sanctuary) has managed to survive in excellent condition. In an attempt to decorate the temple in traditional Egyptian style, the Romans carved a procession of stiff, oddly deformed figures marching solemnly across the walls. The ceiling designs are among the more interesting aspects of the temple: the signs of the zodiac are portrayed just right of the last pillar on the left as you enter the hallway. Faint blue and red hues topping the 24 columns hint at the interior's former brilliance. *(Open daily 6am-6:30pm, in winter 6am-5:30pm. E£8, students E£4. Don't buy tickets from hawkers in the* souq.*)*

EDFU ادفو ☎097

Only 50km south of Esna, Edfu is more than worth the short trip. Even the most templed-out traveler won't be able to resist Edfu's intricately detailed **Temple of Horus.** The vast, stunningly preserved temple is one of Upper Egypt's most spectacular sights, rivaling the serenity of Kalabsha and even the awesome scale of

Abu Simbel. Mysteriously, the temple hasn't made such a big impression on locals. When archaeologists began excavating the temple in the mid-19th century, they had more than sand and rubble to clear; the people of Edfu had also built a number of homes on the half-buried temple's roof.

▛ TRANSPORTATION

The **train station** is remotely positioned on the east bank, away from town. The **service station** sits just right of the small square where the bridge reaches the west bank. Trains run north to Luxor (9:30, 11:30am, 1:30pm; E£1.50) and south to Aswan (9:30, 11:30am, 5:30pm; E£1.50) These times change often, so make sure to check within the train station for up to date information. **Kalishes** (E£2-3) or **private taxis** (E£3-5) can take you from either station to the temple. When facing the mosque in Temple Sq., follow the street on the mosque's right side to the **bus station,** 50m up the street. Buses run to Luxor (6pm, E£8) and Aswan (6, 7, 8am; E£2.50). Another set of buses bound for Luxor (7:30, 8, 9, 10, 11am, 1:30, 2:30, 3, 5, 7pm; E£8) and Aswan (9, 10, 11am, noon, 2, 3, 5, 6, 9:30pm; E£5-7) stop across the river in front of the train station. Schedules change often, so ask around for the latest developments.

✷▐ ORIENTATION AND PRACTICAL INFORMATION

Edfu lies on the west bank of the Nile, roughly halfway between Luxor and Aswan. The center of town, **Temple Sq.,** lies about 1km inland, while a bridge crosses the Nile at the northern edge of town. The **Bank of Cairo** is on the west bank, 200m east (towards the river) of Temple Sq. on the right. (☎71 36 97. Open Su-Th 8:30am-2pm and 3-9pm.) Across the street from the bank is **Ezzat Pharmacy.** (☎71 38 60. Open M-Sa 7:30am-11:30pm.) About 100m from Temple Sq. is a tourist bazaar, the **temple,** and the **tourist police.** (☎70 01 34. Open 7am-7pm, in winter 7am-4pm.) The **post office** is on Tahrir St., 50m south of Temple Sq. (Open Sa-Th 8am-2pm.) From the bridge, the riverfront road runs 100m south to the **central telephone office** (☎71 17 77; open 24hr.) and another 200m to **al-Maglis St.,** which links the Nile with Temple Sq. The **telegraph office,** on the south side of Temple Sq., can help with **calling card calls** (about E£1 per 3min. to call Cairo). Several **telephone offices** line the riverfront where the cruise ships dock.

▐▐ ACCOMMODATIONS AND FOOD

The cleanest budget hotel in town—though that's not saying much—is the musty **al-Madina Hotel,** just off Temple Sq. The included breakfast, however, is impressive. (☎71 13 26. Singles E£20, less without bath; doubles E£30, with bath E£40; triples with bath E£45.) The cheap but run-down **Semiramis Hotel** is near the bank; at E£6 per bed it's not hard on the pocketbook, but you get what you pay for. A handful of restaurants lie in the square by the bridge. The **New Nesma Tourist Restaurant** serves up large portions of chicken and kebab (E£6-10) with heaps of potato chips (Stella E£6). Edfu's produce **souq** encompasses the streets off Temple Sq.

◔ SIGHTS

The spectacular ▨**Temple of Horus** took almost 200 years to construct and wasn't completed until 57 BCE, making it one of the last great Egyptian monuments. The Ptolemies designed this temple and the temple to Hathor at Dendera (see p. 253) as a matching set. Several important religious festivals dealing with the life of Horus were celebrated at Edfu. During the annual Union with the Solar Disk, Horus's earthly form was brought to the roof of the temple to be rejuvenated by the sun's rays. In another important ritual, the Festival of the Happy Reunion, the god's icon (once held in the polished black granite shrine in the temple's inner sanctuary) was removed from the temple in a ceremonial boat, then taken to Dendera to escort gal-pal Hathor back to his humble abode for some play. In a chamber behind the sanctuary there is a modern reconstruction of the ceremonial boat used to carry the statue during festivals; the original is in the Egyptian Museum in Cairo. *(Open daily 7am-6pm, in winter 7am-4pm. E£20, students E£10. Bring a flashlight.)*

The path from the ticket office takes you to the temple's shapely rear end. Wind your way around the complex to the front, decorated with inscriptions galore and a large depiction of Horus on either side of the entrance. Enter through the 12 gargantuan columns of the **Great Hypostyle Hall** and look to the right for the small **library,** where papyrus was found indicating the dates of the temple's festivals. A symmetric doorway on the left served as a **purification chamber** for the pharaoh. On the left-hand wall, inscriptions show Ptolemy building the temple—first digging the foundation and then opening his grand edifice. Proceed to the second hypostyle hall, outfitted with a similar arrangement of smaller pillars. Doorways on either side lead to the **ambulatory,** a narrow exterior passageway running between the temple and its protective wall. Charred ceilings mark the period when Christians used the temple to store and burn their garbage. The doorway on the right side of the second hall leads to a side **chapel** with a celestial ceiling depicting the sky-goddess, Nut, reaching around the Zodiac (see **Meet the Gods,** p. 75). Sadly, monotheists of later eras chiseled away most figures' faces, but the rest of the temple's reliefs remain untouched.

Outside the temple, directly in front of the main entrance, is a well-preserved Roman **mammisis** (birthhouse), where the birth of Horus was reenacted annually with appropriate hoopla. How many breast-feeding scenes can you count? Copt later defaced the images of the growing god on the *mammisis* columns. Note the images of **pot-bellied pygmies,** brought to court for the royalty's entertainment, atop the exterior side columns.

▣ DAYTRIPS FROM EDFU

AL-KAB الكاب

From Edfu, the cheapest way to al-Kab is a one-way service (75pt), though some will say that service don't go there. If traveling by felucca, your captain might not know where al-Kab is; give him the distances indicated below and watch for the Roman wall on the east bank of the Nile. It's best to leave early before the sun is high. To get back to Edfu, hail a pickup taxi.

Don't go out of your way to see the temples at al-Kab (20km north of Edfu and 3km south of the village of al-Mahamid) unless you have time and energy to spare. The temples are intriguing, but not on the order of Middle Egypt's other ancient sites. The distance you have to walk between the two temples and the roadside tombs will make you empathize with the ancient Israelites: 2-4km separates the sights from each other and the decrepit visitors center. Bring several bottles of water—there's not a leaf of shade. The site was once occupied by the ancient city of Nekheb, which was dedicated to the vulture-goddess Nekhbet, protector of the pharaohs and lady of the mouth of the desert. City remains consist of several temples and the rather unimpressive ruins of old tombs dotting the highway.

TOMBS. A guard will lead you up the staircase to the four most important tombs along the highway, dating from 1570 to 1320 BCE. The best preserved is the **Tomb of Paheri.** Paheri was chief priest, royal tutor to Prince Wadjmose (son of Pharaoh Thutmoses I), and scribe for the pharoah's corn accounts. This tomb features brightly colored illustrations: Egyptians sniffing lotus blossoms, cultivating crops, fishing, shipping, and making wine. At the rear of the tomb stands a statue of a happy Paheri flanked by two female figures. The **Tomb of Setau** belonged to the powerful high priest of Amun under Ramses III - IX (20th dynasty). Setau's digs are not as well preserved as the Tomb of Paheri, but they have some colorful pictures of the lotus-sniffers. The **Tomb of Aahmes** is the resting place of a warship captain who suppressed a rebellion in Upper Egypt and led 18th-dynasty forces under Amenhotep I and Thutmoses I against

Syria and Nubia. Unfortunately, a wall of hieroglyphs is about all that remains of the mighty captain's tomb. The **Tomb of Renini,** superintendent of priests under Amenhotep I, contains a geometrically painted ceiling and eyes staring out from a broken statue. Decorations are quite worn, but some colorful paintings of farming practices adorn the tomb's walls.

TEMPLES AND CHAPELS. An unpaved but passable track brings you 2.5km to the tiny **Chapel of Thoth** (1320-1200 BCE), built by the high priest of al-Kab for Ramses II and dedicated to Nekhbet, Thoth (the god of wisdom), and Horus. Inside a small statue shows the three seated gods. Fragments of inscriptions and hieroglyphs remain. The much larger **Ptolemaic Temple,** in the same complex, was built under Ptolemies IX - XI. It is notable for its ramped entryway, leading to a forecourt with a few nice broken capitals and a chamber with ceiling paintings. The stagnant pond within the compound was once considered a sacred lake. Wake up the guard in the shack across the road to open the locked gates; he'll walk or ride with you another 1.5km to the small **Temple of Amenophis III,** with well-preserved colored paintings and carvings of Nekhbet, coiffed with a retro 60s bob. Four columns topped with Nekhbet's face support the temple ceiling. Caravans to and from gold mines deeper in the desert once stopped here to pray. *(All sites open daily 7am-7pm, in winter 6am-6pm. E£10, students E£5.)*

GABAL AL-SILSILAH جبل السلسلة

Reaching the quarries by land is a time-consuming challenge. Only those with a sense of adventure and time to kill should make the journey. First, take a service 25km from Kom Ombo to Kalabsha (E£1), where you can catch another service to the riverside town of Faris (50pt). A small ferry crosses the river to the east bank where you can hire a "special" taxi (E£10) for the round-trip ride to the temple. Make sure to ask for the **Temple of Horemheb** *(requesting Gabal al-Silsilah will land you in the speck of a town by the same name on the east bank). The boat ride over the Nile to the temple should cost no more than E£2. Temple and quarry open 7am-6pm; 7am-4pm in winter. Tickets E£15, students E£7.50.*

The quarries at Gabal al-Silsilah are a fascinating treat for *felucca* travelers who succeed in persuading their captain to stop here. There are sandstone **quarries** (in use from the 16th to the first century BCE) on both sides of the Nile, but boats only dock on the west bank. A guard can unlock the well-preserved **Temple of Horemheb,** built by General Horemheb, the last king of the 18th dynasty, who seized the throne after King Tutankhamun's death. Numerous pharaohs after Horemheb made additions to the temple, including Ramses II and III. A picture of Horemheb being led by dancers and acrobats during the festival adorns the left side of the back wall. From the temple, a path leads 200m south along a bluff 15m above the Nile, ending in the cavernous belly of the quarry. Huge blocks of sandstone were cut from the cliff, loaded onto boats, and transported along the Nile to construction sites; note the boat and ostrich graffiti etched into the wall's face. Small temples were also carved into holes in the granite walls; climb around and explore what remains of paintings and inscriptions. Well-worn statues rest inside the first cave-like temple on the right.

KOM OMBO كوم امبو

Where the temples at Philae, Kalabsha, and Abu Simbel once stood, only water now remains (see **Moving a Mountain,** p. 252). But Kom Ombo still stands in its original spot, 45km north of Aswan, cutting the same striking figure today as it did during Ptolemaic times. The beautiful temple ruins make Kom Ombo worth the visit, but finding a parking spot may be difficult: Nile cruisers carrying an assortment of European tourists and their translators barge in on every available inch of the coastline. One look at the adjacent town will make most travelers want to make like a temple and relocate.

A series of temples has occupied this spot since the Middle Kingdom, and parts of the older versions of the **Temple of Kom Ombo** now rest at the Louvre in Paris and the Egyptian Museum in Cairo (see p. 125). The current edifice dates only to 150

BCE and was built by Ptolemy VI. Later, Ptolemy XIII added the outer and inner hypostyle halls. In 30 BCE, Caesar Augustus left his own mark—though his additions lie in ruins today, as the rising waters of the Nile buried the lower part of the temple in silt. In later years, the above-ground portion was used as a quarry for new construction projects; as a result, the side walls have vanished.

Nevertheless, the temple that remains (open daily 7am-9pm, in winter 7am-7pm; E£10, students E£5) provides more deity for your dollar than you will get anywhere else. **Sobek,** patron of the many crocs that lurked in the waters nearby in ancient times, came to **Horus** the elder, avenger of Osiris and the source of the pharaohs' divine power, asking for food. Horus apparently complied, and the two gods subsequently agreed to share this temple. Kom Ombo is therefore rigorously symmetrical throughout: double halls and double colonnades lead to double doorways which open onto double chambers and double sanctuaries. The right side of the temple honors Sobek, and the left Horus. (Sobek's crocodiles have since relocated to Lake Nasser.) On the ceiling of the left vestibule, bright blue images of Horus still hover protectively over the chamber. A tunnel in the floor of the inner sanctuary allowed clergy to climb in so they could overhear entreaties to the gods. Ask the guard to show you the reliefs of **Cleopatra II and VII,** and take it upon yourself to decipher the risqué hieroglyphs: can you spot the two dripping phalluses and the dismembered bodies?

Predating the Catholic tradition of confessionals by several centuries, a window in the west wall opening into the sanctuary, decorated with ears and eyes, is where the plebeians came to confess their sins to the gods and ask for forgiveness. This section of the temple also houses reliefs honoring yet another deity: Aesculapius, the Greek god of medicine.

West of the temple are remains of a Roman *mammisis*, and adjoining the northern edge of the temple are now-putrid Roman water supply tanks, once crawling with crocodiles. The **Chapel of Hathor,** to your right as you enter the compound, has crocodile mummies which were unearthed near the road leading to the site. Cleopatra's bubble bath is also rumored to be nearby.

DARAW CAMEL MARKET دراو

*Service careen to Daraw from Kom Ombo (8km, 10min.) and Aswan (37km, 1hr.), but check with local authorities to make sure they take non-Egyptians. Trains and buses running between Luxor and Aswan may also stop in Daraw. The taxi stand, bus station, and train station lie along the main highway. To reach the camel market from the stations, walk 300m north, cross the tracks, and head down the road for 15min. Take a right after you pass the open fields. You've arrived when you see 200-odd people smacking the rear ends of bound, groaning camels to display their vigor. If you're gliding by on a **felucca,** have the captain stop at the Daraw ferry landing and a pickup truck will take you to the market. Market open Sa-Tu 7am-2pm; slows down after 11am. Ask around for most up-to-date market days.*

Sudanese merchants, Bishari tribespeople, and Egyptian *fellaheen* gather Saturday to Tuesday mornings in Daraw for the unforgettable **camel market.** Waking up very early in Aswan, you can visit the market and move on to the temple at Kom Ombo. Saturdays and Sundays are the best days to scope out camels. On Tuesdays, various other livestock are sold as well.

The Bishari (Saharan nomads with their own language and culture) purchase camels for the equivalent of E£1000 in the Sudan, where camels are as plentiful as sand, and take them by caravan through the desert from the Sudan to Abu Simbel on the Forty Days Road. From Abu Simbel, trucks take the camels to the vet in Daraw before the Saturday market. Look for the occasional businessman in full traditional dress: flowing pants, a sword and dagger, and a cloak draped over the shoulders. Typically, a Sudanese camel owner will pay a Sudanese or Bishari shepherd to drive his camels north to Egypt The owner then flies up to oversee the sales, coming away with big profits. Camels are used for work, tourism, racing, and meat (the meat is said to be quite tender). Prices range E£2000-4000, savings of E£1000 over Cairo prices. A camel's hump size determines its health and value.

ASWAN اسوان ☎ 097

Aswan, one of the southernmost cities in Egypt, lies at the junction of the Middle East and Africa, evinced by the city's ethnic and cultural pluralism. In 1971, the completion of the Soviet-designed High Dam created nearby Lake Nasser (the world's largest reservoir) and boosted Egypt's agricultural and energy potential. The dam flooded most of Nubia, forcing large-scale migrations to Egypt and Sudan. Darker-skinned Nubian immigrants now thrive in Aswan, giving the city its African flavor. The city's name comes from the Nubian phrase *assy wangibu*, meaning "too much water," although the high daytime temperatures will often make you wonder if there could ever be enough water. This far south, the fertile strip nourished by the Nile is not very wide, and often there are only a few trees separating the desert from the river. Though summer temperatures average over 40°C (104°F), the thermometer dips to a chilly 35°C (95°F) in winter. During this time, the city becomes an all-out resort.

Aswanis' gentle charm makes up for the stuffy weather. Somehow tourists are coaxed into extending their stay, whether by the pesky street vendor stopping passersby mid-stride to hawk his wares, or by the friendly old lady giving directions in broken English. The cool breezes along the corniche in the evenings are a welcome surprise for those foolish enough to go out during the day. Women, however, should experience Aswan's pleasures with company; women traveling alone will get loads of catcalls, suggestive glances, and more-than-friendly hellos.

Aswan is a convenient base for exploring southern Egypt and deserves a spot on any itinerary. Plan on four days if you want to see the sights and stay sane. You can take *felucca* trips to Kom Ombo, Edfu, and Luxor (see **The Nile Valley: Getting Around,** p. 205). Summer, when temperatures are high and captains are desperate to capture the few tourists, is the best time for a *felucca* trip. Not only may prices be lower, but drifting on the Nile provides escape from the sun-soaked sands.

▐ TRANSPORTATION

Flights: The airport (☎ 48 03 20) is 23km south of town, near the High Dam. E£20 one-way by taxi, less if you haggle. Served by **EgyptAir** (☎ 31 50 00; fax 31 50 05), on the southern end of the corniche near Ferial Gardens. Office open daily 8am-8pm. Another EgyptAir office at the airport (☎ 48 05 68), but tickets are not sold there. 4 flights daily to Cairo, 8 during the winter (E£577 one-way). Daily flights to **Abu Simbel** leave at least twice a day Apr.-Sept.; more frequently Oct.-Mar. (E£275 round-trip). MC/V. **Airport Police:** ☎ 48 05 09.

Trains: Station (☎ 31 47 54) at the northern end of al-Souq St. 1st- and 2nd-class A/C trains depart for **Cairo** (14hr.; 1st-class E£73, student E£49; 2nd-class E£42, student E£33) and **Luxor** (3½hr.; 1st-class E£27, student E£20; 2nd-class E£17, student E£15). Frequent trains run to the **High Dam** (30min.; 8, 9:30, 11:30am, 1:45, 3, 4:45pm; 70pt) and back (11:30am, 2, 2:30, 4pm). Prices and schedules subject to the whim of the Egyptian Transportation Department. Morning trains tend to be about E£5 less. The tourist office can provide current fares.

Buses: station (☎ 30 32 25) on Abtal al-Tahrir St. behind Abu Simbel Hotel. To: **Abu Simbel** (4hr.; 8, 11:30am, 5pm, returns to Aswan 7am, 2, 5pm; only four non-Egyptians allowed per bus; E£40 round-trip); **Asyut** (9hr., 7am, E£20); **Cairo** (12hr., 3:30pm, E£55); **Edfu** (2hr., E£5); **Hurghada** (7hr.; 6, 8am, 3:30, 5pm; E£35); **Kom Ombo** (1hr., E£1.50); **Luxor** (3½hr., E£6.50); **Qena** (4hr.; 6, 7, 8, 9, 11am, 12:30, 1:30, 3:30, 5pm; E£13) via **Daraw** (45min., E£1.50); **Suez** (13hr.; 6, 8am, 5pm; E£50).

Ferries: Range from large *feluccas* to small motor boats. Local ferries depart for **Elephantine Island** from the al-Shatii Restaurant on the southern end of the corniche, or even farther south across from the EgyptAir office (every 15-20min. 6am-8pm, E£1). Hotel Oberoi's cheap ferry floats to the northern part of Elephantine Island from a ramp on the

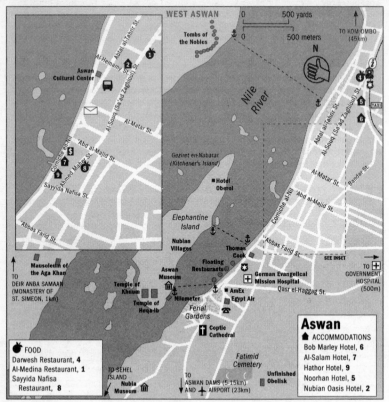

Tombs of
the Nobles

Aswan
Cultural Center

TO KOM OMBO
(45km)

N

Nile River

Geziret en-Nabatat
(Kitchener's Island)

Hotel
Oberoi

SEE INSET

Elephantine
Island

Nubian
Villages

Thomas
Cook

Aswan
Museum

Floating
Restaurants

German Evangelical
Mission Hospital

Qasr el-Haggag St.

TO
GOVERNMENT
HOSPITAL
(500m)

Mausoleum of
the Aga Khan

Temple of
Khnum

Temple of
Heqa-Ib

Nilometer

AmEx

Egypt Air

TO
DEIR ANBA SAMAAN
(MONASTERY OF
ST. SIMEON, 1km)

Ferial
Gardens

Coptic
Cathedral

Fatimid
Cemetery

Aswan

⌂ ACCOMMODATIONS
Bob Marley Hotel, 6
Al-Salam Hotel, 7
Hathor Hotel, 9
Noorhan Hotel, 5
Nubian Oasis Hotel, 2

● FOOD
Darwesh Restaurant, 4
Al-Medina Restaurant, 1
Sayyida Nafisa
Restaurant, 8

TO SEHEL
ISLAND

Nubia
Museum

TO
ASWAN DAMS (5-15km)
AND ✈ AIRPORT (23km)

Unfinished
Obelisk

south side of the corniche gardens (E£1; see **Sights**, p. 244). The **Seti** ferry (not Seti
Tours) departs from the north end of the corniche across from the park to the northern
part of the western bank (every 20min., 6am-8pm, 25pt). Ignore captains who tell you
the ferry is not running.

Service: As of Aug. 2001, buses and *service* were unavailable to tourists due to road clo-
sures and safety concerns, but they may be available later in the year. *Service* leave
from the covered station 1km south of the train station (every 15-30min. 4am-6pm,
depending on demand). To get there, take the overpass just left of the train station,
make a left at the end of the road, then take another right. To: **Daraw** or **Kom Ombo**
(40min., E£1); **Edfu** (1¼hr., E£7); **Esna** (2-3hr., E£8); **Khazan/Old Dam** (25pt); **Luxor**
(3hr., E£10); and **Qena** (4hr., E£9). *Service* also occasionally depart from the corniche
and Abtal al-Tahrir St. across from the bus station.

Taxis: Pick up a taxi anywhere along the corniche. Not more than E£5 within the city.

Bike Rental: Abtal al-Tahrir St., past the Arab Land Bazaar next to Poste Restante office.
Open daily 10am-10pm. E£18 per day, E£3 per hr. Haggle if prices are not posted.

Kalish: After haggling, a horse-drawn *kalish* should cost E£5 for a short ride, E£10 for a
30min. tour.

▨ ORIENTATION

In Aswan, you're rarely more than two blocks from the Nile. The northern half
of the city lies along three long avenues that run parallel to the Nile. The riverfront **Corniche al-Nil** ("the corniche") is the most picturesque, featuring several

hotels, shops, banks, floating restaurants, and docks. Two blocks inland, the market-lined **Sa'ad Zaghloul St.** showcases everything from watermelons to water pipes. Also called **al-Souq St.**, it begins at the train station at the northeast corner of town and runs south 2km to **'Abbas Farid St.** For the block-long stretch behind the al-Salaam and Hathor Hotels, this path of many names curves to the right, narrows, and changes its name to **Ahmed Maher St.** At this point, a crowded shopping street called **al-Sayyida Nafisa** runs perpendicular to al-Souq St. In the southern half of town, the corniche continues for another 1km and ends at the **Ferial Gardens.** South of the *souq*, inland streets form a labyrinth of alleys. Sandwiched between the corniche and al-Souq St., **Abtal al-Tahrir St.** begins at the youth hostel in the north and culminates in a small cluster of tourist bazaars, resuming as a narrow lane farther south. Unless you're an expert at reading signs in faded Arabic, don't plan on being able to identify streets. Asking for directions or using a map is your best bet.

🛈 PRACTICAL INFORMATION

TOURIST AND FINANCIAL SERVICES

Tourist Office: (☎31 28 11). Domed structure on the right as you exit the train station, at the northern end of al-Souq St. Few brochures, but knowledgeable and multilingual staff can help you. Open daily 9am-3pm and 7-9pm; in winter 9am-3pm and 6-8pm.

Tourist Police: (☎30 31 63). On the south side of the train station. Open 24hr.

Passport Office: (☎31 22 38). On Corniche al-Nil, on the 3rd fl. of the police building. Registers passports and extends visas. Open Su-Th 8am-2pm.

Currency Exchange: Banque Misr, 103 Corniche al-Nil (☎31 66 92 or 31 66 93; fax 31 66 94). MC and V advances. Open Su-Th 8:30am-2pm and 6-9pm. **ATM** on the corniche next to Banque Misr takes MC/V, PLUS, and Cirrus cards. Next to Memnon Hotel, the **National Bank of Egypt** also has an ATM that takes PLUS and Cirrus.

American Express: (☎/fax 30 29 09) At the south end of the corniche, on the 2nd fl. of the New Cataract Hotel. Arranges itineraries, cashes traveler's checks, and holds mail for cardholders. Open daily 8am-5pm.

Thomas Cook: 59 Corniche al-Nil (☎30 40 11; fax 30 62 09), just north of the police building. Travel and financial services. Discounts on tours and hotels if you book through Cook. Open daily 8am-2pm and 4-8pm; in winter 8am-8pm.

LOCAL SERVICES

Bookstore: Large hotels usually have small bookstores carrying European newspapers. Books in Arabic, English, French, and other languages can be found in shops along al-Souq St. and Corniche al-Nil.

Laundromat: Most hotels do laundry for E£1-2 per garment. Laundry and dry-cleaning service under the Nubian Oasis Hotel (see p. 242). Open daily 8am-2pm.

Swimming Pools: The Oberoi Hotel pool is a swanky but expensive option (E£21). Other 4- and 5-star hotels may allow use of their pools during the slow summer season for E£20-30. The rooftop pool at the Hathor Hotel is cheaper (E£5; free if you stay at the hotel) but it is only about 4ft. deep.

EMERGENCY AND COMMUNICATIONS

Emergency: Few places have English speakers, so call the **tourist police** (☎31 43 36 or 31 40 15) or **tourist office** (☎31 28 11) first. **Medical Emergency: ☎**123.

Pharmacy: Aswan Pharmacy (☎30 31 65), on the north end of Abtal al-Tahrir St., between the bus and train stations. Open daily 9:30am-1am. Numerous other pharmacies line the corniche and *souq*.

Hospitals: In decreasing order of English proficiency: **Mubarak Military Hospital** (☎ 31 79 85), in the flamingo-pink building behind the Nubian Museum. Clean new facility offers everything from family planning to emergency gynecological care. Travelers pay in cash. **German Evangelical Mission Hospital** (☎ 30 21 76 or 31 21 76), 100m south of the police station down an alley on the left. Look for steel doors with flower symbols. Recommended by the tourist office. The **Government Hospital** (☎ 30 28 55 or 24 19), on Qasr al-Hagga St., should be a last resort. Every hotel reception can provide the name of a **doctor.**

Internet Access: Enter **Oriental Cafe Garden** at the youth hostel sign and head to the outdoor garden cafe. In the back right corner is a pleasant A/C room with 3 computers. E£15 per hr., E£5 min. Open daily 9:30am-2am. **Rohab Internet Cafe,** inside the Aswan Rowing Club, charges E£5 for 15 min. Open daily 9am-midnight.

Post Office: On the corniche, toward the north end of town, right before the park. Offers **EMS** and **telegraph** services. Open Sa-Th 8am-2pm. For **Poste Restante,** walk south from the main post office and turn left down Salah al-Din St., then immediately right. In the yellow building with black columns. Open Su-Th 8am-2pm.

Telephones: Telephone office (☎ 31 06 10), two doors down from EgyptAir on the south end of the corniche near Ferial Gardens. Calls to US E£20 for 3min. Open 24hr. **Telegraph service** and **fax** available 8am-9pm. **Information:** ☎ 16.

⌐ ACCOMMODATIONS

Prices are higher in winter and lower in summer; rates listed are approximate. If you have the energy when you arrive, you may be able to play hotel hawkers off one another to land a better price. All listed hotels have laundry service and breakfast unless otherwise stated, but none dance the credit card tango. Spend the extra money in the summer and get air-conditioning, unless you want to wake up in the morning to find half your body mass evaporated. Be sure to ask for student and group discounts, but be careful of discounted group tours and *felucca* trips, which are often rip-offs. Do not agree to anything until you have checked out the competition on your own.

▨ **Nubian Oasis Hotel,** 234 Sa'ad Zaghloul St. (☎ 31 21 23; fax 31 21 24; nubianoasis@infinity.com.eg). From the train station, turn left on Sa'ad Zaghloul and then right 2 streets after Cleopatra Hotel. Simple and clean, with great views from the rooftop sitting area. The restaurant serves inexpensive meals and the management organizes reliable tours at good prices. TV lounge with cable and pool. Internet access E£15 per hr. Rooms come with fans, soap, and toilet paper. Check-out noon. Singles E£10; doubles E£15; private bath and A/C E£5 each.

Noorhan Hotel (☎ 31 60 69), on Sa'ad Zaghloul St. From the train station, turn left onto Sa'ad Zaghloul and take 2nd left, at the Noorhan sign. When the sun goes down, sip a Stella (E£6) on the pleasant rooftop terrace. Check-out noon. Rooms without A/C come with fans. Singles E£12, with A/C and private bath E£20; doubles E£12/E£25; triples E£18/E£30.

Hathor Hotel (☎ 31 45 80; fax 30 34 62), in the middle of Corniche al-Nil, next to al-Salaam Hotel. It's all about the rooftop pool (free for guests, E£5 for visitors), a perfect spot to chill. All rooms have clean, fully-tiled baths and A/C. Lunch E£12. Dinner E£15. Check-out noon. Singles E£30; doubles E£45; triples E£60. In winter add E£10 to room rates.

Queen N. Hotel (☎ 32 60 69). From the train station, walk to your right and towards the Nile. In a pink building 100m down the road. Brand new and super clean, this small, homey hotel offers rooms with comfortable mattresses, refrigerators, private baths, and A/C. The lobby offers welcoming chairs, TV, and a cafe. Plans for a small rooftop swimming pool by winter 2001-02. Laundry service available. Singles with huge double bed E£25, doubles E£35. Add E£5 for in-room TV with limited channels.

Horus Hotel, 89 Corniche al-Nil, 4th fl. (☎30 33 23; fax 31 33 13). Half the rooms are marvelously renovated and tiled, complete with bathtubs. The other half are shabby, but spacious. All include A/C and private bath. Try to secure a room with a balcony overlooking the corniche and Nile. The cafeteria upstairs offers meals during the winter and tremendous views of the Nile year-round (Stella E£6.75). Check-out noon. Renovated singles E£40; doubles E£50; triples E£65; un-renovated rooms are E£5-10 cheaper. In winter prices add E£10.

Al-Salaam Hotel, 101 Corniche al-Nil (☎30 36 49; fax 30 26 51). Carpeted hallways, an elevator, and clean rooms (some with balconies over the Nile). All rooms have pristine bathrooms and A/C. Check-out noon. Singles E£35; doubles E£50; triples E£65.

Memnon Hotel, (☎/fax 30 04 83), on Corniche al-Nil. Entrance on the street parallel to the corniche, behind the National Bank of Egypt A dim but homey throwback to the early 60s, with yellow walls and views of the river. Basic rooms have A/C, private bath, red shag lamps, and 18th-century French curtains. Lunch and dinner E£10. Singles E£30; doubles E£40; triples E£50; suites E£75.

Bob Marley Hotel (☎30 18 39). From the train station, turn left onto al-Souq St., and take a left at the sign for the hotel. Low on cash? Don't mind lumpy beds? Bob's is your place, mon. No private baths or A/C. Check-out noon. Breakfast E£1. Singles E£5.

◖ FOOD

Aswan's **souq** sells fruit, vegetables, bread, and pigeon (a local specialty)—not to mention *ta'amiyya*, liver sandwiches, *fuul*, falafel, and *kushari*. Vegetarians may find their choices limited to a few rice dishes. For legendary legumes, **vegetable souqs** are tucked away across the tracks from the train station and on the east end of 'Abd al-Majid St. Come in the morning for a full range of options. Small restaurants hide in the corners of al-Souq St. and Abtal al-Tahrir St. At the other end of the price spectrum, wallow in huge buffets and gourmet cuisine at luxury hotels. The Oberoi offers an elegant E£44 **breakfast buffet** (6-10:30am) in its cupola-covered ballroom restaurant. Don't leave Aswan without trying *karkadeh*, a sweet purple drink made of hibiscus. Local legend says downing a glass before bedtime mellows you out.

Sayyida Nafisa (31 71 52). Turn left on al-Souq St. from the train station and continue onto Ahmed Maher St. As you approach the restaurant, the ground in the *souq* turns rosy red from colored wood shavings. Named after a relative of Muhammad, this restaurant has both indoor and outdoor seating. Chicken and beef dishes E£6-11, refreshing juices E£2. Add 10% for service. 10% student discount. Open daily 7am-2am.

Al-Medina (30 56 96). On al-Souq St., across from the Cleopatra Hotel. Street vendors and tourists lunch here in A/C comfort. Beef, chicken, and vegetarian dishes served with rice, veggies, and salad (E£7-18) fill you up, and the speedy service won't slow you down. Add 15% for service and tax. Open daily noon-midnight.

Al-Masry (☎30 25 76). Head south from the train station and turn left on al-Matar St. Treat yourself at this tidy, relatively upscale establishment. Big portions and snappily uniformed waiters. Meals include main course, sides, and dessert (E£20-25). Open daily noon-midnight.

Darwesh Restaurant, on Sa'ad Zaghloul St., opposite the south end of the train station. All meals (E£6-10) come with vegetables, soup, rice, and salad. Add 13% for service and tax. Open daily noon-midnight.

FLOATING AND RIVERSIDE RESTAURANTS

More popular with locals and tourists alike, these pseudo-aquatic eateries offer decent meals and the perfect setting to watch the sun go down over the desert hills of the west bank. All serve basically the same array of meat dishes, salads, tahini, drinks, and desserts. They are all relatively close together along the corniche, starting across the street from Thomas Cook and running down to about 100m north of the EgyptAir office. Expect an additional 15% added to all bills for tax and service.

NILE VALLEY

Aswan Moon Restaurant (☎31 61 08). Popular with locals and tour groups alike, the atmosphere at this floating restaurant can't be beat. Oriental red drapes provide shade and a relaxing setting. Main dishes E£8-18.

Panorama (☎30 61 69). "The best food money can buy" is the motto of this riverside restaurant, set amidst luscious fruit trees. Delicious food and garden seating are worth the walk down the corniche. Try the Bedouin coffee served on coals, filtered with dried grass, and flavored with cardamom, cinnamon, and cloves (E£4). Main dishes E£7-9. Open daily noon-9pm.

Monalisa, with pleasant outdoor and indoor seating and a comfortably covered garden patio. The overbearing heat outdoors might wipe the enigmatic smile off your face, but turn that frown upside down with a Monalisa fruit cocktail (E£2). Well-prepared meat and fish entrees E£7-12. Breakfast E£3.50. Open daily 6am-3am.

Emy (☎30 43 49). The top level of this floating barge is filled with locals enjoying the pleasant view and good food. Watch your step—the boat leans severely to the left. Main courses E£9-12, set dinner menu E£14. Breakfast E£3. Beer E£5.25. 15% tax and service surcharge. 20% student discount. Open daily 8am-2am.

⊙ SIGHTS

Most of Aswan's attractions can be found on the isles in the middle of the Nile. Although some of Aswan's ancient Egyptian ruins are only second-rate compared to those of Giza and Luxor, its Nubian artifacts can't be found anywhere else. Just a short train ride away, the Aswan High Dam and Lake Nasser demonstrate the continuing Egyptian penchant for grandeur.

To reach the sights on the west bank of the Nile, it's easiest to hire a *felucca*. The official rate for *felucca* transport in the vicinity of Aswan is E£15 per hr. regardless of the number of passengers, but getting this price may take some negotiation. A complete tour of Elephantine Island, Kitchener's Island, the Aga Khan's Mausoleum, St. Simeon's Monastery, and the northern tombs goes for E£18 per hr. per group and takes 3-4hr. A cheap alternative is to break the west bank and Elephantine Island into two trips and trek between the sights on foot. Take the local ferry to the west bank (25pt) and back to Aswan and then take the other ferry over to Elephantine Island. From the west side you can hire a small rowboat (E£2-3) to take you to Kitchener and back. Then hop back on the local ferry to Aswan (E£1). Just make sure you don't get stranded late in the day, or you will be at the boatmen's mercy.

MAUSOLEUM OF THE AGA KHAN. The most placid attraction on the Nile's west bank is the Mausoleum of the Aga Khan, a short climb from the *felucca* dock. Aga Khans, the hereditary titles of Isma'ili Muslim *imams*, are believed to be direct descendants of Muhammad and the inheritors of his spiritual responsibilities of guidance. Aswan became the favorite winter retreat of **Sultan Muhammad Shah al-Husseini,** Aga Khan III (1877-1957). Upon his death, the Aga Khan's wife Begum oversaw the construction of the mausoleum, where the feisty nonagenarian still spends part of her year. Unfortunately, the mausoleum has been closed by the Egyptian government since June 1, 1997, due to a dispute with Begum over entrance fees. It sports an imposing fortress-like exterior, while the interior has a quiet simplicity modeled after Cairo's Fatimid tombs. Opposite the entrance stands a beautiful marble sarcophagus inscribed with passages from the Qur'an. *(Once the mausoleum re-opens, hours will be Tu-Su 9am-4pm. Call the tourist office for updates. Dress conservatively and remove shoes.)*

MONASTERY OF ST. SIMEON. The isolated and majestic **Deir Anba Samaan** (Monastery of St. Simeon) is a 1km walk up the stone path from the ferry landing. Built in the 6th and 7th centuries, the monastery is on a terrace carved into the steep hills. With its 6m-high turreted walls, it looks more like a fort than a religious sanctuary. The original walls stood 10m high but were not strong enough to keep the 300 resident monks from being driven out by 14th century Arab conquerors.

KISS MY AS(WAN)

The top ten ways to get rid of *felucca* captains and other undesirables:

10. *"La, shukran."* (No thank you.)
9. *"Ultilak la."* (I said no.)
8. *"Bas."* (Enough.)
7. *"Imshee."* (Go away.)
6. *"Haraam 'alayk."* (Shame on you.)
5. *"Kib nafsik."* (Scram.)
4. *"Iza arabit minni, badribak."* (If you get any closer, I'll hit you.)
3. *"La hawla wa la quwata illa billah...la!"* (By all the force and power of Allah...no!)
2. *"Ya haywan."* (You animal.)
1. *"Ibn kalb."* (You son of a dog.)

Let's Go does not recommend using phrases 1 or 2.

Upstairs, the monks' cells and stone beds (with Bible and *galabiyya* wall slots) are currently occupied by bats. Simeon's chamber is open to visitors, complete with remnants of the baptismal font and drain pipe, well-preserved paintings of Mary and Joseph, Communion wine-making facilities, and a slot in the roof for a rope he tied around his beard to keep him on his feet during all-night prayer vigils. The dining room and kitchen are outside, to the west of the main hall. The monastery had a church and enough accommodations for several hundred pilgrims and their camels (the domed stables are outside to the south of the main hall).

To get to the monastery, follow the paved path that starts in front of the Mausoleum of the Aga Khan or, if you don't mind a chafed rear, hire a camel near the *felucca* stop (E£20 per camel for a 20min. ride for 2 people). Despite what the camel driver says, women do not need to cling tightly to him for safety, nor should he need to grab his passengers' legs to ensure stability. If you feel at all uncomfortable, forget the drivers' beastly manners and leave their camels behind. *(From the Tombs of the Nobles, head down the stairway towards the Nile and turn right. Walk 1.5km through the sand to the camels by the ferry landing. Hitch a camel or continue on up the hill. Open Tu-Su 7am-4pm. Tickets occasionally required.)*

TOMBS OF THE NOBLES. The Tombs of the Nobles lie farther north along the west bank of the Nile, carved into the face of desert cliffs. These tombs of governors and dignitaries date from the 23rd to the 18th century BCE and are significantly better preserved than those on Elephantine Island. Climb up the 100-odd stairs to ogle the bright color and detail of the reliefs in the **Tomb of Sarenput II,** a garrison commander during the 12th dynasty. Note the sacrificial stone slab with a blood drainage spout. The mummy was taken to Cairo, but there are plenty of other things to see. If you ask nicely, the guard will move the grating and let you peer into the enclave where baskets of yummy camel bones are stored; or, you can take a moment to examine the altar where meals were offered to the gods. The interconnected 6th-dynasty **Tombs of Mekhu and Sabni,** father and son, have images of the ancients getting high on lotus blossoms. The cheapest way to visit the tombs is to take the ferry (E£1) from the corniche, across the small park from the tourist office. Once across, walk uphill and to the left to the shack-like office on the left. *(Open daily 7am-5pm, 7am-4pm in winter. E£12, students E£6. Camera privileges E£10.)*

NUBIAN MUSEUM. Nubian culture is more alive and prominent in Aswan than anywhere else in Egypt Ten years in the making, Aswan's Nubian Museum is a magnificent sandstone building south of the Old Cataract Hotel. It features a vast collection of Nubian artifacts from all over Egypt, described in detailed Arabic and English (a rarity in Aswan). Also check out the wonderful models of Abu Simbel and Philae, as well as the interesting exhibit on the High Dam and the numerous temple relocation efforts associated with its construction. If you have to choose, the Nubian Museum is a better deal than the Aswan Museum on Elephantine Island. *(Open daily 9am-1pm and 6-10pm. E£20, students E£10.)*

NUBIAN VILLAGES. For a more authentic and enjoyable taste of Nubian life, the central section of Elephantine Island has several Nubian villages, where you'll find friendly residents, adoring youngsters, and brightly painted homes. The ferry to the west bank tombs (E£1) can take you to **Gharb Aswan,** a series of Nubian villages less touristed than Elephantine Island's. From the ferry dock walk 500m or take a pick-up truck (about E£1) north to the villages.

The large Nubian houses, made of Nile mud, consist of six rooms around a courtyard; each cluster of rooms has its own dome or cylindrical roof. When the High Dam threatened to destroy this traditional style, architect Hassan Fathy whipped up these reconstructed and relocated villages. Just as many Arab Muslims take pride in having made the *hajj* (pilgrimage to Mecca) by adding the prefix "hajj" to their last name, Nubian families celebrate this accomplishment by painting their huts in bright colors.

You may even be invited to join the celebrations and ululations of a wedding ceremony; Nubians consider it a mark of honor to have guests from far-flung villages attend their nuptial festivities. Nubian weddings traditionally involved 15 days of partying, but the demands of modern life have trimmed the celebration down to a mere three or four. Nubians feel slighted if you reject their offers of hospitality, so be diplomatic if you must decline. At all times, be modest in your dress and behavior. Women traveling alone will feel more comfortable amongst polite and hospitable Nubians than with the harassing men on the east shore.

FATIMID TOMBS. Built during one of Islam's earliest eras, this cemetery is spooky, especially when it seems as though it's just you and the ghosts wandering around in the dark. By this time the Egyptians had clearly gotten over their obsession with death, and the abandoned tombs are simply squat stone buildings with crescents on their roofs. *(The tombs are near the camping area, 300m east of the main road at a turnoff 1km sout of Aswan. You can walk or take a kalish for E£5-7.)*

UNFINISHED OBELISK AND GRANITE QUARRIES. The obelisk was abandoned at its site because of a flaw in the granite; it was to have soared to a whopping 41.7m on a base 4.2m on each side. In its unadorned, supine state, the obelisk looks—well, unfinished, but it provides a rare behind-the-scenes look at the mammoth effort that went into its creation. Notice the channels along each side with curved indentations just big enough for a man to sit in and pound away with a ball made of diarite, a rock harder than granite. The earthbound side of the massive shaft would have been cut free either with copper or bronze chisels, or by pounding passages with diarite balls, inserting wooden beams, and flooding the channels so that the expanding wood would break the remaining stone. The adjacent **granite quarries,** best seen from the window of a passing train or taxi, supplied ancient Egypt with the stone that was favored for temple and monument building. *(Across the street from the Fatimid tombs. Obelisk and quarries open daily 7am-6pm, in winter 7am-5pm. E£10, students E£5.)*

🎵 **ENTERTAINMENT**

Nightclubs in Aswan feature a group of drummers and tambourine players, with a loud organ player and a male singer/emcee, plus the hip-notizing gyrations of a sequin-clad belly dancer enticing men into tossing bills. The action starts around 1am and lasts almost until sunrise. Check out the scene at **Salah al-Din Restaurant** or **Isis Hotel.** There is often a cover charge or minimum for discos and nightclubs, but prices change frequently (usually E£13-25 cover or two-drink minimum). The **Oberoi Hotel** has a piano bar where even you can sit down and play (drinks E£18), and a mini-disco during the winter with a pounding dance mix. The bastard love child of Eastern and Western dance scenes can be found at the dank pub and disco at the **New Cataract.** (Open daily 7pm-2am, E£15 cover for disco. Pool table E£20 per hr. Stella E£12.40.) The Pullman Bar in the **Old Cataract** is a more legitimate alternative with no cover. For more subdued enjoyment, try the pool and snooker tables at the **Basma Hotel** on the corniche, just behind the Cataract Hotels (no charge to play if you buy drinks).

For even more laid-back entertainment, join locals for tea, *sheesha*, or a mean game of dominoes at one of the many cafes scattered throughout town. Spontaneous football (soccer) games occasionally spring up around the stadium in the northern part of town past the New Abu Simbel Hotel. For more introspective relaxation, walk south along the corniche and around the Ferial Gardens to the elegant Old and New Cataract Hotels. Stroll through the gorgeous gardens, past the pool, and into the outdoor terrace cafe overlooking the river. (☎31 60 00 or 31 60 17. Open daily 9am-11:30pm. Juice drinks E£6.50, cocktails E£25 and up. No shorts on the terrace after 3pm. Guards at the gate say no visitors, but you can call reception to see if they are welcoming outside guests.) Report to the Hotel Oberoi's health spa for relaxing and rejuvenating treatments and exercises. (☎30 34 55. Services priced individually from E£50-75.)

SHOPPING

If you want more authentic souvenirs than hieroglyph-emblazoned t-shirts—or even if you do want hieroglyph-emblazoned t-shirts—take a stroll down **al-Sayyida Nafisa St.**, where tailors measure and cut with lightning speed. (Pants E£10-25, shorts and shirts E£10-15, shirts with collars and buttons E£25-40.) For traditional Egyptian clothing, there are numerous *galabiyya* (the Egyptian name for the ubiquitous Arab gown) and *qaftan* merchants in the *souq*. A tailor will make one out of his cloth for E£30-50. If you have the time, buy high-quality government cloth (at posted government prices) from one of the government shops on the corniche, then have garments made to order by the tailors on Sa'ad Zaghloul St. To tell if the tailor is experienced or not, look at his right hand. If the fingers are callused, he's authentic; if they're soft, he's probably just a salesman. For authentic papyrus, head down the stairs by the waterfront to **Dr. Rayab's Papyrus Museum,** across from the Horus Hotel. (Open daily 8am-midnight.) Papyrus ranges from E£20 to E£1200, depending on whether you want a sketch of a hieroglyph or an elaborate picture of an ancient Egyptian ritual. From October to May, the **Aswan Palace of Cultures** on Corniche al-Nil, north of the post office and across from the Rowing Club, features Nubian dancing and crafts. (Open Sa-Th 9-11pm. E£10.)

DAYTRIPS FROM ASWAN

An excellent road follows the Nile from Aswan to Khazan (a village near the Old Dam), providing access to both the dam and the motorboat launch to the Temple of Isis at Philae. The route to Khazan is serviced by **service** (50pt-E£1, depart from *service* stand) and by public **bus** (50pt-E£1). Both run until about 9:30pm.

> **TOURS.** The tourist office and most hotels in Aswan arrange minibus trips to the ruins there. The trips generally cost E£40-55. Options usually include a short trip to Abu Simbel (E£40, E£45 with A/C) or a long trip that also includes Philae temple, the High Dam, and unfinished Obelisk (E£50, E£55 with A/C). Entrance fees are not included in tour prices. If your hotel charges more than the price listed here, shop around, as hotels pool their guests into the same tour, regardless of the price you are paying. Arranged tours generally leave at 4am and return to Aswan by 2pm; overzealous authorities insist that tourist groups travel in a police convoy. You'll be miserable if your minibus doesn't have air-conditioning, since blowing sands may preclude opening the windows for much of the trip. A roundtrip flight to Abu Simbel booked through EgyptAir costs E£275.

ELEPHANTINE AND KITCHENER'S ISLANDS

The local ferry drops you just north of the museum on Elephantine Island. From the landing, walk left towards the green metal gate. To continue to Kitchener's Island, find a rowboat from the west side of Elephantine Island: make your way through the gardens and fields to the water's edge, where you should be able to spot a rowboat along the shore. **Elephantine Island** *open daily 8:00am-6pm, in winter 8am-5pm. E£10, students E£5; includes the museum, the adjacent ruins, and the Nilometer. Camera privileges E£15.* **Kitchener's Island** *open daily 8am-5pm. E£5.*

While historically very significant, Elephantine Island is not quite as exciting as the west bank. The island got its name from the black and (you guessed it) elephant-shaped stones at its southern tip. The remains of the ancient settlement on the southeast corner of the island, directly behind the museum, have been excavated. The local ferry from the corniche provides the cheapest transport to Elephantine Island (E£1, see p. 239).

The **Aswan Archaeological Museum** houses a rather small collection of ancient artifacts, either hand-labeled or completely unmarked. Even the "Head of a Man Mummy," resting on a cloth sack in the museum's sarcophagus room, looks bored. An annex augments the collection with a wide array of items recently excavated from the nearby ruins. Outside the museum, past the gardens, the **Nilometer** near the waterfront is nothing more than a staircase with a few engravings on the banister. The most interesting sections of the island are the temples behind the museum. The **Temple of Khnum** lies mostly in ruins, but you can see the remains of the temple door covered with pictures of the ram-headed god Khnum and his wife Seti. Several different **Temples of Satet** also sit amongst the ruins. The temples were built over the course of several dynasties. One displays a picture of 11th dynasty ruler Monthuh II. The **Temple of Heqa-Ib** houses several interesting statues in its courtyard, and a Ptolemaic temple among the ruins is dedicated to Alexander II. Make sure to bring a ball of string to trail behind you; some of the chambers are labyrinth-like, complete with dead ends and false doors.

Behind Elephantine Island and not visible from central Aswan, Kitchener's Island (*Geziret al-Nabatat*, or "Island of the Plants") is a lovely botanical garden planted by British General Kitchener, best known for crushing the Sudanese rebellion of 1898. Flamboyant birds congregate among the tropical plants that flourish here. To reach the island, hire a *felucca* to combine an island visit with stops along the west bank and Elephantine Island (a full afternoon rental runs E£15-18 per hr.). It is also possible to hire a rowboat from the west side of Elephantine Island (about E£3 for 1-2 passengers only). Make sure boats will wait for you or come back to pick you up by withholding payment until the end of the trip. If you're a real cheapskate, you can still get a gorgeous bird's eye view of this miniature paradise from the south face of the Tomb of the Nobles on the west bank.

PHILAE فيلة

Visited most easily by **minibus** *as part of a tour organized through your hotel. A* **taxi** *will take you to Philae for E£20 or as part of an itinerary including other sights.* **Bus** *service for foreigners is prohibited. After paying admission, you must hire a* **motorboat** *to reach the island at the official round-trip rate of E£20 per boat or E£2.50 per person when the boat is full. Prices may drop in the off-season. Find a few travelers to share the expense of a boat. The captain will try to con you into paying more, but be firm. If there are serious problems, complain at the tourist office in town. The boat captain is obligated to wait for you as you tour the site, so there is no need to rush.*

Called "the pearl of Egypt" by one of Napoleon's soldiers, the beautiful Temple of Isis at Philae has attracted the pious and the curious since classical times. The completion of the Old Dam in 1902 partially submerged the buildings only a few years after their resurrection as a popular tourist destination. Victorian vandals then gathered around the pillars and chipped their names into the protruding columns; the graffiti now mark the earlier water level. Archaeologists feared the waters would eventually undermine the foundations of the temples and hasten their collapse, and the construction of the High Dam would indeed have utterly destroyed Philae were it not for the efforts of UNESCO and the Egyptian Antiquities Department. Between 1972 and 1980, the entire complex of temples was transferred from Philae Island to higher ground on nearby Agilkia Island. In 1980, the new site of the temples re-opened to tourism (see **Moving a Mountain,** p. 252). Philae offers a sound and light show. (English performances M, F, Sa 6:30pm, and Tu, W at 7:45pm in winter; M, F, Sa at 8pm and Tu, W at 9:15pm in summer.)

TEMPLE OF ISIS. The Temple of Isis, dominating the island's northern edge, is the last bastion of ancient Egyptian religion. Isis was a goddess in the truest sense: mother of nature, protector of humans, goddess of purity *and* sexuality, and sister-wife of the legendary hero Osiris (see **Meet the Gods,** p. 75). It was on Philae that she supposedly found her husband's heart after he was dismembered, making the island the most sacred of Isis's homes. Her cult following continued long after the establishment of Christianity, fizzling out only in the 6th century during the reign of Justinian, who successfully replaced her with the Virgin Mary. Nearly all the structures on Philae date from the Ptolemaic and Roman eras, when Egyptian art was in decline—hence the inferior quality of the decorative relief work. *(Open daily 7am-5pm. E£20, students E£10.)*

PORTICO OF NECTANEBO. From the landing at the southern tip of the island, climb the short slope up to the temple complex past Philae's oldest structure, the **Portico of Nectanebo,** with several pillars and numerous inscriptions that once formed the vestibule of a temple. A great colonnade with pillars on either side runs from the portico to the massive main walls of the Temple of Isis. The outermost courtyard in Philae was for commoners, while each successive inner courtyard was reserved for increasingly important people—the innermost for High Priests. The larger edifice has been washed away, but the eastern side of the colonnade remains. Ptolemy, Isis, and Horus are depicted on the **first pylon,** which rises 18m on either side of the temple's main entrance. Note the channels cut into the face of the pylon on either side of the doorway, where brightly painted square-cut cedar flagpoles once stood. The space on the left side of the threshold was for hinges that once supported an enormous door.

Through this entrance is the **central court,** with a Roman *mammisis* (birthhouse) devoted to Horus, its columns emblazoned with the head of his consort, the cow-goddess Hathor. The walls depict the falcon god in the marshes of his birth. On the temple wall opposite the *mammisis* (to the right as you enter the central court), Horus is transported in a boat on the shoulders of servants en route to visit another member of the divine family.

To the north is the slightly off-center **second pylon,** marking the way to the temple's inner sanctum. The *pronaos* (vestibule) was converted into a church by early Christians, who inscribed Byzantine crosses on the chamber walls and added a small altar. Farther north is the *naos,* the temple's innermost sanctuary. With a little *bakhsheesh* it may be possible to climb to the roof of the temple or enter a trap door on the interior right side leading to an inscribed crypt

OTHER SIGHTS. Behind the temple to the left is a **Nilometer** with a stairwell and the grooves used to measure the depths of the water during the river's yearly floods. The stairwell is across from a French inscription from Napoleon's expedition. Because Egyptian gods supposedly liked to make house calls, to the right of the temple is **Trajan's Kiosk,** a beautifully columned, open-air garage/divine carport (mistaken as a pharaoh's bed by the Victorians), which housed the barque of whichever god-icon came to visit Isis.

ASWAN HIGH DAM السد العالى

*Until tourists can once again use the buses and service, the best way to get to dam is the frequent **train** or a taxi which can take you by the dams and Kalabsha (E£30). Train stops are not labeled, so make sure to ask veteran-looking passengers for help identifying stations. Neither vehicles nor pedestrians are allowed to cross the dam after 6pm.*

The best-known attraction in the area is modern Egypt's greatest monument, the High Dam (al-Sidd al-'Ali), completed in 1971. The dam is interesting intellectually as well as incredibly impressive visually. It lacks the aesthetic magnificence of ancient Egypt's colossi, but it could teach them a thing or two about size: 1km thick at the base, 3.6km long, and 100m high, the dam contains more than 17 times the material used in the Great Pyramid of Cheops. The construction of the dam created **Lake Nasser**, the world's largest artificial lake, and covered all of Lower Nubia in waters as deep as 200m. Because of it, thousands of Sudanese and Nubians were forced to relocate, and ancient Nubia's archaeological treasures were threatened. The Egyptian government sent out an international plea for help—many countries responded, both individually and under an ambitious UNESCO plan. A rise in the Sahara's water table has been noticed as far away as Algeria, and archaeologists suspect that this effect has damaged the necropolis at Luxor and the base of Giza's Sphinx. Another danger of the dam is the possibility of sabotage. Should the dam be destroyed, the flood that would follow would wipe out 98% of Egypt's population. Nearby hills have radar installations and anti-aircraft missiles to guard against such a disaster. On the brighter side, the dam's 12 turbines doubled Egypt's electrical output, agricultural productivity has been enhanced, and the acreage of Egypt's arable soil has increased by 30%. The dam enabled Egypt to enjoy a healthy water supply during the drought of the past decade, and in August 1988 it saved Egypt from the floods suffered by Sudan when the Nile overflowed after heavy rains. For a few extra pounds or a little sweet talk, have a taxi go behind the gates to the **power plant** where itsy-bitsy workers crawl around the base of the dam like industrious ants.

SOVIET-EGYPTIAN FRIENDSHIP MONUMENT. Crossing the dam to get to this monument is a bit of a pain. The soldiers at the eastern end won't let you walk across, but they will stop passing vehicles and make them give you a ride—but you have to pay E£5. On the other side is the towering Soviet-Egyptian Friendship Monument, arguably premature given the alacrity with which the Egyptians spurned their Soviet benefactors once the dam was complete. A stylized lotus blossom sitting in its own pond, the monument would fit perfectly into a museum of modern art. Amid Egypt's ancient wonders, however, it looks a little out of place. Due to the rise in terrorist activity, tourists should secure police permission to go to the top, either in Aswan or in the large yellow gift shop and cafeteria west of the monument, although some have been known to *bakhsheesh* (E£5) their way to the top if the dam authorities are closed. *(Open daily 6am-6pm, in winter 5am-5pm.)*

NEAR THE HIGH DAM. Built by the Brits between 1898 and 1902, the **Old Dam** supplied most of Egypt's power for years. Cab-oglers can fully appreciate the impressive sheer granite wall; there are no tourist facilities here. The fertile area known as the **First Cataract** is one of the most idyllic spots in the Aswan area. Viewing what is left of the rapid waters, churning around rocky outcrops north of the Old Dam, gives some idea of the perils of early Nile expeditions (when ships were hauled past this dangerous spot with ropes). In the village of **Khazan** on the south side of the Old Dam, 90-year-old British villas (now Brit-less) sit peacefully within walled gardens.

KALABSHA كلبشة

The well-preserved temple at Kalabsha is considered by many Egyptologists to be second only to the temple at Abu Simbel, but the building—situated dramatically above the placid waters of Lake Nasser—is more impressive on the outside than on the inside. Dedicated to the Nubian god Mandulis, renowned for his hundreds of wives and legions of children, the temple was built by Amenhotep II, augmented during the reign of Augustus, and used as a church during the Christian era. In 1962-63, the West German government paid to have the entire temple dismantled and transported in 13,000 pieces from its Nasser-flooded home to the present site, 50km north of the original (see **Moving a Mountain**, p. 252).

The temple is somewhat difficult to reach and poorly publicized, but it offers a relatively peaceful and quiet (if dimly lit) temple experience for those intrepid travelers wary of the pesky crowds at Abu Simbel. The cheapest way to reach Kalabsha is to take the **train** to the east end of the dam, ride to the west end (you'll have to pay the dam E£5 fee), then walk to the boat landing for the temple. To get to the landing from the western checkpoint, continue straight ahead for 100m, then veer left through the shipyard, following the curve of the water for 1km. A **taxi** from Aswan to the boat landing is less of a hassle but more expensive; try bargaining down to E£25-30 (even less for large groups). Adding this stop to your taxi tour of the High Dam, Philae, and the Unfinished Obelisk should cost around E£5. At the dock, a **motorboat** (E£20 for a load of 10 or so) takes you to the temple's island. Remember to bring lots of water, cover your head, and watch your step on the dock. (High Dam open until 6pm.)

TEMPLE CAUSEWAY. An immense causeway of dressed stone leads from the water to the temple's main entrance. The first pylon is off-center from both the causeway and the inner gateways of the temple itself. The grand forecourt between the pylon and the vestibule is surrounded by 14 columns, each with a unique capital. On the wall to the left of the doorway in front of you, baby-god Horus is nursed by his mother Isis. A small picture of St. George slaying the dragon is carved into the bottom left side of the right-hand wall.

HOLY OF HOLIES. Because the temple faces east, light flows into the Holy of Holies (innermost chamber) only in the early morning. Bring a flashlight at other times and be prepared for bats. A passageway leads north through the vestibule to an inner encircling wall; around the wall to the south is a **Nilometer.** Extraordinary carvings of Mandulis, Isis, Horus, and Osiris cover the outside walls.

NUBIAN SHRINE. Outside the huge fortress-like wall, the remains of a small shrine are visible to the southeast; the present structure is largely a reconstructed facade. Nubian reliefs, including pre-dynastic elephants, a large giraffe, and gazelles, grace large boulders on the southern side of the temple. The double-image technique, characteristic of Nubian art, is used to portray motion in some of the drawings. Carcasses of enormous desiccated fish are surrealistically scattered on the sand, as are disembodied stone heads.

TEMPLE OF KERTASSI. Slightly southwest of the Temple of Kalabsha are the ruins of the Temple of Kertassi. Two Hathor columns remain, as well as four columns with elaborate floral capitals and a lone monolithic architrave. A stone pathway leads up the hill behind and to the right of the Temple of Kertassi to the **Rock Temple** (*Beit al-Wali* or "House of the Holy Man"), rescued from the encroaching waters of Lake Nasser with the aid of the US government. Ask the guard to let you in. One of many Nubian temples constructed by Ramses II, it features typically humble scenes of Ramses conquering foreigners, Ramses receiving prisoners, and a particularly understated scene of Ramses storming a castle half his size. Like a miniature Abu Simbel, this cave-temple was hewn from solid rock. Examine the bas-relief scenes closely: political and social history are portrayed in everything from chariot battles to squabbles over whose turn it is to walk the camel.

ABU SIMBEL أبوسمبل

*Abu Simbel is 50km from the Sudanese border and a treacherous 297km south of Aswan. Due to political tensions, the Sudanese border is not passable and should not be approached by tourists for any reason. The government shut down ground transportation to Abu Simbel in 1997 due to terrorist threats, but it has been reopened and is considered quite safe. The easiest and most popular way to travel to Abu Simbel is by **microbus*** *arranged through hotels in Aswan. Prices may vary but the service is the same (hotels pool their guests together), so shop around. There are two options: Abu Simbel on its own (4am-1pm; E£40, with A/C E£45), or Abu Simbel plus stops at the **High Dam, Philae**, and the **Unfinished Obelisk** (4am-3:30pm; E£50, with A/C E£55). Two local **buses** travel between Aswan and Abu Simbel (11:30am and 5pm; returning to Aswan 7am, 2, 5pm; E£40). The morning bus gives you 2½hr. to explore the temple. Public buses are only permitted to carry four non-Egyptians per trip, so buy your ticket at the Aswan bus station a day ahead of time. **Planes** fly to Abu Simbel daily (E£275 roundtrip). Book a flight through EgyptAir at least 2 days in advance. Airline buses meet you at Abu Simbel Airport and shuttle you to and from the sight free of charge. Another option is to take a **ferry** from Aswan to Abu Simbel (4 days/3 nights or 5 days/4 nights; US$100-120 per person per night). Site open 6am-5pm. E£36, students E£19.50; includes admission to Temple of Hathor. Flash photographers will be escorted out.*

Swiss explorer John Lewis Burkhardt happened upon the Great Temple of Abu Simbel in 1813. Until then, its mighty statues had been buried by the desert sands that had built up over the centuries.

BIG HEADS (COLOSSI). The grandeur of the pharaonic monuments reaches its peak at Egypt's southernmost tip. Four 22m tall statues of **Ramses II**, carved from a single slab of rock, greet the sunrise over Lake Nasser and guard the entrance to the Great Temple of Abu Simbel. Each statue wears Old and New Kingdom versions of the crowns of Upper and Lower Egypt An earthquake in 27 BCE crumbled the upper portion of one of the colossi. Modern engineers were unable to reconstruct the figure (and there were debates about whether they should—if it's been broken for 2000 years, don't fix it), so they left it in its faceless state. There are (much) smaller statues of wife Nefertari and some of the kids at the feet of Ramses. A row of **praying baboons** stand above the statues, framing the top of the temple entrance nearly 30m above the desert floor. Ancient Egyptians admired the baboons' habit of warming themselves in the sun's rays, thinking the beasts quite pious to pray to the sun god every dawn.

GREAT TEMPLE OF ABU SIMBEL. This is Ramses II's masterpiece. The temple is supposedly dedicated to the god Ra-Hurakhti, but as in all of Ramses' monuments, the focus is clearly on the great pharaoh himself. Ramses II couldn't seem to get enough self-celebrating statues, and the large first hall is lined with two rows of statues of the king. The walls vividly depict battle scenes of Ramses's Nubian victories. Proceeding through the temple, Ramses undergoes the characteristic

MOVING A MOUNTAIN As the water level of Lake Nasser rose in the mid-60s, Egypt realized that flooding would claim a large piece of the country's heritage if quick action was not taken. The United Nations and individual governments responded by funding a US$36 million relocation effort. The international concern was not entirely selfless: any country that assisted could claim half of the antiquities it helped to rescue and receive concessions for future archaeological research. As a result, the Temple of Dendera is now enclosed in New York's Metropolitan Museum of Art, Debed Temple can be found in Madrid, and al-Lessiya was claimed by Turin. The initial plan was to raise each temple, remove the surrounding mountain, and encase the structures in protective concrete boxes. The boxes would be slowly jacked up, and a thick concrete base would be built beneath them. Another possibility was to build a second small dam around the temples to keep the water at bay. Both of these schemes were deemed too expensive. To the chagrin of Egyptologists, the cheapest method was chosen—cutting the temples into pieces. The mountain had to be cut away, a job that endangered the sandstone statues below. Bulldozers covered the facade of Abu Simbel with sand, forming a mound that was penetrated with a steel tunnel so that workers could set up supportive steel bars inside. It took months to saw the temple apart and move the 3000 pieces to higher ground. When it was reassembled, hollow concrete domes were engineered to support the new artificial mountain.

god-king metamorphosis: near the entrance he is depicted as a great king, then as a servant of the gods, next as a companion of the gods, and finally, in the inner sanctuary, as a card-carrying deity.

Off the main temple chambers are **antechambers** that once stored implements of worship. Inscriptions on the walls show Ramses making sacrifices to the gods. At the rear of the temple, in the inner sanctum, four seated statues facing the entrance depict Ramses and the gods Ra-Hurakhti, Amun, and Ptah. Originally encased in gold, the statues now wait with divine patience for February 22 and October 22, when the first rays of the sun reach 100m into the temple to bathe all except Ptah (the god of darkness) in light. February 21 was Ramses' birthday and October 21 the date of his coronation, but when the temple was moved, the timing of these illuminations shifted by one day (they just don't build temples like they used to). A door to the right of the temple's facade leads into the dome that supports the new and improved mountain.

TEMPLE OF HATHOR. Next door to Ramses's temple was a temple dedicated to his favorite wife Nefertari and to Hathor, the young fertility/sky goddess. Six 10m statues of Ramses and Nefertari (as Hathor) adorn the façade. Along with the temple of Hatshepsut in west Thebes (see **Deir al-Bahri,** <u>p. 228</u>), this is one of the only temples in Egypt dedicated to a woman. Vivid pictures depicting the voluptuous queen and offerings to the gods adorn the walls of the main chamber. Still, images of Ramses abound—scenes on the walls depict his coronation, with the god Horus placing the crowns of Egypt on his head. The temple was constructed in the typical three-room style: the first chamber was open to the public, the second to nobles and priests, and the inner sanctuary only to the pharaoh and the high priest.

SUEZ السويس

One of the most ambitious feats of engineering ever attempted, the Suez Canal was once just a glimmer in the eye of Napoleon Bonaparte, who considered digging a canal between the Mediterranean and the Red Sea but feared that the waters of the latter were too high. Years later, another Frenchman, Ferdinand de Lesseps, persuaded Sa'id Pasha (the *khedive* of Egypt) to give the idea a shot. Excavation started on April 25, 1859, and took 10 years to complete. On August 18, 1869, the canal was opened in a grand ceremony attended by over 6000 dignitaries. A man, a plan, a canal—Suez.

Spanning 195km and reaching a maximum depth of 15m, the canal connects Port Said on the Mediterranean to Suez on the Red Sea. The average transit time for ships through the canal is 15hr. Because it allowed for rapid travel from Europe to the Indian Ocean, the canal became a crucial element in the infrastructure of the British Empire. Nasser nationalized the canal in 1956, precipitating a British-French-Israeli invasion (to read more about the **Suez Crisis** and the rise of **Pan-Arabism**, see p. 69). During the 1967 Six Day War with Israel, Nasser blocked the canal with sunken ships. It remained closed through the 1973 Yom Kippur War and was finally cleared and reopened in 1975.

PORT SAID بور سعيد ☎ 048

Founded in 1860 upon the start of the Suez Canal's construction, Port Said *(Bor Sa'id)* became Africa's gateway to the Mediterranean once the canal was finished. Since the city was declared a tax-free zone in 1976, Port Said has developed into a shopping resort for Egyptians cashing in on duty-free deals. The main streets are saturated with clothing stores fronting styles (mercifully) unseen in the West since the '70s, while the scene near the waterfront faintly reflects the days when even the most hedonistic of sailors could get more than his fill of hashish and prostitutes. Port Said doesn't really come alive until nighttime, when everyone takes to the streets to window shop and enjoy the cool breeze and twinkling lights of the canal. The men of Port Said are well-known for their politeness, and women here (at least, those who are not prostitutes) will experience noticeably less harassment than in other parts of Egypt

▐ TRANSPORTATION

Trains: The **station** is on Mustafa Kamal St., ½km from the southwest end of al-Gomhoriyya St. Trains run to **Cairo** (4½hr.; 6, 8am, 7:30pm; 2nd-class E£14) and **Suez** via **Isma'ilia** (1¾hr., 2nd-class E£6).

Buses: The **East Delta** bus depot is on Salah al-Din St., on the northern side of Ferial Gardens, 2 blocks west of al-Gomhoriyya St. Daily buses to: **Alexandria** (4hr.; 7, 9am, 2:30, 4:30pm; E£15-20); **Cairo** (2hr., every hr. 6am-7pm, E£12-15); **Suez** (6, 10am, 1, 4pm; E£7.50). The **Superjet** depot is next to the train station on Mustafa Kamal St., also with daily buses to **Alexandria** (8:30pm, E£22) and **Cairo** (10 per day 7am-7pm, E£15). A 3rd station is on al-Nasr St. (ask for "Mubarak"), with buses to **Isma'ilia** (1½hr., every hr. 6am-7pm, E£4).

Service: Near the train station and the Superjet depot. Ask for *"taxi ugra."*

Bike Rental: Bikes are a great way to get around the city. Rent them on the south side of Hafiz Ibrahim St., between Palestine and al-Gomhoriyya St. E£5 per hr.

✦ ▐ ORIENTATION AND PRACTICAL INFORMATION

Port Said is 343km east of Alexandria and 220km northeast of Cairo. The town is surrounded by water on three sides: the Mediterranean to the north, the Suez Canal to the east, and **Lake Manzala** to the south. The point at which the canal

Mediterranean Sea

Suez Canal

PORT FOUAD

TO PORT FOUAD

TO CAIRO (220km)

TO ALEXANDRIA (343km)

Port Said National Museum

Thomas Cook

Palace Gardens

American Express

Al-Salaam

West Delta Bus Company

Ferial Gardens

Tourist Police

Memorial Monument

Military Museum

Port Said Stadium

Sadke St.

Palestine St.

Memphis St.

Al-Gomhoriyya St.

Muhammad Mahmoud St.

Hafz Ibrahim St.

El-Geish St.

Ramses St.

Salah al-Din St.

Salah Salem St.

Mustafa Kamel St.

Oraby St.

Atef al-Sadat St.

Al-Madha St.

Safia Zaghloul St.

Sa'ad Zaghloul St.

Sa'ad Zaghloul Garden

Al-Nasr St.

Muhammad al-Sayed Sirhan St.

23 July St.

Beni Swef St.

El Mina St.

Aswan St.

El Giza St.

El Dakhlia St.

El Gory St.

El Roda St.

Ismail St.

Fahmy El Nokrashy St.

Ahmed Maher St.

Mohamed Farid St.

Hamed El Aly St.

Abu El Hassan St.

Nabil Mansor St.

Shohada St.

Nasr St.

Salam St.

Sabah St.

Salim St.

Buses to Isma'ilia

Superjet

Buses to Isma'ilia

SUEZ

Port Said

🏠 **ACCOMMODATIONS**
Akri Palace Hotel, **9**
Hotel Delaposte, **6**
Youth Hostel, **2**

🍴 **FOOD**
El-Borg Restaurant, **1**
Galal Restaurant, **4**
Gionala Restaurant, **8**
Lord's Pastry, **3**
Popeye Restaurant, **7**

● **SERVICES**
Deliurand Hospital, **5**
Service Station, **10**

N

0   400 meters
0   300 yards

meets the Mediterranean is Port Said's northeastern corner. **Atef al-Sadat St.** runs along the sea, and **Palestine St.** follows the edge of the canal. **Memphis St.** and **al-Gomhoriyya St.**, one and two blocks inland, respectively, run parallel to Palestine St. Another important thoroughfare, three blocks inland, is **23 July St.**, which runs parallel to Atef al-Sadat St.

Tourist Office: 5 Palestine St. (☎23 52 89), 2 blocks from the south end of the street. Gives out a good map, and information about restaurants, hotels, and sights in the area. Open Sa-Th 9am-2pm. Another branch at the **train station** keeps similar hours.

Currency Exchange: Small offices abound. The most convenient is **Thomas Cook,** 43 al-Gomhoriyya St. (☎33 62 60; fax 23 61 11). Open daily 8am-5pm. **ATM** at Banque Misr, 30 al-Gomhoriyya St.

American Express: 83 al-Gomhoriyya St. (☎23 98 31), across from al-Salaam Mosque. Cash advances and traveler's check exchange. Open daily 10am-4pm.

Emergency: Ambulance: ☎123. **Police:** ☎122.

Tourist Police: (☎22 85 70). Stationed on the 5th fl. of the abandoned post office building on al-Gomhoriyya St.

Pharmacy: Hussein (☎33 98 88; fax 33 97 77), on al-Gomhoriyya St., a block south of Muhammad Mahmoud St. Open daily 9am-midnight. Many other pharmacies also line al-Gomhoriyya St.

Hospital: Delivrand (☎22 36 63 or 22 56 95), on al-Shaid al-Gaya St.

Telephones: (☎22 01 66; fax 32 57 05), 2 blocks north of the tourist office on Palestine St. Phone cards available for E£15, E£20, and E£30. Direct international dialing (E£10.50 per 3min. to the US). Open 24hr.

Internet Access: Internet and Information Club, on al-Gomhoriyya St. Entrance next door to Popeye Restaurant, 3rd fl. US$3 or E£ equivalent for 1hr.

Post Office: In the southeast corner of the Ferial Gardens, at the intersection of Muhammad Mahmoud St. and al-Geish St. For **Poste Restante,** take the 1st left south of the post office and walk 30m. Both open Sa-Th 8am-5pm.

▀ ACCOMMODATIONS

Most accommodations in town are either on or near **al-Gomhoriyya St.** There are many mid-range and luxury hotels, but super-cheap hotels are hard to come by, especially near the beach.

Youth Hostel (HI) (☎22 87 02), on Muhammad al-Sayyid Sirhan St. opposite the stadium. Your only budget option if you want to roll out of bed and onto the beach every morning. Modern and sterile. Large bathrooms. Fans. 20min. walk or E£2 taxi ride from the town center. Breakfast included. 6-bed dorm E£17.50; nonmembers E£1 extra.

Akri Palace Hotel, 24 al-Gomhoriyya St. (☎22 10 13). 2 blocks from the south end of the street. Owned by the friendly Greek Nicolandis brothers. A 19th-century elevator transports you to charming but run-down rooms, with high ceilings, wood floors, sinks, and desks. Ask to see what you're getting before bedding down. Balcony doors provide a nice breeze. Singles E£13; doubles E£26; triples E£31; add E£10 for private bath.

Hotel Delaposte, 42 al-Gomhoriyya St. (☎22 96 55 or 22 40 48). Look for the English "Hotel" sign with Arabic underneath, next door to a pastry shop. Deserves its 2 stars for rooms with private baths, TV, and fridge. Singles E£38; doubles E£47; triples E£53; with A/C add E£14.

◖ FOOD

▨ **Lord's Pastry** (☎23 52 02), just south of the intersection of al-Gomhoriyya and 23 July St. You'll thank your sweet Lord for the sweets. Friendly staff. Pastries E£1.25.

Popeye Restaurant (☎23 94 94), on the corner of al-Gomhoriyya and Safia Zaghloul St. Your deck may be pooped after a long day shopping or swimming, but you'll be strong to the finish after a meal here. Zesty chicken kebabs E£17. Banana splits E£5.70. No spinach. Open daily 8am-midnight. MC/V.

Gionala Restaurant, 15 al-Gomhoriyya St. (☎24 00 01). Across Safia Zaghloul St. from Popeye. Clean, sophisticated setting. Pasta E£11-15. Fish and meat dishes E£20-35. Generous sandwiches E£4-14. Open daily 8am-2am.

Galal Restaurant, 60 al-Gomhoriyya St. (☎22 96 68). Serves up seafood and standard Egyptian fare at reasonable prices. Fish starts at E£17. Large, plastic crustaceans above the tables make charming dinner companions for the solitary traveler. The after-midnight crowd comes primarily for the Stella (E£6). Open daily 7am-2am; closed during Ramadan. V.

Al-Borg (☎32 34 42), on the beachside corniche. A local favorite for fresh seafood. Full meals around E£30. Open 24hr.

👁 SIGHTS

PORT SAID NATIONAL MUSEUM. This museum houses a fine collection of items from all periods of Egyptian history, ranging from exquisite mummy cases to Coptic icons and Qur'anic calligraphy. See the carriage from which Khedive Isma'il presided over the 1869 opening of the canal. With labels alongside each of the artifacts, not to mention air conditioning, this museum is a must-see. *(At the northern end of Palestine St. ☎23 74 19. Open Sa-Th 9am-5pm, F 9am-noon and 2-5pm; Ramadan 8:30am-1pm. E£12, students E£6. Camera privileges E£10, video E£20.)*

OTHER SIGHTS AND EXCURSIONS. Free **ferries** to Port Fouad leave every few minutes from the southern tip of Palestine St. The shell-covered **beach,** cleaner and quieter than Port Said's, lies along the Mediterranean shore to the north. Beach umbrellas can be rented for E£3 per day, and showers are every 100m. If the words "duty-free" make your wallet tremble, **shopping arcades** stretch three blocks inland from Palestine St. For more affordable goods, hop on a minibus (25pt) and ask to be taken to **al-Souq al-Togary** further inland. Here you'll find street after street of local merchants with cheap clothing, fabric, shoes, and other goods.

ISMA'ILIA الاسماعيلية ☎064

Once known as Timsah Village, Isma'ilia was renamed after Isma'il, the last independent *khedive* of Egypt, and is now the capital of the Suez Canal District. Since it sustained heavy damage during the Arab-Israeli wars of 1967 and 1973, Isma'ilia has been completely rebuilt, and today one can relax in sprawling gardens, stroll down wide, palm-lined boulevards, or swim at the nearby beaches. The absence of attractions keeps away tourists, as well as the hustler culture that tends to follow them. Those coming from one of Egypt's larger cities will find the greenery refreshing, while those newly arrived in the country or coming from the Sinai will find Isma'ilia a good introduction to the Suez region.

📧 TRANSPORTATION

Trains: The **station** is on Sekkat al-Hadid St. in Orabi Sq. Locomotives chug to: **Cairo** (2½hr., 5 per day, 2nd-class E£11); **Port Said** (1¾hr., 5 per day, 2nd-class E£4); **Suez** (2hr., 6 per day, E£3).

Buses: There are 2 **bus stations.** The smaller one in Orabi Sq. serves **Alexandria** (4½hr., 2 per day, E£14-17) and **Cairo** (2hr., 4 per day, E£6). The main bus terminal in Salam Sq., about 2km out of town (best reached by minibus; 25pt), has buses to: **al-'Arish** (3hr., 5 per day, E£7); **Port Said** (1½hr., 8 per day until 6pm, E£4); **Suez** (1½hr., until 6pm, E£3); **Nuweiba** via **Taba** (5-7hr., 10pm, E£40).

Service: Opposite the main bus station in Salam Sq. Frequent *service* to: **al-Arish** (E£7); **Cairo** (E£5); **Port Said** (E£4); **Suez** (E£4). For excursions within town, orange **taxis** are available (E£1-3 is enough for any distance), as well as **minibuses** (25pt).

✴ 🛈 ORIENTATION AND PRACTICAL INFORMATION

Midway along the Suez Canal, Isma'ilia is linked by road and the Isma'ilia Canal to the Delta, and by highway and railroad to Alexandria (280km) and Cairo (140km). While you can't see the canal from the center of town, Isma'ilia's main avenue, **Sultan Hussein St.,** runs roughly perpendicular to the waterway and is lined by restaurants and shops. **Orabi Sq.** is 500m west of Sultan Hussein St., four blocks north of **Salah Salem St.,** which forms the town's southern border. **Mallaha Park** stretches along Salah Salem St. toward the canal.

Currency Exchange: Bank of Alexandria (☎ 33 79 21), in Orabi Sq. next to Travel Misr, gives cash advances on AmEx/MC/V. Open Su-Th 8:30am-2pm and 6-9pm; in winter 5-8pm; during Ramadan 10am-1:30pm. Next door, **National Bank of Egypt** has an **ATM.**

Emergency: Ambulance: ☎ 123. **Police:** ☎ 122. The station is 1 block west of the Governorate Building on Salah Salem St.

Pharmacy: Isma'ilia Pharmacy, 24 Sultan Hussein St. (☎363 29 09), is a well-stocked apothecary. Open daily 9am-5pm and 6:30pm-midnight.

Hospital: 2 private clinics, **al-Shafa Hospital** (☎22 29 20) and **Karin Hospital** (☎22 75 59), serve the area.

Telephones: Office in Orabi Sq. Open 24hr.

Post Office: In Orabi Sq. Open Sa-Th 8am-5pm.

🛌 ACCOMMODATIONS

Isma'ilia Youth Hostel (HI) (☎32 28 50; fax 33 14 29), on 'Omara Rd. A good choice despite being a 3km hike or a E£2 taxi ride from the center of town. Sandy beach and comfy common room of this spotless 266-bed hostel make it a backpacker's dream resort. All rooms except dorms have private bath. Breakfast included. Lunch and dinner E£5 each. 6-bed dorms E£17; doubles E£24; triples E£26; non-members E£1 extra.

Nevertary Hotel, 41 Sultan Hussein St. (☎32 28 22; fax 32 11 08), three blocks north of Bank Misr. With its bright purple exterior and pastel green rooms, Nevertary wins the Miami Vice award for hotel color coordination. Comfy rooms with A/C and private bath. Sitting area and fridge on each floor. Breakfast E£6. Singles E£30; doubles E£40; triples E£50; add 12% service tax.

New Palace Hotel (☎32 63 27), in Orabi Sq., next to the Bank of Alexandria. Clean, quiet rooms with high ceilings. Some include private bath, A/C, and TV. The kindly old manager or his son will show you to the cafeteria and kitchens. Breakfast included. Singles E£40; doubles E£65.

🍴 FOOD

Vendors line the streets with cheap Egyptian fare, but for excellent seafood, try Isma'ilia's sit-down venues. The main streets in Isma'ilia are as notable for their lack of *ahwas* as they are for their cleanliness. For tea and *sheesha*, try the brightly lit cafe on Orabi St. opposite the train station.

King Edward Restaurant, 171 Tahrir St. (☎32 54 51). Off Sultan Hussein St., 1 block south of the Nevertary Hotel and left at the obelisk. Excellent meals for E£20, accompanied by the charismatic King Ed himself. Becomes a nightspot around midnight and occasionally hosts live music. Open daily noon-2am.

Nefertiti's, 11 Sultan Hussein St. (☎22 04 94), south of the Nevertary Hotel. Cozy and romantic. Royal portions of seafood (E£11 and up) and meat (E£15) appease the hungriest carnivore. Beer E£7. Open daily 10am-midnight.

George's Restaurant (☎33 73 27), next door to Nefertiti's on Sultan Hussein St. In business over 50 years. Fish, meat, and pasta meals E£10-30. Owner recommends the fried calamari. Open daily noon-midnight.

👁🎵 SIGHTS AND ENTERTAINMENT

The **Isma'ilia Regional Museum,** on Salah Salem St., near the canal at the east end of town, has a collection of pharaonic, Islamic, and Roman artifacts. (Open W-M 9am-3pm. E£3, students E£1.50.) Near the museum, the **Garden of the Stelae** contains sphinxes from the age of Ramses II. Ask for permission to visit at the museum entrance. **Mallaha Park** is worth a frolic, with its 500 acres of rare flowers and trees. Just 100m south of the Youth Hostel, the **beach club** along Lake Timsah has restaurants, boats for rent, and kiddie amusement park rides. (Open daily 10am-10pm. E£2.)

SUEZ CITY السويس ☎062

Suez (al-Suweis) sits at the junction of the Red Sea and the Suez Canal. Besides counting the unnatural number of dead cats by the roadside, there's not much to see or do here. The young men of Suez are prolific marijuana smokers, and they don't seem to care who knows it. There are, nevertheless, some ways to kill a few hours between buses. **Port Tawfiq** provides an excellent perch from which to watch the canal at work, and it's probably the only place you can dangle your toes in the canal waters. A promenade running parallel to the Suez-Port Tawfiq road provides a great view of the Suez bay and is a good place to meet the exceptionally friendly locals, many of whom will offer you a joint as a sign of their goodwill. (*Let's Go* does not recommend going to jail.)

Most travelers pass through Suez en route from Cairo to the Sinai by way of the **Ahmed Hamdi Tunnel** (which runs under the canal 17km north of town), or on their way south along the Red Sea coast. Others stay a few days looking for passage on a boat at the Yacht Club. Nearby **'Ain Sukhna** is downright spectacular; its proximity to Cairo provides a convenient sun-swim-snorkel option.

▐ TRANSPORTATION

Buses: There are two bus stations around al-Geish St. in the north part of town. Both stations are easily accessible by **minibus.**

East Delta Bus Station: On Salah al-Din St., 1 block west of al-Geish St. Buses leave to: **'Ain Sukhna** (1hr.; 6:30, 7:30, 8:30, 10, 11am, noon, 1, 2pm; E£2); **Alexandria** (5hr., 7am and 2:30pm, E£23); **Cairo** (2hr., every 30min. 6am-8pm, E£7); **Isma'ilia** (1¼hr., every 30min. 6am-4pm, E£4); **Port Said** (3hr.; 7, 9, 10:30am, 3:30pm; E£9). Reserve tickets to Alexandria a few days in advance. Suez is also the main launching ground for forays into the Sinai. Buses leave for: **Dahab** (7hr., 11am, E£30); **Nuweiba** (11am, 1, 5pm; E£29); **Sharm al-Sheikh** (6hr.; 8, 11am, 1:30, 3, 5, 6pm; E£20); **St. Catherine's** (2pm, E£20); **Taba** (3pm, E£25); **'Uyoun Musa** (8, 11am, 1:30, 2, 3, 5, 6pm; E£6).

Superjet Bus Station: 2km north, near the train station. Buses go to **Hurghada** (6hr., 8 per day until 10pm, E£22) and **Upper Egypt.** Reserve tickets to Hurghada a few days in advance.

Service: *Service* travel to most of the destinations reached by bus (except Alexandria) at similar prices: **Cairo** (E£7); **Hurghada** (E£22); **Isma'ilia** (E£4); **Port Said** (E£7). *Service* don't go to the Sinai, and **private taxis** are generally prohibitively expensive.

Minibus: For transport within the city, flag down a blue **minibus** and see if it's headed your way. Common destinations include: Port Tawfiq, the East Delta bus station, the Superjet bus station, and the train station. A flat fare of 25pt gets you anywhere. A few drivers may try to claim that you're destination is "special" and overcharge, but most are very honest and will help you find another minibus if theirs is going somewhere else.

✴🗗 ORIENTATION AND PRACTICAL INFORMATION

Al-Geish St. runs roughly north-south through the center of Suez, from the **bus stations** all the way down to **Port Tawfiq,** where the **tourist office** stands at the westernmost end of town. The tourist office is one of the most knowledgeable and helpful in Egypt and provides a map of Suez and Port Tawfiq, plus a useful listing of local restaurants, sights, and services. (☎33 11 41 or 33 11 42. Open daily 8am-8pm.) **Bank Misr,** at the intersection of 'Amr ibn al-'As and al-Geish, has an **ATM** that accepts MC and V. (☎22 05 71. Open Su-Th 9am-3pm.) **American Express** services are available for all travelers at Menatours (☎22 88 21), next to the tourist office in Port Tawfiq. The **tourist police** (☎33 11 40) share a building with the tourist office. Suez's main house of medicine is the **General Suez Hospital** (☎33 11 89), just west of the East Delta bus station. The **telephone office** is about three blocks west of al-Geish St., on the corner of Shohada'a St. and Sa'ad Zaghloul St. (Open 24hr.) The **post office,** on Hoda Sharawi St., one block east of al-Geish St., offers **Poste Restante.** (☎22 39 17. Open Sa-Th 8am-3pm.)

🛏 ACCOMMODATIONS

Even if you're not planning to continue to the monasteries of St. Anthony and St. Paul, the budget hotels of Suez will give you a taste of the monks' ascetic lifestyle. The city's importance as a transportation hub means that even the grottiest hotel often has no vacancies. Single rooms in particular seem to be in short supply, so call ahead (all hotels listed here accept reservations).

Sina Hotel, 21 Banque Misr St. (☎33 41 81). A mirrored and gilded lobby and friendly management welcome travelers. Unsullied rooms sport fans and may have a balcony and 1-channel TV. Shared bathrooms have hot water. Many rooms are defective in some way (the fan doesn't work, the balcony door locks automatically behind you, etc.), so ask to see the room before signing off on it. Singles E£15; doubles E£26.

Star Hotel, 17 Banque Misr St. (☎22 87 37), 1 block south of the Sina. Large, clean rooms with turbo fans. Stellar showers and balconies. Singles or doubles E£20, with bath E£25; triples E£30, with bath E£35.

Hotel Madena (☎22 40 56). Walk 3 blocks east on Tahrir St., take a right, and proceed to the next street; the hotel is on the left. Rooms are bare and tiny, but functional and decently priced. Singles E£13, with bath E£18; doubles E£26, with bath E£30.

🍴 FOOD

Eating cheaply is no problem in Suez. There's a good **fruit market** near the East Delta bus station. Near the intersection of al-Geish and Tahrir St., there are sandwich stands, small bakeries, and vendors selling kebab and roast chicken. Some recent additions have bolstered the city's formerly meager middle-range options.

Senator Restaurant (☎34 87 35), on al-Geish St., 2 blocks south of Tahrir St. The best of the new joints. Slick exterior. The food is high quality and reasonably priced. Thick-crust pizza E£7-14. Pasta E£7-10. Seafood E£15-25.

Mahmoud Rawash Restaurant, on Tahrir St. just off al-Geish St. Falafel or *fuul* sandwich 25pt.

Seaside Restaurant (☎22 32 54), 1 block west of the telephone office on Sa'ad Zaghloul St. Seating in an A/C interior (with satellite TV) and on a rooftop terrace. Sandwiches E£2. Grilled fish and shrimp E£25.

Teama Restaurant (☎34 14 90), next to the Renaissance Cinema toward Port Tawfiq on al-Geish St. Outdoor cafe with basic Egyptian food like kebab (E£18), rice, and salads (E£3-5).

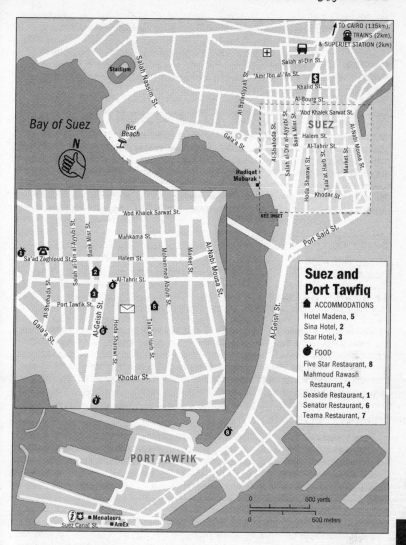

Five Star Restaurant, on al-Geish St. in Port Tawfiq. Neither five stars nor a restaurant, but they do have desserts (E£1.50) to snack on while watching the ships roll in.

SIGHTS AND ENTERTAINMENT

If you get stuck here for any length of time, there are few sites to keep you entertained. **Hadiqat Mubarak,** on the corniche, displays American-made Israeli tanks captured in 1973 and other military vehicles. The dirty water from the many ships at **Rex Beach,** in town near the stadium, isn't very regal, but the beach at **'Ain Sukhna** (Hot Spring), 60km south along the Red Sea, rivals those of the Sinai. **Buses** go there early in the day (1hr.; 6:30, 7:30, 8:30, 10, 11am, noon, 1, 2pm; E£2) and return about 1½hr. later. The hot spring (35°C), originating in the Ataka Mountains, empties out onto a gorgeous sandy beach. Get off the bus when you see the large green-and-white sign for the **'Ain Sukhna Hotel** (☎32 84 88). Daytrippers can pay the hotel a E£15 fee for chairs and umbrellas if they only plan to visually enjoy the crystal-clear water, though the mouth of the hot spring is also available for prolonged soaks. The hotel offers an expensive but incredible fish, salad, and hummus meal (E£30). It's not just the best choice, it's the only choice—bring your own food if you'd rather not put your money where your mouth is.

MONASTERIES OF ST. ANTHONY & PAUL

These centers of faith, dating from the early Christian monastic tradition, are inhabited by monks whose austere lifestyle has changed remarkably little over the past 16 centuries. They warmly welcome visitors, and some speak excellent English. While a few hours suffice to see the monasteries, spending the night can be transcendent (although you'll need a letter of recommendation). Men and women of any religious persuasion can stay in the dorms at both St. Anthony's and St. Paul's. The monasteries are not tourist attractions; rather, they are functioning centers of worship where most guests take religion seriously, so be prepared to field questions about your own beliefs. The monks provide water and generous portions of food (simple fare from their own gardens and orchards). There is no charge, but donations are welcome (even the most ascetic life requires some financing) though not actively solicited.

▐ TRANSPORTATION

Reaching the monasteries is a serious endeavor without a car, since no organized tours go there. Plenty of patience and water are required, as travelers are completely dependent upon **pilgrims** for transportation. Of the two possible options for getting to the monasteries, the safer and more hassle-free is to contact the **monasteries' administration offices** in Cairo and ask when local Coptic churches are planning pilgrimages to the monasteries so you can tag along. A group may be leaving as soon as tomorrow or as late as a month from next Sunday. (St. Paul's ☎02 590 02 18; St. Anthony's 02 590 60 25. Call daily 10am-noon or 8:30-9:30pm.)

The less desirable option is to take public transportation as far as you can. The closest stop to St. Paul's (12km from the monastery) from a Hurghada-bound bus from Suez is by the **St. Bola sign,** near a road running directly to the monastery. Pilgrimage groups have been known to pick up travelers along the way and take them to the monasteries and back. Although pilgrims tend to be friendly, catching a ride can be difficult. Hitchhiking, especially in the desert, is an inherently risky proposition, and *Let's Go* does not recommend it.

✴❷ ORIENTATION AND PRACTICAL INFORMATION

The isolated monasteries of St. Anthony and St. Paul lie 30km apart (84km by road), near the Red Sea. You must have a **letter of recommendation** from the administration office in Cairo (see below) to stay overnight at either of the two monasteries, though the monks certainly won't make you spend the night in the desert if you straggle in late in the day without a way back to where you came from. Both monasteries are open daily 9am-5pm.

◉ MONASTERIES

ST. ANTHONY'S MONASTERY

St. Anthony was raised in the Nile Valley in the 4th century CE and became the first famous ascetic of the Christian Church when he scorned worldly concerns and retreated into the Eastern Desert. Anthony's dramatic move reflected the restlessness that overtook some Christians after Constantine made Christianity the official religion of the Roman Empire—a disturbing development for those who felt that the church had gained worldly security and wealth at the expense of its spiritual focus. In Egypt, some of these Christians (mostly educated upper-class men) sought to escape the secular world by retreating into the desert where they could pray in solitude and render their lives unto God rather than Caesar.

St. Anthony was victimized by his own success: his desert hermitages became popular pilgrimage sites, and crowds of the pious and the curious deprived the recluse of precious penitent isolation. Frustrated in his quest for solitude, St. Anthony came up with the solution of organizing his most persistent followers into a loose-knit group that prayed and ate together once a week, creating the model followed by many Orthodox monasteries to this day. Soon after the saint's death, his disciple St. Athanasius told the story of St. Anthony's choice of poverty and hardship, his wild battles with demons, and his wise counsel to monks and laymen. Athanasius's *Life of Anthony* became the prototype for much of later Christian hagiography (biographies of saints). Around the same time, Anthony's followers settled at the present site and established the first Christian monastery. The Monastery of St. Anthony served as a refuge for some of the monks of Wadi Natrun when their own sanctuaries were attacked by the Bedouin in the 6th century. During the 7th and 8th centuries, the monastery was occupied by Melkite monks, and in the 11th century it was pillaged by the army of Nasser al-Dawla. About 100 years after the sacking, it was restored and transferred to Coptic hands.

The **Church of St. Anthony** and the monastery's southern walls are the only remains predating the 16th-century construction of the present monastery. With ancient frescoes embellishing each of their sections, Anthony's church and its small chapel are the most impressive parts of the monastery. The monks are still awaiting permission from Orthodox Pope Shenouda III before the church can be consecrated and opened to visitors. Inquire at the Cairo office if this fortuitous event has occurred. East of the Church of St. Anthony is the **Church of the Apostles.** Like other early Coptic churches, it is divided into three sections, the closest to the altar reserved for the baptized who can receive communion, the farthest for transgressors, and the middle for those falling somewhere in between. Morbid visitors will appreciate the glass-encased remains of an early 19th-century bishop to the right of the altar. The monks claim his body lies perfectly preserved, though a cloak precludes verification. During Lent, the monks cantillate the liturgy in the 18th-century **Church of St. Mark.** As in the Wadi Natrun monasteries, the **Chapel of St. Michael** is on the top floor of the keep. The extensive **library** contains more than 1700 manuscripts.

The major religious attraction in the vicinity of the church is the **Cave of St. Anthony,** where the ascetic himself is said to have lived. The vista from the cave, 276m above sea level, rewards the requisite 45min. of hoofing and huffing. Before entering the fissure, remove your shoes or risk offending nearby Copts. Inside, a small nook at the end of the cave is stuffed with written supplications for divine assistance. The best time to start the climb is when the sun is low (before 7am or after 4pm). Try to return before dark and bring a bottle of water. The **spring** at which St. Anthony drank resurfaces within the monastery and still delivers a healthy 100 cu. m of water daily. A monk will unlock the gate built around it and allow you to taste the water—it's safe to drink. St. Anthony's also has several **shops**—a snack shop selling soda and cookies, a bookstore, and a gift shop.

ST. PAUL'S MONASTERY

St. Paul (not the Apostle) was born into an affluent Alexandrian family in the 3rd century CE. When his father died, he left his estate to young Paul and his brother. Naturally, this caused squabbling between the two, and when the family had heard enough, the brothers were sent off to consult with a judge. In the

WHEN TONY MET PAULIE According to Christian lore, St. Anthony and St. Paul met in one dramatic encounter at the end of Paul's life. Wanting to reveal the holiness of St. Paul, God led St. Anthony to his cave. As the two conversed, Paul's crow dropped a whole loaf of bread for them (double what the bird usually brought). Paul, realizing that he was talking to another holy man, told Anthony that he was nearing death and made one final request: to wear the robe of Pope Athanasius. Anthony immediately departed to fetch the garment. On his return, he had a vision of angels carrying St. Paul's soul to heaven, and arrived at the cave to find Paul dead. While Anthony pondered what to do with the body, two lions descended from the mountain, mourned for their lifelong companion, and dug a grave. Anthony wrapped Paul in the papal robe and buried him. He then carried St. Paul's palm leaf garment back to Athanasius, who wore it every Christmas, Epiphany, and Easter.

end, the two young men took separate routes. Paul happened to pass the funeral service of a wealthy man and was, for some reason, profoundly affected (why he wasn't so moved at his own father's funeral no one knows). Like St. Anthony, St. Paul cast off all worldly concerns and—guided by an angel—headed for the hills. He lived in a cave near Mt. Nemra and made his garments from palm leaves and branches. Legend has it that his strict diet of half a loaf of bread per day was dropped to him by a crow, and water came from a secret source high in the mountains. These divine provisions enabled St. Paul to live alone for over 80 years.

The original monastery was built on the cave site not long after St. Paul's death—probably before 400 CE. St. Paul's has been attacked by Bedouin throughout its history, most notably in 1484, when the churches were burned, the library destroyed, and all the monks killed. When the Bedouin left 80 years later, Coptic Patriarch Gabriel VII sent new monks to rebuild the churches, but the buildings were destroyed again. Finally, at the end of the 16th century, Patriarch Ioannis ordered St. Anthony's monks to reconstruct and inhabit St. Paul's. These monks built a five-story tower with a drawbridge leading to the fourth story. The first two floors of the tower were for food and water storage and allowed the monks to endure sieges of up to three months. The monastery was most recently renovated in 1974, but—aside from the addition of electrical generators and a guesthouse—it remained the same.

St. Paul's gets fewer visitors than its neighbor, and the monks are even friendlier to guests. The highlight of the monastery is the **Church of St. Paul,** built in the cave where the famed hermit dwelt. Many of the church's 4th- and 7th-century **frescoes** have somehow survived. Ostrich eggs symbolizing the Resurrection hang from the roof. Past the gardens, you can fill your Baraka bottles with holy water coming from the same secret source St. Paul depended on. If you're spending the night, you may be allowed to attend evening prayer, which is most interesting when a large group of pilgrims is in attendance. Amid thick clouds of incense, believers grasp and kiss icons paraded around the chapel by monks, as ancient chants are punctuated by the occasional ululating woman overtaken by religious fervor.

HURGHADA الغردقة ☎ 065

The Red Sea near Hurghada ("al-Ghardaqa") is dotted with small islands and chains of coral reefs where schools of tropical fish swim through the sun-dappled, tranquil cobalt waters. Since the early 1980s, when peace with Israel opened Egypt to foreign investors and tourists, scores of resorts have sprung from the sands of Hurghada. The town continues to expand along the coast at a rapid pace that shows no signs of slowing down. The underwater splendors find their skewed counterparts on land in a profusion of tourist bazaars selling gaudy souvenir dreck to the foreign visitors who flock here for the superb diving and snorkeling.

⌐ TRANSPORTATION

Flights: Hurghada Airport (☎ 44 28 31 or 44 37 94), 3km south of town and about 1.5km inland, is served by **EgyptAir,** with flights to **Cairo** (2 per day 8:50am and every evening at varying times, E£480) and **Sharm al-Sheikh** (M and F 10:40am, E£320). Tickets should be booked in advance through **Karnak Travel** (☎ 54 78 93), opposite the mosque on al-Nasser Rd. Open daily 8am-8pm.

Buses: Upper Egypt Bus Co. launches from al-Nasser Rd., 300m from the southern end of town. Buses to: **Alexandria** (10hr., 7pm, E£60); **Aswan** (7hr.; 10am, 3:30, 10:30pm, midnight; E£25-30); **Cairo** (6hr., 14 per day 8am-2am, E£35-50); **Luxor** (4hr.; 12:30, 1, 2:30, 9am, 1, 3:30, 7, 10:30pm; E£15-20); **Sharm al-Sheikh** (10hr., 9pm, E£65); **Suez** (5hr., 12 per day 10am-1:30am, E£21). Schedules vary with the seasons; consult the station for the most up-to-date timetable.

Ferries: To **Sharm al-Sheikh** from the "New" Harbor (1½hr.; M, Tu, Th, Sa 8am, returning at 6pm; US$40). Reserve at least one day in advance through a hotel manager, at the ferry office, or with **Sherif Travel** (☎ 54 51 47) near the Sand Beach Hotel.

Service: From Dahar, through Saqala, south to the resorts, and back (50pt-E£1). Al-Nasser Rd. and the corniche are the best places to catch one. **Intercity service taxis** congregate off al-Nasser Rd., beside the rotary just south of the telephone office, and go to: **Cairo** (5hr., E£30); **Qena** (2½hr., E£10); **Suez** (5hr., E£20).

Taxis: Local destinations E£5-15 depending on distance. Intercity private taxis can be found at the *service* taxi station. Prices are per car; it's best to form a group and bargain. Taxis travel to: **Cairo** (5hr., E£300); **Luxor** (4hr., E£200); **Suez** (4hr., E£200).

✴🛈 ORIENTATION AND PRACTICAL INFORMATION

Paved highways link Hurghada with other cities, but the town itself is remote. Suez lies 410km north at the end of the Gulf of Suez, and Cairo is another 130km west. Hurghada extends along the coast in a narrow strip. Downtown Hurghada (known as **Dahar**) lies 2km north of **Saqala**, the original fishing town out of which Hurghada grew. Buses and *service* arrive in Dahar, where budget hotels and restaurants await. Saqala has a more authentic Egyptian flavor with plenty of dive shops, cafes, and bars—but few budget hotels. South of Saqala, the five-star resorts preside over private beaches.

Al-Nasser Rd. begins inland from the coastal road and connects the town and harbor. Almost everything, from the passport office in the north to the bus station in the south, lies along a 2km stretch of this street. Smaller streets to the east of al-Nasser Rd. contain budget hotels, restaurants, tourist bazaars, and the **souq,** all separated from the sea by a sandy mound posing as al-Arish "mountain."

Tourist Office: (☎ 44 44 21; fax 44 44 20), just south of the airport on the corniche. From Dahar, get on a microbus headed towards Saqala and ask for Marine Kalab. The poshest tourist office in Egypt is on the right. Open Sa-Th 8am-8pm.

Passport Office: (☎ 54 67 27), on al-Nasser Rd. at the north edge of town, 2km from the bus station. Behind the Red Sea Security Dept. building. Provides visa extensions. Open daily Sa-Th 8am-2pm.

Currency Exchange: National Bank of Egypt, on al-Nasser Rd., 500m north of the bus station, changes traveler's checks and has an **ATM.** Open Su-Th 8:30am-2pm and 6-9pm. Next door, **Bank Misr** also changes money and has an **ATM** (MC/V, Cirrus, PLUS links). Open daily 8:30am-2pm and 3-9pm. **Thomas Cook** (☎ 54 18 71) is just past the bus station on al-Nasser St. Open 10am-2pm and 6-10pm.

Police: (☎ 54 67 23), on al-Nasser Rd., at a bend 900m north of the bus station. The **tourist police** (☎ 44 77 74) is past the telephone building on the left.

Pharmacy: Talat Pharmacy (☎ 54 43 14), on 'Abd al-'Aziz St. just past the Sherry Hand Restaurant. Open daily 10am-1am.

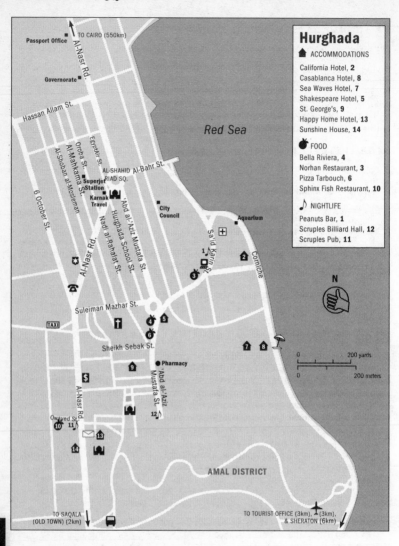

Hurghada

🏠 ACCOMMODATIONS

California Hotel, **2**
Casablanca Hotel, **8**
Sea Waves Hotel, **7**
Shakespeare Hotel, **5**
St. George's, **9**
Happy Home Hotel, **13**
Sunshine House, **14**

🍎 FOOD

Bella Riviera, **4**
Norhan Restaurant, **3**
Pizza Tarbouch, **6**
Sphinx Fish Restaurant, **10**

🎵 NIGHTLIFE

Peanuts Bar, **1**
Scruples Billiard Hall, **12**
Scruples Pub, **11**

Hospital: General Hospital of Hurghada (☎ 54 67 40), on Sa'id Karin St., around the corner from Three Corners Empire Hotel. **Ambulance:** ☎ 54 64 90 or 54 67 40.

Telephones: Office on al-Nasser Rd., on the left after the road turns at the police station. Calls to US, Europe, and Australia: E£7 per min. Open 24hr. Send **faxes** from a hut across from the phone office (☎/fax 54 88 45). E£14-20 per page to the US or Europe. Open Sa-Th 8am-2pm and 8-10pm.

Internet Access: Prince Cafe (☎ 54 43 50), 1 block before the Three Corners Empire Hotel as you head towards the ocean on Sa'id Karin St. 2 computers in the back. E£8 per hr. Open daily 9am-11pm. **Malibu,** inside the tourist bazaar next to Peanuts Bar on Sa'id Karin St., has 4 computers. E£10 per hr. Open daily 10am-12:30am.

Post Office: On al-Nasser Rd., 300m north of the bus station, on the right. **Poste Restante, EMS,** and orange international **phones.** Open Sa-Th 8am-2pm.

ACCOMMODATIONS

Hurghada is a piaster-pincher's paradise, but watch out for spontaneous price inflation, especially during peak season. Many of the cheaper hotels work with diving centers and get hefty commissions for the customers they bring. This either means that you'll be strongly encouraged to dive or snorkel or that you cannot stay in a hotel unless you book a trip through them. It is far more convenient to book through your own hotel than through another establishment, so look at hotels' trip prices before checking in. All hotels listed below have ceiling fans. In the summer it's a good idea to reserve a room in advance.

NEAR THE BEACH

California Hotel (☎ 54 91 01). Friendly owner 'Abdul is justifiably proud of his hotel amd its cozy muraled rooms. Breakfast E£2.50. Singles E£10; doubles E£20, with bath and breakfast E£25; triples with breakfast E£30. California dreamin' on the roof E£5.

Sea Waves (☎ 54 50 71), across from the public beach. Take a right by the Golden Dolphin Dive Center. Clean rooms, shiny floors, and a cute cafe-style dining room. Breakfast E£2. Singles E£10; doubles E£20; triples E£30. Add E£5 for private bath.

Casablanca (☎ 54 82 92), on the corniche opposite the public beach. Enter through the side door of the Cowboy Restaurant and it'll be lookin' at you, kid. Some rooms have beautiful ocean-view balconies, but the private bathrooms have been known to smell. Guests get 20% discount at Cowboy, but some rooms hear the hee-hawing all night long. Singles E£10; doubles E£20; triples E£30.

DOWNTOWN (DAHAR)

Happy Home Hotel (☎ 54 96 11), on Mosque St. behind the post office. Amiable manager makes sure that his hotel, though not in the center of town, is where the heart is. Discounts at the building's diving center. Singles E£15; doubles E£30; triples E£45.

Sunshine Hotel (☎ 54 51 13), 2 blocks north of the bus station. Small hotel with a homey feel and well-maintained single-sex bathrooms in the hall. Friendly and knowledgeable Hassan arranges snorkeling (E£40-45) and dive (US$35-45) trips. Breakfast E£2.50. Singles E£10; doubles E£15; triples E£25.

Shakespeare Hotel (☎ 44 62 56), at the corner of 'Abd al-'Aziz Mustafa and Sa'id Karin-General Hospital St. Tangled in a copse of weather'd trees/This taintless inn entices families/Its fragrant garden sweetens as it blooms/As do the pink and private bathing rooms. Some rooms have A/C. Checkout 11am. Singles E£25; doubles E£35; triples E£45.

St. George's (☎ 54 82 46), 1½ blocks behind Bank Misr, off al-Nasser St. Charming rooms, a friendly owner, and bathrooms as clean as St. George's conscience. Singles E£20; doubles E£30; triples E£45. Add E£5 for private bath and breakfast.

FOOD

In terms of grub, Hurghada is a veritable Little Italy. Other than the usual street fare, it appears that the only foods that have made their way to the coasts of the Red Sea migrated here from a boot-shaped peninsula in the Mediterranean.

Bella Riviera (☎ 54 89 85), south of the Shakespeare Hotel on 'Abd al-'Aziz Mustafa St. One of Hurghada's best deals, with A/C to boot. Watch the waiters scamper in and out of the secret door in the wall. Cheap drinks, lasagna (E£4), salads (E£2-3), meat dishes (E£8-12), fish (E£10-40), and pizzas (E£12-25). Open daily 9am-1am.

Pizzeria Tarbosh (☎ 54 84 56), on 'Abd al-'Aziz Mustafa St. past the Shakespeare Hotel. No relation to the fez-like hat. Owner 'Amir cooked pizza in Italy, and it shows in some of the best crusts in Egypt. Over 20 types of pizza served in generous personal pies (E£9-20). Special student menu: salads E£2.75; meat dishes E£8.

Sphinx Fish Restaurant, under Scruples bar on the corner of al-Nasser and Owayed St. (no English sign). This tiny eatery serves up great fish dinners complete with 2 whole fish, rice, and salad (E£10). Calamari dinners E£15.

Felfela (☎ 44 24 11), south of Saqala on Sheraton Rd., 10min. from Dahar by minibus. This installment of the national chain has the best ocean view in town from its clifftop terraces. *Fuul* E£2-4. Salads E£2.25. Meats E£15-35. Open daily 9am-12:30am.

Norhan Restaurant, on Sa'id Karin-General Hospital St., between Peanut's Bar and the Shakespeare Hotel. Look for the green-and-white awning. Spaghetti (E£7.50-11), meat (from E£15), and fish (E£15-20). Open daily noon-midnight.

SUNKEN SIGHTS

DRY AND MIGHTY. Landlubbers rejoice! Hurghada's underwater splendor can now be enjoyed without even getting your feet wet. Aspiring Captain Nemos can go a couple of leagues under in the **Sinbad Submarine** (☎ 44 46 88). US$50 buys a seat aboard a real 44-person sub for a 1hr. undersea voyage. Sign up at any luxury hotel and leave from the Sinbad Resort. Many of the larger hotels run **glass-bottom boat tours** for E£15-20 per hr. Make reservations at any luxury hotel or over the phone. Get an inkling of the subaquatic splendors at the **Hurghada Aquarium,** which features a variety of fish accompanied by remarkably informative descriptions. (Open daily 9am-10pm. E£5.)

ON YOUR MARK, GET WET, GO! There are a variety of beaches to choose from around Hurghada. **Public beaches** next to the Geisum Hotel and just past the Beirut Hotel on the way to Saqala are the smelliest and most packed. Local rumor has it that sand is buried beneath all the dirt. Women will feel uncomfortable baring anything more than toes. Head to the hotels for more liberal bathing fashions. Just north of the public beach downtown, the **Shedwan, Three Corners,** and **Sand Beach Hotels** all open their beaches and pools to non-guests for E£15; **Geisum Hotel** charges E£10. **Shellghada Beach,** between Safir and Le Meridien hotels, charges E£10 for a day on their soft sand and use of their showers. These beaches can be reached by minibus (E£1 from Saqala) or taxi (E£5-10).

DIVING DELIGHTS

Hurghada's real attractions are silent and submerged. Red Sea creatures will astound you with their array of colors, shapes, and sizes. Buck-toothed triggerfish, iridescent parrotfish, rays with blue polka dots, sea cucumbers, giant clams, and a million others star in this briny show. The shimmering, variegated blues of Hurghada's waters have been spared the horrors of oil exploration (see **Sinai: Underwater Tips,** p. 272, for information on snorkeling and scuba diving).

GEFTUN ISLAND. There are a few reefs you can reach without a boat, including one near the Sheraton, but to reach Hurghada's most brilliant aquatic scenery you must take a barge. Hotels offer an all-day trip to Geftun Island, usually including two 1hr. snorkeling stops near the island and a fish meal prepared on board. Most hotels advertise the trip at E£40, but bargaining often works wonders. Some Geftun-bound boats are as crammed as cattle cars and stop only once for snorkeling. There is a US$1 environmental tax here, so many snorkeling boats are heading to different destinations.

SNORKELING. Snorkeling from a dive-boat might give you access to better underwater sights, but is a bit more expensive (US$10-15). The best reefs are north of Hurghada. The northern waters aren't shielded by islands like the southern ones, so calm weather is a must in order to go. To save money, a group can make independent arrangements with a boat owner—perhaps a fisherman in Saqala—or with one of the sea-trip offices around town. Excursions to other locales can be less crowded and cheaper. For information, talk to: Sayad of **Sunshine Dive Center**

(☎54 51 13), on al-Nasser Rd., between the post office and bus station; Bart or Sylvie of **Blue Paradise Diving Center** (☎54 43 54), a block past the Casablanca Hotel on the corniche; or **Son Bijou Diving Center** (☎54 46 80), behind the Casablanca Hotel. Rent your own gear (E£10-15 per day for mask, snorkel, and fins) at any office in town. ISIC or IYTC (GO 25) discounts are available.

SCUBA DIVING. While Hurghada may have some of the best scuba diving in Egypt, it also has some of the worst dive shops. Many of the shops that have sprung up to profit on rising tourism don't have very much experience, so choose your shop carefully. Inspect the equipment to make sure it has been maintained properly, then ask to see the workshop (a reputable dive center should have a workshop where they repair equipment). Ask about the number of guests per dive boat; any boat with more than one guest per meter is overcrowded. Also check into the diver-to-guide ratio, and be wary of any shop that requires advance payment. Be sure to check your instructor or guide's certification and experience, as well as the ship's gear, and especially its emergency equipment. Dive shops that are members of HEPCA, a marine protection organization, are often more environmentally conscious underwater. **Subex** (☎54 86 51), on the corner next to the California Hotel; **Blue Paradise Diving Center** (☎54 43 54); and **Sea Ray Diving Center** (☎54 33 90), one block past Subex, are all reputable and experienced establishments with full-day diving excursions including two dives, transportation to and from your hotel, equipment, buffet lunch, dive boat, and guide for US$40-50.

Hurghada is also a great place to earn open-water dive certification (for more tips on choosing a dive center, see p. 272). Belgian-run **Blue Paradise Diving Center** offers a reliable 4- to 5-day PADI course for US$280 (PADI book is US$40 extra). Manager Bart brings years of diving experience and an easygoing teaching style to to his small classes. **Subex** is a well-established professional dive center offering open-water certification for US$460. Their high price is worth it, as the instruction is top-notch, all dives are in the ocean, and everything is included in the price.

⬛ DRUNKEN NIGHTS

Just like the reefs, Hurghada's active nightlife attracts creatures of all shapes and sizes. The area's best bars are in Saqala, a quick 10-15min. minibus ride south of Dahar. Conveniently, minibuses operate well past midnight, so you can party it up and then ride back to Dahar. Dutch-run **Papa's Bar,** past the McDonalds in Saqala, is the most happening place in town (Stella E£11). Two blocks south is the beachfront **Chill.** Relax with a Stella (E£10) in one of their hammocks, or groove to the guest European DJs on the dance floor. **Peanut's Bar,** next to Three Corners Empire Hotel on Sa'id Karin-General Hospital St. in Dahar, fills its patio every night. The Stellas (E£10) come with complimentary all-you-can-eat shelled peanuts. **Scruples** pub and steakhouse, on al-Nasser Rd. near the center of town, buzzes and pops with neon lights and beer bottlecaps. Scruples also has a classy **billiard hall** near the southern end of 'Abd al-'Aziz Mustafa St. with several pool tables and a full bar. (Pool E£10 per hr. Stella E£8.50. Cocktails E£11.50.) Bars in town are supplemented by the resorts, which have their own pubs, bars, or nightclubs. **Kalaboush Disco** (☎54 50 87), at the Arabella Hotel on the corniche, is a popular club with a different theme every night (E£10 minimum).

SINAI
PENINSULA السيناء

The Sinai is literally the collision point of two continents—an enormous tectonic summit—not to mention the place where stay-with-the-herd package tourists intent on a resort experience collide with turned-on, tuned-in, dropped-out beach bums. A handful of small towns and a major road occupy the sandy shelf where the mountains meet the sea, but only Bedouin brave the rest of the Sinai's dry, rough landscape. Notwithstanding the wide array of tourists, the greatest diversity of life in the area thrives below the sea: the Gulf of Aqaba's warm waters support a carnival of brilliantly colored coral reefs, tropical fish, and other subaquatic life. In sharp contrast to the earthy hues of the rest of the Middle East, the underwater environs explode with color—the reds and greens of coral broken by the flashes of yellow, blue, and orange fins, set against the sparkling turquoise backdrop of the so-called Red Sea.

For a desert wasteland, the Sinai has had a surprisingly long history of war. Since the pharaohs' troops first trampled the broad plains of the northern Sinai on their march to Syria and Canaan, the favor has been returned by marauding Egypt-bound Hyksos, Assyrians, Persians, Greeks, Arabs, and Turks. In 1903, the British drew the borders of the Sinai from Rafah to Eilat in an attempt to keep soon-to-be World War I collaborators Turkey and Germany at a safe distance from the Suez Canal. On the fourth day of the Six Day War of 1967, Israel seized control of the Sinai from Egypt and began to capitalize on the region's potential for tourism. The Israelis were first to establish the numerous Sinai hotels and dive centers, including those in Dahab and Sharm al-Sheikh. The new development altered the lives of many Bedouin, who began to work in the tourist industry, giving camel tours and staffing hotels, often abandoning their traditional nomadic lifestyle.

In the 1973 Yom Kippur War, Egyptian forces crossed the canal in a surprise offensive to recapture the Sinai. The Egyptian army broke through the Israeli defense line, but later Israeli counterattacks recaptured most of the peninsula. Israel retained the Sinai until it was returned to Egypt in two stages under the terms of the Camp David Accords—the first half in 1979 and the second in 1982. The more recent Israeli-Palestinian violence, dating back to September 2000, has not threatened to spill over onto the peninsula, yet it has had a profound impact on the tourism industry. In many areas, especially those closest to Israel, camps that were once filled to capacity now lie virtually abandoned. On the bright side, the Sinai has become a haven for budget travelers. Some resorts, faced with near-zero occupancy, have reduced rates by half or more. With a little bargaining, it shouldn't be too difficult to score additional discounts. Should the peace process get back on track, it won't be long before tourism and prices increase. Until then, the few who come may enjoy the region's wonders cheaply, and in solitude.

◪ HIGHLIGHTS OF THE SINAI PENINSULA

Secluded **al-'Arish** (p. 273) is the jewel of Egypt's most inviting shore, while the world-renowned **Sharm al-Sheikh** (p. 282) hides beauty beneath its waves.

Even if Dopey's not your favorite of the Seven Dwarves, visit the Bedouin camps of **Dahab** (p. 289) and you'll put on a Happy face.

Moses made the hike up **Mt. Sinai** (p. 278); now thou shalt too. Tackle some of the tougher desert hikes of the **Central Sinai Desert** (p. 280) with a Bedouin as your guide.

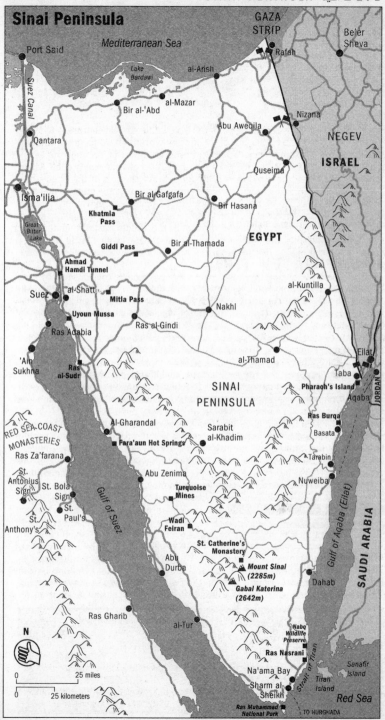

Sinai Peninsula

Mediterranean Sea

Port Said

GAZA STRIP

Beer Sheva

Suez Canal

Lake Bardawi

al-Arish

Rafah

Bir al-'Abd

al-Mazar

Nizana

NEGEV

Qantara

Abu Aweqila

ISRAEL

Isma'ilia

Quseima

Bir al-Gafgafa

Bir Hasana

Great Bitter Lake

Khatmia Pass

EGYPT

Giddi Pass

Bir al-Thamada

Ahmad Hamdi Tunnel

al-Shatt

Mitla Pass

Nakhl

al-Kuntilla

Suez

Uyoun Mussa

Ras al-Gindi

Ras Adabia

'Ain Sukhna

Ras al-Sudr

al-Thamad

SINAI PENINSULA

Eilat

Taba

Pharaoh's Island

Aqaba

JORDAN

Ras Burqa

RED SEA COAST MONASTERIES

al-Gharandal

Sarabit al-Khadim

Basata

Ras Za'farana

Fara'aun Hot Springs

Tarabin

St. Antonius Sign

St. Bola Sign

Abu Zenima

Nuweiba

Gulf of Suez

Gulf of Aqaba (Eilat)

St. Paul's

St. Anthony's

Turquoise Mines

SAUDI ARABIA

Wadi Feiran

St. Catherine's Monastery

Abu Durba

Mount Sinai (2285m)

Gabal Katerina (2642m)

Dahab

Ras Gharib

al-Tur

Nabq Wildlife Preserve

Ras Nasrani

Sanafir Island

N

Na'ama Bay

Strait of Tiran

Tiran Island

0   25 miles

0   25 kilometers

Sharm al-Sheikh

Red Sea

Ras Muhammad National Park

TO HURGHADA

⌐ TRANSPORTATION

BY BUS. The noble machines of the **East Delta Bus Company,** battered cruelly by the rocks, ruts, and dust of Sinai roads, heroically tread the scorched highway, traversing the long distances between the Sinai's spread-out towns. Unfortunately, bus timetables are really no more than an administrator's *(sheesha)* pipe dream. At Sinai bus stations, patience is more necessity than virtue.

BY SERVICE. *Service* are a reasonably priced and convenient alternative to buses. Weathered old Peugeot 504s piloted by Bedouin cabbies are ubiquitous. Hop in with other passengers or negotiate with a driver and wait while he recruits more travelers to your destination. Women should avoid riding alone. *Service* are comparable in price to buses under ideal circumstances, but only with a full load of seven passengers. You'll get to where you're going a lot faster, but this speed has its perils: traffic laws do not apply, and the laws of physics are only grudgingly acknowledged. The law of supply and demand is in effect, though—*service* prices will drop just before the arrival of a bus, then skyrocket after the bus has departed.

ABOVE-WATER TIPS

Travel in the Sinai Peninsula is far easier than in the rest of Egypt. Women can comfortably wear shorts and sleeveless shirts in most places, and professional con artists are rare. However, a number of **regulations** govern travelers to the Sinai. Unguided travel is restricted to main roads and settlements, but you may visit parts of the desert interior with a Bedouin guide. Sleeping on the beach is prohibited in some areas (notably Na'ama Bay), and the police often harass dozing backpackers. Since these areas are not always marked, ask around before settling down for the night. **Nude sunbathing** is illegal, as is the oft-hawked **marijuana.** You cannot bring a rented car or any four-wheel-drive vehicle into the Sinai from Israel. **Prices** tend to be higher and currency exchange rates poorer than anywhere else in Egypt. If you're coming from the Nile Valley, change money before arriving. **Bug season** descends upon the Sinai in the spring and early summer. Dahab is periodically clouded by mosquitoes and flies with killer munchies. Some travelers rig mosquito nets; others advise sleeping near the beach. The Sinai is a laid-back place: in summer, no one wears or carries much, and it takes only a few days before travelers begin to reexamine conventions of hygiene and appearance.

UNDERWATER TIPS

Without question, the Red Sea has some of the greatest coral reefs and marine life in the world. Diving was not very big in the Middle East until Jacques-Yves Cousteau made his voyage through the Red Sea aboard the good ship *Calypso,* later chronicled in his famous book and movie *The Silent World.* Now that diving is a major part of many trips to the Sinai Peninsula, the regional administration has begun to face the serious problem of **irresponsible ecotourism.** All coral reefs from Dahab to Ras Muhammad are under the jurisdiction of the Ras Muhammad National Park. Regulations forbid the defacement or removal from the sea of any animal, plant, or shell—living or dead. The park is fighting a difficult battle with developers waiting to exploit the region. You can do your part to preserve the reefs by observing a simple rule: look, but **don't touch.** Ras Muhammad, like many James Bond movies, has underwater police that will chase you out of the water if they see you breaking this rule. Even accidentally bumping the coral can damage it (and you), so listen to Ice Cube and check yo' self before you wreck yo' self.

Diving, though cheaper than most other places in the world, can still be expensive—but you're paying for safety. The sites along the Gulf of Aqaba coast listed below emphasize safety above all else. **Snorkeling gear** can be rented anywhere, while **dive shops** are concentrated mainly in Dahab and Sharm al-Sheikh. Divers must be certified to rent equipment. Most five-day courses provide certification and cost around US$300. The only decompression chamber in the area is in Sharm al-Sheikh. If you're rusty, take a check-out dive for US$35.

Beginner divers should make sure their instructors speak their language flawlessly, as small misunderstandings can make a big difference underwater ("Tanks!" "You're welcome!"). The instructor must also be certified to teach your particular course, whether it's PADI or SSI—always ask to see his or her card. Some clubs are active in protecting the reefs, participating in annual clean-up dives, and making sure their operations have minimal impact on the marine ecosystems. The size of the club also matters: larger centers often have more scheduled dives and more extensive facilities, whereas smaller ones give you personal attention and will usually run a course for just one or two people rather than waiting for six to sign up. Quality of equipment and safety records are important; ask other divers for advice.

NORTHERN SINAI

AL-'ARISH العريش ☎ 068

Al-'Arish is caught in the cultural vortex between the *sheesha*-smoking Mediterranean and the *who-knows-what*-smoking Sinai—yet manages to avoid the worst of both. Because it is only accessible through Isma'ilia, al-'Arish is much less touristed than the High Sinai and is free of the acres of concrete vacation complexes that line the Mediterranean coast near Alexandria. Al-'Arish is a favorite spot for vacationing Egyptian families, and Western tourists will find themselves a bit of a curiosity but less hassled here than in many parts of Egypt. Currently the capital of the North Sinai Governorate, al-'Arish was once an important stopover on what was perhaps the oldest military route in history. It has since given up military slogans and has settled down with a more mellow one: life's a beach. Some say the beach here is the best on Egypt's Mediterranean coast; it is clean, inviting, and the only one in Egypt dotted with palm trees.

⌐⌐ TRANSPORTATION AND ORIENTATION There are two roads to know in al-'Arish: **Fouad Zekry St.**, which runs along the beach, and **Tahrir St.**, perpendicular to Fouad Zekry. The **bus station** is at the south end of Tahrir St., 2km from the beach. Buses run daily to **Cairo** (5hr.; 8am and 5pm, E£25) and **Isma'ilia** (3hr., every 30min. 7am-5pm, E£10). **Service** (E£5) run to the **Israeli border** at Rafah. Getting around the downtown area is easy on foot, but it's a long walk to the beach—catch a *tut-tut* bus or one of the ancient Mercedes that serve as shared taxis (E£1). City **minibuses** run along the beach on Fouad Zekry St. (50pt). A private **taxi** within al-'Arish shouldn't cost more than E£5.

⁊ PRACTICAL INFORMATION The **tourist office** is just off the beach. Coming from the downtown/Tahrir St. area, bear left at the intersection with Fouad Zekry St.; the tourist office is on the right. The friendly staff speaks English but is short on hard information. (☎34 05 69. Open daily 9am-2pm and 4-8pm.) The **tourist police** (open 24hr.) is in the same building as the tourist office. There are banks along Tahrir St., including the **Bank of Cairo,** which exchanges traveler's checks or cash and gives cash advances on credit cards. (☎35 30 32. Open Su-Th 9am-2:30pm.) The **police station** is at the northern end of Tahrir Sq., but you're better off paying a visit to the tourist police. **Pharmacies** in the downtown area are generally open daily 8am-1am. The **government hospital** is on al-Geish St., just off Tahrir St. (☎34 00 11. Open 24hr.) The 24hr. **telephone office** is three blocks north and two blocks east of Tahrir Sq. Al-'Arish's **post office,** across the street from the telephone office, sends **faxes** for E£5.50 plus the cost of the call. (☎35 15 03; fax 35 15 01. Open Sa-Th 8:30am-2:30pm.)

☎☐ ACCOMMODATIONS AND FOOD Most of al-'Arish's beachfront hotels are reasonably priced. In summer, reservations are strongly recommended. The **Moon-light Hotel** is on the beach, just west of the tourist office, off Fouad Zekry St. The shared baths could use a hosing down, but on the other hand, the hotel has a pleas-ant cafe on the beach. (☎34 13 62. Singles E£20; doubles E£35.) The **Green Land Beach Hotel** is east of the tourist office, just off Fouad Zekry St. Walk toward the beach on the road that angles behind William's Restaurant; the Green Land is on the beach side of the road. (☎34 06 01. Doubles and triples with fan, balcony, bath, breakfast, and the occasional TV E£30.) The airy **al-Salaam Hotel** is on Tahrir St., off the square and near the bus station. Ask for a room away from the street. (☎35 42 19. Private bath. Doubles E£20; triples E£25.)

Food is mostly standard Middle Eastern fare, with the exception of **William's** on Fouad Zekry St. near the Green Land Beach Hotel. Minimalist decor doesn't detract from the fish and meat entrees, complete with french fries and salad. (Entrees E£10-20. Open daily 8am-2am.) **'Aziz,** next to al-Salaam Hotel on Tahrir St., featuring a variety of grilled foods (E£5-15) and rice or noodle side dishes (E£1-3), wins the award for the best budget meal in town. (☎35 43 45. Open daily 9am-1am.) At the western end of al-'Arish, about 3km from the intersection of Fouad Zekry St. and Tahrir St., is the pleasant **Basata,** roofed and furnished with palm fronds and filled with palm frond furniture. (Full meals E£10-20. Open daily 11am-1am.) The part of the beach nearest town is lined with cafes and stands sell-ing everything from *fuul* to pizza.

☑☐ SIGHTS AND ENTERTAINMENT Life in al-'Arish revolves around the Medi-terranean. The entire length of the **beach** is pristine and, except for brief sections in front of the Semiramis and Egoth Oberoi Hotels, there is no private shoreline. Women bathing in al-'Arish should still be fully clothed. There are a few **Bedouin craft stores** at the north end of Tahrir St. Every Thursday, **Tahrir Sq.** comes alive when local Bedouin sell silver, rugs, garments, and camel accessories at the weekly *souq.* A few kilometers east of town on the road to Rafah is the **Sinai Heri-tage Museum,** which details traditional Bedouin life on the Peninsula and has an excellent collection of clothes and jewelry. (Open Sa-Th 9:30am-2pm. E£2. Camera privileges E£5, video E£25.) In the evenings, many locals take to the *sheesha* par-lors of Tahrir Sq., while the cafes along the promenade attract both locals and tourists. The expensive drinks (Stella E£12) sometimes outnumber the people at the **bars** of the Semiramis and Oberoi hotels.

Near al-'Arish is **Zaranik Protected Area,** a nature reserve where thousands of birds migrate in the fall. The park has a birdwatching area, nature trails, and campgrounds. (US$3; camping US$5 per person.) Get there via *service* running between Isma'ilia and al-'Arish.

WESTERN SINAI

The Sinai Peninsula's west coast is a mixed bag. The industrial wasteland of the shallow Gulf of Suez doesn't compare to the stunning beauty above and below sea level all along the Gulf of Aqaba coast. If you see the oil rigs and flame-belch-ing smokestacks of the Suez coast out the window of the Cairo-Sharm al-Sheikh bus, you've probably seen enough. Most Western tourists avoid the Western Sinai, leaving its few memorable attractions uncrowded and peaceful.

'UYOUN MUSA عيون موسى

*Daily **buses** from Suez will drop you off, but it could take a couple hours to find a bus going back. Set off early in the day and bring a backpack full of food and water. A **taxi** from Suez costs E£40-50. Insist on seeing the wells—your driver may deny their existence.*

Moses buffs everywhere will be enthralled by this locale, 15km south of Suez, where the prophet devised an early water purification system with the help of a tree branch. 'Uyoun Musa continues Moses's work in several wells, some of which are open for swimming. When Napoleon visited in 1798, he discovered a canal linking the wells to the sea, used to resupply ships with fresh water.

RAS AL-GINDI راس القندي

*50km inland from Ras al-Sudr, where any **bus** running from Suez to the south Sinai will drop you off. You must then hire a **taxi** (at the petrol station after the turnoff for Ras al-Sudr) to Ras al-Gindi (E£80-100), so get a group together. To get back, flag down one of the **buses** which pass by regularly on the south Sinai-Suez route. Bring gallons of water, a camera, and a solid pair of hiking shoes.*

Ras al-Gindi features the ruins of Salah al-Din's 800-year-old "Fortress of the Soldier," or **Qal'at al-Gindi.** The ruins stand atop a small mountain (a 1hr. climb). Be careful going up, as the path drops off considerably on either side; one misstep and you'll wind up next to your sleeping taxi driver below.

FARA'UN HOT SPRINGS نبوض الفرعون

Just off the main highway, 80km south of Suez. Hire a taxi from Suez for E£100.

Though the hot springs and beach at this southern spot are attractive, their remote location makes them more trouble than they're worth. The beach at 'Ain Sukhna is infinitely more convenient.

SARABIT AL-KHADIM سرابت الخديم

*Despite its location, Sarabit al-Khadim has become a popular destination from Sharm al-Sheikh and Na'ama Bay—the easiest but least exciting way to get here. Independent travelers have to rent or hire a 4WD vehicle for the 1½hr. drive and get permission from the military to venture into the desert. The best place to start is the Suez tourist office, see **Orientation and Practical Information**, p. 260. They can inform you of the latest regulations.*

This remote spot is the site of an ancient temple that extends over 200m of desert. During the 12th Dynasty (c. 1900 BCE), a small chapel was dedicated to the goddesses Sodpu and Hathor, "Mistress of Turquoise." In the 18th dynasty, the temple was elongated and expanded. Ramses VI, the last pharaoh to visit the temple, dropped by around 1100 BCE. The stones of the ruins are decorated with religious inscriptions and accounts of mining expeditions. Around the temple are ancient turquoise mines waiting to be explored.

CENTRAL SINAI

"Hear me! All hear me! All pay heed! The Lord, the Lord Jehovah has given unto you these 15...[crash]...oy...10! 10 commandments for all to obey!"
   —Mel Brooks, *History of the World, Part I*

The central region of the Sinai Peninsula, also known as the **High Sinai,** is worlds away from the lazy daze of Dahab. Cosmopolitan coastal life may cause you to forget that you're on the outskirts of over 60,000 sq. km of arid desert, but savvy hikers know that high times can be had in the High Sinai. Nestled in this rugged desertscape are the biblical locales of **Mt. Sinai,** the mountain on which Moses received the Ten Commandments, and **St. Catherine's Monastery,** near the Burning Bush. The **High Sinai desert** is an ideal place for unforgettable hikes.

ST. CATHERINE'S ☎069

St. Catherine's rich history of monasticism started in the 3rd century CE when Christian hermits, attracted by the tradition designating the valley below as the site of the Burning Bush in the Book of Exodus, migrated here in search of holiness and freedom from Roman persecution. Living in complete poverty and isolation (except on holy days, when they gathered at the Bush), these hermits often fell victim to harsh weather and raiding nomads. In 313 CE, Constantine the Great officially recognized Christianity, and soon afterward the monastery was founded by Constantine's mother, Empress Helena. The monastery thrived under the continual protection of rulers from the Prophet Muhammad to Napoleon Bonaparte over the next 1600 years. As a tribute to the monks' tradition of hospitality to Christians and Muslims alike, it has never been conquered. Modern pilgrims and curious tourists of all faiths visit St. Catherine's throughout the year. Though much of the interior of the monastery is closed to the public, its beautiful architecture and mountainous setting can be enjoyed just as well from the outside.

▐ TRANSPORTATION

Buses: The bus station is at the main square; it's less a station and more a midtown parking lot where the bus is assumed to stop. Buses are notoriously scarce, but they do run to **Cairo** (9hr., 6am, E£35) via **Suez** (6hr., E£25) and **Dahab** (3hr., 1pm, E£25). Check the times with the bus driver who brings you and with someone at the Rest House—buses stop right in front of the establishment, and the staff seems to have a good grasp on the schedule. Should you need to leave in the afternoon, take a **taxi** to the crossroads between al-Tor and St. Catherine's 100km away (E£120 per carload; find an English speaker and say you want to go to the "crossroads" or "checkpoint"). East Delta **buses** stop (or at least slow down) at the military checkpoint on their way to Cairo and Suez about every hr. until 6pm, though not all have seats available. A rest house at the checkpoint sells water and snacks if you get stranded for any length of time.

Minibuses: Red minibuses leave daily to **Cairo** (E£50) via **Suez** (E£40) at 11am. Drivers meet most buses to advertise their service and will pick you up from your hotel.

Taxis: As a last resort, taxis are always available but very expensive; you will have to bargain hard. Popular destinations include: **Cairo** (E£500); **Dahab** (E£120-150 per car); **Nuweiba** (E£200); **Sharm al-Sheikh** (E£200).

▐▐ ORIENTATION AND PRACTICAL INFORMATION

At an elevation of about 1600m, **St. Catherine's Monastery** is hidden away in the mountainous interior of the Sinai. Good roads run west to the Gulf of Suez and east to the Gulf of Aqaba, each about 100km away. Tiny **St. Catherine's town** lies about 3km east of the monastery. St. Catherine's town is home to the office of Sheikh Musa, the starting point for all tours and hikes in the area (see p. 281).

Bank: Banque Misr (☎47 04 63), in an arcade on 1 side of the main square. You can exchange money or traveler's checks and withdraw cash. Open daily 8:30am-1:30pm and 6:30-8:30pm. V.

Police: The **police station** (☎47 03 13) is up the hill near the mosque. The **tourist police** (☎47 00 46) are opposite the bus station in the main square. Open 24hr. Tourist police are also posted on the access road near the monastery.

Hospital: (☎47 03 68), opposite the bus station. Open 24hr.

Telephone Office: (☎47 00 10), opposite the mosque. International phone service. Open 24hr. The monastery also has 2 Menatel phones, 1 in the Auberge and another on the outside of the northern wall. **Supermarkets** in the village sell phone cards.

Post Office: (☎47 03 01), a few doors from the telephone office. Open daily 8am-3pm.

ACCOMMODATIONS AND FOOD

Apart from the free **camping** on Mt. Sinai, **Fox of the Desert Camp,** 1km from St. Catherine's town, provides the cheapest accommodations. Walk out of town toward the monastery, sticking to the main road at the fork. The signless camp is the last building to the right before the four-way intersection. Run by friendly Bedouin brothers Farag and Soliman, the camp offers tidy concrete huts. Prices include blankets, mosquito nets (upon request), and nightly tea around a campfire. (Camping E£5; single huts E£10; double huts E£20.) The closest place to the monastery and the mountain is the monastery's **St. Catherine's Auberge.** To get there, turn right at the fork just before the monastery. Clean rooms have private baths, and the location justifies the price. Delectable dinner and breakfast are included. Reservations are recommended if you intend to arrive after 11pm, or anytime in August or April. (☎47 03 53. Singles US$35; doubles US$60; triples US$75.) Bearing left at the fork outside the village and walking 5min. brings you to a row of hotels, including **al-Fairouz Hotel.** (☎47 03 33 or 47 03 23. Camping in the sand courtyard E£5; 10-bed dorms E£20; rooms with private baths E£35 per person.)

Gift shops, supermarkets, and **restaurants** surround the bus stop. Restaurants are virtually identical, all offering good, simple food (usually E£7-10 for a dish of spaghetti or rice and chicken) with a side order of flies. Some places will even cook food you've purchased from a supermarket. (Markets open daily 8am-11pm.) The most popular place is the **Rest House Restaurant,** right in front of the bus stop, where E£8.50 buys a hearty meal of chicken, rice, bread, and soup. (Open daily 6am-9pm.) Opposite the mosque is a brick-oven **bakery.**

ST. CATHERINE'S MONASTERY

*To get to the monastery from town, follow the road between the tourist police and the telephone office for 1km (going straight at the fork), then turn right at the 4-way intersection. Present your **passport** to the tourist police shortly before another fork in the road, where you bear left to reach the monastery's entrance. Spend the night on the mountain, watch the sunrise, and hike down at 7am and reach the monastery just as the doors open at 9am (to avoid the heaviest crowds). No shorts or bare shoulders allowed, though the monks keep sheets on hand for the benefit of the immodestly dressed. Open M-Th and Sa 9-11:45am; closed on Orthodox Christian holidays (Jan. 6; Feb. 26-28; Apr. 7, 12, 14, 16; May 24; June 4; Aug. 28; Sept. 27; Nov. 14; Dec. 8). Call in advance. Free. For more information, contact Father John (☎47 03 43) or the monastery's Cairo office, 18 Midan al-Dahr, 11271 Cairo (☎02 482 85 13; fax 485 28 06).*

St. Catherine's is believed to be the oldest example of unrestored Byzantine architecture in the world. The complex was named after the martyred Alexandrian evangelist, Catherine, whose body was found on top of Gabal Katerina to the south. About to be tortured on a wheel of knives for converting members of the Roman emperor's family, Catherine was miraculously saved by a malfunction in the wheel (they slit her throat anyway). Her body showed up centuries later atop the isolated mountain. Once home to hundreds of monks, the monastery now houses only a handful. These ascetics are members of one of the strictest orders; they never eat meat or drink wine, and they wake up each morning at 4am when the bell of the Church of the Transfiguration tolls 33 times.

Unfortunately, the most famed and accessible of Egypt's monasteries seems like little more than a photo opportunity from the inside. The occasional passing monk is immediately besieged by the religious and curious alike, while guards patrol the small part of the monastery open to visitors to control crowds. Those looking for a little solemnity should try the Red Sea monasteries (see **Monasteries of St. Anthony and St. Paul,** p. 262).

ICONS. The monastery houses many treasures, including over 2000 exquisite 5th-century icons. The icons with brushed gold halos have a holographic effect, an artistic style unique to the Sinai. In the 7th century, the Prophet Muhammad granted the monastery protection and exemption from taxes; a copy of this directive still hangs in the icon gallery, near a similar letter penned by Napoleon in 1798.

LIBRARY. The monastery's library, containing over 8000 books and manuscripts, is said to be second only to the Vatican library in the number and value of its religious texts. The collection is currently being copied onto microfiche in order to make it available to scholars everywhere.

BURNING BUSH. Upon entering the monastery, turn left to reach a thorny shrub, resting in a wire enclosure at about eye-level. This plant is alleged to have descended from the Burning Bush where God spoke to Moses. Tourists and pilgrims have the (bad) habit of snapping off tendrils within arms reach.

CHURCH OF THE TRANSFIGURATION. The first permanent structure in the monastery was erected in 330 CE, when the Empress Helena (Constantine's old lady) built a small church and tower (dedicated to St. Eleni) at the site of the Burning Bush. Around 530, Emperor Justinian ordered a splendid basilica within a walled fortress to be constructed on top of Mt. Sinai. When Justinian's trusted architect Stephanos found the mountain's peak too narrow, he built the Church of the Transformation next to St. Eleni's chapel instead. This structure became known as the Church of the Transfiguration, so named for its spectacular almond-shaped mosaic depicting this event in Jesus's life. The peeved emperor ordered Stephanos's execution, but the builder lived out his days in the safety of the monastery and eventually attained sainthood (his bones are in the **ossuary**). Both St. Helena and Justinian dedicated their churches to the Virgin Mary, since Christian tradition asserts that the Burning Bush foreshadowed the Annunciation, when the archangel Gabriel heralded the birth of Christ.

CHAPEL OF THE BURNING BUSH. Only the central nave of the Church of the Transfiguration is open to the public. On tiptoe you can see mosaics of a barefoot Moses in the Chapel of the Burning Bush, behind the altar. Should you manage to visit the icons back there, you'll have to remove your shoes, as the roots of the sacred shrub extend under the floor (a living descendant resides just outside). Such privileges are only accorded to true religious pilgrims, who are traditionally allowed to ask God for one favor. The monks themselves, with the help of the local Bedouin population (descended from Byzantine slaves), built a **mosque** within the fortress to convince advancing Ottoman armies that the complex was also Muslim.

MOSES'S WELL. Outside the main entrance of the Church of the Transfiguration is Moses's Well, where the prophet reportedly freshened up after his holy ascent. The **ossuary,** a separate building outside the walls, houses the remains of monks.

MT. SINAI جبل‌موسى

The holy peak of Mt. Sinai, or as locals call it, Mt. Moses (Gabal Musa), stands 2285m above sea level. The Bible describes a mountain engulfed in fire and smoke that Moses ascended to receive the Ten Commandments while the Israelites built a golden calf at its base. Mt. Sinai is one of only two places in the Old Testament where God revealed himself to the people, making the desolate peak sacred for both Christians and Muslims (Jews do not universally identify the modern Mt. Sinai as the peak made famous by the Bible). In the Book of Exodus, God warned the people, "Take heed that you do not go up into the mountain or touch the border of it; whoever touches the mountain shall be put to death" (Exodus 19:12). This prohibition seems to have been long forgotten—busloads of tourists climb the peak each day. God should have included an 11th commandment: "Thou shalt not trash holy places"—maybe then climbers would think twice before leaving litter on the trail and the peak. Nevertheless, despite the Baraka water bottles, the view from the summit is awe-inspiring.

HOLY MT. SERBAL? In some religious circles, the debate still rages over whether Mt. Sinai is actually the site where Moses received the Ten Commandments. Though most believe that Mt. Sinai is the real McCoy, some maintain that the actual mountain referred to in the Bible is Mt. Serbal, 20 miles to the west. According to most biblical scholars, however, the Mt. Serbalists are fighting a losing battle. The Bible mentions three characteristics of the mountain in question: it is surrounded by a vast plain, the summit is visible to all below, and it is accessible to all who surround it. All three describe Sinai, none Serbal. It is also doubtful that the Israelites would have chosen to camp for a year in the valley beneath Mt. Serbal—the site of fierce floods, little drinking water, and hordes of mosquitoes. Besides, who's going to tell 18 generations of pilgrims they've been climbing the wrong mountain?

🚩 PRACTICAL INFORMATION

You don't necessarily need a guide, but for safety neither men nor women should hike alone at night. Most people hook up with **organized groups** from the Gulf of Aqaba resorts and begin their climb (via the camel path) around 2am in order to catch sunrise at the top. Alternatively, you can take the bus to St. Catherine's and start the hike late in the afternoon. Sunset on the mountain is just as spectacular as sunrise, and there isn't a crowd. For a few hours after nightfall, the snack peddlers and blanket hawkers may turn off their lights and music and take a much-deserved nap, leaving you with a real chance to have the summit to yourself. No matter when you make the hike, bring a flashlight and wear walking shoes, or at least a sturdy pair of sandals. If you explore the small ravine between the peaks during daylight hours, you'll discover an ancient Byzantine **cistern** where water was stored during the summers.

Overnighters should bring ample **food,** and everyone should bring two or three bottles of **water** for the ascent. The cheapest places to buy these amenities are the supermarkets in St. Catherine's town (p. 276). The monastery **rest house** also sells snacks and water at reasonable prices. There are refreshment stands on the way up, along the camel path, but prices increase with altitude. A stand on the summit sells tea (E£3), water (E£5), and various snacks (E£5-6).

🏕 CAMPING

Secluded campsites protected by stone windbreaks are available on Mt. Sinai's secondary peak, just a few meters to the west. However, the National Parks administration that oversees the St. Catherine's Protectorate actually prefers that visitors not camp on this peak. Try Elijah's Hollow instead (see **Hiking: Mt. Sinai,** p. 279), which is quieter and a little warmer, anyway.

If you plan to spend the night on the mountain, bring a **sleeping bag** and **warm clothes.** Even in summer, it's often only 8-10°C (46-50°F) at night, and the breeze makes it feel even cooler. Those without the necessary gear can rent blankets (E£5) and mattresses (E£10) at the top. There are also "toilets" west of the summit (holes in the ground with more flies than privacy). Hikers should bring a warm change of clothing—sweaty shirts will quickly turn to shirtsicles.

🥾 HIKING

The hike to the top is not very challenging, but you should still leave all but the bare essentials behind. The monks of St. Catherine's (p. 277) will allow you to leave your bags in a room (E£5 per piece per day). There are two paths up the mountain: the **Steps of Repentance** and a **camel path.** To find either trail, walk up the hill to the monastery, bear left at the fork, and continue to the back of the monastery. From here, the camel path continues down the valley while the Steps start to the right, at a gap in a low external wall at the southeast corner of the monastery. The National Parks Administration publishes *Mount Sinai: A Walking Trail Guide*, a tract describing sights along the trails and on the summit, available at the monastery bookstore and the refreshment stand in Elijah's Hollow (E£10).

Most visitors experience only the small fraction of the mountain visible from the two paths and the peak. But for those without the time or money to make a full-blown desert trek, the mountain provides a unique opportunity to see the High Sinai. A Sinai-only or tourist visa grants access to the entire mountain. Hidden away around the mountain are enough hermitages, chapels, springs, and sights of natural beauty to occupy days of exploration. The sun beats down on wild herbs, releasing their scents into the air, while lizards and bees flit around flowers that somehow survive among the rocks. Start your hike at Elijah's Hollow; the owner of the snack stand there will point you in the direction of a couple of paths and let you store unnecessary baggage in a room. As always, bring tons of water.

STEPS OF REPENTANCE. Of the two paths up the mountain, this one is shorter and also more difficult, but you probably deserve it. It is said that the 3750 steps were built by a single monk in order to fulfill his pledge of penitence. The monk cut corners here and there, making many of the steps extra high. Though it requires more physical exertion, this route has fewer crowds and less trash than the camel path, and great views of the monastery below make it far more rewarding. The Steps take you past a number of interesting sights, which (in the order you see them when descending the mountain) include **Elijah's Hollow,** the 6th-century **Elijah's Gate,** the **Shrive Gate** (where pilgrims until the late 19th century had to confess their sins to a priest before continuing their ascent), and a small white **Byzantine chapel.** Stone walls, smoothed into graceful panels by eons of wind, hem in the Steps on either side. Do not chance the Steps at night—they are treacherous and difficult to follow even with a flashlight. *(Bedouin fly up and down the steps in a matter of minutes, but it will take the less sure-footed 1½- 2hr.)*

CAMEL PATH. The longer route, built in the 19th century, begins directly behind the monastery. **Camel rides** up the mountain usually cost E£35 during peak hours, but if you can stand the sun and the heat, you can get a ride up in the middle of the day for E£20. Unfortunately, the camels are not always available when you need them—you may arrive at the dispatch area at the beginning of the path and find only dung. The path forks a couple of times at the beginning; it doesn't matter which way you go, as the diverging paths always meet up later. There is one juncture that confuses hikers: near the top, the camel path intersects the Steps path after passing through a narrow, steep-walled stone corridor. Turn left to reach the summit; the camel path ends here. Riders will have to get off their high humps and huff up the rest of the way. *(At night about 2½hr. by toed foot, 1½hr. by cloven.)*

ELIJAH'S HOLLOW. After 3000 Steps of Repentence, you'll reach the plain known as Elijah's Hollow. To get there via the camel path on the way up, turn right at the intersection with the path leading to the Steps. The hollow, marked by a 500-year-old cypress tree and a half-dozen of its younger peers, is visible from the north side of the summit. This is where the prophet Elijah is said to have heard the voice of God and the sound of silence after fleeing Jezebel (I Kings 19:8-18). The small **Chapel of Elijah** occupies the site. Another chapel inside is dedicated to Elijah's successor, Elisha. Neither is open to visitors. The **cave** by the chapel supposedly concealed Elijah during his flight.

CENTRAL SINAI DESERT

The natural wonders of the Sinai Peninsula will win you over if nothing else will. *Wadis* shrouded in misty heat lead in every direction, snaking their way around mountain ranges, lush oases, and Bedouin homesteads. The region is fairly untouristed, meaning you'll have all the time and space you want to explore.

⁊ PRACTICAL INFORMATION

WHEN TO GO

Spring and fall are the most temperate seasons for hikes. In summer you'll spend most of the day resting in the shade until the sun calms down, and in winter you'll freeze. The nights are frigid year-round. You may be able to rent blankets from Bedouin, but don't count on it—bring a warm sleeping bag.

PLANNING YOUR TRIP

To venture into any of the mountains other than Mt. Sinai, you must be accompanied by a **Bedouin guide** and have a regular **Egyptian tourist visa**—the Sinai-only visa won't do. **Organized tours** can be arranged in Israel through **SPNI**. The Israeli travel outfitter **Neot Ha-Kikar** specializes in Sinai tours, with trips beginning in Eilat and Cairo. (Offices in Tel Aviv, Jerusalem, and Eilat. 6-day circuit US$360). No matter where in Israel you book your tour, however, you'll eventually end up at Sheikh Musa's office; you'll save a lot of money by starting there, too.

Sheikh Musa, head of Mountain Tours, has a monopoly on all the hikes in the mountains, and trips must be arranged through him. (☎06 947 04 57. Reservations accepted.) You are required by law to leave your passport with Musa—he will notify the army of your whereabouts. To get to his office in St. Catherine's town, walk from the town square past the petrol station. Take the second right; Mr. Musa's office is straight ahead up the hill.

Sheikh Musa will procure both a guide and permit for you. His price, which includes guide, food, camels, and equipment, is US$20-30 per person per day, depending on the size of your party and where you go. The minimum total charge is US$90 per day, making individual travel very expensive. If you're willing to wait a few days, you may be able to join a group. Surplus gear can be stored in Musa's house. You'll leave for your hike within 2hr. of arriving at his office (15min. if you've made a reservation). You and your guide will camp with the Bedouin, so be prepared for long nights by the fire smoking "Bedouin tobacco," drinking tea, and learning a great deal about a little-known culture. Tell Sheikh Musa what you want to see and how quickly, and he'll tailor an itinerary.

⚑ HIKING

Routes include the following possibilities. For most of these trips, you need bring nothing more than a sleeping bag and warm clothes; some of the more difficult journeys require a rope.

Al-Galt al-Azraq: Currently the most popular destination for High Sinai treks, a 7m deep spring-fed pool shaded by a willow tree (2 days).

Gabal Banat: A mountain north of St. Catherine's town overlooking a vast desert (2 days).

Gabal Bab: From this peak you can see west all the way to the Gulf of Suez (2 days).

Gabal Katerina: The highest mountain in Egypt (2642m), 6km south of Mt. Sinai. The path to the top is more difficult, secluded, and beautiful than Mt. Sinai's. A chapel rewards you with shade at the summit (11hr. round-trip).

Gabal 'Abbas Pasha: A rock with palace ruins and excellent views (2 days).

Gulat al-Agrod: A deep, crystal-clear mountain pool where you can swim in the shade of overhanging trees and dive off the surrounding rocks (3 days).

Wadi Talla: There are two wadis, one large and one small. Go to the big one for some swimming in spring-fed pools (3 days).

Wadi Nogra: A rocky valley with a natural dam (Nogra Dam). The water trickles off moss-covered boulders to form a natural shower (3 days).

Sheikh Owat: A picturesque oasis with palm trees, a deep well, and a lot of goats (3 days).

Farsh Romana: A campground equipped with showers, on the way to Gabal Banat (2 days).

Wadi Feiran: An amazingly lush oasis 50km west of St. Catherine's Monastery. Islamic tradition holds that Hagar fled there when banished from Abraham and Sarah's camp in al-Tantawi. Today there is a convent at the center of the valley. The best way to get there is by taxi from St. Catherine's (E£100 round-trip); hiking overland is prohibited by the military. Although buses to and from Cairo pass by, the schedules are unpredictable, and you might get stranded.

GULF OF AQABA COAST

SHARM AL-SHEIKH شرم الشيخ ☎069

In the words of a wise Dahab dive master, "Sharm sucks." The people who stay in Sharm al-Sheikh are not merely package tourists; they are package tourists gullible enough to pay large sums of money to spend their vacation at a resort that appears to have been built on the site of a nuclear blast. The hotels are a fairly wretched bunch, gathered around a bay polluted by constant boat traffic. Still, a couple of factors partially redeem the city. Accommodations, however wretched, are cheaper here than in Na'ama Bay, and the area around the old market is crowded with cheap coffee shops, fruit stands, and butcher shops displaying hanging sides of meat—tails still attached. The diving, also, is pretty amazing.

▐ TRANSPORTATION

Flights: The **Egypt Air** office (☎66 10 58) is along the road leading to Na'ama Bay, not far from the bay. It's easily identified and makes a good landmark. Open Sa-Th 9am-2pm and 6-9pm. Another **branch** at the airport (☎60 06 40).

Buses: From the East Delta station behind the Mobil station between Na'ama and Sharm al-Sheikh, buses leave daily to: **Cairo** (7-10hr., 10 per day 7:30am-midnight, E£50-65); **Dahab** (1½hr., 8 per day 6:30am-11:30pm, E£10); **Nuweiba** (2½hr.; 9am, 2:30, 5pm; E£15); **Suez** (7hr., 9am and 2pm, E£26-35); **Taba** (3hr., 8 and 9am, E£25). To get to **St. Catherine's,** take the earliest bus to Dahab, from where a bus leaves for the monastery at 9:30am. Some buses to Cairo and Suez also leave from a smaller station, down the street from EgyptAir.

Ferries: The ferry to **Hurghada** (☎66 01 66) leaves three times per week from the port just west of Sharm al-Sheikh bay (6hr.; M, W, Th 9am; E£125). From the Sharm Marina, keep walking around the harbor and over the hill at the southern end. Book tickets a day ahead, either through a hotel or at **Thomas Cook** (☎60 18 08), 50m south of the Pigeon House Hotel in Na'ama.

Local Transportation: Take a green and white **minibus** to any destination up to and including Na'ama Bay (50pt). You can catch a minibus going up or down the hill. Other destinations include the Old Market and the marina west of the bay. **Taxis** (☎66 03 57) are much more expensive, charging E£10-15 to go to the main East Delta bus station.

✦🛈 ORIENTATION AND PRACTICAL INFORMATION

Sharm al-Sheikh is divisible into two parts: up-the-hill and down-the-hill. If you are arriving by minibus from the bus station, get off when the bus makes a right off the main road near EgyptAir. You are now down the hill. The hill in question is marked at the top by the sign of the Aida Hotel. A road leads up the hill—continue straight and signs will direct you to the bank area.

Banks: Bank of Alexandria (☎66 03 55). Allows cash withdrawal with MC/V. Open 8:30am-2pm and 6-9pm. **National Bank of Egypt** and **Banque du Caire** have **ATMs** that accept MC/V.

Supermarket: Sharm Express Supermarket (☎60 09 24). From the hill, turn right at Safetyland and left just past EgyptAir to reach the Old Market entrances. Take the 2nd entrance on the right. Open daily 9am-2am. To get to **Supermarket al-Sheik Abdallah,** follow signs less than 100m past the International Hospital. Those serious about cooking for themselves will find the low prices and wide selection of this western-style market well worth the minibus trip. Open 7:30am-3am.

Police: (☎66 04 15), 300m from the banks. **Tourist police** (☎60 03 11 or 60 05 54) are open 24hr.

Pharmacy: Pharmacy Sharm al-Sheikh (☎66 03 88), next to the Bank of Alexandria. Open daily 9am-1am. **Pharmacy Nada'a** is near the Sharm Express Supermarket.

Ambulance: ☎60 05 54.

Hospital: (☎66 04 25), down the hill, just north of EgyptAir. Open 24hr. **Sharm al-Sheikh International Hospital** (☎66 08 93; fax 66 09 81), halfway between Sharm al-Sheikh and Na'ama Bay. Better-equipped than the hospital in town. Open 24hr.

Telephone Office: (☎66 04 00), just before the banks. Open 24hr.

Post Office: (☎66 05 18), in the same complex as Pharmacy Sharm al-Sheikh. **Poste Restante** and **EMS.** Open Sa-Th 8am-3pm.

ACCOMMODATIONS

Youth Hostel (☎66 03 17), at the top of the hill and to the left. The cheapest place to stay in the region. Old dorms are more cramped and running water is unreliable, but breakfast is included. New section sparkles, but breakfast costs E£8. Both sections have A/C. Old section E£19; new section E£40. Non-members add E£1.

Al-Kheima Camp (☎/fax 66 01 66), 1.5km past Safetyland along the road that rings the bay. The "camp" has spacious rooms with A/C and bath, as well as a bit of greenery in the almost-pleasant courtyard. Bungalow singles E£40; bungalow doubles with portable fans E£60; single rooms E£80; double rooms E£120.

Safetyland (☎66 34 63), at the bottom of the hill at the intersection of the road leading to Na'ama Bay and the road running along the bay. The only hotel on the beach and a last resort. Stuffy concrete bungalows are situated in what looks like a construction site. Breakfast included. Open tent sites E£20 per person; singles E£40; doubles E£80.

FOOD

Restaurants are concentrated in the Old Market. Turn left off the Sharm-Na'ama highway at EgyptAir to find Sharm's finest asset: a small, unmarked **liquor store** that sells beer (Stella E£5, Sakara E£5.50) and the usual assortment of dodgy wine and spirits. You'll be hard-pressed to find beer for less than twice those prices elsewhere. (Open daily 11am-3am.)

La Trattoria Restaurant (☎66 22 40), opposite the liquor store. Standard Italian fare. Pizza E£10-18. Pasta E£7-10. Ostrich E£40. Open daily 10am-1am.

Sinai Star Restaurant. Take the 2nd entrance into the Old Market, then the 1st right. Fish and calamari both E£15. All meals include rice, salad, and *tahina*. Open daily 11am-midnight.

SCUBA DIVING

The Sharm al-Sheikh and Na'ama Bay area is undoubtedly the mecca of Red Sea diving and the epicenter of the Sinai's tourism. Despite the large number of wealthy Germans and Italians in five-star hotels, Sharm al-Sheikh still has several unexplored gems in and around the Straits of Tiran, Ras Muhammad National Park, and the wreck of the *Thistlegorm*.

DIVE CENTERS

■ **Camel Dive Center,** P.O. Box 10, Na'ama Bay, Sharm al-Sheikh, South Sinai, Egypt (☎60 07 00; fax 60 06 01; reservations@cameldive.com; www.cameldive.com), in the Camel Dive Hotel. One of the oldest dive centers in the area, and probably the friendliest. Offers an average of 6 boats, state-of-the-art equipment, and highly trained multilingual guides, as well as inexpensive accommodations by Na'ama's standards (dorm rooms US$30). 2 guided dives US$60; full equipment US$25; O/W course US$350. Reserve ahead for a 10% discount on all services. MC/V.

Sinai Divers (☎60 06 97; fax 60 01 58; info@sinaidivers.com; www.sinaidivers.com), next to the Ghazala Hotel on the promenade. Offers a huge variety of courses, liveaboards, excursions, and an ironclad reputation. English, Arabic, French, Italian, and German spoken. PADI or SSI O/W course US$330; 3 days with 6 dives US$160. Accepts traveler's checks, MC/V.

Oonas Dive Club (☎60 05 81; fax 60 05 82), at the northern end of the bay. Slightly cheaper rates and much better after-hours camaraderie than the other centers. 5-day PADI course US$295; certification US$30. Intro dives US$50-65 including equipment. Full gear rental US$24. Full day at Ras Muhammad with 2 dives US$60.

DIVE SITES

■ **RAS MUHAMMAD NATIONAL PARK.** Sticking out into the Red Sea at the tip of the Sinai peninsula, Ras Muhammad National Park is the most famous dive site in Egypt and one of the most spectacular in the world. The tiny neck of land is bordered on the west by the Gulf of Suez and on the east by the Gulf of Aqaba. The waters of Ras Muhammad contain over 1000 species of fish, many of which are unique to the Red Sea. The aquatic wonders found here far outweigh the time and expense of the trip, making it by far the best daytrip from Sharm al-Sheikh or Na'ama Bay. The most famous sites in the park are the **Shark** and **Yolanda Reefs.** The latter includes the wreckage of the freighter *Yolanda* (the actual ship has slipped off the continental shelf and lies 220m below the surface). This surreal sight is possibly the only place in the world where you can swim with sharks among broken toilets.

In the early 1980s, it became clear that tourist and fishing traffic was destroying Ras Muhammad's underwater treasures, so the Egyptian government declared the area a national park. Most of the fragile underwater habitat is now closed to the public, and it is against Egyptian law to remove any material, living or dead, from the park. Diving, snorkeling, and swimming are only permitted in specified areas, mostly around the very tip of the peninsula. On rough days, snorkeling at Ras Muhammad can be difficult. (For underwater advice and warnings, see **Scu-better Watch Out,** p. 287.) Camping is permitted in designated sites; check with the park's Visitors Center for details. Call the Sharm al-Sheikh info office (☎66 06 68 or 66 05 59) for further information about the park. *(The park is accessible by boat and taxi for E£100. Since it is beyond the jurisdiction of a Sinai-only visa, you must have your passport and a full Egyptian tourist visa. Park open daily 8am-5pm. US$5 per person, additional US$5 per car.)*

■ **THISTLEGORM.** The World War II cargo ship *Thistlegorm* was sunk in 1941 by long-range German bombers off the southern coast of the Sinai. Discovered years later by Jacques-Yves Cousteau (who kept the location secret until it was rediscovered in the early '90s), the *Thistlegorm* has become legendary among divers and is widely considered the best wreck dive in the world. Quite far offshore, the *Thistlegorm* requires at least one day and two dives to explore. The cargo bays are crammed full of tires, rifles, motorcycles, aircraft wings, tanks, trucks, and railway carriages. The commander's deck and outer shell are downright eerie. Although a more expensive dive (US$120-150), it is simply unforgettable.

JACKSON'S REEF. Of the four reefs extending down the center of the spectacular **Straits of Tiran,** this is the best and northernmost dive. The strong current is particularly challenging to negotiate, but it also encourages the growth of some of the most beautiful and abundant coral in the entire Sinai. The current brings enough nutrients to feed the coral and schools of fish that congregate on the reef, as well as a variety of sharks and turtles. Schools of hammerheads are seen frequently during July and August.

RAS GHOZLANI. In the area just north of the famous Ras Muhammad National Park lie many peaceful and often overlooked local dive sites. Many of the sites are incredibly beautiful and tranquil; Ras Ghozlani is the best. Divers here are less likely to see the big predators found prowling the deep at other sites, but this location is rarely crowded, uniquely preserved, and full of colorful fish.

NA'AMA BAY خليج نعمة ☎069

This five-star hotel nexus is the center of Egypt's anti-backpacker sentiment—the budget traveler is about as welcome in Na'ama as a narcotics agent in Dahab. However, if you look clean-cut (and act like you own the place), you can freely roam the waterfront shops and hotels. As soon as you don your hip new tie-dye from Dahab, however, you invite stares along the promenade and may be barred from certain areas. Many budget travelers do flock here each year, drawn by the world-class diving and snorkeling as well as the most active nightlife in the Sinai. Travelers have been known to get jobs at hotels or dive centers, where the pay is just enough for food and entertainment (see **Working & Volunteering,** p. 48). If you work for a hotel, you usually get free accommodations; if you work at a dive club, you get free diving lessons or courses. Knowledge of Arabic is not necessary, but French and Italian are helpful.

▐ TRANSPORTATION

By far the best way to go from Sharm al-Sheikh to Na'ama (and anywhere in between) is to hail one of the countless green and white **service minibuses** (50pt) along the main highway. They go both ways, run constantly, and will stop anywhere. Any taxi driver who tells you otherwise is lying and—even after intense bargaining—will charge no less than E£10-15 for the same journey. **Intercity buses** leave from behind the Mobil station halfway down the road to Sharm and from the Sharm bus station.

▐ ORIENTATION AND PRACTICAL INFORMATION

Na'ama Bay is one long strip of resorts on both sides of the highway, which is the town's main street. Virtually all of the beach is owned by five-star resorts. Between the beach and hotels is a **promenade,** where most restaurants, bars, and diving clubs cluster.

Banks: National Bank of Egypt, in the Marina Sharm, Ghazala, and Mövenpick Hotels. Exchanges money. Open Sa-Th 9am-1pm and 6-9pm, F 9-11am and 6-9pm. **Banque Misr** (☎60 16 67), at the Marriott Hotel. Cash advances on MC/V. Open Sa-Th 9am-2pm and 7-10pm, F 10am-12:30pm and 7-10pm. **Commercial International Bank** has 2 locations—next to the Camel Dive Center and across from the Mövenpick Hotel. Both open daily 9am-2pm and 6-9pm.

ATMs: In the Mövenpick Hotel lobby and along the promenade in front of the Ghazala Hotel. MC/V.

Ambulance: ☎123.

Tourist police: (☎64 03 01), just north of the Helnan Marina Hotel.

Pharmacy: Towa Pharmacy (☎60 07 79), in the bazaar south of the Mövenpick. Open daily 10am-1am.

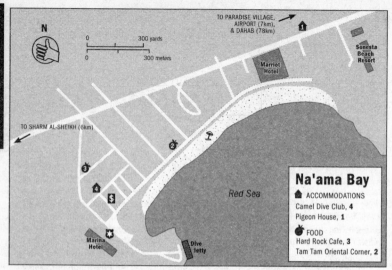

Na'ama Bay

ACCOMMODATIONS
Camel Dive Club, **4**
Pigeon House, **1**

FOOD
Hard Rock Cafe, **3**
Tam Tam Oriental Corner, **2**

Hospital: The closest hospital is the Sharm al-Sheikh International Hospital between Na'ama and Sharm (see Sharm al-Sheikh **Practical Information,** p. 283).

Telephones: Menatel card phones stand between the promenade and the highway.

Internet Access: Neama Internet, on the 2nd fl. of a building next to McDonald's. E£20 per hr. Open 10am-3am.

Post Office: In Sharm al-Sheikh, but most hotels will drop off mail.

ACCOMMODATIONS

If you have the money, opt for accommodations in Na'ama rather than in Sharm. Hotels are nicer, restaurants and clubs are nearby, and you won't have to take a minibus to and from the beach.

Pigeon House (☎ 60 09 96; fax 60 09 95), on the highway in the north end of town, past Thomas Cook. The only relatively cheap place to roost in Na'ama. Happening courtyard is *the* place for a Stella or *sheesha*. Comfortable rooms. Breakfast included. Singles E£65, with A/C E£105; doubles E£85/E£120; extra bed E£20.

Camel Dive Club (☎ 60 07 00), in the center of the small bazaar near the cliffs that overlook the southern end of the bay, a block in from the promenade. This slightly pricey option is worth it for the location as well as the A/C rooms, private baths, and views of a flowery courtyard with pool. The hotel is wheelchair-accessible and features 5 rooms designed for disabled guests. Breakfast included. Dorm rooms US$30; singles US$91; doubles US$108. Reserve ahead for a 10% discount. MC/V.

Oonas Dive Club (☎ 60 05 81), at the north end of the promenade. Look for the red neon sign at the top of the building. With a beach, access to a neighboring hotel's swimming pool, A/C, and a lively bar, this dive hotel offers everything the slightly over-budget traveler could want. Singles US$40; doubles US$60. MC/V.

Shark's Bay Camp (☎ 60 09 43; fax 60 09 44), 4km north of town. A ship-shape Bedouin camp that overlooks a quiet bay. Features a breathtaking view of Tiran Island, an excellent restaurant, and a dive club, but the cost of a taxi (E£20) to Na'ama makes these clean bungalows an expensive choice. Bedouin tent on the beach E£125. Singles E£50-60; doubles E£65-75; triples E£90-100.

FOOD

Food in Na'ama Bay is high in quality, a fact underscored by correspondingly high prices. Only a few places offer low-cost meals, but a little extravagance pays off with a first-rate dining experience.

Seahorse Restaurant (☎60 01 51), also part of the Ghazala Hotel complex, next to Sinai Divers. If you're going to blow the budget, you may as well do it at this excellent Swiss restaurant. The steaks (E£40-42) are considered the best in the Sinai by those who keep track of such things. They also serve veg. entrees (E£22-25), while the daily-changing lunch special could even be considered a borderline budget meal (E£20). Open daily noon-1am. Reservations strongly recommended for dinner. MC/V.

Tam Tam Oriental Corner (☎60 01 51), attached to the Ghazala Hotel. The best Egyptian restaurant in town. Enormous bowl of *kushari* E£8. *Fuul* and falafel E£3-5. Salads E£3.50. Open daily noon-midnight.

Viva Restaurant (☎60 09 64), next to the Red Sea Diving College. The cheapest meal on the promenade. Tasty pizzas E£10. Open daily 10am-midnight. AmEx/MC/V.

Pigeon House Restaurant, in the hotel of the same name. Excellent pork, meat, and fish. Pasta E£10.50-16.75. Kebab E£19.75-22.75. Open daily until 11pm.

Tandoori (☎60 07 00 ext. 329), at Camel Dive Club. Serves good Indian cuisine in a relaxing outdoor courtyard. Lamb and chicken dishes, as well as a number of veg. entrees (E£28-32). Open daily 6:30pm-11:30pm. Reservations encouraged. MC/V.

Hard Rock Cafe (☎60 26 65 or 60 26 66), around the corner from the Camel Dive Club. There had to be one somewhere in the country, and here it is. Caesar salad E£23. Hamburgers E£19-25. Serves liquor. Open daily 1pm-4am. AmEx/MC/V.

WATERSPORTS

CORAL REEFS. Na'ama Bay itself has no spectacular reefs, but a veritable colossus of coral lies just outside the bay to the north and south. Dive centers have maps of the reefscape; pick one up and put on your flippers. The closest free site is **Near Gardens** at the northern tip of Na'ama Bay, a moderate walk down the

---

SCU-BETTER WATCH OUT... Scu-better not die! Hidden among the crevices in the coral reefs around the Sinai Peninsula are creatures capable of inflicting serious injury and even death. If you see something that looks like an aquatic pin cushion, it's probably a **sea urchin** or a **blowfish,** both of which should be touched only in sushi form. Avoid the feathery **lionfish** as well—its harmless-looking spines can deliver a paralyzing sting. The well-named **fire coral** can bloat a leg to mammoth proportions, leaving welts the size of croquet balls. The **stonefish** is camouflaged flawlessly to resemble a mossy lump of coral or rock; if you step on one, you'll puff up and may die within hours. Reach into a hole and a 2m-long **moray eel** may lock its jaws onto your hand. The list goes on. Before plunging in, ask at any dive shop for a look at one of the picture cards that identifies these underwater uglies.

When snorkeling, try to enter the water in a sandy area to avoid damaging underwater plants and animals. If you have no choice but to enter where sea creatures and coral may dwell, wear foot protection. **Sharks** are attracted by blood, so never enter the water with an open wound or if menstruating. Panicking and thrashing tends to excite sharks. If you see one, calmly climb out of the water and casually share the news. Most sharks, however, are not aggressive and wouldn't give you the time of day even if they could; most marine animals become aggressive only if *you* have done something threatening or irritating. If you see an animal getting defensive, simply back away slowly. *Let's Go* does not recommend messing with sharks.

beach. The nearby **Tower** and **Sodfa** are a decent walk south of Na'ama Bay, but both require a E£10 fee, payable at the Tower Hotel. Ask at a dive center which sites are accessible by land; some are tricky to reach.

SNORKELING. Many swear that boat-based snorkeling is the best. For US$15-25, spend a day on a boat and explore spectacular waters. Arrange trips through the dive clubs. The legendary reefs of the **Straits of Tiran** are distant and accessible by boat only. **Ras Nasrani** and **Ras Umm Sidd** are good sites a little closer to town.

OTHER AQUATIC SPORTS. Water activities are not restricted to diving. **Sun-n-Fun** booths (☎ 60 01 37 ext. 170; open 9am-7pm) at the Hilton and Aquamarine beaches rent equipment for **windsurfing** (E£50 per hr.; lessons E£65 per hr.), **water skiing** (E£40 per 15min.), and **sailing** (E£50 per hr.; lessons E£55). Try a **glass bottom boat** ride (every hr. 10am-4pm; E£25 per person) or ride the big **Discovery** (every 2hr. 11am-5pm; E£55, children E£30). Frolic for free at the tiny **public beach** just south of Gafy Land Hotel.

▲ OUTDOOR ACTIVITIES

Landlubbers can throw on some plaid pants and tee off in a game of **miniature golf** at the Hilton. (E£10 per game, E£55 deposit on clubs.) **Horseback riding** (E£60 per hr.) is available across from the Novotel Hotel. **Safari Tours,** next to the Pigeon House, offers **ATV** trips (US$35 per hr.) out in the desert. Most leave before sunset.

WADI KID. Here's looking at you: this *wadi*, 40km north of Na'ama Bay, is a deep, fertile canyon where you can hike among rock formations and fruit trees. Most hotels are affiliated with a tour company that goes once a week. *(Mövenpick Hotel organizes half-day trips to Nabq and Wadi Kid for US$30 per person, with a 4-person minimum.)*

NABQ WILDLIFE RESERVE. On the coast 20km north of Na'ama Bay, Nabq's most notable site is a strip of coastline where the largest **mangrove forest** in the Sinai flourishes, attracting herons, ospreys, foxes, and hard-to-spot gazelles. The mangroves sprout in a few feet of warm, clear water with a sandy bottom, ideal for swimming and relaxation. The problem of maintaining traditional Bedouin lifestyles in the modern world is being actively addressed in Nabq: a Bedouin "reservation" attempts to preserve the culture and openly welcomes visitors. *(Most hotels organize daytrips to Nabq. Wandering off the path in the park is extremely dangerous, as there are still a number of **landmines** in the area.)*

DESERT EXCURSIONS. Na'ama, first popular with divers and snorklers, then with European sunbathers, is now taking aim at the adventure market—teeming with companies promising "a genuine Bedouin experience." A jeep will take you to St. Catherine's or the Colored Canyon for US$50, while a couple of hours on a camel usually costs about US$20. The people who take these overpriced trips are generally package tourists, so unless you relish being stranded in the desert with insipid whiners ("Do we *have* to eat this?"), start your journey in Dahab or Nuweiba.

♫ LIBATIONS 'N' GYRATIONS

Na'ama nights are usually spent tossing back Stellas and swapping diving stories.

Pirate's Bar (☎ 60 01 36, ext. 850), in the Hilton. With cutlasses and rigging hanging from the wall, the bar attracts an appropriately ridiculous mix of swashbucklingly tan diving instructors and suave Europeans. Stella E£10. Imported draught beer E£18-20. Free bar munchies. Open daily 11am-1:30am.

Camel Dive Club, upstairs from the dive center of the same name. Local dive masters congregate here. The 1st fl. is packed and often features live music; the low-key rooftop patio overlooks the main street. Stella E£12, E£9 for divers.

Bus Stop Disco (☎ 60 01 97 or 60 01 98), between McDonald's and the Camel Dive Club. Open daily noon-3:30am.

Hard Rock Cafe (☎60 26 65 or 60 26 66), around the corner from the Camel Dive Club. Transforms into an extremely popular disco at midnight, with a line snaking out the door most nights. Open until 4am.

Casino Royale (☎60 17 31), opposite the Mövenpick Hotel. Give the roulette wheel a spin at this Las Vegas-style joint. 18+. No shorts. Open daily 8pm-4am.

Jolie Disco (☎60 01 00), also opposite the Mövenpick Hotel. Mix of American, Arabic, and Euro pop/disco beats. No relation to Angelina. Open daily 9pm-2am.

DAHAB دهب ☎ 69

Like Kathmandu or Amsterdam, Dahab is one of those places that has grown larger than life in the minds of travelers. For most, it conjures up images of glossy-eyed, tie-dyed hippies lounging on the shore, blissfully asphyxiating themselves in blue clouds of marijuana smoke. Now, Tommy Hilfiger is more popular than tie-dye and cell phones more prominent than joints. As long as you don't look too hard, you can stay here for a week without seeing a proper Deadhead or detecting a rumor of hash. Dahab is now a resort for backpackers and budget travelers, a kind of Club Med on US$10 a day—though clumsy attempts to recapture the tripped-out past remain in the names of shops (you can check your email at the Rasta Business Center) and the ridiculous Jamaican accents sported by restaurant touts. More than any other factor, the diving industry has driven the changes in Dahab. The most common story around is that of the backpacker who means to stay a few days and wakes up a dive instructor six months later (so think hard before you take that introductory dive). Regardless of how long you plan to stay in Dahab, "Bedouin" camps are the cheapest, most social places to crash, though travelers seeking more comfort can choose from a number of more expensive, middle-range hotels with air-conditioning and a family atmosphere.

▐ TRANSPORTATION

Buses: East Delta Buses leave daily from the station in Dahab city to: Cairo (8hr.; 8:30am, 12:30, 10:30pm; E£55-70); Nuweiba (1½hr., 10am and 6:30pm, E£10); Sharm al-Sheikh (1hr.; 8:30, 10am, 12:30, 3:30, 5:30, 10:30pm; E£10); St. Catherine's (3hr., 9:30am, E£15); Taba (3hr., 10:30am, E£20). An Upper Egypt bus leaves daily at 4pm from the same place, stopping by Sharm al-Sheikh (E£15), Suez (E£40), Hurghada (E£76), Luxor (E£90) along the way. Most camps post current bus schedules. Prices fluctuate depending on departure time—the last bus of the day usually costs about one-third more than earlier buses.

Service: If you get a group together, you can convince a driver to go to almost any destination. Service end up being more expensive, but the rides are much faster.

Taxis: Pickups are the cheapest and most common way to get from the bus station to the village. The ride can cost as little as 50pt per person if there are multiple pickups in attendance, or the driver may ask for as much as E£5 if he is alone. You can always bargain him down to E£1-2 by threatening to walk or wait for another ride. Taxis charge E£5 for the same trip. Many drivers of both taxis and pickups are paid commissions by some of the less desirable camps to deliver customers, so don't believe anyone who claims the camp of your choice is closed, inferior, or expensive.

❊ ▐ ORIENTATION AND PRACTICAL INFORMATION

Dahab city is of almost no significance to the budget traveler, who only glimpses it between climbing off the bus and getting into a pickup headed for the village. A quick glance around should provide enough in the way of orientation. The more relevant part of town lies 3km to the northeast, along the coast. The village is sickle-shaped; the curved part that rings the bay is called

Masbat, and the handle to the south is Mashraba. Even farther north (and rarely frequented by tourists) lies the current Bedouin settlement of 'Aslah, home to acrobatic goats, tethered camels, and the occasional dive instructor.

Banks: National Bank of Egypt (☎ 64 02 42), down the road from the bus station to the left. **ATM** accepts MC/V. Open daily 8:30am-2pm and 6-9pm. **Banque du Caire** (☎ 64 04 44), on the bay. Withdraw money with MC/V or change **traveler's checks** with an outrageous commission. Open Sa-Th 9am-2pm and 6-9pm. **Western Union** (☎ 64 04 66), a few doors north of Tota (see **Food**, p. 292). Open daily 10am-midnight.

Supermarket: Near the National Bank of Egypt. Open daily 6am-2am.

Tourist Police: (☎ 64 01 88), opposite the Novotel Resort near the beach. Open 24hr.

Medical Assistance: Dr. Adel Shafey (☎ 012 33 07 97) and Dr. Ahmed Sadek (☎ 012 348 62 09) both have **clinics** in Mashraba.

Telephones: The **telephone office** is across the street from the supermarket. Open 24hr. Another office next to the Muhammad 'Ali Camp provides international **phone** and **fax** service. E£7 per min. for calls to the US.

Internet Access: The bay boasts more than a dozen Internet cafes, most of which charge in the neighborhood of E£10 per hr.

Post Office: (☎ 64 02 23), opposite the supermarket. **Poste Restante.** Open Sa-Th 8am-3pm. Down the road from Western Union, a shop next to Neptune Restaurant has an airmail dropbox and sells stamps.

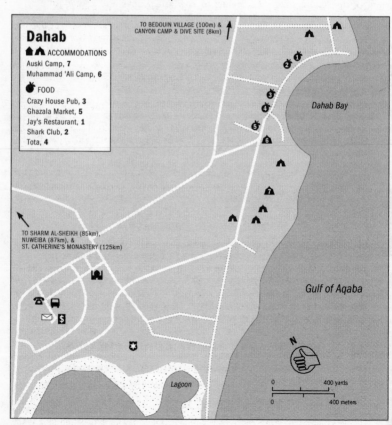

Dahab

🏠🏕 ACCOMMODATIONS
Auski Camp, **7**
Muhammad 'Ali Camp, **6**

🍅 FOOD
Crazy House Pub, **3**
Ghazala Market, **5**
Jay's Restaurant, **1**
Shark Club, **2**
Tota, **4**

TO BEDOUIN VILLAGE (100m) & CANYON CAMP & DIVE SITE (8km)

Dahab Bay

TO SHARM AL-SHEIKH (85km), NUWEIBA (87km), & ST. CATHERINE'S MONASTERY (125km)

Gulf of Aqaba

Lagoon

0   400 yards
0   400 meters

ACCOMMODATIONS

Several dozen **camps** crowd all parts of the village. Dahab camps are an unfortunate bastardization of the thatched beach hut—someone came up with the brilliant idea of casting the huts in concrete, connecting them in rows around a central courtyard, and creating bare cells with minimal ventilation. Fortunately, the huts mostly serve as storage space for your belongings while you lounge outside in one of the restaurants. Rooms with only a mattress are cheapest (E£5-10); those with private bath are a bit pricier (E£15-30). Thatched huts, rare nowadays, provide the best ventilation but also the least resistance to mosquitoes. Camps on the beach south of the bay are the quietest and most relaxed places to stay. Make sure huts have wire screens on the windows; otherwise, you may have to choose between stifling heat and mosquitoes.

Bedouin Moon Hotel (☎64 06 95; bedouinmoon@menanet.net), about 3km north of the village, just past the Bedouin settlement. Owned and operated by 2 Bedouin brothers, the Bedouin Moon is a beautiful hotel situated at the foot of the mountains with a sandy beach and the dive center Reef 2000 (see **Scuba Diving,** p. 293). Rooms have private bath and attractive brick dome ceilings. 3-bed dorm rooms US$14; singles US$20-30; doubles US$35-45 (depending on whether you want a fan or A/C, mountain view or sea view). 10% *Let's Go* discount.

Auski Camp (☎64 04 74), on the beach south of the bay, near the Sphinx Hotel. Friendly owner keeps rooms fresh-smelling and spic-and-span. Doubles E£15.

Venus Camp (☎64 08 38), 50m south of the bay. Clean and laid-back, this camp features an outdoor lounge on the beach—perfect for reading that novel you've been carrying around. Huts E£7; single thatched bungalows E£20; double bungalows E£25.

Cleopatra's (cleopatra140@hotmail.com). A camp in Mashraba whose thatched huts are hot commodities in the Dahab market. Rooms with shower and toilet E£25-30; 2-person huts E£15; 4-person huts E£25.

Oasis Fighting Kangaroo (☎64 00 11; bedouinn@yahoo.com), down a small alleyway across from Napoleon's Restaurant in the middle of the village (don't confuse it with the Fighting Kangaroo Camp). The OFK has some of the best huts in Dahab (E£5) and a Bedouin-style TV room (with hammocks) outside. Singles E£5; doubles E£10. Nicer rooms cost up to E£60.

Muhammad 'Ali Camp (☎64 02 68), in Mashraba, not far from the bay. The camp has its own supermarket, coffee shop, dive club, and laundry facilities. Breakfast E£10; dinner E£20. Singles resembling huts E£10, much nicer rooms with private bath and balcony E£20; doubles with bath and balcony E£40.

FOOD

If you find yourself with the munchies, fear not: Dahab is home to some of the best cheap food in Egypt, but quality varies in the extreme. The beach is lined with inexpensive restaurants which—when they're not harassing passers-by in an attempt to drum up business—serve good, simple dishes like pancakes with chocolate and fruit. However, many travelers report becoming ill after consuming fish at some of these places. Be wary of ordering anything slightly undercooked, especially meat. (For more information on how to minimize the risks of food poisoning, see **Food- and Water-borne Diseases,** p. 21.) For anything ambitious, try one of the restaurants listed below. If you want complete control over food preparation, try **Ghazala Market** at the southern end of town.

Jay's Restaurant (☎335 33 77; julie_jays@yahoo.com), just north of the middle of the bay. You have to step out of the Dahab daze and think ahead if you want to eat at this excellent restaurant. Stop by before 6pm to order dinner for that night (the menu changes daily, and always includes veg. options), and Jay's will have the food ready when you come back. The food is not only some of the best in Dahab, it is also among the cheapest. A main dish, side, and beverage usually amounts to less than E£10. Open for dinner 6-10:30pm. Open for reservations at 10am.

Tota (☎ 64 92 71), near the southern end of the bay. A *Let's Go* favorite for 17 years. Despite the tugboat architecture and the waiters' sailor costumes, Tota specializes in pasta (E£7.50-9.50), not seafood, but you can drink like a fish—the restaurant has a liquor license. Cocktails E£7.50-8.50. Stella E£6. Open 8am-12:30am.

Tarabouche's (☎ 012 235 63 38), on the pathway past the Banque du Caire and the Sunrise Camp, across the small parking lot. 3-course, home-cooked Egyptian meals (E£25-50) include salad, choice of fish or meat, and dessert. Food is known to be hygienically prepared. Reservations necessary.

Shark Club, on the beach south of Jay's; look for the shark emblem on the restaurant's kitchen across the beach. Featuring shakes that will leave you speechless, this restaurant wins the Dahab dessert title. The owner speaks perfect English, and the gigantic portions may cause feeding frenzies among patrons. Small pasta E£3-6, large E£5-10. Shakes E£3-5. Open for dinner only 6pm-"when the last customer leaves."

🎵 SHAKE 'N' BAKE

SHAKE. The social event of the week in the village is the Friday night dance party at the Nesima Resort's **Roof Bar,** where the crowd forms around 11pm and persists until closing time at 2am. The Helnan Hotel in Dahab city is the site of the **Zanzibar Disco,** which can draw quite a crowd on weekends. On Wednesday nights, rock out to a live local band at the **Hilton Hotel** (also in the city) until dawn. Free hors d'œuvres ease the pain of pricey Stellas (E£10).

BAKE. Alcohol is widely available in Dahab and, like most other things, relatively inexpensive. There are six main sources of booze: the restaurant at the Nesima Dive Club, the Sphinx Hotel, Green Valley, , Tota (p. 292), Neptune Billiards, where pool sharks can rack up a game (E£10 per hr. Open 10am-2am), and the **Crazy House Pub** (next to Tota), which also has a billiards table. (☎ 64 02 81. Beer E£6. Mixed drinks E£7-8. Open noon-3am.)

Though the **dope scene** is less noticeable nowadays, marijuana is known to be available. People generally do not actively advertise what type of smoke is coming out of their *sheesha*. The possession of drugs is illegal in Egypt, and Egyptian jails rate low on the Michelin system. Dealers may win an all-expenses-paid trip to the hereafter via firing squad. *Let's Go* just says no.

🌀 SCUBA DIVING

DIVE CENTERS

The Dahab diving scene has unfortunately turned into a cutthroat operation in which inexperienced and ill-equipped dive centers cut corners on services and prices. There are very few dive centers in Dahab, aside from those listed here, that offer safe and first-rate services at relatively inexpensive rates. Some others charge substantially less, but you're paying for the peace of mind of knowing that air will keep flowing. Keep in mind that a change in management—which happens regularly in Dahab—can turn a reputable establishment in the wrong direction. **Certifications,** by the way, mean next to nothing, though the Egyptian tourist board has plans to institute a more rigorous inspection process sometime in the next year. When choosing a club, there's no substitute for local expert advice. You'll find the entire Dahab diving community—instructors, masters, owners, and managers—congregated on the Nesima's beach on Friday evenings after 6pm for their weekly volleyball tournament. Ask around, and try to get a feel for the consensus as to which clubs are currently the best.

■ **Reef 2000** (☎64 00 87; reef2000@intouch.com, www.reef2000.com), at the Bedouin Moon Hotel in its own bay, just north of the Bedouin village. Run by a British couple who offer low prices and a safe atmosphere where even the most inexperienced will feel comfortable (especially since most of the guides and instructors are English-speaking expats). One guided dive with full equipment US$45; PADI O/W courses US$315. **Camel safaris** to Ras Abu Galum include full equipment, lunch, water, and two dives (US$100). 15% *Let's Go* discount. MC/V.

Nesima Dive Club (☎64 03 20; nesima@menanet.com; www.nesima-resort.com), in the Nesima Resort south of the bay. One of the best reputations in the village. Equipment is well cared for and regularly replaced. PADI O/W course US$315. MC/V.

Fantasea (☎64 04 83; ☎/fax 64 00 43; fdc@intouch.com), at the northern end. Offers everything from open-water dives to assistant instructor courses. PADI O/W courses US$295. Three days of guided dives US$120. AmEx/MC/V.

DIVE SITES

Dahab offers some of the best dives reachable by land. The dive sites, on the Red Sea, are all accessible by car (usually four-wheel-drive vehicles) and cover the areas both north and south of the main lighthouse region.

ISLANDS. The most plentiful and beautiful supply of coral and aquatic life in Dahab is here. The labyrinth of pathways, valleys, and coral peaks can make it a difficult but rewarding site to visit, as divers often navigate new and different routes while weaving through delicate cities of coral. Many guides believe that this is the best-preserved coral in the entire Sinai area.

CANYON. Most of the coral have now died due to over-tourism, but the long, narrow canyon ranging in depth from 18-50m still thrills divers looking for deep adventure. At the end of the canyon, divers move through a man-sized crack into the "fish bowl," an enclosure almost completely filled with schools of glass fish.

BLUE HOLE. The most famous site in Dahab is well known for all the wrong reasons. The site should be recognized for the incredibly blue dive, starting at the Bells and continuing along the cliff of coral to the Blue Hole. Every year, though, some of Dahab's best (or just most reckless) divers try to swim through the arched passage (52m below sea level) or even touch the bottom (160m) of this Hole on Earth. Some are successful; others lose their lives. *Let's Go* does not recommend being stupid.

▲ OUTDOOR ACTIVITIES

OVERLAND DAYTRIPS. Daytrips to nearby natural wonders, offered by most camps, are great ways to escape the haze of Dahab. Four-by-four trips to the **Colored Canyon** cost E£50 per person for a group of six. You can travel by camel or truck to the brackish oasis of **Wadi Gnay** (E£30 per person). A one-day camel trip to **Nabq** (see p. 288) is also an option (E£35-50). Hamed the Lobster Man runs **Crazy Camel Camp** (☎64 02 73) and organizes jeep and camel safaris. He also takes people on night **lobster hunting** trips that culminate in lobster feasts on the beach. **Blue Hole Travel** (☎64 02 36; blueholetravel@n2mail.com), across the street from the Sphinx Hotel, runs camel safaris, trips to St. Catherine's, and daily snorkeling excursions to the company's namesake. If you want to go anywhere nearby, ask around the Bedouin community; the Bedouin know these hills better than anyone and will often be happy to organize a trip.

SNORKELING. The snorkeling in Dahab is excellent; enter at either end of the bay where the waves break on the reefs (just be sure to wear shoes or flippers, because if the sea urchins don't get you, the coral will). Trips to the **Blue Hole** and the **Canyon** are arranged every morning by most camps, and you can rent snorkel gear at camps or on the beach (E£5-10). Before paying, make sure the flippers fit, the mask is air-tight, and the snorkel is unobstructed. **Paddleboats** are available for rental near the northern part of the village (E£15 per hr.); use them to explore some of the more secluded spots.

NUWEIBA نويبع ☎ 69

One of the Sinai's natural oases, Nuweiba lies at the mouth of an enormous *wadi* that is filled with drifting sand for 10 months of the year. About the only excitement in town occurs in winter, when sudden, rampaging walls of water 3m high charge down the *wadi*. Nuweiba resembles a younger version of Dahab: a town with no inherent appeal or style that happens to be blessed with a cheap, carefree Bedouin camp and a great beach (complete with its own friendly dolphin; see **A Tale of Two Dolphins,** p. 295). Nuweiba's importance rests primarily on its role in interstate travel: a ferry shuttles tourists and workers to Aqaba, Jordan. Its proximity to Israel and former popularity with Israeli tourists means that Nuweiba has suffered a more severe decline in trade from recent regional unrest than any other Gulf of Aqaba resort city. Aside from Dolphin Beach, you are not likely to encounter many other travelers in the area.

◧ **TRANSPORTATION** Nuweiba, named after the Bedouin tribe whose territory reaches Taba, is divided into a **port** and a **city.** The city lies 10km to the north of the port; a taxi between the two costs E£10. **Ferries** to Aqaba, Jordan leave from the port. The **bus stop** is in the port, in front of the post office. **Buses** are supposed to leave daily to: Cairo (6hr., 10am and 3pm, E£50); Sharm al-Sheikh (2½hr., 6:30am and 3:30pm, E£15) via Dahab (1½hr., E£10); St. Catherine's (6:30am, E£15); Suez (7hr., 7am, E£25); and Taba (1hr., 6am and noon, E£10). Reality is more complicated, and since there is rarely anyone on duty at the station, you'll have to arrive early and ask around.

◨◪ **ORIENTATION AND PRACTICAL INFORMATION** For credit card cash advances, use the **Banque du Caire** in the Hilton Hotel. (Open Su-Th 9:30am-noon and 6-9pm.) Across the street from the bus station in the port is **Bank Misr,** with a MC/V **ATM.** Most stores are in either the **new** or the **old commercial center**—both of which are in the city, neither one larger than a few blocks. The new center is near the Helnan International Hotel; the old is north, closer to Tarabin. Both have **supermarkets,** but the old center keeps longer hours. A **newsstand** next to Dr. Shishkebab in the old center has English-language newspapers, international telephone service, and mostly accurate bus schedule information available. Next to the Helnan stands the **tourist police** (☎50 02 31). The old center also houses the **Nuweiba Pharmacy.** (☎50 06 05. Open 24hr.) Across the street from the old center and clustered around the communications antenna are a handful of other services: The **hospital** is inferior to Israeli health care just over the border, but it's there if you need it. (☎50 03 02. Open 24hr.) The **telephone office** is open 24hr. The **post office** has **Poste Restante** and **EMS.** (☎50 02 44. Open daily 8am-3pm.)

◧◪ **ACCOMMODATIONS AND FOOD** Budget travelers are better off staying in nearby Tarabin. The camps are cheaper and more plentiful, the restaurants closer to the beach, and the landscape unmarred by socialist buildings. The only budget accommodation in Nuweiba city is **al-Waha Village,** 500m south of the Helnan, which sports garden shed-style bungalows. (☎50 04 21; fax 50 04 20. Breakfast E£10. Singles E£25; doubles E£35; triples E£45; camping E£8 per person.) The **Helnan International Hotel,** near the old commercial center, offers relatively cheap rooms with access to a private beach. (☎50 04 01. Breakfast included. Single huts E£46; double huts E£62; triple huts E£78. Pitch your own tent for E£15.)

A TALE OF TWO DOLPHINS Uleen is one of 12 dolphins in the world that have chosen to live and play with humans. While the exact details of her decision remain mysterious, the competing versions of this fish tale are like fatuous episodes of *Flipper*. One story is that in 1994, Awda, a Bedouin fisherman, noticed that Uleen's mother was beached on the shore. Attempting to save her, Awda pulled the dolphin back into the water; but she didn't survive the transition. The next day, Uleen followed Awda and his deaf-mute brother, Abdullah (who could only make one sound: "Uleen"), on their daily fishing trip. Abdullah jumped into the water to swim with her, forging a bond that neither would soon forget. Another version has it that Uleen's male companion was caught in a net and shot by soldiers who mistook him for a shark. Grief-stricken, the lovelorn female lay crying in the water while Abdullah stroked her silvery skin to calm her—again, forging that special interspecies bond. Scientists assign more, well, scientific reasons to her behavior: she was ejected from her pod (perhaps due to some illness or weakness) and sought social interaction, which she eventually found with humans. Whatever the explanation, Uleen has not left the vicinity of the beach, where visitors swim with her every day. It became clear, however, that humans were not meeting her every need: in 1996, Uleen became the mother of a bouncing baby, whom she lost to natural causes. Though the mother entertains visitors everyday with smiles that would make any delphine dentist proud, her second calf, Ramadan, has mysteriously disappeared, leading many to ask exactly what price Uleen has had to pay for human interaction.

Dr. Shishkebab, in the old commercial center, has the best budget meals in the city. (☎ 50 02 73. Sandwiches E£3-4. Meat entrees E£15-25. Veg. dishes E£3-5. Open daily 10am-1am.) **'Ali Baba,** around the corner from Dr. Shishkebab, serves up meat dishes for E£12-15. (Open daily 9am-midnight.) Also around the corner, the bakery **Sugar** has pastries for E£1-2.

◙ **SIGHTS AND SAFARIS** Nuweiba's most rewarding sight is **Dolphin Beach,** named for the friendly dolphin who lives there (see **A Tale of Two Dolphins,** p. 295). Dolphin Beach is a 20min. walk south of Nuweiba Port or a E£5 taxi ride. Tell your driver "Dolphin." Bedouin will charge you E£10 to swim, and another E£10 for mask, snorkel, and fins. The beach is open until 6pm.

Nuweiba is an excellent starting point for **camel** or **jeep safaris** through the desert terrain. All camps in Tarabin either offer their own trips or can refer you to someone else's. It generally costs E£40-50 to go to the Colored Canyon. Camel tours of the interior are in the range of E£80-100 per day; four-wheel-drive tours are about E£20 per day less. You may save E£10-15 per day by dealing directly with a guide—look for one at Tarabin if none approach you. Guides here are generally trustworthy. Desert trips require a **permit,** achieved by some mysterious passport fermentation process at your friendly neighborhood police station (your guide will take care of it for you). Tour prices always include food but not necessarily **water.** The price of bottled water rises dramatically during the safari, so start off with a large supply.

◙ **SCUBA DIVING** Like all towns on the Sinai coast, Nuweiba is surrounded by beautiful coral reefs, but unlike Dahab, Na'ama Bay, and Sharm al-Sheikh, there are only three dive clubs on Nuweiba's shores. **Emperor Divers,** in the Hilton Hotel, opened in 2000. (☎ 52 03 20 or 52 03 21, ext. 900. Two suited dives with full equipment and transport US$70. PADI O/W training and certification around US$325. Open daily 8am-6pm.) **Diving Camp Nuweiba** is in the Helnan Hotel. (☎ 50 04 02. 2 dives with vehicular transport US$60, with boat US$65; introductory dives US$45. O/W training US$325. Open 10am-6pm.) Divers can arrange trips to Ras Abu Galum through either center. **Sinai Dolphin Divers** is in the Nakim Inn. (☎ 50 08 79; sinaidolphin@yahoo.com. Dives with full equipment and transport US$40.)

NEAR NUWEIBA: THE ROAD TO TABA

The 70km stretch between Nuweiba and Taba—the main point by which you can cross into Israel (see **Border Crossings,** p. 38)—is one of the most magnificent parts of the Sinai: mountains tumble to the sea, reefs and sand turn the water a magnificent shade of turquoise, and the peaks of Saudi Arabia tower in the distance. Unfortunately, the view will soon be ruined by the five-star resorts that are popping up like weeds along this beautiful stretch. The coastline is dotted with **Bedouin camps,** which are accessible by bus or *service* from Taba or Nuweiba. East Delta buses leave Taba for Nuweiba at 9am and 3pm (1hr., E£10). Drivers may not know the names of some camps, so keep your eyes peeled for signs. The camps follow a standard layout: a couple of huts, a central lounge, and a restaurant. Some huts do not have electricity (and those that are electrified rely on sputtering generators), so bring a flashlight. It's quiet out here: people spend the days reading and swimming, while night brings on backgammon, stargazing, shagging like rabbits, and all that good stuff.

TARABIN طربين

> **Taxi** drivers try to extort a completely unjustified E£10 from Nuweiba to Tarabin and E£20 from the port. If you bargain, they may accept as little as ¼ of the asking price. To **walk** from Tarabin to Nuweiba, simply follow the road south. When you see Dr. Shishkebab on your left, you're in the old center.

Within spitting distance of Nuweiba, Tarabin is a miniature Dahab in spirit. Unlike Dahab, however, Tarabin actually has a beach, and the water is warm and clean. There is only one road, and camps, restaurants, and bazaars line the shore. At present, very few people stay here, and Bedouin children far outnumber foreigners at the beach. Except for the drug-smuggling four-wheel-drives that occasionally speed by at night, there is little to detract from the stunning natural scenery. The quality of the huts varies from camp to camp. Most charge E£10-15 and have their own Bedouin-style restaurant. Muhammad, who runs **Carmina Camp** at the southern end of town, will make you feel right at home. The cafe here is one of the better restaurants in Tarabin. (☎50 04 77. Two-person huts E£20 for one night, E£15 per night for two nights or more.) **Blue Bus Camp** is the only place with a remnant of a social scene, likely due to the free camping on the beach. It also has a popular restaurant. (Single huts E£10; double huts E£20.) **Soft Beach,** at the southern end of the village, is a quiet place right on the beach. (Single huts E£10; double huts E£15.) A few of the camps have **supermarkets** attached. A cheaper supermarket option, north of the main cluster of camps, is **Safari,** which has a limited selection but boasts a computer with **Internet access.** (E£20 per hr. Open daily 8am-10pm.)

BEACH CAMPS

Some of the most beautiful camps lie 10-15km north of Nuweiba. All camps should cost E£10-20 per person per night. Prices go down the longer you stay, the larger your party, and the fewer the people already staying there. Always **bargain;** camps will probably take less than the prices quoted here. All accommodations are fairly basic, with few amenities to distract you from the neighboring natural splendors. **Magana Beach,** a Bedouin camp near colorful rock formations 10km north of Nuweiba, has reefs and a restaurant. **Devil's Head** *(Ras Shaytan),* named for a rock formation 3km north of Magana, contains four camps. The southernmost, **Moon Island,** is the most simple and secluded. (Bamboo hut singles E£20; doubles E£40; triples E£50.) Moving north, the second and fourth camps offer more huts and consequently more people. Farther north, and close to the Basata camp, the ritzy **Bawaki** has a few budget-priced, non-air-conditioned sheds for US$20 (including use of pool).

SINAI PENINSULA

BASATA بسطة

Basata means "simplicity" in Arabic, and this environmentally conscious camp midway between Nuweiba and Taba is unlike anything you will encounter on the Sinai coast—a gorgeous place you can enjoy without pangs of ecological guilt. Glass, metal, and plastic are all recycled, water is desalinated, organic trash is used as livestock feed, and there are plans to have electricity generated by solar panels. Owner Sharif Ghamrawi cultivates a family-oriented atmosphere with communal dinners, a comfy common area, and lots of **rules:** no nudity, no drugs or alcohol, no sleeping in the common area, and no dirty dishes. A vegetarian (E£20) or fish (E£25) **meal** is prepared every evening, though you can save money by cooking for yourself. The kitchen runs on trust: take what you want and write down what you take. All prices are subject to a 10% tax. Sharif also organizes **tours** by camel (E£75 per day) and jeep (E£60). At the moment, huts are almost always available, but make reservations just in case. (☎069 50 04 81. Camping E£18; bamboo hut singles E£40; doubles E£56.)

Between Basata and Taba is a remote and beautiful spot called the **Fjord,** where a small inlet cuts into the steep hills. The **Salima Restaurant and Camp** is right off the highway on a small ledge overlooking the sleepy bay. There are a few rooms crammed between the restaurant and the rock slope behind it. (☎069 53 01 30. E£25 per person). **Camping** is also available on the beach.

PHARAOH'S ISLAND

Ferry to the island E£15, JD25 from Aqaba. Castle admission E£20, students E£10. Taxis from the ferry terminal to Taba cost E£20.

The rocky outcrop of Pharaoh's Island (called Gezirat Fara'un by Egyptians, Coral Island by Israelis), 8km south of the Taba border crossing, holds the ruins of a Crusader castle built around 1115 CE. Salah al-Din took the fortress in 1171 but abandoned it in 1183 after European counterattacks. The ruins have towers and passageways as well as a large water cistern. En route to the island, the view of Sinai from the castle is ruined by the five-star Salah al-Din Hotel (the best view is from the mainland). The coral reef formations off the northeastern tip of the island draw divers and snorkelers, but neither the reefs nor the wildlife compares to that of the lower Sinai. Meals on the island are overpriced and often unavailable when few other tourists are around.

PETRA البتراء ☎ 03

Follow the ancient path of Nabatean priests hauling the rectangular stone vessels of their gods through a deep and narrow fissure eroded from solid rock. Ghostly images of wind-worn carvings hide in the darkness until—suddenly—the shadows yield to a brilliant pink flash, the first light of the lost city of Petra seeping between the canyon walls. Discovered in 1812, Petra is a city hewn from raw mountain, blood-red cliffs manipulated by a skillful chisel into impossibly delicate structures that were somehow lost for over 1000 years. Petra ("stone" in ancient Greek) is perhaps the most astounding ancient city left to the modern world, and certainly a must-see for visitors to the Middle East—not to mention an incredibly popular (and nearby) excursion from Egypt's Gulf of Aqaba coast.

For decades after Petra's rediscovery, the Bedouin adapted to the influx of tourists by providing them with food and accommodations in the ancient city itself, a practice outlawed from 1984-85 out of concern for Petra's monuments. While many Bedouin have been relocated to a housing project in the hills outside of **Wadi Musa** (the modern town near the ancient site), a large portion still make their homes in the more remote caves and hills of the city (which spans 50km, most of which tourists never see). Some Bedouin sell souvenirs and drinks amidst the ruins, and others herd goats—don't be surprised to smell a barnyard stench emanating from an ancient tomb. If you venture on paths that go beyond the standard one-day itinerary, you will notice stones piled into neat columns; as long as these cairns are in sight, you're near a trail, and Bedouin will pass by.

HISTORY

For 700 years, Petra was lost to all but the few hundred members of a Bedouin tribe who guarded their treasure from outsiders. In the 19th century, Swiss explorer Johann Burkhardt heard Bedouin speaking of a "lost city" and vowed to find it. Though initially unable to find a guide willing to disclose the city's location, he guessed that the city he sought was the biblical Sela, which should have been near Mt. Hor, the site of Aaron's tomb. Impersonating a Christian pilgrim, Burkhardt hired a guide, and on August 22, 1812, he became the first non-Bedouin in centuries to walk between the cliffs of Petra's *siq* (the mile-long rift that was the only entrance to the city). In the nearly two centuries since Burkhardt's discovery, Petra has become a featured tourist attraction, admired by visitors from all over the world, including the crew of *Indiana Jones and the Last Crusade*.

Humans first set foot in the area in the 8th millennium BCE, but the region's occupants didn't enter the written record until Edomite King Rekem unwisely denied Moses and his followers passage through his territory on their way to the Promised Land. The Judean kings held a grudge, and they ultimately enslaved and exterminated the Edomites. The fall of the Edomites (which was literal as well as figurative, as many were thrown off cliffs within Petra), made room for the Nabateans, who arrived in the 6th century BCE. Originally nomads attracted by Petra's abundant sources of water, the Nabateans settled down upon realizing they could control the trade routes between the Mediterranean Sea and Fertile Crescent. Over the next three centuries, the Nabateans

PETRA

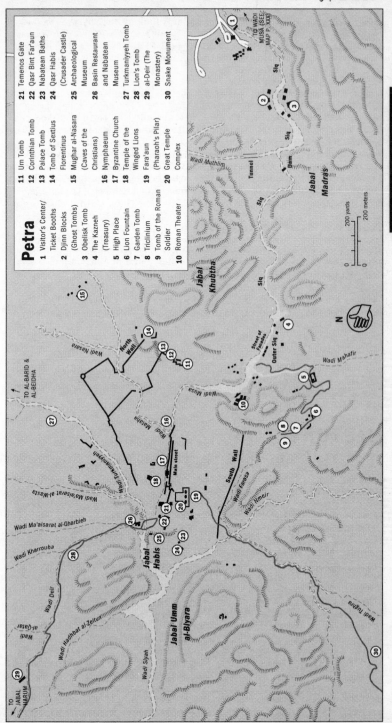

Petra

1 Visitor's Center/
Ticket Booths
2 Djinn Blocks
(Ghost Tombs)
3 Obelisk Tomb
4 The Kazneh
(Treasury)
5 High Place
6 Lion Fountain
7 Garden Tomb
8 Triclinium
9 Tomb of the Roman
Soldier
10 Roman Theater

11 Urn Tomb
12 Corinthian Tomb
13 Palace Tomb
14 Tomb of Sextius
Florentinus
15 Mughar al-Nasara
(Caves of the
Christians)
16 Nymphaeum
17 Byzantine Church
18 Temple of the
Winged Lions
19 Fara'aun
(Pharaoh's Pilar)
20 Great Temple
Complex

21 Temenos Gate
22 Qasr Bint Far'aun
23 Nabatean Baths
24 Qasr Habis
(Crusader Castle)
25 Archaeological
Museum
26 Basin Restaurant
and Nabatean
Museum
27 Turkmaniyyeh Tomb
28 Lion's Tomb
29 al-Deir (The
Monastery)
30 Snake Monument

PETRA

carved their temples out of the mountains, looking to Assyrian, Egyptian, Greek, and Roman styles for inspiration. Their most distinctive symbol is an evolution of the Assyrian crow-step pattern. The crow-steps so closely resemble inverted staircases that the people of Meda'in Salih in Saudi Arabia claimed that God had thrown Petra upside down and turned it to stone to punish its people for their wickedness.

More historically verifiable evidence suggests that the Nabatean King Aretes defeated Pompey's Roman legions in 63 BCE. The Romans controlled the entire area around Nabatea, however, prompting the later King Rabel III to strike a cowardly deal: as long as the Romans did not attack during his lifetime, they would be permitted to move in after he died. In 106 CE, the Romans claimed the Nabatean Kingdom and inhabited this city of rosy Nubian sandstone. In its heyday, Petra housed as many as 30,000 people, but after an earthquake in 363 CE, a shift in trade routes to Palmyra, Syria, expansion of the sea trade around Arabia, and another earthquake in 747, much of Petra deteriorated to rubble.

▉ TRANSPORTATION

The best way to get to Petra from Egypt is to take a boat across the Gulf of Aqaba. A **ferry** shuttles to **Aqaba, Jordan** from the port at **Nuweiba** (see p. 294). Nobody really knows what time the ferries leave, but the latest schedule had them both leaving daily at 3pm. **Taxis** from Nuweiba or Tarabin to the port cost E£5. The ticket office for the ferries is in a small white building 100m south of the port, past a bakery. The slow ferry takes 3hr., barring technical difficulties, and costs US$33, payable in dollars or Egyptian pounds; a faster, less crowded, and more punctual **speedboat** takes 1hr. and costs US$43. Show up a few hours before the earliest possible departure time to deal with customs and ticketing. For general ferry information, call 52 00 52 or 52 03 60. Jordanian **visas** can be obtained on board (Australia JD16, Canada JD36, Ireland JD11, New Zealand JD16, South Africa free, UK JD23, US JD33). There is no departure tax from Egypt.

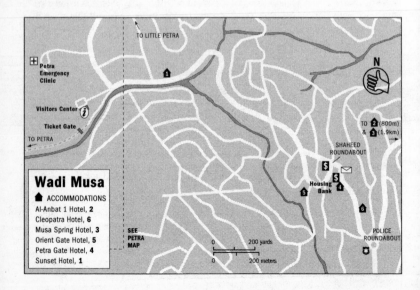

TO LITTLE PETRA

✛ Petra Emergency Clinic

Visitors Center ⓘ

Ticket Gate

← TO PETRA

N

TO ❷ (800m) & ❺ (1.9km)

SHAHEED ROUNDABOUT

$

$ ✉
❹
Housing Bank

❺

❻

Wadi Musa

▲ ACCOMMODATIONS

Al-Anbat 1 Hotel, **2**
Cleopatra Hotel, **6**
Musa Spring Hotel, **3**
Orient Gate Hotel, **5**
Petra Gate Hotel, **4**
Sunset Hotel, **1**

SEE PETRA MAP

0 ___ 200 yards
0 ___ 200 meters

POLICE ROUNDABOUT
✚

From Aqaba, it is an easy **minibus** trip to Petra. The Aqaba **minibus station** (☎201 63 78) is uphill past the post office; turn right onto King Talal St. and walk two blocks. Daily minibuses to **Petra** leave when full (2hr.; 8:30, 10:30am, noon; JD3); sometimes another bus departs in early afternoon. Alternatively, you can rent a **car** in Aqaba and drive to Petra. Rentals longer than three days include unlimited mileage; otherwise, the first 100km is free and each additional 100km is JD10. Daily rates for compact cars hover around JD25, mid-size cars around JD35; prices on four-wheel-drives vary greatly. **Avis** (☎202 28 83), on King Hussein St. next to Nairoukh 2 Hotel, has the best deals on four-wheel-drives (JD60-90 per day). **Hertz** (☎201 62 06), in front of the Aquamarina II Hotel, may have better rates on other cars, depending on what is available.

 SIGHTSEEING STRATEGY. For a "low-tour" of the city center, hire an official guide (2½hr., JD8). More comprehensive tours include the city center and one "high" site: options are al-Madbah (JD22), al-Deir (JD22), and Jabal Harun (JD35-60, half-day city-center tour and 5-6hr. hiking). For more remote areas, arrange trips directly with a guide (full-day tour JD35). You can rent a horse (JD7) for a short trip to the entrance of the *siq*, or a two-person carriage (JD20) for a longer ride all the way to the Treasury. Horses, donkeys, and camels are available inside the site for more negotiable prices, sometimes useful as a means of transportation, but most often hired for the ability to say, "I have ridden a <your mammal here> in Petra." If you have a guide tagging along, you are responsible for renting his ride as well. Without much effort, you can hook up with another guided group or form your own. However, groups of 10 or more are required to hire a guide, so split up before buying tickets if you want to avoid the extra cost. Various guidebooks are available at the Visitors Center, but there's no substitute for the expertise of an official guide on the remoter hikes to al-Barid or al-Madras.

To leave Petra, catch a **minibus** or **service** to Aqaba (JD3) at the center circle of Wadi Musa or at the Musa Spring Hotel. Buses leave early in the morning (6-8am); ask your hotel to reserve you a spot on the morning bus, and the bus will pick you up from the hotel (even budget hotels offer this service). From there you can catch a noon ferry back to Nuweiba.

🛂 PRACTICAL INFORMATION

The town of Wadi Musa stretches along the switchback road starting at **'Ain Musa** ("Spring of Moses," a bountiful spring and the main reason that ancient Petra became a raucously wealthy trade center), passing **Shaheed circle** at the center of Wadi Musa village, and bottoming out near the **Petra Visitors Center**. The Vistors Center houses an excellent (and expensive) gift store, stocks the best selection of books about the site, and arranges all the (official) guide services. (☎215 60 20. Open daily 7am-10pm.) Next to the Visitors Center are the **rest house** and the swinging gate that mark the beginning of the trail down to the *siq*.

Banks: Not surprisingly, banks are conveniently located near the hotels in Wadi Musa, with a few near the entrance to the site. The 2 largest, the **Arab Bank** (☎215 68 02) and the **Housing Bank** (☎215 70 75), are uphill from Shaheed circle and have international **ATMs.** Both open Sa-Th 8:30am-3pm. **Cairo Amman Bank** is in the Mövenpick Hotel, just outside the entrance to Petra. Open daily 8:30am-3pm. All banks extract exorbitant commissions for exchanges and **cash advances.**

Tourist Police (☎215 64 41), opposite the Visitors Center, munching on cigar ends.

Pharmacy: Wadi Musa Pharmacy (☎215 64 44), 10m downhill from Shaheed circle. Open 8am-10pm.

Medical Assistance: The **government health center** (☎215 60 25) is a 15min. walk uphill from the circle. Open 24hr.

Internet Access: Rum Internet Cafe (☎215 79 08), just downhill from Shaheed circle. JD2 per hr. with a 1hr. minimum. **Petra Internet Cafe** (☎215 72 64), off the circle and well marked by signs. Sells computer equipment. Fast connections. JD2 per hr. with a 30min. minimum.

Post Offices: (☎215 62 24), next to the Musa Spring Hotel. **Poste Restante.** Open Sa-Th 7:30am-7pm, F 7:30am-12:30pm. A 2nd branch (☎215 66 94) is behind the Visitors Center, by the entrance to the *siq*. Open Sa-Th 8am-7pm.

☗ ACCOMMODATIONS

When Jordan and Israel signed a peace treaty in 1994, visitors from all over the world invaded Petra, and the once quiet town of Wadi Musa erupted in a hotel construction frenzy, building some 40 new hotels in the past seven years alone. Unfortunately, the recent resurgence of violence in the region has taken its toll on tourism in Wadi Musa, and the city routinely finds itself with more beds than paying guests. This makes for a favorable situation for budget travelers, making some nice rooms available for JD2-3 per night. However, economic woes have also contributed to some less desirable practices, such as taxi drivers (particularly from Amman) recommending a hotel to passengers and then taking a hefty commission. Also, women travelers should be weary of super-cheap rooms (JD1 or less) offered by men advertising hotels around the streets of Wadi Musa. There have been a few instances where accepting an amazing bargain has been taken as an implicit invitation to unwelcome advances. **Camping** inside Petra is illegal, but lingering explorers (especially women) may receive invitations for overnight stays from Bedouin; use your judgment and be sure you'll be staying with a family. Others pick off-the-beaten-path caves for the night. Camping is available in Wadi Musa at some hotels.

■ **Al-Anbat 1 Hotel** (☎215 62 65; fax 215 68 88; alanbath@joinnet.com.jo), downhill from the spring, about 1km uphill from the center of Wadi Musa. The staff, the view, and the meals are wonderful, making al-Anbat the most popular hotel in Petra. Single and double rooms upstairs have private baths and big TVs; some have balconies. Breakfast and transport to Petra included. Dinner buffet served every evening draws as many non-guests as guests (6-9pm, JD4). Mattresses in the scenic and breezy "greenhouse" and campsites with pink-walled bathroom facilities JD2 per person. Student dorms JD4; singles JD14; doubles JD16.

■ **Al-Anbat 2 Hotel** (☎215 72 00; fax 215 68 88; alanbath@joinnet.com.jo). From the center of Wadi Musa, follow the sign downhill from Shaheed circle. Same great service as its older brother, but no dorm/budget rooms, and the view is of the "cityscape" variety. Super-clean rooms have private baths, fans, and TVs. Breakfast and transport to Petra included. Dinner buffet JD4. Singles JD14; doubles JD16.

Petra Gate Hotel, P.O. Box 120, Wadi Musa (☎215 69 08), 40m up the hill from Shaheed circle in Wadi Musa, on the right, overlooking the valley. A homey atmosphere with smallish rooms and home-cooked dinners. Helpful employees live up to the "funky and friendly staff" slogan. Free billiards plus free laundry equal backpacker heaven. Breakfast JD1.5. Dinner buffet JD3, vegetarian JD2. Rooftop mattresses JD1.5; dorms JD2; singles JD7; doubles JD8; triples JD10.5.

Orient Gate Hotel and Restaurant, P.O. Box 185, Wadi Musa (☎/fax 215 70 20), left of the traffic circle, facing downhill. Cozy rooms, some with downhill view and balcony, house backpacker clientele. 2 nearby mosques and their competing *muezzins* create an interesting aural experience. Breakfast JD1-2. Dinner buffet JD2.5-3. Rooftop mattresses 500fils; singles JD3, with bath JD8; doubles JD8-10; triples JD15.

Sunset Hotel, P.O. Box 59 (☎215 65 79; fax 215 69 50), 200m uphill from the Visitors Center. A good value, especially considering what you would pay elsewhere to stay this close to the entrance to Petra. Clean rooms and a helpful staff. Breakfast JD2. Singles JD8, with bath JD15; doubles JD10, with bath JD20. V.

Cleopatra Hotel, P.O. Box 125 (☎/fax 215 70 90), 50m uphill from the main traffic circle, on the left. Colorful, small rooms offer backpackers a more mellow atmosphere than Petra or Orient Gate. Friendly manager gives maps and info. Breakfast included. Rooftop mattresses JD2.5; singles JD8; doubles JD12; triples JD16.

Musa Spring Hotel and Restaurant (☎215 63 10; fax 215 69 10), downhill from 'Ain Musa, the 1st hotel as you arrive from Amman. Big, clean rooms with satellite TV and decent views of the valley. Free shuttle to Petra and free use of the kitchen. Breakfast JD1.5. Dinner buffet JD3. Rooftop mattresses with hot showers JD2; dorm beds JD4; doubles JD8, with bath JD10.

◘ FOOD

The farther you go from the ruins, the less you'll pay for falafel. Wadi Musa boasts the best bargains, especially in the streets off Shaheed circle. Many hotels have all-you-can-eat buffets at reasonable prices, and after an exhausting day of hiking, the ability to stumble from the dining room table to your bed is sometimes worth a few extra dinar. **Star Supermarket,** on the left and uphill from Shaheed circle, has cheap water (300fils) and reasonably priced basics for bag lunches. Even if you can't afford to eat dinner there (buffet JD14), the **Mövenpick** offers affordable ice cream (JD1.5 per scoop), an excellent salad lunch buffet (JD4.5), and a deliciously air-conditioned interior. The Mövenpick and its rival, the **Petra Forum Hotel,** also house the most pleasant bars in town. The former is in a tea garden on the roof of the hotel, while the latter sits on a lobby-level terrace at the base of the Petra hills, offering the best (and closest) view of the sunset over Petra (drinks JD3-5).

Al-Wadi Restaurant (☎07 979 56 26), in the city center on Shaheed circle. The popular breakfast omelets (JD1.5) have energized many a ruin-hungry tourist. Minibuses to and from Wadi Musa stop in front of the restaurant, and the English-speaking manager is helpful in transportation matters. Soups and salads 500fils. Meals (including dessert) JD1-3. 10% student discount. Open daily 6am-midnight.

Red Cave Restaurant (☎215 77 99; fax 215 69 31), up the street from Petra. A long hallway (or "cave," if you like) leads to this beautiful, breezy, bamboo-covered restaurant. Delicious food matches elegant setting. Daily specials and *mensaf* (JD4-5). Grills JD4. Appetizers JD1. Open daily 9am-midnight.

Al-Arabia Restaurant (☎215 76 61), next door to al-Wadi Restaurant. A little more stylish than al-Wadi, with a fountain spewing colored water and retro-modern furniture. The restaurant draws a good crowd of locals, quite an accomplishment for tourist-infested Wadi Musa. Kebab JD2. Appetizers JD1. Drinks 500fils. Open 6am-midnight.

Cleopatra Restaurant (☎079 68 39 47), to the left of the main circle when facing downhill. Friendly cooks serve rice, salad, bird, and bread (JD2.5). Arabic breakfast JD1.5. Kebab or mixed grill JD2.5. Buffet JD4. Soda 75fils. Free Middle Eastern sweets with any meal or sandwich purchase. Open daily 6am-midnight.

Rose City Restaurant (☎215 73 40), just uphill from the site. Pick up a sandwich lunch for the park at this diner and souvenir shop. Hummus 600fils. Sandwiches 400fils-JD1. Grills JD3. Soda 400fils. Open daily 6:30am-11pm.

Petra Pearl (☎079 81 01 85), across the street and 10m uphill from Cleopatra. Serves up a chicken buffet (JD3) and *ad hoc* Arabic lessons. Falafel 150fils. Shawarma 500fils. Open daily 6am-midnight.

◎ SIGHTS

It is possible to see Petra's top monuments in 1 (very full) day, usually via a tour of the city center and a hike up to al-Deir, but there are enough longer hikes and remote ruins to occupy 3-4 days of exploration. Guides are expensive but recommended for distant sites. Bring water bottles from outside; Bedouin sell water throughout the park, but at JD1-1.5 per bottle, you'll need to empty the Treasury to stay hydrated. Open daily 6am-6:30pm, in winter 6am-5:30pm; but hours loosely enforced. If you stay to see the sunset, you should have no problem getting out. 1 day JD20; 2 days JD25; 4 days JD30; children under 15 free.

Officially, the Nabateans had only two deities—Dushara, the god of strength, and al-Uzza (Atargatis), the goddess of water and fertility—but worship of money was by far the most common practice. If the size of a man's tomb truly does reflect his wealth, Petra was once home to a lot of very wealthy people. Tombs and temples clog the brightly colored sandstone cliffs, stretching deep into the diverging valleys away from Petra's main attractions. Climbing into these hills will quickly remove you from the waves of tourists, but it is nearly impossible to find even one breathtaking vista that escaped the skillful manipulations of a Nabatean chisel.

OBELISK TOMB. If you head toward the canyon-like *siq*, large *djinn* monuments (ghost tombs) and caves will stare down at you from the encroaching rocky hills. The Obelisk Tomb is built high into the cliff on the left, a testament to the architectural influence of Ptolemaic Egypt. Closer to the entrance of the *siq*, rock-cut channels once cradled the ceramic pipes that brought 'Ain Musa's waters to the city and the surrounding country. A nearby dam burst in 1963, and the resulting flood killed 28 tourists in the *siq*. While engineers designed the new dam, the Nabateans' ancient dam was uncovered and used as a model.

▨ KHAZNEH. As you enter the *siq*, 150m walls on either side begin to block out the sunlight, casting enormous shadows on the niches that once held icons meant to hex unwelcome visitors (you should be safe if you've paid the admission fee). The *siq* winds around for 1.5km, then slowly emits a faint pink glow at the first peek of the Khazneh (Treasury). At 28m wide and 39m tall, the Khazneh is the best preserved of Petra's monuments, though bullet holes are clearly visible on the upper urn. Believing the urn to be hollow and filled with ancient pharaonic treasures—hence its modern name, Khazneh—Bedouin periodically fired at it, hoping to burst this petrified *piñata*. Actually, the Treasury is a royal tomb of distinctly Hellenistic style, leading some to believe that monument was actually designed by foreign architects. The Khazneh's rock face changes color as the day progresses: in the morning, the sun's rays give the monument a rich peach hue; in late afternoon it glistens rose; and by sunset it drips blood red.

ROMAN THEATER. Along the road to the right as you face the Khazneh, rows of tombs line hillside, sporting the traditional crow-step facade. The older tombs have one row of steps, while the younger tombs have more. At the end of this **Street of Facades**, Wadi Musa opens up to the 7000-seat Roman Theater. The (once) three-story, fully enclosed theater is carved into the red stone beneath a Nabatean necropolis, and the ancient cave tombs still yawn above it. The theater has been restored to its 2nd-century appearance, and audiences are returning after a 1500-year intermission. A marble Hercules (now in the museum) was discovered just a few years ago in the curtained chambers beneath the stage.

ROYAL TOMBS. Farther down the *wadi*, high up on the face of Jabal Khutba, are the Royal Tombs. The **Urn Tomb,** with its unmistakable recessed facade, commands a panoramic view of the valley. The two-tiered vault beneath the pillared facade is known as the **prison,** or *sijin.* A Greek inscription on an inner wall describes how the tomb, originally dedicated to the Nabatean King Malichus II in the first century CE, was converted to a church 400 years later. Nearby sits the **Corinthian Tomb** (allegedly a replica of Nero's Golden Palace in Rome) and the **Palace Tomb** (Tomb in Two Stories), which juts out from the mountainside. Workers completed the tomb by attaching preassembled stones to its top left-hand corner. Around the corner to the right is the **Tomb of Sextus Florentinus,** who was so enamored of the hewn heights that he asked to be buried in this ultimate outpost of the Roman Empire.

CARDO MAXIMUS. Around the bend to the left, a few restored columns are all that remain of the paved Roman main street. Two thousand years ago, columns lined the full length of the street, shielding markets and residences. At the beginning of the street on the right, the **Nymphaeum** ruins outline the ancient public fountain near its base, where the waters imported all the way from 'Ain Musa finally resurfaced. On a rise to the right, before the triple-arched gate, recent excavations have uncovered the Temple of al-Uzza (Atargatis), also called the **Temple of the Winged Lions.** In the spring you can watch the progress of US-sponsored excavations that have already uncovered several workshops and some cracked crocks.

BYZANTINE CHURCH. A team of Jordanian and American archaeologists has excavated an immense Byzantine church, home to a wealth of mosaics. The site lies several hundred meters to the right of the Roman street, near the Temple of the Winged Lions (from which some of the church's column bases and capitals were probably lifted). Each of the church's side aisles is paved with 70 square meters of remarkably preserved mosaic, depicting people of various professions, representations of the four seasons, and indigenous, exotic, and mythological animals. Recent studies attest that the church was the seat of an important Byzantine bishopric in the 5th and 6th centuries, an assertion that challenges the belief that Petra was in decline by 600 CE.

GREAT TEMPLE COMPLEX AND ENVIRONS. A team from Brown University in the US has recently unearthed the remarkable remains of a 7000-square-meter **Great Temple.** The Nabatean temple's short, wide columns were constructed of many cylindrical sections (unlike the slender Roman columns along the Colonaded Street). White hexagonal paving stones cover an extensive tunnel system that marks the importance of this holy site. Farther along, the triple-arched **Temenos Gate** was once the front gate of the **Qasr Bint Fara'un** (Palace of the Pharaoh's Daughter), a later Nabatean temple built to honor the god Dushara. Like many of Petra's monuments, the walls of Qasr Bint Fara'un were once decorated with elaborate designs of colored plaster, the bleached remains of which can still be seen today. On the left before the gate are the **Nabatean Baths.** On a trail leading behind the temple to the left, a single standing column, **Amud Fara'un** (Pharaoh's Pillar), gloats beside its two fallen comrades.

MUSEUMS. To the right of the Nabatean temple, a rock-hewn staircase leads to a small **archaeological museum** holding the spoils of the Winged Lions dig as well as carved stone figures from elsewhere in Petra. On the way to the monastery, next to the Basin Restaurant, the **Nabatean Museum** has well-documented exhibits and air-conditioned restrooms with what is probably the ■**world's best toilet seat view.** *(Both museums open daily 9am-4pm. Free.)*

⚑ HIKING

HIKE	DURATION
Wadi Turkmaniyyeh	30min.
Al-Habis	1hr.
⚑ Jabal Harun (Mt. Hor)	4-6hr.
Jabal Umm al-Biyara	10-12hr.
High Place of Sacrifice	1½hr.
Al-Madras	4-8hr.
Al-Barid	6hr.

Many people rave about Petra's most accessible 10 percent, content with what they can see in one day. The Bedouin say, however, that in order to appreciate Petra, you must stay long enough to watch your nails grow long. The following seven treks fill two strenuous days, but you can easily spend a week wandering, especially if you venture beyond the ancient city limits. Four of these seven hikes require a guide (officially JD35, but good luck finding one who charges less than JD50): **Jabal Harun**, the **Snake Monument, al-Madras,** and **al-Barid**. It's unwise to hike the remote hills alone. If you feel lost, keep a sharp eye out for remnants of donkey visits, which can serve as a trail of crumbs.

WADI TURKMANIYYEH وادى تركمانية

The shortest and easiest of the hikes leads down the *wadi* to the left of and behind the Temple of the Winged Lions. Fifteen minutes of strolling down the road running through the rich green gardens of Wadi Turkmaniyyeh leads to the only tomb at Petra with a Nabatean inscription. The lengthy invocation above the entrance beseeches the god Dushara to protect the tomb from violation. Unfortunately, Dushara took a permanent sabbatical, and the chamber has been stripped bare.

AL-HABIS الحابس

A second, more interesting climb begins at the end of the road that descends from the Pharaoh's Pillar to the cliff face, a few hundred meters left of the museum. The trail winds up to al-Habis, the prison. While the steps have been restored recently, they do not lead up to much. A path winds all the way around the mountain, however, revealing gorgeous canyons and (you guessed it) more tombs, on the western side. The climb to the top and back takes less than 1hr.

⚑JABAL HARUN (MT. HOR) جبل هارون

This climb begins just to the right of Jabal Habis, just north of the Nabatean Museum. Winding staircases lead panting tourists up the narrow ravine of Wadi Deir, passing shrewd Bedouin selling expensive water (JD1). A sign marks a trail diverging off to the left that leads to the **Lion's Tomb**. The anthropomorphic hole in the tomb's facade is the skilled work of Mother Nature and her persistently eroding breeze.

Back on the path, keep climbing to reach the most rewarding summit in all of Jordan, which the Nabateans have sculpted into **al-Deir** (the Monastery), Petra's largest monument. Larger (50m wide and 45m tall) but less ornate than the Khazneh, al-Deir has a single inner chamber that dates back to the first century CE. Most scholars believe that al-Deir was originally either a Nabatean temple or an unfinished tomb dedicated to one of the later Nabatean kings. It picked up its orthodox appellation in the Byzantine period. Straight across the *wadi* looms the highest peak in the area, **Jabal Harun** (Aaron's Mountain or Mt. Hor). On top of the mountain, a white church reportedly houses the **Tomb of Aaron**. The hike straight up to al-Deir (no side trips) takes 30min., but the whole trip takes a few hours. Expect to spend a couple more hours if you detour into **Wadi Siyah** and visit its seasonal waterfall on the way back.

JABAL UMM AL-BIYARA جبل أم البيارة

It takes a grueling 3hr. hike to ascend **Jabal Umm al-Biyara** (Mother of Cisterns Mountain), which towers over the Crusader castle on Jabal Habis. Follow the trail from the left of the Nabatean temple past the Pharaoh's Pillar and down into the *wadi* to the right. A 50m scramble up the rock chute to the left of the blue sign leads to the beginning of a stone ramp, which leads to the top. Exercise caution on the ramp, as the footing is fickle. It was here, at the site of Petra's original acropolis and the biblical city of Sela, that a Judean king supposedly hurled thousands of Edomites over the cliff's edge. The gigantic piles of shards, over 8000 years old, are the only remnants of the mountain's first inhabitants.

If you continue south along Wadi Tughra (which runs by its base) instead of climbing Umm al-Biyara, you'll eventually reach the **Snake Monument,** one of the earliest Nabatean religious shrines. From here, it's about 2hr. to the **Tomb of Aaron** on Jabal Harun. The path meanders around Jabal Harun before ascending it from the south. When it disappears on the rocks, follow the donkey droppings. As you start to climb Jabal Harun you'll see a lone tent. Inside, a Bedouin (the official holder of the keys) will escort you the rest of the way and open the building for you to explore. The entire trek takes 5-6hr.

HIGH PLACE OF SACRIFICE المكان العالى

One of the most popular hikes is the circular route to the **High Place of Sacrifice** on **Jabal al-Madhbah,** a site of sacrifice with a full view of Petra—even the tourist police come here to watch the sunset. A staircase sliced into the rock leads to the left just as the Roman Theater comes into view. Follow the right prong when the trail levels and forks at the top of the stairs. On the left, **Obelisk Ridge** presents obelisks dedicated to Dushara and al-Uzza. On the peak to the right, the High Place supports a string of grisly sights: two altars, an ablution cistern, gutters for draining away sacrificial blood, and bleachers for an unobstructed view of animal sacrifices. Head downhill past the Pepsi stand, leaving the obelisks behind you, and backtrack under the western face of the High Place. A hard-to-find staircase leads down to a sculptured **Lion Fountain.** The first grotto complex beyond it is the **Garden Tomb.** Below it is the **Tomb of the Roman Soldier** (named for the tough guy carved in the facade) and across from it a rock **triclinium** (feast hall), which has the only decorated interior left in Petra. The trail then leads into Wadi Farasa and ends near the Pillar. The circle, followed either way, takes about 1½ hr.

AL-MADRAS المدرس

Tourism beyond Petra disappears rapidly. The isolated antiquities can only be reached by donkey or foot. All roads lead back to the King's Highway.

A trail branching to the left just past the Obelisk Tomb and before the entrance to the *siq* leads to **al-Madras,** an ancient Petran suburb with almost as many monuments as Petra. On the way, watch for the short-eared desert hare and a full spectrum of small lizards in dazzling purple, fuchsia, and iridescent blue—one camouflage for each color of Petra's sandstone. Come with water, a snack, and a guide. The round-trip takes 4-8hr.

AL-BARID البارد

Past the Tomb of Sextus Florentinus and the **Mughar al-Nasara** (Caves of the Christians), a trail chisels into the rock that leads to the northern suburb of **al-Barid**, affectionately known as "Little Petra." A road passing the new hotel in Wadi Musa also approaches this archaeological site. Al-Barid is a fascinating miniature of Petra, complete with a short *siq* and several carved tombs, but almost no tourists. If you don't feel like hoofing it, a Wadi Musa **taxi** will take you there and wait at the entrance for 1hr. (JD7). Also off the new road past the hotel is **al-Beidha.** Excitement runs high among the members of the excavating expedition here—they've uncovereld make al-Beidha, along with Jericho, one of the oldest known farming communities in the world. A Bedouin guide can lead you here via a painless trail, about 3hr. each way. Bring an extra JD2-3 or some trinkets (such as cigarettes) to trade.

Check out our new
City Guides

Barcelona 2002

photos

walking tours

service directory

amusing anecdotes

detailed map coverage

Amsterdam 2002

&
you know you love
our special Let's Go Thumbpicks

APPENDIX

AVERAGE TEMPERATURES

AVG. TEMP., PRECIPITATION	JANUARY			APRIL			JULY			OCTOBER		
	°C	°F	mm	°C	°F	mm	°C	°F	mm	°C	°F	mm
Alexandria	15	59	52	19	67	4	26	80	0	24	76	8
Aswan	17	62	0	27	81	0	34	93	0	29	84	0
Cairo	14	57	5	21	71	25	28	82	0	24	75	1
Hurghada	16	60	0.1	22	72	0.1	30	85	0	25	77	0.2
Luxor	14	57	0	26	78	0	33	91	0	27	80	0.8

MEASUREMENT CONVERSIONS

The metric system is used throughout Egypt and the Middle East.

1 inch (in.) = 25.4 millimeters (mm)	1 millimeter (mm) = 0.039 in.
1 foot (ft.) = 0.30m	1 meter (m) = 3.28 ft.
1 yard (yd.) = 0.914m	1 meter (m) = 1.09 yd.
1 mile = 1.61km	1 kilometer (km) = 0.62 mi.
1 ounce (oz.) = 28.35g	1 gram (g) = 0.035 oz.
1 pound (lb.) = 0.454kg	1 kilogram (kg) = 2.202 lb.
1 fluid ounce (fl. oz.) = 29.57ml	1 milliliter (ml) = 0.034 fl. oz.
1 gallon (gal.) = 3.785L	1 liter (L) = 0.264 gal.
1 acre (ac.) = 0.405ha	1 hectare (ha) = 2.47 ac.
1 square mile (sq. mi.) = 2.59km^2	1 square kilometer (km^2) = 0.386 sq. mi.

TELEPHONE CODES

To call within Egypt, in addition to coin-operated public phones, you can buy **pre-paid phonecards,** which carry a certain amount of phone time depending on the card's denomination. Phone rates tend to be highest in the morning, lower in the evening, and lowest late at night. When calling within the country, add a **zero** in front of the dialing prefix; when calling internationally, drop successive zeros. For more information on staying in touch by phone, see **Essentials,** p. 30.

CITY	PHONE CODE	CITY	PHONE CODE
EGYPT	**20**	Kharga	092
Alexandria	03	Qena	096
Aswan	097	Luxor	095
Asyut	088	Port Said	066
Bahariya	010	Sinai	062
Cairo	02	Sohag	093
Dakhla	092	Suez	062
Hurghada	065	Tanta	040

APPENDIX

ARABIC PHRASEBOOK العربية

Arabic (al-'Arabiyya) is the official language of Egypt. Dialects of Arabic vary from country to country—it is not uncommon to see a Lebanese and a Moroccan speaking French with each other because their Arabic dialects are so different. Egyptian Arabic is the most widely understood dialect because of Egypt's prolific film and television industry (it's also considered to be the best dialect in which to tell jokes). However, there are even different dialects within Egypt. In Upper (south) Egypt, the Nubians (also called Sa'idis) replace the q sound (ق) with a hard g. In Lower Egypt and in most other dialects, q is dropped completely and replaced with a glottal stop (a sound similar to that of the middle syllable of the word "butter" pronounced with a Cockney accent), indicated with a ' in transliteration. The Levantine j sound (as in fudge) becomes a hard g (as in gulf) in Egypt.

Arabic is read from right to left, but numerals are read from left to right. Arabic uses eight sounds not heard in English. Kh (خ) is like the German ch; gh (غ) is like the French r. There are two h sounds; one (ه) sounds like the English "h" and the other (ح, in Muhammad) is somewhere between kh and plain h. The letter 'ayn (ع) comes from the throat; it is ' in transliteration. R is trilled, as in Spanish. Dh (as in this), d, t, k, and s all have emphatic equivalents. Vowels and consonants can be long or short (it means the difference between a hammam, bathroom, and a hamam, pigeon). The definite article "the" is the prefix al. When al comes before the sounds t, th, j, d, dh, r, z, s, sh, or n, the l is not pronounced, and the l elides to become the letter which follows it (e.g., al-noor is properly pronounced an-noor).

EMERGENCY

ENGLISH	ARABIC
Help!	Saa'idoonee!
Stop!	Waqif!
I'm ill.	Ana marid (m), Ana marida (f)
It hurts me here.	Bituga'ani hina
I'm tired.	Ana ta'aban (m), Ana ta'abana (f)
Water	Mayya
Hospital	Mustashfa
Doctor	Duktoor
(Tourist) police	Bolees (al-seeyaaha)
I'm calling the police.	Agiblak al-bolees
Go away!	Imshee!
Passport	Gawaz
(American) Embassy	Safara (al-Amrikiya)

GREETINGS

ENGLISH	ARABIC
Informal hello	Marhaba
Formal hello (response)	As-Salaamu aleikum (Wa Aleikum as–salaam)
Goodbye	Ma' as-salaama
Good morning (response)	Sabah al-kheir (Sabah al-noor/Sabah al-ishta)
Good evening (response)	Masa' al-kheir (Masa' al-noor)

ENGLISH	ARABIC
How are you?	Izzayyak? (m), Izzayik? (f)
I'm fine	Kwayyis (m), Kwayyisa
Yes (informal); Yes (formal);	Aywa; Na'am
No	La
Maybe	Mumkin
Never mind, no big deal	Ma'alish
Thank you (very much).	Shukran (jazilan)
Please...	Min fadlak/Law samaht...
I'm sorry.	Ana aasif (m), Ana aasfa (f).
Excuse me (to get attention)	'An iznak (m), 'An iznik (f)
Pardon me (to apologize)	'Afwan
God willing; Praise God	Inshallah; Al-hamdu lillah
I don't know.	Mish 'aarif (m), Mish 'aarifa (f).
What is your name?	Shoo ismik?
My name is...	Ismee...
Student	Talib (m), Taliba (f)
Tourist	Saayih (m), Saayiha (f), Suwwaah (pl)
I don't understand.	Mish faahim (m), Mish faahima (f).
I don't speak Arabic.	Ma bahki 'arabi/Mabatkallimish 'arabi.
Do you speak English?	Tatakalim inglizi? (m), Tatitkalimee inglizi? (f)
What is that?	Eh da?
Where?; What?; Why?; Who?; When?	Wayn?; Shoo?; Leysh?; Meen?; Imta?

DIRECTIONS AND TRANSPORTATION

ENGLISH	ARABIC
Let's Go!	Yallah!
Can you tell me how to get to [Tahrir] Street?	Shaari'a [Tahrir] fein?
Straight	Dughree or 'Ala tool
Right, Left	Yameen, Shimal
North, South, East, West	Al-shamal, al-gunoub, Al-sharq, al-gharb
I'm lost.	Ana tuht.
Station	Mahatta
Public Square	Midan
I would like a ticket for...	'Aayiz (f: 'Aayza) tazkara rayhah...
One way/Round-trip	Bass/Rayih gayeh
What time does the (bus) leave?	Biyitla' imta (al-bus)?
Bus	Autoobees
Train	Atr
Automobile	'Arabiyya
Airport	Mataar

SIGHTS AND SERVICES

ENGLISH	ARABIC
Room	Oda
I'd like a (single/double) room.	'Aayiz (f: 'Aayza) ghurfa (bisrir wehid/litnein).
How much is a room?	Al-oda bikam?
Is there ___ ?	Fee ___ ?
There is no ___.	Mafeesh ___.
Hotel	Funduq or (h)otel
Lunch; Dinner	Al-ghada; al-'asha
Coffee; Tea	Ahwa; shay
Bathroom	Hammam/twaleet
Restaurant	Mata'm
Telephone	Tilifon
I'd like call [the US].	'Aayiz (f: 'Aayza) atasil bi [Amrika].
Pharmacy	Saydaleeya or 'Agzakhena
Post Office	Maktab al-bareed or Bosta
Street	Shaari'a
Market	Souq
Museum	Mat-haf
Mosque	Masgid/gaame'
Church	Kineesa

DATE AND TIME

ENGLISH	ARABIC
What time is it?	Al-saa'a kaam?
Hour, Time	Saa'a
Day; Week; Month; Year	Yom; Usbuu'; Shahr; Sana
Yesterday; Today; Tomorrow	Al-yom or Al-nahar da; bukra
What time do you open(close)?	Bitiftah/(Biti'fil) al-saa'a kam?
Sunday/Monday/Tuesday	Yom al-ahad/Yom al-itnein/Yom at-talaat
Wednesday/ Thursday /Friday/Saturday	Yom al-arba'/Yom al-khamees/Yom al-guma'a/Yom as-sabt

MONEY

ENGLISH	ARABIC
How much is this?	Bikam?
Will you take half?	Taakhud nuss? (m) Taakhdee nuss? (f)
I want...	'Aayiz (m), 'Aayza (f)
Is there a student discount?	Fi takhfid lit-tulaab?
Cheap/Expensive	Rikhees/ghaalee
No way! Impossible!	Mish mumkin!
Money	Fuloos
Change	Fakka

GLOSSARY

'ain: spring
ankh: Egyptian symbol for life, Coptic cross
bab: door, gate
bakhsheesh: tip, bribe
bir: well
booza: ice cream
caretta: donkey-drawn taxicart
corniche: from the French, long avenue along the water
deir: monastery
djinn: ghost
emir: prince
felucca: Egyptian sailboat
gabal: hill, mountain
galabiyya: long gown worn by men
hammam: hot baths; bathroom
hantour: horse carriage
hibis: plow
hijab: traditional women's head-covering
hurriyya: liberty; freedom
iconostasis: icon-covered screen in a mosque separating the nave from the sanctuary
imam: Muslim leader
irwan: arcaded porch in a mosque surrounding the central open courtyard
kalish: from the French *calèche,* a horse-drawn carriage
kefyeh: traditional black-and-white checkered headscarf
khan: caravanserai, courtyard inn
khanqah: home for Sufi mystics
khedive: Turkish for viceroy
khuttar: tradition in which Bedouin families host any visitors that cross their path
kuttab: Qur'anic school
lakaban: marble basin
madrasa: school or college of Islamic law
margunah: large, decorated woven basket
mashrabiyya: interlaced wooden screen
mawlid: festival celebrating events from the Qur'an or birthdays of saints
mayda'a: ablution fountain
midan: square
mihrab: richly decorated prayer niche in a mosque pointing in the direction of Mecca
minbar: pulpit in a mosque next to the mihrab where sermons are delivered
muezzin: person who sounds the call to prayer
papyrus: ancient Egyptian paper made from reeds
pronaos: vestibule
qala'a: fortress, citadel
qasr: castle
Ramadan: Muslim holy month of fasting
sabil: water dispensary
saha: central open courtyard in a mosque
service: group taxi
siq: narrow passageway in rock (see Petra, p. 298).
souq: market
tarfudit: veils
umm: mother
wadi: small river or riverbed

FOOD AND DRINK

ahwa: coffee (also, qahwa)
'araq: strong anise liquor
argileh, sheesha: water pipe, hookah
'asab: sugar cane juice
aseer: fruit juice
baba ghanoush: pureed eggplant with lemon juice, mayonnaise, and spices
ba'laweh: pistachio- or almond-filled filo dough (baklava)
basbouseh: wheat pastry with syrup

burma: shredded, fried dough with pistachios
farooj: roasted chicken served with chilis and onions
fattoush: salad of lettuce, tomato, and cucumber with small pieces of toasted pita.
falafel: fried chickpeas, shaped into balls
fuul: cooked fava beans with garlic, lemon, olive oil, and salt on bread and vegetables
hummus: ground chickpeas with oil and spices
jamid: tangy yogurt-based sauce
jellab: raisin syrup with pine nuts
kibbeh naye: raw beef and spices
kofta: spiced ground beef grilled on skewers
kushari: starch-laden Egyptian dish of pasta, rice, lentils, and onions in tomato sauce
lagbi: sweet, palm tree juice
mahshi: grape leaves stuffed with mincemeat, rice, and onions
mana'eesh: pizza with za'tar
marqooq: paper thin baked bread
mensaf: rice on a large tray of flat bread, topped with pine nuts, lamb or goat, and a tangy yogurt-based sauce
mezze: appetizers
musakhan: chicken baked with olive oil, onions, and spices, served on bread
mujeddra: lentil stew with sautéed onions and spices
mulukhiyya: green Egyptian vegetable
na'na': mint
shawarma: fatty lamb rolled onto pita
shay: tea
shish kebab: skewered lamb
shish tawouq: skewered chicken
ta'amiyya: Egyptian version of falafel, discus-like in both shape and hardness
tahina: sesame-based sauce
tabbouleh: parsley, cracked wheat, onions, tomatoes, lemon juice, and spices mix together
tawila: backgammon
zaghlouta: ululations (perform when served. Lather. Rinse. Repeat.)
za'tar: hyssop (thyme mixed with sesame seeds and spices)

APPENDIX

Travel Cheep.

Visit **StudentUniverse** for real deals on student and faculty airline tickets, rail passes, and hostel memberships.

INDEX

ABOUT LET'S GO

FORTY-TWO YEARS OF WISDOM

For over four decades, travelers crisscrossing the continents have relied on *Let's Go* for inside information on the hippest backstreet cafes, the most pristine secluded beaches, and the best routes from border to border. *Let's Go: Europe*, now in its 42nd edition and translated into seven languages, reigns as the world's bestselling international travel guide. In the last 20 years, our rugged researchers have stretched the frontiers of backpacking and expanded our coverage into the Americas, Australia, Asia, and Africa (including the new *Let's Go: Egypt* and the more comprehensive, multi-country jaunt through *Let's Go: South Africa & Southern Africa*). Our new-and-improved City Guide series continues to grow with new guides to perennial European favorites Amsterdam and Barcelona. This year we are also unveiling *Let's Go: Southwest USA*, the flagship of our new outdoor Adventure Guide series, which is complete with special roadtripping tips and itineraries, more coverage of adventure activities like hiking and mountain biking, and first-person accounts of life on the road.

It all started in 1960 when a handful of well-traveled students at Harvard University handed out a 20-page mimeographed pamphlet offering a collection of their tips on budget travel to passengers on student charter flights to Europe. The following year, in response to the instant popularity of the first volume, students traveling to Europe researched the first full-fledged edition of *Let's Go: Europe*. Throughout the 60s and 70s, our guides reflected the times—in 1969, for example, we taught you how to get from Paris to Prague on "no dollars a day" by singing in the street. In the 90s we focused in on the world's most exciting urban areas to produce in-depth, fold-out map guides, now with 20 titles (from Hong Kong to Chicago) and counting. Our new guides bring the total number of titles to 57, each infused with the spirit of adventure and voice of opinion that travelers around the world have come to count on. But some things never change: our guides are still researched, written, and produced entirely by students who know first-hand how to see the world on the cheap.

HOW WE DO IT

Each guide is completely revised and thoroughly updated every year by a well-traveled set of nearly 300 students. Every spring, we recruit over 200 researchers and 90 editors to overhaul every book. After several months of training, researcher-writers hit the road for seven weeks of exploration, from Anchorage to Adelaide, Estonia to El Salvador, Iceland to Indonesia. Hired for their rare combination of budget travel sense, writing ability, stamina, and courage, these adventurous travelers know that train strikes, stolen luggage, food poisoning, and marriage proposals are all part of a day's work. Back at our offices, editors work from spring to fall, massaging copy written on Himalayan bus rides into witty, informative prose. A student staff of typesetters, cartographers, publicists, and managers keeps our lively team together. In September, the collected efforts of the summer are delivered to our printer, who turns them into books in record time, so that you have the most up-to-date information available for your vacation. Even as you read this, work on next year's editions is well underway.

WHY WE DO IT

We don't think of budget travel as the last recourse of the destitute; we believe that it's the only way to travel. Our books will ease your anxieties and answer your questions about the basics—so you can get off the beaten track and explore. Once you learn the ropes, we encourage you to put *Let's Go* down and strike out on your own. You know as well as we that the best discoveries are often those you make yourself. When you find something worth sharing, please drop us a line. We're Let's Go Publications, 67 Mount Auburn St., Cambridge, MA 02138, USA (feedback@letsgo.com). For more info, visit our website, www.letsgo.com.

Will you have enough stories to tell your grandchildren?

Yahoo! Travel

Do You YAHOO!?

CHOOSE YOUR DESTINATION SWEEPSTAKES

No Purchase Necessary.

Explore the world with Let's Go® and StudentUniverse!
Enter for a chance to win a trip for two to a Let's Go destination!
Separate Drawings! May & October 2002.

GRAND PRIZES:
Roundtrip StudentUniverse Tickets

✓ Select one destination and mail your entry to:

☐ Costa Rica
☐ London
☐ Hong Kong
☐ San Francisco
☐ New York
☐ Amsterdam
☐ Prague
☐ Sydney

* Plus Additional Prizes!!

Choose Your Destination Sweepstakes
St. Martin's Press
Suite 1600, Department MF
175 Fifth Avenue
New York, NY 10010-7848

Restrictions apply; see offical rules for
details by visiting Let'sGo.com or sending SASE
(VT residents may omit return postage) to the address above.

Name: _____

Address: _____

City/State/Zip: _____

Phone: _____

Email: _____

Grand prizes provided by:

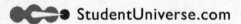

StudentUniverse.com   Real Travel Deals